TRANSACTIONAL ANALYSIS AFTER ERIC BERNE

Eric Berne
1910–1970

Transactional Analysis after Eric Berne

TEACHINGS AND PRACTICES OF THREE TA SCHOOLS

Graham Barnes, Editor

President, Southeast Institute
Adjunct Lecturer, Department of Psychiatry,
University of North Carolina School of Medicine

Contributors

Michael Brown   Ken Lessler
Robert C. Drye   Ruth McClendon
John M. Dusay   John R. McNeel
Fanita English   John J. O'Hearne
John Gladfelter   Jacqui Lee Schiff
Robert L. Goulding   Jon Weiss
Martin Groder   Laurie Weiss
William H. Holloway   Terri White
Kristyn Huige   Jerome D. White
Lois M. Johnson   Kenneth L. Windes
Vann S. Joines   Stanley J. Woollams
Taibi Kahler

Harper's College Press
A Department of Harper & Row, Publishers
New York / Hagerstown / San Francisco / London

Sponsoring Editor: William D. Eastman
Project Editor: Renée E. Beach
Designer: Emily Harste
Production Supervisor: Kewal K. Sharma
Compositor: Ruttle, Shaw & Wetherill, Inc.
Printer and Binder: The Maple Press Company
Art Studio: J & R Technical Services, Inc.

TRANSACTIONAL ANALYSIS AFTER ERIC BERNE
Teachings and Practices of Three TA Schools

Library of Congress Cataloging in Publication Data

Main entry under title:

Transactional analysis after Eric Berne.

    Includes index.
    1. Transactional analysis. I. Barnes, Graham.
II. Brown, Michael, Date—
RC489.T7T69   158   77-4754
ISBN 0-06-168412-0

Most teachers and practitioners of transactional analysis neither march to the sound of a drummer—real or imagined—nor are they inclined to make anyone their master. Eric Berne is appreciated and lauded for the contributions he made through his teachings and for the reliable maps he drew of the ways to reach personal and professional autonomy. He set an example for rigorous scientific scholarship in a spirit that would be amused by any attempt to hear him in some distant meadow beating a drum for others to march to, or by any attempt to make him a final authority. In this spirit, it is appropriate to honor him by dedicating this book to his memory.

CONTENTS

Eight
The Three "C's" of Corrections: Cops-Cons-Counselors
Kenneth L. Windes
138

Nine
A Graduate Program in Psychotherapy
Ken Lessler
146

PART III
PROGRESS IN TRANSACTIONAL ANALYSIS

Ten
Groder's 5 OK Diagrams
Martin Groder
161

Eleven
Transactional Analysis: An Integrative View
William H. Holloway
169

Twelve
The Miniscript
Taibi Kahler
223

Thirteen
An Integrated Systems Perspective
Vann S. Joines
257

Fourteen
The Implications of Cultural Scripting
Terri White and Jerome D. White
273

PART IV
BEYOND SCRIPT ANALYSIS

Fifteen
What Shall I Do Tomorrow?:
Reconceptualizing Transactional Analysis
Fanita English
287

PART V
TRANSACTIONAL ANALYSIS
IN CLINICAL PRACTICE

Sixteen
From 21 to 43
Stanley J. Woollams
351

Twenty-one
Pilgrim's Progress
John J. O'Hearne
458

PART VI
OVERVIEW OF TRANSACTIONAL
ANALYSIS

Twenty-two
What Transactional Analysts Want Their Clients to Know
Stanley Woollams, Michael Brown, Kristyn Huige
487

PREFACE

This book is for psychotherapists and other professionals, for students and trainees in transactional analysis (TA) and other disciplines, for social scientists, and for the many nonprofessionals who have an interest in transactional analysis.

It is presented to transactional analysts with the hope that the sharing of ideas will further understanding among them. The authors expect neither uniformity nor agreement. This book is addressed to others as an advanced introduction to TA.

Those readers not familiar with subtle differences in emphases and approaches will, undoubtedly, see more resemblances than differences among the authors.

Contributors accepted the invitation to pursue the following goals through this publication: (1) to engage publicly in a theoretical and clinical introspection of TA; (2) to document the diversity of TA orientations; (3) to advance TA theory; (4) to record new clinical directions; (5) to encourage and further dialogue among major TA schools and approaches; (6) to provide a summary of where we are with TA at this point; and (7) to publish a readable and understandable reference work on TA that may demand cerebrating but not require deciphering.

Most of the authors are well known to transactional analysts, although virtually unknown to others. Even professionals who attempt to keep abreast of new developments by reading the scholarly journals and through participation in conferences have not had the opportunity to examine in depth the clinical and theoretical insights of many of the teachers and practitioners of TA whose works are included in this book.

Eric Berne, MD, the founder of transactional analysis, introduced TA to a wide audience through the publication of his best-seller, *Games People Play*. His other books have continued to engender both popular and professional interest in TA. The International Transactional Analysis Association (ITAA) came into existence on October 20, 1964, to promote an understanding of TA and to provide appropriate training and certification of teachers and practitioners of the discipline. Public excitement about TA as a method of psychotherapy and a model for solving problems was generated by Thomas A. Harris, MD, in his book, *I'm OK—You're OK: A Practical Guide to Transactional Analysis*. When Berne died in 1970, there were only a few other well-known transactional analysts, most of them in California. There were about 500 regular and advanced members of the ITAA, including 58 Teaching Members. During the early 1970s the number of advanced members of ITAA grew to over 500. These professionals form a body of competent TA practitioners. The roster of regular members of ITAA has now swelled to almost 10,000 with members in more than 35 countries.

Concomitant with the rapid growth of TA, many theoretical and personal controversies developed among transactional analysts. A positive result of the controversies and conflicts was the awareness that conformity could never be demanded of practitioners of TA. This awareness was followed by the recognition that, over the years, schools of transactional analysis had developed. The ITAA was faced with the problem of how to respond to the new clinical and theoretical approaches. With Eric Berne dead, there was no one to say which approaches were and were not TA. The ITAA responded to this crisis in 1973 by requiring all candidates for advanced membership to have a working knowledge of the teachings and practices of the major TA schools and orientations.

In this book, representatives of the schools share their teachings and practices. Represented here are also those transactional analysts who have broken through the boundaries of schools to synthesize and integrate the techniques and practices of TA.

I have a secret hope that this book will contribute to the demise of nascent sectarianism, including any possible competitive drives to prove that one approach is better than another, or the assumption that a new approach to TA will set the future course of the human race or even that of transactional analysis.

The reader who does not have a working knowledge of the language and theory of transactional analysis is invited to begin this book by turning to the final chapter, "What Transactional Analysts Want Their Clients to Know," for an overview of TA. Others may also find this chapter helpful since it provides an integration of basic TA theory usually presented to beginning trainees in TA and to many clients in TA treatment and growth groups.

In the Introduction, I present the model that I use to identify the schools of transactional analysis. This is followed by presentations from the leader of each school: John Dusay discusses the phases of TA's development and shares emphases of the Classical School; Jacqui Schiff tells how the Cathexis School came into existence through her work with young people with diagnoses of schizophrenia, and how they were involved with her in the development of an approach to cure schizophrenia;

and Robert Goulding describes how he and Mary Goulding use marathons for treatment and training and shares the advances in the theory and techniques of the Redecision School.

The chapters by the other authors reveal how they have, in their own personal and professional development, drawn upon, gone beyond, or ignored the teachings and practices of the schools.

My extended family, especially my sons, Chris and Jamie, have offered understanding throughout this undertaking. I thank Chris for suggesting that the title be simple and to the point. I take this opportunity to express my deep gratitude to my colleagues at Southeast Institute for their invaluable encouragement during all stages of the preparation of the book. I am greatly indebted to Theda Callaway, who has given careful attention to the progress of this work. I have also profited from her advice. Pat Reefe has been involved in the production of this book from the beginning. I appreciate her assistance with many aspects of the book, especially for typing the manuscript. Chellie Steel and Sheryl Scrimsher also offered invaluable assistance. I am deeply indebted to my friends and colleagues who reviewed sections of this book, especially Barbara Page, who read all the chapters, and Dorothy Gullen and Jerrold Paul, who read selected chapters.

To all who contributed to this volume I give my thanks and appreciation for their original chapters. Their contributions make possible the publication of a number of the innovations in transactional analysis since the death of Eric Berne.

GRAHAM BARNES

Chapel Hill, North Carolina
March 1977

Schools of Transactional Analysis

ONE

INTRODUCTION
Graham Barnes

In a recent article Robert Goulding lists four major schools of transactional analysis but gives no criteria for what constitutes a school.[1] Several institutes, seminars, collectives, and other groups can be classified as schools if no clear criteria are used to define what a school is. Any innovative theory or technique introduced by a charismatic teacher can be called a school. Almost all teachers of TA can be considered leaders of schools. But, properly speaking, the term "school" should describe a social group and not be used to classify the assumptions of popular teachers, leaders, and authors who use methods that are new to transactional analysis.

WHAT IS A SCHOOL OF TRANSACTIONAL ANALYSIS?

A school of TA is a body of persons under a common personal influence who hold a common theoretical position and follow the same clinical methods. A school can be identified by its unique leadership, canon, and group culture.[2] (Figure 1)

LEADERSHIP A school has a leader who is a Teaching Member of the International Transactional Analysis Association. Leaders of the schools occupy the leadership slot in the imago (mental picture) of the persons who have studied and trained extensively with them. These leaders are also seen by others as occupying the leadership slot in the imago of those persons.

Schools have *charismatic* leaders whose leadership was recognized before they became founders of schools. They demonstrate attributes of unusual "gifts" and exemplary character; they are set apart from "ordinary" persons and treated as though they are endowed with exceptional qualities and powers. Some persons see them as "gurus." Their leadership is natural; they are not appointed and they cannot be dismissed. Individuals accept their challenges to break with traditions and the establishment. If they are

3

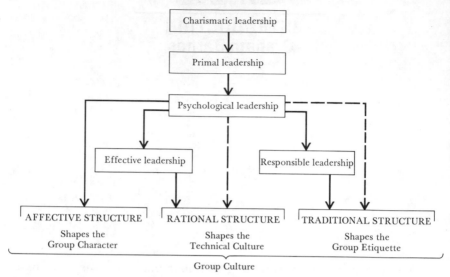

Figure 1
Leadership and Group Culture Diagram

successful, they often produce "elitist" movements. These leaders seek influence and continuity.

Charismatic leadership alone is unstable and temporary. It is a style of
leadership that exists only in the process of originating. Successful charismatic leaders organize their followers into a social structure. The structure
retains the psychological aspects of the leader's personality and it tends to
become traditional or rational or both.[3] (Most teachers of transactional
analysis are charismatic leaders. Most of them have not made, or attempted
to make, the breakthrough to the established pattern of behavior that is
discussed below.)

After a school is established, the charismatic leader becomes the *primal*
leader who is recognized as the founder of the school. Primal leaders are
the canon makers and they give the canon existential reinforcement and
meaning. The group culture is made possible by them. Others recognize
them as being agents of change, as having set new directions in TA and
psychotherapy, and as having established a school. They provide new role
models for doing transactional analysis. Other transactional analysts often
quote them.

A school requires psychological, effective, and responsible leadership.
The primal leader usually becomes the school's psychological, effective,
and responsible leader.

A TA school has a *psychological* leader to whom individuals turn in
times of crisis. This leader is responsive to the personal crisis of others.
She or he has also identified defects in TA theory and technique, has
sought to correct them, and is acknowledged as having done so. The psy-

chological leader is *creative* and develops new theories and techniques. In comparison to those who prefer stability and appeal to tradition, this leader is *spontaneous*. Her or his leadership is *unusual* and differs radically from the routine in traditional psychotherapy.[4] (Treatment groups also have psychological leaders, but not all psychological leaders will demonstrate all the qualities described here. However, their leadership will be seen by members of their groups as creative, spontaneous, and unusual. Members of a group always turn to the psychological leader when there is a crisis.)

A series of crises during the late sixties and early seventies led many students of TA to respond to the teachers who exemplified these qualities of leadership. TA developed in a context that was highly competitive. A competitive spirit often leads people to call attention to their differences or to their unique contributions. There was also the issue of what practices and techniques were consistent with TA and whether certain other modalities could be integrated with TA.[5] TA was blessed and at times cursed by its widespread public and professional acceptance. A few major TA theorists were geographically remote from San Francisco where basic theory was being developed. Their contributions did not quickly become part of the canon. Occasionally there were challenges to Berne's leadership and his unexpected death precipitated the most serious crisis. Some individuals had conflicts with Berne that were unresolved at the time of his death. While they were working through these conflicts and they and others were dealing with their feelings toward Berne for dying, the situation remained potentially volatile. No leader was immediately available to help resolve the theoretical differences among various teachers or to reconcile personal disputes. The emergence of schools created stability and helped resolve most of the crises. Gradually an acceptance by most transactional analysts of the diverse approaches of various leaders led to equilibrium.

A school of TA has an *effective* leader whose technical competence is acknowledged. She or he has developed theories and methods that are copied and used by others. Indications of the effective leadership of founders of TA schools can be seen in the following:

1. They have set new theoretical directions in transactional analysis.
2. They have developed theories and/or methods that go beyond TA as formulated and presented in the works of Eric Berne.
3. They have developed theoretical models that are clear and easily understood.
4. Others use and follow their clinical approaches and get similar results.
5. Their influence on transactional analysis has been direct.
6. People outside their schools have heard their names and know about and cite their work.
7. They are the transactional analysts whose clinical work people hear the most about.
8. They continue to develop new clinical and theoretical material.

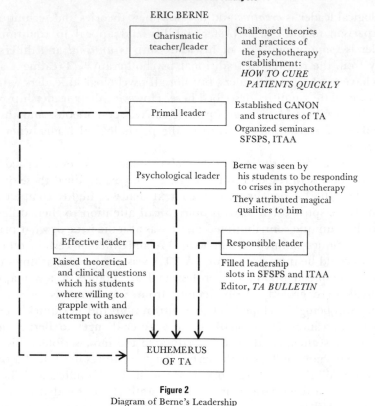

ERIC BERNE

| Charismatic teacher/leader | Challenged theories and practices of the psychotherapy establishment: *HOW TO CURE PATIENTS QUICKLY* |

| Primal leader | Established CANON and structures of TA. Organized seminars SFSPS, ITAA |

| Psychological leader | Berne was seen by his students to be responding to crises in psychotherapy. They attributed magical qualities to him |

| Effective leader | Raised theoretical and clinical questions which his students where willing to grapple with and attempt to answer |

| Responsible leader | Filled leadership slots in SFSPS and ITAA. Editor, *TA BULLETIN* |

EUHEMERUS OF TA

Figure 2
Diagram of Berne's Leadership

9. Their theoretical and clinical approaches have had national and international influence.

Each school has an organizational or *responsible* leader. The founder of each school has established an institute and/or has an official position in an institute or a seminar. This leader has also received the formal recognition of the International Transactional Analysis Association as the recipient of the Eric Berne Memorial Scientific Award for his or her work.

Eric Berne, as the founder and first primal leader of transactional analysis, has a special place in all schools of TA. Most transactional analysts have made him the *euhemerus* (the dead primal leader) of TA. Already for some he has taken on mythical qualities. To give cohesiveness to their groups or to strengthen their positions during controversies, leaders of some schools have been heard to appeal to Berne's works or to quote a statement that he made to them (Figure 2).

THE CANON   Each school has established its own canon which gives it form and assures its orderly existence by regulating the work of the school and its internal group process. The basic canon for each school comes from Berne. Not only was the euhemerization of Eric Berne essential for the survival of ITAA, it is necssary for the survival of each school. Eric Berne established customs which have now become traditions in TA. Berne's influence on the canon of each school is what makes it a TA school.

Although the canon of each school comes from Berne, each school has made its own variations and alterations of the canon. For instance, Berne first called his group of followers the San Francisco Social Psychiatry Seminars. When the charter of the Seminars was amended in 1964 to form the ITAA, the name of the group in San Francisco was changed to the San Francisco Transactional Analysis Seminars. The Seminars function as an "educational institute." When Berne reported on the organizational history of the SFSPS, he noted. "The title of the organization was carefully chosen to avoid pretentious words like 'Institute' and 'Society.' "[6] Leaders of schools and other teachers of TA have not been reluctant to call their groups institutes.

The founder of each school has significantly influenced the canon of his or her school. The canons of the schools, as with many of the teachings and assumptions of TA, are often unwritten but they are well known within the TA community (Figure 3).

Each school has an unwritten constitution that makes major assumptions about people. There is also a formal organization incorporated by the state. The school has a formal name that distinguishes it from the others. The constitution and laws of the ITAA influence many of the activities of each school, especially in the setting of rigorous standards for training. The major activities of each school of TA are training and treatment.

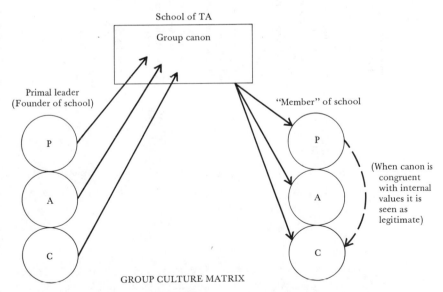

Figure 3
Origin, Organization, and Transmission of Canon of TA School

	TRADITIONAL STRUCTURE	AFFECTIVE STRUCTURE
TRADITIONAL STRUCTURE	Framework of meaning (Pattern of beliefs) Analogous to Parent ego state in personality structure (Nurturing Parent Functions) Elicits Parent and Child activities and responses RESPONDS TO POSITION HUNGER GOAL: Maintains structure	Pattern of behavior (Includes ethics) Analogous to Parent ego state in personality structure (Critical Parent Functions) Elicits Parent and Child activities and responses RESPONDS TO STRUCTURE HUNGER GOAL: Prescribes behavior in response to member's capacity for adjustment
RATIONAL STRUCTURE	Technologies (Theories and methods) Analogous to Adult ego state in personality structure Elicits Adult activities and responses RESPONDS TO HUNGER FOR NEW EXPERIENCE GOAL: Sets standards of competence and defines situation	Pattern of emotions (Includes aesthetics) Analogous to Child ego state in personality structure Elicits Child activities and responses (expressions of group life in response to archaic needs and wants) RESPONDS TO STIMULUS AND RECOGNITION HUNGER AND TO LEADERSHIP HUNGER GOAL: Offers gratification and strokes
	Technical culture	Group character

Figure 4

Elements of the Group Culture

THE CULTURE OF EACH SCHOOL IS IN MANY WAYS UNIQUE
Each school has its own pattern of human behavior. The culture of a
school consists of three segments: Group Character, Group Etiquette, and
Technical Culture (Figure 4).[7] The group *character* originates in the emotional and archaic elements of the primal leader's personality (Figure 5).
It is also the expression of the group life that arises out of the archaic
needs and wants of the individuals. The character of a school includes expressions of behavior not established or made legitimate by the social
contract (see below). The goal of the school's character is the gratification
of the individual. The group character of the school is one of the things
that makes it attractive or unattractive to others. Some motivations that
originate in the Free Child are considered proper expressions of behavior
by a school, while others are considered improper. In some instances, the
group character arises out of substitute behaviors and the motivation is
to get needs and wants met through behaviors and feelings that have been
learned (Adapted Child). Every school has ways of responding to these
two motivations. It also has its own theory of what constitutes archaic
needs and wants, and its own methods for eliciting and responding to
emotions.

A school has a prescribed *etiquette* that includes standards of behaviors
and a framework of meaning. For the individual it includes a social contract that is enforced by the group etiquette. The social contract prescribes
ways of presenting an acceptable persona and how the persona of each
person is to be respected and reinforced. The etiquette is traditional and

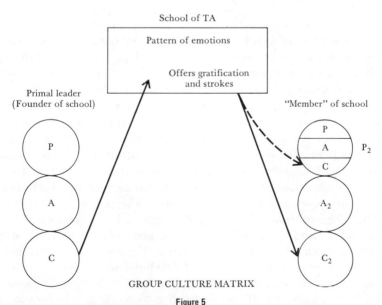

Figure 5
Origin, Organization, and Transmission of Group Character of TA School

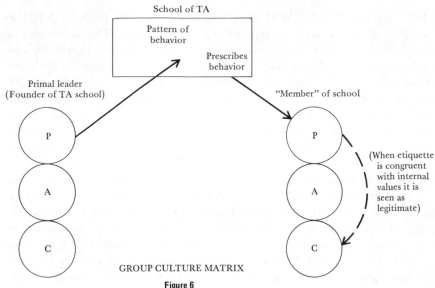

Figure 6
Group Etiquette of TA School
Origin, Organization, and Transmission of Pattern of Behavior

has both nurturing and controlling aspects. It responds to the organism's capacity for adjustment by prescribing patterns of behavior (Figure 6). The patterns may be either positive or negative or both. The school prescribes behaviors that will be reinforced and behaviors that will be confronted. It also has standards of responsibility for both therapists and patients.

The school's framework of meaning brings together those patterns of the culture that are seen by the primal leader (and other persons in the group culture) as normative (Figure 7). The values that are seen as normative assure the maintenance of structure. These values usually specify what it means to be human. They become the basis for both nurturing and critical behavior. Whether meaning is derived from psychobiological principles or philosophical precepts, or both, the same issues are usually at stake: what it means to be human, what is meant by "human nature," "biological inheritance," or "the limiting influences of the organism." Definitions of autonomy and the place of human freedom in the life of the school are decisive here. It may be useful to note that a school's point of view on OKness and basic life positions is also part of its etiquette.

The *technical culture* of a school is seen in its use of logic, how it defines reality, how it identifies, defines, and solves problems, organizes information, and determines competence (Figure 8). Its techniques, treatment methodologies, and theoretical developments evolve out of the technical culture. The technical culture of a school includes its response to the following: (1) the definition of the situation, (2) the influences of the environment on an individual's script, (3) how the personality develops, (4) definitions and explanations of psychopathology, (5) the part indi-

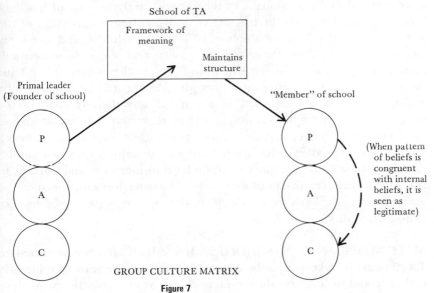

Figure 7
Group Etiquette of TA School
Origin, Organization, and Transmission of Pattern of Beliefs

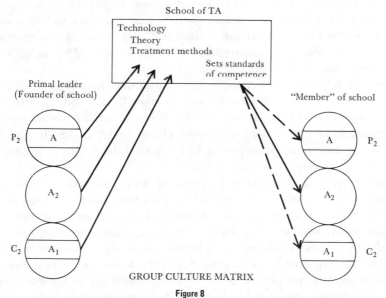

Figure 8
Origin, Organization, and Transmission of Technical Culture of a TA School

viduals play in shaping their own destiny, including their own treatment, and (6) the goals of treatment. (Some of these items are also influenced by a school's etiquette.)

A SCHOOL TENDS TO BECOME RATIONAL AND TRADI-TIONAL As a school develops it tends to become less charismatic and more rational and traditional. As the theories and methods of a school become institutionalized the innovative and spontaneous activities of the primal leader may become absolutes. The primal leader and the early members of a school use their intuitive powers and reason to understand what is going on both in the world and among themselves. They trust their definition of the situation although it may conflict with what the establishment says about reality or about the way therapy ought to be done. However, the followers may not trust their ability to intuit and to think creatively. If they make what the primal leader says and does into a norm, then they extend what started out as a definition or a new understanding of the situation, move it to the level of meaning, and attempt to make it the way everyone must see reality. The behaviors sanctioned by the leader become the basis for a code of conduct that may have no relevance to new situations.[8]

AUTONOMY AND TA SCHOOLS   Individuals who are attracted to TA may use it to keep from becoming autonomous. Persons who identify with a school of TA may do the same thing. Most transactional analysts emphasize the importance of autonomy, although they have various points of view on the possibilities of owning or attaining it. Berne saw the attainment of autonomy as the goal of life. A person begins life in an autonomous state and gives up autonomy when he or she decides to follow negative or destructive parental influences. But the decisions are reversible and the individual can regain his or her autonomy. The struggle for autonomy continues throughout life.[9]

Some individuals in TA make the assumption that their teacher or therapist has the truth, knows the way to right living, and uses the only correct methods. They do not see the diversity of TA approaches as something to be appreciated; they must choose one and then turn it into the way to conceptualize and do TA. They talk about "the TA way," or they authoritatively claim that "TA says. . . ."

Most people are attracted to TA because of the emphasis on autonomy, but when they make TA an external support they use it to avoid autonomy. To join the ITAA or to be a member of a school does not mean that one has to give up one's autonomy. The crucial issue is whether one joins and then becomes a conformist or whether one uses involvement in TA to develop the capacity for autonomy.* Walter Kaufmann has delineated ten strategies that people use to avoid autonomy. Four of these strategies can apply to the use of TA: allegiance to a movement, allegiance to a school of thought, exegetical thinking, and the faith that one is riding the wave of the future.[10]

---

* Autonomy is recaptured when friendship is made with one's internal Parent, when parents are forgiven and then divorced on friendly terms. The autonomous person is aware, spontaneous, and joyful and can be close to others without being enslaved by any individual or institution. Freedom calls for autonomous people to join groups and organizations to confront and change heteronomous (Parent-dominated) structures.

Many people become members of a TA school by training with someone in that school. Often they have not made a *decision* to be identified
with the school. After they begin training in the school, however, some
tend to emphasize the differences between the schools rather than the
similarities. They may view the group culture of their school as superior
to that of others, instead of seeing the culture as one they feel more comfortable in. Some claim that the techniques of their school are more effective than those of other schools. New developments do not interest them
unless they originate in their school. The work of other teachers of TA
are ignored. The leader of their school is their guru. Though they may
have started out with an allegiance to the "TA movement," they now have
found the truth. Members of the school may reinforce each other with the
belief that their leader has led them to the truth. Their work is not as
important as the truth. They are riding the wave of the future. If they
engage in intellectual activity, they do what Kaufmann calls "exegtical
thinking," or what Groder calls "picture-straightening." They read Berne
or the leader of their school and treat the text as authority. Rather than
interpret the text, they read their own ideas into it and "get them back
endowed with authority."[11]

Many teachers of transactional analysis refuse to be identified with
any school of TA. They call for an integrative approach that gathers theories and techniques from all the schools and from other sources also. Although this approach may resolve some issues, it cannot prevent individuals from doing the same thing with the integrative approach that they do
when they join a school. They can even endow the integrative approach
with more authority, especially when there is an implication that integrative TA includes everything and can solve all problems.

TEACHINGS AND PRACTICES OF THE THREE SCHOOLS OF TA

When the criteria previously described for a school of TA are followed,
the following three schools can be identified: the Classical School, the
Cathexis School, and the Redecision School. The teachings and practices
of each school will be outlined briefly (see Figure 9). This overview will
be followed by a tentative effort to set forth a challenge to transactional
analysts to continue to build new and more effective models for exploring
previously uncharted areas for the application of TA.

THE CLASSICAL SCHOOL   The Classical School is difficult to describe
because there is almost as much diversity within this school as there is
within TA itself. The Classical School was founded by Berne and its
existence antedates ITAA and all the other TA groups. San Francisco has
been the center for this school since its beginning. Since Berne's death
many leaders of branches of this school have emerged. They have established their own seminars and institutes in the United States and in other
parts of the world. The approaches of the following teachers of TA in the

	Basis for Therapeutic Intervention	Target for Intervention	Ego State Locus of Primary Pathology	Techniques or Treatment Methodologies	Interventions in response to client who vigorously begins tapping fingers	Possible Interventions in response to suicidal patient	Goal of Treatment
CLASSICAL SCHOOL San Francisco Group	Contract	Interpersonal	P_1	Decontaminate Adult (A_2) of Parent or Child (P_1) interferences; 3 P's; Analysis of transactions; insight into games and script	Note what client is saying and possibilities of incongruity (Confront Drivers) May or may not confront the behavior	Parent-To-Child transaction: "DON'T!" (Use 3 P's)	Autonomy
Radical Psychiatry	Contract	Interpersonal to help people overcome the oppressive social situation	P_1				Autonomy
Asklepieion Foundation	Contract	Interpersonal to help clients create alternative groups within existing systems	A_1	In prison situation help inmates clean up and create their environment, then do decontamination and use a variety of techniques	Ask the client (often with Little Professor embellishment), "Why are you tapping your fingers?"	A_1 intervention unique to each patient	Autonomy
CATHEXIS SCHOOL (Schiff Family)	Contract (if patient is able to make one)	Intrapsychic and Interpersonal to help clients change intrapsychic conflicts to conform to expectations of a healthy social structure	A_2, or A_1 (A_0)	Confrontation of pathological behaviors, thinking and feelings; help client get C_1 needs met and overcome early developmental problems; with some severely emotionally disturbed clients replace old ineffective Parent with new Parent	Confrontation of the agitation: "Stop agitating and think!"	Therapist takes charge from P_2 and A_2, enters into a symbiosis with client, nurtures and cares for client, gets client to move to a level of C_1 necessary to get needs met	Autonomy
REDECISION SCHOOL	Contract	Intrapsychic	A_1	Use gestalt therapy, imagery, and emotional reworking of client's childhood experiences in present tense; client emotionally reexperiences early scene of pathological decision and makes redecision, and practices new feelings, clear thinking and problem-solving behavior in here and now	Say to client, "What are your fingers telling you? Increase your tapping and find out."	Make Adult (A_2) no-suicide contract with client, then do redecision work to get client to reverse early decision (A_1) in response to "DON'T EXIST" injunction	Autonomy

Figure 9

Comparison of Schools

United States have a classical orientation: John Dusay, Stephen B. Karpman,[12] Claude Steiner,[13] Muriel James,[14] Martin Groder, Franklin H. Ernst, Jr.,[15] Fanita English, Dorothy Jongeward,[16] Hedges Capers,[17] Pam Levin,[18] Melvin Boyce, Kenneth V. Everts, William J. Collins, Viola Litt Callaghan, Joseph P. Concannon, W. Ray Poindexter, Pat Crossman,[19] Solon D. Samuels,[20] Jerome D. and Terri White, Morris L. and Natalie R. Haimowitz,[21] and Taibi Kahler. Some of these teachers are leaders of a branch of the Classical School; others have gone beyond an explicit classical approach.*

The three branches of the Classical School that are distinctive are the Eric Berne Seminars of San Francisco or the San Francisco Group, the Radical Psychiatry Movement, and the Asklepieion Foundation. The culture of each group is unique, but all three groups share a classical orientation clinically.

Claude Steiner, Ph.D, is the originator of radical psychiatry and was in a position of leadership at the Berkeley Radical Psychiatry Center from 1969 through 1973. He is a Clinical Member and a Teaching Member of the ITAA. His association with Berne began in 1958 when he joined the San Francisco Seminars. In 1971 he received the first Eric Berne Memorial Scientific Award for devising the script matrix which Berne had described as one of the most useful and cogent behavior diagrams of the 20th century.

Martin Groder, M.D., founder and chairman of the Asklepieion Foundation, is a Clinical Member, a Teaching Member, and a vice president of the ITAA. Shortly after he was assigned to practice psychiatry at the federal penitentiary, Marion, Illinois, in the late sixties, he organized a therapeutic community based on the Synanon Community Model that used TA as its basic treatment technique. The Asklepieion Foundation grew out of the therapeutic community at Marion.

Since the death of Berne in 1970, the Classical School has not had one person who was concurrently the psychological, effective, and responsible leader. These three kinds of leadership have been shared by different people. Leadership of the San Francisco Group has been shared by both John Dusay, M.D., and Stephen Karpman, M.D. (Both have won the Eric Berne Memorial Scientific Award.) Various other people have served as the responsible leader of this group.

Berne is the euhemerus for the San Francisco Group more than for any other TA group. As founder of the San Francisco Social Psychiatry Seminars, he was their primal leader and members of the Seminars had personal contact with him for many years. (Following Berne's death the Seminars were renamed the Eric Berne Seminars of San Francisco.)

John M. Dusay, M.D., has contributed this book's chapter on the Clas-

---

* This list is not exhaustive. It is included to give the reader unfamiliar with transactional analysis an idea of some of the teachers of TA the author has in mind when discussing transactional analysts who share a classical orientation. The author is aware of some of the risks involved in such a categorization.

sical School. He practices psychiatry in San Francisco and is a Clinical Member, a Teaching Member, and immediate past president of the ITAA. In 1973, he received the Eric Berne Award for the development of the egogram. In his chapter, he traces the evolution of TA through four phases. There is a consensus among transactional analysts on the first three phases, but a lack of distance and perspective makes it difficult for many to identify the state of the art in the present phase. As Dusay implies, work on the earlier phases continues and many exciting new developments are taking place.

The character of the Classical School is seen in its therapeutic use of humor, imagery, imagination, intuition, and hyperbole. Fun, play, and creativity are encouraged as part of the group life.

Patient and therapist are equally responsible for their actions: the patient is responsible for his actions because his problems are the result of his script, and the therapist is responsible for his behavior toward the patient and in their work for a speedy cure. The therapist asks the patient for a treatment contract; the patient enters into a contract with the therapist for behavioral change.[22] The emphasis, however, is on what the therapist is to do for the patient; he is to cure the patient.

Group treatment is generally preferred to individual sessions. Patients are not stroked when they display their rackets. Therapists use TA to tell their patients what they see. They attempt to dispel the magic of psychotherapy by sharing their thinking and TA theory with their patients.

The framework of meaning of the Classical School retains Berne's idea that "children are born princes and princesses and their parents *turn* them into frogs." Steiner (following Erikson's terminology) sees the basic position of the infant as one of trust and describes this as the existential position, "I'm OK, You're OK." When the relationship of mutual trust is interrupted, the youngster may decide that he or she is not-OK, or that the other is not-OK, or that neither is OK.[23]

Individuals are seen to have at least partial responsibility for deciding their life script. Dusay (see Chapter Two) notes that Berne said that anything that is decided can be redecided. The therapist's focus of attention is on the Parent in the Child (P_1), which Berne called the "Electrode."[24] However, not all classical transactional analysts rigidly adhere to this position.

Several classical transactional analysts follow Erikson's theory of personality development; others use both Erikson and Piaget (see Chapter Fifteen by Fanita English). Nonorganic psychopathologies are seen as "transactional disturbances" that result from the Child's response to ulterior transactions (injunctions) of parents.[25]

The initial thrust of the Classical School was social psychiatry and included control of P_1 influences, permanent modification of behavior, and cure. Treatment begins with structural analysis and progresses to transactional analysis proper, game analysis, and finally to script analysis.

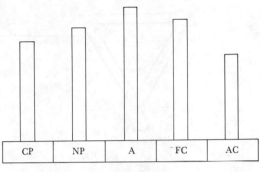

Figure 10
An Egogram

Primary attention is given to the analysis of units of social discourse or action that takes place in the group. Although script analysis is used, the therapist is concerned with what the patient is doing in the here and now rather than with what might be discovered in an archaeological search for the early injunction or decision behind the behavior. Cure takes place when the patient can effectively use the Adult ego state (A_2). This calls for Adult decontamination. For this reason the Parent in the Child (P_1) is given special attention. P_1 is referred to as the Witch Parent not to blame parents but to indicate the nature of its messages and the source of contamination. The patient experiments in the group with new expressions of behavior toward others. Along the way the patient gains new insight into his or her games and scripts and receives positive strokes for thinking creatively about new behavioral options. Therapists use the egogram (Figure 10) to help clients change the internal flow of energy from, for instance, the Adapted Child and Critical Parent to the Free Child and Adult. The Karpman drama triangle (Figure 11) is used to analyze and break up games. Emphasis is placed upon the use of the 3 P's in therapy: Permission, Protection, and Potency.[26] Permission is seen as a specific transaction whereby the therapist gives the patient a command (a Parent-to-Child transaction) backed up by information (an Adult-to-Adult transaction) to free the patient from an early injunction from the patient's parents that is now lodged in the Electrode. Potency is a measure of the therapist's competence. The therapist demonstrates potency with his or her ability to give effectively at the proper moment a permission that is more powerful than the parental voices in the patient's head. The therapist who gives permission without offering sufficient protection acts irresponsibly. Protection is offered by the therapist as the patient accepts the new permission instead of following the parental injunction. For this reason the therapist has to be more potent than the parental voices coming from the patient's Child (P_1).

Autonomy means that an individual is script-free. It is gained by over-

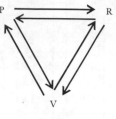

Figure 11
Drama Triangle

coming the harmful programing from parents and society. Autonomy is not only a goal of treatment, it is the goal of life. The issue is how to raise children so they will grow up to be autonomous persons.[27]

Claude Steiner was a key participant in the development of most aspects of basic TA theory. In the late sixties he went far beyond the practice of most transactional analysts and became the founder of the Radical Psychiatry Movement. In 1969 he taught a course on radical psychiatry at the Free University in Berkeley. He considers this one of the decisive events in the development of radical psychiatry. Later the RAP ("Radical Approach to Psychiatry") Center was started to work with people who were confronting various social injustices and to conduct a training program in radical psychiatry. Out of this developed the Berkeley Radical Psychiatry Center.

In 1969 Steiner wrote a pamphlet entitled "The Radical Psychiatry Manifesto" which was distributed by various social action groups at the annual meeting in San Francisco of the American Psychiatric Association. The Manifesto urged psychiatry to "return to its non-medical origins." All competent psychotherapists "should be known as psychiatrists." (Elsewhere Steiner asserts that medical practice is not related to the practice of psychiatry.[28]) Psychiatry is an oppressive institution. It fails to recognize that people's problems are the result of their alienation from others. Psychiatry should encourage the liberation of people. "Personal liberation is only possible along with radical social reforms."[29]

In recent years Steiner has concentrated his work on the theoretical and practical aspects of cooperation as an alternative to oppression, competition, and the abuse of power, especially psychological power. He is concerned about transactional analysts who demonstrate financial immodesty and greediness and who depart from the rigor of scientific understanding and investigation by making TA a business enterprise, a pseudo-religion, or a new form of orthodoxy.

Although Steiner's therapy orientation is classical TA, he seems to place more stress on changing the external problems in the society that negate autonomy than on doing psychotherapy with individuals who are having the problems. Whereas Berne saw TA as a way to help adolescents and adults overcome their history and become free, autonomous people,

Steiner sees TA, combined with the principles of radical psychiatry, as a way to help people overcome the oppressive social context which produced their history. This context creates and is created by the Pig Parent (P_1); it does not give enough warm fuzzies (positive strokes), it encourages competition and power plays, and forces children to give up their natural desires and wants. This Pig Parent element of society leads to stroke deprivation, fears of scarcity, and capitalism. The goal of radical psychiatry is to help people who are alienated change their contexts. When their social situation is changed, then they no longer have to be helped to the same degree by psychotherapy.

In contrast, Martin Groder developed a model that stressed both the need to make psychotherapy available to troubled individuals and to work with them to create a new social situation. Any therapeutic approach, according to Groder, has to give equal emphasis to both the culture and the individual. "I see myself as combining the truly classical TA approach, which shows individuals how to clean up psychologically, take charge of their destiny, and become autonomous, and the Synanon approach which shows a group of individuals how to create and maintain a clean environment."

When Groder began his work in Marion, he was concerned that most psychotherapy programs in prisons did not seem to work. He began an intuitive investigation of the real forces that were operating both among the inmate population and within the authority structure of the institution. The marriage of classical TA with Synanon type therapy provided a combination that was not easily corrupted by the inmates. Synanon provided a context for people different from any of their previous contexts, and through the use of psychotherapy in that context people could reshape their destiny. Groder has discovered that a successful program with inmates has to combine at least three methods of psychotherapy to enable them to give up their destructive scripts and become winners (see Chapter Seven).

The Asklepieion Foundation invites therapists and students into the prison environment to receive training in TA and Asklepieion techniques from the inmates. Kenneth L. Windes, a graduate of the Asklepieion program at Marion and a Teaching Member of the ITAA, describes the group culture of the Asklepieion Foundation in Chapter Eight.

As a result of his work in the prisons, Groder developed techniques for the treatment of character disorders. He is also developing a model for understanding and changing organizations. Another aspect of his work is the clarification of script theory. The following is included from Groder to illustrate his current theory on scripts:

> Each of us has the task each morning to re-create the universe from our central focus and this responsibility is unavoidable. Unfortunately, we tend to be habit-ridden and do the same lousy job of it every morning. This is what scripts are all about. I arbitrarily define seven areas of investigation that usually intersect and interlock with one another in script theory:

1. *Counterscript* is that part of the person's universe which is civilized, that is, adapted to survival in a culture or cultures.
2. *Script Proper* is that part of the person's universe which would be better left unstated, or at least kept secret. It is not necessarily bad but it is something you would not want the neighbors to know right away. The script proper consists of an idiosyncratic set of ideas, decisions, and behaviors that resulted in survival in the family of origin.
3. The *Antiscript* was devised by the rebellious Child and belongs to the demon inside. It is basically related to the highly energetic part of the personality that is pushed away and still very eager to get its day in court, its shot at making up the universe. If the opportunity is given, it will make the universe backwards, inside out, upside down with time running in reverse.
4. The *Episcript* has to do with specific concrete tasks that are handed down to others with a "do it or else" message. It is the incorporation of other people's universes and what they would be doing if they were looking at the task from the universe they had created. The Episcript does not occur in every individual.
5. The current *Plan* is those operational decisions and strategies that are currently in awareness (A_2). These plans need to be reviewed and updated periodically to see how realistic they are (their probability of achievement) and to see how well the actual needs of the Child are being met.
6. The *Non-Script* activities, usually friendships and hobbies, are an important base for expansion of a Script Proper-free stroke economy. Further, Non-Script facilitates coping with the grief and despair of letting go of the strokes and hopes of the Script Proper.
7. The *Center* or Self, described poorly by Berne, is clearly by definition script-free. This center commits itself by decision to the delusional everyday world and has the power to re-create its universe.[30]

THE CATHEXIS SCHOOL   Jacqui Lee Schiff, MSSW, is the founder of the Cathexis School or "The Schiff Family School." Schiff is a Clinical Member, Teaching Member, and member of the Board of Trustees of the International Transactional Analysis Association. In 1974 she and Aaron Schiff, her son, received the Eric Berne Memorial Scientific Award for their development of the passivity material. She is the founder and director of the Cathexis Institute in Oakland, California. She works primarily with young people who have been diagnosed as schizophrenic. In her chapter in this book she shares the work of the Cathexis School.

Schiff's psychological leadership is seen in her rejection of the Freudian and Bernian point of view that "the Parent ego state was irrevocably fixed in the consciousness of mature individuals." She believes that the Parent continues to develop and incorporate new messages or values throughout life. This makes social change possible. She also challenged the establishment's entrenched view of schizophrenia, that it was "hopeless and incurable and probably not accessible to psychotherapy." Schiff is willing to engage in practices that are controversial if she thinks there is any possibility that they will be effective in her work with individuals who have severe emotional disturbances. Her motto is, "There is *no right way* to solve a problem."

The theories and methods developed by the Schiff Family School are widely known. They are used by psychotherapists in Europe, India, Australia, Canada, and the United States.

The work of the Cathexis School takes place in an environment modeled after a family. Schiff is willing to deal with the regressive tendencies and the passivity of persons who are virtually incapacitated. She elicits a transference with her clients (children) and enters into a countertransference to establish a (healthy) symbiotic relationship. "I am as much a part of the symbioses and as vulnerable as any parent," she writes. Nurturing is an integral part of the group culture at Cathexis.

Schiff does not comment on her view of OKness in her chapter. However, she participated recently in a panel on schools of TA and said the following:

> OKness is socially derived. No one is born OK or not-OK. The question of whether one is born OK or not-OK is irrelevant. Between age two and age three, children get a concept of themselves which is derived from social feedback as to whether they are OK or not-OK. What is OK and not-OK has to do with what is developmentally appropriate in the particular culture in which children live. As persons grow older their OKness and not-OKness has to do with whether they are culturally flexible and how they adapt to the demands or changes going on in their culture.

She also explained her views on scripts:

> A script can be either a satisfactory or unsatisfactory life plan, and develops out of a script protocol: early conditioning that influences the various options with which the child approaches the script decision. Games are a reenactment of things that went wrong in relation to the script. If the script is unproductive, the person reenacts the conditions of the original problem and attempts to establish the original symbiosis over and over again. The game players hope that each time they play a game they will find a new option for an old problem.[31]

The unresolved symbiosis from which games originate was not resolved because of some interference with the healthy maturational process. (This is a major difference with other schools of TA.) A racket is an attempt to resolve internal conflicts when the Parent and Adult are in conflict with the Natural or spontaneous reactions of the Child. Pathology occurs at the level of A_2, A_1, or A_0. In a psychosis the conflict is at the level of C_1. (For a description of personality development consistent with this view, see Chapter Six by Jon and Laurie Weiss.)

In the Schiff Family there is a "respectful, goal-oriented cooperation between the patient and the therapist." Parenting of patients was begun in response to a patient's request; "he elicited it." Patients are included in discussions of theory and method. When a patient is unable to assume responsibility, the therapist does. The therapist—and the patient if he or she is thinking clearly—identifies the behaviors that are destructive to an individual. Contracts are not necessary when the patient is involved in issues that are life-threatening.

The goal of psychotherapy is to cure—to rear oversized infants into healthy adults. Schiff says that her goal is to give her clients "a new background experience of symbiotic resolution." The psychotherapist in the Cathexis School takes power and works with the patients and restores their power when the patients can assume responsibility. When the patients are able to function, their autonomy is reinforced.

Major contributions to TA from the Cathexis School include: (1) reparenting, (2) use of touch-stroking, (3) passivity material, and (4) frame-of-reference material. At present the Cathexis School is dealing with the theoretical issue of energy: "TA is a system based on social stimulus and it ought to have a response to Freud's position that energy is always generated internally."[32]

THE REDECISION SCHOOL   Robert L. Goulding, MD, and Mary M. Goulding, MSW, are codirectors of the Western Institute for Group and Family Therapy, Watsonville, California. The Gouldings share the leadership of the Redecision School of TA. Both are Clinical and Teaching Members of the ITAA. In 1975 they were awarded the Eric Berne Memorial Scientific Award for their work on Child redecisions and twelve injunctions. Robert Goulding is president of the American Academy of Psychotherapists. He contributed the chapter for this book on the Redecision School.

John R. McNeel's chapter, "The Seven Components of Redecision Therapy," describes many of the elements of the group culture of the Redecision School as well as aspects of the Gouldings' psychological and effective leadership.

Most of the Gouldings' clients at the Western Institute are psychotherapists who go there for both intensive training and therapy. (Other members of the faculty treat patients from the community.) From the beginning their clients are asked to experience themselves as in charge of their own thinking, feelings, and behavior. They may be confronted when they attempt to play games or get into a racket. Usually when clients play games the Gouldings work with them on their bad feeling payoffs and rackets and use these feelings to get clients in touch with early pathological decisions. They then work with the clients to resolve these decisions.

The Redecision School differs from the other schools on the issue of life scripts. An individual makes a decision as a child in response to injunctions (behaviors and feelings) of his or her parents. The decision was made so the child could survive. Rackets and games are then used to support the early decision. The focus of treatment is on the Little Professor (A_1) rather than on P_1. (P_1 is not seen as an Electrode.) Goulding has discovered three degrees of impasses that relate back to early decisions. He sees phobias as related to early injunctions.

In the case of a suicidal patient, Bob and Mary Goulding do not use the Permission transaction ("Don't"). Rather, they ask the patient, "Will you make a contract not to kill yourself accidentally or on purpose?" They also ask the patient to give himself or herself the necessary permission and protection to experience his or her autonomous potency while working in the treatment sessions. Their work continues with the individual until he or she has made an affirmative life redecision to live. (The initial no-suicide contract with the patient is an Adult decision. A redecision is seen as an emotional, thoughtful, behavioral decision made by the Child and reaffirmed by the total personality.)

The Gouldings' assumption is that games and early-adopted scripts deny autonomy. The emphasis of their work is on the emotional, the intuitive, and the subjective. The focus is on the intrapsychic process. (They do not deny the logical, the intellectual, and the objective, but they use them as outgrowths of the emotional, the intuitive, and the subjective.) They protest any emphasis on the Parent-dominated approach in psychotherapy, because it interferes with the patient's ability to be his own law and decide for himself. Because the patient is responsible, he or she cannot be made to feel by someone else. Hereditary, biological and environmental influences do not excuse the individual from responsibility. Autonomy is a reality to be experienced and is within a person's reach if he or she will but grasp it. The patient is confronted to face choices, make decisions, and accept responsibility for them.

The Gouldings emphasize the power of the patient and de-emphasize the "all knowing" role of the therapist. They do not tell people what to do. They rarely even make suggestions to a client except to "test out both sides of an issue and see what is right for you."

They begin treatment with a contract and work in the present tense. When a client starts talking about her father, Goulding will suggest, "Imagine your father in the room and talk directly to him."

The Gouldings believe that since individuals are brought into the world without their consent and since they are not responsible for their own birth, they do not have to accept the messages from their parents that they are a burden. They encourage their clients to stop experiencing themselves as powerless and to take responsibility for their own lives. "I'm OK, You're OK" is the only real life position. The other positions are fantasies that people experience as real. The goal of therapy is to help individuals become what they really are.

A TASK FOR THE FUTURE   Groder noted in 1974 that the clinical development of TA is virtually complete:

> TA has increasingly moved from being a theory and practice of social psychiatry to being a particular branch of psychotherapy. . . . I have become convinced that TA is rapidly approaching a peak of integration in the area of individual psychology. We have now, in a convincing way, demonstrated rapid and efficient methods of training masses of competent, ethical clini-

cians, efficient treatment for most psychological problems and, importantly, cures for some selected cases of schizophrenia and psychopathy. There are probably not more than a few years left until the integration is fairly well worked out. The picture straighteners, however, will, I am sure, continue to spend many happy years at their trade.

But transactional analysts are urged to retranslate TA back into a social psychiatry:

> If TA is to continue to have the impact on general affairs that it appears to now be having, finally, on psychotherapy, we shall need to retranslate it back into a social psychiatry. TA has the potential to be a curative and comprehensive system for understanding, dealing with, and maximizing the goodness, sense and fun of people, and their organizational contexts. This effort will need to come from an organizational base quite different from that of the private office practice of psychotherapy or even the training institute or professional communes.[33]

Dusay notes in Chapter Two that social movements have arisen in TA to deal with oppressive institutions. The task, however, of integrating theoretical and practical aspects of personal autonomy with social justice remains.

Models have been developed for the use of TA in organizations and various institutions (the Asklepieion Foundation), for the use of TA to create alternative institutions, including new large extended "families" (the Schiff Family), and for the use of TA to confront oppression in organizations (the Radical Psychiatry Movement). Models are needed for working with people who are not in institutions or who do not need alternative social structures but who are also alienated from themselves, from others, and from nature. TA has opened up the possibility and availability of psychotherapy to many who probably would not have sought out traditional forms of psychotherapy. These clients deserve more from TA than what they could have received from traditional psychotherapy.

A task for the future is to find a nexus between psychotherapy and social justice, and to explore how the institutions and profession of psychotherapy, especially the discipline of TA, can reduce the impersonal forces that contribute to destructive personal experiences, alienation, and human oppression. Psychotherapy that does not enhance awareness of the pathological aspects of economic, national and social groups encourages a distorted view of reality. But psychotherapy must do more than enhance awareness. People also need help in finding ways to influence the policies and actions of the major institutions that encroach upon their lives daily. Many workers are alienated from the means of production or from the instruments they use to carry out their work. Transactional analysts need to find tools to help workers tap their spiritual and emotional resources for the creative enjoyment of life instead of being driven by a compulsion to work, or a compulsion to engage in commercially prefabricated leisure activities.

This future task for transactional analysts will require the creation of new forms of group culture. It is legitimate in group treatment to deal with personal and interpersonal problems both in response to what happens in the group and to accounts from clients of their experiences outside the group. Two additional activities also seem legitimate. Group treatment needs to help clients attain aesthetic fulfillment. Psychotherapy as an art as well as a science can include cultural enrichment without doing violence to its purpose. Art and music are already used by some therapists to expose their clients to these formal expressions of human emotions that enable them to explore new options for feelings and to gain appreciation for diverse cultural expressions of transcendence.

Treatment groups also need to provide opportunities for social action that include options for clients to experiment with different forms of problem-solving behavior. Participants in treatment groups could be invited to develop a group contract to change some aspect of an organization or to influence community issues as well as to work on their personal treatment contracts. Members of the group could agree to remain together long enough to complete a mutually agreed upon activity that would involve the group in eliminating some form of institutional or social oppression. The group could decide by consensus what social problem they wanted to solve. They could also decide what actions they would take, what activities each member would engage in, and how long they would devote themselves to the problem. At each meeting members of the group could spend part of their time working on their personal and interpersonal problems and part of their time on their joint project. Each member of the group could also be encouraged to participate as an autonomous citizen in a *controversial* voluntary association actively concerned with issues of social justice. This could be done without neglecting each group member's peculiar needs and problems, including somatic difficulties, unresolved script issues, unpleasant relationships with family and associates, and vocational or professional problems. Although this proposal may appear radical, these activities do not seem radical when compared with what that courageous physician did years ago when he invited patients to lie on a couch and say anything that came to their mind, or when compared with what that brave psychoanalyst did later when he invited most of his patients to get up off the couch and join a therapy group.

A new group etiquette is called for if transactional analysis is to assume a responsible role in society. A framework of meaning that begins with one's essential OKness offers possibilities for expansion of the concept not only to involve the *Other* but also the *We,* the *They,* and the *It* (for an original discussion of this concept see Chapter Ten). TA is built on the premise that all members of the human race have the fundamental right to be the masters of their own destiny and not its objects. People are autonomous and in control of their destiny to the extent that they intuit themselves in a world that they have created.

Models of behavior that are informed by social ethics as well as the

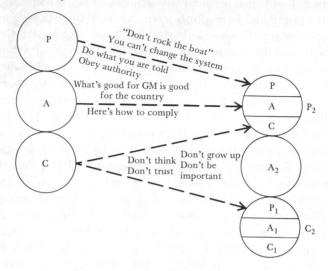

Many messages are communicated from one generation to another that encourage political passivity.

Figure 12
Political Passivity Matrix

discoveries of social scientists are also needed. Many patients (and therapists) have not incorporated principles of social ethics in their Parent ego state (Figure 12). They need to be taught social concerns that may have been neglected by their cultural traditions. Parenting through persuasion and influence appears to be a legitimate role for therapists when it is done explicitly. By doing this therapists consciously accept their responsibility to transmit and transform the best of the culture and to critique cultural scripts that breed privatization and political quietism and that leave incipient totalitarian forces unchecked.[34]

Issues such as coercion, power, and conflict require special attention. Groups and organizations by their very nature do not have the capacity that their individual members have in their personal relationships to control demonic influences and to comprehend and respond to human needs. Large groups and organizations tend to be coercive and to be dominated by a few individuals who often seek to impose their will upon others. Nor do institutions yield power voluntarily. Power has to be challenged by power.[35] Consequently, conflict is inevitable and it has both positive and negative elements. Both of these elements of social conflict are essential for the persistence of group life.[36] Transactional analysts generally work effectively with their clients to help them gain their power to resolve intrapsychic conflicts between their script and their natural needs and wants. They often help their clients use interpersonal power as a basis for the healthy growth of a relationship. Therapists also need to look for effective and ethical ways to extend their work to enable groups of people to use their power to confront and change oppressive institutions.

It seems worth noting in this context that Berne did not see psychotherapy as an end in itself, but as a tool to better living.[37] In 1969 he wrote that transactional analysis is "sufficiently well established to undertake one, or even two crusades. . . ." "It is the fashion among psychotherapists to disclaim moral judgments, but this does not sit well with all of us. There must be *something* worth fighting for." He suggested that the "first crusade is against The Four Horsemen, War, Pestilence, Famine, and Death, which no matter how much they may ennoble the characters of those who survive them, are nevertheless bad because they increase the infant mortality rate." The second crusade proposed by Berne "is against the Fifth Horseman of the Apocalypse, Bare Walls in our Social Agencies, and its slogan is that no room or cubicle in any social agency should be without at least two art works on its walls." Rather playfully he envisioned a decrease in "the infant mortality rate among the clients of those social agencies" meeting this demand.[38]

To complete the development of a more responsible role for transactional analysis, its technical culture needs to be changed. Transactional analysis developed within the matrix of social psychiatry. It still has the potential to become a viable form of social psychotherapy. Transactional analysis has the potential to offer a radical critique of culture. It can help overturn heteronomous social structures that contribute to estrangement to the point where people lose touch with reality.

TA has at least three tools that will probably be invaluable in the development of its new technical culture and in the creation of a synthesis of autonomy and social change. Game analysis helps people to become aware of and predict their destructive behavioral patterns and then, if they choose, to modify them. The script matrix diagram (which includes the ego states of each person in the matrix) shows how individuals reflect what the culture has given them, how they have become persons in their transactions with other persons, and how they have used their power to react to these stimuli by deliberation and decision (Figure 13). Treatment contracts provide a tool whereby people can specify the social as well as the personal problems they want to solve.[39]

Most teachers of TA therapists have developed training programs that place emphasis upon both the personal and professional growth of transactional analysts. As with most other training programs in psychotherapy, however, not many TA training programs have shown concern for the development of the social responsibility of transactional analysts. Unless this trend changes, future transactional analysts could become specialists with their "minds in a groove" (Whitehead), lacking sensitivity to the idea of compassion and to the principle of social justice.

This calls for new models for training transactional analysts. Psycho-

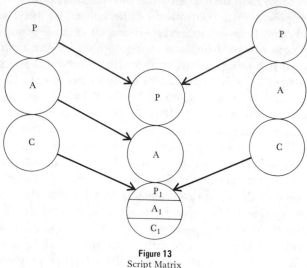

Figure 13
Script Matrix

therapists need to be trained, on the one hand, to assist people with personal exploration and change that lead to increased awareness of social injustices which demand to be corrected lest they render personal exploration and growth worthless. On the other hand, psychotherapists need to learn how to help people participate as citizens in solving social problems such as poverty, racism, sexism, and environmental damage. This will require an understanding of the pathology of groups, institutions and cultures, including possibilities of thermonuclear war, collapse of cities, world starvation and famines, infant mortality rates, and totalitarianism on a global scale. Such training will encourage the development of a new breed of transactional analysts.

The commitment in TA to the scientific method has produced simple, yet fairly reliable, models for predicting and changing the behavior of individuals and small groups. As transactional analysts muster the courage to devise models to make organizations and institutions more responsive to human needs, they must keep in mind that TA is an endeavor to bring about personal, aesthetic, and communal fulfillment.

References

1. Robert L. Goulding, "Four Models of Transactional Analysis," *International Journal of Group Psychotherapy, 26* no. 3 (July, 1976), pp. 385–392.
2. Eric Berne, *The Structure and Dynamics of Organizations and Groups,* Philadelphia, J. B. Lippincott Co., 1963.
3. Max Weber, *The Theory of Social and Economic Organization,* New York, The Free Press, 1964, pp. 358–364.

4. Thomas F. O'Dea, *The Sociology of Religion,* Englewood Cliffs, New Jersey, Prentice-Hall, 1966.

5. Stephen B. Karpman, "The Bias Box for Competing Psychotherapies," *Transactional Analysis, 5,* no. 2 (April, 1975), pp. 107–116, offers some helpful models for the integration of various psychotherapeutic approaches. See also, Richard Gordon Erskine, "The ABC's of Effective Psychotherapy," *Transactional Analysis Journal, 5,* no. 2 (April, 1975), pp. 163–165, for a discussion of the affective, behavioral and cognitive approaches of various psychotherapies. Erskine notes that TA incorporates all three approaches.

6. Eric Berne, "Organizational History of the SFSPS," *Transactional Analysis Bulletin, 2,* no. 5 (January, 1963), p. 45.

7. Berne, *Structure and Dynamics;* Talcott Parsons, "An Outline of the Social System," in Talcott Parsons, *et al.,* eds., *Theories of Society,* New York, The Free Press, 1965, pp. 30–79.

8. William I. Thomas, "The Four Wishes and the Definition of the Situation," in Talcott Parsons, *et al.,* eds., *Theories of Society,* New York, The Free Press, 1965, pp. 741–744.

9. Eric Berne, *Games People Play,* New York, Grove Press, 1964.

10. Walter Kaufmann, *Without Guilt and Justice,* New York, Peter H. Wyden, Inc., 1973.

11. *Ibid.,* p. 16

12. Stephen B. Karpman, "Fairy Tales and Script Drama Analysis," *Transactional Analysis Bulletin, 7,* no. 26 (April, 1968), pp. 39–43; and "Options," *Transactional Analysis Journal, 1,* no. 1 (January, 1971), pp. 79–87.

13. Claude Steiner, *Games Alcoholics Play,* New York, Grove Press, 1971; and *Scripts People Live,* New York, Grove Press, 1974.

14. Muriel James and Dorothy Jongeward, *Born To Win,* Reading, Addison-Wesley Publishing Company, 1971. This is a basic introduction to TA and is recommended and used by most teachers of TA. The reader is referred to the following works by Muriel James: *Born To Love,* Reading, Addison-Wesley Publishing Company, 1973; *What Do You Do With Them Now That You've Got Them?,* Reading, Addison-Wesley Publishing Company, 1974; *The OK Boss,* Reading, Addison-Wesley Publishing Company, 1975; and with Louis M. Savary, *The Power at the Bottom of the Well,* New York, Harper & Row, 1974; and *The Heart of Friendship,* New York, Harper & Row, 1976.

15. Franklin H. Ernst, Jr., *Who's Listening?,* Vallejo, California, Addresso'set, 1973; and "The OK Corral: The Grid for Get-On-With," *Transactional Analysis Journal, 1,* no. 4 (October, 1971), pp. 321–340.

16. Dorothy Jongeward's major contributions to TA have been in its non-clinical application, though most of her discussion of theory is relevant to the clinical practitioner as well. In addition to *Born To Win, op. cit.,* see *Everybody Wins: Transactional Analysis Applied to Organizations,* Reading, Addison-Wesley Publishing Company, 1973; and with Dru Scott, *Affirmative Action for Women: A Practical Guide,* Reading, Addison-Wesley Publishing Company, 1974.

17. K. Hedges Capers, "Spurious and Authentic Stroking," *Transactional Analysis Bulletin, 6,* no. 24 (October, 1967), p. 104.

18. Pam Levin, *Becoming The Way We Are,* San Francisco, Trans Pubs, 1974.

19. Pat Crossman, "Permission and Protection," *Transactional Analysis Bulletin,* 5, no. 19 (July, 1966), pp. 152–154; and "Position and Smiling," *Transactional Analysis Bulletin, 6,* no. 23 (July, 1967), pp. 72–73.

20. Solon D. Samuels, "Games Therapists Play," *Transactional Analysis Journal, 1,* no. 1 (January, 1971), pp. 95–99.

21. Morris L. Haimowitz and Natalie R. Haimowitz, *Suffering Is Optional,* Evanston, Haimowoods Press, 1976; and Chapter 44, "Introduction to Transactional Analysis," in Haimowitz and Haimowitz, eds., *Human Development,* New York, Thomas Y. Crowell Company, 1973, pp. 318–352.

22. Steiner, *Games Alcoholics Play, op. cit.,* p. 159.

23. Steiner, *ibid.,* p. 36; Steiner, *Scripts People Live, op. cit.,* pp. 71*ff.*

24. Eric Berne, *What Do You Say After You Say Hello?,* New York, Grove Press, 1972, pp. 115–116.

25. Steiner, *Games Alcoholics Play, op. cit.,* p. 158.

26. Steiner, *ibid.,* pp. 143–155; Steiner, *Scripts People Live, op. cit.,* pp. 258–269.

27. Steiner, *ibid.,* pp. 303–309; see especially ten rules for raising children for autonomy, pp. 308–309.

28. Steiner, *ibid.,* pp. 233–234.

29. Claude Steiner, *et al., Readings in Radical Psychiatry,* New York, Grove Press, 1975, pp. 3–6.

30. Martin Groder, Participant on panel, "Schools of Transactional Analysis," Third Annual Spring Conference of the Southeast Institute (March, 1976).

31. Jacqui Lee Schiff, Participant on panel, "Schools of Transactional Analysis," Third Annual Spring Conference of the Southeast Institute (March, 1976).

32. Schiff, *op. cit.*

33. Martin Groder, "Editorial," *Transactional Analysis Journal, 4,* no. 4 (October, 1974), p. 6.

34. Hans H. Strupp, *Psychotherapy: Clinical, Research, and Theoretical Issues,* New York, Jason Aronson, Inc., 1973, notes that psychotherapists indoctrinate patients with both their personal values and those of the society whether they intend to or not. Seymour L. Halleck, *The Politics of Therapy,* New York, Science House Inc., 1971, is required reading for all therapists who want to be informed on these matters. James Luther Adams, "The Political Responsibility of the Man of Culture," *Comprendre,* no. 16 (1956), gives consideration to "the social forms by means of which the man of culture, as well as other citizens, translates the consciousness of political responsibility into objective reality." This work is relevant to psychotherapists as is his essay, "Social Ethics and Pastoral Care," in James Luther Adams and Seward Hiltner, eds., *Pastoral Care In The Liberal Churches,* Nashville, Abingdon Press, 1970, pp. 174–220. Social psychiatrists will appreciate his call for the joint advancement of sociotherapy and psychotherapy; his aphorism explains the connection: "Every personal problem is a social problem, and every social problem is a personal problem."

35. The classic discussion of the differences between individual and group morality is by Reinhold Niebuhr, *Moral Man and Immoral Society,* New York, Charles Scribner's Sons, 1932.

36. See Lewis A. Coser, *The Functions of Social Conflict,* New York, Free Press, 1956, for the positive as well as the negative elements of social conflict.

37. Eric Berne, *Principles of Group Treatment,* New York, Grove Press, 1967, p. 359.

38. Eric Berne, "Editor's Page," *Transactional Analysis Bulletin, 8,* no. 29 (January, 1969), pp. 7–8.

39. My booklet on problem-solving lends itself to helping clients formulate contracts for both personal and social change, *Steps for Developing and Implementing Problem-Solving Contracts,* Chapel Hill, Southeast Institute, 1974; San Francisco, TA Press, 1977.

TWO

THE EVOLUTION
OF TRANSACTIONAL ANALYSIS
John M. Dusay

A simple, yet literal definition of transactional analysis is: TA is an analysis of the transactions that go on between human beings who are interacting with each other. Eric Berne, the originator of TA, spent long hours in his early groups and in his consulting room watching what people do and say to one another. From these beginnings TA has developed into a complete system of psychotherapy which actively incorporates useful techniques for facilitating human growth and change. Because TA is now a total theory of personality, it explains why people differ from one another and why they behave the way they do with each other. TA has become ensconced in a vast organization, the International Transactional Analysis Association, which is comprised of educational and professional leaders. The ITAA's membership is dedicated to practicing, strengthening, and furthering the aims of its theory and its techniques. Persons who are effectively practicing and teaching TA generally exhibit a lively, inquisitive spirit and a professional attitude.

AN HISTORICAL PERSPECTIVE

From the beginning TA has been continually developed, researched, and expanded. It would have become old and decrepit if its devotees had staunchly defended its earlier phases as being the final product. Instead, TA's process of growth and challenge lives on, with the viable older ideas providing the necessary foundation of stability and substance to both theory and practice. I have found it difficult to define "classical" or "orthodox" transactional analysis, and have resolved this by entitling the early beginning phases of TA as "classical." These initial phases comprise a vital part of the total TA movement, and they include the early discoveries and vigorous thinking of the San Francisco school during the 1960s. Although most major components of TA theory were derived then, virtually no one practices TA as it was practiced during its conception. TA has taken diverse directions since then, and it is continually being honed and polished.

The Eric Berne Memorial Scientific Awards were designed to commemorate outstanding contributions and innovative thinking in the field of TA, and they have been presented to worthy recipients of the International Transactional Analysis Association. The first three awards were presented to members of Dr. Eric Berne's inner circle, three of the original pioneers of TA theory. Claude Steiner received the first award for his work with the script matrix; Stephen Karpman acquired the second one for the drama triangle; and I was given the third award for the egogram. Although influenced by the San Francisco Seminars, the following recipients did their major work outside of the Berne milieu: Jacqui and Aaron Schiff, who received the fourth award for their discoveries on passivity confrontation and the four discounts; and Mary and Robert Goulding, given the fifth award for their contributions on childhood decisions and redecisions.

Many popular, contemporary TA authors such as Muriel James and Thomas Harris were influenced by the early San Francisco Seminars, as well as by Eric Berne himself. Some of the original pioneers of TA theory still attend and contribute to the San Francisco Seminars (now called the Eric Berne Seminars of San Francisco). This seminar continues its tradition of weekly Tuesday night meetings and has continued to meet regularly for the past eighteen consecutive years; it has the distinction of being the longest ongoing seminar about group psychotherapy in the world.

During the past five years, my own personal approach to the practice of transactional analysis has developed in a rewarding way. I have continued to synthesize new observations from my clinical practice and combine them with new techniques. In addition, I have incorporated techniques from both Moreno's psychodrama and from Perls' gestalt methods. Other TA therapists develop and formulate personal techniques for themselves which enhance their styles of therapy and can be incorporated into the body of TA theory.

FUNCTIONAL ANALYSIS

Throughout this brief history of the development of transactional analysis, I will emphasize my personal approach to TA at the time of this writing. This is meant to imply that my own methods will continue to grow and change, while being solidly based upon the early theoretical foundations. At this time I am focusing on the *functional* aspects of ego states rather than on their *structural* properties. I have chosen the term "functional analysis" to describe both one's personality forces and the way one's psychological energy shifts between the different ego states. Berne titled his own study of ego states "structural analysis," and he depicted the action between ego states by the well-known arrows or vectors that illustrated the transactions. Both structural analysis and functional analysis maintain different, although valid positions of distinction in TA theory.

Functional analysis became possible only because of the evolution of TA theory. A major criticism of TA in the past, especially the decade of the 1960s, was that it appealed only to the intellectual faculties and that it ignored the emotional or feeling aspects. This may have been an appropriate criticism ten years ago; however, TA has continued to appeal to persons' emotional development by utilizing concepts from the action, growth, and behavior schools of therapy. Observing today's TA practitioners at work, one can readily feel the focus on emotions.

Medically oriented readers can quickly understand the difference between structural analysis and functional analysis by comparing it to the dichotomy between human anatomy and human physiology. Anatomy is concerned with the basic building blocks of the human body, such as the heart muscles; physiology is concerned with the life processes, such as the blood's flow and action. Anatomy and physiology are interdependent; there is neither function without structure, nor structure without function.

The visual symbol of my work is the *egogram*. Visual symbols have been an integral part in the development of TA, in that they provide an observable and symbolic shorthand of what is happening. Symbols are far from being mere gimmicks; they imply that the user is making a definite commitment to understanding his or her own situation and also that he or she is responsible for what he or she is saying. A diagram can clearly be seen by others and it does not become lost in clouds of mystic verbosity. A symbol quickly "hooks" the thinking properties of the Adult. Both therapist and client realize that they are accountable for their positions. I contend that any future breakthrough in TA will be accompanied by either a new symbol or by an old symbol which is used in a new and creative manner.

I was intimately involved with Eric Berne and remember his oft-repeated question, "Does this work to get my patients better faster?" Berne's rhetorical question emphasized his continual quest for treatment aids that would enable his patients to get better. I will present my approach to TA in the form of an historical synopsis in which I identify the four primary phases that TA has undergone, all of which adhere to Berne's admonition. The first and second phases are viewed as the traditional foundations of TA; the third and fourth phases encompass further dramatic advances. Because most of my own ideas and contributions have evolved directly from my clinical practice, I will use an actual, but camouflaged, case presentation to illustrate the evolution of TA. Daisy will be taken through the four phases of TA, and she will serve as the clinical prototype.

FIRST PHASE: EGO STATES (1955–1962)*

Daisy, a bright, bubbly, pretty 27-year-old woman, acted quite confused during her appointment. She asked me, "Is this the right day and time

---

* Dates of the phases are approximate with some overlap.

for my appointment?" As I was confirming that it was, she interrupted me and said, "Is this the right place?" I nodded my affirmation and Daisy, still looking bewildered, proceeded to tell me that she was a frustrated professional actress who was relegated to "bit" parts. She felt that people did not take either her or her talents seriously. She confessed that she usually felt slighted in both her social and private life. Neither her ex-husband nor her current boyfriends took her seriously. Daisy whined that she felt like a dumb child who couldn't get what she wanted. She continued to speak in a helpless, little-girl voice and threw me occasional furtive glances which seemed to be aimed at eliciting my approval. I observed her to be behaving like a helpless, tearful child. At the same time, Daisy was providing me with some logical data about how others viewed her. She had demonstrated her thinking abilities by finding my office on the right day and time, yet she continued to ask me "dumb" little-girl questions, to which she obviously knew the answers. My encounter with Daisy reminded me of Eric Berne's cowboy story, which has become a classic in TA literature.

In the mid-1950s, Berne was treating a patient with an excessive gambling habit. His patient used both a logical system and a superstitious system to increase his chances at the Nevada gambling casinos. His superstitions took the form of many rituals: he would take meticulous showers at his hotel after winning streaks; he carefully avoided stepping on the sidewalk cracks as he walked between the casinos; and he would employ a peculiar rationale to explain his losses. If he lost $50, he would say that since he brought $100 to gamble with and only lost $50, he was therefore $50 ahead. However, his everyday logical thinking was entirely different from his superstitious thinking, and it was this dichotomy that led Berne to a dramatic revelation in a later session with this patient. During this session, the patient recalled an incident that happened to him when he was a boy of eight. He remembered vacationing with his parents at a dude ranch and being all dressed up in a cowboy outfit. As he was helping a real cowboy unsaddle a horse, the cowboy looked at him and said, "Why, thanks, cowpoke!" The patient answered, "I'm not really a cowpoke; I'm just a little boy." The patient had then looked at Berne and said, "That's just the way I feel now. Sometimes I feel like I'm not really a lawyer; I'm just a little boy." To Berne it was evident that his patient was employing two types of thinking in his everyday life. One was the effective, logical system that he used in his successful law practice, and the other was a nonrational system that was more appropriate for a little boy. This system involved avoiding cracks, taking showers, and using unusual arithmetic formulas that changed his losses into gains.[1] One personality state dealt with his business functions, and the other dealt with his fantasies. Both Berne and his patient could see that these two distinct behavior patterns were phenomena that could be readily identified by voice tones and facial expressions.

Berne labeled each of these phenomena an ego state. Each state portrayed a distinct, conscious way of thinking, feeling, and behaving. The logical,

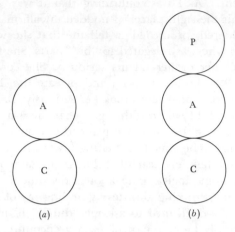

Figure 1

rational part was analogous to "grown-up" thinking, and Berne called this the Adult ego state. The other was creative and childlike, and Berne symbolized this one as the Child ego state. In order to show that each ego state was separate, complete, and total, Berne drew a circle around each one (Figure 1a). It wasn't until later that the Parent ego state was delineated, thus completing the three ego states that constitute the total personality (Figure 1b).

Berne was primarily concerned with the boundaries that separated each of the three ego states; he was less involved with the amount of energy which would emanate from each of them. Berne primarily focused upon the structure of ego states. Briefly, Berne in 1961 made a reference to ego-state energy in his discussion about the monkey on the tree.[2] Berne probably remained with the structural aspects because of his scientific background and his formal medical training. Some of Berne's associates considered him to be too intellectual, too thinking, and too Adult. However, I consider Berne's detailed and well-thought-out contributions to be the most significant in the entire field of psychotherapy and psychological theory in this century. Berne's childlike and inquisitive probing have catalyzed both the feeling and action approaches. The merger of thinking and feeling can be easily observed by contemporary transactional analysts.

If I had applied early structural TA with Daisy, I woud have encouraged her to separate her Adult ego state from her Child ego state. For example, her Adult consulted with me as the doctor, and her Child ego state naively asked me about the date and time. This first phase of TA occurred with the discovery of separate and distinct ego states.

SECOND PHASE: TRANSACTIONS AND GAMES (1962–1966)

During the 1950s, Berne was influenced by the cyberneticists, including Alfred Korzybski and Norbert Weiner. Throughout the 1960s, Berne encouraged semanticists and systems theorists to give presentations at the San Francisco Transactional Analysis Seminar. During this period, Berne actively explored the various communication theories. In essence, there are two basic types of communications—the latent and the manifest. A radio exhibits both types of communications. When it is turned on, the manifest communication (i.e., the six o'clock news) is delivered; the other type of communication—the latent—is embodied in the pops, whirrs, static, and other sounds which reflect the mechanical workings of the radio rather than the messages and music being transmitted. A whirr or a pop may indicate that a tube is burning out. Berne observed two types of communications in humans as well. After he delineated the three separate ego states and combined them with his knowledge of cybernetics, he was able to apply this information to the two different levels of communication that humans frequently share with one another. He represented these duplex transactions with corresponding solid and dotted-line vectors. The solid line revealed the verbal social message; the dotted line indicated the hidden nonverbal message (Figure 2).

On a verbal level, Daisy transacted with the therapist mostly by using her Adult ego state. However, in a hidden, psychological way, her little girl (Child) asked the doctor for reassurance as well as a confirmation that she couldn't think. If Daisy and the doctor had continued to follow an orderly series of transactions along with the corresponding double levels of meanings, they would eventually be entitled to receive their psychological payoffs. Daisy could have ended up feeling stupid, inadequate, and discounted. The therapist could have felt like either a rescuer or a wise doctor who would save a "poor damsel in distress." Instead, Daisy's game of *Stupid* was interrupted. Many psychological games have been identified according to their payoffs and they follow the same basic paradigm. Berne and the early transactional analysts identified, studied, and classified

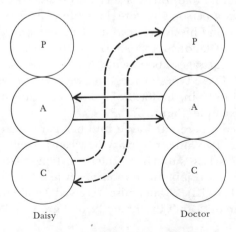

Figure 2
A Game Diagram

games* throughout the mid-1960s, and transactional analysis was publicly introduced to the world through the best-selling book *Games People Play* in 1964.

The first two phases of TA—ego-state structural analysis and the duplex transactions of games—covered a ten-year span and attracted the general public and the mental-health professionals alike. These early phases of TA gave rise to the inception of TA seminars and TA therapist training groups throughout the world. In 1964, the International Transactional Analysis Association itself was formed as an offshoot of the early San Francisco Social Psychiatry Seminars, and the name of these was changed to the San Francisco Transactional Analysis Seminars and finally to the Eric Berne Seminars of San Francisco after Berne's death in 1970.

Because the initial mode of early TA treatment was based primarily on thinking rather than feeling, the therapist and the patient would diagnose and separate out the different ego states by using the "Martian" position. One would stand "outside oneself" and observe oneself interacting with others. (This may be likened to Theodore Reik's "listening with the third ear.") By both awareness (diagnosis) and analysis (transactional analysis), one could gain personal insight into oneself, break off games, and attain a better level of social control. During the third phase, the thinking aspects remained but there was a definite shift to the feeling aspect as well.

THIRD PHASE: SCRIPT ANALYSIS (1966–1970)

TA's third phase began in earnest when transactional analysts began to explore why different persons choose various games to play, and why they exhibit specific types of personalities. How did Daisy acquire her unique personality and why did she choose *Stupid* as her favorite game? To answer such questions, attention was focused on *scripts*. Berne initially defined the script as a person's unconscious life plan. However, during the third phase Berne and his associates found a more workable and practical definition through Claude Steiner's script matrix. Daisy, for instance, had received parental messages about what her behavior should be since she was a small girl. These types of messages were viewed as the *Values*. She was told how not to be in the form of *Don'ts,* and shown How to grow up by her parents' example (Figure 3).

Daisy was given a Parental Value into her Parent ego state and this is labeled the Value (I). Values may vary between persons; Daisy's value was a standard middle-class, suburban American type—"Go to college, make good grades, get a good job, make money, get married, and have two children (a boy and a girl)." Daisy also received Don't messages from her father in the form of "Don't think and "Don't grow up" (II). Daisy looked

---

* In addition to the ulterior or dual-level transactions, other types were defined and found to be useful in the science of human communication.

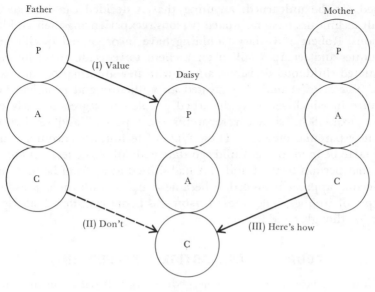

Figure 3
Daisy's Script Matrix

to her childlike, helpless mother for assistance on how she could achieve all of this. Daisy's mother was helpful in showing her how to act stupid by dropping dishes, asking dumb questions, and looking helpless around her husband (III). These three aspects, the Value, the Don't Injunction, and the Here's How comprise the vital elements of a person's script. The script matrix explains where each individual's personality is derived from and why the person acts and interacts the way he or she does. Life scripts are an orderly and well-defined series of transactions between parents and their children throughout the generations.

Between 1966 and the time of Eric Berne's death in 1970, there was much excitement about scripts and script theory. Minute details about life scripts were filled in, connections to fairy tales and myths were explored, and the various types of Parental injunctions were outlined. Several script check lists were compiled, and Berne himself devised an elaborate one in his final book, *What Do You Say After You Say Hello?*

Script analysis provided a vast new method for enabling people to experience their feelings. While there is detail and intellectual work still to be done in script analysis, some exciting new experimental techniques were developed. Reversing of clients' life scripts took the direction of the person reexperiencing his or her Child ego state. The implication was that the client had at least partial responsibility for deciding his own script and life plan. The Child part of each person was bombarded with Parental Values and Injunctions throughout his early development. Some children may have rejected certain messages and others may have decided to "buy into" them. Long ago Berne had stated that anything that is learned can be unlearned; anything that is decided can be redecided. Gestalt techniques have facilitated persons reexperiencing their childhood decisions. Robert and Mary Goulding have incorporated specific gestalt techniques and set up a milieu for a client to redecide about his earlier antiquated childhood decisions, armed with new information and experiences. The Schiff Family has created an authentic and complete family structure in which seriously disturbed people can regress to early childhood. Jacqui Schiff actually reparents these persons and reraises them with new parental messages. These types of techniques encourage the individual to be in his or her Child ego state with all of the feelings and emotions that pertain to the Child. TA had shifted away from being a purely intellectual approach; instead, it became rampant with the expressions of all types of feelings. The whole person was being considered, along with his or her thoughts and feelings.

FOURTH PHASE: ACTION (1970–PRESENT)

The fourth phase of TA has emerged: energy distribution and action. The egogram was created in order to symbolize the amount of energy that a person exudes in each of his or her ego states at any time. After considering his or her egogram, a person becomes clear about what he or she wants to change, raise, lower, or develop in certain ego states. My own intuitive and logical assessment of Daisy's egogram follows (Figure 4).

Daisy's egogram portrays her relative amounts of psychological energy in her ego states; they are the equivalent of a psychological fingerprint, except that they can be changed. An egogram is arrived at in both an intuitive and a scientific manner. Because egograms serve as a map of the personality, treatment contracts are frequently made around them. Daisy said that she wanted a higher Adult ego state. The egogram is highly advantageous when it is constructed in groups, in that it is a valid measurement of how an individual's energies line up. There is usually an 80 to 90 percent agreement about the way a person's egogram lines up when an informed group is constructing it. The egogram is likewise reliable,

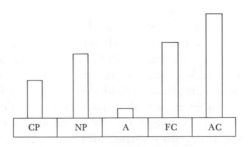

Figure 4
Daisy's Original Egogram

meaning that another informed group will draw the same egogram for that same individual. The egogram is a potent psychological tool which illustrates both consensual validity and reliability.

Daisy's Adapted Child was her highest ego state, and she used it at every opportunity when she came into my office. She acted dumb and giggled frivolously about being stupid and helpless. Daisy also had a tremendous amount of Free Child, and her creativity was evident as she responded quickly and colorfully to questions I asked. Her Critical Parent was low; she seldom complained about other people's faults and she blamed her mishaps on herself in an Adapted Child fashion. Her Nurturing Parent was evident when she told me, "You probably get kind of tired listening to problems like mine." She offered her concern in a genuine and believable manner. The lowest ego state she exerted was her Adult. Although she had a good memory and a quick associative ability, she sabotaged her Adult by playing *Stupid*.* Adult ego state functioning is not equated with a person's IQ measurement. Rather, the Adult is a reflection of how much time and energy a person spends in problem solving and logical assessments. In the Adult area, Daisy lacked commitment, decision, and direction in her thinking. Daisy's total personality composite, or mosaic, is summed up in her egogram, and it reflects the way that the world sees her.

To me, functional treatment is a term that I apply when one shift's one's energies from the "old" characteristic personality, the "status quo," into a more compatible balance, a shift reflected in the successful achievement of a well-chosen contract. The egogram represents both the forces of energy which emanate from the different ego states** and the total amount of energy. When one of the columns goes up, another will therefore come down. This is the simplest statement of the "constancy hypothesis." The constancy hypothesis provides the *growth model* as well as the *medical model* with functional and theoretical bases. Therapists who adhere to the growth model would approach Daisy's problem by encouraging her to raise an underdeveloped part such as her Adult, and they would not concentrate on lowering a high ego state, such as her overdeveloped Adapted Child. The medical-model approach is designed to cut out or remove the pathology, and those who adhere to this approach would work at lowering overdeveloped states, rather than raising the lower ones. Although I was schooled in the medical model, I find that using a combination of both models is advantageous when working with egograms. If Daisy were to raise her Adult at the expense of her Free Child, she would be a more logical person who did adaptive and daffy things. Likewise, if a therapist used only the medical model and encouraged the person to lower the Adapted Child and not raise any other states, one may end up with a client who resembles the "cured" alcoholic who says he is cured

---

* *Stupid* is usually played by people who have a reasonably high IQ.
** This is an *a priori* definition.

of drinking because he takes antabuse.* He feels bored and burned out. When a person has an operation, the pathology is cut out but nothing substantial replaces the pathology. In other words, an effective therapist will employ a discriminate combination of both models in order to arrive at the optimum treatment.

Over the last five years, there has been a veritable cornucopia of techniques devised inside and ouside of the TA family for the purpose of raising various ego states. Deciding which techniques to use can be facilitated by constructing the client's egogram, which will provide a map of what the person wants and needs. Thereby the client and the therapist can avoid haphazard treatment.

Each use of transactional analysis can be view as working at one of these four phases, regardless of the particular techniques or school of thought that the practitioner uses. Some therapists may focus upon action techniques to shift energy, with or without using the egogram as a treatment map. Other practitioners may work with the script itself, others may look to the games which reinforce the scripts, while still others may focus on the structural aspects of the personality. TA is not confined to any one of these areas; there are differences in the ways each therapist may choose to direct his or her attention and energy while still practicing TA. In addition to the historical phases, there has been a corresponding shift in the modes of treatment. With the ego state dealing with issues during the first two phases, the predominant mode was thinking (mainly Adult); with script redecision and reparenting, the mode was feeling (NP and FC). During the fourth phase, the mode is action (low ego state raised).

CLINICAL CONSIDERATIONS

The question arises as to why Daisy has come into treatment in the first place. She, like all other human beings, is a complex individual who has different forces going on inside her. Each and every person has at least a smidgen of each of the five psychological forces that are represented in the egogram. Daisy used her Adult and her Nurturing Parent to bring herself into treatment. However, her Adapted Child was adept at resisting changes in strong, dramatic ways. I differ with Berne's idea that people come into treatment in order to advance their scripts and to play their games better. I disagree with Perls' statement, "Very few people go into therapy to be cured, but rather to improve their neuroses." I believe that many people enter treatment because their lower or weaker parts want to grow, to develop, and to enrich their lives. There is a natural human drive towards health and growth which stimulates persons who are suffering, as well as curious and creative persons who want more for themselves and their lives. The egogram, the constancy hypothesis, and the techniques developed to strengthen personality force areas comprise an energy

---

* A chemical that produces nausea when taken concurrently with alcohol.

model. In my view, the clinical goal in transactional analysis is for the client to experience new and different parts of his or her personality, to develop the weaker areas and, finally, to explode with authentic new action. Authentic contracts between the client and the therapist have this goal in mind.

There are major differences between authentic treatment contracts and pseudocontracts. A pseudocontract may be made over and over again in unenlightened treatment groups, and it may be exemplified by an individual who is highly angry and hostile and who wants to contract with a therapist to become more aggressive toward others. Naturally, this would be an ill-chosen contract, because this person already has a well-developed Critical Parent which will protect him in both a street fight and a group therapy confrontation. A well-chosen, authentic contract for this person would be one which emphasizes *doing something different,* such as raising the weaker parts of his personality—his Nurturing Parent, Free Child, or perhaps his Adult, depending upon what he wanted. If he wanted to have a more lusty and rewarding sexual life, I would see this as a well-chosen, authentic treatment contract. The cognizant therapist will direct appropriate techniques for clients; techniques are dependent upon individual considerations. Correct choosing separates the true professional from both the well-meaning scout master at best and the selfish opportunist at worst. Untrained persons may learn a few clever gimmicks and techniques, then apply them in haphazard and possibly destructive ways, thinking that these techniques will work for everyone. These persons may attempt to mold their clients to make them fit the treatment which the therapist has to offer, rather than finding the appropriate way of handling the clients' needs. Authentic action provides a bridge between what went on in the past and all of what's happening in the present. Authentic change requires authentic action, which is fresh, applicable, and expressed in a well-chosen treatment contract. A hard contract means that a permanent shift in the egogram balance has occurred, and the client has made a script redecision, has abated games, and made a shift on the egogram.

When Daisy regarded her egogram, she said, "I guess I should raise my Adult some because it's so small and I don't think very much." I agreed with her and said that a shift in ego-state energy would be a well-chosen contract. Daisy, looking like a little girl, asked plaintively, "How can I raise my Adult?" I almost answered her question, when I became aware that she was already *slipping* back into her Adapted Child by barraging me with questions. After a few more abortive attempts which were aimed at getting me to do her thinking for her, she tucked in her chin and raised her fluttering eyes up to me in her characteristic little-girl state, began to squirm and said, "I just can't think of anything. Will you please help me?" I reached for a folding chair and placed it upright, about equidistant between us, on the line that went from Daisy's eyes to my own. I invited Daisy to switch to this empty chair, at which time I directly gave her permission to think, using her Adult ego state; and I encouraged her to describe what she saw happening between the two of us. Daisy sat up straight, stopped squirming, and looked thoughtful. I was not expecting Daisy to have a breakthrough of some great awareness; rather, I was hoping that she would experience as well as utilize her Adult ego state. This type of situation is the essence of an energy shift. For Daisy, the actual exercising of her Adult ego state is more important than answering questions correctly, because once the weak parts become strong, the person is finally able to handle new situations, both inside or outside the therapy room.

Raising the Adult ego state was applicable only for Daisy in this situation, as it is for others who have low Adult ego states. Many people who consult with me have plenty of Adult or even too much, which may cause them to be accurate but rather boring as well. Too much Adult at a cocktail party is not in demand. There are innumerable techniques for raising each ego state. Suicidal persons with low Free Child ego states are encouraged to strengthen their Free Child so that their spirits will be encouraged. Blemish players often have low Nurturing Parent and they are actively encouraged to nurture both the therapist and themselves. Impotent men and pushover women can profit by raising their Critical Parent. Those who are experiencing blocks in forming human relationships because of poor abilities to compromise with others are encouraged to strengthen their Adapted Child. Having people strengthen their weak parts is called *redirection* of energies, which means a shifting of attention to the underdeveloped ego states. Persons are given permission to exercise their newly developing skill in the "here and now" of the therapy group. My position as a therapist is not to use my energy in supplying all the answers, or even to consider that "great" answers are important. Rather, I am an interruptor of a client's habitual behavior patterns. Interruption is one of the more important functions of treatment; I am also a catalyzer of the new and adventuresome uses of ego-state energy that the person is developing. A particularly useful technique in raising a weak ego state is to have the client oppose the weak force with another.

When Daisy was trying to involve the group members in her game of *Stupid,* I had her choose two people: one to play the role of herself and the other to play the role of her favorite partner in the game, the doctor. I asked her to be the director of her own psychodrama, TA style—an excellent Adult facilitator technique. She was directed to coach these two individuals on how to play her as she usually behaved in ordinary life, and how to play the therapist. Her directing facilitated her ability to look at herself to the extent that she instructed others how to behave exactly as she and the doctor did. Once this had happened, she was told to have the person playing her act differently under her direction. In essence, she used her Adult ego state to outline and then show different behaviors for herself. She later mentioned that she had never experienced more excitement than when she was actually directing and redirecting her own psychodrama. Daisy had taken charge, and she told the actors how to behave, what facial and bodily expressions to use, when to inflect certain words, and how to behave just like her. She then set up actual situations from her own life and had them turn out the way she wanted. Since Daisy's Adult ego state was her lowest, she used specific exercises that would strengthen it. Now she was able to redirect her own life, long after the group was over.

Daisy and I contracted to work with her "flabby" undernourished Adult. Her situation can be compared to that of a weak person who yearns to have big strong biceps. The person initially begins by flexing his arms several times until he get the feel of doing something new. Although he may be uncomfortable at first, he eventually gets used to it until finally his biceps are developed to the extent he wants. People can strengthen their underexercised ego states in much the same way as the person with the low biceps. In the protective and permissive environment of the therapy group, persons can practice exercising their newly developing ego states. After Daisy developed her thinking abilities in the group, she created a new tool, a new structure, and a new force to use outside of the group. Supplying answers for someone else is like lifting a log for a person with underdeveloped biceps—the log gets "raised," but the weakness remains for that person.

Naturally, what happens outside of the treatment group is also important, and these situations may be focused upon. A client may make suitable prescriptions to handle the daily problems in life. The client learns specific skills in the formal treatment setting, and she or he can practice these evolving skills elsewhere. I asked Daisy what new Adult endeavor she would be willing to undertake in her everyday life. Had Daisy decided to think of an Adult strengthening endeavor and actually directed her energy in that way, things would have proceeded well. But, alas, this seldom seems to happen with persons who are strengthening deficient ego states. Resistance tends to creep in. Daisy's resistance emerged when she looked quizzical and mystified about how she would raise her Adult. As could be expected, an unsuspecting group member "bit" on her game "bait" and suggested that she could take an algebra course at the local college. Reflexively, Daisy responded that she couldn't because she was lousy in math. Another member offered a chemistry course, and Daisy, with a laugh, said that she couldn't even spell it. Daisy continued to reinforce her early life decision—that she "couldn't think"—with the group members. Math, chemistry, and other strong Adult activities were foreign to her—as much as her parachuting naked into Afghanistan. The process of Daisy's resistance continued in the form of a game, *Why Don't You— Yes, But . . .*

The principle of resistance can be simply stated: the big gals work to keep the little gals down. With Daisy, her egogram revealed her Adapted Child was the highest (the big gal). When the little gal, her Adult, decided to emerge, Daisy would reflexively lower her head and look up at the therapist with wide eyes and beg to be treated like a little girl. Daisy viewed her Adapted Child as being her "real self" and her Adult as being phony at first. Resistance to change comes on four levels:

1. Inner psychological (personal resistance)
2. The family (intimate social resistance)
3. On the job (institutional resistance)
4. Fairy tales, myths, TV, advertisements, etc. (cultural resistance)

Daisy was experiencing inner psychological resistance, and I turned to the redecision processes. One evening in her TA group, Daisy directed a psychodrama between herself and another group member, and she began to plan an especially heavy game of *Stupid*. After she described the roles to her two actors, she turned to me, looked confused, and then said that she couldn't go on because she couldn't think of anything else. This seemed to be an opportune time to go back into her script for redecision work. I encouraged her to fully experience the feelings she was having right now, and right away Daisy said she felt like a very confused little girl. I told her to close her eyes and I used both a guided fantasy and an hypnotic technique while I had her trace that feeling of confusion back to one of the earliest times in her life that she felt that way. I encouraged her actually to be there, and when she was, to slowly open her eyes. I told her, "Describe where you are, how old you are, who is with you" (reinforcing her to stay in the present tense, as if the scene were just happening). In a little-girl voice, Daisy said, "I'm almost seven and I'm sitting at the dining room table. It's late and the light is on, my daddy is in the other room, and I am trying to do arithmetic problems that my teacher gave me for homework. I am asking my daddy for help and he is mad at me because he wants to read his newspaper. But now he is helping me and I am very happy. I am getting him to pay attention to me. He is solving my arithmetic problems, and now he is saying that I can't think very well."* I asked Daisy what she was deciding about herself, and she replied, "I am deciding not to think and solve problems because if I do, Daddy won't pay any attention to me." I asked Daisy if she was willing to view this situation in a different way. She nodded her affirmation and I provided another chair and placed it in front of her. Daisy was instructed to sit in that chair and to be in her Adult ego state. I invited her to use her Adult because it was her lowest ego state on the egogram. I usually pick a lower ego state when I do redecision work, and this underexercised ego state is crucial in attaining the contract. An even better situation is for the clients to choose for themselves. This becomes advantageous in subsequent sessions. The most common choices are the Adult, the Nurturing Parent, and the Free Child. Occasionally, either a constructive Critical Parent or an Adapted Child may prove an effective catalyst in the empty chair.

Daisy did not stay in the Adult ego state very long; it is inevitable that

---

* This was probably a hyperesthetic memory.

people will switch out of ego states that are unfamiliar to them. The process of redecision was proceeding and would have been culminated when her Adult ego state talked to her Child and facilitated a redecision about her acting stupid. However, resistance frequently occurs, and it usually is in the form of *slippage,* by which I mean that a person has slipped out of the intended ego state. This happened to Daisy when she was sitting in her Adult chair and then suddenly slipped into her Adapted Child ego state. Her conversation between her two ego states resembled a discussion with two little kids getting nowhere. In her Adult chair, Daisy began to ask questions such as, "Am I doing this right?" She also began to giggle nervously and glance at the other group members in her characteristic little-girl manner. She was no longer an Adult in the Adult ego state, but rather, she had slipped into her Adapted Child, asking approval of what she was doing. Slippage provides the therapist with an excellent opportunity once again to oppose the ego-state forces. I provided a third perpendicular chair for her to sit on with her Adult, and then I asked her to describe what she saw going on between the other two chairs. Daisy had the opportunity to reconstitute her Adult, and she provided an accurate description. "My Child was sitting in that chair believing that she could not think. My Adult started out in that other chair. However, the Adult shifted into the Adapted Child and soon both chairs sounded like two little kids saying the same thing over and over." The other group members congratulated her for her clear Adult observations, and we enthusiastically hugged her and praised her for her clear thinking. Daisy was then in a solid position to talk to her opposing Adapted Child, her resisting ego state which masqueraded as her Adult. Daisy continued to use her Adult ego state, to slip out of it, catch herself, and start over again. Through this process, she strengthened her Adult and became aware each time she slipped. Her Adult finally became the impasse breaker. Daisy talked to the Adapted Child ego state that robbed her of her Adult energy. Her Adapted Child told her that the reason she slipped was so she wouldn't have to worry about changing. She said, "I really like being a cute and bouncy little girl; however, I guess it would be OK if I could think too." The group congratulated her for her logical thinking and Daisy went back to her Adult chair in order to talk with the "deciding little girl," the Adapted Child. The redecision process concluded with the little girl explaining, "I really don't have to be stupid or act stupid to attract attention; I'm going to start getting attention for being smart." Daisy appeared to be tremendously relieved and joyful upon saying this.

Whenever the resistant ego state creeps into the Adult chair, I will use a third chair and, occasionally, a fourth in order to confront the resistant force that slips in. This has been more useful to me, rather than labeling the slippage an impasse and then telling the client that we will work on it at a later time. However, after confronting the slippage two or three times, I will inform the client that I want to stop, and then resume at a later date when the client is more willing.

I encourage ego-state opposition work in groups for two main reasons. I think that the group setting is superior to one-to-one treatment, because in group there are plenty of people to both congratulate and reinforce a person's new decisions as well as encourage the person's new behaviors and actions. Group members also confront slippage as it occurs, and they have an opportunity to learn more about themselves as they are observing another person go through the process. I use multiple chairs which serve as an ego-state sorting system. Mental conversations between the ego states go on daily in people's heads as they make decisions, whether they be mundane or profound. When a person becomes confused, a spatial separation may prove hepful, even though it may seem awkward. The separation symbolizes that there are several ego states involved, and this in itself helps to sort out the confusion. Another distinct advantage is that the person is active rather than passive in his or her treatment process and will be expected to do the moving.

In my experience, even the most powerful redecision experiences which have combated the resistant ego states are not enough for a lasting change. One needs to be able to *practice* one's newly developing ego states. After the person leaves the group and goes out into the world, he or she needs to redirect new ego-state energy with either old friends or by developing new relationships. Treatment does not end with the redecision or the combating of the slippage process. The question, "Where do I go from here?" is appropriate. After one writes a prescription about one's new goals, it may be difficult to put it into effect because of old resistances as well as new resistances that may arise in order to keep the person in his "place." Husbands, wives, family members, and others maintain an intimate investment in their systems and they usually are not willing for their members to change. Family therapy can be particularly effective in both shifting the energies and maintaining the balance in such closed systems. As Daisy decides to redefine her relationships with her boyfriends, her remaining in therapy over the next weeks and months becomes especially critical and analytical. An important consideration is that Daisy's boyfriends are also human beings capable of growth and change, although they may not choose to grow. I frequently recommend that the spouse, parent, or crucial family member also enter treatment, either indirectly or conjointly, about the same time as the individual who is seeking change. If this is not possible, I remind my client that he or she needs to make a clear-cut statement (and I consider it my responsibility to take this position), that treatment may affect relationships with the other persons who are significant in his or her life, and that these persons are entitled to know it. Special problems usually arise with parents who are paying for their children's treatment; they may prematurely jerk the children out of therapy (usually when their children are attaining change and growth). Another social resistance may be observed when a spouse is opposed to the mate being in treatment, knowing that they got together in the first place with their "old" personalities, and being angry or afraid that the mate might change. These special problems illustrate that intimate relationships may frequently resist and even bar potential changes in a member of the system. When dealing with families or couples, I have found the anticipatory interpretation to be useful. This term refers to a technique whereby the therapist tells a client or the partner what he or she is going to do beforehand. By analyzing both games and script theory, one may see that the client's close social contacts will work to prevent him or her from changing, even though they may want the person to be in treatment. Daisy was warned in advance about the potential resistances which she might encounter from her family and friends.

I have found it useful to classify resistances as coming in three volleys: the first is innocuous and hardly noticeable, while the third one frequently involves a separation in the relationship. The second volley is somewhere in between. After a group treatment session, Daisy told her boyfriend that she wished to engage in a serious discussion about what happened in her therapy session that evening. He appeared interested and said that he had been reading a TA book. When they began to talk, Daisy applied her intellectual capabilities, and her boyfriend began to look unhappy. He told her that she looked too serious and that he would prefer her to be her usual bouncy self without all of the information stuff. The more Daisy began to express her intellect, the more her boyfriend attempted to reestablish the old, comfortable Parent-to-Child relationship that he was used to. This irritation is the first volley of resistance and is quite predictable. The second volley usually involves an increased expression from the other person's strongest ego state. This may erupt as an escalation of anger with well-chosen insults of the nature of "You're not the person I married." The third volley, if it occurs, may involve an actual split in the relationship. In Daisy's situation, the third volley did not occur, because her boyfriend decided to explore his own feelings about himself and to look at their relationship in a new light. After a few months, he told Daisy that he actually preferred their new ways of relating to each other. He appreciated being able to problem-solve *with* her rather than *for* her. He revealed that he enjoyed her complexities and did not view her as the "cute, dumb, Daisy" of before. While her boyfriend's resistant forces to Daisy's change came from outside of her head, they tended to reinforce the resistances that Daisy was feeling inside her head. Her specific resistances became evident in her redecision work, which was discussed earlier. Her boyfriend had resisted her earlier attempts at strengthening her Adult by using his Adapted Child with her. He had tantrums, he mimicked her, and he treated her as if she were not able to think. He also tossed in a few Critical Parent prejudices such as "women are dumb." When clients remain in ongoing therapy groups, they have the opportunity to discuss the resistances (internal and external) that they are experiencing, and they are able to receive group support for achieving their treatment contracts by strengthening their previously unused ego states.

The final two levels of resistance, the institutional and the cultural, are less amenable to psychological treatment. The institutional resistance may be viewed as pertaining to people's jobs and livelihoods, and these institutions are sometimes oppressive. An an actress in an institution where the game of "casting couch" was rampant, Daisy was chosen to play sexy, ignorant, bouncy little-girl parts. The directors, producers, and writers expected this type of behavior from her. Daisy easily fit herself into this niche and was rewarded with jobs, money, and pats on her fanny. Unfortunately, treatment becomes more difficult when social institutions are involved. The theories and the techniques of transactional analysis, however, are useful in analyzing oppressive institutions. Also, various social movements have arisen to deal with oppressive institutions, most noticeably the radical therapy movement, the antiracism movement, the feminist movement, the gay liberation movement, the Asklepieion movement (for reform in prison), and others. The movements, rather than single individuals acting alone, have been more effective at blasting oppressive institutions. An individual who is working in an oppressive institution may reassess the authority structure under which he or she works and then decide whether or not to go along with it. Frequently, the person's reward of a newly changed personality becomes more important to the person than the job, and she may choose to leave the situation. This is far easier than making the necessary changes in the institution itself, although institutional change is not impossible.

The fourth level of resistance to change is cultural opposition, which manifests itself through themes on television, through the popular entertainment media, as well as through more esoteric ways such as in novels, folk tales, and mythology.[3] Daisy incorporated a personal model for herself which was the "dumb blond." Her favorite heroines in fairy tales were helpless victims who could not take care of their needs. Daisy followed a classic oppressed-woman's script, that of the woman who does not think but is a great playmate. After Daisy overcame her internal resistances to change, handled her boyfriend and family, recognized the underlying dynamics of her acting job, and analyzed her heroic models in fairy tales

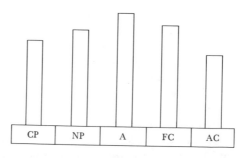

Figure 5
Daisy's After Egogram

and myths, she emerged as a potent person with a well-functioning Adult ego state. She took control of her life and gave herself permission to think. At this time, she and the group members redrew her egogram (Figure 5). Daisy qualifies for my definition of "cure," and this means that she shows at least one major shift in an ego state, as portrayed in her after-egogram. Her Adult and her Critical Parent rose, while her Adapted Child fell dramatically. Outside as well as inside the consulting room, she behaved as an intelligent, exciting woman who stood up for her own rights.

THE COSMIC WHISTLE

The major thrust of psychotherapy is to raise the ego states that are low, so that the individual will be able to experience himself more fully and have many behavior options for dealing with everyday situations. Daisy strengthened and raised her Adult ego state. An important consideration in egogram work is for the client to recognize which ego state is deficient. I arrived at the egogram concept by working with Mary (see "Mary's Orgasm"),[4] to effectively raise her low Nurturing Parent. The ego states themselves have both positive and negative functions which are characteristic of them. It is not a matter of an ego state to be either good or bad; rather, the important consideration is that there be a balance between them in order that a person will have a comfortable access to each of his ego states. Because each person is different, one can readily see that a good district attorney will have an egogram different from that of a creative artist, an executive accountant, or a burlesque performer.

Many techniques have been devised to raise specific ego states, and various techniques are being continually refined in order to be more effective.[5] Specific Critical Parent-raising techniques have been derived from Synanon and from assertiveness-training courses. Physical hugs, verbal strokes, and taking care of others' needs are indicative of Nurturing Parent-raising techniques. The Adult can be strengthened by utilizing the Tavistock method of group process. Group psychotherapy may also aid the Adult through intellectual analysis. The Free Child has been raised by encounter groups, permission groups, musical therapy, art therapy, and other modes of Free Child activity (including the extreme end, the Sexual Freedom League). The Adapted Child may be raised through techniques that involve compromise. Because people seldom enter therapy to raise their Adapted Child, there have not been many treatment models devised to raise the Adapted Child. However, therapists may inadvertently raise a client's Adapted Child with injudicious use of prescribed drugs that tranquilize the person and cause him to be psychologicaly habituated to them, thereby foiling the client in handling his responsibilities. The Adapted Child is frequently high in those persons who do not take full responsibility for their lives and themselves. Most important is that no particular technique is right for everyone; each person needs to take into account the ego states she or he wants to raise.

This is where the cosmic whistle comes in. It is an inspirational tool that I have developed in this phase of action therapy and treatment for the shifting of psychological energies. Many people lie on their psychoanalysts' couches on any given morning and use their Adult ego states while they think and interpret their dreams and their free associations. Other people romp around the California countryside, experiencing their feelings as they laugh, cry, shout, and beat their pillows. The major problem for these two groups of people is that those persons who obsess on their analysts' couches are already thinkers and have been problem-solving with Adults for years. Likewise, those persons who cavort in the countryside have been letting out their emotions for years. The cosmic whistle would provide the following function. Each Monday morning at 11:00 o'clock all around the world, I will blow the cosmic whistle loud and clear. The whistle will cause people to switch—the obsessives on the couch will take off their neckties and shoes, and they will start frolicking through the countryside, and those emoting persons in the fields, who haven't had their shoes on in years and who don't figure out things for themselves, will appear on the analysts' couches to get down to work and do some good hard thinking. The cosmic whistle will facilitate these switches, so that the feelers will think and the thinkers will feel. This Monday, listen and see if you hear that whistle blowing!

References

1. John M. Dusay, "Eric Berne's Studies on Intuition," *Transactional Analysis Journal, 1,* no. 1 (January, 1971), p. 40.
2. Eric Berne, *Transactional Analysis in Psychotherapy,* New York, Grove Press, 1961, pp. 37–43.
3. Catherine M. Dusay, "Recurring Themes Throughout World Literature," Master's Thesis, San Francisco State University, 1975.
4. John M. Dusay, "Egograms and the Constancy Hypothesis," *Transactional Analysis Journal, 2,* no. 3 (July, 1972).
5. John M. Dusay, *Egograms,* New York, Harper & Row, in press.

THREE

ONE HUNDRED CHILDREN GENERATE A LOT OF TA: HISTORY, DEVELOPMENT, AND ACTIVITIES OF THE SCHIFF FAMILY
Jacqui Lee Schiff

The first question we might appropriately address here is, why transactional analysis? What makes this particular theory preferable to other ways of viewing the internal and external gyrations of humanity? And secondly, why do we have various schools of transactional analysis?

In regard to the first question, it is not our impression that we of transactional analysis have all the answers, or even very many of them as yet. However, we do think certain concepts in transactional analysis were essential as a starting place for the theoretical and clinical work we have done and are continuing to do; and we believe that other theoretical frameworks could not have resulted in the same accomplishments. Without the idea of ego states as they were defined by Eric Berne, we could not have accomplished what we have with schizophrenia. Without the concepts of games and scripts, we could not have carried out our theoreticcal research in passivity, symbiosis, redefining, child development, and diagnosis. Without the argumentative model developed at the old San Francisco Seminars, where transactional analysis began in the 1950s, our theories would have been less dynamic, less potent. And the basic formula of respectful, goal-oriented cooperation between patient and therapist has made it possible to arrive at theory and achieve success in acquiring data and developing programs we could not have otherwise.

We are the leaders of one of several schools of transactional analysis. Probably many of our differences are due to a relative isolation from the mainstream of theory development in the 1962–1968 period. That time was important in terms of theorizing, both in California and in our smaller community on the East Coast. However, the emphasis was different. Although we, like most of the other schools of transactional analysis, have integrated the theoretical developments that came out of our differences during that period, our emphasis at Cathexis Institute has continued in the directions charted then.

Another important factor in our development has been our political situation. Through a period of social unrest which has permeated psychotherapeutic circles as well as other aggregates in our society, we have been in the forefront as innovative and controversial, with many young people actively participating in our programs. We have naturally attracted a circle of bright and energetic young therapists looking for new ideas and answers. They, in turn, have enriched our outlooks and lent their energies to promoting our development. Many of them are now working independently in various parts of the world and have carried our techniques and philosophies beyond the boundaries of our own contacts.

Something that we say frequently to our patients when they are rigid or negativistic about how they want to solve problems is that there is no one right way. It is important to keep open as many options as possible to maintain optimum chances for success. I'm delighted that in transactional analysis we have maintained ourselves sufficiently flexible to include many, varying, and opposed points of view and have as an organization committed ourselves to that model. I hope that in the future we do not succumb to a dogmatism that would limit our capacity to react spontaneously to new ideas. We do not have all the answers or even very many of them as yet. We do have confidence that answers are available, that continued seeking for them is desirable, and that we all share a common goal of alleviating human distress.

OUR HISTORY

My first exposure to transactional analysis was in the late 1950s, when I had an invitation from Vi Litt Callaghan to visit a meeting she was attending and discuss my experiences working with groups. I was a caseworker for a public welfare agency, with no training as a psychotherapist, lacking even a college degree. Overwhelmed by the demands of a swelling workload and the incredible paper bureaucracy which reigns throughout public agencies, I had begun to see my clients in groups. At the time there was little or no significant theory of group dynamics as related to personal change, nor was there any substantial concern about my activities on the part of the agency; the idea of serving larger numbers of welfare recipients more frequently was pleasing to my administration, and there was no expectation that my efforts would yield any particular results. In the social climate of the period, mass migrations of blacks from the Deep South had stretched community resources in California beyond any hope of organized response or meaningful confrontation of the issues presented by the dependent poor; concerned involvement on nearly anyone's part was applauded.

Nor was I aware of how little I knew. My group sessions were fairly successful, meaning that they were gratifying to me, the clients attended them willingly, and they alleviated the tedium of clerical detail. Occasionally it may have occurred to me to wish that I knew more, but I had no particular expectation that any available knowledge would yield results and serve the needs of the population inhabiting the California slums. The education I had to prepare me for the experience consisted of some classes in experimental psychology, and I perceived that Guthrie and Skinner knew little about the problems I encountered. Nor was clinical training much available in California then. My concept of psychology as related to helping people was very shallow; I saw psychotherapy as neither a science nor as an art but rather as something of a mishmash of archaic conjecture.

I don't remember why I went to that first seminar. (Probably because Vi's invitation was enthusiastic and I had nothing better to do.) Nor do I remember the first meeting. Anyway I went back, at first occasionally and then, as I got acquainted, more frequently.

In analyzing past events it is difficult to view them without adding judgments and shifts in perspective which came about later. I remember the participants of those early seminars, which met at Eric Berne's apartment, as roughly divided into three groups. By far the most impressive and attractive to me were the older professionals. Many of them were psychiatrists, but other disciplines were represented. They seemed to be established in their fields, and to my unsophisticated view they possessed a remarkable amount of information.

A second group consisted of much younger people, mostly men who were students or young professionals, quick-tongued, witty, and very competitive. I puzzled somewhat about what might be the goal of their competitive efforts and arrived at no answer. I would have liked to be part of that group but never experienced myself as sufficiently clever to participate in their dialogue.

The third group, which was really not a group at all, I thought of as hangers-on, people who were there because of some personal interest— women seeking to make out with an established middle-aged doctor, needy individuals looking for therapeutic insights, or lonely professionals wanting to belong. While they swelled the attendance of the seminar considerably, they rarely contributed.

People came and went. The first two groups I have described made up sort of a nucleus for the seminar and involved perhaps 12 to 15 individuals. Most of those people developed a real commitment to transactional analysis, and many are still active contributors. They were not, as commonly believed, a remarkably warm or intimate group, and viewing them in the light of my present sophistication, I would see them as a group of professional dissidents, not intellectual giants but probably representative of the range of dissatisfied therapists of that period. Many of them were frustrated at the narrowness of acceptable professional practice, somewhat at odds with the establishment, and without clear goals about what they would like to see changed or how to go about it. They were not particularly comfortable with themselves or with one another, and sometimes they immersed themselves in a kind of frenetic playfulness which did little to bring any of us to the kind of intimate encounters we purported to be seeking.

Eric Berne's creative genius permeated the group: I did not perceive him as the warm, grandfatherly, humanitarian that others seem to remember; as a human being he seems lost in legend even though it is only a few years since his death. He was sharp-tongued, competitive, and endlessly argumentative, his tenderness often obscured by unexplained moods and unexpected hostilities. Irritability sometimes took precedence over assurance and potency; he lacked many of the characteristics a group usually seeks in a leader and did not actively seek a leadership role. Nevertheless, he inspired and gave loyalty and affection, and his lively curiosity, impatience with affectation, and respect for intellectual accomplishment gave structure to the group.

Although I don't remember that first seminar meeting, I had an encounter with Eric Berne after the meeting which I have always remembered as important. At the end of the meeting Vi asked me to step into the next room. A few moments later Eric entered, bringing with him a stool. I identified him as one of the leaders of the group I had just attended; otherwise he was not known to me. He sat down in front of me, and without speaking leaned forward and began to stare into my face. I was conscious that Vi was still in the room but was reluctant to shift my gaze away from him. I was not particularly frightened, suspecting that it was some sort of experiment, and was determined that I would not look away, that someone else must make the next move. We gazed at one another for a long while, and eventually Vi, who reported she was alarmed at the passing of time, interrupted us. The intimacy experiment is described in the early literature of transactional analysis,[1] and I have often used it as an exercise, but never after the first time did the experience have the same intensity of engagement. I don't know if that was because it was the first time or because it was related to the force of Eric's personality.

I don't remember myself merging into any of the three groups I have described, although others have remembered me as "one of the smart-mouth kids." I could not enter into the competitive repartee but since I always like to be active and involved, I used my naiveté and lack of background to establish a role for myself. I listened carefully to what was said, and asked questions. Sometimes the response was critical and condescending, but my questions were on target often enough that people began to notice me as being perceptive. It has also been said to me by a number of other women who drifted in and out of that situation that I was the only woman from that period whose intellectual contributions were treated with respect.

One of the views held strongly by the individuals indoctrinated to the Freudian point of view was that the Parent ego state was irrevocably fixed in the consciousness of mature individuals. I argued against this, maintaining that what had been environmentally imposed usually could be extinguished, and that new Parent messages or values were incorporated throughout life or else social change would not be possible. The others believed that psychotherapy necessarily involved working through the Adult, and their response to my arguments were eventually impatient; then I would give way to the force of their shared position, but without believing them to be correct.

Because of my exposure to the seminar and also as a result of continuing college on a part-time basis, I began to develop some sophistication about psychotherapy. Soon my work reflected the skills I was acquiring, and somewhat to my astonishment there began to be changes in the attitudes of the welfare clients with whom I worked. As their depression was broken down, motivation increased and participants in my groups began to explore options they previously would have rejected. I was excited and gratified by our mutual achievements and began to consider becoming a therapist. In this I was encouraged by several of the seminar participants, particularly Eric Berne, Joe Concannon, and Frank Ernst, and I began to look around for a graduate school.

The circumstances of my moving to Virginia are not significant to this account. What is relevant is my exposure to the stifling bias of conventional views of psychotherapy at the time, my irritation and frustration at the lack of involvement and coping, the too prevalent philosophy that treatment consisted of assisting the client or patient in accepting and adapting to limitations. The therapists I was exposed to, with only a few exceptions, maintained no expectations for achievement or success either for themselves or for their patients; and success as a social worker seemed dependent on subscribing to a remarkable standard of mediocrity. Undoubtedly the climate of conservatism was exaggerated in the locale to which I was exposed; the South was close to crisis over social change and the more traditional groups with vested interests in the old ways were clinging frantically to remnants of their stability and values. However, I believe that the state of the treatment arts that I found in Virginia was not unlike that to be found in other places, and as a student I found the lack of enthusiasm or intellectual competence surprising and disappointing. For the first time, as I held back in order to conform to expectations for a student, I became aware that my own skills compared favorably with those of individuals who had considerably more background than I, and that the exposure to transactional analysis had yielded meaningful results. The school I attended viewed my situation with some consternation and surprising tolerance, trying to understand and adapt to me as one of that mysterious changing population of students with whom they were learning to cope, even though they did not accept or approve of many of our activities or values. I have never understood the reasons for their supportiveness and can only recall their efforts with appreciation.

Following my graduation in 1964 with an MSSW degree, I undertook employment in a children's program in Virginia and began making decisions about the next stage in my personal and professional life. During that year I decided not to return to California and married Morris (Moe) Schiff, also a social worker. Following my marriage I continued to work part time in a rural community clinic, did some teaching of transactional analysis, and began a small private practice. I envisioned that during the next few years I would devote a lot of time to my three sons, participate actively in the social-action politics that were rocking the South, and maintain some limited professional involvement.

I had, at that time, no more than the casual exposure to schizophrenia that came about through graduate training and my previous seminar contacts. My husband's work, however, involved him with one of the state hospitals in Virginia; he became interested in some young schizophrenic patients, and my part-time employment included some prepsychotic and after-care patients. Thus, 1965 was for me another year of gathering data which had little impact on me at the time but which later became useful. Through my interest in social action I began to teach transactional analysis, and my improved financial circumstances enabled me to return to California for conferences and to reestablish contacts with old friends from the San Francisco seminar. I was astonished and pleased at the growth of interest in transactional analysis at the time, although awareness had not yet extended to Charlottesville, Virginia. Nevertheless, my activities did result in some interest and I began to teach an extension course at the University of Virginia and also participated in training vocational counselors for the Psychiatry Department at the medical school. I was aware that this period was a period of dramatic growth for transactional analysis; I was excited at the generation of new ideas and frustrated by my isolation.

SCHIZOPHRENIA

In 1965 I took into my home as a mother's helper a young woman who, following the termination of her marriage, was having an acute upset, apparently schizophrenic. I tried to be supportive of her and was aware of the urgency with which she sought parenting and how readily she established transference. Compliant to my traditional training, I resisted responding to the transference, and she left at the end of the year, improved, but not well, disappointed and angry at my withholding.

In 1966 my husband and I took into our home a very disturbed young man diagnosed schizophrenic, paranoid type. Within a few months we had a whole household of severely disturbed youngsters, mostly schizophrenic, and were frantically attempting to have an impact against the devastating disorganization of their thinking and the intense urgency of their needs.

Crucial to our eventual success was the unusual responsiveness of the first of these patients. Dennis, who later was adopted by me and became Aaron, did not look particularly promising in the beginning. He was an exceptionally large and powerful boy with a stupid, slack face; he was incredibly dirty and had a severe scalp rash. However, I had seen him a year or so earlier, before he became so very sick, and remembered him as potentially bright although unpleasant. Our original idea was to take him into our household for a month, hoping to support him through a period of crisis and to avoid hospitalization. We were particularly concerned about his situation because the hospital available to him was lacking in resources and we knew the chances for a youngster like Aaron, once committed to a state hospital in Virginia, were very poor.

The first month extended into a second and then a third. We were excited and pleased with Aaron's progress, and we found that it was not possible to circumvent his desperate eliciting of parenting. When confusion overtook him, it became natural to move into parent roles in order to avoid escalations of violence dangerous to us all, and it was apparent that his response justified at least experimenting with supporting the transference. Thus, we began actively to support the formation of a symbiosis, where he would cathect his Child in response to our Parent directives, as a way to maintain control through the escalations of rage, the endless hassling, and the sullen withholding that are characteristic of this pathology.

I thought a lot during this period. Utilizing my transactional analysis background, I thought about ego states, and about child development and healthy parent-child symbiosis as compared with the obviously pathological symbiosis which we were establishing with our six-foot houseguest. And I began exploring the things I was thinking with Aaron, trying to get information on how he perceived the situation and what our involvement meant to him.

Aaron was mostly resistant to these discussions. As was typical of instances when he didn't want to listen or think, his face would become slack and his responses would be slow, laborious, and unintelligent. With considerable persistence I elicited enough response from him to discover that he was viewing us as his family and was not at all appreciative of our interest and efforts; rather, that he considered what we were doing to be the correct and responsible thing for us to do—what parents were supposed to do! However, he did not view the situation optimistically; rather, he anticipated that we would fail him as parents had always failed in the past. We would have joint responsibility for the failure: he would fail because he was not-OK, and we would fail because we were inadequate.

Thus, I began at least dimly to comprehend the problem we were facing and were going to face, to understand the script, and see how it would work.

However, when we talked about ego states, Aaron's response was quite different. His face came alive and his contributions were enthusiastic and intelligent. Eagerly he reached out for tools by which he might understand and describe his experience, the de-energizing internal conflict which beset him. His memory was very impaired and he was unable to describe the sources of the deviant structures inside his head, but he could define what they were and how they were located within ego states. He could readily cathect ego states *in toto,* excluding any input from irrelevant ego states. Thus, he could become a snarling werewolf (restrained so he could not kill anyone), which he ascribed to his Parent ego state; or a crawling, drooling infant (his Natural Child); and he had available also a number of Adapted Child structures which seemed distinct from each other (including a new one he was incorporating from us).

In his normal state Aaron appeared to be a conglomeration of all of these. I was aware that always the crafty werewolf watched and waited, while the unattractive baby clung desperately or amused itself with infantile exploration. I began working with the fragmented parts of his personality, having him cathect directly into those ego states which seemed to be costing him energy and eliciting a ventilation of the distressed feelings; in this way I hoped to restore equilibrium as a means of avoiding episodes of uncontrolled rage or such behaviors as smearing feces. The exercise seemed naive to me, ridiculously simple, and there seemed no way to screen out whether what was happening was truly therapeutic or whether it was a new development in Aaron's adaptive repertoire (a question still unanswered). However, it seemed obvious that the externalization of the inappropriate behaviors did stabilize functional cathexis to Adult, and while later we came to question instances of wholesale ventilation of feelings as practiced in some encounter-type techniques at this stage, we depended heavily on this means of enhancing patient management.

The werewolf Parent was by far the most disruptive of the various fragments that seemed to make up Aaron's personality. The constant threat of cathexis to this homicidal state seriously disrupted our interactions; I learned how to avoid encounters, how not to stimulate that part of him, but the spontaneity of our interaction was sacrificed to caution. In discussing this problem with Aaron, it became apparent that the werewolf was an introject, a distortion of how he perceived his father, and that it seemed to serve no Natural Child function. It appeared that there was no support for it anywhere else in the personality system (a situation I have never found in nonschizophrenic patients). I began to consider the possibility of decathexis, going back to my thesis of years past that what had been environmentally acquired could be extinguished, but I proceeded cautiously because of my lack of understanding and information and because of Aaron's apparent fragility.

When I approached Aaron with the idea he reacted with surprise and enthusiasm. He perceived the werewolf as a threat to his survival, that its bizarre and violent behavior might on some occasion result in the police or someone else killing him, or that he might kill someone else. He reported that he believed he could eject it totally or kill it internally. He thought he then would have no protection against external attack or abuse but decided to trust that Morris and I, as parents, would and could provide that for him. Assured that we understood, he proceeded to try.

And he succeeded! Unexpected changes were almost immediately apparent. He stopped hallucinating, Child contaminations cleared up spontaneously within a few days, and a whole defensive structure, presumably constructed to defend against cathexis to Parent, dissipated as the problem ceased to exist. It was in this work with Aaron, which we soon after initiated with other young schizophrenics, that the process which came to be called *reparenting* was developed. From our point of view, reparenting does not involve the changing of specific Parent messages; that is more in the line of traditional psychotherapy. Rather, it involves a drastic, dramatic intervention which is likely to incapacitate the individuals in some ways but leaves them more available in others. It is only safely attempted as described here, within a protected and supportive environment, and it should only be utilized as a last resort with severely psychotic individuals.

Thus began the job of finding out how ego states work, when and how and by which patients they may be manipulated or de-energized (excluded) for therapeutic intervention, and what the consequences and advantages are of practicing the various possibilities. Results had to be checked and rechecked before we could eliminate the possibility that any particular effect was the result of an hysterical response unique to that individual. Moreover, the internal dynamics unique to particular diagnosis and the critical introjected messages for each kind of pathology had to be examined. This task, which is still underway, is generally referred to as the *Frame of Reference* aspect of our work.

One significant difficulty was the instability of the diagnostic system utilized throughout the medical establishment in this country. Usually patients arrive with many recorded diagnoses, frequently contradictory to one another. Before we could undertake any significant studies, we had to begin to sort out the different defensive structures individuals develop in pathological attempts to integrate their internal and external experience. Fortunately, there was no shortage of patients; as soon as it became known that we were interested in working with individuals who were diagnosed schizophrenic we were deluged with referrals.

CONTROVERSY

While the success we were having was known locally, we were cautious about how it was presented, hoping to have tangible results before we challenged the establishment—entrenched as it was in the view that schizophrenia was hopeless and incurable and probably not accessible to psychotherapy. Within a year after Aaron came to us we were engaging in practices which we knew might outrage conventional psychotherapists. We were openly eliciting transference and deliberately entering into countertransference in an attempt to establish symbiotic relationships with the patient. We were actively and intimately touch-stroking our schizophrenic children. And, in a southern community rocked by integration strife, we took into our family a black 16-year-old girl.

Transactional analysis was, at this time, exploring the ideas of winners and losers, looking at ways in which individuals are driven by their scripts to enter into ill-advised kinds of activities. I took in the new information and examined what I was doing with trepidation, wondering if some kind of kink in my own head were leading me along the road to disaster.

Eric Berne, who was kept posted on what I was doing, also advised reticence, watched our ups and downs anxiously, and on occasion threw caution to the winds to lash out angrily at our critics. "You young residents better just keep your mouths shut," he once said, in introducing me to a group, "because she *cures* schizophrenia!" His support throughout the early period of our development was personally very important to me, and while in private he actively disapproved of many of our methods, in public he was uncritical. An important memory of Eric Berne is the visit he paid to us shortly before his death and knowing how important our success was for him toward the end of his life.

In late 1966 our family moved to Fredericksburg, Virginia, where we settled with our schizophrenic children into an upper-middle-class housing area. The only psychiatrist who practiced locally, Donald Reed, was supportive to our working with young schizophrenics in our home, although not interested in the theoretical aspects of our activities. Fredericksburg is a college town, more liberal and more middle class than most of Virginia, and it seemed a quiet place in which to take temporary refuge. Moreover, it was within easy driving distance of Washington, D. C., where I hoped I might find companionship and stimulation. I continued to have some private practice during this time and by 1968 I was spending one day a week in Washington, where I founded a Transactional Analysis Seminar.

Out of this experience I made friends with a Maryland secondary school principal, Harry Rose, who became my first cotherapist and who has contributed enormously to the development of theory. We began to explore the possibilities of out-patient reparenting, utilizing exclusion rather than decathexis. What we found was that, although with out-patients we did not accomplish the same immediate and dramatic alleviation of pathology, such interventions were not so urgently needed with an out-patient population, typically made up of people who were less sick than the patients who came into the residential program; the long-range results were approximately the same. Since that time out-patient reparenting has been practiced and is being practiced by many therapists throughout the country with considerable success, but in 1968 the manipulation of ego states as a means of therapeutic intervention was a very new concept even in TA, one that we explored timidly at first and then with increasing excitement.

In the beginning in the residential program we experienced considerably more success than failure. Partly that was because every small success came as a major achievement and often as a surprise, partly because neither we nor anyone else had ever before done what we were doing. Thus, our expectations were limited and were greatly exceeded. Most of the youngsters who came to us demonstrated significant improvement, often very quickly. Others presented positive changes within a year or so. It was not until the second year was well along that we began to experience failure.

The most difficult thing I have faced is the feeling connected with the loss of those kids with whom we were not successful. Often people say, "But look at how many have succeeded," as though the successes and failures can be balanced against one another. For me each loss has been uniquely painful, sometimes as if the individual had been a natural child. I am as much a part of the symbiosis and as vulnerable as any parent. While my attachments don't occur at the same kind of depth with each youngster, they have not been selective in favor of those kids who were successful, and several times I have experienced tremendous loss and grief as it became necessary to give a child up. Almost equally painful have been the instances where success seemed partial, the individual overcame that pathology which would traditionally be considered schizophrenia but still demonstrated some defect of personality or character, so that in spite of the apparent success, I felt unhappy about the outcome.

By 1969 we were well under way. There no longer seemed any doubt that we were having significant results. While it was premature to call what we were accomplishing cures, people *were* calling them cures and certainly cure was our goal. Aaron, a presentable and sociable young man, was attending the University of Virginia. Shirley, our only black child, had also left for college. Michael, who had come to us at age 22 looking nonhuman after ten continuous years of hospitalization, was working part time. Eric Berne had proposed that we begin to publish—cautiously, of course—and then in his excitement he threw caution to the winds and devoted a whole issue of the *TA Bulletin* to our work.

The *Bulletin* had a limited distribution, mostly on the West Coast, so the effects reached us slowly. Nevertheless, we had come out of hiding.

And we weren't ready. In spite of how good the kids looked out in front, we simply didn't have all the answers we needed for facing the onslaught of scrutiny and criticism. There were things we didn't know, problems as yet unresolved, even for those kids who seemed to be doing the best. And of course there were the failures, those individuals against whose pathology we seemed unable to have any impact.

Two major problems were definable. One was that we had not yet learned to deal with the regressive tendency that is characteristic of schizophrenia. Each of the previously schizophrenic kids still experienced sudden cathexis at times of stress into an unhappy, not-OK, pathological Child, relatively untouched by the efforts we had made so far. At such times the kids managed to maintain a façade of appropriate behavior reinforced by strong injunctions against acting crazy, so the problem was their internal discomfort. However, it was apparent that for at least some, their Child ego states were still fragmented; one or more parts of them still didn't belong to the internal system or relate effectively to external stimuli. The other problem was passivity. With some of our failures that was the major issue, and even for those who had done very well there were unresolved issues having to do with motivation and capacity to organize energy in a goal-directed way.

My professional advisors offered no help; I was already beyond the range of their imaginations. Thus the kids and I and the participants in the Washington, D. C., seminar struggled with the problems. Aaron had, early on, demonstrated an unusual capacity for theoretical operations. It was initially because of my investment in the practice of discussing the theoretical issues with him that we initiated a practice which became an important part of our program, that of including patients in discussions of theory and method. As Aaron became active in seminar discussions others joined also, and the participation and insight contributed by those individuals whose welfare was most at stake was and is indescribably valuable to us. Another person whose contributions were very valuable during this period and even more useful later on was Bob, who joined the family in 1969 and whose name was later changed to Shea when he was adopted. Shea quickly decathected his Parent and moved into a compensation of pathology, convinced that he could resolve the problems through incorporation of a new Parent. In 1970, when it became apparent to us that his efforts were not going to be successful, we began to put pressure on Shea to look at the situation of his Child and he left; however, he maintained contact with us from a distance and emerged later as an important member of our community.

The impressive participation of the kids in public presentations and private discussions had a significant effect on the philosophy of the developing organizations of transactional analysts. Eric Berne's initial philosophy that the patient could and should be an active and equal participant in treatment was broadened substantially when patients began to intrude upon the private places where therapists formulated their theories and planned their interventions. Aaron and Shea, and later Eric and others, were certified as advanced members of the newly formed International Transactional Analysis Association, much to the disconcertion of some of the more conservative members.

Of the problems we faced, we considered the passivity problem as probably the most urgent, since it was most disruptive to those who were struggling to break out of the symbiosis and become independent, and they were a fairly vocal group. I considered it possible and even likely that resolution of the passivity issues might resolve the regressive problems. However, a newcomer to the family, who was by far the most energetically regressive patient we had seen so far, tipped the scales in the other direction. Until that time we had supported the regressive tendency with touch-stroking, giving occasional baby bottles, and permitting short-term cathexis to Child (Infant). Our newcomer maintained that this would never be enough to quell the urgency of his needs and punctuated his demands with outbursts of violence, refusals to eat, and frightening weight losses. Decathexis resolved some of the issues but his frantically rampaging Child presented a management problem that exceeded all we had encountered previously. What he needed, he insisted, was to be a baby *all the time.*

We agreed to try it—and suddenly all the older kids, those who had been complaining about regressive problems, were back home saying, "Hey, me too! That's what I need!"

So we began to take care of babies. Added to everything else we were doing, now we were diapering and giving bottles to six-foot infants, trying to discipline and toilet train enormous two-year-olds, and attempting to find out what regression is all about.

And, while we certainly don't yet know what regression is all about, we now know quite a lot.

We believe that all of us experience cyclic patterns in our lives in which we reenact sequences of psychological events which are like developmental stages in a child. Because children are undefended, these cycles of affect and behavior are more apparent in them than in adults. Thus, a regression simply involves cathecting energy into some part of the personality common to all of us but which is more pronounced in certain individuals because that part of them is fragmented from the rest of their personality and as a result of unmet needs is fixated at an early developmental stage. All of us experience instances where we are stimulated by external stimuli to cathect our Child ego states to young ages. However, most of us pause briefly and then pass on to other aspects of ourselves. The regressive individual is likely to find cathexis to a young child state more comfortable than trying to cope with problems of living in the world and so becomes locked into an infantile state. The cathexis is likely to be a time prior to the beginning development of the pathology, a time when the individual was still comfortable and not experiencing more than normal conflict. Regression is a decisional process in the beginning stage, but once undertaken and maintained for a significant span of time (a day or two) it becomes irreversible. Regressed individuals can cathect Adult and Parent (if they are not heavily contaminated), at least for short periods of time, but are reluctant to do so since it requires an excessive output of energy.

Another reason that regression is likely to work out well as a therapeutic technique is that the patient is generally well motivated. Many of the behaviors that the patient feels the need to externalize are bizarre and unacceptable for functioning individuals in our society, but they are normal at some stage in the development of a child and can therefore be approached from a more positive frame of reference.

If the regressed person has a functional Adult and was relatively uncontaminated at the time the regression occurred and received care and nurturing throughout the period of the regression, the outcome can be remarkably therapeutic. The tendency is for the regression to move forward sequentially in a specific time pattern, and the problems present themselves at various developmental stages. Because they come up one at a time, they are more available to resolution. We do not recommend regression for individuals who are heavily contaminated; although supporting a regression for these individuals is likely to alleviate management problems, the outcome in terms of what is accomplished in treatment is not generally worth the energy required to provide care.

It has long been known that many acute upsets occurring with schizophrenics and resulting in hospitalization are caused by regressions. The individual feels helpless, dependent, and reluctant to think. There is likely to be a tendency to sleep excessively. Physical changes such as a cessation of menses and a recurrence of infantile reflexes are not unusual. Some individuals are frightened and confused about what is happening to them and act out during this period; that is most likely to occur if support for the regressive needs is not available. When the regression is not supported, the problem is reinforced because the individual learns again, as has happened many times in the past, that feelings and needs are not-OK and love and nurturing are not available. The problem is made even worse because the frightened-child consciousness is trapped in an oversized body, the individual lacks information or adaptive behaviors to elicit nurturing, and neither the patient nor the caretakers understand precisely what is happening.

When we began to support regressions we decided to proceed as though we *did* know what was happening. We were trying to rear our oversized infants into healthy adults. As our babies matured they presented us with behaviors typical of disturbed children rather than normal youngsters, and we modified our approaches in order to seek resolution of the disturbances. Our overall goal was to give our kids a new background experience of symbiotic resolution.

Our views about working with regression have changed as we have gained experience. We continue to see diagnosis as very important and know what different behaviors to expect from several different diagnoses. Eric, our most regressive patient, was hebephrenic, and we no longer recommend fully supported regressions for those individuals, although we do use regressive techniques to pursue the overadapted and seductive behaviors that are part of this pathology and also to resolve perceptual disturbances. We may someday resume doing more intense regressive work with hebephrenics, but we are currently finding other techniques more useful. Certainly we continue to see regressive techniques as a valuable resource for the treatment of schizophrenia and some nonpsychotic disorders.

MORE CONTROVERSY

In 1969 several publishers approached me about the possibility of writing a book. I was at first reluctant because of the controversy I thought would result and also because of my heavy schedule. However, when one of the publishers proposed providing a coauthor who would do all the documenting, I agreed hesitantly. We were already getting publicity and controversy was piling up; I thought I might as well risk making a public statement. I decided that the book would be an entirely true account of our activities so far, mostly using real names and describing honestly the controversial aspects of our activities, and that the book would be written for popular consumption. I hoped that popular interest and opinion might provide some protection from the professional furor I expected to excite.

A couple of weeks before the book (*All My Children*) came out I attended a workshop held by the Fairfax County—Falls Church Mental Hygiene Clinic (one of the first group-treatment agencies in the country), from whose staff I had experienced much personal support, and there I talked about the book. I remember the leader of the workshop whistling softly. "You're gonna get it now, baby," he said. "You're really in the marketplace now."

The coming-out of the book was almost anticlimactic. At first nothing happened. Then a strange car began to hang around, and we realized we were being watched. Our mail showed signs of tampering, and sometimes we suspected the telephone was tapped. A medical group began to conduct an investigation of whether we were practicing medicine without a license. Referrals dropped off (but didn't stop), and friends who worked for state agencies began to be less friendly and supportive.

Meantime, Aaron was wanting to do a regression, but insisted that we had to finish the passivity theory work first, so I would know how to handle problems he expected to encounter. He and I worked together, motivated by a tremendous sense of urgency on his part. Looking back, I guess he was afraid that everything would fold up before he got what he needed. We worked through the spring and summer of 1970, a period I remember as especially fruitful in terms of new learning. Eric Berne's death in the summer of 1970 was very distressing to our whole community, and we finished the preparation of the passivity material to be published in the Eric Berne Memorial issue of the first *Transactional Analysis Journal*. Then Aaron, confident that I would know what to do about the passivity issues, became a baby, and I spent the rest of the year checking out and validating findings. That theoretical work, which has been a significant influence throughout TA, won the Eric Berne Memorial Award in 1974.

The controversy continued to mount. Morris and I separated and it seemed impractical for both of us to remain in Fredericksburg, so I planned to move to California. I thought more resources would be available there to the kids and believed the medical establishment to be more liberal. Also, I hoped for support from TA activists, who were still more influential in California than elsewhere.

An important person in our structure at this time was Bob Morris, a young clergyman who joined us as a trainee and contributed immeasurably to the survival of the family. In June of 1971 Bob and Aaron (who was nearly through the regression) began the caravan to California with a large number of the kids. A few days after they left (the rest of us were due to leave almost immediately) most of the kids who were left and I were arrested.

The charges were ludicrous. They were misdemeanor charges of assault with a baby bottle based on the proposal that my treatment of schizophrenic individuals in my home was improper, and with contributing to the delinquency of a minor, because my 11-year-old son, Ric, had been exposed to nudity as a result of our supporting regressions in our home. It was made clear to me that the agencies that had initiated the action as a result of pressure from the medical establishment, hoped and expected that I would simply leave the area with the charges unresolved, in which case the charges would continue on the record as convictions. Instead, I stayed to fight and I won the cases.

The controversy followed us to California. For three years after our arrival a man in a car parked down the block kept watch on our activities, and we experienced considerable pressure from both state and local agencies. However, it was true that California was more liberal and we also found friends and protectors, some from within the TA organization and some from outside. In 1972 a schizophrenic youngster who was visiting us was mysteriously injured and later died in surgery relevant to the injury. The boy was too disturbed to give a coherent account of what happened, and there was a great deal of negative publicity and morbid speculation about the whole affair.

The resultant publicity was obviously disadvantageous to transactional analysis and precipitated an open controversy between me and the more conventional transactional therapists, who disapproved anyway of my departures from traditional practices of psychotherapy. However, TA was in a period of change; many young professionals and a few of the older folks were using my methods with good results, and after some ugly and degrading quarrels it became apparent that the support outweighed the opposition and the controversy died down.

In a way, that unfortunate period seemed to be a turning point. Opposition both within TA and beyond seems to have settled down; the medical establishment knows of my work and treats me with respect. I have presented at the American Psychiatric Association and was invited to do so again in 1976, and I often lecture in medical schools. Another unfortunate incident such as the one in 1972 might turn the tide back again, but I doubt if it would. Meantime, the influence of certain aspects of our work is beginning to be felt throughout the country, both within and outside transactional analysis, as well as in Europe, India, and Australia.

TOUCH-STROKING

One of the profound influences we have had on transactional analysis is our support of touch-stroking as a therapeutic measure. Early in transactional analysis, touching patients was strictly unacceptable. In 1969 Eric

Berne was publicly disgruntled with this aspect of my behavior (to my knowledge the only time he criticized me publicly). When I confronted him with, "Eric, do you really want me to stop touching patients?" the question might as well have been, "Do you want me to stop curing schizophrenia?" and he capitulated. After that, when he and others expressed disapproval of touch-stroking, they often said, "Of course that doesn't mean Jacqui Schiff. It's different with schizophrenia." However, even then many of us knew that it really wasn't different with schizophrenia, that touching was crucial to intimacy, and that psychotherapy needed to be integrated into the total life experiences of the patient. If we were going to teach the patients to utilize all of their resources, then we would have to be willing to include all of ours.

Today most practitioners view transactional analysis as a touching therapy. Therapists touch one another and their patients. There is a body of theory to justify this position, beginning with published statements by Eric Berne (how he would have hated that!). Some practitioners who are still committed to the old schools of psychotherapy continue to practice without touching, but many of those who opposed touching in the past now touch frequently and comfortably.

CATHEXIS INSTITUTE

Cathexis Institute, a nonprofit educational corporation founded in 1972, carries on the traditions begun in the Schiff Family of research and innovative approaches to the treatment of psychosis. Under the auspices of this organization, our emphasis has shifted from residential treatment toward support of the current trend of using communities' effective out-patient facilities to serve the needs of severely disturbed individuals while they remain in community. A daily drop-in program, including classes dealing with common issues of daily living as well as treatment programs, has been very successful and can be provided at low cost.

My own major interest has been to investigate and understand the family conditions which result in severely disturbing emotional problems and to further evaluate diagnosis for meaningful categorization. Some important theoretical work was done by an Australian trainee, Ken Mellor, who came in 1973 and stayed on with us as a member of our staff, in conjunction with Eric Schiff. This work is considered to be part of the frame-of-reference material that we began to publish in 1975. Late in 1974 a group of us—Joel Fishman, Ken Mellor, Aaron and Shea Schiff, and me—gathered for a long weekend to bring our theoretical considerations into focus and to write *The Cathexis Reader*, an overview of several years of collecting data, much of which was already significantly affecting the practice of psychotherapy both within transactional analysis circles and beyond those circles.

So how, in 1976, are we different from other schools of transactional analysis? Probably the most significant difference is our view of games.

GAME THEORY

We consider that the traditional transactional analysis methods of analyzing games are correct, as far as they go. Certainly it is true that games are the means by which we all pursue whatever destructive scripts linger outside our awareness; the ultimate goal of the game is to act out feelings and behavior, and this produces the *racket*.

We see the racket, however, as a desperate attempt on the part of the adaptive structure of the Child to resolve the internal conflict experienced when the Parent messages and the Adult information or thinking resources are in conflict with the natural or spontaneous reactions of the Child. The racket was first produced and adopted as a preferred behavior when the conflict was not an internal conflict, but one which the individual, as a child, experienced in relation to the environment and people in the environment. It was only later, after much reinforcement, that the conflict was internalized; however, it continues to be produced in mature life because the individual experiences internal reinforcement and also because the individual does not have other options available.

As a result of perceiving limited options, there is a tendency in all of us to try to redefine conflicting issues in such a way as to enable us to engage in problem-solving, which reduces internal conflict. Ken Mellor and Eric Schiff listed the possible roles as follows:

1. Angry Righteous. Example: "Look what you did!"
2. Angry Wrongdoer. Example: "So what!" (nastily)
3. Woeful Righteous. Example: "If you had only told me." (Jewish mother)

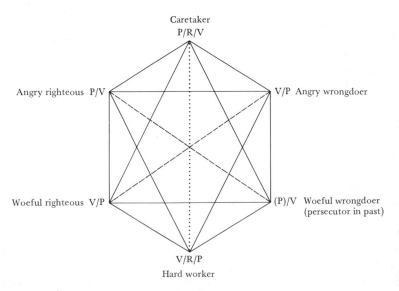

Figure 1

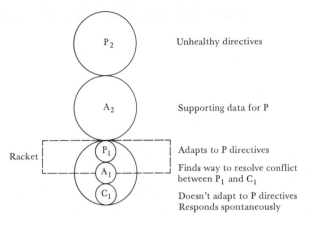

P_2	Unhealthy directives
A_2	Supporting data for P
Racket — P_1	Adapts to P directives
A_1	Finds way to resolve conflict between P_1 and C_1
C_1	Doesn't adapt to P directives Responds spontaneously

Figure 2

4. Woeful Wrongdoer. Example: "I'm so sorry!"
5. Caretaker. Example: "Let me give you some advice."
6. Hard Worker. Example: "Is there anything I can do?"

The individual engages in subtle shifts of frame of reference, re-creating the archaic situation in which the game is acted out (Figure 1).

We view games as a desperate attempt on the part of a struggling individual to re-create an environment in which archaic problems can be reenacted and resolved. Unfortunately, the players are frequently too successful in setting the stage, and the action runs its course with no alteration in the script; the same old outcomes are re-created and the same unhappiness is reexperienced. True, we believe that the individual may actually enjoy his or her discomfort at one level, but we are convinced that it does not end there, that people with destructive life patterns would prefer to be rid of their misfortunes.

Utilizing conventional second-order structure, Figure 2 defines our view of the dynamics of games.

PASSIVITY AND SYMBIOSIS

As a result of the theoretical work on passivity, we view all games as resulting from unresolved symbiosis. The symbiosis was not resolved because of some pathological interference or nonresponsiveness to the healthy maturational process. The presence of the game is demonstrated by a discount, a transaction in which the initiator demonstrates a redefining of the situation or some other nonrelevant thinking. The response indicates willingness to act one of the roles in the game. In order to avoid cognitive dissonance, the individuals in the game must misperceive reality; consequently there are distortions in thinking which can be demonstrated and confronted in verbal transactions. The distortion, which involves exaggeration of some aspect of the situation, is called grandiosity. Thus, our game formula is:

Problem: Symbiosis
$\downarrow$
Mechanism: Discount
$\downarrow$
Justification: Grandiosity

An example of a game confrontation using the passivity material is as follows:

Jack: I'm planning to marry a wonderful girl. However, there's a slight problem. She's quite a lot younger than me, and a lot of people won't approve.
Therapist: This will be your fourth marriage, Jack?
Jack: That's right. This one will work out though.
Therapist: What will be different this time from the other times?
Jack: Well, you see, we're really in love. (Discount)
Therapist: You didn't answer my question. (Confrontation)
Jack: Oh—yeah—sorry. I don't remember what you asked. (Discount)
Therapist: (*Waits.*) (Confrontation)
Jack: Uh—will you tell me again?
Therapist: What's different this time?
Jack: Uh—well, it's a different situation entirely. Uh—I've learned a whole lot . . . I'm just not the same person I used to be. (Grandiosity)
Therapist: You look like the same person to me.
Jack: Well, I mean I've made a lot of changes. (Grandiosity)
Therapist: What are those changes?
Jack: Well, I understand myself a lot better. My games and all.
Therapist: What else? You said a lot of changes. What does a lot better mean?
Jack: I get along a lot better with people than I used to.
Therapist: Hey, Jack, I'm pretty sure you're into a game. You're discounting a lot and sound really vague when you try to explain what you mean.
Jack: Yes, I can feel the confusion. Maybe I better do some more thinking. (Out of game)
Therapist: If you kept on being confused like that, what would the outcome be?
Jack: I suppose I might get married and not really know what's going on.
Therapist: Think about how that would feel. Get in touch with how that feeling is familiar. When do you first remember the feeling?
Jack: (*Swears.*) When I was a little kid and my parents used to get into fights. My old man would accuse my mother of things. Only I knew they weren't true. He was just making it up. He was always jealous of her.
Therapist: What has that to do with this situation?
Jack: (*Swears.*) I suppose I was just setting it up to be in the same kind of thing. I mean, jealous of my wife. Just like my old man!
Therapist: Why would you want to have that happen?

Jack: I suppose—I guess because I always wanted to be close to him. Only the fights he had with my mother—the way he picked on her—I couldn't ever be close to him. I suppose I'm trying to justify the way he acted. (Symbiosis)

Therapist: What do you need to do to give that up?

Jack: Let me think a minute. Let's see. (*Pauses.*) You know, I don't think I need to do anything more. I think just realizing all that takes care of it.

Therapist: What about your marriage plans?

Jack: Well, I need to do some more thinking about that. I really need to take some time to think it through.

INTERNAL DYNAMICS

To describe the internal dynamics of an individual and the manner in which pathological adaptations occur, Figure 3 illustrates how we use the traditional structural diagram, carried to third-order structure in order to show the interrelatedness between what is biological and what is introjected; the arrows show how the different internal structures interrelate, demonstrating the relationships between the various levels of internal reactions and how they are relayed to the more primitive (biological) parts of the personality where they relate to the various hungers (i.e., stimulus hunger, structure hunger, and position hunger).[2]

The child is born with the shaded-in part of the Child ego state. Everything in Figure 3 above that level is adaptive. Thus, when we talk about Natural Child, we are generally referring to adaptive behaviors that are expressive of natural (biological) responses. We have developed a theory of child development related to ego states to demonstrate when and under

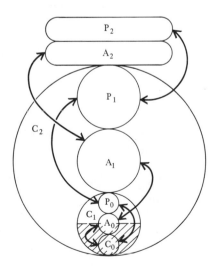

Figure 3

what circumstances pathological adaptations are likely to occur and to relate that to diagnoses, utilizing the traditional medical diagnostic nomenclature.

Pathology is likely to occur at the level of A_2, A_1, or A_0, as the Adult struggles to accomplish resolution of internal conflict. More pathological resolutions occur at the more primitive levels. In psychosis the individual, because the conflict is at the C_1 level and very primitive, is no longer able to discriminate what is internal and what is external.

TREATMENT PHILOSOPHY

Our view of treatment, following this model, is quite simple. First we must identify what behaviors are destructive to the individual patient. Sometimes the patient can participate in this diagnostic process in an active way but often, when the patient is unable to think clearly about the issues, it must be the therapist's responsibility. Once an issue is defined, then it is necessary to identify and alter the internal structures in the Parent and Adult that reinforce the messages. Often this can be accomplished in conversational encounters, but with severely disturbed individuals, or with very primitive issues occurring in the first two years of life, the encounters may need to be experiential.

When the internal structure is altered (that is, replaced with healthy Parent messages and more appropriate Adult data), the next step is to elicit an appropriate adaptive response on the part of the Child. In some cases this may occur spontaneously and readily. However, many issues are such that the original encounters could not have been managed without conflict (toilet training and weaning, for example) and neither can they be conflict-free in the therapeutic resolution. So the treatment contract must include, for these individuals, some way of managing the conflict, the goal being to produce a more appropriate Child adaptation to replace the pathological adaptation.

There are many ways to elicit adaptation when there is resistance. It is possible to use authority, force, unconditional and conditional stroking, teasing, threats, and many others. And we do use them all, to whatever extent we find them useful in accomplishing valid therapeutic goals. While we try to operate on the basis of mutually agreed upon contracts, we perceive that many of our patients are unable to offer contracts. If issues are life-threatening (such as suicide, homicide, anorexia nervosa, self-mutilation), we do not consider that contracts are reasonable or necessary in order to justify taking preventive action. In a meaningful therapeutic contract the patient gives the therapist power; when such a contract is not possible, we believe that the therapist is justified in taking the power, utilizing that power in a constructive and appropriate way, and then restoring the power to the patient as soon as the patient can resume responsibility.

We believe in a reactive environment, a situation in which there is maximum feedback to individuals about their impact on others in their environment. We disagree with the gestalt-influenced philosophy that it is not possible to *make* anyone feel. It seems to us evident that people often do things to other people which *make* them feel, and that manipulating feelings in these situations without eliciting response probably involves discounting and can lead to serious reinforcement of pathology. Rather, we attempt to teach people that no matter what they feel, they can still think and make responsible decisions, that it is not necessary to be incapacitated by feelings.

More than anything else, we believe in people—in ourselves as having a capacity to contribute and be involved with troubled people, and in their capacity to respond, recover, and contribute to others. We utilize group process more than other schools of TA. We believe in using all our resources, in looking beyond the usual cultural ideas of what is "nice" and "appropriate" and "traditional." We look for solutions to problems, and are willing to work with issues such as suicide, violence, and religion which other therapists often try to avoid.

A quote from *The Cathexis Reader,* which sums up our treatment philosophy, is as follows:

> Often what we do matters less than our willingness to be involved, to enter into the struggle with patients, to lend them our resources of energy and thinking when their own fail, and to reinforce their autonomy when they are able to function. We don't think it is necessary to be nice to the patients if niceness interferes with clarity. We doubt if it is possible for anyone to get well while maintaining an unreal investment in comfort, the comfort of either the patient or the therapist. We deal in issues as primitive as vomiting, feces, and violence, and we try to deal with them in sensitive and sensible ways. We use all of our personal resources and are willing to address all of the patients' needs which we can understand and respond to.[3]

SUMMARY

In summary, the Cathexis School of TA (sometimes called "The Schiff Family School") developed separately from the mainstream of theoretical thinking in TA and has had a substantial impact throughout the ITAA. Our emphasis has been on the manipulation of ego states in the service of therapeutic goals. We have developed programs for working with severely disturbed individuals, and among specific interests are passivity, child development as related to diagnosis, frame of reference in thinking disorders, and exploration of innovative treatment techniques. We introduced touch-stroking as a therapeutic intervention and have developed many controversial treatment philosophies. However, as our society has changed in the direction of acceptance and individuation, our work has had increasing impact and success.

References

1. Eric Berne, "The Intimacy Experience," *Transactional Analysis Bulletin, 3,* no. 9 (January, 1963), p. 113; Eric Berne, "More About Intimacy," *Transactional Analysis Bulletin, 3,* no. 10 (April, 1964), p. 125.
2. Eric Berne, *Transactional Analysis in Psychotherapy,* New York, Grove Press, 1961, pp. 83–88.
3. Jacqui Lee Schiff, *et al., The Cathexis Reader,* New York, Harper & Row, 1975.

FOUR

NO MAGIC AT MT. MADONNA:
REDECISIONS IN MARATHON THERAPY
Robert L. Goulding

In this chapter, I will present the history of marathons as we have done them; I will define a marathon as I see the definition; I will present the therapeutic indications for doing marathons; I will present the scene and the format, as I think they ought to be done; I will review what the factors are that seem to establish an environment conducive to change; I will briefly touch on some of the results of our work.

EARLY MARATHON EXPERIENCES[1]

My first marathon, over Labor Day weekend in 1963 at Big Sur, California, was designed at the request of four couples in an ongoing group. These eight people said in effect, "Hey, we are doing great, but sometimes we just seemed to get warmed up on something when the hour and a half is over—and by the time we get back the following week, the desire, or the intensity, or the energy is gone. How about having a longer group once in awhile?" The request seemed reasonable to me, and I arranged for a large house in Big Sur for the weekend. We started Friday night, worked until very late, started Saturday morning, worked until after midnight, then all day Sunday, and part of Monday. Only three couples came, plus my former wife, who came along for the ride. I was greatly impressed, as were the patients, that we did seem to get farther; we stayed with impasses until we were through them, and a great deal of wonderful, warm intimacy was developed which these people never lost in the years afterwards.

My next marathon-like experience was with Virginia Satir, also at Big Sur. There were five families and one divorcee. I believe this was also Virginia's first prolonged experience as a group leader. We started Sunday night, worked until Friday noon, with time out, of course, to eat and sleep.

The results, we thought, were interesting. The divorcee was married a few months later. One couple is still together and has not been in therapy since the week-long experience. One family consisted of a mother and daughter, who had been clashing for eighteen years—ever since the daughter was adopted (the father did not come to the experience); at the end of the week, the mother and daughter had finished out most of their disagreements, made some decisions to change their way of dealing with one another, and they have done well since then. Incidentally, most of the problems between mother and father also were ironed out, even though father was not there.

For several months thereafter I did an occasional weekend marathon, but did not really want to get involved—it was tough doing them by myself, and at that time I had no associate to work with. Later on, I heard George Bach talk about his sleepless marathons. I had by then associated with a psychologist; he and I did several marathons without sleep over a period of several months. These, in my opinion, were horrors. We started Friday evening at 6:00, stayed together working, eating, swimming until 10:00 Saturday night; slept a little, then finished Sunday at 4:00 PM. I was not impressed with results being any better than with reasonable sleep; I *was* impressed with the fact that I lost two or three days' work each week after such a marathon, while I tried to recover from the fatigue. I felt, and the patients did also, that the lack of sleep seriously interfered with their ability to do good intellectual work, that they probably had more emotional crises but were unable to put them together as well. After a few months I decided that sleepless marathons were for those (in the words of Price Cobbs) who are either under 40 or think they are—and, since I am neither under 40 nor think I am, I stopped the sleepless weekends.

Since that time, I have done a marathon almost every fourth weekend; occasionally I have done three a month, always (except once) with a cotherapist. We sleep six to nine hours Friday and Saturday nights. This does not meet the definition of a marathon as George Bach describes it, but in my opinion an intensive therapeutic experience which lasts through two nights, with approximately 18 hours of time spent in therapy, is a marathon. (People are on the grounds for 56 hours, 18 of which are spent in therapy.)

CRITERIA FOR PLACING PATIENTS IN MARATHONS

For the ongoing patient, there are several indications we use for placing him in a marathon. However we do not, at this time, suggest to a patient that he go into a marathon; rather, we allow him or her to volunteer first. At one time we did urge patients to attend marathons, but we began to feel that we were letting our own enthusiasm get in the way of what might be better judgment if we waited for the patient to volunteer. He usually does so at a point where he has reached what Fritz Perls called the impasse—where he is making no gains in therapy, has not reached his most recent contract, and feels he needs a therapeutic experience more intense than that afforded in ongoing groups. Sometimes other patients urge that he get into a marathon, and we do nothing to bridle their enthusiasm. The second indication for the ongoing patient is often his inability to get close to people; he then wants the experience primarily for the opportunity to develop more intimate feelings for other people. Another indication is the impasse arrived at by couples or families, at which point they feel that a weekend together may enable them to discontinue their marital games. Also an important indication is the desire of a patient who has been moving rapidly to get into a marathon in order to finish his contract and discontinue therapy.

For the new patient, or new couple, or new family, we do not wait for the patient to volunteer. Most patients, in the initial interview, are told about the marathons and asked to plan for one in the near future after they start therapy. It has been our opinion that many patients, if they get into a marathon early in treatment, reach their contracts much more quickly, and can get out of therapy with the crisis in question solved. We recognize in this, then, the statement that most of our therapy today is crisis-intervention therapy; not only do we have no objection to this, we heartily endorse this type of psychotherapeutic experience. The gate to our institute opens both ways.

A third category of indications for a marathon concerns training (see section below on "The Therapist-Patient"). The professional who is in training is expected to be in a marathon and to make a therapeutic contract for himself.

CONTRAINDICATIONS FOR MARATHONS

I will not treat in a marathon an alcoholic who is actively drinking or one who has just recently stopped drinking. This decision came after one patient on two occasions had a grand-mal seizure following three or four days of drying out prior to the marathon. I will not treat an acute psychotic in a marathon, nor will I treat a seriously depressed and acutely suicidal patient who has not reached a decision not to kill himself.

This does not mean that we don't treat the chronic depressive in a marathon; but the acute, severely depressed patient who is still ruminating about suicide is too difficult to handle in a marathon and takes too much time from the other patients. We want the hard drug user off drugs for a while before we do a marathon with him.[2] There may be some other contraindications but these seem to cover most conditions. We have made no attempts to eliminate patients because of physical disabilities. If another physician did not want his patient to go to a marathon because of cardiac disease or other contraindications, I would honor his decision.

For the above reasons we will take no patient in a marathon unless he is our own patient, or has been referred to us by a professional who has, preferably, been to one of our marathons. We do take professionals into marathons without referral. We have had professionals who fell into the contraindicated categories, and we have dealt with each of them on an individual basis. I believe that the reason we have had almost no untoward reactions in 14 years is because we take seriously our responsibility for the patient. Some workshop and marathon leaders have written that the professional (or patient) arrives under his own steam, is responsible for doing so, and is responsible for himself. I do not feel this position is medically responsible and would not allow a distraught participant to leave without some definitive plans for his immediate care.[3]

THE MARATHON FORMAT

Let me now describe the physical setting we have and the format of the marathon itself. We hold most of our intensive experiences on a 30-acre farm in the mountains outside Watsonville, California. The house is big enough to sleep 20 participants comfortably, although we seldom have more than 14. We have a good kitchen, a good cook, and good food. Everyone sleeps in beds, although at one time when we first did marathons everyone slept on the floor in the living room on sleeping bags and air mattresses. We have a swimming pool, because we feel that swimming, exercise, and some play are important to encourage the participants to have fun together as well as to work. (We have treated many patients with phobias about water by teaching them to swim while we were concurrently working on the source of the phobic feelings in the therapeutic environment. See below.)

We start the weekend at 9:00 AM Friday with a theoretical presentation on transactional analysis. Patients seem to be able to put things together much better with the orderly presentation of the theoretical material, and this emphasizes the view of the TA therapist that he share with the patient all his theoretical and practical ideas, so that the patient is not in the dark regarding the therapeutic process.

We break at noon for lunch; unlike Bach, we allow the participants to eat wherever they like—with each other in the dining room, or around the pool, or by themselves. We feel that a patient should have the opportunity to withdraw for a while if he wishes. Formerly we picked up the theoretical material again at 1:00 PM, but now we start therapy at 1:30 and continue working until about 5:00. In the past, we had the participants take small groups under our supervision to begin to get some experience in the use of the theory; we have discontinued this, because we found it somewhat disjointed and often not productive.

At the start of the marathon, we announce the rules of the marathon. They are as follows:

1. The use of alcohol, drugs, and marijuana is prohibited, and anyone having any illegal drugs on the premises is asked to take them across the road and bury them. Anyone taking a prescription is asked to notify me of the nature of the drug.

2. No physical violence will be permitted, and no breaking of furniture is allowed unless it is first paid for.
3. No one is permitted to leave the property, but anyone can withdraw at any time if he wishes; there are 30 acres and 20 rooms to withdraw to.
4. No sexual intercourse is allowed except between married couples or partners who have been living together.
5. Any food or nonalcoholic beverage found in the house may be eaten or drunk at any time.

If anyone questions the reasons for the rules, we explain why we have made them. We want people to be in the best possible shape to work—and neither alcohol nor drugs are conducive to good work. I don't want pot on the place because it is against the law. Physical violence is not therapeutic. Furniture costs money. Sex between participants not married to one another or previously living together often is pure rape and ends in difficulty.

At 1:30 we start the formal work of the marathon. During the afternoon of Friday we obtain contracts for the weekend from each participant—patient and professional alike. A therapeutic contract is one of the most important tools of the group therapist. If the therapist and the patient know where the patient wants to go, then they can tell when they get there, and the therapist will usually be able to check out the sideroads down which the patient goes as not in the interest of the contract.

To get the contracts usually takes all of Friday afternoon. This does not mean that no therapeutic work is done; frequently, at the time a contract is made, some work is done which is most important towards achieving the contract. The work we do includes several therapeutic tools. We are basically transactional analysts and use TA as our primary theoretical position; we also use a great deal of gestalt therapy and our own brand of psychodrama. Our marathons are designed to afford an opportunity for the patient to contract to have new experiences for himself. Unlike many other therapists, we are discriminating in the use of nonverbal and verbal techniques; the particular technique has to fit the needs of a particular patient at a particular time. In other words, we don't suddenly say to the patients, "Now let's everyone do Technique 23A," or use gimmicks or sensory awareness or other such ploys unless they fit in the therapeutic scheme for a particular problem. These marathons are intensive therapeutic experiences and not sensory awareness weekends.

We formerly stopped work at about midnight, but have since found it wiser to quit at 9:00 PM. Saturday morning we start at 9:00, with breakfast being served about 7:30. We usually work for about one and a half hours, then break for an encounter-group session made up of three or four small groups. This is done to allow the less assertive patients to have more of a chance to transact and interact, and often some good experiences come out of the encounters. When we meet again, a half-hour later, we ask for unfinished business from the encounters so that if there were any loose ends we can work them out. We break at noon for lunch and a swim, and at 5:00 for dinner and a swim, then work until everyone is satisfied with where they are at the moment. Usually we quit at about 8:30 or 9:00 PM and then have a dry party, with music, dancing, and games if the group wishes. Mary, my wife, and I usually take part in the party for a half-hour or so, then leave and allow the participants some time together without us, and us some time without them! We have noticed that they usually have more fun after we have left.

Sunday morning we start again at 9:00 and work until noon. Usually Sunday is the time for dream work, and this is one of the many therapeutic reasons why I prefer doing marathons in which patients can sleep. Frequently some very important dream work is done, which really crystalizes the weekend experience for a number of patients. We prefer to do active, in-the-present, dream work, in which the patient relives the dream, takes the various parts in the dream, and then retells it the way he wants it to finish and be.

Beginning at 11:00 AM on Sunday we wind up that marathon with a discussion of redecisions, in which each participant reviews what he is going to do differently in the future. This frequently is a most important part of the marathon: for instance, when the depressed patient states that he is not going to kill himself, and that he is going to enjoy himself in the future; this is often the start of a new life for him, in which he will check out what he does day in and day out against that decision.

Following the redecisions, the patients are allowed time to say goodbye to each other. Many patients have been working all weekend on saying goodbye to old figures in their lives and to old feelings. The experience of saying goodbye to the group members, and their group transferences, is often extremely important.

EFFECTIVENESS OF MARATHON GROUP TREATMENT

If we assume that this method of treatment is effective, and perhaps more effective than individual or group psychotherapy in the classical sense, then we need to postulate what the effective factors are. In our opinion, there are at least three reasons for what we feel to be more effective therapy in many cases. The first is the time factor itself; patients are exposed to intervention and self-discovery and to redecisions in a prolonged period, where they are not as likely to use their common defenses, and where they cannot so easily withdraw or delay until the hour is up. Although they may withdraw and although we always give participants a chance to stop at any point if they wish, the recognition that others have made changes without disaster, that others have broken through some old patterns without the walls falling down encourages each one to do more for himself. This last point brings home the second issue: the patient is stimulated by the intensity of peer pressure and peer encouragement over a prolonged period of continuous time, and rewarded by the recognition that he or she gets for doing a particularly important piece of work. Thirdly, the degree of intimacy that builds up in 60 hours makes it easier for patients to feel safer in working through impasses. Thus it would seem that the prolonged time involved, with difficulty in withdrawing, the increased stroking, and the awareness that others are making immediate changes all add up to increased opportunity for change for each patient.

The results of marathon group treatment are difficult to evaluate scientifically, but we do have two specific pieces of research that are supportive. One is the work done by Yalom, Lieberman, Miles, and Golde, reported in the book *Encounter Groups: First Facts*. The other is the dissertation done by John McNeel for his PhD on one of our weekend marathons.[4] We have enough feedback from both patients and professionals to feel that our participants very often make changes in their behavior as well as changes in their feelings after attending marathons. We have feedback from organizations such as the O. H. Close School, an agency in the California Youth Authority, that their staff members, after attending a training marathon, seem to work better together, to stop their institution games faster, and to be generally happier. Many of our patients tell us that they accomplished more in a marathon than they had in several months of group treatment. All these reports are somewhat intangible, and I can't and won't claim that we have proof positive that marathons are better than weekly group sessions, or individual sessions, or prolonged psychoanalysis. It is even difficult to evaluate whether the marathon is the primary agent, or whether it is our technique, our enthusiasm, and our abilities that set the stage for the possibility of change. McNeel's work cites four major areas which the clients in his research of one of our marathons stated were helpful:

1. the environment—physical and personal;
2. positive recognition;
3. the therapists' modeling behavior; and
4. the techniques—experimental and cognitive.

This brings me to Eric Berne, who was more interested in working with patients to change (he called it "cure") than to find out why. He said, "Cure the patient, then analyze."

I first met Eric in Carmel before my residency, played poker a few times with him, but had no professional contact. I had intended to finish my analysis with him, since my analyst in Baltimore had died. I phoned him in January of 1962, on my way to Roseburg, Oregon, where I had been assigned for two years as part of my Veterans Administration contract, and made an appointment to see him the following Saturday. During that week, Carl Bonner asked me if I had read a book on transactional analysis by ". . . a fella named Eric Berne."[5] "Wow," said I, "I'm going to see him Saturday. Let me borrow it." So I read it, and turned on. When I saw Eric, I told him right off that I wanted to both finish my analysis and learn TA from him. "Waal," he drawled, "that would be kinda sticky." I can still hear him. I was in supervision with him almost every Saturday for two years—driving down from Roseburg to Carmel (600 miles) on Friday and back on Sunday. In June, 1963, I was transferred to Palo Alto, so I only had to drive 60 miles to Carmel and I was able to attend most of the Tuesday night seminars in San Francisco. Sometime during those two years I started the Carmel Institute for Transactional Analysis to train some of the professionals in Carmel as well as non-professionals who were interested in mental health from a community standpoint.

FROM A WEEKEND TO A MONTH   Later we (Mary and I) expanded the training offered by the institute to include intensive month-long workshops, and for the past several years professionals from all over the world have trained with us and our associates. We also changed our institute's name to the Western Institute for Group and Family Therapy and moved to Mount Madonna, near Watsonville, California, overlooking beautiful Monterey Bay.

RACKETS

From the very first moment, the trainee/patient at Mount Madonna is confronted with the awareness that he alone is in charge of his thinking, behavior, and feelings. He possesses the power. If he chooses to feel angry, or sad, or anxious, or confused, that is his choice, and he has other options. This concept is the very core of our work. Furthermore, he looks for his original power in being anxious, or angry, or sad, and for what that feeling originally got him. The feelings, appropriately called *rackets* by Berne, were developed in order for him to manipulate his parents into giving him what he wanted, and he is still doing something, and feeling something, so as to manipulate other people. Unfortunately, most of the anger he may still have is also designed to change the past, as well as the present. Of course, since this can't be done, the bad feelings are maintained so as to perpetuate a myth and are totally without any good return.

INJUNCTIONS/DECISIONS

The patient is confronted with the *decisions* he made early in response to his injunctions, and which he still is maintaining in the present. This was *his* decision in response to the behavior and feelings of his parents; the injunctions were not stuck in his head like electrodes, but he responded to them in order to survive both psychologically and physiologically. He had the power to make the decisions, and he has the power to make new ones now, in this time, in this place, if he doesn't like what he is doing, what he is feeling, what he is thinking now. His rackets, his games, his pastimes, all support this original decision, and he has the power to change. This is the essence of what we do.

GAME CONFRONTATION

The patient has the power to do whatever it is he wants to do. We create an environment in which the patient may recapture his autonomy. We supply surroundings that are most conducive to that purpose; the patient has little to do each day but work on himself and play. His food is supplied, everyone around him is giving him positive strokes, no one is parenting him, no one is bossing him. At the same time, whenever he gives an indication that he is staying in a bad place, or feeling badly inappropriately, he is confronted by staff and by other patients. If he laughs while talking about feeling badly while at the table, I will say, "That's not funny," or "I'm not laughing." If he arrives before the stated time of seven and finds the gate locked (as it is), and if he feels anger, or chagrin, or whatever, we immediately ask him how come he set himself up to feel badly when he knew the gate would be locked. If he calls to say that he would like to come early, and we say no (of course) and he gets angry, or feels we have rejected him, we immediately confront him with his game of *Kick Me*.

The confrontation of the game is done very simply. The patient is asked what he is feeling. In this case—coming early and finding the gate locked—he usually is angry that we won't let him in until seven o'clock. We ask him if he wants to know how he did it—how he set himself up to get angry. Usually he is willing to find out. Then we draw the game out using the Goulding-Kupfer representation of the game (Figure 1).

His ostensibly straight message is "Please open the gate" (#1 in the diagram). His secret message is "Say no so that I can be angry" (#2). We of course say no, because we have already written everyone a letter with directions and the explicit statement not to come early because the gate will be locked; his Child must know that, even though he is keeping it out of the awareness of his Adult (#3). He then takes his payoff, which in this case is anger (#4), and says inside his head, or out loud, "No one ever gives me what I want" (#5), and "Everyone in the world is sons of bitches" (#6). Of course, the entire process is out of his Adult's awareness —the process that he sets up so that he can maintain his anger at a world that won't give him what he wants.

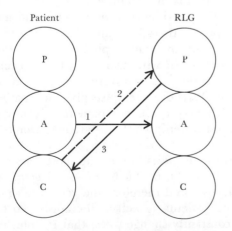

Patient   RLG

4. Anger
5. Statement about self
6. Statement about others
7. Not in adult awareness

Figure 1

We then may ask him what he will do if he continues to make himself angry in this manner for the next five years. What will be his predictable behavior? He may say that he will kill someone in anger and go to jail. He may say that he gets so disgusted that he will kill himself in anger. He may say that people get tired of his anger, and he will end up alone. Whatever he says, this is his *script payoff*, and we ask him if this is what he really wants out of his life. If it is not, we ask him whether he is willing to stop playing the game and willing to stop taking the payoff. We usually get an "Of course." Then we want to know what he predicts he will do if he plays again. He'll usually say that he would angrily kick himself—thus, of course, continuing to play all by himself. We then ask him if he is willing, at the moment he recognizes he has played, to refuse the anger and instead feel good that he has recognized the game. A little practice is all he needs, for if he doesn't get the payoff, his Child will stop playing after a while.

REDECISION

The next piece of work, at some point, is to get him into an early scene in which he gets angry, and in which he says the things he said above about himself and others, including "I never get what I want" and "You're a son of a bitch." Then we give him the opportunity to make a *redecision* about getting what he wants appropriately.

THE THERAPIST-PATIENT

Recognize, of course, that in our current work 90 percent or more of our "patients" are therapists.[6] We take no nontherapists in our one-week, two-week, or four-week workshops, and no patients in our ongoing training; only a few make the marathons because therapists often have signed up for them a year in advance. However, almost everyone who comes here has problems to work out. My position is that training *must* include therapy; a depressed therapist has a difficult time treating anyone, and more particularly, depressed patients; phobic therapists (and there are a lot of phobic therapists) have great difficulty in treating phobiacs. Male *Rapo* players get involved over and over again with female hysterics. Female therapists of any age who are still little girls have very little potency and find it difficult to confront patients. Psychotic therapists give their patients many negative injunctions, which may cause the patient to get worse instead of better. Suicidal therapists often give their patients "Don't be" injunctions.

Thus, to train without treatment neglects one of the most important issues in training—the trainee. He or she has to be of sound emotional stability in order to be most effective, and therefore the very core of our training is that the therapists are patients as well as therapists. To take the magic out of therapy, they constantly change roles; that is, John may be Susan's therapist at 9:00 AM and Susan's patient at 10:00 AM. At the time I am writing this, I am just completing a two-week advanced workshop and, by the time the group got to the last weekend when Mary and I were to do a marathon, most of the members of the workshop were finished with their work. Advanced therapy, conducted by good therapists in this environment, leads to very rapid resolution of all kinds of archaic impasses and to the beginnings of substantial permanent changes. That doesn't mean that, after a week, a depressed therapist gives up all his depression forever; it does mean that he usually gives up all thoughts of suicide, and begins to take charge of his own sadness and to stop playing games and fantasizing in order to feel depressed. He gets in touch with his own power, and claims it.

That may sound simple and it is, but there is no magic in it. It takes very careful work, and it takes a lot of practice. The patient has to *know* that he is in charge, and he has had years of conditioning which tell him that he is not in charge, that other people *make* him feel angry, or sad, or anxious. He reads this in books, his culture believes it, even the songs he hears say that people make other people hurt, or fall in love. Remember the song, "You made me love you, I didn't want to do it"? How naive can we get? Mother says, "You were a very difficult birth, you tore me up!" Or, "If it weren't for you, I wouldn't have had to marry your father!" My God, who fucked?

That is the kind of trash we were raised with, and 95 percent of the world believes it. Mother controls behavior by saying, "You make me so angry," or "You give me a headache," or "You make me worry so when you are not in by nine." So part of the work is in behavior and thinking and feeling modification—operant conditioning. Every time someone says "How does she make you feel?" or "He made me feel bad," we holler "Tilt." Every time. We constantly recondition our patients. Every time they say "Try," as "Yes, I'll try not to say 'make me feel,'" I ring a huge cow bell. We teach people how to be in touch with their immediate surroundings instead of harrassing themselves by thinking of what they did yesterday that was wrong, or being anxious about what they are going to do tomorrow. Most of the difficulty people have is in not staying in the here-and-now, but instead of anticipating the future or rehashing the past. There is usually no way of feeling bad if I stay in the present, in this place, unless this is a bad place, and then I need to get the hell out of it. If I can't get out of it—like the prisoners at Marion Federal Penitentiary —then I must find a way of making it a better place, as Martin Groder has done in his work with prisons.

DEGREES OF IMPASSES

Thus we keep up a constant modification of the behavior and thinking and feeling that is inappropriate to the present and to the idea of autonomy. We use gestalt work to facilitate people getting through impasses, and we see impasses as being of only three basic kinds: Between A_1 and P_2, between A_1 and the Child of the parent in the Parent of the Child—P_1—

which Berne called the Electrode, or between the Adapted Child and the Free Child. All impasses relate directly to the Little Professor having decided something in order to get along, and now not wanting to do that anymore. Decisions cannot be made in the Adult to produce comfortable change, they must be made from the Adult of the Child (A_1).[7]

For example, in the first-degree impasse (degrees refer to type, not severity), the patient decided at one time, from his Little Professor, to listen to and obey a counterinjunction—a message from the Parent ego state of his parent—to "Work hard" or "Whatever you do, do it well or don't do it at all." All therapists probably received one or the other or both of these. No one would get to be a professional therapist if he hadn't worked hard to get through college, get through graduate or medical school, get through clinical training in psychotherapy. At some point, the therapist says to himself, "I don't want to work so hard anymore; I am going to cut down to 40 or 50 hours a week" (A_2). And so he does, and perhaps he will get away with no problems, and resolve the impasse simply. The impasse is the conflict between the introjected Parent saying "Work hard" and the Child saying "I don't wanna anymore." The Adult making the decision not to work hard is probably not enough; the Child feels deprived because he wasn't consulted about something that had gotten him a lot of strokes (for working hard), and he rebels. The rebellion may be in the form of anxiety and restlessness, with difficulty in structuring time; it may be in headaches, or insomnia, or a feeling of despair (Figure 2).

More work then needs to be done to resolve the first-degree impasse.

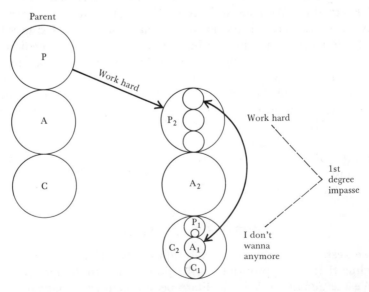

Figure 2

For instance, the therapist may complain that since he decided yesterday not to work so hard, he has a headache. I may say: "Think of a scene in which your mother or father told you to work hard."

> *Patient:* I was seven years old and . . .
> *I:* Be in the present tense.
> *Patient:* I am seven years old and I want a bicycle. My father says, "You can't have a bicycle unless you do something for it." I say, "What?" "Well . . ."
> *I:* Move over in the chair and be your father.
> *Patient:* (*As Father.*) If you are going to get anywhere in this world, you are going to have to work for it, and work hard.
> *I:* Switch.
> *Patient:* (*As self, switching.*) I'm just a little boy, and I want a bike, and I don't want to work hard. You give me a bike for Christmas.
> *Patient:* (*As Father.*) No, you have to work hard to get anything; bikes don't grow on trees.
> *Patient:* What do you want me to do?
> *I:* OK, you gave in. What would you really like to tell him? *Be* there.
> *Patient:* You son of a bitch, I'm not going to always work hard to get what I want. All you think of is work. I'm playing more, working less from now on. (Headache stops.)

A day or two later, the patient may say, "OK, my headache is gone, but now I'm beginning to feel depressed. It seems like I keep hearing in my head my mother's voice saying, 'If you are not going to work hard and make me proud of you, you might as well be dead."

Now we are working through the injunction "Don't exist," and the Child's response to the injunction could be "If I'm not working hard, no one will stroke me, and I might as well go out and eat worms." The second-degree impasse relates to the Child's awareness of the "Don't be" injunction, and his uneasiness with not resolving it at this time (Figure 3). "Respond to your mother," I say.

> *Patient:* I remember your saying things like that.
> *I:* Be there.
> *Patient:* How come you don't want me unless I work hard?
> *Patient:* (*As Mother.*) I never wanted you. It was your father's idea; if you must be here, you're going to have to work.
> *Patient:* (*As self.*) Well, to hell with you. I'm not going to work hard, and I'm not only going to stay alive, I am going to start living, not just existing for you to be proud of. I'm going to play, and have fun, and enjoy myself and my life. Furthermore, I'm going to buy my own damn bike (*laughing*).

It is even possible that he may return in a couple of days and say, "Well, I don't feel depressed anymore, but I sure am uncomfortable somehow. I feel worthless. As a matter of fact, I have always felt worthless unless I was doing something. I can remember helping my mother when I was only a little tiny kid, and I felt worthless then."

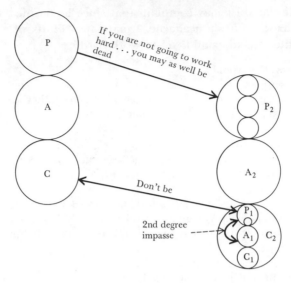

Figure 3

Now we are dealing with the third-degree impasse, the Adapted Child feeling that has "always" been there. Always worthless, always clumsy, always nervous, always stupid. (The second-generation Mexican-American in California is called and feels stupid because he doesn't speak much English, but nobody calls the teacher stupid for not speaking Spanish. Nobody calls the other kids stupid for not speaking Spanish either.) The Adapted Child does not experience the injunction as coming from outside; rather he experiences that any comments coming from mother, or teacher, or other students were justified because he *was* stupid, or clumsy, or worthless.

In this, the third-degree impasse, the conflict is not between the Child or Parent of the parent and the Child's Little Professor; it is between the Adapted Child and the Free Child (Figure 4). Now, instead of the dialogue being an I-Thou dialogue, it is comprised of two statements; one from the Free Child, one from the Adapted Child. For instance:

> *Adapted Child:* I have always felt worthless. I remember feeling worthless when I was a little kid, and I had to keep doing things not to feel worthless.
>
> *Free Child:* I don't know what to say from this side.
>
> *I:* Stand over here near that chair. Pretend you are just born there on the chair, and tell you why you're worthless.
>
> *Patient:* I won't do that. He's not worthless at all; he's just born, and he's cute.
>
> *I:* Sit in the chair and say that for you.
>
> *Free Child:* Heh, I'm a great little kid, and if those other guys don't appreciate me that's their problem. (*Switches.*)
>
> *Adapted Child:* Yeah, I'm tired of feeling worthless. I think I'll give it up.

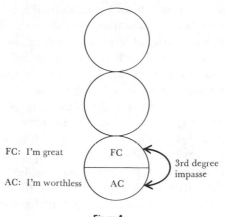

Figure 4

Free Child: I know I'm giving it up. (Note the use of the future tense in the Adapted position, the use of the present tense in the Free position.)

Adapted Child: Now I'm feeling great. I am great.

We use behavior modification, gestalt, Wolpe's desensitization, psychodrama, anything at all that will facilitate the patient getting into his Child ego state in an archaic scene, making sure that he or she is there with affect, reliving the scene, and then making a new decision.[8] We use TA as a structure of thinking for ourselves, asking ourselves the same questions over and over again: What is the racket? What kinds of games does the patient play? What were the decisions that he made as a child? What were the injunctions and counterinjunctions? We move as rapidly as possible to get the patient to work through the impasse, and *then* we give him cognitive feedback by word of mouth and by visual imagery, using the script-matrix drawings and diagrams of games (both Karpman's triangle and the Goulding-Kupfer drawings). The moderate affective experience, the maximum cognitive feedback, the maximum caring, and the entire operation done in an environment that is moderately executed will bring about the best results, as long as the patient maintains his *own* autonomy. Any attempt to discount the autonomy of the patient will end eventually in either a psychotic or a neurotic symbiosis.

TREATMENT OF PHOBIAS

We are particularly interested in fast work. Berne said long ago that every time he started a group, he spent a few minutes before entering the room planning on how he could cure everyone that day. That is a fascinating concept, and we use it as the primary goal in our therapy. We ask ourselves what kind of a situation we can develop that will enable the patient to get to the very heart of his impasse, get through the impasse, and change today. Now, we know that he won't make a complete change today, but perhaps we can do something so that he makes a substantial, powerful redecision that will enable him to look at the world through a different pair of eyes and see himself in the world differently. The treatment of phobias is an example of this kind of work, and I know that in most cases we can facilitate a patient losing his phobia in 20 to 30 minutes. For instance, we work with many therapists who are phobic of heights, of water, and of insects. Some of the most fun we have is in facilitating them not to be phobic after one session of work.[9]

Our basic position about phobias is that the phobic response is the result of an injunction and that, in such phobias as fear of high places or fear of drowning, the Little Professor said at one time, in response to a "Don't be" injunction, "That's pretty scary, I had better be careful" (of high places, water, etc.). As he grows up, he forgets the original injunction, but he has incorporated it in the Parent of his Child, and he responds as if it were still being said and stays scared in order to avoid the scary places.

We first came to this realization when we heard patients say, "I am afraid, if I get close to an edge of a hill, cliff, building, that I will fall off or *jump* off." Now, the only reason the person would jump off is if he were going to commit suicide, but for all we can find out, there is no evidence of depression or suicidal ruminations in him. (Sometimes there is, but often there is not.) The only reason why he would jump off, if not suicidal, is that he would be responding to some internal message, and when we started looking for it, we found it. Perhaps her father didn't catch her once when he threw her up in the air, or his father let him slide down the slide into the water without catching him, so that mother had to jump into the pool to pull him out. These kinds of behavior on the part of parents were interpreted by the patient as "Don't be" injunctions, and he developed a defense by becoming phobic.

It is further perfectly logical that, if such was the case, then the patient should be able to lose his phobia by deciding he would *never* fall off, jump off, slide off, slip off. After all, if he is reasonably careful, he doesn't need to be scared to save his life—he just needs to operate from A_2 rather than from P_1, where the original scare is. We do this by a combination of desensitization and redecision work. Sometimes we do the desensitization in fantasy, sometimes in reality.

For instance, if the patient is willing, I will put a ladder against the barn. I will ask the other patients to hold it firmly. I will ask the phobic patient to climb the first step and then tell the others that he is not going to fall off, jump off, slip off. If he says he is scared, I ask him to step back down on the ground immediately, breathe deeply, get back into not being scared, then climb the first step again. Each time he climbs a higher step without being scared, he repeats the phrase before he climbs higher. When he has reached the top rung, before he climbs onto the roof, I ask him to climb back down, and I go up the ladder onto the roof. Now he is asked to climb up again, and to repeat the phrase again, this time imagining that his parents and his whole archaic family are below; he is to tell *them* that he is not going to fall off, jump off, slip off, slide off, lose his balance. I then ask him if he wants to climb on the roof by himself, or wants me to help. I do whichever he wishes, and we now repeat the desensitization as he climbs higher and higher on the sloping roof, until he is standing up on the ridge, looking at the view. He only goes as far as he wants each time, and if he reaches a scary place he goes back, then does it again. In NO CASE has the patient failed to climb up and to drop his fear. If he says that it was too easy, that he wasn't scared of things that low, then we find a higher place, such as our log cabin, and do it again. We also do things to hook his Child, so that he is saying the phrase from his Child; for instance, I might ask him to quack at the ducks down on the pond; the ducks will almost always quack back. The patient laughs, and then I ask him to tell the ducks!

Swimming phobias are equally simple and quick. Here the patients are sometimes so scared that they won't go into the water; others are only scared of deep water. In any case, the technique is to teach them to float, and then to turn over from a prone to a supine float, and then to swim on their backs after they have stabilized. Many patients are afraid of getting water in the mouth, nose, and throat; if so, we play noisy games with face under water, gargle, spit at each other with a mouth full of water, until they laugh and drop that fear. I teach them to float by stabilizing them with two hands in the water, asking them to breathe from deep inspiration to *half*-expiration, and to be aware of how they float on their back off my hands as I am holding them. Then I take one hand off (asking them first if that is OK), then hold them with four fingers, three, two, one, and finally letting them be aware that they are floating off my finger. This is usually enough for them to drop their fear—especially if the whole workshop is there cheering each move they make. This all may take only five minutes or, in some panicky patients, it may take a little longer. If they can't float because they are particularly skinny, it is not quite so easy, and I ask them to wear a life belt at first.

At some point I ask them to talk to the water and tell the water that they are in charge, and they will not let the water drown them. Then I ask them to direct these words to their parents, their siblings. They then swim in from the edge to increasing depths until they are swimming the length of the pool.

If they are sinkers rather than floaters—and very, very few people are sinkers—then I suggest that they always wear some kind of a life belt, padded bra, cork jock strap, or something that will give them the buoyancy they need to float. Otherwise, stay out of the water, but stay out by assessment of the danger by the Adult, not because of fear or panic. Usually even the sinker will lose his phobia once he decides not to drown himself or let anyone else drown him.

SUMMARY

In general, we use the same basic methods no matter whom we are treating—the method of getting to the basic impasse as rapidly as possible. Some of the techniques include always using I-Thou transactions: if someone is talking about his wife, about her father, we ask him or her to pretend the other is in the room and to talk to him or her. No matter what was happening, it is difficult to get to affect with stories *about* the past, but easy when we bring the past and the person into the room in the now. Of course, we get contracts, but we are not as obsessive about spelling it out as we once were; once we are sure that we and the patient are on the same course, and not in a Parent contract, we start the process for getting to early scenes rapidly, finding the impasse, working through the impasse, and stopping.

We rarely ask, "When was the first time you felt depressed, anxious, phobic, confused?" Rather, we go back in time progressively as, "What were you depressed about last year?" then, "How about in medical or graduate school?" then, "Before that?"—each time getting a short statement in the here-and-now. For instance, the patient says, "When I was in medical school, my father . . ." We stop him. "Tell him this as if he were here." Each time we get the story as if it were happening and by the time the patient gets to an early scene, he is in the affect of the scene, is remembering it clearly, and may say, for instance, "If you don't change, I'll kill myself" (if he has been depressed). "What do you say knowing what you know now?" we may ask. In the same Child ego state the patient may say, "You'll never change, and I'm not going to kill myself just because you won't change. I'm not going to kill myself at all."

And so the redecision is made, and the patient is off to a new start. He, of course, won't give up everything he has done at once, but each time he plays another game and comes to the payoff, he recognizes his part in it and gives up the bad feelings. He also restates the statement that almost always goes with the payoff, about himself and others.

For instance, it might have been, "I'm worthless, and you all are a bunch of bastards to pick on me," which he may change to "Wow, I played *Kick Me* again, and I see how I did it, and I'm not going to take any payoff; I'm excited about my awareness."

References

1. Robert L. Goulding (Chairman), "Panel VI: Marathons," *Transactional Analysis Bulletin, 6,* no. 24 (1967), pp. 87–88.
2. See Robert L. Goulding, Mary E. Goulding, and Paul McCormick, "TA with a Marijuana User," in Morris L. Haimowitz and Natalie Reader Haimowitz, eds., *Human Development: Selected Readings,* 3rd ed., New York, Thomas Y. Crowell Co., 1973, pp. 412–426.

See also Robert Goulding, "New Directions in Transactional Analysis: Creating an Environment for Redecision and Change," in Clifford J. Sager and Helen Singer Kaplan, eds., *Progress in Group and Family Therapy,* New York, Brunner/Mazel, 1972, pp. 105–134, also Appendix A, "Annotated Transcript of a Group Therapy Weekend Marathon," pp. 125–134, which includes work with Tim who had been hospitalized previously for treatment of a drug-induced (LSD) psychosis.

3. Robert Drye, Robert Goulding, and Mary Goulding, "No-Suicide Decisions," *American Journal of Psychiatry, 130,* no. 2 (1973), pp. 171–174.

4. Morton A. Lieberman, Irving D. Yalom, and Matthew B. Miles, *Encounter Groups: First Facts,* New York, Basic Books, 1973; and John McNeel, "Redecisions in Psychotherapy: A Study of the Effects of an Intensive Weekend Group Workshop," Doctoral dissertation, The California School of Professional Psychology, August, 1975.

5. Eric Berne, *Transactional Analysis in Psychotherapy,* New York, Grove Press, 1961.

6. See Robert L. Goulding, ed., "The Training of Psychotherapists in Transactional Analysis," *Voices, 10,* no. 3 (1974), pp. 29–34, for a statement of the training at Western Institute for Group and Family Therapy.

7. Robert Goulding, "Thinking and Feeling in Psychotherapy: Three Impasses," *Voices, 10,* no. 1 (1974), pp. 11–13; Robert Goulding and Mary Goulding, "Injunctions, Decisions, and Redecisions," *Transactional Analysis Journal, 6,* no. 1 (January, 1976), pp. 41–48.

8. Joseph Wolpe, *The Practice of Behavior Therapy,* London, Pergamon Press, 1969; Robert L. Goulding, "Gestalt Therapy and Transactional Analysis," in Chris Hatcher and Philip Himmelstein, eds., *Handbook of Gestalt Therapy,* New York, Jason Aronson Inc., 1976.

9. Robert Goulding, "Curing Phobias," *Voices, 11,* no. 1 (1975), pp. 30–31.

II

Transactional Analysis in Action

FIVE

MY MOTHER DRIVES A PICKUP TRUCK
Ruth McClendon

My mother really does drive a pickup truck. And when the man down the street calls to say his toilet is plugged, she goes down and fixes it. What I find strange is that when I was little—really little—she wouldn't have dreamed of fixing that toilet. She would have stood back and simply screamed "Jimmy!!" Then, of course, Dad would move in and take over. At that point Dad usually had a big smile on his face, obviously pleased to be in charge. When there was a crisis with one of us in our growing up, it seemed that Dad would always be the one to handle it. Now as I look back, however, I can see how Mom and Dad together would create the situation: purposely Mom would sit back and look meek so Dad could be in control and "know it all." And when we were very little, Jan, Linda, and I also learned how to fit into that system. We three kids played it very well so that we could get what we needed and wanted. We played it in our different and special ways. Jan was best at making herself and what she did "look right"; I stamped my feet and said "No, I won't"; and Linda, who was the smallest and often sick, got herself well taken care of by moaning loudly. It's very clear to me now how Mom and Dad drew the outline, and then each one of us filled in our parts with our own colors and details. Even back then, when my grandparents visited, I began to see why Mom and Dad were the way they were. Today, it makes sense to me that Mom and Dad teamed up together. More interesting, though, is that I can now see how George and I got together. Even before much of our family therapy work came about, George and I used to do our own version.

Mom is different now, though. She drives a pickup truck, and with a smile she even fixes Mr. Murray's toilet. I'm different too, and when we are together my family is very diffrent. This chapter is about how I believe family relationships are made and how they change. It's about all families, whether they have big problems or just the normal hassles which come along with growth and change.

From our viewpoint,* a family is a whole made up of different parts; the parts fit and interconnect into the whole and the whole into the parts. In considering the family, we think of the whole as a three-generational unit and treat in person at least two generations. We see the parents as architects of the current family unit and take into account that they learned their architectural skills from their own parents. In other words, parents had parents too. We see families as beginning with a relationship involving two persons and then continuing to grow as children are produced and take on their roles.**

Our approach to families is both interpersonal and intrapsychic. We work with the interpersonal relationship, or the exterior system, and with the intrapsychic self or the interior system. We use transactional analysis, gestalt, and systems theory as our theoretical bases and conceptualize what we do into three different phases.

In order to illustrate more specifically how families develop, I will consider in detail the Puffin family.† Sarah Puffin is 32 years old and has been married to Tom for 16 years. She is tall, slender, and physically attractive. She has recently completed her high-school education and, up to this point, her primary occupation has been that of housewife and mother. Tom is 37 years old, short and husky. He is a well-known public personality from the Midwest. Tom and Sarah currently have three children. Karl is 11 years of age and in the sixth grade. He is attractive but physically small for his age. He has been taking Ritalin medication for the past three years. He is labeled a "hyperactive child." As you can probably guess, Karl is the identified patient. Marcia and Connie are seven-year-old twins in the third grade. Each is a "bundle of energy and needs little sleep." Marcia whines and has a tendency to get herself hurt. Connie is cooperative and fun to be with. The Puffin family was referred for treatment because of Karl's hyperactivity and Tom's insistence on getting help away from home because "someone in the community might find out."

NATURE OF THE MARRIAGE CONTRACT

The nature of the marriage contract between Sarah and Tom is essential to consider as we look at the development of the Puffin family. Eric Berne talked about three different elements of the marriage contract.[1] In our

---

* This chapter was written by me alone. However, all of the concepts included herein have been developed by both my husband, George, and me. They are used by both of us in the training we do, which accounts for my use of "we" and "our" in this chapter.

** In referring to marriage we are speaking of all forms of coupling, not only legalized marriage.

† From this point on I will be referring to the Puffin family. This is a family treated in one of our week-long family therapy workshops. The identity of the family has been disguised. The family problems and dynamics, along with the course of treatment, are actual. The week-long multiple family workshops consist of several families coming together to live, work, and play. During the week individual family therapy, multiple family group therapy, parents' groups, children's groups, male groups, and female groups are held.

understanding of marriage contracts, we have expanded this to five elements.

The first element of the marriage contract is the explicit *formal contract* which Berne said took place between the two Adults and which we believe takes place between two Parent-contaminated Adults. This contract is contained in the marriage service in such phrases as "love, honor, and obey until death do us part," and it is derived from a moral and cultural base. By it the partners make promises to each other in various situations.

The second element is the *Adult contract*. It is an explicit agreement between two Adult ego states. This agreement includes buying the marriage license, deciding where to live, when to be married, and so forth.

The third element is what Berne called the *relationship contract*. This is an implicit agreement of symbiosis, where each partner secretly expects the other to be Parent and Adult in areas where he or she is Child, and Child in areas where he or she is Parent and Adult. In the Puffin family Tom expected Sarah never to ask about money matters, and he stated that she certainly would never be able to make any money on her own. Sarah was, of course, queen of the kitchen and Tom would enrage himself if Sarah wasn't there to fix dinner. Due to its secret nature and the tendency for partners to switch roles, thus making new demands upon each other, this third contract element is often the area of overt marital discord. Many couples will ostensibly seek therapy because of switches in this contractual area. Mary Goulding identifies this as the arena where the "wall of trivia" is built.

The fourth element in the contractual basis is what Berne called the *contract of script*. This is the essential basis of a marital relationship— Sarah's choosing of Tom, and Tom's choosing of Sarah so that each may perpetuate his or her own life script. It is an implicit agreement between Tom's Child and Sarah's Child. Sarah got married at 16 to get away from her mother and stepfather. Sarah was in the third round of trying to live with her mother and a new stepfather, and in her seventh different home. Sarah had been physically and sexually abused many times by the men in her life. When she was three years old, she had made a decision: "I am just an ugly old rag to be used by other people. Someday after I am wrecked enough I will get you to kill me." Sarah chose Tom, who had been called a puny little boy by his alcoholic father. He had been asked by his mother to be big and to protect her from her horrible husband. Tom had made an early decision which said, "I'll show you, Dad, that I can do the man's job you're not doing. I'll show you both I'm big enough even if it kills me." Tom had lived at home with his mother until marrying Sarah. In order to make life predictable and to continue what had once been functional and lifesaving for them, Tom and Sarah had chosen each other.

In addition, Tom and Sarah chose each other out of what we call the contract of *creativity*. This fifth element of contract is both an explicit

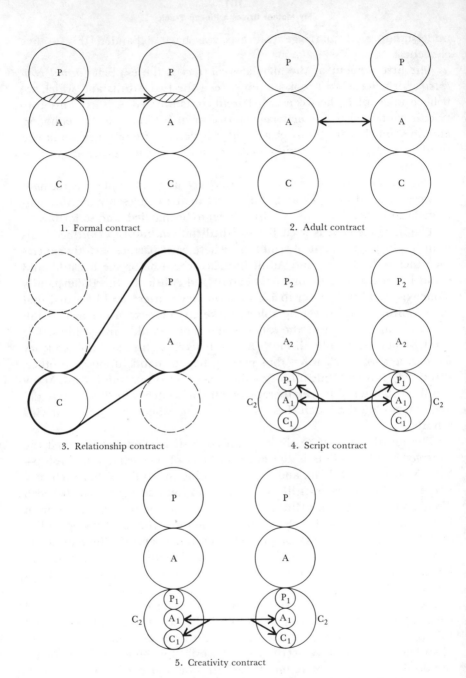

1. Formal contract

2. Adult contract

3. Relationship contract

4. Script contract

5. Creativity contract

Figure 1
Elements of the Marriage Contract

and implicit agreement between Tom's Child and Sarah's Child to get together for neat, creative, exciting, and nourishing reasons (Figure 1).

After five years of marriage Sarah and Tom had their first child, Karl. They had been trying to have a child for four of those five years but had been unable to conceive earlier. At the time of Karl's birth, Tom was working 12 to 14 hours each day and staying away from home more and more. He said, "I had to succeed in my profession, and after all, Sarah just bitched at me and would hardly let me touch her." Sarah described herself as depressed and unappreciated: "All Tom wanted from me was sex." When Karl was born, he immediately became Sarah's "little energetic man." She wanted him to fill her void. When he didn't, she became frustrated with him and physically beat him as she had been beaten. Sarah remembered believing and often saying, "If it weren't for Karl, I could leave Tom. Why was he ever born?" Tom was pleased to give Karl to Sarah but he was also jealous. He delighted when Karl would upset Sarah and, at the same time, he punished Karl for being disrespectful to her. When Tom left for work, his parting words to Karl were usually (with a smile on his face), "Now take care of your mother."

When Karl was three years old, Connie and Marcia were born. Connie, who was eight minutes older than Marcia, was to have everything that Sarah never had. Connie was the apple of her dad's eye. Marcia, when asked about her birth, said, "I wasn't supposed to be around. They had a bed for Connie and none for me." Marcia was delighted when people confused her with Connie and was the one who wanted to dress alike. She was adept at getting Karl to beat on her. She had many allergies.

When Marcia and Connie were born, they had to find their places in the family with Sarah, Tom, and Karl. Reality is that children have to take what they get (are born into) in the parent and family department. They have no initial choices. Karl, Marcia, and Connie each watched, looked, and listened, then decided on the best way to be in order to stay alive and get what they needed in the Puffin family. Sarah and Tom themselves had done that. Sarah and Tom then passed on to their children all that they had learned about doing, being, feeling, and thinking. Karl, Connie, and Marcia decided about themselves as best they could.

STAGES OF FAMILY THERAPY

In the field of family therapy, there is a general lack of theoretical and practical consensus. As a theory, family therapy is not a well-integrated approach, but is diffuse in its focus. As a treatment modality, there are numerous and very different approaches to family work. Often family therapists intervene only on an interpersonal or systems level. They focus on the operation of the family system and effect changes in the family by altering the functioning of the system. Different therapists have different ways and means of doing this. Some choose to approach the family through changing communication patterns, while others play with the power dynamics in the system. Essentially, family therapists who intervene only on a systems level are not concerned with the intrapsychic dynamics of the individual who is advancing his or her own script by participating in the system.

George's and my work with families is done in three different stages. Briefly, the first is an interpersonal phase where the aim is to identify the shape and form of the family system and to discover how each individual (whether two or 82 years old) identifies with and is identified by that family system. The second is an intrapsychic stage. Here, individuals are encouraged to do their own intrapsychic work in the TA framework that we use. Stage II most often takes the form of redecision therapy. The third is a reintegration phase. At this point family members realign themselves into a new and more functional family pattern. The purpose in using these three stages in therapy with families is to integrate interpersonal and intrapsychic elements. Thus, our model takes into account both the family as a unit and each individual within that family. It is a model which offers family members the opportunity to adjust better to their current environment and to their own personal history.

STAGE I: DIAGNOSIS OF THE FAMILY SYSTEM

The process of Stage I is diagnosing the system and finding out how the whole family works. At this point, many of you reading this chapter are likely to be asking yourselves, "What does she mean when she talks about system? What does she mean when she asks how the whole works?" General systems theory is a body of knowledge originally developed by a biologist, Ludwig Von Bertalanffy. He first presented his theory in 1945 and later went on to show how it related to psychiatry.[2] He was interested in wholeness and organization rather than reduction, and thus he described systems as "complexes of elements in interaction."[3] Von Bertalanffy, furthermore, described the complexes of elements in interaction as being of two kinds—closed and open systems.[4] He said that closed systems are characterized by a continuous circular flow of original component material. Closed systems thus tend toward maximum disorder. On the contrary, open systems continually allow for the intake and output of matter and energy in an interchange with the environment. The elements of any system are known to relate through a feedback process which maintains the system's functioning. The feedback is a circular model where (a) affects (b) affects (c) affects (a).

To put this simply and into TA terms: At Stage I, a family is a unit sustained through multiple interlocking symbioses or multiple interlocking game patterns (triangles). The functions of feeling, thinking, and doing are intertwined, and a movement by one person in the family necessarily commands countermovement by others. All members of the family thrust to support and advance their own scripts. This is done through interacting, balancing, and counterbalancing, one with another. Thus the family system as a whole maintains a homeostasis and furthers the family script. The family as a unit guards against intervention from the outside, because such would be threatening to the advancement of the family script and each individual script.

There are several important indicators of Stage I position for families. Some of them are as follows: the use of "we think" or "we feel"; or "you have made me feel this way"; the use of "can't" or "it just happened"; a family member listening briefly and immediately "correcting" the other person, frequent defensive interruptions; assuming rather than checking out; always trying to change the other or asking the therapist to change the other; high levels of verbal and nonverbal interference; a negative feedback loop or negative-stroking system; everybody talking at once.

Stage I of family therapy is figuring out what is happening in the system *now* and seeing how each person as well as the whole supports what is happening and is supported by it. Involved in the process of first-stage work is decontamination of the system. Our main focus is to help each individual accept responsibility for his or her own—and *only* his or her own—thinking, feeling, and doing. For us, dealing with a family by intervening at the systems level is somewhat like dealing with an individual by intervening on the social-control level. Berne described the aim of transactional analysis as social control. He saw social control as structural readjustment and then reintegration. Structural readjustment according to Berne, has two phases: the anatomical phase, which consists of "clarification and definition of ego boundaries by such processes as diagnostic refinement and decontamination"; and the physiological phase, which Berne said is "concerned with redistribution of cathexis through selective planned activation of specific ego states in specific ways with the goal of establishing the hegemony of the Adult through social control."[5] Such is the task of Stage I.

Assessment of the family to determine whether or not the systems or Stage I approach alone will provide the most appropriate treatment for the family is important. As with individuals who work only on a social-control level, it is important for some families to work only on a systems level. This is true in families where there is a high level of individual pathology (one or both of the parents is psychotic), and the treatment time is relatively limited. In this case, we would complete family social control and not proceed into Stage II work. The goal of treatment here is to decontaminate the family system and support appropriate functioning without regressive work. For most families, however, we believe in the combined three-phase approach—changing what goes on between people, and changing what goes on within each person. The Puffin family as a unit and each member of that unit clearly changed.

THE FAMILY WORKSHOP IN ACTION   In order to accomplish the task of Stage I, it is necessary to establish an atmosphere where it is safe for people to shake loose from others and to be themselves. Offering the protection and permission for each member of the family to be and express himself or herself is essential. Techniques for doing this include stroking, caring, confronting, supporting, and providing structure. Each member of the family must have the freedom for differentiation without fear of retaliation from other family members. Sometimes necessary are contracts assuring no punishment outside the therapy room for what goes on in the family session. When each person feels it is safe to accept responsibility for herself without fear of retaliation or fear of not getting what she needs, the family mass is beginning to separate and movement is made toward Stage II. In other words, it becomes OK for individuals to differentiate themselves from the family script and transact with the outside environment. Pulls toward the old balance are minimized.

When the Puffin family arrived for the workshop, Karl was in charge of the system. Tom had relinquished his role as parent in the family, and Sarah parented from an Adapted Child position. These systems issues became clear after I asked the first question, "Who is the boss in your family?" Karl quickly and energetically replied, "I am." Tom smiled and said nothing. Sarah mentioned how lonely she was, and that Tom was never home and refused to be involved with her or the kids. Marcia pushed Karl, got kicked in return, and had to be taken to the bathroom to put cold water on her hurt. Connie crawled into her father's lap.

This quick sequence revealed how the Puffin family system was operating. Sarah returned from the bathroom with Marcia and began in a soft little voice to talk about how bad Tom was. Tom hung his head and guiltily agreed. As this was happening, Karl was physically sitting in a chair high above both of his parents. I intervened and asked Tom if he would change chairs with Karl. Tom turned to Karl and helplessly asked, "Is it OK? Can I have your chair?" Karl angrily replied, "No" and Tom looked back at me saying, "He's a little like me. Isn't it OK for him to be big there?" As all this was happening Sarah was crying and saying how scared she was. Connie was wiggling on her father's lap while looking straight at her mother. Marcia was trying to sneak out of the room and fell down the stairs.

Several interventions were necessary to separate out this mass and overall sequence of interaction. First, it was necessary to stop the interference of Marcia and Connie. I retrieved Marcia and held her, telling her it was not OK to leave, and that it was especially not OK to hurt herself for any reason at any time. I asked Connie to move off of her father's lap and sit on the other side of me. Sarah (while working with George) changed her words and frightened crying from "It's getting me down" to "I am scaring myself." Second, it was necessary to help Tom reassume his position as father. I coached him to tell Karl to get down from his chair and to tell him that he, Tom, was the father in the family and that he would be the boss. Tom also told Karl that he was important as his son, and that he didn't have to be the dad. Karl reluctantly left his high place and challenged his father on the way down with, "No, you can't do it."

At the end of the session, Sarah and Tom were sitting and facing each other, talking about why they had come to the workshop. Karl was getting his head rubbed by George. Connie and Marcia were sitting quietly with me. The natural order of the parenting and childing systems had been temporarily established. George and I were able to help family members move into their own autonomy rather than remain interlocked with one another. We intervened in their game relationship (or support system for each other's pathology) and helped establish clear boundaries around new roles for family members.

Our main therapeutic principle is that each person is responsible for her or his actions and feelings. Thus, the interventions mentioned above are to encourage each person to take responsibility for her or his own feelings and behavior.

STAGE II: SCRIPT ANALYSIS AND REDECISIONS

Movement into the intrapsychic work with each family member is done by singling out script issues and doing the most important process of redecision work. Berne described games as originating in childhood, and scripts and basic life positions as being the result of early decisions made from the Adult ego state in the Child (A_1). He then said, "The optimal situation for the readjustment and reintegration of the total personality requires an emotional statement from the Child in the presence of the Adult and Parent."[6] Bob and Mary Goulding went on to further develop and clarify the concept of the redecision as a way of dealing directly and effectively with patients for script change.[7]

Redecision work is based on the principle that every person has a choice about her life when a child. This choice is made based on a working combination of: the material resources of the child; the information made available to her by parenting figures; the irrational demands made upon her (injunctions); how she interprets the information and demands; and the support she gets for her interpretation. Each child makes decisions about her life in order to survive psychologically, and sometimes physically, in her environment. She had the power to make early decisions about herself, and right now in this time and place each person has the power to choose to make new decisions. One's rackets, games, pastimes, and existential position all support the original early decision. The power to change the early decision, and the behavior that supports it, is in the person.

In family therapy it is important to emphasize the above concepts of original decisions as a device for survival. It is important to underline that nobody is a bad guy and that parents had parents too—parents who also made early decisions for themselves. These early decisions then became the basis of the parents' interaction with each other and with their children. In doing intrapsychic work with family members, we emphasize also that it is possible for both young and old to make redecisions. In fact, central to the way we work with families is the concept that even three- and four-year-olds have already made life-script decisions for themselves. They are part and parcel of the family system or script.

After watching the system and initially working with the Puffin family, many of the areas for intrapsychic work with each member became clear. The workings of the injunction-decision complexes had been played out in dramatic form before our eyes. Marcia was clearly receiving "Don't exist" messages from both Sarah and Tom. At that time her decision about herself was: "There is no room for me in this family. I must be bad, therefore, I will hurt and someday kill myself in order to get out." Connie was receiving "Don't be you" messages from Sarah and "Don't grow up" messages from Tom. She had decided, "I'll stay the good sweet little girl so that I can get lots of things for me around here." Sarah was showing Marcia how to get herself hurt by men. She was showing Connie how to stay a scared, good little girl. Karl was clearly hearing "Don't exist" and "Don't be a child" from Sarah. From Tom he was seeing how to handle himself by being superaggressive to overcome his puniness, and he was hearing "Don't be you, take my place." Karl had decided, "I'll try hard to stay alive and be the someone you want, but I know I'll never be able to do it." It was more difficult to see exactly what the injunction-decision complexes with Sarah and Tom were. After all, their parents weren't physically in the room. "Don't exist," "Don't think," "Don't grow up," and "Don't be angry" messages seemed to be present for Sarah. Her decision was made around being no good and letting herself be used by people in order to end up dead. Tom had received "Don't exist," "Don't make it," and "Don't be close" messages. His decision was to feel angry and be unsuccessful at showing his parents.

HOW FAMILY REDECISION WORK IS DIFFERENT   The process of redecision work has been described by Bob Goulding.[8] The process of our work with families is very similar and yet somewhat different. In family therapy our pacing is different. We are continually having to balance between confrontation and support. We are alternately intervening in the system and then supporting the individuals to create a new and more functional balance. If our confrontation is too scary, family units tend to return to *Go* and collect their $200 for not changing. Our pacing is also related to protection and to archeology. It is not possible to facilitate redecision work when old decisions are still operative. In other words, children *can't* (here it is not a question of won't) give up patterns of feeling, thinking, and doing, if those patterns are still functional in the family. Karl could not give up his boss slot until one of his parents was willing to take charge. Karl could not decide to stop playing *Kick Me* and move out of his Victim slot as long as Sarah still needed him to use her as an old rag, and she still needed to have him to kick around. The family system was such that Karl's only alternative was to stay script-bound. As long as Sarah was still giving him injunctions, he simply couldn't change.

THE INTERNALIZED FAMILY   Another difference in our therapy technique is related to our theoretical view concerning the internalization of P_2 and the content of P_1. Essentially P_2 is not a tape recording of mom and dad. We agree with R. D. Laing when he talks about an internalized family system with a space-time dimension and a temporal sequence. Laing states, "As in a *reel* of a film, all elements are co-present, pre-set to unfold in sequence in time as a *film* on the screen. *The reel is the internal family.*"[9] This is what we see as P_2. In addition, we believe that the family as a system is also what the Little Professor (A_1) in us sees when deciding on how best survive in this family. Thus, in the redecision work which we do, we have persons work with the old scene that was operative when they responded to the injunctions. Simultaneously, we invite them to transact with both of their parents plus other participating family members. People don't make decisions in relation to only one parent figure. Sarah, for instance, was just as angry at her mother for allowing her father and stepfather to physically and sexually abuse her as she was at either one of them for doing it. Her decision that she was just an ugly old rag to be used by other people grew out of both of her parents' interactions with one another as well as her parents' reactions to her. In marathon work which we recently completed, one man was relating to and sorting out his relationships with 20 different parent figures and their crisscrossed intertwinings. The impact of this man's entire family had been phenomenal. His prior dealing in therapy with just one part of his family unit at a time had been insufficient.

THE ENVIRONMENT The third way that the process of our redecision work differs is in our use of self and the environment. I am particularly comfortable in doing therapy from my Child. Toys and teddy bears are integrated into the environment. Because families include little people as well as grownups, much play therapy is done. Frequently I lie on the floor in order to meet a three-year-old face on.

Second-stage redecision work is generally done with all family members present. This creates some new aspects. When Tom is dealing with his parents, those same two persons are his children's grandparents. "I didn't know Grandma was like that" was Karl's comment after Tom had exhibited some of his anger at his parents. While Tom was involved in this particular sequence of anger work, all three children were quiet and attentive. In second-stage family therapy, children allow themselves to see and hear. The work proceeds much as in a group of adults. Our process is one of focusing on intrapsychic changes within one member and then working immediately with the others in the system to establish their concurrent intrapsychic changes. When separate subgrouping (parents' group or kids' group, etc.) is done, information and changes by individuals from each subgroup are fed back into the family group at the next session. Secrets are not kept.

REDECISION WORK WITH THE PUFFIN FAMILY

The process of the second-stage work with the Puffin family began with Sarah. During the first day of the workshop, she had moved out of her helpless, scared little girl slot. Her Adult was now in charge of her mediation with the current family environment. The system was disengaged enough so that interference by Tom or any of the children was at a minimum. Thus, the next time Sarah got herself into the scared, helpless, "I'm-no-good" spot, I began by asking her to rehearse the situations last year where she had felt the same. I then asked about the year before and so on back. (As Sarah was doing this, George was holding Connie and Marcia and touching toes with Karl.)

Through this process, Sarah reached a scene when she was three years old. I asked her to be three years old and to put herself into that scene. Sarah saw herself in her room lying on the floor by the crack in the door. She had just been sent there by her mother because she had spilled her milk. I asked Sarah to see her father. She described him as enraged and "out of control." She saw him come bursting through her bedroom door, slamming her across the floor on her stomach. He then picked her up, shook her, and shouted, "You are nothing but a dirty dust rag, look at your dress now. Stop crying! You shouldn't be alive at all. You're nothing but dirt." Sarah became rigid and stiff, stopped crying and responded to my question of, "What did you decide about yourself then?" "You're right," she said looking at her father with tears in her eyes, "I am just an ugly old rag and I deserve to be wrecked and killed." At this point I was touching Sarah and said, "You are worthwhile, Sarah. You deserve to be alive and your dad should not have done that. Your mother should not have allowed you to be hurt." Sarah cried violently for several minutes. I moved closer to her and said, "Knowing what you know now, Sarah, what would you say and do differently?" In a quiet and meek voice Sarah said to her father, "You can't kill me." With some prompting from me, she said in a louder voice to both of her parents, "I won't let you kill me and I won't kill myself either!" After repeating this several times, Sarah was obviously back in the here and now. I then had her turn to Tom and to her three children and repeat the same thing. By this time Sarah's speech was flowing easily, her face was smiling, and she was standing straight, no longer hunched as though waiting for someone to hit her. The tenseness in the other Puffin family members had also changed to relief and smiles.

In the workshop session following this, Tom began by saying how angry he was at Sarah. She had been so distant and he couldn't keep up with her. As he said this, Tom looked liked a frightened little boy in grownup clothes. I asked him how old he felt and he replied about four. In response to a question from me, Tom then related the following scene. He was sleeping in his mother's room as usual when his father stumbled in drunk. Yanking Tom by the arm and flinging him out of bed, his father yelled, "You're no good, you're not big enough, get away!" Tom's mother screamed, "He's all I've got." Tom sneaked to his room and as he lay there listening to his parents fight he said to himself, "I'll show you I can do a man's job. I'll show you I'm big enough, even if it kills me."

In working with this scene Tom realized he no longer needed to keep trying to show his parents how big he was. They were never going to change and notice him. Also, no matter how big he was, he couldn't stop his dad from drinking, and thus get his mother off his back. Tom claimed his anger from the past and dropped it. He decided he was worthy of being alive even though he couldn't change his parents. Following this piece of work, Tom took his mother's face off of Sarah, stopped encouraging Karl to act out for him, and accepted Marcia for herself. He stopped seeing her as his little sister who was favored by his father.

In further second-stage work with the Puffins, Sarah decided to accept her sexiness without being afraid of hurting other women (on whom she had put her mother's face) or setting herself up to be hurt. She stopped the second-degree *Rapo* game. Karl, in one of the children's groups, decided not to ask others to hurt him and never to kill himself. Karl was able to do this only after Sarah decided to see Karl as himself and no longer to beat him or ask him to take care of her. In other words, Karl was not her father. Both Tom and Sarah told Karl of their changes, told him they wanted him to be alive, and gave him permission to be himself. After Tom, Sarah, and Karl had made their redecisions, Karl's hyperactivity decreased significantly. His ability to attend to himself, to others, and to his activities greatly increased. (Karl's medication had been discontinued at the beginning of the workshop.)* Karl, his anxiety reduced, was beginning to get the stroking and attention he needed for being alive and for being himself. His parents were seeing him differently. He was being different. Marcia decided that there was a place for her and that she would not hurt herself for any reason. This, of course, followed Sarah's and Tom's acceptance of her. By the fourth day of the workshop it was, for the first time, OK with Marcia that she and Connie dress differently. Connie moved from being the good little girl to allowing herself more feelings. She decided she wouldn't get hurt if she got dirty. Sarah told Connie that she had decided that she, Sarah, was Tom's wife, and that Connie was their little girl. Tom decided and shared similarly with Connie, Marcia, and Karl. Tom was Sarah's husband. Mom and dad were the bosses and they would take care of the kids.

STAGE III: INTERPERSONAL REINTEGRATION

Stage III, reintegration, is our final phase of family therapy. It is again an interpersonal phase. We are back to looking at the exterior system. We are interested in how each individual with a new interior system will

---

* Following consultation with parents and our own diagnosis of the family and the hyperactive child, often we will discontinue the Ritalin medication during the week. Karl had not been on medication since early in the workshop.

facilitate her integration into a new external system. The question of Stage III is: how can I enter into a system with other I's and still maintain my I? To use a familiar political phrase, Stage III is "a choice not an echo." It is a choice of how I am relating to you in the present so that my relating to you is not merely a repetition of past decisions about my life. In TA terms, Stage III is "I'm OK, You're OK, We're OK." Individuals retain their own identities in relationship to one another, and get their needs met without merging. The family system is a positive feedback loop which now reinforces health, individual power, and autonomy.

The signs of reintegration in a family are essentially the opposite of the signs for Stage I. Family members have learned that they have neither the ability nor the responsibility to change others. Mind-reading and assuming are no longer the patterns; facts are continually being asked for and checked out. "I think that you think that I am" is no longer the basis for doing. The discounting level is low. People, and what they say, are counted as important merely for themselves. The process of listening, hearing, and seeing the other is safe. Differentness is accepted. Feelings count without having to be turned into reasons.

Reintegration is a natural outgrowth of redecision work. It answers the question, "What will be different for me now?"

In reintegration the entire drama of the family and each individual has changed. There is a new stage, a new script, and new actors to play the parts. Rehearsal begins as the family continues with us, and soon a completely new show is ready to open. The new show is due to have a winning run for many, many years. It will have many variations as the family's life continuously changes. The internal producers and directors, however, will know how to incorporate the variations into a winning performance. On occasion an outside expert might still need to be called in for consultation. Knowing that is one of the signs of a well family and a winning production.

Much of the reintegration with the Puffin family has already been described in conjunction with the redecision work. Their new and functional relationship was manifested when Tom and Sarah chose to take their places with each other as husband and wife, and to assume responsibility as parents with the children. Neither Tom nor Sarah nor Karl nor Marcia was going to die, so they were no longer reacting and interacting to further their own abuse and death scripts. Each was asking for positive connections with the other. A ceremony was held and the huge bottle of Ritalin pills was dumped down the toilet to the tune of "Auld Lang Syne." Karl didn't need those pills any longer—he could fit into the new family model without the capsuled crutch. At the time of writing, now eight full months following the workshop, Karl remains without any medication. Connie and Marcia decided to rearrange their room, and Sarah and Tom promised to buy them new beds which they could pick out themselves. I recently received a letter from Marcia saying:

DEAR RUTH
I LiKE yOUR HAiR.
I HAVE My BED. ME
AND My FAMiLy
LOVES yOU.

LOVE

MARCiA

References

1. Eric Berne, *Transactional Analysis in Psychotherapy*, New York, Grove Press, 1961, p. 214.
2. W. Gray and N. Rizzo, eds., *General Systems Theory and Psychiatry*, Boston, Little, Brown and Company, 1969, pp. 7–31.
3. Ludwig Von Bertalanffy, "The Meaning of General Systems Theory," *General Systems Theory*, New York, George Braziller, 1968, p. 33.
4. Ludwig Von Bertalanffy, "General Systems Theory and Psychiatry," in S. Arieti, ed., *The American Handbook of Psychiatry*, New York, Basic Books, 1966, vol. 3, pp. 702–721.
5. Berne, *op. cit.*, p. 224.
6. *Ibid.*
7. Robert Goulding and Mary Goulding, "Injunctions, Decisions, and Redecisions," *Transactional Analysis Journal, 6*, no. 1 (January, 1976), pp. 41–48; Robert L. Goulding, "Decisions in Script Formation," *Transactional Analysis Journal, 2*, no. 2 (April, 1972), pp. 62–63.
8. See Robert Goulding's chapter in this book. See also Robert Goulding, "New Directions in Transactional Analysis," in Clifford J. Sager and Helen Singer Kaplan, eds., *Progress in Group and Family Therapy*, New York, Brunner/Mazel, 1972; Robert Goulding, "Thinking and Feeling in Psycotherapy: Three Impasses," *Voices, 10*, no. 1 (1974), pp. 11–13.
9. R. D. Laing, *The Politics of the Family*, New York, Vintage Books, 1972, p. 17.

SIX

CORRECTIVE PARENTING
IN PRIVATE PRACTICE
Jon and Laurie Weiss

We are Jon and Laurie Weiss; we share an out-patient private practice in Littleton, Colorado. We are both senior staff members at Rocky Mountain TA Institute, teaching and consulting with TA both locally and nationally, alone and together. We have two children—Brian, nine, and Linda, six.

We use TA as a clinical model, as an educational tool, and as the basis of a lifestyle. Our use of TA has evolved since we were first introduced to it in 1967. Jon was a psychologist and read *Transactional Analysis in Psychotherapy* out of curiosity; I was a teacher and read *Games People Play* because it was a best-seller.[1] Our personal evolution with TA has largely paralleled the general development of TA during this period.

We have worked, played, and explored with this tool since we first encountered it, and our present uses of TA are the current sum of our experience with it. Jon and I had very different early experiences, primarily because at that time we were both still operating from typical banal scripts.

EARLY EXPERIENCES WITH TA

Our immediate reactions to TA books were similar; each of us was interested and excited by the tool. Jon's interest was in how to use the tool with people as a therapist, and mine was a vague and passing interest in how to understand what was happening with me and other people. Jon pursued his interest and participated in an introductory course offered by Dave Kupfer and Bob Goulding in October, 1967, in Chicago. He was eager to increase his professional skills and joined the Chicago TA Seminar. When he arranged to study with Kupfer and Goulding in California in August, 1968, I went along to vacation in Carmel with our nearly two-year-old son. At that time, we both defined TA as a tool for professionals; we defined me as a nonprofessional (and, therefore, somewhat not-OK).

Kupfer and Goulding were no longer working together by the time we reached California. Jon was unwilling to choose between them and spent two weeks with each of them. His two weeks with Bob Goulding included work with Mary Goulding. This was the start of a persistent pattern with Jon and later with me. We have consistently worked with members of different schools within TA, and have utilized and interpreted the work of these practitioners to create our own style.

I became really interested in TA during the 1968 Summer Conference of the International Transactional Analysis Association, which I attended as a "wife." I listened to Steiner, James, Dusay, and others discuss "advanced" TA concepts. I easily understood what they were saying and my mind raced with ideas for applying the concepts in my sixth-, seventh-, and eighth-grade science classes. I also experienced the personal impact of an "I'm OK and You're OK" orientation at that conference. The dawning awareness that all those smart people considered me OK and treated me accordingly prodded me to reorganize my own view of my life and my experiences.

While we were in California, Jon was enthusiastic at seeing professionals combine their personal and professional lives. His Parent was impressed by the quality of the professional people he saw, and his Child was intrigued by the fact that they were having so much fun at the same time.

When we returned to Chicago, I joined the TA Seminar there to learn more concepts and to spend time with people who assumed other people were OK. I also enjoyed the Child-to-Child play of the seminar members. I participated in training workshops as they became available and thoroughly enjoyed learning for the fun of it.

As a teacher I was always attracted to educational models that imply that children are exciting, growing creatures, and that education is primarily intended to channel that growth. I recognized the powerful possibilities of deliberately creating an "I'm OK, You're OK" atmosphere in my classrooms. I experimented with introducing different TA concepts to my classes, with different stroking patterns, and with simply operating from my own changed awareness of "OKness." The results were encouraging. The children learned the subject matter at about the same rate as before, and problems in classroom management almost disappeared. I was also able to help my students use TA to figure out how to solve some of their own interpersonal problems.

When I was teaching in Chicago, I had no plans to become a therapist. The concepts I was experimenting with then are central to the way our therapy groups operate now. These concepts are also vitally important to the way we live our lives and to the establishment of the TA community in Denver, where we live and work.

Jon studied cycles of human growth while earning his PhD in Human

Development at the University of Chicago. His therapy training there was the client-centered approach developed by Carl Rogers. Jon also trained with Carl Whitaker, who was a consultant at the Mental Health Center where he worked, and had some time at the National Training Laboratories concurrently with his TA training. As a graduate student and young psychologist, he was exposed to many different models for understanding human behavior, and was attracted to TA because of its simplicity. Using TA, he was able to clearly understand at least a part of what his patients presented to him, and to *do* something about what he understood.

Our use of TA in 1968 and 1969 was already paralleling the different approaches to TA nationally. Jon, the trained mental health scientist, was studying how to use this tool to work better with his clients. I, with no background in mental health at all, was attracted to TA because I felt good with TA people. I participated in some random training activities and experimented freely with applying TA in new areas, with minimal or no supervision. This theme continued with many modifications during our early careers in TA. Jon approached each new technique carefully and scientifically, while I jumped in to experiment with it, without really considering what the implications of my action might be. When we worked together, particularly when doing public presentations, we worked symbiotically, with Jon usually supplying the controls for my creativity.

We moved to Denver in August of 1969, with our two-year-old son and infant daughter. Another Chicago TA couple, Warden and Carolyn Rimel, moved to Denver at the same time. Our experiences in establishing TA there are described in detail in *A Transactional Analysis Community: The Denver Experience.*[2] We worked together and separately to acquaint people in the Denver area with TA. When Jon and Warden established a training group, I joined for the fun of it. I was learning TA by hanging around. I didn't seriously consider becoming a therapist until the Summer Conference of 1971. Natalie Haimowitz asked me when I was going to take my exams for clinical membership in ITAA. My first response was "Who, me?" and my next response was to count my hours of training.

Meanwhile, Jon had trained with Fanita English, Natalie Haimowitz, and Bob and Mary Goulding. He passed his clinical membership exams in January, 1970, and earned his teaching membership in August, 1971.

I decided to finish the clinical requirements for advanced membership in ITAA, and when we returned to Denver, I organized groups and had regular supervision sessions with Jon. Our symbiotic relationship began to break down when I discovered my own Adult strength. We began to do treatment groups together in mid-1972, and again challenged the symbiosis, influencing and moderating each other's approaches. This has been an engrossing, rewarding, stimulating, growth-enhancing, and sometimes frightening experience. We have continued to borrow from other TA leaders while developing our own therapy style together. While engaging in this process professionally, we found the implications so far-reaching for us personally that it became almost totally necessary to reorganize our personal lives as well. In the process of doing this we have also influenced and been influenced by our community.

CHANGING LIFESTYLE Our family life is now a reflection of our professional partnership. Logically, since we both do the same work professionally and provide about the same amount of income for family support, it made sense to share our home responsibilities. Disengaging from the symbiosis at home was somewhat more traumatic than at work. In the professional situation, the rewards to both of us for me using my Adult and Jon using his Child were quickly apparent in increased efficiency. I wanted recognition for my intellect and Jon wanted more freedom to use his Child professionally, so that task was seen positively by us both. We were each adding to ourselves.

At home the situation was viewed negatively. I wanted to stop taking all the responsibilities for structuring family maintenance tasks, and Jon didn't want to give up his freedom from responsibilities. We shared an intellectual commitment to the reorganization, but we were each committed emotionally to the traditional American family structure. We did restructure with support from both women's and men's consciousness-raising groups and a commitment to growth. We now share in the responsibilities of family life and child rearing. As we learned to share, to our surprise, we also learned that there were many rewards of closeness and warmth available to us. We have also experimented with each of us assuming total responsibility for both home and practice while the other travels. Each does fine alone, but we much prefer to share!

INFLUENCES AND SUPPORT

Our major theoretical and personal support from 1972 to 1975 came from two sources. The first was the Schiff Family—Jacqui, Aaron, Eric, and others—who generously shared their theoretical orientation and personal experience with us. The second was the feminist movement and its implications for people's liberation. Pam Levin influenced us in many ways, both professionally and personally. We learned from Claude Steiner, Hoagie Wycoff, and Dorothy Jongeward through their writing and presentations at conferences.[3] *Ms.* magazine and other feminist writings helped raise our consciousness. Friends and colleagues helped us become aware of how the theoretical issues impacted on us personally in ways we were very ambivalent about recognizing.

THE SCHIFF FAMILY Our personal connection with the Schiff Family was established when I visited the Family briefly in March, 1971, when they lived in Fredricksburg, Virginia. I invited them (20 or so Family members) to stay with us in Denver while they were traveling to their new home in California. When they stayed with us in July, 1971, we were exposed in our own home to the warmth and caring that is an integral part of a passivity confrontation structure. While they were with us, Jacqui and her sons, Aaron and Eric, did a workshop explaining passivity and developmental theory. We arranged for them to demonstrate their theory at the mental health center where Jon worked. We decided that passivity confrontation was probably a useful therapeutic tool which we would experiment with, but that reparenting as practiced by the Family required an investment of far more time, energy, and commitment than we were willing to make. We also decided to keep our personal life separate from our work as therapists.

Jon and I and the children, Brian and Linda, accepted an invitation to visit the Schiff Family in their new home in Alamo, California for a week in December, 1971. While we were there our children were integrated into the family structure and thrived in it. We were free to observe and participate as guests in family functions. During this visit we learned how the Schiffs used passivity confrontation to help people solve developmental problems, change script decisions, and eventually function effectively and independently. Our understanding was enhanced by visiting one of Pam Levin's groups, where she was experimenting with using passivity confrontation and parenting methods in an out-patient structure.

Jon and I started working together regularly as cotherapists with an ongoing group in March, 1972. This accelerated our awareness of our own symbiotic relationship, and we used frequent encounters with the Schiffs and with Pam Levin as opportunities to work out personal problems. During the summer of 1972, we agreed to reparent a schizophrenic woman who was a member of a treatment group we did together. In the fall of 1972 we established a second group. We continued to experiment with combining passivity confrontation and other techniques we were familiar with, and we talked with other therapists about what we were doing. Colleagues also experimented with these methods, and gradually our current structure evolved. We have continued our association with the Schiffs, sometimes directly integrating their new materials into our current practice, sometimes modifying them, and often developing ways to integrate these concepts into nonclinical areas.

THE FEMINIST INFLUENCE   Our exposure to the feminist movement and to Steiner's new views about the stroke economy began in 1970. Jon and I did not immediately see the relevance of this material to our own practices. We watched the struggle of the Women's Caucus at the 1970 ITAA Summer Conference and wondered what the fuss was about. We invited discussion of feminist issues at the Denver TA Seminar, and very gradually we became aware of how sexism subtly influenced our own lives. When we began recognizing discounts in the summer of 1971, the discounts inherent in the way men and women were supposed to relate to each other became more and more apparent. Pam Levin was aware of the problems of sexism and helped us highlight some areas we had been reluctant to expose.

An incident occurred in the fall of 1972 which helped us understand the difference between intellectually supporting principles of personal equality and actually recognizing and practicing those principles under stress. One evening it appeared that our three-year-old daughter would be too sick to attend preschool the following day, when I was scheduled to do a long-anticipated presentation on TA to about 50 women. We both assumed this was my problem but checked schedules to see if Jon could help me out. Jon had two clients scheduled, and offered to help me find someone to do my presentation. CLICK! We both realized how that proposal was tied to sexual stereotypes, so we regrouped and he decided to cancel his clients and stay home with the sick child. This incident disorganized us enough to lead us to take a new look at many assumptions we were making about ourselves and our clients.

We began to recognize that some of our assumptions about the options our clients had for solving problems were subtly and unnecessarily limited by sex-role expectations. In many instances, we changed our position from a supporting "Of course that can't be changed" to a thought-provoking "Why can't it?" We began to distinguish between cultural scripting and personal scripting of individuals.

CHANGING CULTURAL SCRIPTING   We use the individual script principle that children accept injunctions from their parents and devise life plans to limit their behavior according to those injunctions. We view much of what we do in treatment as giving clients an opportunity to examine the validity of their scripts, and providing protection for clients to experiment with giving up their self-imposed limitations. When we view the injunctions as coming from only one or two parenting figures, it seems reasonable that one or two therapists can have sufficient potency to provide protection for clients to resolve personal script issues.

We believe all scripting cannot be explained according to this model. Our understanding of the subtle issues of sexism led to the concept of a Cultural Parent which prescribes certain behaviors for females and other behaviors for males. These influences have been widely documented.[4]

The injunctions children accept from a Cultural Parent may either reinforce, contradict, or be irrelevant to personal injunctions they accept from their own parents. When a client understands and discards personal injunctions in treatment and still has difficulty changing behaviors, the internal pressure to conform to cultural norms may be what is getting in the way. This problem is especially severe in instances when personal programming matches cultural programming. It is very difficult for any therapist to provide sufficient protection for a client to make lifestyle changes when many people the client associates with oppose those changes. In our experience, the potency to provide this protection can most effectively come from a group of people who support the changes and from exposure to people who model the new behavior patterns.

ADJUNCTS TO THERAPY   We encourage clients in our groups to provide additional support (and an approving new Cultural Parent) for each other when making lifestyle changes. This Group Parent phenomenon has also been useful in helping clients identify new options which go beyond those commonly acknowledged by our majority culture. Gradually, our clients began to use some parts of the evolving open TA community to provide parental protection for their experiments in breaking cultural norms and trying new autonomous behavior.[5] More experienced members of the community serve as role models for new members, who incorporate from the new Cultural Parent permission to change which supports the new behavior.

Providing information about alternatives is one way of providing permission to examine and change cultural scripting. Using a treatment group for this purpose seems to be an inefficient use of our time and our clients' money. Acquainting people with cultural issues seemed more educational than therapeutic, so we began to explore other models for dealing with issues of cultural scripting. Since we were both resolving these issues for ourselves in leaderless consciousness-raising groups, we wanted to experiment with using such groups as an adjunct to therapy. However there were very few groups to refer people to. We eventually devised low-cost Public Education Workshops in which participants were exposed to a great deal of information about issues in scripting, parenting, communications, and playing, with plenty of time to discuss and share personal implications of this information. We encouraged people who participated in these workshops to continue to meet in leaderless groups after the workshops ended, and many did.

Clients who attended these workshops and leaderless groups appeared to use them for support in solving current problems, and continued to identify and solve developmental problems in treatment groups.

Our increasing awareness of sex role stereotyping provided an additional diagnostic and therapeutic tool. We began to watch for and confront instances when clients related differently to similar behavior in one or the other of us. We discovered frequent instances where women would play *Stupid* with Jon and appear intelligent and effective with me. We also observed instances where men would attack me for being controlling when I was potent and effective in group, while they would respond quite differently to similar behavior from Jon. When this occurred we learned to ask, "What would you have done if Laurie/Jon had said that to you?" Frequently, clients recognized how they responded to sexual stereotypes instead of real people in other areas of their lives and used that information to make important changes for themselves.

OTHER INFLUENCES Our treatment style has evolved partly from our own personal experiences with other therapists.

I, Laurie, owe a special debt to many of the women who have been centrally involved with ITAA for long periods of time. They have been very influential in my development as a therapist, teacher, and independent professional. They have served as role models of how women can combine effective professional and personal functioning. I think the importance of modeling how to live and work is often neglected in designing educational and therapy programs; actually seeing possibilities had more influence on me than any abstract discussion of them. Many trainers (male and female) and colleagues have provided noncompetitive support, encouragement, acknowledgment, and love, in large and small ways. Over and over again they have helped me to shift my frame of reference from "Who, me?" to "Yes, me!"

I encountered Fanita English and Natalie Haimowitz in 1968 and 1969 in the Chicago TA Seminar. Each provided an outstanding model of how women can both think and feel, and each stroked me warmly for my own growth in those areas.

Mary Goulding, a person who had much impact on Jon early in his TA experience, also had a major impact on me from 1972 to 1974. Mary and Bob Goulding have made important theoretical contributions to TA.[6] We use redecision theory as an "of course" background to work. Mary's impact on me was personal as well as theoretical. Over the years I have watched Mary choose promising people, create space for them to demonstrate their ability, and then quietly challenge them to grow and meet the situation. She did this for me. I have used her spaces to grow personally, and her methods as another way of helping my own students to grow.

PERSONAL PARENTHESES   I am aware that in writing this chapter we are again playing out the pattern of my (Laurie—the female part of the pair) sharing the personal, feeling information, and Jon (the male intellectual) writing the theoretical "Adult" material which follows. We have each edited the entire chapter. We are each whole and each have our own special strengths.

THE MECHANICS OF PRACTICE

Before describing the theoretical framework around which we organize our approach, I, Jon, will describe some of the mechanics of our practice so the reader can see the context in which we operate.

Our offices, which we share with ten other therapists and with the facilities of our training institute, are in a commercial building in a suburban area. The thickly carpeted group rooms are furnished with large pillows and boxes and cabinets full of toys. Laurie and I do three two-hour groups per week with each other, and each of us does an additional weekly group with a different cotherapist. We do weekend residential marathons every eight to 12 weeks. Group membership is usually about ten but can range from eight to 12; marathon groups are usually ten to 14.

Some clients attend more than one group, and it frequently happens that people will attend a group other than their regular one, if they have a temporary schedule conflict. All clients in all groups have a contract to confront and to accept confrontations on discounting and passive behavior; the structure is, consequently, quite consistent from one group to another.

In addition to the group members, therapists, and possible extra clients, groups typically have one or two assistants. These may be people who are former members of the group and who have fulfilled their contracts but are invested in the group and attend without paying so as to help maintain the group culture. The assistants may also be people who are in the institute's training program, who are there in a kind of apprentice capacity for a specified period of time. Finally, there are, from time to time, other professional people who are visiting and observing groups as part of the institute's Visiting Therapist Program.

We typically see new clients two to four times before putting them in a group. We rarely see anyone for individual treatment over an extended period without having them in a group. We will see someone individually as well as in group if a person asks for it and presents some good Adult reasons for the request; we would not consider fear of or unwillingness to talk about some topics in group to be Adult reasons for an individual session.

During the individual sessions, the new client gets an exploration of the presenting problem, a script analysis,[7] and a great deal of information —both verbal and printed—about what we do and why we do it, what will be expected of him or her, and how all that relates to his or her presenting problem.[8]

New clients get a substantial amount of the information presented in the following sections, but in a less formal way. In addition to the readings, many of the concepts are explained verbally, using the clients' own behaviors for illustration. In this manner, we get some early assessment of the clients' responsiveness to information about their problems, and can see how well they are likely to react to an expectation to think.

THE HEALTHY MODEL

When people come for psychotherapy we usually perceive that they are being ineffective in solving problems for themselves and in getting what they need in the world. Clients will usually accept this definition and then proceed to locate the cause of their ineffectiveness either in the external environment ("If it weren't for . . .") or in some constitutional and immutable inadequacy of their own ("I just can't . . ."), or in both.

At this point, we tell the client that problems are solvable: "It is possible to get what you need; you are being ineffective because you have not learned *how* to be effective, not because you are *incapable* of being effective, and you can learn to be effective if you are willing to."

A healthy, effective person, man or woman, we define as one who takes initiative to solve problems to get what he needs in the world in a manner that takes into account: his own needs, feelings, thoughts, and behavior; the needs, feelings, thoughts, and behavior of other persons; and the relevant aspects of the reality of the situation in which he operates.

A person who does not take into account his own needs is not likely to be effective in getting what he needs. A person who discounts the needs of others is operating from a position that he is the only one in the world whose needs count. Such a person is rarely liked by others and is frequently discounted. A person who discounts the situation will not recognize the availability of resources for meeting needs, or will attempt to meet needs in ways that do not fit into the reality of the situation. Many people, for example, get into competitive struggles in situations where there are ample resources which could easily be shared with cooperation.

The way in which the treatment process is organized is that the clients are placed in a situation—the group—in which everyone is expected to transact with others in a manner that matches the definition of a healthy person; when they do not operate in this fashion, they are then helped to recognize the fact, encouraged to look at what is getting in the way of their doing so, and expected to change their behavior in accordance with the healthy model. At the same time, all clients are told that the group is one place to get what they need, and all they have to do is ask for it.

It is important to recognize and acknowledge that this procedure is, in fact, a parental way of structuring the treatment process. There are a number of reasons for using this approach. First of all, as Eric Berne pointed out, the client perceives therapy as a Parent-Child situation in the first place,[9] and, to the extent that the therapist is successful in influencing him at all, he will incorporate the therapist's Adult into his Parent. We see this as being quite accurate, and deliberately go with this tendency by specifying that we are, in fact, offering parental structures for the client to incorporate in order to be more effective at getting what he needs for the Child.

Secondly, many people are more likely to experience their emotional problems in situations where it is necessary for them to cope with the task of integrating their own needs with the expectations of others. In our structure, their methods of attempting to solve this fundamental problem are quickly exposed.

Our assumption is that the way in which a person learns to solve problems in a healthy, effective manner is by having experienced appropriate and effective parental or environmental responses to his or her own expressed needs, feelings, thoughts, and behaviors as they arose throughout childhood. The adult person's problem-solving will be affected to the extent that responses were lacking, inappropriate, and/or ineffective.

When the client transacts with others in the group, he will soon begin to display the various impairments in his problem-solving ability. As these occur, they are pointed out, and the client is asked both to change the immediate behavior and to look at the source of the problem behavior. The client is also asked to exercise Adult control of these behaviors outside of the group.

We find that this practice has several distinct advantages. First of all, there seems to be a very rapid decrease in symptomatic behavior and a simultaneous increase in responsible behavior outside of the treatment sessions. People seem to generalize their ownership of and control over problem behaviors. Secondly, the demand to change the passive behavior in the treatment groups frequently meets with resistance which is also confronted. This gives the client an opportunity to experience the amount of investment she or he has in maintaining the passive behavior. At this point, we frequently use Pam Levin's Think Structure for identifying archaic problems; it provides clear information regarding the underlying motivation for the behavior and shows what steps need to be taken to correct the archaic problems.[10]

Probably the most important advantage of a confrontation structure is the degree to which clients experience safety and protection. The Child in each person associates the passive behavior and discounting that others engage in as directly associated with his or her own needs not being met. People learn to discount by being discounted. Since discounting is a frequent social operation, most people perceive social situations as places where, if they expressed needs directly, they would (again) be discounted. In the group, the implementation of the mutual contract to confront discounting is perceived by the Child as proof that expressed needs will not be discounted. The message to the Child is, "This is a safe place to do what you need to do."

The most frequently used techniques for responding to displays of non-problem-solving behaviors are derived from the Schiffs' passivity confrontation methods,[11] although gestalt techniques, game analysis, and script analysis are often used in addition. Treatment interventions are described more fully below.

THE NEED-RESPONSE CYCLE

Needs arise continuously and repeatedly, simply as a function of being alive. A need mobilizes and organizes the person's energy and resources until the need is met; at that point, there is a closure or completion, and the energy is released to be organized around the next need that arises. Both biological needs (air, food, strokes, etc.) and transactional needs (information, separateness, differentiation, etc.) follow a natural sequence of experience, expression, and resolution, unless something interferes with the cycle. I'm hungry (need), I go to the kitchen to look for something and find it (expression), and I eat it and no longer experience hunger (resolution).

A person who functions according to the healthy model described above will respond to needs as they arise by: (1) experiencing the need (Adult awareness of Child feeling), and (2) expressing the need in some manner appropriate to its nature and intensity and to the situation the person is in (Adult and Parent assessment of relevant information, with energy and initiative supplied by the Child motivation to get the need met). I'm hungry, I look for food, and, at some point, remember that I'm going to be having a big meal very soon, so I don't eat or eat only a small amount.

Only when the behavioral expression of the need has been made is there any kind of impact on the environment. This may seem simple, but many people operate as if they think that others know what they need or feel, even though they have done nothing to express it. If the impact is effective, there will be a response from the environment that will meet the original need; for example, in a restaurant, I tell the waiter what I want to eat and he brings it.

When the need is met, the person experiences a sense of closure and satisfaction, a release of energy, and a freedom to move on. The specific behavior that succeeded in eliciting a response from the environment is reinforced, and it remains in the person's repertoire as something to do when that need is experienced again. In addition to the satisfaction of getting the need met, the person also experiences a sense of "OKness": "I am adequate to get what I need, and the world is responsive to my needs."

The situation becomes more complex when we recognize that the world does not always respond to the person's needs as soon as they are expressed: the impact of the behavioral expression of the need on the environment may well be such that it does not work. When this happens, the person experiences something new, a reaction to not getting the need met. We are calling this reaction "anger."

Anger, rather than being a problem in itself, is a Natural Child response to not getting needs met. If we remove other connotations from the word, we can see that in its Natural Child form, anger is simply an increase of energy directed towards getting a need met. Just as the original need mobilizes energy in the direction of taking initiative to do something to get the need met, anger *adds* energy to the original push. Anger appears to function to motivate the person to find alternatives to the original behavioral expression of the need. Thus, anger can be viewed as another need or feeling, logically comparable to, but in addition to, the original frustrated need. Its natural behavioral expression is either to repeat, with more energy, the original behavior, or to move to an alternative behavioral expression of the same need. Gwendolyn, age 14 months, is attracted to the brightly colored flakes inside her clear plastic block; she pulls at the block to get it apart. When it doesn't open, she pulls harder, starts to yell, and bangs it on the floor. Oblivious to mother bearing down on her with the brush and dustpan, she happily pokes the little flakes around amid the fragments of the block.

Producing an alternative behavioral expression of the need implies that the person has alternatives available in his or her repertoire. There may be a greater or lesser number of such alternatives, depending on the level of maturity of the person. In response to hunger, for example, an infant can only cry; anger at not getting fed can only be expressed directly by persisting or by crying louder. An older child can ask for food with words in several different ways; she can ask someone else. If the first person doesn't respond, she can get food herself or cry with or without words, and so on.

Each time the person puts forth another behavior in an attempt to meet the original need (or to express the anger at not getting the need met), there are the same two possibilities as before: either the environment will respond so that the need gets met, or it will not. If the need does get met, the person experiences all the satisfaction, closure, reinforcement, etc., described above; if the need does not get met, the person adds some more anger to the pot and goes to the next available behavior in his repertoire, continuing the cycle until the need gets met.

SUBSTITUTE BEHAVIOR

When the person has exhausted all of his or her behavioral alternatives, adding as much angry energy as possible to those behavioral expressions, and finds that the need is still not met, he or she creates a totally new behavior. This new behavior, which we call a substitute behavior, is a disguised or indirect expression of the original need; its impact on the environment is typically such that either some portion of the original need gets met, or there is some relief from the pain and discomfort of not getting the need met, or both. For example, an infant cries for food, and is responded to by being slapped. She quickly learns to stop crying, to do nothing in the face of hunger; if she is passive long enough, she sometimes will get fed.

Since there is some reinforcement of the behavior, it is likely to be repeated and soon becomes part of a separate behavior repertoire of Adapted Child responses, as distinct from the Natural Child repertoire of direct behavior. With sufficient repeated experiences of the failure of the environment to meet needs directly, and with sufficient reinforcement of the substitute behavior, this new behavior will get attached directly to the original need. Once this connection is made, the person is likely to bypass the Natural Child repertoire completely and express the original need whenever it arises by means of the substitute behavior. Thus the battered infant described above responds to hunger by being quiet and passive. In fact, such an infant, when grown up, is likely to respond to *any* needs with passivity.

Since the substitute behavior is a compromise, the person never really experiences an entirely satisfactory meeting of the need. There always remains some sense of "This isn't right"; "I should feel better, but I don't"; "This is the best I can do," etc.; in short, some sense of not-OKness. In addition, since the substitute behavior is created because angry energy doesn't help, there usually is an incompleted expression of anger attached to the expression of the substitute behavior. This anger is often converted to some racket feeling.

Since there is neither a complete satisfaction of the need nor a resolution to the anger, the energy mobilized originally to accomplish these ends remains in flux. Here the gestalt concepts of "closure" and of "unfinished business from the past" are most useful. If the need is not met, it does not go away; the energy from it is channeled into other behaviors and keeps pushing those behaviors in an attempt to get closure. The experience of closure or satisfaction of the need, however, is only possible when there is an environmental response that meets the original need. Although it is possible that such response may come accidentally, at random, it is far more likely to come in response to the direct, Natural Child expression of the need. This Natural Child expression, however, is exactly what gets bypassed in the creation and continuation of substitute behavior, so the person is left with continuously and repeatedly unmet needs, driving behaviors that don't work to get the needs met.

We have been describing the process by which substitute behaviors are originally created in childhood. It is important to emphasize that, once established, a substitute behavior tends to become the characteristic method a person uses throughout life in an attempt to meet the underlying need. For example, a four-year-old, who needs to learn how to deal effectively with sad feelings, can get taught that "big boys don't cry," while getting strokes for being tough and aggressive. As an adult needing to express grief, this person is likely to discount being sad and act angry and tough instead. The grief remains unexpressed and unexperienced, and the force of it pushes more tough (substitute) behavior into other situations.

A large proportion of the behaviors that are described by TA theory fit into the category of substitute behavior. Games, rackets, stamp collecting, passive behavior, ulterior transactions, script decisions, not-OK positions, and Adapted Child behaviors can all be seen as substitutes for the direct experience and expression of needs. These behaviors are created in response to situations in which the direct expression of needs and feelings did not elicit the kinds of responses from the environment that would meet the needs. It is our view that these substitute behaviors can be dealt with directly by identifying them as such and by helping the client to identify and express appropriately the original needs underlying them.

DEVELOPMENTAL AND ARCHAIC NEEDS VS. CURRENT NEEDS

In the description of the healthy model, we characterized the healthy person as one who takes initiative to get his or her needs met in a way that does not discount the needs of others or the reality of the situation. A person learns to behave in this manner when he has experiences in childhood that are responsive to his own needs.

More specifically, each developmental stage of childhood contains a task, a problem for the growing child to solve, which, if resolved effectively, provides him with another piece of the structure needed to function effectively as a healthy adult.

Many authors have detailed the various stages of child development from a TA point of view, and this material will not be duplicated here.[12] The point that needs to be emphasized here is that the needs of each stage are expressed via the need-response cycle described earlier, with the same possibility, in each case, of the occurrence of some failure to meet the need. If the particular developmental problem of a given stage is not solved because of a failure of the environment—usually parents—to respond appropriately to the natural expression of the developmental need, then the ability of the person to meet that particular need in a healthy way in the future will be impaired.

In our approach to treatment, the expectation to conform to the healthy model quickly exposes whatever impairments there may be in the client's problem-solving abilities. This information is combined with our knowledge of the client's individual contract, her or his script, cultural script influences, and developmental stages. Taken together, these sources of information help pinpoint the particular developmental needs that were not met, and that are still driving the substitute behaviors.

CONFRONTATION VS. REINFORCEMENT

Any response to a substitute behavior that does not recognize that behavior for what it is, and that does not deal with the need underlying the behavior, will tend to reinforce the behavior—at the least with strokes, and possibly with some semblance of meeting the need. A therapeutic strategy, therefore, necessarily involves providing as little response as possible to substitute behaviors, and as much response as possible to genuine needs.

In our approach to treatment, we make it clear to clients that, when they identify what they need and ask us directly to meet that need, we will usually agree to do so, or at least to problem-solve with them about how to get the need met if we are not willing to meet it. In general, we will contract to meet archaic developmental needs directly. At the same time, we tell people that we will confront substitute behaviors and will do what we can to minimize their getting any rewards from those behaviors. We find that once people see that the energy they are putting into substitute behaviors is actually interfering with their getting needs met, they are willing to accept confrontation of the substitute behaviors.

The form of confrontation varies a great deal from one situation and client to another. The intent of any confrontation is, first of all, to help the client experience what his or her real need is and then to take appropriate initiative to get the need met and achieve closure. Secondly, the intent is to help the person distinguish between and respond differently to current needs and unresolved developmental needs. In order to achieve these ends, one or more of three different types of interventions may be used: (1) we may ask the person to identify the need or feeling and do something about it; (2) we may suggest a particular behavior for the person to experiment with, in or out of the group; or (3) we may elect to initiate doing something to meet the person's need. As a frequent compromise, we may suggest what the need or feeling might be, based on our own observation, and ask the person to check to see if we are correct. If so, we then suggest the person do something about the need or feeling.

Clients do not always respond to these interventions, and continue to display the same substitute behavior that is being confronted. Under pressure, they may also switch to some other substitute behavior in order to avoid the confrontation. When we recognize these maneuvers, we usually confront them as well, keeping in mind the intent of the original confrontation.

When and how much to push a person who is not accepting confrontation is a complex issue, and one which is more profitably explored in supervision than in a text. There is a line between effective confrontation and a competitive power struggle, just as there is a difference between deciding to de-escalate a confrontation and giving up and adapting to the client's refusal to solve a problem. Our preference is to define the problem clearly, then leave the initiative for solving it up to the client. Pushing is done if the client identifies that he needs that kind of response from us in order to solve the problem.

When a client continually refuses to accept confrontation of any kind, and insists on maintaining his self-defeating substitute behavior, we define this as a refusal to operate within our contract and terminate the relationship. We run an out-patient practice with limited access to hospital facilities, and we make it clear to clients that we can only be effective for them within our structure. Any escalation outside of group that leads to psychiatric hospitalization or to encounters with the police is treated as a decision not to solve problems within our structure, and the relationship is immediately terminated and the client referred to another source of treatment. Some other therapists in our community are willing to deal with such escalations without terminating the client.

APPLICATIONS

Here are several examples of the way in which we diagnose developmental problems, plan a treatment strategy based on the diagnosis, and carry out the plan. The discussion is linear, while the actual process may not be. Diagnosis and treatment planning may, for example, be carried out in just a few transactions, which might take place early in treatment or after considerable time in the group. The implementation of the plan can take anywhere from several minutes to several months or years. For many people, just being in a simultaneously confronting and nurturing structure is a significant intervention all by itself.

The information presented in the following examples is accurate for each case, but some of it has been edited for the purpose of keeping the illustration clear. Certain features of each case have been emphasized so the reader can see the entire mosaic of theory, diagnosis, intervention, and outcome.

1. A six-year-old needs to argue, to demand to know the reasons for rules in order to incorporate a Parent ego state that can work with his Adult to know when to be strong, when to be flexible, and what to do if a rule doesn't work. Kurt was six during World War II, in Belgium. When the shooting and bombs came, survival depended (he was told) on immediate and unquestioning obedience: if you wait to ask "Why do I have to turn out the light?" before turning it out, you could get killed. Nobody was ever sure if there would be food for another meal: "Eat everything on your plate, and don't complain." Frightened adults were trying to control their own fear by controlling a frightened child.

As an adult, Kurt does what he is told immediately and expects others to do the same. At work, he berates his colleagues for not doing their duty. He flies into a screaming rage when his children do not eat everything on their plates. In quiet moments, he knows this is irrational but has no available Adult at all when the situations occur. He doesn't understand the group; the "rules" are not clear to him, he is frightened, and we are not "strong" enough to protect his Child; he leaves after two sessions.

2. Gerry is a good girl; she was taught to be sweet, cute, polite, and well-behaved, starting when she was crawling around the house. Instead of getting to explore and find out what things felt and tasted like, she was cleaned, shined, polished, displayed, and taught tricks. When she got to the "terrible two's," when most children get negative and stubborn (so they can later think for themselves), Gerry simply continued to be sweet and obedient.

After many weeks of cautious experimenting, playing with toys like a two-year-old and saying no, she threw a screaming tantrum and refused to pick up her toys. She was told she could choose between picking up the toys or standing in the corner while someone else picked up after her. She refused to choose, and so she was put in the corner. The following week, she came in excited and enthusiastic about having finished several projects that she had been putting off for months. By expressing the "I won't—you can't make me" position in group and having it responded to appropriately, she did developmental work that a two-year-old would normally do. This drained the energy from her acting out the "I won't" in a passive-aggressive manner outside the group.

3. Jack is a new client, a middle-aged banker, who is sent for psychotherapy by his physician. There is no organic cause for his dizziness, belching, chest pains, and other "disabling" symptoms. He is disabled from going to work occasionally, from social life, from being active with his family. What does he want to change? He not only doesn't know, he has a great deal of difficulty saying *anything* about what he wants; he is full of what he should do, what is right, what is expected of him, and has trouble even conceiving of the idea that what he needs is a relevant question.

When Jack was exploratory, he was spanked for being "bad"—that is, exploratory, active, getting into what he could reach. The exploratory phase is critical for connecting "I want" with "I do something to get what

I want." When he was two, he was spanked for saying no, and was told to respect his elders instead of having his negativism accepted so he could later decide to think for himself. When he was four, he was "so smart" that he was sent to a strict religious school. A four-year-old's developmental task is to give up magical thinking. He has yet to learn that thoughts and feelings and wishes are not actions; he needs accurate information in order to learn this. Jack was taught that "the evil thought is as wicked as the evil deed," and that the thought or deed of saying no to other people's expectations is un-Christian; he already knew it was dangerous. So Jack has things in his life he would say no to, sometimes, if he dared even to think it. When he is sick, however, nobody, not even the Parent in his head, hassles him about *doing* "no" and he doesn't have to say it. I suggest he experiment by thinking to himself "I don't wanna. . ." when he gets his symptoms. He returns for the next session and reports progress. I think he's going to do fine. The immediate treatment plan is to continue to focus on the negativism, and to provide him with a lot of nurturing for identifying his own needs.

4. Sally is doing a gestalt technique, feeling like a five-year-old and pounding on pillows, expressing her anger toward her mother, who doesn't listen. "Listen to me!" she screams, shrilly, flailing away with all her might. "Why don't you listen to me?" she wails. One of us asks, "Suppose you do everything there is to do, and find out that you still can't control her, that she still doesn't listen." Sally pauses with fists upraised, and collapses into huge sobs of grief. After a while, one of us asks her if she is "suffering," i.e., being a Victim. "No, I'm *not* suffering!" she snaps. "I ought to know whether I'm suffering or not! I'm just being sad 'cause I can't make her do what I want. Stop telling me I'm suffering when I'm not!" "Okay, let us know if you need anything."

In our view, Sally suddenly resolved the key issue of the three- to five-year-old stage by giving up her magical thinking. Her whole script had been based on trying to please her mother, and what held it together was not unexpressed anger but the four-year-old position that "I can control people with my feelings, if I just find the right way to go about it." We have frequently seen people experience grief when they give up magical thinking, after which they are ready to move on. Sally moved on dramatically, getting immediately into the argumentativeness of the next developmental stage.

5. Sid is depressed, feels that he can't do anything right. When he was eight, his father would give him jobs to do and then take over himself, telling Sid that he was too slow, clumsy, too stupid to learn, etc. Sid identifies a specific problem area at work: he is afraid to present ideas to his superior, because he is afraid there might be an argument. "What would happen when you argued with your father?" "I never argued with him, I didn't dare." "Sounds like you need permission and practice; how about arguing with me?"

Sid wants to argue about using the car, having me (J.W.) role-play his mother; I think this is way off the point but am willing to start here. We have a "playacting" kind of argument. The following week, Sid says that the arguing seems to help, and wants to do some more role-playing. This time I object, telling him that we need to have a real argument, not a make-believe one. He persists, pointing out that the way we did it last time worked well for him. After a few rounds, he convinces me that his point of view is valid, and I agree to the role-play. He grins and says he doesn't need to now; he feels good about having handled a real one. Subsequently, he reports presenting ideas to his boss with no difficulty. Incidentally, he is significantly less depressed, since the substitute behavior of the depression and inadequacy racket is no longer being pushed by the archaic need to argue and be heard.

We have a usable and effective roadmap, with the combination of TA theory and developmental stage theory. It enables us to recognize the significance of current behavior patterns and helps to guide us as we pick our way among the many different bits of information that clients present. The map is not the territory, however, and we always need to keep in mind that it is the client, not the map, that ultimately tells us where we are going.

References

1. Eric Berne, *Transactional Analysis in Psychotherapy*, New York, Grove Press, 1961; Eric Berne, *Games People Play*, New York, Grove Press, 1964.
2. Laurie Weiss, *A Transactional Analysis Community: The Denver Experience*, Littleton, Colorado, Rocky Mountain Transactional Institute, 1975.
3. Claude Steiner, *Scripts People Live*, New York, Grove Press, 1974; Dorothy Jongeward and Dru Scott, *Affirmative Action for Women*, Reading, Massachusetts, Addison-Wesley, 1974.
4. Steiner, *op. cit.*; Betty Friedan, *The Feminine Mystique*, New York, W. W. Norton & Company, 1963; Phyllis Chesler, *Women and Madness*, Garden City, New York, Doubleday, 1972; Caroline Bird, *Born Female*, New York, David McKay, 1968.
5. Weiss, *op. cit.*
6. Robert Goulding, "New Directions in Tranactional Analysis," in Clifford J. Sager and Helen Singer Kaplan, eds., *Progress in Group and Family Therapy*, New York, Brunner/Mazel, 1972; Robert Goulding and Mary Goulding, "Injunctions, Decisions, and Redecisions," *Transactional Analysis Journal*, 6, no. 1 (January, 1976), pp. 41–48.
7. We use a variation of the McCormick Life Script Questionnaire. See Paul McCormick, *Guide for the Use of a Life Script Questionnaire*, San Francisco, Transactional Pubs, 1971.
8. Muriel James and Dorothy Jongeward, *Born to Win*, Reading, Massachusetts, Addison-Wesley, 1973; Eric Berne, *What Do You Say After You Say Hello?*, New York, Grove Press, 1972; Jacqui Lee Schiff and Beth Day, *All My Children*, Philadelphia, J. B. Lippincott Co., 1970.
   The printed material given the client is usually selected from the following items based on the level of sophistication of the client:
   Paul McCormick and Leonard Campos, *Introduce Yourself to Transactional Analysis*, San Francisco, Transactional Pubs, 1974.

Paul McCormick and Leonard Campos, *Introduce Your Marriage to Transactional Analysis,* San Francisco, Transactional Pubs, 1972.

Aaron Wolfe Schiff and Jacqui Lee Schiff, "Passivity," *Transactional Analysis Journal, 1,* no. 1 (January, 1971).

Fred L. Wollerman, "A Layman's Guide to Passivity," Unpublished paper.

Laurie Weiss, "Confrontation," Unpublished paper.

H. Close, "On Parenting," *Voices, 4,* no. 1 (1968), p. 94.

Bill Falzett and Jean Maxwell, *"OK Childing and Parenting,"* El Paso, Texas, Transactional Analysis Institute of El Paso, 1974.

Stanley Woollams, Michael Brown, and Kristyn Huige, *Transactional Analysis in Brief,* Ann Arbor, Michigan, Huron Valley Institute, 1974.

In addition, it may be recommened that clients read *Born to Win, What Do You Say After You Say Hello?,* and/or *All My Children.*

9. Eric Berne, "In Treatment," *Transactional Analysis Bulletin, 1,* no. 2 (1962), p. 10.

10. Pamela Levin, "A Think Structure for Feeling Fine Faster," *Transactional Analysis Journal, 3,* no. 1 (January, 1973), pp. 38–39; Schiff and Schiff, *loc. cit.;* Jacqui Lee Schiff, *et al., The Cathexis Reader: Transactional Analysis Treatment of Psychosis,* New York, Harper & Row, 1975.

11. Schiff, *et al., op. cit.*

12. Pamela Levin, *Becoming the Way We Are,* Sacramento, California, Jalmar Press, 1974; Falzett and Maxwell, *op. cit.;* Dorothy E. Babcock and Terry D. Keepers, *Raising Kids OK,* New York, Grove Press, 1975.

SEVEN

ASKLEPIEION:
AN INTEGRATION OF PSYCHOTHERAPIES
Martin Groder

When working with psychopaths, I found that there was no one method that was good enough; or, to put that another way, there was nothing they couldn't corrupt if they got wind of how it worked. They were very adamant to get wind of how it worked, because they were very interested in corrupting it. Inversely, of course, they were also trying to see if it was really worth changing, because if the method was corruptible, then everything in the world was a bad joke anyway, as they already knew. This testing process is a very advanced form of "Do me something."

In the Butner project I was doing, I ended up realizing that there are six major points of view about what it is that's wrong with or what needs to be changed in people who are "unhappy." They are represented by the six points of an octahedron. (Figure 1).

GRODER OCTAHEDRON

There are two pyramids, one on top of the other. The central surface is a square. The central square has the four major types of psychotherapeutic techniques and assumptions about people. The first point is a body, a physical assumption which says essentially that what's wrong with people is their bodies. If you can just get their bodies straight, everything else will be fine. To me, these absolute statements sound absurd; I hope they sound absurd to you, too, but there are real people running around stating such principles as truth. They are the basis for Hatha Yoga, drug therapies of various kinds. bioenergetics and other neo-Reichian offshoots, Rolfing, and all kinds of physical training. These body techniques say that if you get your body straight, you'll be OK.

The next point on the square represents an emphasis on feeling or affect. Gestalt therapy, primal therapy, and reevaluation counseling are widely known. The basic assumption is that if you get your feelings

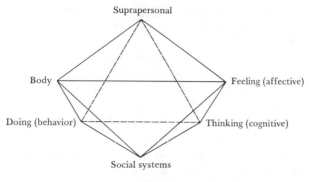

Figure 1
Groder Octahedron

straight, everything else will fall into place; you'll think straight, you'll act straight, and your body will be cleansed of all poisonous feelings.

The next point is that of cognitive or thinking processes, of which classical TA is an example as are rational therapy and reality therapy. The essential assumption is, "If you get your thinking straightened out, then your feelings will straighten out and then you'll act decent and you'll be a good, productive citizen." Psychoanalysis, theoretically, is a cognitive-affective treatment. (Recently TA has become a feeling therapy as well as a cognitive therapy.)

Finally, at the fourth point, the behavioral people assume that all that's real is behavior. Thus, if behavior is straightened out, who cares what people think about or feel like inside the "Black Box." The two currently widely known schools of behavioral psychotherapy are the Skinnerian and the Wolpe Conditional Response Schools.

Those are the personal-level psychotherapy types. Essentially, they all assume that the problem with people is the person. The task then is to get the people straightened out and then everything else will straighten out, because what's wrong with people is in one or more of these four areas upon which the therapist can use therapeutic leverage for change.

The bottom pyramid consists of methods that are called social-systems methods; these rely essentially on the assumption that what's wrong with people is the system they create and live in. If the system were RIGHT, everybody would fall in line and have good bodies and have clean minds and healthy feelings and act right. Of course, there are a variety of political systems that say this, like communism and democracy, plus a variety of economic systems, and a variety of small-scale living systems of communal types, including therapeutic communities. Thus, Asklepieion, for instance, takes and includes a social-systems approach to psychopaths and others. Social-system believers get very annoyed with the personal therapy people. They say, "Oh, to hell with those personal therapy people, just get the social system right and everything will be all right." Of course, the personal-therapy people of each of the four flavors—physical, feeling, cognitive, and behavioral—say, "Ignore the system; if the people aren't right, they will muck up the system. It doesn't matter what system you've got, get the people right."

The last point on top I'm calling the suprapersonal; here again, there is an extremist view, whether the talk is of a system of ethics or philosophy or some kind of religious movement. The idea here is, "To hell with society and to hell with people and to how they feel, etc. If you just get right with the universe (The All or The Nothing), or with this system of ethics or philosophy or whatever, everything will be cool. You'll feel right and think right and be right." Sometimes this position means you won't feel or think anything—which is fine since there is no one really there to feel or think anyway (egoless), and furthermore there are many very interesting trips for the egoless ego to take while discounting very heavily the reality of the other levels. If you're personally interested in the suprapersonal, you can probably expand this octahedron out to a cube and make four corners and have ethical, philosophical, religious, and enlightenment corners. When I talk to sociologists, they say, "Oh, one point isn't enough for social systems; what you need to do is break it down to economics and politics and systematics of one kind or the other." It's an octahedron because I'm a psychotherapist; I guess it would be a cube if I were less narrow-minded. Anyhow, the point I am making with this talk is that however many points you want to designate, obnoxious purity is idiotic. At Asklepieion, we are moving into filling out our methods to each of the six corners so that we can use an interwoven tapestry of understood and effectively practiced methods to solve the problems that people bring, either singly or in groups.

When I first presented this material in our first annual Asklepieion conference back in February, 1975, one of the ministers in our bunch came out and said, "Thank God." I said, "Thank God for what?" He said, "I've been secretly practicing religion for all of these years in Asklepieion. Now I can come out and talk about it. I'm sorry I felt I had to practice it secretly." So he felt much released by the idea that the suprapersonal has a valid dimension within Asklepieion.

In looking into what methods can cure psychopaths, I discovered an interesting thing: that there seemed to be no method that could reliably cure psychopaths which didn't include at least three corners or assumptions in a very solid way. Now, I'm not sure whether this was because three ways were more than the guys could figure out to corrupt, or whether the kind of leadership that would go to the trouble to learn three sets of methods really well was the kind that they couldn't corrupt, or some combination of both. Further, the more additional methods that were integrated, the more solid, reliable, and uncorruptible was the process and outcome. Psychopaths who want to test foolproof methods by "making fools of" the practitioners seem to require both diversity and strength. We could not find at Butner any usable, reliable, or generally applicable method not using at least three methodologies.

COMMENTS AND QUESTIONS

Question: You've got a line under TA. Would you explain that?

Groder: TA started off as a cognitive method, moved into using behavioral methods (contract) and later the feeling work of gestalt. Recently bio-energetic methods are being introduced so that TA is starting to move over and pretty well cover the personal plane. TA, until recently, had done almost nothing with social systems, except for Eric Berne's book on organizations, which is 13 years old. That's the direction where Asklepie-ion and recently others are adding. In addition, most people in TA secretly practice religion or ethics and/or philosophy.

Question: What does this diagram say to us as therapists?

Groder: What I'm saying is this: when patients present problems to us that are not obviously solvable by the methods we now know, we have three choices:

1. To fake professionalism or "Only try to help."
2. To discount the problem as presented, redefine the problem into a similar problem that we can solve, solve the newly created problem, and then sell that "cure" to the patient as a cure of his original problem. This remarkable method has a history of thousands of years and millions of successful trials. Unfortunately, the grandiosity of the therapist leads to the eventual downfall of the therapist and the therapy, and later patients grow wise (resistant) to the ruse.
3. Invent a new form of psychotherapy for each client, using elements of the known methods and such new ideas as are fostered by the encounter between therapist and patient. This is the hardest and most rewarding, both long and short term, for both therapist and client.

EIGHT

THE THREE "C'S" OF CORRECTIONS: COPS-CONS-COUNSELORS
Kenneth L. Windes

It is generally agreed among those involved in any facet of the prison system in America that this corrections system has been a failure since its inception 200 years ago. The reason for its failure have not been agreed upon. The development of transactional analysis by Eric Berne[1] and its application to sociopathic personalities by Martin Groder[2] have provided the first adequate technology for treating the personality disorders that underlie losing criminal behavior. Berne's contribution to the theory of group and organizational dynamics[3] and Groder's later work expanding on these concepts[4] provide the tools for analyzing the structure and function of correctional institutions and programs, and insight into why they fail.

CHECKING OUT WHAT THE SIGN SAYS

In discussing the success or failure of an organization, it is first necessary to define failure and success. As Groder has pointed out, a "clean organization" is one that is doing what the sign on the door says it's doing.[5] The sign on the front of the Gizmo Manufacturing Company says, "We make Gizmos." To determine whether or not it is a clean organization, you need only walk around to the back of the plant and see if gizmos are actually coming out. If there is a significant output of gizmos, you know that what is happening inside the plant is what the sign on the door says is happening. On the other hand, if no gizmos are being produced, the organization is "dirty," that is, it is not meeting its stated goals. Berne states that the failure of a group or organization to meet its stated goals is due to the energy of the group being dissipated in maintaining its internal or external boundaries.[6] This can occur in our example by radicals attempting to blow up the gizmo plant, which disrupts the work or group activity and turns the energy of the organization towards protecting its external boundary. A strike by the workers creates a conflict across an internal boundary between labor and management, again taking energy away from the making of gizmos. Groder carries this one step further by pointing out that in a "dirty organization" the energy of the organization is being diverted toward fulfillment of the covert or unstated goals. An example of this would be if the Gizmo Manufacturing Company were more interested in maintaining a worker caste system than in producing gizmos.

The sign on the door of a correctional institution says, "We correct offenders." If you walk around to the back and check the output, you find that upwards of 60 percent of the total output is made up of rejects, uncorrected offenders. The output does not support the stated goals. The next step is to look inside the organization to see what is actually going on. If the energy of the organization is not being used to produce "corrected offenders," what is it being used for?

PRISON CULTURE

Each organization develops its own customs, rules of behavior, value system, and allowable roles. This is the culture of the organization. The structure of ineffective correctional programs and institutions assigns a limited number of social roles, each of which has its own code of thinking and behavior. Figure 1 shows CONS, COPS, and COUNSELORS in their major game positions on the drama triangle.[7]

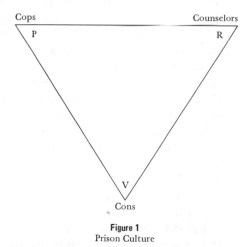

Figure 1
Prison Culture

CONS:

	Drama Position	Victim
	Life Position	I'm not-OK, You're OK (*haha*)
	Social Role	Penitent
	Psychological Role	"Make fools of"
	Major Messages	"Don't trust cops"
		"Don't snitch" (Support cons)
		"Do your own time" (Mind own business)
		"Keep a good front" (Be strong)

COPS:	Drama Position	Persecutor
	Life Position	I'm OK—You're not-OK
	Social Role	Custodial
	Psychological Role	"Keep 'em in their place"
	Major Messages	"Don't trust cons"
		"Support your fellow officer"
		"Counselors are fools"
		"Don't make waves"

COUNSELORS:	Drama Position	Rescuer
	Life Position	I'm OK—You're not-OK
	Social Role	Helper
	Psychological Role	"They're incurable"
	Major Messages	"Don't make waves"
		"Sociopaths are incurable"
		"They're out to get you"
		"Don't trust cops or cons"

Persons entering the institution or program are pressured by the group culture to assume one of the approved roles. A felon entering the institution through the criminal court system is expected to assume a role that reinforces the attitudes and behavior that caused him to lose in the first place. A person joining the custodial force is expected to assume a role that prevents him from transacting with inmates as OK people and forces him to treat them like CONS. Young college graduates with new social-science degrees enter the institution and are covertly invited to join the welfare ranks, write their reports, and not expect too much.

The sanctions against deviant behavior can be severe or mild. Most commonly, refusal to join the covert culture means that a person loses status, the protection of the culture, and major stroke sources. In third-degree institutions such as San Quentin or Marion, Illinois, refusal to join may result in death or disfigurement. Correctional personnel who refuse to buy into the COP role are targets of verbal abuse from fellow officers and superiors, who brand them as weak. Interesting, except for violent retaliation, the power plays used by the culture on both COPS and CONS are the same: name-calling, withdrawal of stroking, and lack of protection. Additional pressure comes from the fact that only COPS, CONS, and COUNSELORS can transact within the prison culture. Persons initiating autonomous transactions are first invited to assume one of three roles. Refusal to do so is viewed as threatening by the entire culture. Major games played between COPS and CONS are: *Now I've Got You, You SOB—Kick Me,* and *Cops and Robbers.* Major games between CONS and COUNSELORS are *I'm Only Trying to Help You* and *How Do I Get Out of Here.* COPS and COUNSELORS like *Mine's Better Than Yours* and *Now I've Got You, You SOB—Kick Me.* Three-handed games involving the entire culture are *Blemish* and *Let's You and Him Fight.* The latter is commonly initiated by CONS who set up Custody (COPS) and Treatment (COUNSELORS) to fight. This is usually easy to do because their respective roles include gimmicks for the game.

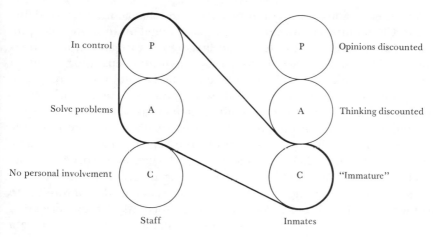

In control — P

Opinions discounted — P

Solve problems — A

Thinking discounted — A

No personal involvement — C

"Immature" — C

Staff   Inmates

Figure 2
Symbiosis

SYMBIOSIS

As I have pointed out in an earlier paper,[8] the symbiotic structure of correctional institutions and programs defeats most treatment or educational efforts before they get started. The inmates are defined as immature (Child) and their thoughts and opinions (Adult and Parent) are discounted, while the staff is defined as being in control (Parent) and responsible for problem solving (Adult), while avoiding personal involvement (Child). This sets up the symbiotic structure diagramed in Figure 2. The message to the cons is "Don't think" (just follow the rules), and to the cops and counselors "Don't feel" (just maintain order and get the paperwork done). Again, this structure limits the members of the culture to a few sets of ritualized transactions. Autonomous, nonsymbiotic transactions are met with escalated demands to reestablish the symbiosis.

TREATMENT CONSIDERATIONS

It is important to note that rehabilitation, treatment, and educational efforts take place within the context of the prison culture. Most programs are defeated at the outset by not taking the culture into account. One way of viewing this is to analyze the way time is structured inside an institution. Assume one hour is spent in a treatment group each week. This leaves 167 hours of the week that are spent outside of the treatment culture in an environment that is totally antithetical to the values, behavior, and attitudes that are being taught in the group. Cultural pressure, combined with the limited options available, serves to negate the efforts of the best psychotherapists. Personal redecisions to healthy, autonomous functioning cannot be actualized without life-threatening consequences.

In order for a correctional program to function effectively, the following minimum criteria must be met: (1) the environment must allow change (Permission), and (2) reinforcement for change must be available to the Child (Protection). Since most correctional institutions and programs fail to meet these criteria, the first step is to establish a counterculture. This may be accomplished by physically separating program members from the rest of the institution or by establishing a strong psychological counterculture. Physical separation is usually impractical because of limited resources. It is often undesirable because of the spotlighting effect it has on the program and its members. A more workable solution is partial isolation by housing program members in the same unit or dorm while they continue eating, playing, and working in the general culture. This enables members of the program to have a place to learn and practice new behavior and attitudes while continuing to deal with the old culture. Combining partial isolation with the formation of a strong psychological counterculture enables a program to become a major force in the institution culture as a whole. Program members begin to function more effectively in the institution to get needs met in direct ways. They feel better about themselves, and they stop playing institution games and yet still survive. This "role-modeling of winning behavior" is directly antithetical to the losing prison culture and has a side effect of giving others in the culture permission to think about changing.

ASKLEPIEION: A MODEL COUNTERCULTURE

Asklepieion is a total learning environment which began as a therapeutic community in 1969 at the U.S. Penitentiary, Marion, Illinois. This community, under the direction of Martin G. Groder, MD, began by utilizing the principles of transactional analysis in a traditional one-hour-a-week setting, but without success. Subsequently, Groder began using the principles and techniques of the Synanon Foundation[9] as a means of negating the prison culture. The Synanon methodology is based on the Synanon Game, a highly confronting type of group therapy. The Game is an emotional battlefield where an individual's delusions, distorted self-images, and losing behavior are confronted at a very high level. It is best represented as a miniature arena of life into which a person can only bring himself or herself. Past experience, status in other cultures, levels of academic attainment mean nothing in the Game, where the only usable criteria for status is here-and-now functioning.

The Game was introduced into the community by Groder, who had learned it while attending sessions at Synanon in San Francisco just prior to his assignment as staff psychiatrist at Marion. It was found that the Game was potent enough to begin treatment of the negative lifestyles of the inmates who then constituted the therapeutic community. Along with the Game, the Synanon community lifestyle was introduced into the community and served to reinforce the attitudes, values, and behavior being learned in the Game. The initial members of the community were veteran CONS with "cast-iron guts" who were serving long sentences for major crimes. The majority of the men had previously served time in either state or federal prisons.

The initial treatment goals for the community consisted of establishing a clean environment with a positive stroke economy, straight talk, and commitment to growth and change as its basis. These were met by confrontation of the men on gross behavior patterns that were causing them to come into conflict with others (such as gambling, carrying weapons, fighting, homosexual activity, etc.). The behavior was confronted in the Game and followed up by an environment in which the status system did not support that kind of behavior. The initial establishment of the clean culture took approximately five months using a straight Synanon model. During this time the literature on TA was available and read by some of the men participating in the program, and didactic sessions were held frequently to acquaint the men with the concepts of personality structure. This gave them a frame of reference for viewing their behavior and explaining why things went the way they did for them, but the TA treatment model was not used. At the end of five months following the establishment of a clean culture, TA was introduced as a treatment model and proved successful. The Synanon Game is still used as the primary tool for maintaining the positive culture and for out-escalating high levels of discounting. The TA groups are led by older residents who are also able to serve as role-models for the culture. Role-modeling to develop a new lifestyle plays an important part in the Asklepieion culture. An inmate entering the prison culture looks to others in the culture to show him how things are done: who's OK and who's not-OK, how to transact with cops, cultural rituals and mores, etc. He assimilates the culture from those who have previously assimilated it and are in a position to pass it on.

The growth program in Asklepieion programs is based on an educational model rather than a medical treatment model. This serves to make the residents responsible for the behavior by taking away the Wooden Leg of "mental illness," while at the same time communicating the message that it is OK to learn new things and to change as a result of the new learning.

The Total Learning Environment concept provides a model for learning how to win under conditions ranging from ideal to severely adverse. A Total Learning Environment (TLE) approximates a complete society as closely as possible, and the learning is designed around the residents taking roles in the mock society and striving to get their needs met. This brings into play all of the coping behaviors they have incorporated from previous environments, and they are able to see in this laboratory setting what works and what doesn't work. Every aspect of an individual's functioning is continuually tested under conditions of simulated stress. Stress is simulated in the sense that failure does not carry tragic results but provides an opportunity to learn how to win.

Emphasis is placed on the following three principles: (1) winning for oneself is dependent on others winning too; (2) winning personally is much easier in a society that functions well and has productive participation from all of its members; and (3) thinking and planning is necessary if one is to exercise control over one's own life, and not to think and plan is to turn one's destiny over to those who do think and plan. These three principles actively counter the dynamics of alienation and impulsivity that characterize typical sociopathic functioning.

Woven throughout the design of the Asklepieion Program is the concept of family. This permits the formation of a cohesive group culture and provides a model for caring and loving other human beings. Residents are encouraged to take care of others, allow themselves to be taken care of, and to develop an investment in each other's growth and welfare. This, again, counters the "Get lost" and "Don't be" script messages that result in alienation.

Upward and downward mobility within the status structure of the community enables each man to use every tool at his command to achieve success and status, including those he used previously—cheating, lying, stealing, conning, conniving, withdrawing, etc. Immediate, on-the-spot confrontation from the environment and a man's peers determines what works and what doesn't. Thus, old behavior and coping mechanisms are discarded, not because they are illegal or immoral but because they are dysfunctional and nonproductive.

Since the program exists as a miniculture within the greater prison culture, keeping the environment clean requires continual effort. Attitudes, behaviors, and thinking that are modeled on the old lifestyle are confronted at all levels. Stealing a cookie from the dining hall inside prison is equal to robbing a bank outside prison and is confronted at the same level. First-degree *Cops and Robbers* rapidly becomes third-degree once institutional restraints are gone. Thus, even first-degree game-playing is confronted as though it were third-degree. The convict lifestyle is not permitted within the TLE. Residents are expected to learn to speak English without cursing five times per sentence, to quit snarling at each other when they're angry and, instead, to use the energy generated by the anger to solve the problem, to relate thinking and feeling to behavior, and to give up prison games and pastimes. It is noted that giving up prison pastimes ("I've served time at. . . ," "This jail is better/worse than . . . jail") cuts off the social advantages of *Cops and Robbers* and makes the game less attractive. One way of determining whether a program is clean or dirty is to spend some time with the residents during their free time and listen to their pastimes. If the pastimes are formulated around prison, crime, drugs, and the like, it is probable that the covert prison culture is defeating treatment efforts. Conversely, lack of that kind of pastiming is indicative of the success of the program. The Asklepieion program confronts even mild pastiming around criminal issues, and the status structure withholds stroking from persons who are exhibiting behavior reminiscent of the prison culture.

A comprehensive training program is incorporated into the design to enable residents to develop their problem-solving skills to a high level. Most of the treatment groups in the community are led by residents who have greatly increased their own level of functioning and are training to become clinicians. The training program is geared to ITAA requirements and can eventually lead to advanced membership in the ITAA. Residents who are not interested in working in the "people business" are encouraged to define professional/vocational goals for themselves and to use institution and community resources to meet these goals.

References

1. Eric Berne, *Transactional Analysis in Psychotherapy*, New York, Grove Press, 1961.
2. Martin Groder, "Asklepieion—An Effective Treatment Method for Incarcerated Character Disorders," Unpublished manuscript presented at Summer Conference, International Transactional Analysis Association, San Francisco, 1972.
3. Eric Berne, *The Structure and Dynamics of Organizations and Groups*, Philadelphia, J. B. Lippincott Co., 1963.
4. Martin Groder, "Effective Organizations," Unpublished manuscript presented at Winter Conference, International Transactional Analysis Association, Scottsdale, Arizona, 1975.
5. *Ibid.*
6. Berne, *The Structure and Dynamics of Organizations and Groups. Op. cit.*
7. Stephen Karpman, "Fairy Tales and Script Drama Analysis," *Transactional Analysis Bulletin, 7,* no. 26 (1968), pp. 39–43.
8. Kenneth Windes, "TA With Addicts," *Transactional Analysis Journal, 3,* no. 3 (July, 1973).
9. Lewis Yablonski, *Synanon, the Tunnel Back,* Gretna, Louisiana, Pelican, 1965.

NINE

A GRADUATE PROGRAM IN PSYCHOTHERAPY
Ken Lessler

A graduate program in psychotherapy and social change was initiated and conducted by Southeast Institute in Chapel Hill, 1973-1975. The core residential faculty consisted of a Teaching Member and a Provisional Teaching Member of the International Transactional Analysis Association, a psychiatrist and a psychologist. All were psychotherapists and all had a desire to create a graduate program which was professional in orientation and responsive to social issues. This chapter will describe the development and evolution of that program.

The first section will discuss the ideas and ideals on which the program was based. Section two will describe the program itself. The third section will discuss the natural history of the program and the reactions of the students and faculty. An analysis of some of the stresses experienced by students and faculty, using Eric Berne's models of group leadership, will comprise section four. Finally, some thoughts for future training of therapists will be presented.

IDEAS AND IDEALS

The initiators of the graduate program in psychotherapy and social change wanted a training sequence that would provide the trainees with the information, practice, and values they would need to become effective psychotherapists. In addition, there was a common desire among the initiators for psychotherapy to be used not only as a tool for personal change, but also as a vehicle for social change.

Among the initiators, there was a shared excitement about therapy training. Each had experienced the powerful training techniques developed by Robert and Mary Goulding of the Western Institute of Group and Family Therapy. There was a common desire to use this model in a formal graduate program in therapy.

The involvement in social change was also a strong motivational factor for all members of the core faculty. For each person there was a somewhat different emphasis, although racial justice and equal opportunity were important to everyone. All the faculty members were interested in a therapy for persons without financial resources and for persons of diverse cultural backgrounds. All had a sense of mission and a concern that patients be treated with respect by encouraging them to share the responsibility for their treatment. The faculty saw therapy as a tool for both individual and social change.

Through the earlier work of Graham Barnes, founder of Southeast Institute, on racial prejudice and discrimination, it was clear that the tools of psychotherapy could be used effectively in challenging values that previously had been based on parental prejudice and Child delusions. Barnes found that once individuals dealt with issues related to their fears (early decisions) and stereotypes (parental messages), they were able to communicate more positively and openly with people who had previously been the object of their prejudices, and to work with others to devise solutions to problems of racial discrimination within their institutions.

THE PROGRAM

IDEALS AND GOALS   The program was initially conceived as a training program in psychotherapy and social change. This version of the program is well stated in the first bulletin, which described the program to prospective students:

> Our objective is to create a graduate school in which persons can prepare themselves adequately and directly—without detouring through medicine, psychology, religion, or social work—to become competent psychotherapists who command the respect of the various professional associations and who can help meet the social need for well-trained therapists.
>
> We propose the following goals for the projected graduate program of the Southeast Institute:
>
> 1. To train a new professional whose expertise encompasses biological, social, psychological, and political aspects of behavioral change. The graduate would be a generalist rather than a specialist and would be familiar with diagnoses, treatment, and prevention.
> 2. To train students who demonstrate a natural ability in the art of therapy.
> 3. To offer a degree in psychotherapy which cuts across the disciplines of other professsional fields such as medicine, psychology, the social sciences, theology, and philosophy.
> 4. To offer a degree inclusive of intensive training in the biomedical sciences, educating students to work under the direction of clinical professionals in the diagnosis of somatic, psychosomatic, and psychological disorders.
> 5. To offer a flexible and practical program capable of training talented and committed clinicians, keeping in mind economy of time.
> 6. To serve career persons whose jobs require specific skills in effecting personal and social change.

7. To maximize the use of internship and apprenticeship experiences along with a sound academic program.
8. To emphasize training and problem-solving to effect the changes necessary for furthering personal growth and social justice.

When the pragmatic issues of granting a degree in "psychotherapy" and obtaining recognition for the new profession were confronted, it was decided that it was not feasible to grant a degree in psychotherapy and social change at that time, because there were no licensing laws to allow persons without roots in a helping profession to practice psychotherapy. Instead, a Master of Arts in Clinical Psychology was offered through a joint program by the Southeast Institute and Lone Mountain College in San Francisco. The acceptance of psychology as the parent profession and the acceptance of Lone Mountain College as a degree-granting institution added two new dimensions to the program: psychology with its traditions, and an established academic department with its requirements and traditions. What began as a practical solution to the problem of finding an acceptable home for a therapy training program in time created its own harvest of problems.

At its inception, the program was based historically and professionally in transactional analysis and was designed to meet the requirements of the International Transactional Analysis Association for clinical membership. The change to psychology and the concomitant de-emphasis on transactional analysis was a major one. The shift in allegiance required a change in leadership to affirm the basis in psychology. The psychologist on the faculty was appointed the program director. At that point, the tradition of psychology, the required coursework and knowledge expected of psychologists, the code of ethics of the American Psychological Association, and the North Carolina state licensing laws for psychologists all became a source of program evaluation and attention. Students were now viewed as psychology students and were compared with persons in other psychology Master's programs. At the same time, it was clear that psychologists were not heavily represented on the faculty. There was instead a mixture of helping professionals and others who were specialists in the subject matter of the courses that were presented.

ENTRANCE REQUIREMENTS   An entrance screening procedure was designed to provide the candidates with an opportunity to learn new material, participate in discussions, experience being a client and a therapist, and receive supervision. These experiences provided a three-week microcosm of the MA program, during which time the faculty and students were able to observe each other learn and work, share ideals, and cooperatively plan the initial stages of the program. This screening technique allowed an emphasis on the skills, attitudes, and behaviors which were important for the program itself, and de-emphasized the less direct traditional indicators of competence, such as academic history and scores on achievement tests. If the candidates were able to deal with the material presented to them, able to relate well to others, willing to look at how they affected others, then they were offered the opportunity to participate in the graduate program. Of those thirty-five who were candidates, twenty-five successfully passed the screening process. The resulting student body was energetic, outspoken, bright, and a bit older than most Master's students in traditional graduate programs.

TRAINING SEQUENCE   The program differed in emphasis from traditional Master's-level psychology programs. The courses in psychological assessment, statistics, and research design were all de-emphasized. More time was invested instead in directly relevant theory courses, including personality theory, methods of psychotherapy, and family therapy.

The faculty wanted didactic material, patient contact, supervision, and personal and professional growth to occur concurrently in such a way that there could be an immediate interplay among such elements as didactic presentation, theory, practice, personal growth, and supervision. To create this interaction, the substantive material was presented in intensive blocks, followed by periods of time in which the students were immersed in the clinical application of the course material.

Coursework was divided into three categories: therapy theory and practice, general psychology, and social issues. The courses included such traditional titles as "Methods of Psychotherapy," "Psychoanalytic Theory," "Theories of Psychotherapy," and "Human Development." The course selection represented the beliefs of the staff about what knowledge an individual needed to provide sound therapy service. A knowledge of medicine sufficient to alert the therapist to medical issues, including the awareness of the use of prescription drugs and the ability to communicate with physicians, was incorporated through a medical science course and in clinical supervision by a physician. The need of the psychologist to relate to others of a more traditional background was accomplished through survey courses in basic psychology, statistics, and psychological assessment. Courses on social theory and social issues were designed to broaden and deepen the students' perspective and allow them to use the psychotherapy tools meaningfully to aid individuals interested in changing practices in their institutions.

PRACTICE AND SUPERVISION   Each student had a field placement concurrent with his course work in which he had an opportunity to participate directly in tasks about which he was learning. Although many of the usual practicum sites (such as hospitals and clinics) were not eager or willing to take students from this unusual program, all of the students did eventually get placed. Most of the students were placed in mental health centers, some in mental hospitals, and a few in out-of-state agencies. A total of 900 hours of clinical work (including 300 hours of psychotherapy) was required. Each student was required to have 100 hours of personal therapy experience in group or individual therapy and was responsible for obtaining this treatment. The bulk of the supervision for this work was performed by the same individuals who taught the clinically related course work.

It was important to the faculty that part of the therapy practice take place in their presence so that they would be able to provide instant feedback to the students. This was accomplished by working with the students in small groups in which they took turns as therapists, and in which the instructor was present to comment immediately and, if necessary, to intervene. One moment the student would be a patient, and the next he or she would be leading the therapy group. This training model, taken directly from the Gouldings, provided the core of the supervision. In addition, tape supervision of the students' therapy was an important part of the program.

NATURAL HISTORY OF THE PROGRAM

The 18-month program will be divided into four phases: the start-up phase, formalization phase, functioning phase, and termination phase.

During the *start-up* phase, the program was led by Graham Barnes, who recruited faculty to work with him to develop a graduate program in psychotherapy and social change. There was enthusiasm on the part of the faculty, a spirit of working together and moving toward a shared ideal. Students who were recruited during this period had seen the work of Graham Barnes (and later that of Vann Joines) and were excited about the form of treatment that they saw. They were also excited about the program's commitment to social change. At this point the students did not know the other faculty members. Persons outside the program included mentors from ITAA, who were generally encouraging toward the program's development.

During the *formalization* stage, there was a shift in leadership. A psychologist was given the function of developing the program along lines consistent with a Master's degree in clinical psychology. The faculty continued to work together but now there were more rules and expectations—some from Lone Mountain College and some from the need for the program to conform to psychology ethics codes and licensing laws. The differences in the backgrounds of the faculty were more sharply focused during this period. From the students' point of view, this phase was experienced as a time of change from the program as envisioned by Graham Barnes to a program which approximated those ideals but was adapted to practical demands.

The students seemed to go through an evolution as a group. They began as might have been expected. The banner they held against the Establishment was raised against the faculty as soon as it became clear that there were additional academic demands, standards, and responsibilities. There was some rebellion, some foot-dragging, and a few decided, as they had before, to comply and excel as students in the old form. The group split into factions. One group attempted to change the new "system." Another group attempted to defeat it by outdoing or outsmarting it. A third group went along with the system's demands. These groups fought and vied for power.

At the point of the highest levels of anger, when many on both sides were leaving (physically or psychologically), the group pulled together and decided to deal with the task of learning. The faculty provided more structure and made many decisions that were previously left to the students. Many of the students seemed relieved to have a clear structure.

There were two casualties. One student who had had solid psychology training earlier believed that the program did not meet her needs or "deliver" at a level that met her expectations. Another student crossed some ethical boundaries in a way that could not be resolved. The rest got on with the business at hand and completed the program.

Pressures were experienced from Lone Mountain College, which became stronger in its demands that the program approximate a psychology program. Concurrently, there were the first rumblings from professionals in traditional psychology programs and from mental health services within the state which were concerned about the quality and type of training being provided. The responsiveness to ITAA regulations for clinical membership diminished. The program no longer prepared the students to become advanced members of ITAA, although it continued in its orientation toward social change and effective therapy training.

During the *functioning* phase, the faculty and the students came together less frequently for faculty meetings. Each of the faculty had his own primary allegiance to a private practice or to other responsibilities at Southeast Institute. The actual day-to-day operations were left to the administrative assistant and the program director. There was diminished enthusiasm for the program and vastly increased awareness of the day-to-day teaching load which had been accepted by the small faculty. Adjunct faculty, recruited to teach specific courses, added both depth and breadth to the program.

From the students' point of view, the program now seemed more traditional in its requirements, more structured, and less receptive to their input. It was clear that they had settled down to doing the work that needed to be done and, based on their individual preferences, each was relating to one or another faculty member or to the administrative assistant.

At the same time that the program was moving forward, there was increased intensity of negative reaction on the outside, which, in one case, eventuated in an accreditation visit. The visit was stimulated by a psychologist in a North Carolina university who believed that the program was inadequate and should not be supported. The result of the visit was a very positive evaluation by the representative of the regional accrediting association for colleges and universities, which concluded that the program was exemplary. Pressure from the universities and from some of the traditional departments did not diminish, and yet the crescendo was not such that the program had to be disbanded. The relationship with Lone Mountain College was now solid and that part of the program went smoothly.

During the *termination* phase, the MA degrees were granted. The faculty functioned individually, taking their own responsibilities for the program and for course offerings. Dissension and differences in direction increased among the faculty members. The sense was, "Let's finish the job we started, because we owe it to the students." There was general disappointment when the ideals with which the program was started were compared with the reality with which it was ending.

The students were determined to finish the Master's degree for which they had worked a year and a half. Yet dissatisfaction with the program was expressed in differential preference for one faculty member or another, and at one point, it reached such a pitch that a few students tried to oust the president of the Institute.

The final confrontation was a recurrence of the initial ones, very much in the same way a person makes a last display of the symptoms of a pathology before giving it up: who would determine the form of the graduation exercises? Would there be traditional speakers, a dinner, a reception? Or would we sit around and share experiences, read poems written for the occasion and have a guitar accompanying words set to the scene? Both sides met: the "conservative traditionalists" and the "radical do-your-own-thingers." Each came up with a proposal unpalatable to the other. With some power, with some resolve, and with some giving-up, the ceremony took place—no robes, no music, but talks by a dean and the president of the Institute, an address by a distinguished professor who was a member of the adjunct faculty, and the presentation of awards. The program ended with a dance at a student's house and was accentuated by a sense of freedom, joy, and relief. It was over.

Twenty-two students graduated. A few did not complete the coursework in time for graduation. A year later, all but one of the students have completed their work and received their degrees.

Outside agitation decreased as the program finished; however, there was no acceptance of the program from those who were agitating against it. There was a great deal of acceptance of the program from the mental health centers and the hospitals where students had field placements.

ANALYSIS OF THE PROGRAM FROM THE STANDPOINT OF BERNE'S DIAGRAMS

Eric Berne's work, *The Structure and Dynamics of Organizations and Groups,* will be used as the primary reference for the discussion of the authority pattern.

LEADERSHIP ROLES   Berne points out that there are three types of leaders: the person who fills the leadership slot in the formal organization (the responsible leader), the leader who makes decisions (the effective leader), and the leader who is most important in the eyes of the group members (the psychological leader). These leaders may or may not be the same person.

In the start-up phase of the graduate program, Graham Barnes filled all three leadership slots. During the formalization stage, the psychological leader was still Graham Barnes but another faculty member, a psychiatrist, began to share the psychological leadership slot. Barnes was still the effective leader, but he now shared this position with the psychologist who was appointed director of the graduate program. The responsible leader was the psychologist who led the program, but he, in turn, was responsible to Graham Barnes, who was the president of the Institute. During the functioning phase of the program, the psychological leader for the majority of the student body was shared by Graham Barnes and the psychiatrist. The psychologist became the effective leader due to the fact that Graham Barnes chose to take a secondary role. The psychologist was also the responsible leader. Graham Barnes had the next level of responsibility but operated at a distance from the students. During the termination stage, the psychological leader for most of the students was the psychiatrist, and the effective and responsible leader slots were still shared by the psychologist and Graham Barnes.

The story of the program is clearly depicted in the leadership role change (Figure 1). The psychological leadership changed three times and at only one point were the psychological leader, the effective leader, and the responsible leader the same person. Also, the person who was initially the psychological leader was later displaced. The effective leadership was taken over by the psychologist through the wishes of the faculty and administration, but it was typically shared in the background with the president of the Institute.

GROUP IMAGO   The imago of the group, according to Berne, represents how individuals see the leadership structure of the group. Since each

LEADERSHIP

Program phase	Psychological	Effective	Responsible
Start-up	Graham Barnes	Graham Barnes	Graham Barnes
Formalization	Graham Barnes/ Psychiatrist	Graham Barnes/ Psychologist	Psychologist/ Graham Barnes
Functioning	Psychiatrist/ Graham Barnes	Psychologist/ Graham Barnes	Psychologist/ Graham Barnes
Termination	Psychiatrist	Psychologist/ Graham Barnes	Psychologist/ Graham Barnes

Figure 1
Leadership Profile for Each Stage of Program Development

person's group imago may be different from each other person's, and since these imagoes change as time passes and in different settings, it is hazardous to assume the group imagoes of the students. It is instructive, however, to build an estimate of the modal group imago to understand the operation of the program. The modal imago of the students will be compared to the faculty's view of the program leadership (also as estimated by the author).

The group imago as seen by the students in the start-up phase (the provisional group imago, Figure 2) depicts Graham Barnes as the leader and the other leadership slots as undifferentiated. The student body was

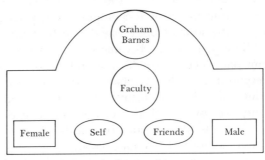

A. Start-up phase

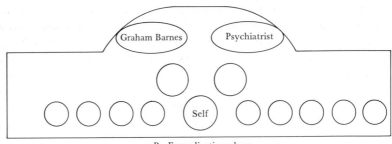

B. Formalization phase

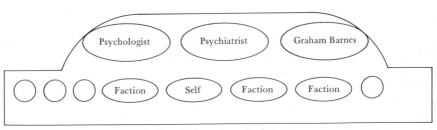

C. Functioning and termination stage

Figure 2
Group Imago Diagrams of Each Stage of Program Development

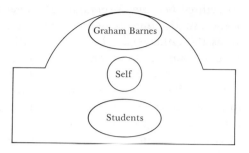

Figure 3
Faculty Group Imago

only partially differentiated with a self slot and a few friends who were selected for the program during the same screening round (one that was conducted several months before the second and final screening workshop). During the formalization stage, there was a partially differentiated group imago with the leadership slot shared by the psychologist and Graham Barnes, and a differentiated picture of the other two leadership slots, involving two faculty members. During the functioning and termination stages, there were fully differentiated, though unstable, group imagoes with the psychiatrist in the leadership role for most of the students; the three other residential faculty were in secondary leadership roles, and there was a completely differentiated student body.

The group imago of the faculty was interestingly different. During all phases, Graham Barnes was clearly the leader, that is, the individual who each of the other core faculty members saw as the person in whom personal energy was invested (Figure 3).

When the roles of leaders are differentiated according to who was psychological leader, effective leader, and responsible leader, and when the faculty and student group imagoes are viewed, some of the issues stand in relief. There were marked leadership shifts in the view of students (psychological leader). At the same time, the faculty had a different view of the organization than the students had.

CANONS AND EUHEMERI   The jarring effect of the evolution of the program can be seen by identifying the important background works or canons and spiritual/mythical leaders (euhemeri). The initial canons of the program were the writings of Berne, and clearly Berne was the euhemerus of the program (as was, to some extent, Martin Luther King). The works of the social thinker James Luther Adams, who was a member of the adjunct faculty, and the works of Paul Tillich could also be considered important at this point because of the social aspects of the program. In the formalization phase, however, the canons were shared with Freud and diffused, since not only Berne (as the euhemerus) and his writings (as the canons) were important, but now canons in the form of a psychology code of ethics became ascendant. No new euhemeri were established during the functioning phase of the program, and Berne was still clearly present as the euhemerus. The canons still included Berne's writing, the psychology code of ethics, and major books which were assigned in coursework. The works of social theorists took a lesser role for most students, as the emphasis changed from becoming "social change agents" to becoming "psychologists." Even at the termination phase, the canons of psychology were strong; the canons of psychotherapy (including Berne's writings) were strong; and the place of the social philosophers continued to be minimal.

FORMAL ORGANIZATION   During the start-up phase, ITAA and the Southeast Institute occupied the top position in the formal hierarchy. During the formalization stage, Lone Mountain College took the place as the degree-granting institution, and the American Psychological Association and the North Carolina Psychological Association were recognized as parent bodies. Southeast Institute continued throughout to be dominant, while ITAA dropped out of the formal organizational chart. This same formal organizational chart continued for the next two phases.

GOALS   Finally, it is instructive to observe the change in program goals throughout the program. During the start-up phase, the purpose of the program was to train the students to be "psychotherapists" and to be effective in working for social justice. In the formalization stage, the goal was to train "psychologists" with an emphasis on social change. During the functioning and termination stages, "psychologist/therapists" were trained.

Once the program has been viewed from these various organizational perspectives and program goals, it is easily observed that the changes in leadership, the changes in canon, the changes in provisional group imago, and the changes in the goals of the faculty all led to unrest which was often expressed as hostility, dissatisfaction, irritation, or dissension. The power of the program's thrust together with the commitment of the faculty and the students kept the program together. The outside agitation helped to create group cohesion, which had been previously weakened by the leadership changes and by the activity across major (students and faculty) and minor (among students) internal boundaries.

The program has been completed and the staff are back at their regular jobs with business as usual. There were not enough funds from student fees to continue the program and to hire the level of faculty to meet the program standards. Tentative commitments for other funds for the program did not materialize. Clearly, the program could not be operated again with the donated time and support from the Southeast Institute alone. The program has been suspended until adequate funds are found.

Were the ideals achieved? Some were and some weren't. Students and faculty alike were disappointed at the erosion of the social-change emphasis of the program. In the end, the program was much more a psychotherapy training program and offered, specifically, a professional Master's degree in clinical psychology with some emphasis on social issues. We could not do both in the time allotted. We could not nod to the ancestry of psychology without sacrificing something, and that something was the social-change coursework. Most of us would do the program again, but we would do it differently.

A year after the completion of the program in 1975, most of the students are working as mental health workers in mental health agencies. About a quarter of the students are pursuing PhD's in clinical psychology programs throughout the country. One student has applied for North Carolina licensure at the Master's level. The students are functioning as psychotherapists in responsible institutions.

The experiment was a success. The will to succeed, the faculty commitment to the students, and the student commitment to advanced training were supraordinant to the forces inherent in a new program that created disintegrative pressures.

THOUGHTS FOR THE FUTURE

A ladder (vertical) and a lattice (horizontal) progression of professional training is envisioned for the future (Vail Conference on training of psychologists). Persons with a BA degree could enter for training at the Master's level. They could get a Master's degree or a professional doctor's degree. Horizontally on the lattice, they could, in addition, use the centers for postdoctoral training to deepen or continue their knowledge or to broaden their training in therapy and/or social issues (see Figure 4).

The learning environment which would provide the opportunities for the "therapists/social activists" could be constructed in three places. First would be a center for didactic work, reading, and relaxation, to include classrooms, a library, some small gathering spaces and, in my fantasy, an invigorating outdoor environment. This would be the Academic Training Center.

There would be a second place which would look more like a clinic—the Therapy Activities Center. At the clinic, there would be rooms to work with small groups, with individuals and families and training aids. The center would be located in an area accessible to the community folks who would come for educational growth or treatment activities.

There also would be an Action Center. Here is where the activities directed at primary intervention, at social change, and community impact would be concentrated. The Center could house community meetings and workshops, political activities, and programs designed to have impact on the human environment and to involve the people in identifying and in solving their problems.

The people who work in each of these centers would be the models for

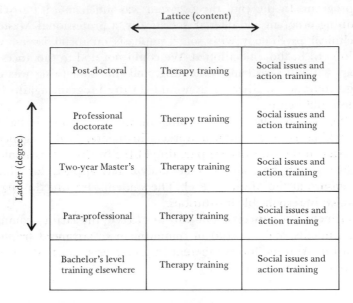

Figure 4
Career Growth Ladder and Lattice

the students. Their commitment, their ethics, and their ways of dealing with the stresses, struggles, and gratifications of their work would demonstrate possibilities and provide instructions and a place to participate.

Most important of all, there would be six months to a year lead time with all the faculty present, in which goals, programs, rules, and leadership could be worked out so as to avoid some of the problems described in this chapter.

Progress in Transactional Analysis

TEN

GRODER'S 5 OK DIAGRAMS
Martin Groder

In the last few hundred years, we have started to get into a process of conscious evolution. I define conscious evolution as human beings getting together a plan for the evolution of the race. A few major figures—Thomas Jefferson, Adam Smith, Marx, Mao Tse Tung, Freud—thought through what the human race should be like, how it should relate to itself, and succeeded in getting versions of their ideas directly on-stream in their lifetime. This process of conscious evolution is qualitatively different as well as quantitatively faster than the cultural evolution of previous history. Genetic or biological evolution is by comparison infinitely slow. In order to help measure the effect of an individual, an organization, and their transactions on the course of human evolution, I have added a minimum of three additional types of OKness or not-OKness.

1. We are OK (or We are not-OK) refers to the primary group of which the person transacting is a member (the family, team, unit, etc.). The action or position is rated as to how it fosters or hinders the achievement of the goals of the unit.
2. They are OK (or They are not-OK) refers to the largest social unit affected by the transaction (General Motors, business, U.S.A., capitalism, the human race). Clearly, additional points may need to be specified for special cases leading to 6 OK, 7 OK, etc. evaluations.
3. The degree of conscious evolution fostered by an individual or organization can be described as "It's OK." "It's OK" means that your being alive is making a positive change in the direction of human evolution. The criterion that I use for human evolution essentially is our general therapeutic one of whether people's needs are being met. Eric Berne half facetiously claimed that the infant mortality rate determined societal OKness. Thus, if your effect on the infant mortality rate was positive, the world was better for your being around. So, "It's OK" has to do with leaving your mark in the world—and you leave some kind of mark, either a positive mark or negative mark, unless you are just the wind passing over the snow.

To be really, really, really OK, one must pass the test of an "I'm OK, You're OK, We're OK, They're OK, It's OK" analysis. This 5-OK analysis can be very chastening, especially for OK therapists who don't care what effect they have on the world at large. Thus, I can say nasty things like, "Well, what have you done for the organization lately. How will you advance human evolution?" If the answer is "Nothing," then I can say, "Well, you're not-OK," which may motivate the self-centered miscreant.

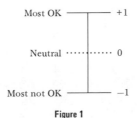

Figure 1

The scale I use goes from 1 to −1: 1 being full OKness, which is very rare in any dimension; 0 being neutral; −1 being totally negative. The most negative thing you can do to yourself is destroy yourself, and the most negative thing you can do to somebody else is destroy them. The most negative thing you can do organizationally is to destroy the group, the organization, or the history of the people.

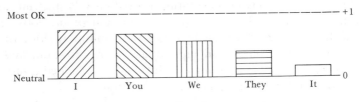

Figure 2
OKness of One Highly OK Transaction across 5 OK Diagram

The probable impact of any transaction gets less and less as you move to higher organizational levels. So, no matter how OK you are, your effect on other people is less than whatever you've done for yourself, and less on your group, and so on down the line. The good thing, luckily, is that no matter how not-OK you are, the negative effect you have is also decreasing down the line. Exceptions to this rule, other than accidental, are created by high-leadership people, who can have far-reaching effects. Actually, even for high-leadership people, the effect of each transaction still goes down, but the effect doesn't diminish at quite the rate of regular folk's actions.

At this point, we start to get into some energy-dynamics concepts which I want to show you by using the 5-OK diagrams. What we in Asklepieion did was to take a whole group of people and make a clinical diagnosis, slightly different than DSM II[1] but a clinical diagnosis nonetheless, and observe how people generally function in organizations and in the world from that diagnostic position. We presumed *a priori* that we have effective methods to change any type of person to any other type of person and then we looked at the energy input needed. Further, in order to simplify the data, we performed the following operations:

1. Looked at a person's transactions in a given time period in the five-dimensional 5-OK space as a cloud of points of equal weight.
2. Allowed the center of gravity of this cloud to represent the individual's OKness space.
3. Grouped people of like diagnosis.
4. Took the cloud of points of similar people and took that cloud's center of gravity to represent that diagnostic category.
5. Arbitrarily arranged the diagnostic points in projected two-dimensional curves, preserving their order and adding metaphorical information from clinical observation of the change process.

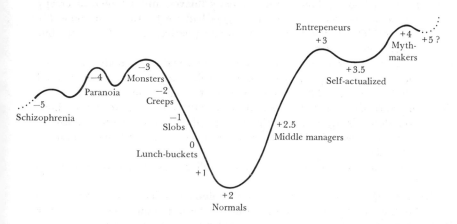

Figure 3
Projection onto Two Dimensions of Diagnostic Space of 5 OK Diagram

Starting at the left, there are the −5 people, who are the chronic schizophrenics, backward types who are wiped out—"They're not-OK, You're not-OK, We're not-OK, It's not-OK, Nothing is OK"—just wipeouts. The next level up is the −4, at which people are more active schizophrenic types who do interact with the world to some extent and who do make some interventions. Minus four (−4) is also the center point for a whole lot of different kinds of people like paranoids, borderline schizophrenics, and other semi-wiped-out people who are still energetic to some degree, who are still interacting, or still trying things out. Up in the −3 peak area are the kings of the monsters, who are psychopathic leaders. Minus three (−3) is a very high energy state and has a very strong effect on the world from the position of "I'm OK, My buddy is OK, You're not-OK, We're not-OK, They're not-OK, It's not-OK, We are going to take the world with us." This position Eric Berne described as that of "I'm going to make the world pay."

Question: Are all psychopaths —3's?

Groder: No, this point represents the center point of a cloud of many high-energy negative people.

Question: Will you review the life positions of a —3 person?

Groder: The —3 person is saying I'm OK, You're OK to his right-hand buddy. Maybe We're OK but very, very strongly They're not-OK at multiple levels and It's not-OK and, boy, are we going to leave a mark, a trench, we're really going to dig it up. I call these people monsters. They often have monster children who are bullies and are very strong and very energetic, very smart, very much into making fools of other people, and very quick to wipe out anything or anyone that gets into their way. Further down the diagram at —2, —1, 0, and 1 levels are the slobs, creeps, and lunch buckets. Slobs are people who really make big messes but they don't have the enormous energy of the monsters. They are not crazy and they often have a lot of counterscript behaviors. So here you find alcoholics, junkies, petty thieves, and a bunch of creepy people finally down to weekend bingers, bad-check writers, and poor TA trainers. The lunch buckets are unimaginative, often desperate, but law-abiding citizens.

At the very bottom of this hill are the normals. Somebody asked what the normals are. Normals are almost totally untreatable by any method I have ever seen. The amount of reinforcement from the environment for normals to remain unchanged is fantastic. They're right about everything already so what's there to talk about? In this culture, normals, however, almost don't exist anymore. They used to be quite common but died out.

Comment: I can go to a fundamentalist college and find a lot of normals there.

Groder: Yes, this is true as long as they don't wander outside. But in the kinds of circles that we go in, normals have just about disappeared. Part of this has to do with the rapid rate of culture change. It's hard to figure out what it is to be normal, and, really, most of what we call normal is what *used* to be normal. So, even normals are now questioning themselves and sometimes they choose to make changes as their culture's cage is rattling. The point is that a normal takes as much energy to become a creep or a slob or a monster or a crazy as it takes someone else to go the other way.

Question: Is that the essence of banal scripting?

Groder: Yes, solid banal scripting. Now, the so-called burn-out phenomenon that occurs with major psychopaths when they grow older is that, as their energy goes down, they move down the hill to become slobs and creeps and drink beer, beat up their kids, and antiscript anybody interested in hearing war stories.

On this next plateau at +3, which is a long pull, are what I identify as entrepreneurs. Entrepreneurs are highly energetic, leader types who win the races their culture provides, especially if the culture is a competitive one. They win the race, they make the million dollars, or whatever it is. Entrepreneurs are quite different from normals. They're cunning and shifty, they cut corners, they're high-energy people, they bowl people over they do a whole lot of Machiavellian stuff. They invest a whole lot of energy in their goals and skills, and the only other people that look very much like them are the psychopathic leaders. The main difference between entrepreneurs and psychopaths is that the entrepreneurs are winner-survivors, and the psychopaths are loser-survivors, and sometimes you will see shifts between the two. Both the winner-survivor and loser-survivor have experienced childhood abandonment and reacted with decisions to survive—get revenge by "showing them," live for drama and excitement rather than for life itself—in the respective cases, decisions to win or lose. Often, later generations who "have it made" from birth do not invest the energy in surviving; they're mostly up here because the money keeps them up. If the money disappeared, they often couldn't make it up again.

The next area up in the diagram is the +4 level—"I'm OK, You're OK, We're OK, They're OK, It's OK"—these I call the myth makers. These are people whose world view is so powerful that other people who come in contact with them choose to adopt their world view instead of their own. These are people who can practice conversion as a method of change. They are different from entrepreneurs in that they have much higher energy, much more charisma, but they are not supported solely by a column of money and power. They are supported by a column of people. Part of the reason that they have more OKness than entrepreneurs is that their OKness involves other people, not just goal achievement.

The +5 level I can't describe, but there are some people so described in famous ancient books.

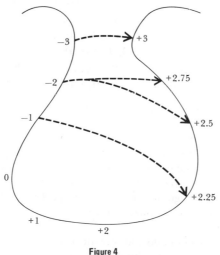

Figure 4
Energy Diagram

So, here is an interesting combination of the 5-OK diagram and an energy gradient map to give you some idea of what it takes to get people from one place to another, and why people are where they are. The thing

I want to emphasize is that each point here is the center of a mass of five-dimensional clouds so that an actual person may be acting at a point quite distant from his diagnostic label point. Further, the script proper, counterscript, antiscript, and episcript (if present) may be quite distant from each other so that a typical counterscript/script shape is a dumb bell with a rubberband connector.

The −3 psychopath and +3 entrepreneur are not only similar in skills but their energy levels are so close as to lead to "spark-gapping" across the gap under proper circumstances. For the psychopath to have a positive transformation, what is required is a bridge, usually a civilizing community of former −3's who are +3's (Asklepieion). For the +3 to jump to a "hope to die" −3 requires severe adversity and the breakdown of civil order (e.g., Lebanon, 1976). Thus, what our experience at Asklepieion has shown is that it is easier to spark a high-energy, high-leadership psychopath into being a high-energy, high-leadership entrepreneur than it is to teach a civilian, especially a normal, how to be an entrepreneur or how to run a program for psychopaths. I have found it much easier to train convicts to cure psychopathy than to train graduate students to cure psychopathy. One reason is that the leap across the spark gap is mortally frightening and bitterly resisted, and only blind faith in the leader lends courage to leap, and the support of a therapeutic community on landing confirms the reality of this leap. To try to push psychopaths down into "normality" is almost impossible. In doing that you have to take all their energy and leadership away and press them down to a pancake and then try to build them up again, and it doesn't work. The omnipresent programs of various types in correctional institutions, in alcohol treatment, etc., universally try to grind their clients down and fail at a high rate. The easiest thing to do is to take clients right straight across the gap and fill in behind them. It is dangerous as hell, but the alternative is failure. After the individual is a stable +3, he still faces the psychotherapeutic task of letting go of drama as a substitute for life and enjoying living.

> Question: What about psychopaths that are not leaders? Aren't there lots of psychopaths that are pretty low energy?
>
> Groder: Yes, they are the creeps and slobs. They go in two directions under pressure. Some go up here to major negative leadership and then we can spark-gap them. Some go down toward normality and never take a leadership role. I've seen people go in both directions. Usually, high leadership aptitude people go up and the potato peelers go down. The potato peelers respond to more usual civilizing, educational, and psychotherapeutic endeavors.
>
> Barnes*: When they jump, do you provide a new counterscript?
>
> Groder: Yes, Asklepieion, its philosophy, ethics, and way of being in the world. The Synanon-Asklepieion game is one of the techniques of spark-gapping individuals. Some techniques are even more artistic, such as

---

* Graham Barnes (named) and other workshop participants (unnamed) asked the questions.

administrative manipulation. For example, every three to six months I would eliminate the entire organization and restructure it.

Barnes: So, what if you have people who take over the organization and work themselves up into crooked leadership?

Groder: On rare occasions, a revolution of corruption would take over. An effective counterrevolution was mounted each and every time. Usually the destructive activity was clipboarding, sometimes known as bureaucracy. The energy level would go down and the program would become ineffective. However, there were usually some hungry people with less experience and power who were still full of energy, raring to go and trying to bite their way up through the other people. Often, I would feed the defunct leadership to the hungry.

Barnes: When you talk about energy, are you talking about energy that is directed toward leadership only, or are you talking about how people experience their energy?

Groder: Both.

Barnes: The people I work with often experience more energy after treatment than before and I don't know where to put them.

Groder: Most ordinary people that I see after treatment are in the range of 2 to 2¾. They are not in the high leadership range; they are not running things in the world, but are competent managers.

Barnes: I am really impressed with what you are doing here because, when I work in an institution on racism, I like to work with the leaders, and my whole theory has been structured on the process of change in the leaders. What often happens, however, is they give me a number of middle managers to work with and the process peters out.

Groder: The middle managers (2½) are not powerful enough to bring about the change; they don't have enough energy.

Comment: Now I can see why that was so important.

Groder: What we do in Asklepieion training is that, when we get a person of the middle-manager type, we boost him up to +3 with great effort.

Question: How?

Groder: By stamping him down first, and then rebuilding him with his newly found motivation and new skills.

Question: What keeps these people from just blowing all to hell with all this pressure?

Groder: Skill.

Question: Whose?

Groder: Ours. The stamping down looks like a very gross process, but it really is very artistic.

Question: How do you jam people in a corner?

Groder: First you have to pick a corner, then you have to pick an approach, and then you have to actually pull it off when they come shooting at you.

Barnes: I take it Maslow is up around +4.

Groder: Self-actualization is a +3½ level. Plus four (+4) is myth-making level.

Barnes: You are being very pessimistic about human beings.

Groder: What do you mean?

Barnes: Well, I hear you saying that not many people get to +4 and that there are not very many people who get to self-actualizing level (3½).

Groder: That has been historically true. However, I am optimistic. I think there are more self-actualized people in this generation than there has ever been in the history of the world. Likewise, there are more scientists alive right now practicing science than *ever* have lived.

Question: Do behavioral changes occur when the guy jumps the gap—do things like IQ change?

Groder: Yes, in fact, recently I got an interesting phone call about an ex-convict graduate who is here in town. The parole officer called me and said, "How can you have a guy hired as a program manager with a 70 IQ?" I said, "Where did you get that from?" He said, "I got it right here, an official report for 1969." I said, "Well, he's been in our program for five years and, on a clinical level, I guess his IQ is 115 or thereabouts. He said, "Well, how do you know that?" I said, "Well, that's my clinical judgment although I didn't test the IQ." Our experience with black guys who go through the program is amazing changes in IQ. Most of this has to do with mastering problem-solving behaviors. Some men have had 30- to 40-point increases in tested IQ.

Question: Have you been accumulating data on that?

Groder: Yes, that's very typical for a black prisoner. The white prisoners do not show that effect.

Barnes: So, Marty, what gives the organization its essence is its +4 leadership?

Groder: The organization is born out of the actualized myth in the mind of the leader and then, during the growth process, maintenance of that essence by that leader is required. The followers often let the organization plateau. Some of the analogies I use are beehives and anthills and stuff like that. Certain conglomerations of organisms have a biological reality and a further reality of their own, above and beyond the biological, called social or cultural. That's why I put up the thing about three kinds of evolution: biological, social, and conscious. Let me talk about small organizations, which is where the essence of organizations becomes very clear. A small organization with a +4 leader is the myth and the essence of that leader written large in the world through the cooperation of the membership. One of the problems with organizations is that, as long as that primal leader is creating his personal myth in the world, the essence is present; however, most organizations that exist are, in fact, degraded sorts of covert housekeeping arrangements among people at a fairly low level of functioning. Thus, the organization, in losing its essence, becomes merely a medium where people ferment. The kinds of organizations I've been interested in do have an essence, and they have a history, and they have an evolution, and that evolution is conscious in the minds of the leaders and those members who choose to be aware and take responsibility for the consequences of their acts.

References

1. *Diagnostic and Statistical Manual of Mental Disorders,* 2nd ed., Washington, D. C., American Psychiatric Association, 1968.

ELEVEN

TRANSACTIONAL ANALYSIS: AN INTEGRATIVE VIEW
William H. Holloway

I both am and am not a transactional analyst. If being a transactional analyst implies the nearly exclusive use of TA concepts, then the title ill-befits me. If it means one who understands Berne's contributions and how they can enhance communication and therapeutic processes, then the term accurately portrays an aspect of me.

THE PERSONAL SIDE

To provide the reader with a brief sketch, I was the eldest child and only son of parents who came from rural Midwest settings. Both were educators and my father remained so until he retired. Both came from devout Christian families with a typical Protestant ethic which valued industry and responsibility. Both also encouraged me to discover and to be interested in everything. Both maintained a dedication to charitable services to others less fortunate than they. I value the experience they provided.

As a consequence, I have lived as a dedicated discoverer of systems and processes. Always intrigued by the psychological function of humans, I experienced a major turning point during my medical internship, when I assisted in a surgical procedure that would have been unnecessary had the patient found a willing and trustworthy person with whom to share inner turmoil. Because of military service obligations, my formal studies in psychiatry were deferred for four years. In the meantime, however, I began listening and counseling and found that patients reported much benefit from our discussions.

For my psychiatric residency I chose the 4100-bed Ypsilanti State Hospital in Michigan, which provided a unique combination of experiences. As was typical in such hospitals, they were understaffed. The population had a preponderance of persons labeled schizophrenic or organically impaired. The hospital superintendent was Oris R. Yoder. His acceptance of me as a person with contributions to make, rather than as a novice needing to be taught, was a major factor in my choice. The formal training was provided mostly by the psychoanalytically oriented faculty at the University of Michigan's Neuropsychiatric Institute, directed by Raymond Waggoner. The total program was well rounded and I completed it with a sense of confidence.

From that training, I moved forward with new determination. My psychoanalytic theoretical studies had provided me with a conceptual framework which gave me an understanding of the psychological aspects of emotional disorders. Since my training also was during the emergence of the modern psychotropic drugs, I had respect for the marked changes which could be effected chemically. I also saw both the rewarding and the crippling consequences of the hospital milieu. I departed with a determination to find ways in which my knowledge and skills could be made available to more people than was likely in a career of one-to-one psychotherapy.

My next move was to directorship of a community mental health center in a large metropolitan area. It was here that I also began a part-time private practice. My acquaintance with Mark Cook encouraged me to explore the use of group treatment. This I found most rewarding, and my interest lead me into the American Group Psychotherapy Association, where I remain active.

After about three years of group-treatment experience, I decided that I wanted to teach group treatment to others, and in 1966 I began the two-year training program in analytic group psychotherapy at the Postgraduate Center for Mental Health, New York. It is difficult to say who had the greater impact on my career, since there were several persons from whom I gained much, including Asya Kadis, Emanuel Schwartz, Helen Durkin, Alexander Wolf, Henriette Glatzer, Harold Leopold, Helene Papanek, Jerome Kosseff, Ruth Cohn, Robert Thorne, and Marvin Aronson. Although the Postgraduate Center for Mental Health is a psychoanalytic center, the diversity of exposure provided me with much stimulation.

During these same years I became more familiar with gestalt therapy and psychodrama. I was involved also in evaluation of encounter-type sensitivity training. All these experiences led me to explore the use of active experiential techniques in the basic analytic groups.

It was also during this time, while attending meetings of the American Group Psychotherapy Association (AGPA), that I first met Eric Berne. I was not especially impressed with Berne as a person and did not have the opportunity to know him as an intimate as did others. I read his material and found some of the ideas useful. My real interest in TA emerged from my contacts with my friend Robert Goulding. Bob and I shared many common interests in AGPA. In the course of organizational activities, we talked of our clinical practice and from that I challenged Bob to convince me of the claims he made for his application of TA. Not being one to hesitate at challenge, he invited me to come and observe his work, which I first did in the spring of 1970. This time I also met Mary Goulding. In the meantime I attended TA 101 courses by the Gouldings and by David Kupfer.

As I have become familiar with TA and with the large group of professionals who identify themselves as transactional analysts, I have been concerned about abuse of TA by persons who seemed to lack understanding in depth. To the extent that such abuse may be corrected by the acquisition of more comprehension of the concepts found in TA, this contribution of mine will be an important message.

I consider it unfortunate that Berne's contributions have been accepted by such a small percentage of mental health professionals. He believed that patients are persons who are to be related to as equals capable of understanding anything that the therapist knows. He saw also how often the jargon of psychiatry and psychology were used by clinicians to maintain an unequal relationship, which he believed antithetical to the attainment of autonomy. Contrary to popular belief, Berne's writings give abundant evidence of his thoroughness in depth and breadth of psychology and related behavioral and social sciences, as well as of philosophy and religion and history. It is only from such a broad base that one can create the communication tools and concepts found within the jargon of TA.

It is my desire to help people to recognize the sophistication that is inherent in Berne's inventiveness, so that there will be an increased and effective use of TA by those who are dedicated to thoroughness and professionalism.

Eric Berne was a master at capturing the essence of complex psychological concepts, mechanisms, and operations and at converting them to colloquialisms with which he cleverly communicated for the benefit of his patients and students. That skill led to the writing of books which the public has found highly stimulating and useful.[1]

All professional and technical groups develop a jargon to facilitate communication as well as to create some exclusivity. While jargon is handy to the well-prepared, there are pitfalls for the novice who desires to be accepted by peers and who therefore learns the jargon without fully knowing its meanings. Then the jargon becomes a cant, the special language of a group with special identifications, such as psychotherapist or transactional analyst. When this jargon is found appealing by the public at large (e.g., TA), it becomes an argot, the special language of a clique. Unfortunately this can lead to the development of persons who abuse their limited knowledge through adroit trickery. Responsible professionals will distinguish between those who abuse and exploit TA and those who by reason of limited opportunity have not yet become well grounded in theory and practice.

A major problem which has existed in the field of TA is the limited availability of literature to provide understanding in depth of the concepts introduced by Berne in his colloquial descriptions of human behavior, development, and psychopathology. It is my intent in this writing to explicate several of these issues. These are areas of theory that are "fuzzy." I find frequently that these fuzzy concepts are questioned by clinicians of other theoretical orientations and defended rather rigidly and somewhat superficially by some clinicians dedicated to TA.

What has resulted from Berne's formulations is a set of operational terms which serve well the clinician who is grounded in psychology, and which are used with only limited success and occasionally abused by those insufficiently prepared. I endorse Berne's emphasis on intuition and its reliability, and at the same time I hasten to add that it is most desirable that the intuitive clinician also be knowledgeable about, and have access to, an uncontaminated Adult.

I find among colleagues practicing TA a not uncommon tendency to be critical and at times derisive of other therapeutic approaches. For me such criticism arises out of personal need rather than fidelity to a Bernian tradition. It may also occur by reason of the individual's lack of familiarity with psychoanalytic and behavioral psychology concepts. Berne himself did not have that lack. His writings evince a great reliance on the utility of both the intrapsychic and interpersonal aspects of the analytic approach. The introductory statement by A. A. Brill in Berne's book, *The Laymen's Guide to Psychiatry and Psychoanalysis,* is most complimentary of Berne's obvious and thorough knowledge of Freudian concepts. I also have no doubt that Berne drew upon his knowledge of the concepts of Alfred Adler and Harry Stack Sullivan. Additionally, he was familiar with the advantage of a goal-oriented treatment method in the context of a living laboratory; this is evident in his utilization of contractual treatment groups. Undoubtedly, he saw the great hazards of a therapist's romantic pursuit of a psychological frame of reference which could result in interminable exploration and progress without sufficient attention to the issue for which the patient originally sought professional assistance.

Based on my acquaintance with various schools of psychology, and on a general belief that therapists are effective because of their commonalities rather than their differences, I shall frequently draw upon the various approaches to show what I believe to have been underlying and within Berne's formulations.

It is my general experience that change occurs most effectively when there is insight or awareness, especially experiential awareness, followed by cognitive reintegration. The pathways to such change vary considerably and may include the approach of social transactional options, the highly structured reparenting systems, and the integration of techniques from varied active experiential approaches such as gestalt therapy; psychodrama; neo-Reichian, bioenergetic, primal therapy; Synanon, and probably others too numerous to mention. I do not believe there is a "pure" transactional analysis any more than there is "pure" psychoanalysis or any other approach. I say this in recognition of the uniqueness of the philosophy and values of therapists even when they have a common investment in a theoretical system.

Eric Berne described transactional analysis as a system of social psychiatry. As a means of understanding communication and interpersonal relationships, its applications are numerous. I shall be focusing on those aspects which, broadly defined, are clinical. Thus I shall be dealing with personality development, personality defect (psychopathology), and the consequent impaired satisfaction in living which is manifested in the areas of thinking, feeling, and behavior.

Berne often and capably made leaps from very complex constructs to a succinct statement with a catchy phrase without ever describing his reasoning process. At one point he even stated that the methodological problems involved in the transition are not relevant. Unfortunately, he did not indicate to whom they were nonrelevant. Personally, I consider the interrelation between the concepts prominent in TA and their antecedents in analytic psychology to be most important. In fact, the failure of many to understand these issues has resulted in an abuse of TA by unwitting and poorly prepared clinicians.

Out of my personal desire to see TA taught with respect in well-established academic centers for psychiatry and psychology and related sciences, I shall clarify and present the comprehensiveness of TA at the present time.

MY VALUES   I believe that the reader will have a better understanding of my theoretical presentations if I explicate my positions and values. Firstly, I value joyful living and believe that it requires that the uniqueness of the individual be directly expressed and appreciated, resulting in fulfillment of personal needs. I also believe that all social systems, regardless of their political designation, do develop and persist by the creation and maintenance of structures which inherently limit unrestrained individual expression. As a result, all social systems have their oppressive and inhumane features which can be readily identified, especially when the individual "feels" oppressed. All political systems and most religious systems offer security, as well as encouragement and reason for accepting some conformity as being for the general good. I believe that it is possible to find satisfaction and joy through creative individual expression even within oppressive systems. To do so requires that the individual recognize and use his or her autonomy while at the same time being responsive to others. The result will be a cooperative lifestyle which to some will appear to be conformity. The difference is that the autonomous and cooperative person will experience interpersonal intimacy rather than the struggle and rivalry of competition. I also realize that those whose lives I touch and who believe similarly will have their impact on existing social systems. It is my experience that both the oppressors and the oppressed often have retained their positions because of scripty choices.

I therefore value life, autonomy, cooperation, and intimacy. I believe that every person has an inherent worth by reason of her or his very existence, and that that worth is not something to be earned or taken away, nor can one person have more than another. For me that is the essence of "OKness" and therefore, in my view, "not-OKness" is a delusion, even though it is a popular one.

I also see personality development and psychopathology as having originated in decisional processes. While admitting that there are possible issues of neurological integration and perception, the practical issues for most persons reside in the interpersonal contexts of the early years of life. Thus early life decisions have great impact on subsequent developments. I believe that the potential for individual change is unlimited because of the human ability to engage in introspection, attain awareness, and grow by decision to a rewarding life. This seems possible regardless of how maladaptive one's behavior may have been.

I hold that we as individuals are uniquely and solely responsible for the creation of our thoughts and feelings and the behavioral choices we make. While I recognize that we are also reactive and responsive to external stimuli, including those symbolized in verbal and nonverbal language, we are not bound inevitably to fixed responses. The tendency toward fixation is a learned process and is subject to modification by new learning. In this belief about personal ownership of internal processes lie both the hope and realization of change. I suspect the reason most persons are reluctant to depart from the belief that others can make them have good or bad feelings is that when one lets go of the belief, there is no longer an opportunity to manipulate others through tactics designed to induce guilt—the ultimate interpersonal emotional weapon.

It seems at times that moralists believe that without guilt there would be no responsiveness to community. Such an attitude discredits the ability of individuals to recognize the benefits of community and its ability to be supportive to all members. It is my experience that people who are accepting and regarding of others, even with their foibles, are also persons who experience joy and intimacy within their caring cooperation. It is possible for children to respect structure without being required to feel guilty.

In the context of psychotherapy I believe that change or cure occurs more rapidly when the patient or client clearly identifies his or her personal dissatisfactions and identifies also a specific goal for change. When the goal is specified by the seeker of change and when the therapist willingly joins the contract, then both can proceed as coequals. This minimizes the likelihood of countertransference interference and enhances the working through of transference processes. I also am biased in favor of group treatment methods for numerous reasons which will not be discussed further in this chapter.

In the treatment setting I confront the incongruities displayed by those seeking change. Effective confrontation requires that one avoid parental pronouncements, which evoke childlike responses and are seldom productive. I have yet to see persons display self-discovery when trying to explain or justify themselves. The other major hazard in treatment is when the therapist believes that his or her way of life is the way others also should be.

I have often stated that my theory represents ways that I explain things to myself. I borrow from and modify at times the theoretical speculations of others as I discover ideas that enhance my understanding. I do not intend to claim that anyone's theory is right or wrong, since the term "theory" as used by me means the way in which I explain things to myself. I understand how theoretical speculation may lead to competitive endeavors. I think it tragic that such competitiveness occasionally leads to destruction of relationships. I shall devote myself to exploratory cooperation with respect for the differences between myself and others.

THE HUMAN CONDITION

In order to construct an understanding of the psychology of the person, it becomes necessary to make certain assumptions and hypotheses. As have many others, I shall present some ideas which are based upon my own personal observations of growing children, the contributions of numerous other authors, my personal experiences in psychotherapy, and my resulting analysis, synthesis, conclusions, and projections.

Humans can be described as naturally responsive, i.e., they can and do respond as an inherent aspect of existence. Furthermore, the response may be to internal stimuli or external stimuli. Persons are able to modify responses, and the factors involved in such modification will be dealt with shortly.

Another way to describe humans is as problem-solvers. The ability to solve problems is easily described as decision making, and there are many complexities of information processing to which I shall attend. The style and effectiveness of our responsive problem-solving constitute our character and personality.

The extent to which anyone understands the environment and persons within that environment is based upon the accuracy of perceptions. Perceptions are seemingly subject to certain constitutional and/or genetic conditions as well as to modification by one's life experience—including opportunity and impairment as from disease or disorder—which influences the perceptual apparatus. Therefore, though we tend to operate as though most persons have had common experiences, it is always necessary to respect the uniqueness of each individual.

In terms of psychological development it is convenient, though perhaps risky, to assume certain experiences and processes as being fairly common and thus to build a model for personality development which has broad applicability. This process permits description of the variances from the norm. When such variances result in impairment of choices and limit the adaptive capacity, we speak of psychopathology with implication that the ability to function and perhaps survive is definably restricted.

There is a general principle in science that function arises from structure. At times it is possible to explore intimately a structure and thus to understand the mechanisms by which it produces the functional display.

When such is possible we can describe the structure pictorially and as having static elements that are productive of dynamic mechanisms. Furthermore, we can describe substructures and their dynamic functions. As yet we have not attained the sophistication necessary to comprehend in a major way the psychological aspects of human function. As a consequence, we theorize to explain that which is functionally displayed.

EGO STATES

Berne chose to base TA on the observable behavior of individuals—the functional display. To describe this he utilized the term "ego state," originated by his mentor Paul Federn. In describing the behavior of an individual, Berne chose to limit the categorization of the ego states to three. Within each category there are commonalities and yet each category will contain a wide range of differences.

I shall make a special emphasis on ego states, since it is my experience that they (along with rackets) are poorly understood by a significant number of clinicians.

My description of an ego state is that it is the observed way of being which is correlated with certain feelings and thoughts and which sets a frame of reference for decision-making. Thus there is an element of predictability as to a person's immediate future actions and responses. Knowledge of ego states and the relative predictability provides a method for more accurate understanding of interpersonal relationships and communication. Consequently, the knowledgeable person is afforded a broader range of options and an opportunity for autonomous function.

When a person behaviorally displayed a manner which either provided structuring or support for another person, Berne identified the ego state as parental and referred to it as Parent (capitalized).

Similarly, he identified ego states which had childlike commonalities displayed in the form of impulsiveness, expressiveness, and stylized reactiveness, and dominated by feeling. Such ego states were labeled Child.

The third way of being, which he labeled Adult, was displayed in a manner demonstrating thoughtfulness and careful concern for goal attainment and the probable consequences of choices. General rules and personal needs were included in the deliberations.

The most common misconception about ego states that I encounter is a belief that there are only three ego states. Actually, there are thousands upon thousands of ego states displayed by each of us. What Berne did to ease understanding of self and others was to note that it is convenient to categorize any ego state into one of the three types: Parent, Adult, or Child.

Berne cautioned that the appreciation of ego states as experiential realities rather than as handy ideas was difficult for both patients and trainees. That statement is profound and ignorance of it is a major source for abuse in the practice of TA.

Berne further identified methods with which one could presumptively diagnose and confirm the presence of Parent, Adult, and Child ego states. The presumptive diagnosis is known as *behavioral* and the confirming methods are three: *social, historical,* and *phenomenological.*

It is possible for a knowledgeable observer to identify ego states with a fairly high degree of accuracy by watching a person's facial and body movements while listening to the vocal utterances. This is known as *behavioral diagnosis.* Even very young children have a capability for such identification because of the consistency of vocal and nonvocal communication patterns. Thus Berne based his concepts on interpersonal experiences readily understood by all. This provides a convenient basis for teaching effective interpersonal problem-solving and ultimately the resolution of internal psychological conflicts. The behavioral diagnosis of an observed ego state relies on accuracy of perception and is conveniently supported by consensual validation with others.

The confirmation of the behaviorally observed and tentative diagnosis of an ego state involves the social, historical, and phenomenological levels of awareness. The *social diagnosis* is useful when one realizes that the experienced way of being has occurred in response to a specific ego state of another individual. Thus the social confirmation of a Parent ego state rests in the recognition that it appeared as a reaction to a perceived Child ego state in another. The social diagnosis of the Adult is accomplished by recognition of the ongoing adaptability displayed by autonomous reality testing.

The third level of confirmation, the *historical diagnosis,* results from the awareness within the person that the present behavior and frame of reference has an historical antecedent, either in the remembrance of similar behavior by significant authority figures in the past (in the instance of Parent ego states), or by recollection of prior similar experiences and behavior in one's own earlier life (in the instance of Child ego states).

The fourth level of confirmation applies most aptly to the Parent or Child ego states. This is the *phenomenological diagnosis,* described as a reexperiencing of an event from early life, or an abreactive experience. In the instance of the Child ego state, it is the reliving of an emotionally charged experience from early life with the full impact of original feelings. In the instance of the Parent ego state, it is reliving the moment when one incorporated a way of being of a significant authority figure; for example, when one changes by expressing now an emotion or thought from one's father or mother.

In the treatment setting as well as in educational contexts, much is accomplished by using only the presumptive behavioral diagnosis. By so doing, it is possible to establish social control and to recognize options in communication. The knowledge of ego states provides persons with a satisfying sense of self-mastery. In common practice the social diagnosis is less often used and the historical and phenomenological are rarely used.

However, if the goal of treatment is autonomy rather than social control, the therapist must be familiar with the history and phenomenology that provide access to the primitive and early experiences of childhood and the decisions resulting from those early experiences. Many of the techniques now used by TA clinicians that were derived from gestalt therapy and psychodrama are actually devices for regressively returning to earlier ego states, by which the client attains awareness of decisions and their consequences.

At this juncture I want to dispel some common misconceptions. I occasionally hear persons state that feelings are in the Child ego states and maybe also in the Parent ego states but not in the Adult ego states. Such a view is not consistent with Berne's descriptions of ego states and is the result of a misunderstanding about the psychic organs, which will be discussed below.

Regardless of the observed ego state, every individual is, in the waking state, simultaneously experiencing and displaying thought and feeling and behavior. It is impossible to exist without the combination and interrelation of these three, even though occasionally there may be a psychological denial of one or another. Consequently, there are feelings, thoughts, and behavior in all ego states. Within this it can be generally stated that Parent ego states are dominated by imitative or instructed styles, Adult ego states by thoughtfulness, and Child ego states by feelings.

THE PSYCHIC ORGANS

The basis for much of the confusion arises out of a failure to understand Berne's hypothesized psychic organs: the archeopsyche, the neopsyche, and the exteropsyche. Berne was apparently in the same position as other behavioral scientists. He could observe behavior but he could not define precisely, in terms of physical structure, the source of the functional display which he defined as an ego state. Yet, based on the principle that function arises from the structure, he elected to describe the total structure as a system or mental apparatus—the mind—and he apparently preferred the Greek term *psyche*. He saw the psyche as an organ, a complex system which receives and orders information and makes the information available so that it is used as an individual relates to all else. In a general sense, the psyche includes perception, intellection, response ability, and initiation of action. He chose to subdivide the psyche into three compartments, each with specialized internal functions.

He named the most primitive part the *archeopsyche*. This part organizes events related to biological needs and is a storage place for experiences related to such needs. As such it is seen as generally functioning at a visceral or essential level and closely tied to one's "hungers." Berne referred to the archeopsyche as the organizer of internal programming. To understand this archeopsychic organ requires that one assume that survival of the human organism is possible only where certain physical conditions exist and when certain chemical substances are provided. It is the need for these conditions and substances that Berne called hungers. In a general sense all receptor systems of the organism, both physical and psychological, must be periodically stimulated and gratified or else the organism functions at an impaired level or ceases to exist. Thus, touching or stroking becomes essential to life regardless of the degree of sophistication of humans. The primitive systems must be adequately fulfilled. When not sufficiently fulfilled, there is "tension" which results in a felt awareness of a need and which will assume increasing primacy in the individual's functioning until that need is gratified.

Once an organism develops an ability or potential for a function, then the periodic expression of that function begins to drive the person in a manner similar to that of the biological hungers. I have found convenience in labeling the biological hungers as acquisitive needs, since they are usually directed at "taking in" or "attachment" behaviors. The other needs which arise as a consequence of developed functions I have labeled as the expressive or inquisitive needs.

Both acquisitive and inquisitive needs will motivate behaviors. However, when survival is an issue for the person, the need which is more important for survival will assume primacy. Most often this is the acquisitive biological need. It is important for those who study behavior to realize that the primitive hungers represented by Child behaviors are always being served even when Parent and Adult ego states are being displayed. If the needs of the Child are not being met, then other ego states will give way and the Child will be dominant. Recognition of this has led many clinicians to say that the Child ego state is most important. Berne indicated that the Adult properly serves the needs of the Child. Some therapists have said that the Parent and Adult ego states are developed by the Child. These statements become much clearer when one understands the differences between the ego states and the psychic organs.

The *exteropsyche* is the organ which orders the structuring of external operations. It handles the rules and regulations, the "how to's" which are taught and internally recorded for use throughout life. In this sense it develops as a rather rigid protective system to assure survival by avoiding the dangers of impulsivity which rest within the archeopsyche. On this basis, the exteropsyche is continually subject to updating as one relates to new authority figures whose rules will modify previous positions. It has been compared to a high fidelity tape with permanently stored messages.

The *neopsyche* is the organ which integrates experiences, constantly striving to maintain a balance of the input from the archeopsyche, exteropsyche, and the environment, and synthesizing a response which is based on estimated probable consequences. In that sense it is an observer, moderator, and regulator of options and has been compared to a computer. Like all computers, the accuracy and adequacy of its functioning are related to the input and data base and also require that all internal connections be operating properly. Neopsychic function will be impaired whenever there is insufficient, excessive, or erroneous input, or when internal connections are awry (as with neurological disease), or when the feedback is distorted.

I have often compared neopsychic function to the servomechanisms in rocketry which provide for inertial guidance. Such a rocket "knows" from where it departed in terms of place, time, direction, speed, etc., and it "knows" the location of its target. It is capable of continuously monitoring the accuracy of its trajectory and of altering its direction and/or speed so as to stay on target regardless of changes which are external, the way a heat-seeking missile chases a maneuvering airplane and eventually flies directly into the exhaust chamber. Finally, the "computer" operations of the neopsyche are infinitely more complex than any machine yet devised by humankind. The neopsyche was described by Berne as probability programed and with objective reality testing.

Now to the issue of confusion about the ego states and the psychic organs. Berne capitalized the words Parent, Adult, and Child and used them interchangeably to refer to either an ego state or a psychic organ. Actually there is need for a very critical distinction to avoid the complications which have arisen in understanding pathology and the "second orders" of structure.

In order to establish a distinction, I shall when referring to the exteropsyche use the term "the PARENT" and when referring to an ego state use the term "a Parent," etc. The reason for the distinction is that structures can be described and categorized by commonalities but functions cannot

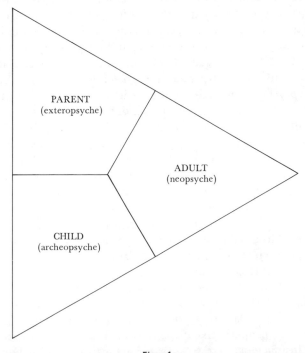

Figure 1
The Psychic Organs

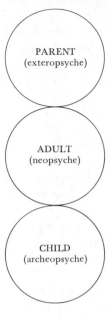

Figure 2
The Psychic Organs

be structurally or pictorially subdivided. A function is a dynamism and it can be subdivided into part processes which are temporarily related. Only a structure such as an organ can be structurally subdivided, thus permitting a description of the functions or dynamics of its subsystems.

Therefore, it is possible to divide the psychic organs PARENT, ADULT, and CHILD into theoretical substructures, which is precisely what Berne did in second- and third-order structural analysis. This subdivision is convenient as a means for explaining psychological function, and it is also the basis for distinguishing the CHILD from the psychoanalytic construct "id" and for distinguishing the PARENT from the psychoanalytic construct of "superego."

Another technical problem was that Berne used the diagram of three stacked circles to pictorialize both the concept of the ego states and that of the three psychic organs. It is my impression that in the field of TA the three circles are now most commonly believed to represent ego states and only rarely does anyone use the diagram in reference to the psychic organs. For these reasons I have chosen to develop a new pictorial representation of the psyche and its structural divisions. In its simplest form it is a triangle, as shown in Figure 1. I shall retain the three circles as useful when depicting communication processes and ego states, as in Figure 2.

RELATIONSHIP BETWEEN THE PSYCHIC ORGANS AND EGO STATES   An ego state is a dynamic functional display originating as a result of the external stimuli, internal stimuli, internal recorded events, and instructions, and the degree of synthesis or integration of which the person is capable and has attained.

Ego states are behaviorally displayed and are the net result of all of one's internal psychic operations. Therefore, in any given moment an ego state represents the activities of and in the PARENT, the ADULT, and the CHILD. During this time certain internal operations and influences will predominate. Thus when the PARENT, with its organization of external programing, is dominant there will exist a Parent ego state, and so forth.

When one describes the "active" Parent, the reference is actually to the parental ego state displayed. When one describes the "internal" influence of the Parent, the reference is to the PARENT exteropsychic internal organ. Thus interpersonal communication occurs between persons in their manifest or perceived ego states. This is in contrast to internal dialogue, which occurs between the psychic organs. Cathexis, the charging with psychic energy, represents an internal shift among the psychic organs which results in a change in the displayed ego state.

The PARENT consists of faithfully recorded instructions based on past relationships with persons in authority, especially mother and father. Because mother and father displayed Parent, Adult, and Child ego states, each will be represented in the PARENT.

It is my belief that all parental influences are stored in the PARENT. Thus counterinjunctions, injunctions, attributions, and programs are all resupplied from the PARENT. This has comparability to the position of Stanley Woollams.[2]

The CHILD, or archeopsychic organ, represents the mental functions of the earlier life periods. In its most primitive aspects are recorded the experiences of striving for direct gratification of the hungers. In this sense there is impulsivity. Because the youngster very early develops a recognition of how to get around obstacles, there is also a quality of cleverness. These two, impulsivity and cleverness, result in the display of Free Child ego states and these experiences are recorded in the CHILD. In addition, because of the stresses of structure imposed by authority there also developed stylized patterns for fulfillment of hungers. While these stylized patterns have a practical utility, they often are accompanied by a sense of diminished worth of self and/or others and also are associated with unpleasant feelings which tend to endure. These styles displayed as ego states are characterized as Adapted Child ways.

The nature of thought processes within the CHILD that are displayed when Child ego states are manifest can be described as prelogical. Prelogical thinking is characterized by holistic, concrete, and/or magical reasoning and is focused on immediate rather than future goals. The CHILD is the repository for the affective experiences of early life and seems to be less subject to modification by experiences of adult life than is either ADULT or PARENT.

The ADULT, or neopsychic organ, is the moderator. Its functions are conveniently divided into data processing and data transmittal, which

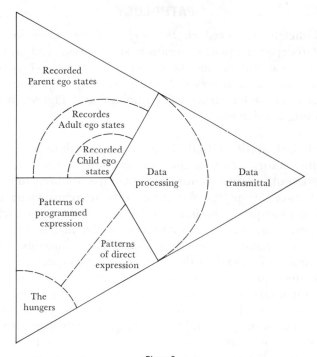

Figure 3
Subsystems of the Psychic Organs

includes intake and output. The intake will be from PARENT, CHILD, and through any stimulated sensory pathway. This information is then processed for the purpose of maintaining survival while fulfilling the hungers. The result is choosing of options based on a prediction of probable consequences. Thus there is sophisticated problem-solving. The function of the ADULT can be impaired by either excessive or insufficient data input. Excesses or deficiencies may occur in numerous ways, such as when there is a demanding PARENT CHILD, or when too many external events occur, or when brain function is impaired by illness or injury. There may also be impairment which is based in limited opportunities for acquisition of knowledge.

The PARENT and ADULT are both continuously updated by reason of new experiences. The PARENT, however, retains with some tenacity the old rules, and therefore "old tape recordings" are heard occasionally by even the most liberated person. I have found that many patients and some clinicians believe that cure means the erasure of old tapes from the PARENT. In my experience, erasure is an improper concept. Rather I think in terms of turning the volume down by reason of newly developed ADULT awareness and choice.

From the foregoing conceptual formulations, I have developed an elaborated diagram of the psyche and its separate organs (Figure 3).

PATHOLOGY

The symbolic three stacked circles originated by Berne were designed originally to depict the psychic organs PARENT, ADULT, and CHILD. As such they present a convenient method to also depict structural pathology and a frame of reference to understand functional pathology. Figure 4a shows my pictorial model for structural pathology and Figure 4b shows the corresponding Bernian model.

STRUCTURAL PATHOLOGY   Structural pathology is defined as either *contamination* or *exclusion. Contamination* means that in relation to some aspect of intrapsychic function there has not been sufficient differentiation between neopsyche and either or both archeopsyche and exteropsyche. The consequence is that in relation to the specific area of intrapsychic operations, there is impairment of the neopsychic probability programing by reason of unresolved issues. These unresolved issues may be due to fixated material in the CHILD or the incorporation of parental excesses or inadequacies in the PARENT. The identification of these developmental intrusions as contamination assists patients to realize that in some sense they are relating to the present and others "as if" they were in another context in the past, and that consequently they are denying themselves optimal choices and autonomy now. It is reasonable to assume that all humans have incorporated into the PARENT and/or CHILD unresolved conflicts which will in some contexts impair both autonomy and effective problem-solving. Contamination in a precise sense properly includes a description of the specific unresolved issues and the resultant impairment. However, since the condition is quite common and usually affects numerous internal operations, the broad general descriptions of PARENT contamination or CHILD contamination have considerable clinical utility.

The concept of *exclusion* has special implications and has been made complex by the views of authors other than Berne. Berne specifically used exclusion to indicate a person who at the time was functioning in a single

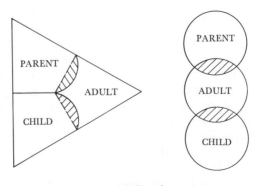

Figure 4
Contamination

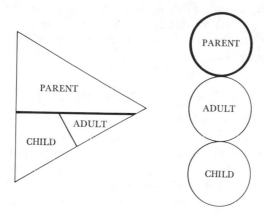

Figure 5
The Excluding PARENT

ego state—Parent, Adult or Child—as a consequence of the cathecting of a corresponding psychic organ, PARENT, ADULT, or CHILD, with the resultant exclusion of the other two. The result was a constant ego state which was well defended. In my experience, such exclusion is more often of short duration rather than an ongoing life experience.

In many ways, exclusion can be more conveniently diagramed using Berne's model, since it is a condition in which functionally one ego state persists and the other two are not seen. Internally, it is probably the result of a major incursion of the PARENT, ADULT, or CHILD on the other areas. In Figure 5, I compare pictorial models for an excluding PARENT.

FUNCTIONAL PATHOLOGY   Functional pathology was described by Berne as of two types: altered flow of cathexis, and altered permeability of ego boundaries. He seems to have used the term "ego boundary" in a specialized way related to his hypothesized psychic organs. Thus with an *altered flow of cathexis* he saw two poles. One was manifested by excessive lability, as though the "viscosity" of the cathexis was low and it flowed too easily between PARENT, ADULT, and CHILD. At the other pole was high "viscosity" resulting in sluggish cathexis because of an impaired flow.

The second functional pathology was described as the consequence of either too rigid or too lax *permeability of boundaries* between PARENT, ADULT, and CHILD. Here he mixed the functional and structural, describing exclusion as the result of rigid boundaries. Laxness of boundaries was seen as related to asthenic persons whose personalities are slipshod.

I have found little clinical applicability for the concepts of functional pathology. I find much more relevance to Berne's observation that psychological symptoms are exhibited by a single ego state or result from conflicts, concerts, or contaminations, that is, from within the psychic organs.

I find the lack of understanding of ego states and psychic organs to be the most troublesome aspect of the TA literature. Few, if any, authors have remained faithful to Berne's careful description and there has been much consequent lack of clarity. I believe a thorough understanding of these terms by clinicians will enhance their effectiveness and facilitate changes for the patient.

THE FUNCTIONAL DISPLAYS

In furthering the understanding of psychic function, Berne identified that the PARENT is functionally *exhibited* in two forms. He identified one as prejudicial and the other as nurturing. He saw the prejudicial as generally prohibitive and arbitrary. His use of the term "exhibited" was rather unusual. There is a lack of clarity in his writings as to whether exhibited means a manifest display as Parent ego state or the internal influence. This has been further complicated in the redefinition and addition of other terms by other authors.

Functionally, and as an observable display, Parent ego states can generally be described as either *controlling* or *nurturing*. I use *controlling* to describe those occasions in which an individual in a Parent ego state engages in communications that are intended to structure another's ways of being. This Parental ego-state display is useful and relevant when and if the other person has clearly displayed a desire for external control. The result is a complementary relationship. Similarly, there may be seen in some situations a nurturing form of Parent ego state which results in unqualified tenderness and concern for the other individual desiring support. I prefer to use the terms Controlling Parent and Nurturing Parent to describe the nature of Parent ego states. I do not equate the terms Critical Parent or Prejudicial Parent with the term Controlling Parent, because I believe they have different interpretations. I do not use the concepts of OK or not-OK aspects of the PARENT, as introduced by Taibi Kahler.[3]

Berne made a clear distinction, as I do, between the functional display of an ego state and the internal influence of the PARENT on the CHILD. This internal influence is related to the functional descriptions of Child ego states. I adhere to Berne's original split of the Child into two types of ego states, Adapted and Natural. I prefer using the term Free Child to that of Natural Child.

Free Child ego states are the direct expressive and creative derivatives of the CHILD and contain much evidence of that which Freud identified as primary process—utilizing the pleasure principle and being evidently narcissistic. Emotionality is immediate and intense regardless of its designation. In pure form it is readily and frequently seen in the very young but only rarely in older persons unless psychotic or when in some altered state of consciousness.

Adapted Child ego states are seen in reaction to the internal influence of the PARENT or to the Parent ego states of another person actual or perceived. The adaptations that are manifested vary greatly. I have found convenience in categorizing three modes of adaptation, which will be described in the section on personality development.

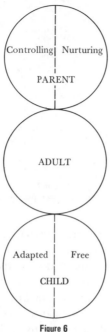

Figure 6
Functional Styles of Ego States

Berne as well as some other authors have occasionally used the term "rebellious" Child ego state. I prefer to avoid the term rebellious because of the potential for misunderstanding. At times "rebellious" is used to describe the assertive "natural" qualities of a child, which may appear as a Free Child ego state. That sort of rebellion seems to me to be healthy and to be encouraged. There is also another form of rebellion which is vindictive and at times destructive and is the result of programing of the Adapted Child. That form of rebellion is only rarely useful and usually undesirable, in fact it is ultimately self-destructive. If the clinician is not very clear about the distinction, there is a hazard that vengefulness and hostile expressions will be supported with eventual tragic consequences. When stroking the "Rebellious Child" one must be certain as to the nature of the "rebellion."

In second-order functional or descriptive analysis the terms I use are Controlling Parent, Nurturing Parent, Adult, Adapted Child, and Free Child (Figure 6).

STRUCTURAL-FUNCTIONAL INTERRELATIONS

There is need for differentiating the functional aspects from the structural, since they have relevance in different contexts. Controversy among TA theoreticians has resulted from failure to differentiate between function and structure. Second-order structural analysis refers directly to the

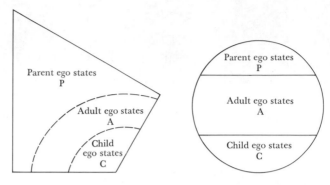

Figure 7
Recordings in the Exteropsyche (PARENT)

substructures of the psychic organs PARENT, ADULT, and CHILD and not to the ego states to which they give rise.

As an exteropsychic organ, the PARENT consists of the introjections and the composite incorporations of the ways of being that are displayed by all persons to whom one grants significant authority. Therefore, when mother or father or parental surrogates display an ego state, especially with consistency, they provide a model to be integrated and subsequently imitated. Thus the PARENT consists of multitudinous discrete displays which are adopted as one's own. Since ego states are categorically divided into Parent, Adult, and Child, one's PARENT will contain numerous examples of each. Some will undoubtedly exert more influence and thus be reproduced more frequently than others. If one were to compartmentalize on the basis of categories, the simplest scheme would be as in Figure 7.

Figure 8 provides a model for subdividing the ego states of mother and father as recorded in the exteropsyche of the offspring.

In actuality, numerous authority figures are rendered in the exteropsyche so that one could use an elaborated model, as in Figure 9, with an

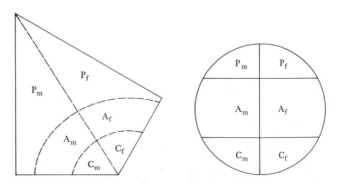

Figure 8
Mother's and Father's Ego States Recorded in the Exteropsyche

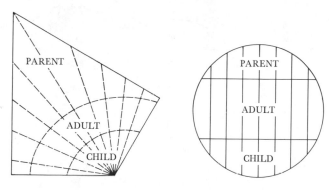

Figure 9
Recorded Ego States of Multiple Authority Figures

unlimited number of vertical divisions and, perhaps, with more space given to the more significant influencing persons.

Figure 7 represents an oversimplified, yet useful model in clinical practice. Figure 8 corresponds generally with ITAA official nomenclature, while Figure 9 is comparable to Woollams'[4] proposal. Figure 9 is useful to the theoretician and will seldom be used in clinical practice. Berne also indicated that one might have occasion to further subdivide the PARENT to a third order as shown in Figure 10.

Second-order structural analysis (and third also) reveals the significant internal influences that have arisen from external sources. An understanding of the external programing and origins of one's own Parent ego states assists in understanding the internal conflicts, contaminations, and exclusions which impair psychological functions and comfort. The awareness that one has faithfully incorporated the scripty patterns of parents and surrogates is an important aspect of cure. It is because I view the PARENT as an early-formed psychic organ and as continuously being updated that I see the injunctions, attributions, programs, and counterscript instruction

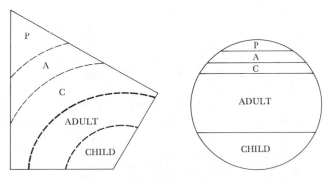

Figure 10
Third Order Structure of Exteropsyche

Figure 11
Second Order Aspects of the ADULT

all as incorporated into the PARENT of a grown person as well as that of the still growing youngster.

Berne at one point subdivided the ADULT into three parts, all related to one's style of relating to objective reality, yet showing the influence of external and internal programing as well. This can be described as in Figure 11.

Ethos refers to ethical qualities possessed by individuals who are demonstrably responsible grownups. Faithfulness, trustworthiness, courage, and justice characterize Ethos. *Pathos* refers to the responsible "feelings" one has towards others. These feelings are integrated childlike attributes. They are also manifested as a captivation and candidness of character. Little else appears in the literature about second-order structure of the ADULT, probably because those who have well-developed and integrated ADULT functions seldom have occasion to explore extensively their sources.

The most difficult subdivision of the psychic organs occurs in relation to the CHILD. Berne clearly indicated that there was progression and that primitive archeopsychic ego states were recapitulated in subsequent childhood experience. For example, a Child ego state at age eight would likely contain a reexperiencing of an event from a younger age, such as five, and that in turn would incorporate the reexperiencing of an event from age two. Each such event also would be manifested in accordance with the qualities of neopsychic and exteropsychic function in existence at each of the earlier periods. In regard to the event at age eight, that event could be reexperienced by a grownup at age 38 as a Child ego state. Likewise the incorporated events of age five and two could be individually cathected as Child ego states. Berne does not clearly state when CHILD is fully formed. On the basis of the studies of J. Piaget,[5] I assume that uniquely new Child ego states diminish rapidly as one acquires the ability to reason abstractly. This generally occurs between age 11 and adolescence.

I will next consider some of the issues and controversies surrounding the designations P_1, A_1, C_1, P_2, A_2, C_2, Little Professor, etc.

The terms P_2, A_2, and C_2 have come to represent PARENT, ADULT, and

CHILD operations in life after the onset of adolescence, when one has developed a capacity for abstract reasoning and the potential for uncontaminated ADULT processing of information. In general, this is the analytic "knowing" of grownups. Berne was rather casual about the earlier psychic operations, and I believe the graded and progressive means of "knowing" one's world as described by Piaget provide a much more comprehensive view.

Clearly A_1 represents the neopsychic operations of a person chronologically younger than when A_2 is present. Although Berne indicated that neopsychic (A_1) functioning began with the differentiation between self and other at approximately two to three months of age, he did not elaborate on the chronologically progressive refinements which take place.

A_1 could therefore represent any level of ADULT function present at a given preadolescent period, and then P_1 and C_1 would represent the concomitantly existent PARENT and CHILD operations. I will say more about the time of origin of PARENT and CHILD in the material about development.

The present speculation of other authors as to the time of origin of what they describe as ego states is compounded by a probable misunderstanding of the distinction between psychic organs and their derivative ego states, and also by an attempt to "force-fit" certain psychoanalytic concepts of child development into a Bernian three-circled pictorial diagram.

PERSONALITY DEVELOPMENT   Berne engaged in minimal written speculation about personality development. When he did, he focused on the interpersonal rather than on the intrapsychic, and this leaves a void for clinicians without other formal preparation. I interrelate the interpersonal and intrapsychic, using the Bernian constructs. I acknowledge but will not discuss here the issues of hereditary and constitutional factors which may impair perception and other intellectual processes. Likewise, I shall not digress into the problems introduced by intercurrent illness and/or neural malnutrition from various sources.

The newborn enters the world as a bundle of desires and/or needs and cannot fulfill those desires himself for a rather long time. At birth, all of an infant's functions are archeopsychic and the ego states are all Free Child and highly narcissistic. When differentiation of self and other results in purposeful seeking, neopsychic functioning has begun and primitive Adult ego states will be briefly experienced and sometimes observed. As soon as the nonverbally transmitted instructions from mother influence the independent primitive decision making of the infant, primitive exteropsychic functioning has also begun. The results of this are seen behaviorally before the child can verbally communicate experience. Adaptation is not simply efforts at preservation and survival, but rather a progressive equilibrium between accommodation and assimilation. In an overly simplified explanation, we learn about our world through our ability to accommodate. In so doing we assimilate and move to a more sophisticated level from which we learn anew—followed by another level of assimilation. Thus, there is a flow in the growth of intellect, which progresses from the primitive of the infant to the very elaborate abstractions of adulthood.

Assimilation describes the process by which the organism incorporates external reality as a part of itself. Accommodation is the change within the organism which occurs as a consequence of the assimilation. Not only does the infant acquire knowledge through primitive exploration but he changes by reason of the acquired knowledge. Adaptation is the progressive change which occurs and is in turn in equilibrium with ever more sophisticated organization of that which has become known or learned.

Piaget's observations lead to these statements. (1) The infant and its environment coexist with a complete interdependence. (2) The infant and its environment are engaged in a continuous process of action on and reaction to each other. (3) A balance or equilibrium of relationship exists.

The environment as described above includes all persons and objects relating to the infant. The discovery of the environment is initiated by the accidents of innate and reflexive behavior patterns. Very soon, however, the reflex repetition is productive of some consistent experiences from which there is early learning. Each discovery results in a new level of function by adaptation and the organizing of experience. While the flow is towards ever-increasing complexity and sophistication, it is also true that the primitive ways of earlier stages coexist and at times the youngster reverts to earlier mechanisms. Thus there is the combination of flow of learning intermixed with primitive modes of learning.

Within the upward flow of the learning process, it is possible to discern epochs within which certain patterns are identifiable. These will be described briefly, using Piaget's observations. I recognize that this is reductionism and does disservice to Piaget's thoroughness and subtleties. While I relate these to chronological age, it should be understood that each child uniquely initiates and completes each in his or her own time or fashion.

The first epoch, from birth to about two years, is that of sensori-motor thinking. The infant has several sensori-motor systems which receive stimuli, and in each there is a response ability which is largely reflex yet subject to repetitive ordering. The consequence is a trial-and-error system which produces a simple type of control. Even at this early age then the infant is engaging in primitive problem solving and decision-making, which is the essence of Berne's model. The infant is not yet engaged in problem definition or problem-stating, which come at later stages. By the end of the first epoch, the infant clearly appreciates the difference between self and other. Objects have permanence. Simplistic causes and effects can be related. Even though there has been tremendous growth, the infant's understanding is still limited to the appreciation of events and the properties of objects which have arisen directly from her or his actions relating to them. There is a practical sort of understanding of the way things behave when handled, but there is no appreciation of why. Public knowledge as conveyed through language is not a part of the youngster's world.

The second epoch begins at about 18 months and ends near five years with the emergence and development of symbolic thought (preconceptual representations). Playing becomes very important and through the process of play a child introduces symbolic representations. Dolls become mommies, babies, brothers, or sisters, paper becomes clothing, and mud becomes food. If the child were stopped from playing, then thinking would be stopped.

With the emergence of the symbolic thoughts the child finds new uses for the older sensori-motor representations. Use of substitute objects aids mental symbolic manipulation. The child can also separate the representation of her behavior from her body and apply it elsewhere. Previously, in the sensori-motor epoch, images arose as the result of internal imitations of external activity. Now internal images arise first and are followed by activity, the beginning of creative expression.

During this period the use of language rapidly increases, since the words are symbols. However, at this stage words are a very private symbolism arising from the child's experiences. Words at this time differ from language as a conceptual symbol system. For example, mommy is mommy; mommy is not lady. Dog is only dog and a toy dog is something else. The fixation of symbols is evident. The child does attempt inferences, but does not possess the concepts necessary to carry out the reasoning process. Space and time are not yet understood.

The third epoch is from four to eight years and is a transitional period in which there is articulated or intuitional representation, the threshold for operational thinking. The major features of this period are seen in the youngster's social relationships where, among peers, the private symbol systems are frequently found in conflict. Through available limited language, realignments are made, thus reorienting the mental model of the environment. The concepts of space and time are still out of reach.

The foregoing second and third epochs, which emerge at about two and end at about eight, are, in combination, labeled the period of pre-operational thinking. It covers the emergence of symbolic thinking through the development of articulated representations. This is probably the period which fits with Berne's description of A_1 as Little Professor, but such functions continue on until later. Following this there is the fourth epoch, the emergence of operational thinking. The characteristics of this period are concrete thinking operations. Within this time there are two periods. From seven to 12 years there is continuing emergence of new operations of concrete reasoning. By age nine, the refinements which are occurring place the youngster on the threshold of formal operations by reason of increased understanding of complex classes and linked statements.

Finally, from about 11 and into adolescence, there is the emergence and development of formal thinking operations with the use of abstract logic in the reasoning processes. This last stage seems to be the attainment of full adulthood in regard to the ability to think. This is clearly related to what is commonly designated as A_2.

Berne's definition of Adult is, "an ego state oriented toward objective autonomous data-processing and probability estimating." By use of that definition, Adult is equated with neopsychic functioning regardless of the age or accuracy. Therefore, I believe an infant engaging in data-processing is in the Adult ego state. The use of the symbol A_1 then becomes a convenience for indicating that the nature and qualities of data-processing in earlier life are different than those seen in adulthood. Specifically, the youngster relies greatly on verbal sounds, gestures, movements, facial expressions, etc., for the purpose of understanding others. It is this ability to "know" without the use of well-developed verbal skills that Berne labeled as the Little Professor. This intuitive skill is present from the time an infant begins to have social exchanges and is not limited to some narrow age period. Furthermore, it is a capacity which all grownups possess even though they may not use it.

I suspect that it is also true that many persons during the developmental years have been told that that which they understood was not accurate. A youngster, for instance, upon seeing a pained facial expression in mother may ask if she feels bad. Mother may respond in the negative even though the youngster was accurate. Mother discounted the youngster's effectiveness in thinking. This kind of prohibition against effective thinking and its reinforcement has been exquisitely elaborated by R. D. Laing.[6]

HOW SCRIPT DEVELOPS

Next, I want to show how the interrelationship with authority figures, especially parents, can result in marked limitations in the intellectual development and thereby preclude autonomous functioning.

The "ideal" child-rearing situation would include the absence of any developmental impairment of the child's nervous system and no intercurrent illness or injury which impairs the opportunity for progressive development of reality-testing. It also presumes a child born to a mother and father who are free from any scripty ways and who are dedicated to the well-being of their child. With no "hang-ups," both mother and father will provide the youngster with structure, nurture, information, and play. They will always protect while at the same time endorsing creativity and growth by actions which are timely and never hurtful.

The child raised in such a situation would not be used by the parents to fulfill their narcissistic needs, and all of the youngster's desires would be gratified in a manner whereby happiness and growth occurred consistently. The parents would recognize that their child was capable of incidental self-injury because of lack of knowledge about danger and they would handle this without any fear on their part. The youngster would be supported and endorsed in all creative and problem-solving efforts and would attain autonomy without contamination.

Having described that ideal situation, it is my observation that such never exists because every youngster has parents with some unresolved conflicts, and often the mother, father, or some other significant authority figure is severely disturbed, either around certain issues or during a special period of the relationship. Under such circumstances, the youngster is not supported and often is actively pressured not to develop his or her full potential.

When those conditions exist, injunctions are transmitted by the parents and the youngster perceives that she or he is expected not to be fully what she or he is capable of being. Traditionally, injunctions have been described as originating in the Child of the parent and as being evoked by the Child of the child.

To understand this, it is necessary to picture a parent—mother or father —who has some specific unresolved intrapsychic conflicts. Thus there will be PARENT and/or CHILD contamination of the parent's ADULT. Eventually the youngster, through the process of natural exploratory activity, will engage in behavior which impinges on the parent's unresolved conflict. By observation and association, the parent's conflict is stimulated, brought to the surface, and intensified. Under such circumstances that parent's ability to respond meaningfully to the youngster's needs will be impaired, at times very seriously.

Take, for example, a mother who was raised in a family context which prohibited and punished overt displays of aggression and hostility. Every one in that family was "very nice." This woman married a man who was also proper, considerate, and nice. They both abhorred violence and saw all energetic activity as potentially violent. They chose to live in a secluded setting, and nearby residents thought of them as eccentric but very pleasant. They finally decided to have their first child and, when born, their son Clare was beautiful and such a "nice baby." They vowed that Clare would never have to face the "ugliness" of life that they themselves had occasionally seen. Clare soon showed signs of robust development. Everything went fine until the day when, in reflexive excitement, mother was accidentally kicked by Clare while changing his diaper. Mother was alarmed by his vigor; she also had an impulse to strike back but instead she picked up the baby and literally smothered him with hugs and kisses. Clare had trouble breathing for a short while and went limp.

Soon after that, baby Clare did other energetic things like throwing toys out of the crib and later the playpen. One day he even bit mother playfully. With each of these perceived "bad, aggressive, and destructive" acts mother became increasingly alarmed. Clare was both intrigued by her alarm and displeased with her smothering responses, which he experienced as interfering with his breathing. Mother "loved" him so. She was determined that he should know that "love" is always the best way. One day when he was three and had taken the stuffing out of the teddy bear and scattered it around the room and while doing so had broken grandmother's picture, mother "loved" him so much that he became unconscious. From that day forward he was never again an aggressive boy. Clare was "nice." Sometimes his stuffed animals were naughty and he "loved" them so they would be good. Mother was very pleased with him because he wasn't rowdy and she never worried that he would hurt anything, even an ant. He spent much of his time rocking in a little chair. When other children he knew did naughty or destructive things he cried and they called him a sissy and said he had a funny name. When he told mother she said, "Don't cry, dear sweet Clare, I love you just like you are, a sweet little boy."

With that vignette it is easy to recognize that Clare was being encouraged not to utilize fully some of his innate potential. On the day he became unconscious he suddenly made a "connection": "If I keep this up I'm going to stop existing." In so doing he assured himself of strokes, and furthermore mother rarely had that terrified look on her face. If she did it would go away when Clare said, "Don't worry Mommy, little sweet Clare is here."

What happened was that with Clare's aggressive acts, mother's own suppressed aggressive desires were stimulated. Her PARENT then sent to her CHILD harsh internal messages and she responded by being in a sweet Adapted Child ego state. While in that ego state she related to Clare as a "smothering mother." Clare sensed her excitement and her scare. He liked the strokes, but he didn't like smothering, especially the day that he thought he had "died."

You may find several possible injunctions in this story. Which is the correct one?

The answer of course is that the outside observer can never determine the injunction, even though by conjecture a percentage of observers might be accurate. Clare's injunction was determined by his own conclusions as to the intended nonverbal message in mother's actions. I want to emphasize that it is the individual living in script who starts the whole plan by decision, and ultimately it is by that person's unique ability to re-experience early events that he will eventually discover the script-setting decision and identify the harsh injunction which he believed was intended.

To complete the picture of Clare, I will describe father, a very ambitious yet gentle man who never uttered an oath. From the time Clare was very young, he noticed how often father reached over and gently touched mother and spoke softly. Later, when Clare understood words, he heard father say, "Don't worry, Mom, I'm here to love you." Eventually Clare realized that father said "Don't worry" whenever she had "that look" on her face, as for example when there was unexpected violence on the TV or during news reports. "That look" was just like the one Clare had seen when he was having fun. Clare's mom and dad both told visitors what a nice son they had and Clare smiled properly in response. One day when Clare was nine, dad said, "Clare, if Mom is upset, just tell her not to worry." In school Clare was noncompetitive and the gym teacher sent home comments. Clare's dad would at such times say, "I know you're strong, son, you have good moral fiber." Clare was strong; he didn't show his feelings. At times, though, he worried and if he revealed his worry to mom or dad they would say, "Well, I guess it runs in the family. I worry too, you know."

With this we have a fairly complete picture of the major influences in Clare's life. Certainly there was a "Don't be X" as an injunction, which he concluded after a number of times when he sensed that he might lose his life by smothering. He also recognized that mother was much happier after the day he decided to obey what she seemed to be directing. It was good to know that mom wasn't going to feel bad and stop taking care of him. Also, father set a model for him to observe from an early age. Later father actually told him how to be helpful when mom was upset. Both of these constituted a program along with other patterns displayed by dad. In part, they came when dad was in an Adapted Child ego state, and the instructions were given as Adult information. Both mom and dad told him to be strong and that he had "moral fiber." This provided his counterinjunctions and was issued from the Parent ego state as showing the way to success. There were also attributions from mother when, out of a desire to impress friends, she in an Adapted Child ego state said, "Meet my nice little Clare, he's really sweet."

Based on the foregoing information, I construct the script-matrix diagram in Figure 12. I have purposely avoided the connection of lines to Clare so as to reveal the dynamic processes. Mom in her scared Adapted Child ego state is sending out messages which contain a plea for help and also represent a childlike attempt at control—a passive behavior which invites Clare to solve her problem. Up until the age of three, Clare sensed

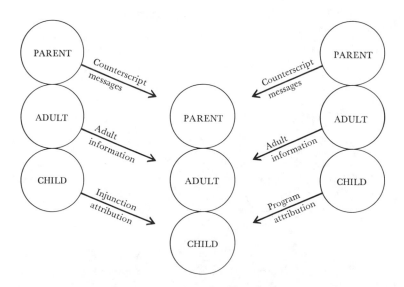

Figure 12
Script Matrix Diagram (ego states and transactional stimuli)

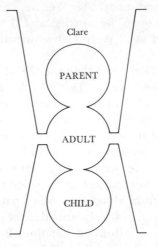

Figure 13

Information Reception of Psyche

that some weird things were happening. On the day that he became unconscious, he used his "professor" and made a decision. To give a better picture of what is going on, I will make another modification of the psychic organ diagram, Figure 13.

The peculiar appendages shown in Figure 13 are Clare's information detectors. These receivers work like finely tuned radio antennas to pick up the weak as well as the strong signals. The detectors are a function of Clare's ADULT because they represent neopsychic functioning. When Clare was being aggressive, mom got upset and sent out those "bad vibes"

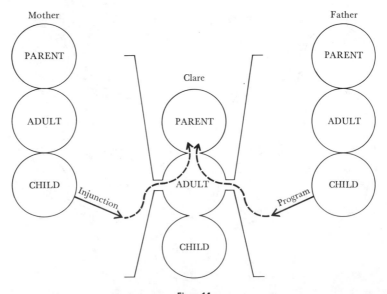

Figure 14

Recording Parental Messages in the Psyche

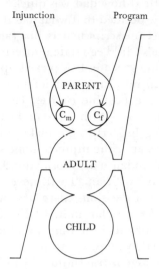

Figure 15
Recording Injunction and Program
(incorporated parental ego states)

and Clare's detectors picked them up. He wasn't sure what they meant until the day he "went too far" and destroyed the teddy bear and grandma's picture; then he knew what the "bad vibes" meant and he understood that they were triggered specifically by his energetic fun activity. He decided "not to be X" in the belief that that's what mom really meant when she had "that look" of alarm on her face.

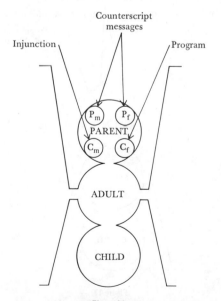

Figure 16
Addition of Counterscript Messages

His detectors also noticed how dad was quick to console mom too and, without knowing why, he decided that what dad did made good sense.

Now I will reconstruct the script-matrix diagram as in Figure 14.

The vector from mom's Child ego state is directed toward Clare's Child-derived behavior, a Child ego state. It is picked up, however, by the detector and the data is taken into his ADULT for processing. In his primitive ADULT, Clare considers the possible choices. He also remembers all the times he saw dad console mom. With this data he makes a decision "never to be X," thus beginning his script. To make sure he will never forget, he records into his own PARENT the injunction message he perceived. Little Clare doesn't have an abundance of information but he is not stupid. He figures out how to survive with an "I will never be X" decision and he means NEVER! After that decision, Clare has two special places in his PARENT (Figure 15). Like a radar unit, Clare's detectors are always in motion, always on the lookout. When mom and dad tell him how to be, he respects them because they know so much.

The counterscript message is transmitted by messages given later, when Clare understands words. After he listens to the counterscript messages and accepts their value, he creates two more special places in his PARENT. Now Clare might be represented as in Figure 16.

When he gets more sophisticated, Clare hears other messages, such as father telling him the best way to take care of mother and then mother's frequent description of her nice little Clare, the attribution. These are also processed by Clare's ADULT and then are lodged in the PARENT. Now the picture looks like that in Figure 17.

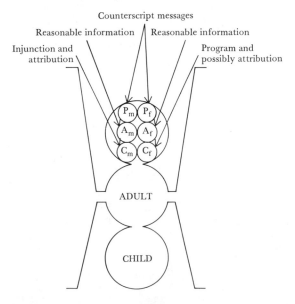

Figure 17
Further Incorporation of Scripty Influences

The foregoing diagrams are much too simple. Clare has been detecting all sorts of additional information from mom and dad in each of their ego states and he has decided to store much of it in his PARENT. The diagrams do point up that all information for the child is processed by the neopsyche, though it may be stored in the exteropsyche. Berne spoke of the automatic hi-fidelity recording, and it does appear that much of the information is stored in unmodified form.

INJUNCTIONS

I have intentionally avoided a specification of the injunction since I am convinced that the conclusions of Clare may be, but are not necessarily, congruent with the intent of the enjoiner. Factors such as the style, intensity, and frequency of transmission of the Adapted Child communications of mother are involved. In addition, the variety of CHILD-derived behaviors of Clare which evoke the injunctive messages will also be involved. Ultimately the intensity, pervasiveness, and restriction that result from the early decision will be determined by Clare.

Other factors include the extent to which there was behavior similar to mother's on the part of other authorities, with which Clare reinforced his decision. Injunctions may originate from more than one parent figure, as may also program, attribution, and counterscript messages. Furthermore, messages from these various sources may be consistent and thus complementary, or they may be discrepant and in conflict. Again, it is the young individual who, under various stresses, synthesizes the mixed messages and refines the decision so as to fit his or her world view. It is in recognition of the growing child's capacity for adaptation and organization that I have chosen to view injunctions in a somewhat different way than have other authors.

I believe that injunctions can be best understood as the conclusion of a young person under stress who is determined to survive. Regardless of what the authority figures intended to communicate, the expectations are perceived by the offspring as a demand that she or he arrest the development of some inherent potential that is just beginning to "blossom." The youngster is faced with a dilemma. On the one hand, the experienced desire is "I want to be me, all of me." On the other hand, there is the issue, "Being all of me is dangerous and I might not survive." The child resolves this with a decision, "For the purpose of my survival I shall not become all that I am capable of being." Thus, purposeful and decisional limitation of potential is the essence of the early decision, which has been described as obeying the injunction.

I therefore refer to all injunctions as represented by a prototypical command, "Don't become that which you are fully capable of being." This can be contracted to a simple "Don't be you." By use of the concept of a prototypical injunction, one realizes that each person in script will refine that injunction to the issues which seem most relevant and this can vary with the stage of development.

There is further material to be considered in the relationship between the perceived enjoining parent and the offspring. While it is true that the early decision reduces the conflict between mother and Clare, it also sets up an internal conflict within Clare. Mother, of course, is relieved by his changed behavior and is again willing to nurture. We now have the ideal setup for perpetuation of an unhealthy symbiotic relationship between mother and Clare. This could be pervasive or it could be limited to a special aspect of the total experience of mother and Clare. Regardless of the pervasiveness, Clare has made a decision to live as a psychological cripple to some extent and he must now build a support system so that whenever his survival requires the use of that suppressed potential, which he has decided not to use, someone else must be available to provide him with the means to solve a problem.

Problem-solving in connection with fulfillment of desire is throughout most of childhood a two-person event. Children, with their limited supply and organization of information, have abundant experience which demonstrates to them how the big people can do almost any job much better. This is often intensified when grownups are intolerant of a youngster's bumbling experiments or when the grownup is in a Child ego state and seems to need to prove superiority.

As a child develops, she or he will be aware of the difference in skills between self and parents, and with this recognition will find ways to have the grownups assist in problem-solving. I find Adapted Child behavior of two types: the utilitarian and the exploitative. By utilitarian adaptations I mean those which are found to be highly useful and which are in response to parental instructions. This would include the automatic behavior of brushing teeth, learning manners, dressing one's self, etc. While they may have originated as an intent to please, if they are utilitarian adaptations the pleasing of others is no longer a significant issue in the activity.

SYMBIOTIC ADAPTATIONS

The exploitative adaptations are quite another story, and in my view they are the critical aspect of scripty living. To describe their development, I will again go back to the very young infant and discuss behavior. As previously mentioned, the infant is born with biological desires and an ability to act motorically. The existence of the desire is accompanied by energization of the muscles and when fulfilled there is cessation of desire. It is also true that prolonged nonfulfillment of desire results in temporary cessation of activity. In an oversimplified way, the infant responds to desire by either "push" or "collapse"; energization or de-energization; "Do something" or "Do nothing."

In the process of experimentation the child learns that both push and collapse can get results that have a consistency. Thus, both push and collapse will acquire purpose within the early interpersonal relationships.

Utter collapse becomes a form of contrived passivity which invites others to take action. Push is combined with compliant behavior which invites others to take action to reward the compliance. Push, in and of itself, becomes aggression which invites others to action by submission. The child discovers the accomplishments of these three behaviors very early in life and begins to refine them so as to have a fine collection of options, all of which invite another person, the parent or parent-surrogate, to assist or to totally accomplish the problem solving.

These behaviors are a part of every child's experience. The actual behavioral choices which are most highly developed will be those endorsed within his or her family system. Even if it were possible to avoid the initiation of scripts, the youngster would have explored these pathways and then later would have abandoned them in the establishment of autonomy.

When a youngster, under stress, decides to create a life script, she also simultaneously decides to forgo autonomy and to pay the price of perpetual dependence, partial if not total—the unhealthy symbiosis. When that occurs, the three modes of exploitative adaptation become the means to perpetuate two-person problem-solving.

What the child discovers as she refines and elaborates these three modes of behavior, in accordance with the reinforcement by reward or punishment, is that escalation to certain critical levels will produce results, i.e., someone will act in her behalf.

When collapse or passivity is escalated, the youngster becomes progressively more helpless, thus inviting assistance. I have characterized this behavior as typical of the *Helpless Adapted Child* mode. Through Helpless Adapted Child behavior one may be cared for by those who wish to nurture. A Helpless Adapted Child recognizes those persons who have an exaggerated investment in caretaking and invites rescue by them. The Helpless Adapted Child is often a skillful victim who has learned well the fine points of displaying inability and confusion.

In a second mode, where compliance is refined, the youngster starts off by doing as instructed. With more development, she does what she usually has been instructed to do in the past, i.e., the expected. With further refinement, the child will do what she anticipates may be desired even without an indication of a wish or request. I have labeled this behavior as typical of the *Helpful Adapted Child* mode. By Helpful Adapted Child behavior one will be cared for by those who reward good deeds, such as mothers or fathers who like dutiful children—children who perform rather than those who explore and make messes in the process. The Helpful Adapted Child will also appeal to helpless victims who say "Thanks a heap," and then the Helpful Adapted Child feels good. The Helpful Adapted Child mode provides for "rescuers" who often see others as "victims" even when they are not.

In the third mode, aggression or push is first refined by the youngster by making louder noises and by being demanding. With more development she will punch or scream or stomp and even break things to show how threatening she can be. I have labeled this behavior as *Hurtful Adapted Child* mode. By Hurtful Adapted Child behavior one invites relationships with those who want to "help" upset people or those who take perverse pleasure in being victimized.

Each of these three modes or styles is contrived and therefore one can attach to each a statement of intentionality. For the dutiful Helpful Adapted Child mode it is, "If I do what you expect, you will do what I want." For the idle Helpless Adapted Child mode it is, "If I appear incapable, certainly you'll do what I want." For the pushy Hurtful Adapted Child mode it is, "If I threaten you enough, you'll do what I want." Behind each of these styles is an unfulfilled CHILD hunger, so each is an elaborated method for fulfilling basic desires. These three modes are coping behaviors which invite or "force" participation by others. They are designed to solve problems, but not autonomously.

Jacqui Schiff and Aaron Schiff[7] and related authors have described all three modes as passive behaviors and have further defined passivity as non-problem-solving behavior. Because I see these behaviors as actively contrived patterns for fulfilling needs, I do not consider them to be passive in the usual sense. I agree that they are nonautonomous patterns, that they are implemented by a discounting operation, and that they serve narcissistic strivings which I would equate with grandiosity as used by the Schiffs.

Discounting, as an intrapsychic operation, is closely related to the psychoanalytic concept of *denial,* wherein the significance of persons, events or operations is diminished or exaggerated. Interpersonally and in problem solving, the scheme devised by the Schiffs provides a useful conceptualization.

It is by means of the discounting or denial that a person repetitively initiates interpersonal actions designed to foster nonautonomous behavior or unhealthy symbiotic relationships. In elaborated forms, these racket become games or miniscript sequences manifested in individual or interpersonal behavior. The Hurtful Adapted Child, Helpful Adapted Child and Helpless Adapted Child are early prototypes for the roles respectively of Persecutor, Rescuer, and Victim initially described by Berne in the Life Game, *Alcoholic,*[8] and later elaborated by Karpman in the development of the drama triangle.[9]

In the exploration of the three modes of exploitative Adapted Child behavior, children test out the amount of escalation needed. In the process they also discover that sudden switches from one mode to another are often more productive of the desired result than escalation. Thus, even in early life, children engage in prototypical "gamey" behavior.

I have not mentioned yet another factor which also seems to be a part of developing these modes of Adapted Child behavior: not only do young sters find their authority figures responsive, they observe that the authorit figures themselves frequently display the same behaviors. Thus, both modeling and shaping, in a behavioral sense, occur as the youngster develops. This could be typified by an internal decision, "If it's good enough for Mom or Dad, it's good enough for me."

Finally, regarding these three exploitative Adapted Child behaviors, I want to emphasize that in the perpetuation of such nonautonomy it is axiomatic that the youngster experiences an alteration of self-esteem in relationship to others which is accompanied and supported by unpleasant feeling states that preclude intimacy. These alterations give rise to the attitudinal sets of OKness and not-OKness, which differ in each of the three Adapted Child modes. The unpleasant feeling states are an aspect of what Berne described as "feeling rackets." Since the three modes are contrived operations, substituted feelings are commonly an aspect of the contrivance, a feature previously described by authors such as Steiner[10] and English.[11]

The perpetuation of these styles means a reliance on more primitive information-processing of a concrete or magical type involving fantasies of the future or the past, as described by Robert Goulding.[12] They can only be perpetuated by denial of the reality of the "here and now" and a reliance on an "as if" relationship to one's world. The predominance of the "as if" qualities gives rise to the distortion of other persons, which is described psychoanalytically as *transference processes*. This same operation has appeared in TA literature in the recent writings about "frame of reference" and "redefinition" by Schiff.[13]

I view the basis for all of this as *narcissism,* an issue which strangely enough has not been emphasized by authors in TA. I have no doubt that Berne chose not to write directly about narcissism, although his analytic training would certainly have emphasized it. Other than Jacqui Schiff's and Aaron Schiff's references to grandiosity, it has been avoided. I believe the issue cannot be avoided when one refers to the satisfaction of hungers as a motivating feature of the human experience.

Within writings in transactional analysis there has been much emphasis on the creative potential of the Free Child aspects of the archeopsychic CHILD. I concur in that emphasis and seek the release of it in the course of treatment. Few if any authors, other than Berne, have acknowledged the destructive potential of the Free Child.[14] In the impulsive seeking of gratification, infants and children operate with naive disregard of the possible consequence of their choices. Because they do not appreciate danger and destructiveness, there is a possibility that destructiveness will result unexpectedly and then they or others may be injured or destroyed. Berne touched on this when he wrote of "The Little Fascist" and "The Demon." I am not suggesting the existence of a purposeful destructiveness or a death instinct, rather I refer to the incidental destructiveness accompanying impulsive behavior. It is precisely because of an awareness of this potential that mothers and fathers, invested in the survival of the offspring, choose to provide parenting. It is the knowledge that the youngster will learn the rules that causes parents to take pride in consistency, since eventually this consistency of structure will be incorporated into the PARENT of the offspring where it will serve as an automatic barrier to injury and destruction until the child develops the logical reasoning, which Piaget described as "formal operations." When that occurs the youngster can provide self-protection, not by rules, but by appraisal of the situation and through abstract reasoning.

There is the need for a thorough understanding of both the intrapsychic and the interpersonal operations, organization, and adaptation, if treatment is to be more than an intellectual exercise.

I believe that we humans are always seeking fulfillment of our basic hungers. Berne included stimulus hunger, and I concur in its inclusion as a biological need. In early life we seek direct gratification by taking or demanding, by showing our frustration readily. As we discover life's processes, we develop devious ways to fulfill these hungers while at times appearing to be invested in something else. The Adapted Child modes, though somewhat devious, have utility. They represent the new directions which our narcissism has taken. For most of us these adaptations have been effective in significant ways, and it is no wonder that we are reluctant to relinquish them even when they are very painful. Even ADULT-derived functions ultimately serve to provide opportunity for gratification of primitive desires. Thus, our narcissism is forever with us and we develop increasingly sophisticated mechanisms for fulfillment.

In the service of fulfilling narcissistic desire we find opportunities to direct our aggression. This may be manifested in compliant, defiant, or obstructionistic patterns, as when one holds tightly to childlike adaptations. Aggressiveness may appear as rigidity when Parental ego states are present. It may appear as effective and accurate action in the Adult ego states. Throughout there is the channeling of aggressive energy.

OTHER TA CONCEPTS

STROKES   Much has been written about strokes. Whether they are positive or negative, conditional or unconditional is determined by the receiver rather than by the originator. I am concerned at times by those TA clinicians who seem to teach patients that the only acceptable positive strokes are those that are provided exactly as desired by the patient. The hazard in this is the fostering of a state of chronic stroke deprivation. People give strokes from the thinking and feeling state that they happen to be experiencing. If I have just stubbed my toe, yet manage a hasty and perhaps weak wave of greeting to a friend, I have actually extended myself considerably. If the friend discredited the stroke because of its briefness and lack of vigor, then he would have missed out. I therefore encourage acceptance of positive strokes always, even when they seem compliantly contrived. The "sugary" stroke may be the only kind a scripty person believes will be accepted, and to refuse it discounts that person who is doing the best she or he knows. I do not concur in the recent attempt at redefinition of strokes and discounts on the part of Kahler and Cooper.[15]

STRUCTURING OF TIME   The structuring of time by the six methods originally described by Berne—withdrawal, ritual, activity, pastime, games, and intimacy—suffices in instances of social relations, which is the context he considered. In my opinion, there are two categories of experience which also must be considered, and I therefore add a seventh and an eighth method of structuring time. Creative Self-Expression is a category I use to account for those periods of time when an individual is absorbed in joyful and thrilling self-expression, especially as typified in artistic endeavor. As examples, one can picture a painter, creatively exploring the blending of color and form, or the musician who is improvising and figuratively "out of his head and into his fingers." These are moments of intense pleasure akin to intimacy with the self and perhaps related to "peak experiences" as described by A. Maslow. They are often solitary experiences yet they are rich and rewarding even in the absence of stroking by others. Those who have had such experiences of Free Child expression value them highly and conduct their lives so as to have more.

The eighth category I add is "Altered States of Consciousness." Initially I thought only about sleep, but now include various other experiences which by some have been labeled mystical and/or religious. The emerging field of transpersonal psychology relates to these states of being which are methods for structuring units of time.

Not uncommonly, I have heard the six categories arranged in a hierarchical order supposedly related to the intensity of stroking available. When that is done, intimacy is usually considered the richest source and games next. I believe that this arises out of an unstated value system, and I am not aware of hard data which supports the premise.

Usually another statement accompanies this ordering, which is, "The richer the supply of strokes the greater the 'risk.' " The implication is that intimacy is risky, although the nature of the risk is not explained. Both patients and trainees have often indicated that if one desires intimacy, one must accept the risk of being hurt. Openness and trust, the antecedents of intimacy, are seen as exposing oneself to danger.

I do not support that view because I believe it endorses a childhood myth. Openness and trust will lead to hurt only when the person who is being "open and trusting" maintains a hidden insistence that others must respond accordingly. Thereby he or she can be disappointed and claim rejection. To offer one's self to others in loving openness and trust is not a potentially hurtful experience. The responses one receives will be related to the other person's freedom from or contamination with scripty mistrust. I believe that the person who is script-free will be candid and trusting and will set a model which will evoke similar responses from many other persons. True openness and trust are *not accompanied by hidden demands.* The greatest gift for one who gives is to have the offerings warmly received by another and no other reward is needed. Unresolved issues remain to the extent that one operates with a strong expectation that others must respond by giving equally.

A perennial question arises! "What is intimacy?" I believe this experience involves two persons and it is as though their individual essences have merged to become as one. There is a sense of warmth and beauty and to a great extent an obliviousness to the environment. Communication occurs, but it seems unnecessary because each almost automatically comprehends the other. I suspect that intimacy has many forms of expression and that one of the reasons it is not easily described is that when persons are in an intimate experience, there is no investment in objectively defining the experience. In fact, to do so would stop it. As a consequence, we know how we are just prior to intimacy with trust, love, and investment and also how we are after the experience with longing, reverie, and fondness. The experience itself is anticipated or recalled as warm and desirable.

DISCOUNTING   Effective communication and interpersonal relationships involve an awareness and accurate appraisal of self, other, and context. Discounting is present when any one of these is distorted by exaggeration, diminution, or denial. Discounting is a mental operation of the discounter. It may also be communicated verbally or nonverbally.

An unfortunate thing which occurs among persons invested in TA is the occasional use of knowledge about discounting as a manipulative or exploitative device. This is typified by the statement "You discounted me," which so frequently carries with it a parental flavor of "You shouldn't do that!" I suspect these occasions arise out of a misunderstanding about the purpose of confrontation. Therapeutically, the confrontation of discounts is done for the purpose of enhancing an individual's awareness of scripty styles. The confrontation is offered as information or identification, not accusation. In fact, if it is offered or responded to as accusation, the information will have little value since it will likely serve to perpetuate scriptness and avoidance of autonomy.

RACKETS   The second area of theory which seems not to be clearly understood is rackets. Berne and other authors have at times described rackets as feelings and at other times as processes or operations associated with feelings. (Steiner,[16] English,[17] R. Goulding,[18] Erskine,[19] and Zalcman have made notable contributions in this area). Rackets are closely related to feelings, generally feelings of an unpleasant type, though triumph and apprehensive glee seem also to qualify. The racket includes an intent to achieve gratification of personal desire through the exploitation of others. The effectiveness of the exploitation is dependent upon the individual's creation, communication, and escalation of feeling states. I label feelings associated with such a design as "rackety feelings," to identify their contrived and exploitative potential. Also, I differentiate such feelings from those that are spontaneous responses to the unexpected, whether the unexpected is threatening or rewarding.

The design aspect of the racket is basically seen in the three modes of exploitative Adapted Child behavior previously described. In fact each of these operations is carried out with a display of rackety feelings.

I concur with Berne that rackets frequently are taught within the family, as could be seen in the description of Clare. I believe, however, that youngsters are versatile and that they also find models in persons other than mother and father or siblings. I do not concur with the view that each person has one racket or one rackety feeling. Each of the three exploitative Adapted Child modes has a different design and each may involve the display of a different rackety feeling. It is not uncommon for an individual to rely primarily on one of the three Adapted Child modes, at times seemingly to the exclusion of others. In such instances one rackety feeling may predominate. An example of this would be the person who commonly operates as a Hurtful Adapted Child with frequent displays of anger.

Racket designs and rackety feelings are most exquisitely elaborated in interpersonal games. Here we see the intensity of feelings escalated and used exploitatively in the beginning, middle, and especially at the payoff. Rackety feelings can, however, exist as a solitary operation, as when in fantasy a person projects himself or herself to some other time or place. Under such fantasized "as if" conditions, the feelings may exist modestly or with great intensity. This is the situation for worriers and has been well described by R. Goulding.[20] I believe that this is also the essence of Berne's formulations of "reachback" and "afterburn."[21]

The importance in rackets is to realize that they are based in nonautonomous styles of mental operations which rely on concrete prelogical thinking methods. They exist with a presumption that problem-solving will be accomplished by competitively forcing some other person's involvement. Thus, it is easy to see how it has been said that games support one's racket.

GAMES Games are basically deceptive and therefore dishonest maneuvers and sequences that are intended to force a dependent relationship and to perpetuate nonautonomy to insure security. They provide predictable strokes, thus fulfilling biological desires and some existential needs related to the person's world view.

It is my personal position that games, as an operation of the game player, are exclusively an Adapted Child activity and directly the consequence of the three exploitative modes previously described. Games occur because of an individual's perpetuation of prelogical thinking and problem-solving, a process related to an internal frame of reference supporting a belief that autonomous functioning is either not possible or is very dangerous.

I also recognize that game playing in a social setting may be the intent and design of only one person in a relationship of two or more people. Generally, however, all parties have an investment in the process, with each doing the best with his or her skills to maintain competitive complementary connection. As with discounting and rackets, processes and maneuvers are perpetuated in belief that it is the "best" way to get what one wants. In this instance "best" means predictable, based on past experience.

Games which are initiated and perpetuated by discounting and rackets are the consequence of transferential "as if" relationships and are a clear indication of unresolved conflicts. They provide a substitute for intimacy in that there is a binding closeness and a predictable supply of strokes. Biological and existential needs are fulfilled also. For persons who have had little skill or practice in autonomous problem-solving and intimacy, games have utility and provide for survival.

Because of my view that games represent Adapted Child behavior, I find only partial compatibility with material written by others. For instance, in the past games frequently have been detailed using two sets of structural diagrams; these show the vectors of stimuli and responses that start with and are perpetuated through complementary ulterior transactions until one party responds with a crossing of the previous response or stimulus. To demonstrate my present view I will first describe a brief game in words and then pictorially.

> *Patient: 1. (Social message)* "I feel so bad, doctor, do you believe there is any help for me?" This statement is an ostensible Adult request for information, but actually is a cover for a hidden plea for caretaking. *2. (Psychological message)* "Will you be my protector and solve my troubles for me?"
>
> *Therapist: 3. (Social message)* "I know you're worried and you can rest assured that there is help for persons like you." This response is an ostensible Adult provision of information with a tone of nurture and protection. It is motivated, however, out of the therapist's desire to be seen as omnipotent and thus be assured of a supply of strokes from the grateful people whom she or he "helps." *4. (Psychological message)* "I'll help you and tell you what to do if you will honor me for being so 'considerate.' "

In this instance patient and therapist are each relating to the other as if the other were a significant person from the past. This typifies transference and countertransference and could be readily diagramed using Berne's description of group imago and persona.[22]

Following these first two exchanges, there may be a series of transactions, all duplex and supporting the myth that each will take care of the other by providing strokes. Eventually one or the other will become impatient of the process and the communication will change. In this instance, I ask the reader to assume that the patient is playing *Do Me Something* so that helplessness is gradually escalated. The therapist is playing *I Was Only Trying to Help You* and is becoming intolerant of the patient's

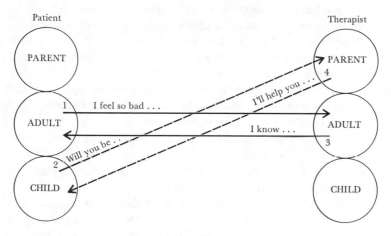

Figure 18
Duplex Transactions in Game

avoidance of change and his increasing passivity. Eventually, then, the therapist responds.

> *Therapist: 5. (Social message)* "You're not really cooperating with me, you're not even trying!" (said with anger and disgust). Client responds by weeping, with an apology and also a promise to do better in the future.

In a fairly traditional way this series of transactions might be diagramed in compressed stages as in Figures 18 and 19.

Figure 18 shows the initial complementary duplex transactions—a pattern which continues. Figure 19 shows what happens at the switch when the therapist suddenly and openly becomes critical. Now the social trans-

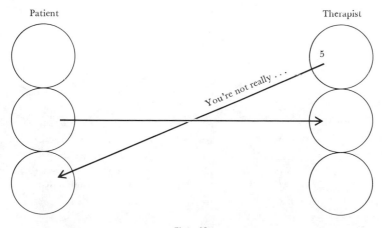

Figure 19
The Transactional Switch in Game

action is crossed and the negative strokes have been given and bad feelings have been escalated for both. The therapist is angry and the client is hurt.

The dissatisfaction I have with such a diagram is that I believe both patient and therapist are operating primarily under the influence of their archeopsychic CHILD. The apparent ego states appear pseudo-Adult and pseudo-Parent because both want the other to provide needed strokes and caretaking, as if they were themselves incapable of directly asking for strokes or believed that by asking directly they would be rejected.

I find that the Helpful Adapted Child is often misperceived as a "Nurturing Parent" ego state. The Hurtful Adapted Child is often misperceived as a "Critical Parent" ego state. The Helpless Adapted Child is occasionally misperceived as a "contemplative Adult" ego state. Game-playing is dependent upon a perpetuation of these misperceptions.

Here is a modification of the usual transactional diagram (Figure 20): (1) Patient (from Helpless Adapted Child, but sounding Adult): "I feel so bad. . . ." (3) Therapist (from Helpful Adapted Child, but mimicking Nurturing Parent while sounding Adult): "I know you're worried. . . ."

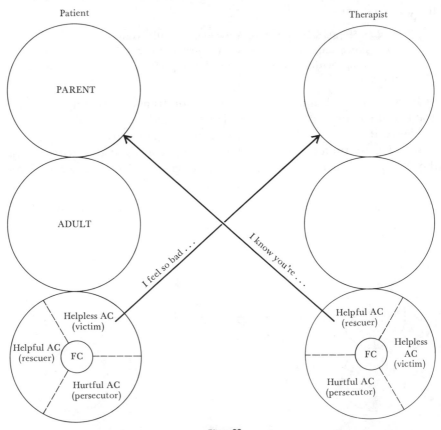

Figure 20
Game Initiated by AC Transactions

Next, I diagram the switch (5) preceding the payoff, when the therapist says angrily, "You're not really. . . ." What the therapist is really intending is an escalation with a flavor of "You ingrate, I'll bet you're never going to show appreciation for my efforts," which is also a shift to the Hurtful Adapted Child mode (Figure 21).

I believe both continue to operate in a Child ego state but that each. is misidentifying the other in a transference process. The attempt to force caretaking eventually breaks down and one of the two players shifts suddenly to a different Adapted Child ego state. In the instance described, the therapist moved from Helpful Adapted Child to Hurtful Adapted Child while the client remains in Helpless Adapted Child.

The game has occurred because the client approached the therapist and was relating to him as if the therapist were going to be a good "parent" who would want to take care of a small waif. The therapist related to the client as if the client were a good "parent" who would reward a dutiful helpful child. In this instance, as the "child" therapist began to be helpful

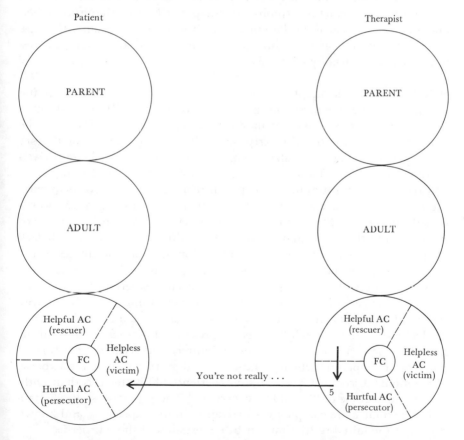

Figure 21
The Gamey Switch (helpful to hurtful AC mode)

the reward was not forthcoming, which soon resulted in the switch to the hurtful childlike way that the therapist previously used when mom and/or dad were not sufficiently responsive to dutifulness. The entire sequence occurs because both therapist and client are relating to the other on an "as if" basis. Had the therapist not made the switch so soon, it is entirely possible that the client eventually would have switched to a vindictive hurtful position with a statement like, "You don't really care about me!" In the latter instance, the client's game would have been *Now I've Got You, You SOB*, instead of the therapist's game of *I Was Only Trying to Help You*.

It would also be possible for the client to pull what I sometimes refer to as the Victim-Victim switch. Had the client, instead of becoming hurtful, ended up saying, "I just knew no one would understand me," there would have been an effective switch while he remained in the Victim position. The switch is from a position of "I'm so incapable" to "I'm so put upon."

It is my position that all games, all rackety feelings, and all discounts of self, are the product of exploitative Adapted Child mechanisms. When one sees what appear to be Parent or Adult ego states in games, they are pseudo-Parent and pseudo-Adult designed to mislead and attempt a restoration of an unhealthy symbiosis.

SCRIPTS   The life script is a self-chosen and personal plan for living which determines the directions and main events that will occur in one's lifetime. While the individual may appear at times to achieve or to be "successful" socially, the life script basically produces an unsatisfactory life experience. The dissatisfaction results from a sense of being driven or restricted and is characterized by repetitive unpleasant-feeling states and recurring difficulties in interpersonal relationships. As a consequence, there is little intimacy experienced and often a diminishing of the worth of self and others. The ultimate outcome may be tragic or vexatious or stagnant, and the individual often fits the cultural stereotypes with lack of spontaneity, creativity, and joy. This scripty life plan originates in the early years of life and is based in decisions made by a child who is determined to survive by making sense of the events experienced. Since the stresses are experienced as coming from the controlling authority figures, the child concludes that certain ways of being are dangerous and thus by decision chooses to exclude direct expression of those ways from his or her life. The expression then becomes indirect and stylized, resulting in patterns of adaptation which produce partial gratification at the expense of emotional discomfort, yet with an experience of "Better this than nothing" or an attitude of "Wouldn't everyone?" The primitive stylized adaptations become more complex with advances in life experience and knowledge, but the initial restrictions on full expression of the self persist.

The script begins in an early and somewhat sweeping decision of a child based on the injunction. The injunction is a command which the youngster concludes is the intended message from a powerful parent. This conclusion derives from the youngster's perception, with all its possible immature inaccuracies, of what the parent's behavior was intended to communicate. The injunction, therefore, is not a statement in words; rather it is the message a child believes the parent intended. The life script is initiated when a youngster decides to follow the injunction.

It does seem likely that harsh injunctions are concluded when one or both parents frequently control the actions of their offspring by resorting to the exploitative Adapted Child styles. This is the craziness that has been referred to in the statement that "The injunction originates in the crazy Child of the parent."

I believe that such Adapted Child behavior on the part of parents is experienced early in life by the offspring and that the stress of such influence, therefore, begins at a preverbal and prelogical time of life. I also believe that the complementary program from the other parent begins early. To the extent that attributions occur, they also seem to have an early existence. Therefore, it is quite likely that in most instances the script-initiating *decision* occurs fairly early in life. Counterscript messages, being verbal, come at a later time. Injunctions, programs, and attributions have major impact because of the primitive emotional overloading that they produce.

The early script-setting decision has these elements:

1. Obey the injunction.
2. Choose an escape hatch.
3. Establish prominent life position.
4. Begin a racket with feelings.
5. Assure perpetuation of dependency by discounting or by game-playing.

Thus, through the process of initiation of scripts, the child, by decision, agrees to permanently suppress personal potential. This results in a psychologically crippled existence which is manifested in continued efforts to establish unhealthy dependency relationships and with consequent loss of autonomy. The person living in script will demonstrate, periodically or consistently, the major Adapted Child styles that were rewarded in the original nuclear family.

Life, then, becomes a repetitive series of rehearsals, each of which is initiated with a belief that "This time things will be different." Nevertheless, the underlying plan eventually comes into play and the sequence ends with disappointment or disaster instead of rewards. These rehearsals may be very brief, lasting only a few moments, or may be elaborated over longer periods of time. Whether one sees them as miniscript as described by Kahler,[23] or as games, or as an extended epoch, the pattern or theme can be readily traced throughout. It is this underlying scheme that I believe to be the true racket. The unpleasant feelings that accompany the racket are an integral part of the scheme and have to do with the perpetuation of the attitudes or life positions.

There has been a differentiation by many authors as to the script destiny. Steiner describes tragic scripts which are different from banal. The essential difference is whether or not the script calls for tissue damage. I consider all scripts to be tragic. The tragedy is not, however, in the potential for tissue damage (which could occur), but rather in the fact that living in script denies one the autonomy, creativity, spontaneity, expression, and joy of which all are capable. In a sense, Steiner seems to have alluded to this when he described three types of script (no-love script, no-mind script, and no-joy script) and then suggested that we are all afflicted by each of the three to some extent.[24] I believe that he was on the right track, and I prefer to describe the three exploitative Adapted Child styles rather than to say we each have a touch of three scripts. Actually, it is the blending of these Adapted Child styles that gives the script its unique nature.

Each of us is familiar with each Adapted Child style. Whenever in life we are faced with a problem situation, if we do not believe we possess the information and skill to solve the problem, we will begin with exploitative Adapted Child behavior. The more frequently we believe that independent problem-solving is not possible, the greater will be the display of Adapted Child behavior.

I have also previously written how, in the extreme, one will see certain "escape hatches" as available.[25] In essence, the escape hatches become the ultimate destinies of the Adapted Child-controlled scripty living. In effect, while there may be a major theme, there can also be secondary themes. The escape hatches correlate well with the three Adapted Child modes. Hurtful Adapted Child can be escalated to homicide, Helpful Adapted Child escalated to suicide, and Helpless Adapted Child escalated to psychosis. The knowledge of this has practical utility in treatment since the decisional closure by the client of one escape hatch may make the other two more likely.

It is my observation that even persons whose lives may be described as banal, when explored will frequently reveal an underlying tragic outcome which is secretly held. Unless that secret tragic outcome is dealt with, all the rest of the treatment can become a superficial exercise. What I am suggesting here is closely related to the degrees of impasse described by R. Goulding.[26]

LIFE POSITIONS The concept of life positions appears early in the TA literature.[27] The implications are that each of us has a fixed position to which we hold tenaciously. The positions are I'm OK, You're OK; I'm OK, You're not-OK; I'm not-OK, You're OK; and I'm not-OK, You're not-OK. The views about which position is first vary between Berne and T. Harris.[28] F. Ernst suggests that the position is a changing phenomenon.[29] The resolution seems easy when I use the exploitative Adapted Child modes as a frame of reference. The Hurtful Adapted Child attitude is "I'm OK, You're not-OK"; the Helpless Adapted Child is "I'm not-OK, You're not-OK"; and the Helpful Adapted Child is "I'm not-OK, You're OK."

With this realization it is easy to see how in the life of most persons in script, one of the three modes tends to dominate interpersonal relationships. To that extent, it would be easy to cite it as the particular individual's life position. Actually, I find more compatibility with Ernst's ideas about the ending of encounters. There may be a preponderance of one attitude, but not an absolute exclusion. Life position then becomes a matter of preponderance rather than an absolute.

CHANGE, CURE, AND GROWTH: THE TREATMENT PROCESSES

The most frequent question that I am asked in professional settings is, "Is TA good for all diagnostic categories?" My common answer is that TA is not a pill given for a condition. In many ways I'm appalled to hear the question, since it reveals lack of knowledge about TA.

All professionally responsible treatment begins with diagnostic appraisal being initiated in the first contact. By diagnostic appraisal I do not intend a labeling process. Rather, it is an appraisal of the person's immediate request and the process of instilling hope for change, which is paramount. I have often stated that the purpose of the first visit is to make a second visit possible. For anyone who elects to continue in treatment, TA has potential utility as does knowledge of any other conceptual framework.

To the extent that people who change in psychotherapy usually like to make sense of themselves, I have found TA highly useful. This is especially true in the training of psychotherapists, who generally are most comfortable in being able to identify a diagnostic entity in the belief that therefore prescription is more readily accomplished.

Because the concept of script focuses on stylistic repetitions manifested in interpersonal behavior, the student readily gains understanding of the dynamic processes of psychopathology by using TA concepts. Furthermore, it is easier to identify what is happening. There is less likelihood of defining something as wrong. Similarly—since the behavior, thinking, and feeling originated in a decisional process—there is less chance that a person will be labeled as incurable.

DIAGNOSIS   I initiate conversation in the first interview with the statement, "What are we here to do?" In so doing, it is my intent to convey the "we-ness" of our future relationship and to immediately test the fantasies of the patient as to what I am expected to do. I proceed from there to gather information about the major features of the person's troubles. While doing so I test the person's access to the Adult ego states and observe the various "cons" presented through denial, projection, and rationalization. I also test the responsiveness to humor and to my responses at a literal level. Before the interview is completed, I am prepared to recommend a next step in the process, which may be for further appraisal on a group or individual basis, entry into a group, referral to another source for evaluation or treatment, or no further treatment. If treatment seems indicated, I make clear that I will function as a friendly detective who will present evidence of incongruities. Here it is important for the patient to understand that the information will not be presented as accusation or condemnation, but rather as identification that is intended to enhance awareness of self-operations.

Provided the patient has reasonable access to the Adult, I will accept him for out-patient treatment after specifying the treatment I am willing to offer. For individuals with evident severe affective, thought, or character disorders I recommend other initial approaches relevant to their specific symptoms and degree of impairment.

In addition to the appraisal of current function, I also collect data regarding historical and current patterns. Using the life script as a frame of reference, therefore, the life-script questionnaire and script checklists provide a frame of reference for initially analyzing the situation. One of the major connections I want to make in the beginning is to identify the schemes by which the client has achieved failure in the past and to see where these same schemes will undermine the treatment process. Early recognition is important since the undermining begins at the same time that curative processes are initiated.

While therapists are approached as helpers, it is also to be realized that for the client the therapist has a scripty role. Since the client has had much more experience in maintaining his or her script, the therapist must be wary not to step into the pitfalls. The most effective way for avoidance of pitfalls is the use of behaviorally specific goal-oriented contracts.

CONTRACT STAGES   The essence of treatment is contained in the establishment of a meaningful contract. Treatment can be viewed as consisting of contract-related stages, as follows: (1) contract negotiation, (2) contract specification, (3) contract performance, (4) contract completion, and (5) contract affirmation.

Contract negotiation begins at first contact and continues until a behaviorally specific terminal point is identified. All the maneuvers between therapist and client at initiation of treatment are for the purpose of clarifying and identifying important issues. It is most important that the contract be focused on goals that are desired and chosen by the client. Therapists who set goals for their clients will be ultimately disappointed.

When the contract is specified, both therapist and client can understand the task ahead and each will proceed with whatever skills they possess. An effective treatment contract defines the working relationship between therapist and client and contains a statement of a goal of change to be attained by a future decision by the client. The goal of change may be described as social control, which can be achieved by decontamination of the Adult. The goal may be a change to script-free autonomous living, to be attained by deconfusion of the Child through detailed script analysis, a process comparable to the "working through" of transference processes in psychoanalysis.

I am wary of descriptions of "soft" and "hard" contracts which I occasionally hear about. The implication is that "hard" contracts are goal-specific, whereas "soft" contracts do not contain a clear statement of change. I think there is great hazard that "soft" contracts are designed by the Adapted Child of both the therapist and the client as a means for each to think that progress is being made while in actuality the life script continues in the guise of "progress" in treatment.

Once the contract is specified, the active exploratory phase of treatment begins, during which time the client is confronted with the incongruities of thinking, feeling, and behavior that serve to perpetuate the scripty ways. There is within this process both an invitation and a challenge to change, and to do so as soon as possible. It is to be noted also that there may be reason to renegotiate a contract in the light of material uncovered in the course of treatment.

Eventually there will come the event or events by which a client makes a clear "connection" as to what purposes the old scripty styles have served. When, simultaneously, there is a realization of what new ways would be more effective, a decision becomes possible which results in change. In effect, these decisional changes must provide that the hungers of the Child be fulfilled predictably and adequately.

It is my experience that change is basically a change in one's "stroke procurement" system and it will not be explored or instituted unless and until there is reasonable assurance that the new system will be equally effective to the old. It is for this reason that when setting contracts, among other details, I ask the question, "What's in it for your Child?" If that question is not answered, I am most dubious that the contract is capable of being sustained after attainment.

Contract completion occurs with the decision to institute new ways of being and is most often the reason for discontinuance of treatment. In a few instances, however, continued contact with the therapist and group are desirable. I refer here to those persons who have instituted extensive changes in their lives and who have not as yet developed a new supportive social network and its predictable supply of strokes.

All persons who have lived in script have over the years developed a social network which consisted of individuals who were willing to support the client in his or her scripty way. That social network will become rebellious and/or coercive as changes are initiated. If the client's life had been quite restricted, then the transitional period may be traumatic if stroke deprivation is a threat. When such a threat occurs, the client may benefit from some additional contact with the therapist and group while developing a new social network.

This is the process which I would identify as contract affirmation. Eventually I would expect the client to terminate treatment relationships with the therapist as autonomy is firmly established.

References

1. Eric Berne, *Transactional Analysis in Psychotherapy*, New York, Grove Press, 1961.
   Eric Berne, *The Structure and Dynamics of Organizations and Groups*, Philadelphia, J. B. Lippincott Co., 1963.
   Eric Berne, *Games People Play*, New York, Grove Press, 1964.
   Eric Berne, *Principles of Group Treatment*, New York, Oxford University Press, 1966.
   Eric Berne, *Sex in Human Loving*, New York, Simon & Schuster, 1970.
   Eric Berne, *What Do You Say After You Say Hello?*, New York, Grove Press, 1972.
2. Stanley Woollams, "Formation of Script," *Transactional Analysis Journal, 3*, no. 1 (January, 1973).
3. Taibi Kahler with Hedges Capers, "The Miniscript," *Transactional Analysis Journal, 4*, no. 1 (January, 1974).
4. Woollams, *op. cit.*
5. Jean Piaget, *The Origins of Intelligence in Children*, New York, International Universities Press, 1952.
6. R. D. Laing, *Knots*, New York, Pantheon Books, 1971.
7. Aaron Wolfe Schiff and Jacqui Lee Schiff, "Passivity," *Transactional Analysis Journal, 1*, no. 1 (January, 1971).
8. Berne, *Games People Play, op. cit.*
9. Stephen Karpman, "Fairy Tales and Script Drama Analysis," *Transactional Analysis Bulletin, 7*, no. 26 (April, 1968).
10. Claude Steiner, *Games Alcoholics Play*, New York, Grove Press, 1971.
11. Fanita English, "The Substitution: Rackets and Real Feelings (Part I)," *Transactional Analysis Journal, 1*, no. 4 (October, 1971); Fanita English, "Rackets and Real Feelings (Part II)," *Transactional Analysis Journal, 2*, no. 1 (January, 1972).
12. Robert Goulding, "New Directions in Transactional Analysis," in Clifford J. Sager and Helen Singer Kaplan, eds., *Progress in Group and Family Therapy*, New York, Brunner/Mazel, 1972.
13. Jacqui Lee Schiff, *et al.*, *The Cathexis Reader*, New York, Harper & Row, 1975.
14. Berne, *What Do You Say . . . , op. cit.*
15. Taibi Kahler and T. Cooper, "An Eightfold Classification System for Strokes and Discounts," *Transactional Analysis Journal, 4*, no. 3 (July, 1974).
16. Steiner, *op. cit.*
17. English, *op. cit.*
18. Goulding, *op. cit.*
19. Richard Erskine and Marilyn Zalcman, Paper in publication on rackets.
20. Goulding, *op. cit.*
21. Berne, *What Do You Say . . . , op. cit.*
22. Berne, *Structure and Dynamics . . . , op. cit.*
23. Kahler with Capers, *op. cit.*

24. Claude Steiner, *Scripts People Live,* New York, Grove Press, 1974.
25. William Holloway, "Beyond Permission," *Transactional Analysis Journal,* *4,* no. 2 (April, 1974).
26. Robert Goulding, "Three Degrees of Impass," *Voices, 10,* no. 2 (1974).
27. Eric Berne, "Classification of Positions," *Transactional Analysis Bulletin, 1,* no. 3 (July, 1962), p. 23.
28. Thomas A. Harris, *I'm OK, You're OK,* New York, Harper & Row, 1967.
29. Franklin H. Ernst, "The OK Corral: The Grid for Get-On-With," *Transactional Analysis Journal, 1,* no. 4 (October, 1971).

TWELVE

THE MINISCRIPT
Taibi Kahler

Why do people go into feelings or thoughts of not-OKness? Are there observable, measurable sequences involved in the process? What are the dimensions of OK behavior? How can people learn to feel and think of themselves as OK? The Miniscript concept was devised in response to these questions and presents itself both as a technique for monitoring OK behavior in self and others and as a theory of human behavior. It is at once consistent with transactional analysis principles and compatible with the main body of traditional psychoanalytical thinking.

THE TECHNIQUE As a technique, the miniscript focuses on behavioral clues to internal processes. Words, tones, gestures, posture, and expressions reflect and reinforce emotional reality. By monitoring these behavioral clues, a person can identify the beginning sequences of not-OK behavior in himself and in others. Decisions to stop these behaviors can then be made, effectively preventing the sequence of not-OK behavior.

Regardless of the particular therapeutic technique being employed by the therapist, use of the miniscript affords both therapist and client a yardstick by which to measure OK and not-OK behavior second by second, transaction by transaction. In the therapist-client relationship, as well as in all relationships, invitations into OK and not-OK thinking and feeling are being issued constantly; hence the critical importance of being aware of ourselves and the signals we are sending moment to moment.

As a concept, the miniscript can be used as a framework in dealing with the broad range of psychopathology, as illustrated below.

The miniscript as a technique is like other tools such as options,[1] script rehearsal,[2] egograms,[3] drama triangle,[4] reparenting,[5] redecisions,[6] and OK Corral work.[7] As with these other tools, it is as valuable as the people who use it. In therapy, identifying drivers and making contracts to stop specific words, tones, gestures, postures, and facial expressions constitute steps one and two. Then the client is encouraged to replace not-OK behavior with any problem-solving or "get-on-with-it" behavior. A contract to do this is made and homework is given.

THE CONCEPT   The miniscript, as a concept, is a system that affords a framework which spans structural, transactional, game, and script analysis. Using miniscript as a concept means thinking within its framework without having to use its jargon. Thinking miniscript will enable us to monitor whether we are in OK or not-OK behavior second by second, regardless of the technique we use. As a technique, miniscript falls within a Bernian approach.

I am writing about *how* we do things, not what we do; *how* to stay in OK behavior and invite it in others, and how to avoid, in ourselves and others, driver behavior that is the beginning of not-OK behavior.

Conceptually, then, a miniscript framework can be used with other approaches because it requires only thinking miniscript, not using it full-blown, in order to guarantee staying out of drivers and monitoring how far into OK behavior we want to go. The best approaches or techniques (content) can be sabotaged by getting into not-OK behavior and feelings (process drivers).[8]

HISTORICAL DEVELOPMENT OF THE MINISCRIPT

REINFORCING THE PROCESS SCRIPT   The term "miniscript" is a misnomer. When I first discovered sequences of behavior that precipitated the fall into not-OKness, I labeled the ideas that formed around my observations "miniscript," thinking that what I had pinpointed was the script within a script to which Eric Berne had referred, using mirror imagery. Later, I saw that such was not necessarily the case. What was happening was that, at the driver level, people were reinforcing their main life or process script. In *What Do You Say After You Say Hello?*, Berne stated his premise that the script (or some diluted version of it) is repeated over and over again in the course of a person's life—in a year, a day, a moment. This repetition compulsion, as Berne called it, is observable to the eye of a watchful therapist and the activity reveals, sometimes in a glance, the story of a client's life.[9]

While I was running a group which met in a state mental hospital, I began focusing on the hunch that people go into their counterscript before they play their script injunctions or feel their rackets. I thought that this insight had possibilities for more effective diagnosis and treatment, yet I realized that there were hundreds of counterscripts, surely too many to incorporate into a useful tool. Thinking that a comprehensive set of counterscripts could be arrived at, I took home several tapes of my group. I listened to them carefully with the intention of identifying the behaviors specifically associated with counterscripts. In this work I consistently consulted Berne (and I continue to find almost every theoretical issue foreshadowed in his work).

| Drivers: | Compliance (inner feelings) | | Words | Tones | Important behavior | | |
	Physical	Psychological: internal discount			Gestures	Posture	Facial expressions
1. Be perfect	Tense	"You should do better"	"Of course" "Obviously" "Efficacious" "Clearly" "I think"	Clipped Righteous	Counting on fingers Cocked wrist Scratching head	Erect Rigid	Stern
2. Try hard	Tight stomach Tense shoulders	"You've got to try harder"	"It's hard" "I can't" "I'll try" "I don't know"	Impatient	Clenched, moving fists	Sitting forward Elbows on legs	Slight frown Perplexed look
3. Please me	Tight stomach	"You're not good enough"	"You know" "Could you" "Can you" "Kinda"	High Whine	Hands outstretched	Head nodding	Raised eyebrows Looks away
4. Hurry up	Antsy	"You'll never get it done"	"We've got to hustle" "Let's go"	Up and down	Squirms Taps fingers	Move quickly	Frowning Eyes shifty
5. Be strong	Numb Rigid	"You can't let them know you're weak"	"No comment" "I don't care"	Hard monotone	Hands rigid Arms folded	Rigid One leg over	Plastic Hard Cold

Figure 1
Driver Chart

Berne suggested that behavioral diagnosis should revolve around awareness of a person's words, tones, gestures, facial expressions, and posture.[10] I followed this suggestion and coupled it with the assumption that there is a finite number of behaviors which every person exhibits before going into not-OK behavior, playing a script injunction, or feeling a racket. By listening carefully to the tapes I came up with four categories of counterscripts: Please Me, Be Perfect, Try Hard, and Hurry Up. Then I presented my ideas to the group and filled out "driver charts" for each member (Figure 1). I was still not convinced, however, that I had covered the counterscript waterfront.

Engineering students who came to the group from a nearby university provided the clue to the fifth driver, or counterscript message. Prone to holding in their feelings and assigning to others power over themselves, they exhibited what I came to call the Be Strong driver. Since then I have presented the miniscript to thousands of people across the country and on three continents. The five drivers are the functional manifestations of not-OK (structural) counterscripts.

THE NOT-OK MINISCRIPT What I had described as the miniscript was actually the not-OK miniscript. I had been concerned with the sequences that lead to not-OK behavior because I had observed that people seem to be in their drivers, or below them and thus into some pathology, most of the time. Several years later, when I moved to California and began working with Hedges Capers, he suggested that I focus also on the OK sequence, even though we may be in it a very small percentage of the time. At my invitation Hedges proceeded to write the section on OK behavior in the article on miniscript,[11] affixing the labels "allower," "goer," and "wower" to the OK sequence I had identified. His permission and consistent invitations to focus on OK behavior, as well as his hypothesis that the Little Professor is the initiator of behavior, were valuable contributions.

One of the chief things I became aware of as I did my group work, lectured, and wrote was the distinction between process and content in therapy. Process refers to *how* we say something; content, to *what* we are saying. Both are integral to human communication. Thus, as a therapist, I may be offering a sterling analysis (content) to a client. Yet at the same time, if I am in driver behavior (process), I am inviting the client into not-OK behavior and sabotaging therapy. Miniscript monitoring is the quickest and most accurate way I know to keep that from happening.

This does not, however, mean that I could not be doing "good therapy."

Functionally, I could be sabotaging by inviting driver behavior; yet, bound energy in the client's structural Adult may be activated later as the client cathects unbound and free energy into his Functional Adult, resulting in an "Aha" as he integrates the content of my message.

The functional analyst is interested in what he can look at and diagnose. Clearly to him, "Don't feel what you feel" is a command expressed from the not-OK Critical Parent. He can defend this by pointing out the not-OK Critical Parent words, tones, gestures, posture, and facial expressions.

Thus, the functional analyst maintains that script injunctions are tapes expressed from Parent. While the structural analyst speculates, the functional analyst can demonstrate. Now that scripts can be identified transaction by transaction, a clear understanding of the difference between structural and functional analysis is crucial.

This does not mean that I believe that the script matrix and structural views of scripts are not valuable. I am saying that script theory advancement can be hampered by a structural referee stopping the play because the quarterback "double dribbled."

I expect that developmental theory will be greatly enhanced by shifting from an inferential structural approach to a demonstrable functional approach. I also believe differences of opinion about cathexis can be integrated easily by understanding the difference between structure and function.

HUMAN DEVELOPMENT

In therapy I was often asked the questions, "If I am responsible for making myself feel racket feelings, why do I make myself feel them? Who sets out to feel bad?" My response is that each of us has varying degrees of investment in positive or negative strokes, and I use the battery concept to explain why this is so.

Picture Rothchild as he emerges from the womb. Inside him he has a system analogous to an OK battery and a not-OK battery.[12] These batteries at this stage are not self-activating and must be charged from the outside. Mother and father have to provide the stimuli, a reality that reflects the behaviorist thrust. Now let us assume that Rothchild's parents engaged in lots of not-OK behavior. Note that they engaged in not-OK behavior; not that they themselves were not-OK. We are OK; sometimes we have not-OK behavior. That means they will have an investment in reinforcing not-OK behavior in Rothchild. Hence, his not-OK battery will receive a good deal of stimulation. Notice that the child, with only a Child ego state at this point, has little choice in the matter. What he does have is, literally, a life-or-death decision. He can resign himself to live with not-OK strokes in a not-OK world and survive; or he can set himself up to shrivel and die by refusing the negative attentions he is offered. A fearful choice indeed!

After a while Rothchild's Little Professor intuits that mother's and father's not-OK Parent ego states will not always be around to charge up his batteries. This he will have to do for himself. He needs a closed system, one that will enable him to live apart from his parents. So he begins to build himself his own parent which becomes the Parent ego state. Functionally, this Parent ego state is a tape recorder. It houses the multi-

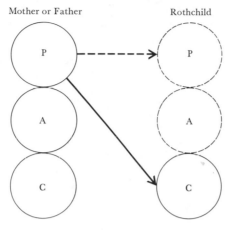

Figure 2

tude of messages, verbal and nonverbal, sent to Rothchild by his biological parents. Equipped with this Parent, Rothchild is ready to launch out into the world of transactions.

Now suppose Rothchild is eight years old. Someone comes along and says, "My, you're a bright young man!" Suppose, too, that at this point his stroke reserve is low and his Little Professor wants to charge up his not-OK battery. The sequence Rothchild will go through to the get the job done is as follows. The Little Professor will use the charge that is left in the not-OK battery to activate a tape in the Parent. In this case the tape might say, "Don't trust people." This is the Parent message, then, that is played and aimed at Rothchild's Adapted Child. On being called "a bright young man," the Adapted Child responds by feeling threatened and wondering, "What's his angle?" The result is that a warm fuzzy stroke has been fended off and Rothchild's not-OK battery has received a unit of charge.

This sequence occurs transaction by transaction with the Little Professor deciding on what payoff will be garnered and at what level of intensity.* The sequence is essentially the same for charging up the OK battery. The tapes are OK life-giving tapes which cause us to feel authentic rather than racket feelings. The only variation is that in the OK sequence the tape might be run through the Adult so that we are aware of what is going on.

The important thing to note in both of these sequences is that it is Rothchild himself, and not the outside stimulus, that caused him to feel the way he felt. In a sense, "stimulus" is an incorrect word, since what another person does can only invite and not "stimulate" in a mechanical sense a particular response in another. In other words, we are in charge

---

* The Little Professor is not diagramed functionally because he or she is a structural component.

Rothchild

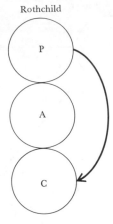

Figure 3

of our emotional lives whether or not we choose to recognize it. It is our self-image that is the significant factor in determining what we will get out of a transaction. In TA language, the payoff emerges from the interaction between the Little Professor and the stroke reserve. The crucial shift is from the external parents to the internalized Parent, from exterior to interior stimulation.

A slightly different way of looking at this dynamic comes from using Berne's concept of the palimpsest.[13] I once thought Steiner's and Gouldings' approaches were mutually exclusive in developmental theory. They are not. I see Steiner's behavioristic emphasis as valuable in understanding mother's and father's Parent ego states activating the Child in Rothchild. This interpretation has as a major premise that the Child ego state requires a Parent ego state to activate it (Figure 2).

When Rothchild has integrated his parents' Parent ego states into his own Parent, he is activating his own Child (Figure 3).

No longer is the environment "making him feel," he now is "making himself feel." He is deciding what injunctions he will accept, and from here on he is responsible for his feelings. People can only invite him to play OK or not-OK internal sequences. The Gouldings emphasize a humanistic decision framework. I see this shift of Rothchild listening to his own Parent rather than to his mother's or father's as the beginning of Berne's palimpsest. Rothchild now has the needed element of the script provided by his own P to be able to put forth his script socially.

STROKE RATIONALE, A PARENT CONTINUUM, AND EGOGRAMS

I agree with Hedges Capers' view that each transaction begins with the Little Professor (LP). The LP selects whether he or she will be initiating an OK sequence or a not-OK sequence, based on battery recognition "requirements."

The internal loop theory suggests a third level of communication (the first two being the social and the psychological), and that is the internal. My hypothesis is that the LP chooses to go through either the negative or positive battery, as he or she is limited by recognition "requirements." The Parent is cathected and a tape is played. The Adult may be the next to be cathected and lastly the Child.

The LP has two not-OK Parent parts and two OK Parent parts to select from (although there will be a sequence there too). The four parts of the Parent (functional) are: the not-OK Critical Parent (−CP), or the Persecuting Parent; the not-OK nurturant Parent (−NP), or the Rescuing Parent; the OK Critical Parent (+CP), or the Protecting Parent; and the OK Nurturant Parent (+NP), or the Permission-giving Parent. Examples of the Parent parts are:

−CP: "You're stupid."
−NP: "Try hard for me, honey."
+CP: "Stop! Don't kill yourself."
+NP: "It's OK to live."

INTERNAL SEQUENCES   Both sets of diagrams (Figures 4–7) reflect the observable sequences of the OK and not-OK miniscript.

The internal loop theory stresses the importance of accepting responsibility for one's own feelings. The battery theory gives rationale for choosing to make oneself feel authentic or rackety, no matter what the psychological invitation.

If the Parent is involved in every transaction as a tape recorder and

Not-OK Internal Sequences

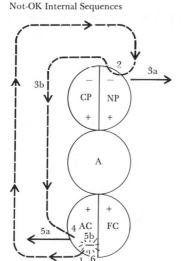

1. LP through −B.
2. −NP tape is activated. Rescuring begins with internal discount about "how to make it" (related to one of five drivers).
3a. Active rescuring (Parent drivers).
3b. Influencing rescuring.
4. −AC is activated.
5a. Active Child drivers.
5b. Internalized Child drivers.
6. −B is recharged.

Figure 4
The Rescue Sequence

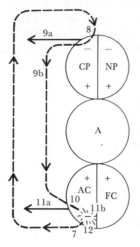

7. LP through —B.
8. —CP tape is activated. Persecuting begins.
9a. Active persecuting.
9b. Influencing persecuting.
10. —AC is activated. Rackets are felt.
11a. Active —AC (or VC).
11b. Internalized —AC (or VC).
12. —B is recharged.

Figure 5
The Persecution Sequence

player of OK and not-OK messages, then it becomes the dependent variable, or the constant. This means that by observing the Parent functioning, we can understand how a person may be treating him or herself. (I believe also that transactions are projections.) (Figure 8).

The way a person cathects his or her active Parent will consistently reflect how his or her influencing Parent[14] is coming on to the person's own Child. This can be a diagnostic tool as well as an educational and therapeutic tool.

While working with Leda, a depressive, suicidal patient, this sequence

OK Internal Sequences

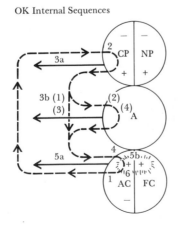

1. LP through +B.
2. +CP tape is activated. Protecting begins.
3a. Active protecting.
3b. (1) Influencing protecting.
   (2) A is activated. Computing begins.
   (3) Active A.
   (4) Internalized A.
4. +AC is activated
5a. Active +AC.
5b. Internalized +AC.
6. +B is recharged.

Figure 6
The Protection Sequence

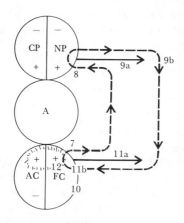

7.   LP through +B.
8.   +NP tape is activated. Permission-
     giving begins.
9a. Active permission-giving
9b. Influencing permission-giving.
10. FC is activated. Authentic feelings
     are felt.
11a. Active FC.
11b. Internalized FC.
12. +B is recharged.

Figure 7
The Permission Sequence

of her influencing Parent was observed. In a parenting technique, Leda expressed what she wanted to feel (authentic feelings).

Therapist: You know what you want to feel. Will you turn on your OK Nurturant Parent and give yourself that permission?
Leda: Yes. (*Into a mirror*[15]) You're really stupid—(not-OK Critical Parent).
Therapist: How do you feel?
Leda: Not any better. Sounded like my father. (*Into the mirror*) Try and feel good for me—(not-OK Nurturant Parent). Still doesn't feel right. I always had to please my mom. (*Into the mirror*) Stop feeling bad! Feel good!—(OK Critical Parent). That isn't warm, yet I'm feeling stronger. (*Into the mirror*) It's OK to be you. It's OK to feel good—(OK Nurturant Parent).

THE SILVER RULE   Such a Parent continuum can reflect several considerations. I agree with what might be called the silver rule of therapy: "A therapist can help clients to help themselves generally just as far as the therapist has helped himself or herself."

The modified egogram[16] is a valuable tool with such a conceptual framework.*

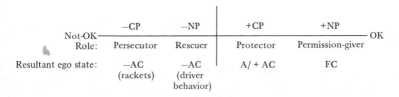

	−CP	−NP	+CP	+NP	
Not-OK					OK
Role:	Persecutor	Rescuer	Protector	Permission-giver	
Resultant ego state:	−AC (rackets)	−AC (driver behavior)	A/ + AC	FC	

Figure 8

* For purposes of focusing on the "−" and "+" parts of the Parent and AC, slight modifications have been suggested.

1. We would predict that a therapist who feels rackets often and exercises his or her not-OK CP (PP) would give frequent invitations to the client to have a similar egogram.
2. We would predict that a therapist who rescued frequently would invite his or her client to be at the not-OK NP level at best. Although there would not be as much gaming and racket payoffs as in (1) above, this example does emphasize racketeering[17] and rescuing. Much not-OK AC behavior without frequent escalating to rackets would be observed.
3. We would predict that a therapist who used the OK CP with directives and imperatives and who used A often would invite a client to have an egogram with low not-OK CP and not-OK NP, low not-OK AC, high OK CP and A, yet still low OK NP and FC. It is as if such a therapist teaches people how to protect themselves by learning OK ways to avoid rackets and to handle drivers, yet does not give them the invitations to permission and Free Child behavior. This is like purgatory—not hell but certainly not heaven. Generally, the greater the pathology the more appropriate it is for the therapist to operate from his protection level. This is because the client needs OK Parent tapes in order to activate his A, +AC, or FC.
4. We would predict that a therapist who operates out of A, OK NP, and OK FC more than OK CP, A, and OK AC will invite the client into the same egogram (modeling). Such a person will smell the flowers and see the birds. This is the "most OK" of egograms, of Parent continua.

This concept suggests a "quality dimension" to transactions. As such, techniques like Karpman's options[18] can be used with more therapeutic selectivity.

THE MINISCRIPT: TRANSACTIONS AND GAMES

The miniscript concept is inclusive enough to cover any transaction and to identify where a person is, existentially, in any transaction. People will be in the OK or not-OK miniscript at every point, since both represent behaviors. The not-OK miniscript is drawn using a triangle (Figure 9). At position 1 are the drivers, reflecting a position of "I'm OK if. . . ." On Ernst's OK Corral,[19]

−+	++
GAF	GWO
−−	+−
GNW	GRO

they are on the line between the I'm OK, You're OK and the I'm not-OK, You're OK quadrants. At position 2 are the stoppers[20] reflecting I'm not-OK, You're OK. When a person is here he is Getting-Away-From (Ernst) and not Getting-On-With. Typical rackets associated with position 2 are inadequacy, confusion, worry, guilt, and sadness. Although I am identifying "rackets," I am referring to results of internal discounting

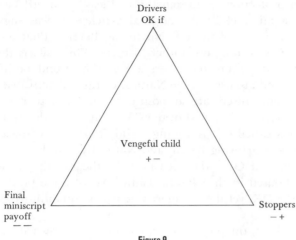

Figure 9

that combines inappropriateness, nonrelevancy, and grandiosity. Payoffs can be collected at this level by playing such games as *Kick Me* and *Stupid*.

Position 3, the Get-Rid-Of position, reflects the Vengeful Child,[21] although it can also reflect the not-OK Critical Parent. Rackets here are anger, hostility, and feelings of triumph. Payoffs come from games like *Now I've Got You—You S.O.B.*, *Blemish*, *See What You Made Me Do*, and from games in the Blameless family.

The Get-No-Where position is 4. There, rackets of depression, despair, hopelessness and the sense of being unwanted and unloved are felt. Corner players, believing they're damned any way they turn, often move to this position.

The flip side of the not-OK miniscript is the OK miniscript (Figure 10). It, too, can be drawn as a triangle, with allowers replacing drivers in the first position. Allowers are commands from the OK Critical Parent which

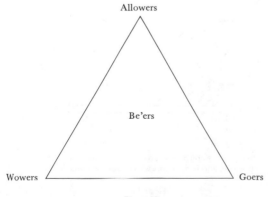

Figure 10

give a person protection to do something: Please yourself! Feel OK even if you make a mistake! In the original article,[22] it was suggested that allowers are the result of the OK Nurturing Parent. That is inaccurate. It is not "It's OK to do," but rather "Do it." This reflects the sequence of protection and permission. Goers are at the second position on the OK miniscript and are used in the Natural Child and activated by the OK Nurturing Parent. Be'ers are at position 3 and are turned on by the OK Critical Parent and housed in the OK Adapted Child. In the original article, this was called OK Affirming Child. This, too, is inaccurate since it is not the OK Nurturing Parent and Natural Child, but rather the OK Critical Parent and OK Adapted Child. In the fourth position are the wowers, also housed in the Natural Child. All of these positions assume I'm OK, You're OK, yet there is more OK payoff, quantitatively, at 4 than there is at 2.

In Figures 11–13, three types of transactions are shown for the purpose of illustrating the internal sequences that are at the heart of miniscript analysis.

OK COMPLEMENTARY TRANSACTION (Figure 11) Social Level: "I feel close to you." This statement is ostensibly Natural Child to Natural Child.

Internal (Little Professor) Level: At this level we learn what projection is about. Person B has a prior investment in charging up his OK battery. He hears the invitation to get a positive payoff in the warm words spoken to him by Person A.

Person B then consults his Nurturing Parent, plays a tape such as "It's OK to be close," and feels the good feeling in his Natural Child. The

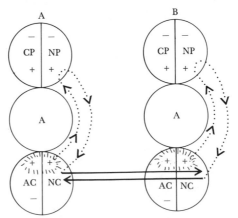

In order for congruence, diagnosis of tones, gestures, posture, and facial expressions must be considered.

Figure 11
OK Complementary Transaction

sequence is completed when Person B responds with a complementary message, "I feel close to you too."

It is important to note here that a position of and investment in OK behavior is essential for anyone to give or receive positive strokes. If OK behavior is not present, discounts will be offered; or, in the case of the person receiving the stimulus, even a positive stroke will be turned into a negative one in some way. In other words, when a person is charging up his OK battery, the natural tendency will be to project that OK behavior onto others.

This is the essence of the message, "It is better to give than to receive." As I give OK behavior, I am in OK behavior, charging up my positive battery. I will continue in this as long as I *don't* believe that I can *make* the other person feel good by what I say.

CROSSED TRANSACTION (Figure 12)   Social Level: Person A, with an investment in not-OK behavior, offers the stimulus, "You're stupid!" Person A is coming from his not-OK Critical Parent and aiming his barb at Person B's not-OK Adapted Child. Person B responds from his Adult: "Sounds like you're angry at me. Are you?"

Internal Level: Person A begins the transaction from his Little Professor, on the lookout to charge up the not-OK battery. He goes through the not-OK battery, using what charge is left in it to activate a tape in his not-OK Critical Parent, a tape that suggests that he is stupid. Some of the feeling of inadequacy will dribble down, as it were, to his own not-OK Adapted Child but most of it will be projected toward the not-OK Adapted Child of Person B.

Person B, however, is in OK behavior and has a stake in remaining there. Hearing the invitation from Person A to feel stupid and inadequate, Person B's Little Professor goes through his OK battery, plays a tape in his

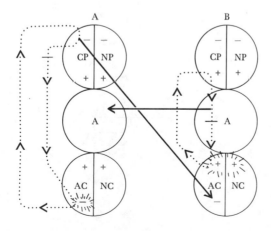

Figure 12
Crossed Transaction

OK Critical Parent that says, "You're not stupid. Think!" Playing this tape activates the Adult, from which ego state Person B responds, "Sounds like you're angry with me. Are you?" This response crosses the transaction. Dynamically, Person B is aiming for Person A's Adult and inviting him to join him in OK behavior.

In Martian, Person A is saying to Person B: "Get into your not-OK Critical Parent and beat on yourself so we can agree that we both have power over each other's feelings." B's Martian response is: "No, I won't join you. I'll stay in my OK behavior, get an OK payoff, and invite you into your OK behavior."

ULTERIOR TRANSACTION (Figure 13)   Social Level: This transaction sounds like Adult to Adult. Person A says, "Where did you hide the TV schedule?" Person B responds: "You're the one who always hides it." Ostensibly, this sounds like Adult to Adult, yet each is coming from his not-OK Critical Parent, aiming for the other's not-OK Adapted Child. The social level of ulterior transactions (and thus games) reflects a structural framework, while the psychological and internal levels are based on a functional approach. Ulterior transactions usually require a structural view, as does contamination and exclusion. Berne's transactional game diagraming then forces a shift from structural to functional as there is a shift from the ulterior to the social.

Internal Level: Person A begins by activating his not-OK battery through the Little Professor. He then goes up to the not-OK Critical Parent and plays a tape like, "You're stupid (for not keeping track of the TV schedule)." Having played that tape, he delivers a message from the same ego state directed at Person B's not-OK Adapted Child. The non-adult word in his question is "hide"; tones, gestures, facial expression, and posture would also have to be noted for a full behavioral diagnosis

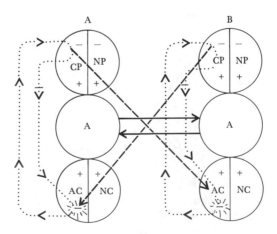

Figure 13
Ulterior Transaction

to be made. The Martian for the message is: "I'm mad and frustrated. Join me in these or similar bad feelings."

Person B, hearing the message and with a similar "need" to charge up his not-OK battery, accepts the invitation to actuate his own not-OKness. Using not-OK battery energy, he goes up to his own not-OK Critical Parent and directs the Martian message "You're stupid." Note that Person B bought into the word "hide" in Person A's message and used it for his own not-OK purpose. Note, too, that some of the energy generated by the playing of the tapes in the Parent in both these cases dribbles down; it is introjected to the not-OK battery, giving it charge. Thus, when we are in not-OKness with others, we are charging up not-OKness in ourselves.

GAME ANALYSIS Game analysis has been an important part of traditional TA. This has been all to the good, since, as Berne described them, games are ways in which people avoid straightness and intimacy, "collect stamps," reinforce unhelpful life positions, further their scripts, and, in general, go into not-OK behavior. Yet game analysis can be cumbersome and time consuming. The sequence of games demonstrates the sequence reflected in the not-OK miniscript. Eliminating behavior at the driver level (position 1) will automatically prevent an individual from entering into games. What follows is a detailed unpacking of this thesis. The game formula includes these elements:[23]

Con + Gimmick = Response → Switch → Crossup → Payoff. Let us use this formula for in-depth analyzing of the first game Berne identified, *Why Don't You, Yes But* (WDYB).

The Con (Figure 14) is represented by the opening gambit, differing in nuance in each case but comprising the basic announcement, "I've got a

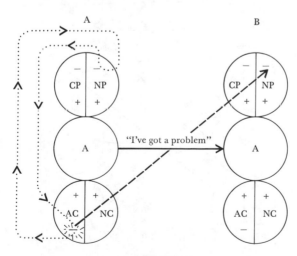

Figure 14
Con

problem." This may very well be a statement of fact; yet it is a Con because the person reporting the fact failed to follow up with a request for help. "Do me something" is the Martian message.

Thus the Con functions as a baited hook thrown out to catch people who have investment in charging up their not-OK battery through the rescuing sequence.

Before the game initiator flings the bait, however, he will have gone through the rescuing sequence. It will start with the Little Professor, who will sense a recognition need and be on the lookout for opportunities to have it satisfied. The Little Professor will use the charge left in the not-OK battery to play a tape in the not-OK Nurturing Parent which may say "The way to make it is to try hard." He will hear that tape in his not-OK Adapted Child and aim the "I've got a problem" message at the not-OK Nurturing Parent of anyone within range. In leapfrog fashion, the game initiator will aim at others so they will go through the same internal sequence he did.

At the Gimmick level (Figure 15), if a person has a similar investment in not-OK battery charging and if he has the driver's Try Hard and Please Me ranking high, he is likely to rise to the bait and hook himself into the game. It is important here to underscore the fact that each person bears the responsibility for his or her participation in games. By contrast, a behavioristic approach, as I have previously described it, tends to invite a person to ask the question, "What do I do to hook another person into a game?" This is an inappropriate question because it suggests that there is something I can do or say which will cause someone else, in an instrumental sense, to respond in a certain way. It takes two people (or more)

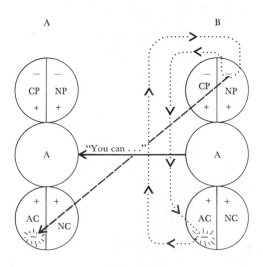

Figure 15
Gimmick

to play a game and each will get his or her negative payoff from the action.[24]

The respondent, then, having recognition needs similar to those of the initiator, will go through a driver, perhaps Try Hard with Please Me behind it, and project "Why don't you . . ." from his own not-OK Nurturing Parent, thus complementing the ulterior transaction of the initiator. While this is going on, the untrained interlocutor will hear nothing but a polite, ostensibly helpful conversation about practical living, presumably Adult to Adult.

At Response (Figure 16) the respondent will offer one or more suggestions to the initiator as to how he might solve his problem. To each of these the initiator will counter with a "reason" why the suggestion is plausible but unworkable, due to certain aspects of the initiator's unique circumstances. This reflects the persecuting sequence. The initiator will go to his not-OK Critical Parent and play a tape like "You're dumb, you're of no help to anyone." This tape releases energy with which the not-OK Critical Parent beats on his own not-OK Adapted Child. At this point he will feel a twinge of racket, perhaps inadequacy or frustration, then trigger his Vengeful Child, who aims the "Yes, but . . ." counter at the not-OK Critical Parent of the respondent, the same ego state from which he had just come in order to be able to feel racket feelings. Had he chosen, the initiator could have stopped at position 2 on the not-OK miniscript, saying something like "That's a good idea" but thinking to himself that he'll never have the time or energy or expertise to carry it out. Instead, in order to set up for the payoffs, he went to position 3.

The next step in the game is the Switch (Figure 17), without which there would be no game. The Switch in WDYB is silence. Actually, how-

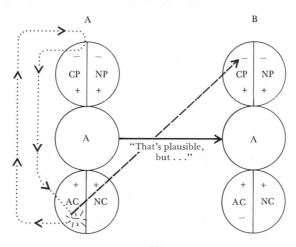

Figure 16
Response

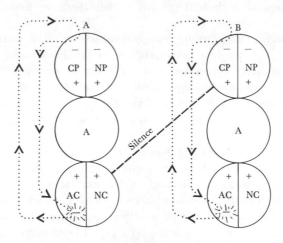

Figure 17
Switch

ever, there are two switches in games: one occurring when the respondent goes from rescuing to persecuting; the other when the respondent goes from projecting to introjecting.

The silence of the switch leads to the moment of confusion identified by Berne as the Crossup (Figure 18) and associated with position 2 on the not-OK miniscript. The respondent becomes aware that the initiator will not accept his not-OK Critical Parent suggestions, some of the energy of which he has been aiming at his own not-OK Adapted Child. At this point he wonders "What happened?" The stage has been set for the payoff.

The Payoff (Figure 19) comes for the initiator as he feels triumphant, having activated his Vengeful Child through his not-OK Critical Parent. "Ha! You can't help me, can you?" he intimates to his fellow gamer.

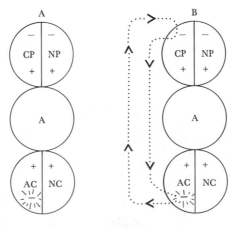

Figure 18
Crossup

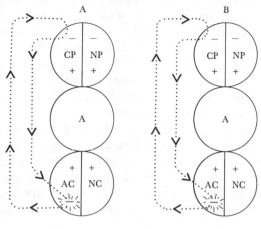

Figure 19
Payoff

His respondent, on the other hand, has several possibilities for payoffs with options for stopping at positions 2, 3, or 4.

Jacqui Schiff contends that all games begin with a discount.[25] I agree with this contention and add that the discounts can be incorporated into what I call driver behavior, which has at its base the internal discount of the not-OK (rescuing) Nurturing Parent. Thus, to repeat, all games can be stopped at their inception by stopping drivers. The drivers are at the Con and Gimmick levels of the game formula. Response, Switch, and Payoff may be represented at positions 2, 3, or 4 while the Crossup lies exclusively at position 2. Note that the Adult, while appearing to be present is actually excluded in both the game formula, as per Berne, and in the not-OK miniscript. It is true that we can argue from a structural point of view that energy is available for Adult cathexis. Functionally, however, the "real Selves" involved are the Parent and the Child.

By viewing games with this precision, we can see that "Good Games" are Cons and Gimmicks without the Response, Switch, Crossup, or Payoff. As such, only the rescue sequence with drivers is involved. This certainly is not from I'm OK, You're OK; nor from I'm OK, You're not-OK; I'm not-OK, You're OK; or I'm not-OK, You're not-OK. The existential position is "OK if." Thus, there are no "Good Games," just less bad ones.

DRIVERS

The concept of drivers can be approached from three aspects: internal discounts, behavioral diagnosis, and script invitations. In terms of internal discounts, I believe that more discounting behavior can be identified by looking at drivers than in any other way. The internal discount comes in the form of a message supporting the driver in the not-OK Nurturing Parent, which says, "The way to make it is to try hard (or be strong, etc.)."

Diagnosis involves monitoring words, tones, gestures, facial expressions, and postures. Each person will exhibit a fairly regularized set of behaviors that will be associated with particular drivers. Thus raised eyebrows in one person may reflect Please Me, while in another they may not.

The script invitation has to do with those behaviors in one person which invite another to exhibit concomitant scripty behavior. This process of inviting corresponding behavior is, I believe, one of the most important dimensions of all human interacting. The reason is the high positive correlation between script invitation and script response. It would seem that the probability is around 90 percent that if Person A is in a driver, Person B will reciprocate with the same or complementary driver behavior. Happily, this principle works the same for OK behavior. There is no third alternative, however. Second by second, transaction by transaction, we are inviting each other into OK behavior or not-OK behavior.

Drivers can be observed from a —NP or a —AC without rackets.

When the —NP is cathected, then the P driver reflects the belief, "You're OK if you Try Hard for me, Please me, etc."

When the —AC [without rackets] is cathected the C driver reflects the belief, "I'm OK if I Try Hard, Please you, etc."

THE TRY HARD DRIVER   Internal Discount: Comes from the not-OK Nurturing Parent. "The way to make it is to try hard." This is internalized as a discount and used when a person says, "If I don't try hard, I'll. . . ." What follows the "I'll" will give a clue to the payoff the person with the Try Hard will receive if he goes through the driver and gets down into pathology.

The therapist working with a client can issue Try Hard invitations that will compromise his work. For example, if the therapist asks the client to "try to get in touch" with his feelings, that is probably what the client will do, i.e., *try* to feel what he's feeling. Or consider this example:

Therapist: What are you feeling?
Client: Same as last week.
Therapist: How were you feeling last week?

Note that the client failed to answer the therapist's question directly. Instead of intervening, the therapist went through a Try Hard and followed the client at his tangent. An appropriate response would have been, "You didn't answer my question. Will you?" The last two words are the key. They constitute an Adult invitation to an Adult decision. When a person is in his Adult, he is automatically not in any driver.

THE PLEASE ME DRIVER   Internal Discount: The person feels that he is responsible for making people feel good; if they feel bad, he is also responsible. Typically, a person in a Please Me will whine, raise the eyebrows, use a questioning tone without asking a question in a straight way, and look away before answering a question. He is more concerned with how he is doing than with what he is doing. Sweethearts and Good Guys usually have heavy Please Me's.[26] The thesis behind Please Me, as it is behind all drivers, is that we're OK *if* we Try Hard, etc. Yet pleasing people, often if not always at the expense of yourself, doesn't work. What works is being responsible for ourselves, making sure we are protected, then being responsible to each other to be the best people we can be, which includes asking straight questions.

Please Me cuts both ways. I please you but I also expect you to please me. If I fail, I can feel sad and inadequate because I didn't please you as I was supposed to do according to the counterscript message that lies behind the driver. Or, I can choose to feel angry at you for not responding correctly to my valiant efforts to be nice and please you. Yet again, I can feel totally worthless as a pleaser and believe that there is no one out there who can help me. In short, I can go through the driver and get to and stop at any of the three positions on the not-OK miniscript.

Conversely, if you fail to please me, watch out! You're breaking the "rules." You're not reading my mind as per the "contract," so you'll know my needs. You're giving me an excuse to persecute you for your thick-headedness or to rescue you from it. I can also feel victimized by it. In all cases, the sequence of not-OK behavior is the same. I first go through the driver and fail to make it. Then I go to the script injunction and feel the associated feeling.

The following question invites a driver response, which means that the client would not be in an OK ego state Getting-On-With-It.

Therapist: Could you get in touch with your feelings?

A book that is helpful in knocking off Please Me and in learning to take care of yourself is Harry Browne's *How I Found Freedom in an Unfree World*.[27]

THE BE PERFECT DRIVER   Internal Discount: If I make a mistake, I'm not-OK.

The Be Perfect involves the belief that if I am less than perfect, according to my own or others' canons, I have to feel bad. Likewise, the more knowledge I have, the more OK I am. I'm like Charlie Tuna, constantly striving to improve myself until finally, one day, I will be accepted.

People in a Be Perfect use big words and long sentences. They cover all the bases, balance every positive with a negative, speak in redundancies. Typical words include "of course," "obviously," "I think." People in a Be Perfect will be anxious that you understand them exactly. They will also want to make sure they understand your question exactly. This is a therapist's Be Perfect invitation: "What are you feeling *right now, inside you?*" Since the client is invited to sabotage whatever technique was being attempted, it is highly probable that he will respond in kind with driver.

THE HURRY UP DRIVER Internal Discount: If I don't hurry up, I am not-OK. Certainly, it's appropriate under many circumstances to move rapidly toward an objective. What is behind the Hurry Up driver, however, is compulsiveness and conditional OK behavior. A person in a Hurry Up will usually talk rapidly, tap fingers or toes, or say things like "Let's get the show on the road." He might also interrupt people as they speak or complete sentences for them.

THE BE STRONG DRIVER Internal Discount: The person in a Be Strong will deny that he is responsible for his feelings or thoughts. He will believe in the emotional vulnerability of people.

Further, he will believe that he has to maintain a strong defense against those who would "make him feel bad." He will appear to be in his Adult much of the time that he is in the Be Strong driver. Yet gross or subtle clues, suggesting he is not in charge of his feelings, will give away the driver. On this point, I don't believe there is a constant Adult (James and Jongeward)[28] or an excluding Adult (Berne).[29] Since the Adult is by definition OK, it makes no sense to say that when one is in his Adult, he can be in not-OK behavior, as the aforementioned authors seem to imply. My experience tells me that people often mistake the Be Strong driver for Adult functioning. When there is doubt, what happens after the behavior is noticed is critical for the diagnosis. If evidence of not-OK payoffs is observed, the chances are great that what was seen was not Adult but Be Strong behavior.

The OK part of the driver is the *allower*. This represents Adult functioning that has been energized by the OK Critical Parent. In the allower, the Adult has seen through the Con of the not-OK Nurturing Parent and realizes that driver behavior does not, in fact, cause one to make it in life. To get out of this myth,[30] a person has to listen to an imperative of protection from the OK Critical Parent. In the case of Please Me, the imperative is "Please yourself!" (The protective imperative is aimed at the Adult or the OK Adapted Child. Permission messages, on the other hand, are aimed at the Free Child.) That message allows us to get on with being ourselves, feeling OK about who we are and avoiding racket feelings.

So what if I *commit* a driver? I'm still OK. I give permission to feel OK one way or the other, and use the experience positively and learn from it. If you get 10 percent of this chapter in first reading, give yourself a big stroke . . . there's a lot here! If we do go into not-OK miniscript behavior 90 to 95 percent of the time, then we are likely to undercut the best of information and rationalize about it.

SCRIPT ANALYSIS

A FAIRY TALE When Fahrquahr was a very little boy, he made a decision to hold his hand over his nose minute by minute, day by day. In his hand he held an icky substance that the not-OK parts of mommy and daddy had placed there just after his birth. Holding his hand to his nose and smelling that awful stuff caused spots to appear on his little lungs each time he breathed. Fahrquahr's whole family and almost everybody he ever met held their hands on their noses too, so he never thought much about it.

One day he felt a big pain in his chest. He told his friends Phoebe and Barnaby about it.

Phoebe said, "Oh, I remember feeling that way once."

"What did you do to get well?" asked Fahrquahr.

"I went to a doctor who told me that I had spots on my lungs, and that they would keep getting bigger because I held my hand to my nose. At first I didn't see how holding my hand on my nose made my lungs hurt, but when I stopped doing it I felt better. I kept forgetting to take my hand away. I must have been holding my hand to my nose a lot, because I had to think about it to stop doing it. After a while though, I was keeping my hand away even without knowing it. I had to practice for months before I could do it without having to think about it. Then when I went back to the doctor and he looked at my lungs, he said that the spots were almost all gone and that I hadn't made any new ones."

"Gee, that's funny, I was wondering why you don't have your hand on your nose like I do, Phoebe," chimed in Barnaby. "I had spots on my lungs too, only my doctor didn't say anything about holding my hand on my nose. He operated on my lungs and took out the spots. I felt better right away and for a long time afterwards. But just last week my lungs started to hurt a little again."

Fahrquahr reflected on what his two friends had said and, being a wise and thoughtful little fellow, he said to himself, "I'm going to go to a doctor who will operate on my spots and who will teach me how to keep my hand away from my nose."

PROCESS VS. CONTENT   Traditional script theory has been organized around the contention that the script is a result of script injunctions. I have been maintaining, however, that scripts are a result of drivers (not-OK counterscripting messages).

The focus of this chapter is the synthesis of these two positions into a consistent theoretical framework that is easily applied in therapy.

In *Sex in Human Loving,* Berne discussed six life (time structure, process) scripts: "Never," "Always," "After," "Until," "Over and over (Almost)," and "Open end."[31]

I have spent the last four years focusing primarily on script and transactional analysis and have concluded that Berne's first five scripts are unique and need not be amended. I believe that the "Open end" is a particular payoff for another script (perhaps the "After").

As a person changes the order of his drivers, he reinforces a different script.[32] He does this by repeating driver-programed sentences. Unconsciously, a person may say such scripty sentences many times a day. His whole life (not-OK) pattern then is reflected and reinforced by his (not-OK) sentence patterns. Making a redecision[33] about a script injunction, game, racket, or not-OK position will not necessarily alter the (process) script. I agree, however, that this does not lessen the importance of redecisions.

Recently I have been viewing scripts in terms of process and content. From this perspective, what originally appeared as two mutually exclusive theories can be embraced simultaneously.

While I have emphasized process, other theorists—working in the area of script injunction, rackets, and redecisions—have emphasized content.

Process has to do with the way that drivers, stoppers, rackets, games, and not-OK life positions are combined and replayed in sequence, second by second, year by year. Content has to do with how deeply a person will buy into the stopper, racket, game, or not-OK life position.

The not-OK miniscript yields more process than content information. We can identify which drivers, rackets, stoppers, games, and not-OK life positions are being reinforced, yet we may not be able to discern the depth of an individual's commitment to them. This process information will provide a key to understanding and predicting how a person will spend his life under the influence of his (not-OK) script. At the same time, it provides less information about the level of pathology he may reach. Content, then, has to do with measuring severity or intensity—the level of obedience to the script injunction (decision). This information forms the basis for a banal (nonwinning) or hamartic (losing) script.

More precise and consistent definitions, as well as greater understanding of script theory, are invited by drawing this theoretical distinction between process and content. If a therapist limits himself to content treatment (redecisions, primals, some gestalt, regressions), he will not have invited total change of the process. Operating on Barnaby to remove his spots was most valuable, yet the process of how those spots were allowed to grow was not stopped. Little Barnaby still held his hand to his nose.

The therapist who utilized process treatment, however, will be teaching patients to nip the sequence of not-OK behavior in the bud. This invites total change of content. Little Phoebe's spots cleared up because she stopped the process that kept the lungs agitated. Similarly, we cannot play a script-injunction tape that we had decided to keep in our library or feel a racket feeling without going through driver behavior.

Working with the racket feeling and making a redecision or allowing a "purging" of the racket has merit, yet it does not prevent the person from going into driver behavior. Since the average person appears to go into drivers a high percentage of time, and since drivers define how the process of a life script will continue, content analysis is not enough.

Content treatment is of great value, however, because it invites lessening and even eliminating the playing of the script injunction. Barnaby immediately felt better after having his spots removed. Eliminating the injunction, however, does not stop the drivers—the zero-to-seven-second behavior that acts as a doorway to reestablishing the content basement of racket feelings. This also does not prevent the drivers from reinforcing the process main life script.

On the other hand, if a therapist emphasizes process by teaching people how to stop the beginning moves into not-OK behavior at the driver behavior (initial discounting) level, the person learns to stop reinforcing his main life script by stopping his drivers. Simultaneously, he is extinguishing his content problem as well. If he stops himself at the driver behavior level consistently, he will not play the script injunction tape or feel the racket.

Content treatment seems to prevent the process script. Process treatment does prevent the content script. Yet, it is wise to use both: for example, getting a no-suicide contract, working through grief, having stroking exercises, giving permissions, doing regressions, and reparenting. Timing and the severity of the problem are important concerns too. Content treatment often fosters a deep feeling of release from the original investment in the decision concerning the script injunction, racket, or not-OK life position. This release often acts as a discharging mechanism on the not-OK battery.

Although Phoebe's lungs had cleared up by her focusing on process, this did take time and much Adult awareness. She guarantees health by preventing her driver behavior. Barnaby felt better immediately, yet the subtle beginnings of the problem remained untouched.

Little Fahrquahr opts for the best of both possible theories.

DRIVERS AND SENTENCE PATTERNS   Imprecise language has hindered our understanding of script theorists' work. Berne himself has invited some confusion by labeling various fairy tales "scripts."[34] The following is a list of expressions which are used, some colloquial and contributing to confusion, together with their technical counterparts:

Colloquial	Technical
A "Be Perfect" script	A driver
A "Don't be" script	A stopper
A "Rescuer" script	A role
A "Depression" script	A racket
An "I'm not-OK, You're OK" script	A position
A "Little Red Riding Hood" script	A fairy tale
A "Lone Ranger" script	A hero
A "Kick me" script	A game
A "Pastimes" script	A time structure

Winner, nonwinner (banal), and loser (hamartic)[35] are content dimensions of script.

Drivers are behaviors that last from a split second to no more than seven seconds. There are no feelings related to them. There is no way to feel a racket or play a stopper tape without first going through driver behavior (this is demonstrated behaviorally).* Just as the stopping of the driver behavior prevents the stopper tape from being played and the racket from being felt, the stopping of the driver behavior also prevents the concurrent script sentence (thought) patterns. Script reinforcement is a four-step process: (1) low stroke reserve causes; (2) driver behavior, which causes (3) different sentence patterns, which reinforces (4) the life script.

A charged-up not-OK battery ("low stroke reserve") precipitates driver behavior as the beginning step in observing not-OKness. The driver causes certain sentence structures. The sentence structure has a fixed pattern which may be repeated, unconsciously, hundreds of times a day.

Consider the elements of script reinforcement. If I "Never" finish my sentences by "Trying hard," and I do that 200 times a day, unconsciously, in a month I would have reinforced a "Never" script 6000 times, in a year 72,000 times, in twenty years, 1,440,000 times—no wonder I believe that I'll never make it. These sentence patterns were the result of a driver.

THE "NEVER" SCRIPT   Thesis: "As a child I was forbidden by my parents to do the things that I most wanted to do."

Life Pattern: A person when in a "Never" script may set himself up daily, monthly, and yearly never to make it in "important ways." Women with "Never" scripts never have orgasms.

Sentence Pattern: A person when in his "Never" script may be entering a Try Hard driver and never finish his sentences. Example:

Therapist: What are you feeling?
Patient: I don't, oh, I was feeling, um, it's just when my husband, oh, last night when I, ah, it's like my aunt . . . .

Drivers: Try Hard is the predominant driver of a "Never" script. Others, except Please Me, are seldom seen.

Case illustration: Tany's two life goals were to find a man who would love her and share intimacy, and to have children; but she had set herself up never to get what she most wanted. She married a man who had strong "Don't trust" and "Don't be close" script injunctions, and who had an "Almost" (Over and over) script, having been married and divorced two times already. He structured his time heavily in activity and withdrawal so as to avoid intimacy with Tany. He avoided being with her and accused her of being oversexed when she wanted to make love more than once a month. She would "try hard" and not have an orgasm herself. (This was also related to having a father who seduced her sister and attempted the same with Tany—it is not uncommon with women who have "Never" scripts that there was some deep competition with a sister or brother, sometimes sexually based.) She thus found a man whose script interlocked with hers.

Therefore, she could "never" make it with him ("Never" script). He

---

* One possible exception is endogenous depression.

almost made it with her ("Almost"), rationalizing that he was "just that way when it came to flying, his 'first love.' "

Before they were married she had told her husband of how she adored and wanted children. He agreed. Once they were married, he disclosed that he had not really meant it, that he actually hated kids and certainly did not want any. Tany became pregnant—"I somehow forgot to take my birth control pills"—and out of a "Corner" game ("I'm damned if I tell him and I'm damned if I don't"), went to a charlatan ("Well, I didn't want to ask him for money"), and got an abortion.

Script payoff: Now Tany can't have any kids—she's 28. The content is hamartic.

THE "ALWAYS" SCRIPT   Thesis: "Well, if that's what you want to do, then you can just spend the rest of your life doing it. You've made your bed, now lie in it."

Life Pattern: Often a person with the "Always" script will describe his or her life as "blah," having neither many highs nor many lows.

Sentence Pattern: Although the person with this script repeats his "Corner" again and again, there does not appear to be a well-defined sentence pattern.

Drivers: Hurry Up and Be Strong are common, yet there does not appear to be a consistent ranking for this script.

Case illustration: This script often has a built-in "Corner" game with a focus on sex. "I can have sex with a woman, but the more I enjoy it the less I'll love her. I can be in love with a woman, yet the more I am the less I want sex with her." Mr. Prides feels cornered because if he gets a divorce, he'll be "losing the best mother he could possibly find" and if he stays married, he "doesn't want sex with her and feels frustrated."

THE "AFTER" SCRIPT   Thesis: "Things can be going well now, but afterwards something will happen. If you have a high, you'll have to have a low to pay for it." Damocles' sword.

Life Pattern: OK ⌐
                ‾‾‾‾‾‾‾
                not-OK ⌐⟶

When in an "After" script, a person will feel OK, then set him or herself up in some way not to make it and to feel not-OK.

Sentence Patterns: Typically, a person with an "After" script will express positive feelings, insert a "but," and end with negative feelings.

Drivers: Please Me ranks number one in this script.

Case illustration: "After" scripts, like all scripts, are repetitive. Scripts are like motifs of a play, which can be seen in an act, a scene, a scenario, a strophe, or a phrase. Mr. McAldoes' life pattern reflects an active "After" script. At 19 he received national acclaim for his artistic talent. Now, at 38, he reports, "I seem to have lost all my ability. The first four years of our marriage were great, but then something happened and now we're divorced. In September and October I get so depressed." McAldoes is an art teacher who has summer vacations in July and August. I saw Mr. McAldoes on a Wednesday night. The night before he had been suicidally depressed. My question was, "What did you do last weekend?" "Oh," replied Mr. McAldoes, "I went to New Orleans and had the time of my life." He then felt depressed.

In an even shorter period of time Mr. McAldoes evidenced his "After" script. One night he rose and ritually stroked each member of the group, sat down, and immediately slouched and appeared sad. "I felt so good, but then I thought of the time I was taking away from the other group members. Now I feel guilty for taking everybody's time."*

THE "UNTIL" SCRIPT   Thesis: "You can't have fun until . . . (you've got your work done, or you've achieved . . .)." Hercules had to clean out the Augean stables and do other labors before he could be free.

Life Pattern: People with "Until" scripts collectively see themselves as "more OK" than people with other scripts. They are achievement and goal oriented, having been given conditional positive strokes.

Sentence Pattern: A person reinforces an "Until" script by starting a sentence, inserting a phrase "so that people understand me just right" (Be Perfect), then finishing the original sentence. Example: "In TA there are three ego states: the Parent, the Adult—and recall this is the part that computes probabilities and mediates between the other two—and the Child.

Drivers: Be Perfect is number one; often Be Strong is ranked high.

Case illustration: Dr. Litun, a physician, "can't take a vacation until he has worked five more years, can't make love until he reads the paper, can't retire until he has earned another $50,000," and so forth. Freemasonry is a common game—"I can succeed, but I can't be content with it."

THE "ALMOST" (OVER AND OVER)** SCRIPT   Thesis: "I almost make it, but not quite . . . if only, if only."

Life Pattern: A person with an "Almost" script is like Sisyphus who almost makes it to the top of the mountain, inevitably faltering. "Over and over" he may repeat: "marriage—divorce, marriage—divorce, . . ."

Sentence Pattern: A person reflects an "Almost" script by making a statement or presenting a question, yet ending with some kind of negative. Examples: "I've really made changes, kind of." "The color of your TV is great. The screen's a little dirty though." (Even though each statement may well be a fact, the order makes it scripty.)

Drivers: Try Hard and Please Me are the first two drivers, in either order.

---

* This clinical example could fit that of a manic depressive.

** I see the script as focusing more on "Almost" making it. Also, each script is cyclical.

Case illustration: Al Most has yet to find a job that he is comfortable with. As a result, Al has a pattern of job—quit—job—fired. He's been married twice. Typically, Al almost makes it. He almost got the raise. He made an excellent financial report to the board of directors, yet left out one variable that invalidated the whole presentation. In college, he once had a tie-breaker free throw, with no time left on the game clock, for a chance to capture the conference title. He made the shot but stepped over the line. The game and title were lost. In hundreds of ways each day Al reflected this life pattern.

THE "OPEN END" SCRIPT   Thesis: "I've made no plans for when the kids grow up, . . . I reach menopause, . . . I retire, . . ."

Life Pattern: The person with an "Open end" script is programed by duty. Although this is a relatively easy script to diagnose, it does not appear to have a cyclical nature or a well-defined driver order. My hunch is that this is not a separate script but an hamartic payoff for the "After" script.

DRIVERS AND SCRIPTS   Drivers are behaviors that reinforce an existential position of "I'm OK if," which is shown by the thick line on Ernst's OK Corral.[36]

Drivers begin functionally in the Parent (−NP, Rescuing) and can also be observed in the Child (−AC). The beginning internal discount of any sequence of not-OKness (discounting), then, will be that of the driver in −NP.

If a person changes driver-formed sentences, he may change his whole life (process) script pattern.

In treatment: if a therapist is in driver behavior, he invites similar behavior.

A man with an hamartic (content) "After" script, replete with a Please Me driver (process), comes to therapy. If the therapist is in Please Me behavior, he invites this patient into his own Please Me driver. An unsophisticated observer may think that "good" therapy is being done because of the therapy "rapport" evident in the smiles and nods. The therapist might also believe that he is doing good therapy. But the more the patient gets "high" by pleasing the therapist, the more he is setting himself up to pay for the "high" with a "low" to comply with "After" script. His hamartic payoff that night might well be suicide. The therapist, then, not only did not help the patient but actually invited him into the suicide payoff of his "After" script. The therapist's choice of techniques is not even relevant. He could have used a "great" technique and even known it very well. The way he used it (process)—through a driver—not only nullifies the results, but may even invite catastrophe.

The miniscript offers a measure and a categorizing of each transaction. It is not so much a new technique as it is an instrument to help us focus on us, whatever the technique we are employing. As a technique, the miniscript can be used to treat a script and to give positive alternatives in group.

MINISCRIPT CONTINUUM

All generalizations are false, advised Mark Twain, including this one. Mindful of that sage dictum, I nevertheless would say that all pathology can ultimately be traced back, in any given individual, to the stroke reserve. A person's inclination to go into not-OK behavior stands in inverse proportion to his stroke reserve. Thus, if the quantity or quality of his strokes is low, he will be more inclined to go into not-OK behavior than when his reserve is high.

The Miniscript Continuum (Figure 20) presents a rationale for this view, integrating as it does second-by-second behavior that can be clinically identified, and bringing together structural and transactional analysis.

On the horizontal line, numbers 1 through 4 represent the positions on the OK miniscript; number −1 through −4 represent the positions on the not-OK miniscript. This is inclusive and can reflect all behavior.

I postulate that each person puts together in childhood a survival package, an important element of which is the recognition requirement, quantified into the number of strokes the person believes he needs in order to keep on living. This quantity can be represented by the absolute value of some number. The term absolute value, "[ ]," indicates that the number can be positive or negative or a combination. Suppose Rothchild's survival number is [10]. Suppose further that Rothchild's Little Professor decides that, each day, he must receive 3 positive strokes. This means that he must also receive 7 negative units to come up with the "necessary" [10]. I put necessary in quotation marks because, while inviting not-OK behavior (getting 7 negative units) may have had a certain survival value at one

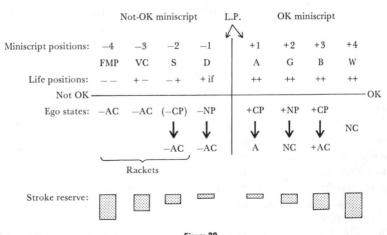

Figure 20
Miniscript Continuum

time, given the home situation of Rothchild, it is never an appropriate response in the present to assume that the way to live (i.e., to get on with it) is to invite oneself and others into not-OK behavior. Anger, for example, is better expressed than suppressed. Yet letting go of anger is seldom an end in itself in therapy. The goal is to invite the Adult to monitor the drivers so that a person doesn't go through one or more of them to get down to the anger.

Individuals will differ widely in terms of the level of pathology they will reach at any given position on the not-OK miniscript. They will also differ in terms of how long they will spend in their pathology. Some people, when they initially become aware of drivers, tend to find them around every corner they turn during the week. Hence, they feel they are regressing, since they are finding so much driver behavior in themselves. What they are doing, however, is admirable. They are becoming aware at the driver level, then choosing *not* to get down into pathology. I teach people to stroke themselves for their cleverness when they identify and stop driver behavior, rather than to beat on themselves for their stupidity.

In the total picture of TA therapy, stopping not-OK behavior and feelings at the driver level is not enough. The goal is to move from negative to positive, from driver to allower, from stopper to allower to goer, from vengeful child to allower to goer to be'er, and from final miniscript payoff to allower to goer, from be'er to wower. In order for this to occur, we need good Parent tapes in the OK Nurturing Parent and Critical Parent. Thus, if these tapes are missing in an individual, it would be inappropriate to get contracts with him to show him his driver behavior using miniscript technique. He has nowhere to go. This is the point at which a reparenting technique would be extremely valuable.

Although we can get heavier payoffs at different life positions, generally the payoffs will be reflected on the miniscript continuum.

Every stimulus or response that I set up will end with either a positive or negative payoff. I do this, as do we all, from our Little Professor, who monitors and is delimited by the battery charges.

Let's say that I need a minus charge and I'm lecturing.* "There are three ego states in TA: the Parent, the Adult, and the . . . the . . . the Child (*trying hard*)." At that point, I get my payoff. My Little Professor sensed that I needed such a minus to recharge my not-OK battery. My payoff was at the Child driver level (−AC), reinforcing "I'm OK if."

Let's say I want more of a negative payoff. "There are three ego states in TA: the Parent, the Adult, the . . . the . . . , oh, I feel so embarrassed . . . I'm supposed to be the expert."

I've now taken my payoff at the stopper level, feeling embarrassed, and reinforcing the I'm not-OK, You're OK position.

---

* Unfortunately, I can only relate to you, the reader, with the words. Hearing my tones, seeing my gestures, posture, and facial expressions would be more enlightening.

Let's say I want to reinforce the I'm OK, You're not-OK position by becoming angry. "There are three ego states in TA: the Parent, the Adult, the . . . the . . . , oh, gosh. I've done it again. I feel so stupid and silly. You're the coleader, Jim, and you're not even going to tell me, are you. Some leader!"

If I wanted to get all the way to feeling hopeless and reinforcing I'm not-OK, You're not-OK, I could do it by going through the same sequence and then adding: "Oh, well, what's the use. You don't care and neither do I."

Generally the more negative the payoff I want, the further along the negative continuum I'll go. I decide how long and how far I'll go, virtually second by second.

The content—what I talk about (lecture, technique, etc.)—matters very little. *How* I talk—my process—is the hard-core basic.

If I wanted a positive payoff, I would say: "There are three ego states in TA: the Parent, the Adult, and the Child." This is a +1 allower level with the Adult.

Since there are also hierarchies in OK behavior, I could go to the goer level by showing my Natural Child: "There are three ego states in TA: the Parent, the Adult, and the Child," and I would draw a face on the board.

If someone said to me, "You're stupid," I could reply from a be'er level with my +AC, "No, I don't feel stupid."

The wower level is that ultimate good feeling—the tingle of hearing a baby's laughter, the rush of first love, the peace of a family having Thanksgiving dinner, the security of feeling loved.

I have the wherewithal to make me as high as I want every single second of the day. WOW!!

CLINICAL APPLICATION

I invite autonomy. When a client comes to a group session, if she puts her name on the board to signify she is prepared to work, if she has a contract that is measurable and in eight-year-old language, if she has chosen a technique and has in mind whom she wants to be her therapist (every client is encouraged to be a therapist), then I can act as supervisory therapist.

In the sessions, we have "tiltees" and "tilters." Any time the working client or therapist is in a driver, two appointed tilters may say "Tilt." This brings attention to the process of therapy no matter what the content (technique). The tiltee has the option of integrating the information within himself or asking straight what the driver was. If he escalates and/or feels overloaded, he can make a "King's X" by raising two crossed fingers, signaling that he does not want feedback on his process but prefers to continue the content and focus later on the process implication.

I use miniscript technique about 20 percent in therapy. However, I "think" miniscript concept 100 percent, no matter what technique is used. Knowing a technique does not insure that it will be delivered in OKness. I knew dozens of techniques when I first started to practice, yet there were still times when I did not even know what ballpark I was in. By thinking miniscript, I know what bases the client and I are on, whatever the technique. *It is much more important how (process) a client says something than what he says (content).*

I use miniscript to monitor the recurrence and escalation of not-OKness in clients. Within 30 seconds to two minutes, I am about 95 percent accurate on what their drivers, games, not-OK life position, decisions about script injunctions, rackets, role in the drama triangle, and scripts are.

I am currently interested in how such a focus can be employed in categorizing a client within a standard diagnostic category. My prediction is that this will facilitate and accelerate accurate diagnosing.

I am also interested in script closure. For example, if a person has an Almost script, look for that client to almost finish, get the point, make the redecision, etc., at the end of the session. If this is not confronted and closure is not achieved, then a "great therapist" with "great techniques" will have just reinforced the script pathology.

References

1. Stephen Karpman, "Options," *Transactional Analysis Journal, 1,* no. 1 (January, 1971), pp. 79–87.
2. John M. Dusay, "Script Rehearsal," *Transactional Analysis Bulletin, 9,* no. 36 (October, 1970), pp. 117–121.
3. John M. Dusay, "Egograms and the Constancy Hypothesis," *Transactional Analysis Journal, 2,* no. 3 (July, 1972), pp. 37–41.
4. Stephen Karpman, "Fairy Tales and Script Drama Analysis," *Transactional Analysis Bulletin, 7,* no. 26 (April, 1968), pp. 39–43.
5. Jacqui Lee Schiff, "Reparenting Schizophrenics," *Transactional Analysis Bulletin, 8,* no. 31 (July, 1969), pp. 49–50.
6. Robert Goulding, "New Directions in Transactional Analysis: Creating an Environment for Change," in Clifford J. Sanger and Helen Singer Kaplan, eds., *Progress in Group and Family Therapy,* New York, Brunner/Mazel, 1972, pp. 118–125.
7. Franklin H. Ernst, "The OK Corral: The Grid for Get-On-With," *Transactional Analysis Journal, 1,* no. 4 (October, 1971), pp. 33–42.
8. Taibi Kahler, "Scripts: Process and Content," *Transactional Analysis Journal, 5,* no. 3 (July, 1975), pp. 277–279.
9. Eric Berne, *What Do You Say After You Say Hello?,* New York, Grove Press, 1972, p. 344.
10. Eric Berne, *Transactional Analysis in Psychotherapy,* New York, Grove Press, 1961, pp. 29–36, 71ff.

11. Taibi Kahler with Hedges Capers, "The Miniscript," *Transactional Analysis Journal, 4,* no. 1 (January, 1974), pp. 26–34.
12. *Ibid.*
13. Berne, *What Do You Say, op. cit.,* p. 444.
14. Mary Edwards (Goulding), "The Two Parents," *Transactional Analysis Bulletin, 7,* no. 26 (April, 1968), pp. 37–38.
15. Taibi Kahler, "Mirror Techniques," presented at Wabash Valley TA Seminar, February, 1972.
16. John M. Dusay, "Egograms," *op. cit.*
17. Fanita English, Lecture on "Racketeering," ITAA Winter Congress, Atlanta, Georgia, January, 1976.
18. Karpman, "Options," *op. cit.*
19. Ernst, *op. cit.*
20. Berne, *What Do You Say, op. cit.,* p. 107.
21. Zelig Selinger, Paper presented at ITAA Ninth Annual Summer Conference, San Francisco, California, August, 1971.
22. Kahler with Capers, *op. cit.*
23. Berne, *What Do You Say, op. cit.,* p. 24.
24. George David, "Zero Sum Fallacy," *Transactional Analysis Bulletin, 7,* no. 26 (April, 1968), p. 47.
25. Aaron Wolfe Schiff and Jacqui Lee Schiff, "Passivity," *Transactional Analysis Journal, 1,* no. 1 (January, 1971), p. 73.
26. Amy Harris, "Good Guys and Sweethearts," *Transactional Analysis Journal, 2,* no. 1 (January, 1972), pp. 13–18.
27. Harry Browne, *How I Found Freedom in an Unfree World,* New York, Macmillan, 1973.
28. Muriel James and Dorothy Jongeward, *Born to Win,* Reading, Massachusetts, Addison-Wesley, 1973, p. 230.
29. Eric Berne, *Transactional Analysis in Psychotherapy, op. cit.,* p. 46.
30. Taibi Kahler, "The 4 Myths," Unpublished manuscript.
31. Eric Berne, *Sex in Human Loving,* New York, Simon & Schuster, 1970, pp. 163–171.
32. Taibi Kahler, "Drivers: The Key to the Process of Scripts," *Transactional Analysis Journal, 5,* no. 3 (July, 1975), pp. 280–284.
33. Robert Goulding, *op. cit.*
34. Berne, *What Do You Say, op. cit.,* p. 45.
35. Claude Steiner, *Games Alcoholics Play,* New York, Grove Press, 1971, pp. 55–56.
36. Ernst, *op. cit.*

THIRTEEN

AN INTEGRATED SYSTEMS PERSPECTIVE
Vann S. Joines

Previously, most branches of psychotherapy have tended to concentrate on only one psychosocial system of the human organism at a time. The psychoanalytically oriented therapists have emphasized the intrapersonal system. The behaviorists and others have dwelt on the interpersonal system. The systems theorists have concentrated almost entirely on the social system. With a concentration on any one of these systems to the exclusion of the other two, much valuable input is lost. A perspective which links these three systems is greatly needed in order to maximize the possibilities for effective change. The purpose of this chapter is to provide such a perspective. Transactional analysis is useful in this process since it focuses not only upon the personality structure of the individual but also upon the transactions between and among individuals and upon the structure and dynamics of the resulting social systems. Therefore, the development of the individual personality structure will be discussed from a TA perspective, the resulting interpersonal relationships examined, and certain characteristics of the emergent social systems predicted. With such a perspective, the change agent can begin to develop models for working with all three systems simultaneously rather than concentrating on only one. The potential effects can thus be multiplied.

DEVELOPMENT OF THE INTRAPERSONAL SYSTEM

Let us begin with an examination of the development of the intrapersonal system.[1] In normal child development looked at from a TA perspective,[2] the natural and necessary relationship between parent and child during infancy is a symbiotic one. This is necessary because the child does not yet have the resources to take care of himself. He cannot feed himself, change his diapers, or adequately stroke himself. Therefore, he is both physically and psychologically dependent upon his parents for survival. The infant must remain within that symbiosis if he is to survive.

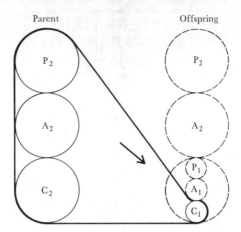

Figure 1

Often the parent or parents can structure that relationship so that their own Child ego state is included and their own needs are being met along with those of the offspring (Figure 1). For example, the parents can feel a great amount of joy, warmth, affirmation, and fun in playing with, cuddling, or feeding the infant.

At times, however, it is necessary for the parents to set aside or postpone gratification of the needs of their own Child ego state and meet the needs of the offspring instead (Figure 2). For example, the baby is crying to be fed at 3:00 AM and the parents want and need to sleep, or the parents have been working all day and want some time to themselves while the child wants some attention from them or needs to be changed, fed, or bathed.

As long as the parents have well-integrated ego states, are aware of their own needs and structure ways for them to be met, the parents' own Child

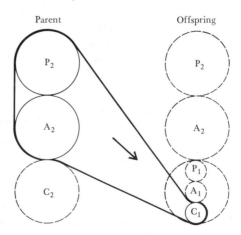

Figure 2

ego states will be satisfied and content to participate in the parenting process for the benefit of the offspring. Since no human parents have reached perfection, however, there are inevitably times when the parents are not aware of their needs, discount them, or do not have adequate information for getting them met. If those times are very frequent or the needs of the parents' Child ego states are very great, then those ego states begin to take over in order to get their needs met rather than those of the offspring. In other words, the survival of a parent's own Child ego state becomes the issue of primary concern for the Child ego state of that parent.

As the parent's Child ego state feels threatened, the parent will increasingly decathect his or her Parent and Adult ego states and cathect Child. The threat is simply that the offspring is feeling, thinking, or behaving in some way that the parent does not think he or she can handle. At that point, a competitive relationship with the offspring is set up in terms of whose needs are going to get met (Figure 3). The Child ego state of the parent may react with resentment, anger, scare, hurt, confusion, withdrawal, violence, or it may act in some other irrational manner. The offspring intuitively becomes aware of the threat to his very existence. He knows he cannot compete with this giant and he cannot survive without this big person's protection and care. He must do something to reduce the threat to his parent so that he or she will provide care and protection once more. Since he has no other frame of reference at that point, the offspring may begin to feel that there is something wrong with his needs or the behavior he is using to get those needs met. In the interest of survival, the offspring may suppress those needs or change the behavior he is using to one to which the parent will respond in a less threatening fashion. Since the situation involves the issue of survival, the child will carefully record it for future reference. The adaptations the child makes may become an automatic program for survival in similar future situations of stress.

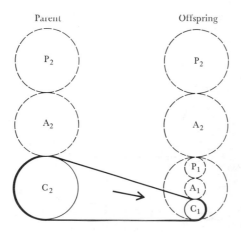

Figure 3

Although the program is psychologically secure since it enables survival, the natural needs of the offspring are not being met. Therefore, the child may set up the same situation again and again in order to attempt to resolve his frustration and get the original needs met. Since the program produces partial satisfaction, the four- or five-year-old child may develop the magical belief that he can get what he wanted originally by continuing to repeat the program with enough intensity. In addition, the program offers intense stroking and less psychological threat than other possible situations, since the child has developed an automatic behavior for handling this situation. As long as the child sticks to the program, there are very few unknowns and the child's world remains very predictable. The only problem is that the behavior involved in the survival program is not the behavior needed in order to get the original needs met.

In structural terms, the offspring, perceiving the competition from the parents' Child and the threat to his existence, cathects his Little Professor (A_1) and Electrode (P_1) in order to take care of the parents' Child (C_2) (i.e., reduce the threat) so that the parents will recathect their Parent (P_2) and Adult (A_2) ego states once again and resume taking care of the Infant (C_1) in the offspring (Figures 4 and 5). In the Electrode are recorded the irrational messages (injunctions) from mother's and father's Child. The Little Professor figures out ways to carry out these messages and develops a fantasy of what he is supposed to do ultimately to please mother and father, thus developing a life script.

An example of this process would be what happens when the parents are threatened by their offspring feeling angry and acting aggressive. A small child wants what he wants when he wants it. If he does not get it, he becomes angry, aggressive, and demanding. If, at that point, mother reacts with scare and withdraws, and father reacts with even more anger than the offspring and raises his hand to spank the child, the child may

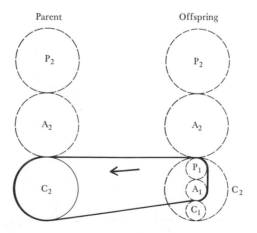

Figure 4

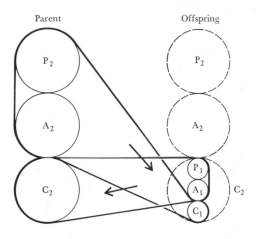

Figure 5

begin to feel scared and withdraw since he faces two immediate threats. Mother might abandon him and father might annihilate him. As he acts out his scare, a very interesting thing occurs. Father begins to back off and mother begins to move closer to take care of the scared child. The child may not get what he was after initially, but at least he gets some intense and exciting stroking as well as protection instead of being abandoned or annihilated. The message he picks up intuitively from father's Child is "Don't feel angry and act assertively," and mother's Child shows him how through her own behavior. If this sequence gets repeated over and over, or even a few times with enough stress, the child may learn to substitute fear and withdrawal for anger and aggression as a survival program for stressful situations. The child may also decide that, if things get bad enough, he will run away (which in later adult life may mean run away from reality). Since the child got his needs partially satisfied by being scared, his fantasy will likely be that if he feels scared enough, for long enough, he will get what he wanted in the first place. Or, if he sets up the same situation enough times, surely mother and father will react differently. If all that doesn't work, then mother and father are bound to change and feel sorry if he runs away. At that point he believes that they will say it's okay for him to act angry and assertive and will give him what he wanted in the first place. In this process, the child writes out a life script which calls for suppressing anger, feeling scared, and running away. Included in that script are games to invite anger (negative strokes) from others and a racket of maintaining scare as a way to get support (positive strokes) from others. During this whole process, the parents may be telling the child verbally to "be brave" but giving him the most attention when he is scared. The counterscript messages such as "be brave" are likely to encourage the child to get into scary situations without adequate protection in order to reinforce the feelings and behavior the script calls for. By

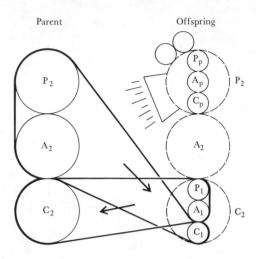

Figure 6

following the script, the child has an automatic program enabling psychological survival, but one which may become very dysfunctional or destructive later on. The ultimate attraction of the script is that it is perceived as a magical way to solve once and for all a problem the child did not solve in infancy.

While the offspring is reacting to mother and father, making decisions and forming a life script, he is also videotaping everything the parents are doing; this the offspring does from the part of him that will later be his own Parent ego state (Figure 6). This means that, in addition to developing his own personality structure as a child, he is simultaneously incorporating their personality structures. Thus, as a grownup the offspring has within his own head not only who he was as an infant but also who

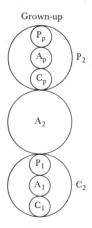

Figure 7

his parents were during that time (Figure 7). For every feeling, thought, and behavior in his Child, there is a supporting structure in his Parent.

The result of this development of ego states is fourfold: *(1)* the individual can operate autonomously on the basis of who he is in his present awareness (P_2, A_2, C_2); *(2)* he can feel and act in the same way and engage others in the same games and rackets he used in infancy (P_1, A_1, C_1); *(3)* he can feel and act and engage others in the same games and rackets he observed his parents using with him (P_p, A_p, C_p); or *(4)* he can play out both parts of the game and set up the rackets within himself intrapsychically.

THE INTERPERSONAL SYSTEM

The reason a grown individual will act out of his archaic ego states, either his own as an infant or those copied from his parents when he was an infant, is that this is the way he automatically knows for getting the most intense strokes and remaining psychologically secure in times of stress. His parents gave him a set of prescriptions (counterinjunctions) for how to "try" to win recognition from others, but they also let him see how threatened they would be if he really succeeded. When mother and father are no longer around, the individual simply finds someone else upon whom he can project mother's or father's face. Then he uses his archaic Parent and Adult (P_1 and A_1) to take care of the other's Child. He sets up the same games and rackets that worked with mother and father so that the other will stroke his Infant (C_1) in the same way that mother and father stroked him when he was little. He can also project his Child onto others and use his P_p and A_p to take care of their infant (C_1) in the same way that mother and father used to take care of him (Figure 8). Thus, he reestablishes the same symbiotic relationship(s) that he and his parents originally perceived to be necessary in order to survive physically or psychologically

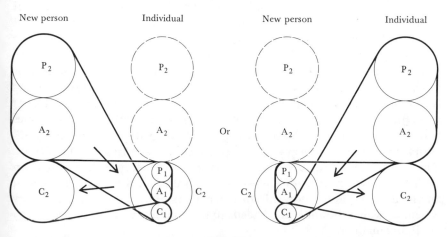

Figure 8

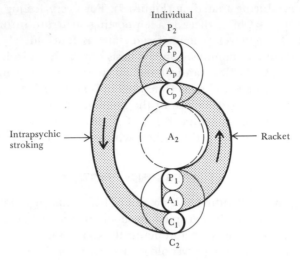

Figure 9

when he was an infant. Either symbiosis will enable him to procure intense strokes in a highly predictable and thus psychologically secure manner.

When no one else is around, he can also establish these same symbioses intrapsychically, since he has inside his own head both who he was as an infant and who his parents were during that time. He simply uses his P_1 and A_1 to set up situations and feelings which will satisfy his parents' Child in his Parent ego state (P_2), so that their Parent and Adult in his Parent will stroke his Infant (C_1) in the same way they did when he was little (Figure 9). This enables him to maintain equilibrium within his own intrapersonal system and thus satisfy his hunger for a psychologically secure position. Therefore, within the intrapsychic system, there is an autonomous structure ($P_2A_2C_2$) and a dual symbiotic structure with each of the archaic personalities partially satisfying the others' needs ($P_pA_pC_1$ and $P_1A_1C_p$) (Figure 10). The significant point here is that ego states are not formed and incorporated as isolated entities but rather are formed and incorporated as part of structures which function either autonomously or symbiotically. The autonomous structures are formed in relation to those issues and situations in which the individual received automatic support as a child. The symbiotic structures are formed in relation to those issues and situations in which automatic support was withheld, and the individual had to discover ways of manipulating support in order to survive. The autonomous structures function as an open energy system which can both create new sources of energy from within and draw new sources of energy from without. The symbiotic structures function as a closed energy system in which the individual feeds upon himself or others in an energy depleting manner.

As a grownup the individual will shift structures according to the issue

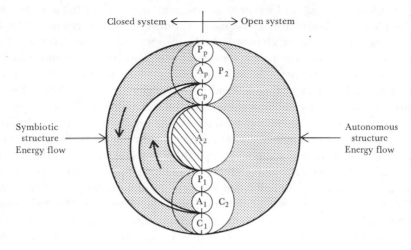

Figure 10
Individual Personality Structure (can function as either)

or situation involved. In nonstressful situations, he will act autonomously and get the strokes he wants directly. In stressful situations he will first "try" to follow the counterinjunctions from his parents in order to procure strokes by acting out his counterscript. As the external or internal stress increases and his need for more intense stroking increases, he will replay the archaic injunctions and shift into his symbiotic script behavior. Through this process, the individual maintains contact with and experiences intense stroking between his archaic parents and his infant, whom he now keeps within himself and at times projects onto others. The individual is aided in this process by other persons whose scripts call for them to act in ways that are synonymous with the first person's projections. This accommodation makes the world very predictable and, in that respect, psychologically secure for all.

Social relationships are most frequently formed and pursued on this basis. They are set up as the archaic Adult or Little Professor in the Child ego state of an individual becomes intuitively aware that the Child ego state of another individual is a willing target for its projections and will correctly accommodate with a similar response. In this way, interpersonal relationships are established as a means to procure strokes and maintain psychological equilibrium by enabling each individual to act out his or her life script while giving the appearance of "trying" to carry out his or her counterscript.

Each individual is maintaining (often outside of Adult awareness) an existential position based on an early decision and a feeling racket which accompanies the position. This existential position can be summed up in a brief phrase such as "I am no good" or "You are no good" or "Nobody is any good." The typical respective racket feelings are guilt, helplessness, or depression; hurt, anger, or scare; and hopelessness, despair, or confusion. Other examples of existential positions may be: "All men (women) are alike," "Nobody cares about me," "I'll never get what I want," "I can't win," or "You'll never change." As Jacqui Schiff has pointed out, these are grandiose perceptions of the Child and involve a maximization or minimization of reality.[3] In order to justify what the individual already believes and is already feeling, and in order to shift responsibility for the problem to someone or something else, the individual will set up psychological games. In that way the phobic situation in which the individual felt most vulnerable as a child is avoided and the racket feeling which can be used to manipulate support is justified. For example, if a child was discounted whenever he attempted to get close to his parents directly, he may have felt depressed and decided, "There is something wrong with me. Nobody can ever love me." Chances are that when he "looked" really depressed his parents would become nurturing or at least pay attention to him. As a grownup, the same individual is likely not to pursue closeness with others directly because he would feel too vulnerable and would fear being discounted as he experienced earlier. By playing games, he can get himself rejected by others, blame them, and justify his belief and his depression. As others see him "looking" depressed, they are likely to become concerned and try to help. Thus, through his games and racket, he can elicit strokes and support from others in a psychologically safe manner.

One of the most significant relationships in which these dynamics are set up is in marriage. The delusion often is that the choice of a marital partner is a rational decision. In reality, the Little Professor (A_1) in each individual picked someone upon whom it could project some figure from the past (usually mother, father, a sibling, or its own archaic Child ego state) and set up the same games and rackets that worked in childhood to get intense strokes. Thus, the two individuals can relate in automatic ways with very little thought involved. They are psychologically comfortable with one another and secretly hope to get resolved the issues that were unresolved in childhood. Each will be setting up a projection screen and transacting primarily with her or his own projected archaic ego states while maintaining the delusion of being in contact with the other person (Figure 11). Other important relationships are picked in much the same way. Bosses, employees, teachers, therapists, friends are all picked in part by the Little Professor on the basis of who knows how to play similar games and use familiar rackets. In that way, the individual has an automatic repertoire of behavior out of which to transact with those others, and he can maintain psychological homeostasis while carrying out his life script.

Thus, what is going on at the psychological level in the structuring of social relationships is that the archaic intrapsychic symbiotic system is projected onto interpersonal relationships, and the various social systems are set up to provide homeostasis in the same way that the individual works intrapsychically to satisfy his or her position hunger. Perhaps the

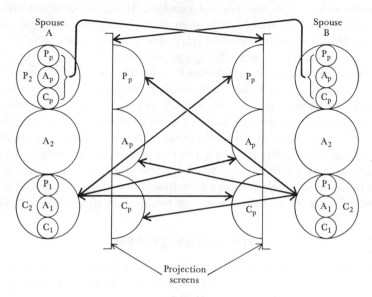

Figure 11
Marital Relationship Involving Mutual Projections

most familiar example of this is again seen in the marital and family systems.

THE MARRIAGE SYSTEM

When two individuals get married, they become not one, as is the popular delusion, but three. There is the husband, the wife, and the relationship. Any change in one of these three, as the systems theorists have pointed out,[4] will produce a corresponding reaction in the other two in order to bring the system back into a position of homeostasis or balance. Think of a seesaw with husband on one end and wife on the other and the fulcrum being the relationship. The relationship has been set up according to a variety of implicit rules resulting from the set patterns of transactions over a period of time. If one spouse does *X*, both know that the other will automatically do *Y*. There is a certain range of movement and a certain intensity of stroking that is psychologically comfortable to both persons, and their behavior will be regulated to maintain those ranges. If one spouse becomes too active or intense, the other will automatically cool off in order that the balance might be maintained.

A second analogy that may be useful is to think of the relationships between individuals in a system as being psychological ropes tied at each person's waist. If spouse A begins to change drastically, then spouse B will experience visceral discomfort and will pull back by escalating his or her behavior in the opposite direction in a frantic attempt to reestablish the homeostasis and thus the visceral comfort. If that does not work, then spouse B will cut off spouse A in order to maintain psychological comfort and security. To say this another way, one spouse alone changing his or her script will leave the other hanging and feeling very threatened. There has been a break in the archaic symbiosis which is still being perceived by one spouse as necessary for psychological survival. Thus, in order for effective change to occur in a marriage, it is important for the individuals to work together on both themselves as individuals and on their marital relationship. In that way, the individuals can make changes in themselves and simultaneously expand their relationship in such a way as to maintain the necessary balance and psychological comfort. Together, they can undo the symbiotic relationships they have been maintaining and achieve autonomy through a process that does not unduly threaten either person.

THE FAMILY SYSTEM

When a child is added to the marital system, a family system results. The child will be taught the necessary roles to play in order to maintain the life script drama of the parents. Thus, the parents as architects will structure the family system in such a way as to enable each of them to live out their own life script. As a child assumes the necessary roles in the drama and receives reinforcement for those roles, he or she will begin to write out his or her own life script which will contain those roles. Thus, the family system will contain a greater complexity of transactions, but ones which again follow the principles of systems theory. A change in any part of the system will produce corresponding changes in the rest of the system. As each additional child joins the family, the complexity of the system increases geometrically. For example, with two persons, there are two individuals and one pair making up a total of three entities. With three persons, there are three individuals, three pairs, and three triads giving a total of nine entities. With four persons, there are four individuals, six pairs, and 12 triads for a total of 22 entities.*

In the family system as in the marital system, each individual has a psychological investment in all the other individuals remaining fairly constant in their behavior. Their knowledge of how to procure psychologically safe strokes depends on it. Thus, there is a built-in inertia to change. Again, if one member attempts to move out too far and too fast, the other members will escalate their behavior in the opposite direction in an attempt to bring that individual back into line and thereby maintain

---

* The mathematical formula for this progression is:

$$E = n \left[1 + \frac{(n-1)^2}{2} \right]$$

where E is the number of entities and n is the number of family members. The formula was derived by R. E. Lee, Professor of Mathematics, University of West Florida, Pensacola, during a workshop I was conducting in family therapy.

homeostasis within the symbiotic systems that have been established. If the individual persists, the family will cut him or her off. That individual no longer plays the parts the other individuals' scripts call for and the symbioses are threatened. Therefore, the individual is gotten rid of in order to continue the old structure. Change in the total system once again requires working with all parts and providing the opportunity for everyone to move a similar amount while expanding the various relationships to offer nonsymbiotic options.

THE LARGER SOCIETAL SYSTEM

Families, in turn, are part of a larger societal system composed of numerous other systems such as additional family systems, legal systems, school systems, business and industrial systems, political systems, religious systems, and therapeutic systems. Once more the principles of systems theory apply; any change in any part of the societal system will produce corresponding changes in all other parts. Again, there is a built-in inertia to radical change. Thus, social change also, in order to be effective and lasting, must involve all the elements within the societal system and must be carried out through a careful process of confrontation, support, differentiation, separation, and restructuring. This fact has both positive and negative aspects. On the negative side, it means that important social change, like the elimination of racism in society, will require a long process, and that men like Martin Luther King who try to move too far too fast will get cut off. On the positive side, it means that social conditions like Watergate can go only so far and that men like Richard Nixon also will get cut off. The larger the system, the more energy required for achieving long-lasting effective change but the greater the potential gains.

As was noted earlier, individuals choose spouses, employers, and societal groups on the basis of what their script calls for. Moreover, each individual, upon entering a new societal group, brings with him or her an "imago" or fantasized psychological structure of the group. This imago provides a mental picture of where the individual stands in relation to the group and how he or she is to relate to the other members of the group. In *The Structure and Dynamics of Organizations and Groups,* Eric Berne describes four phases through which an individual moves in fantasizing his or her relationship to a group.[5] These phases will determine both how the individual will structure time in the group and the degree of relatedness the individual experiences with regard to the group. Each phase will involve a different imago representing the degree to which the individual has differentiated the members of the group. The differentiation will usually be done in terms of who in this new group is like the members of the individual's family of origin or other significant early relationships. The reason the individual will make these identifications is that he or she has already developed a whole repertoire of behaviors with which to transact with these persons and can do so without even thinking. By adhering to these familiar behaviors, there are very few unknowns and the psychological risk is minimized. Therefore, until the individual has made these differentiations and has sufficient information about where he or she fits into the imagoes of other persons, the individual will limit the ways in which he or she structures time in the group. This entire process is often carried out on the psychological level without Adult awareness. The imagoes are essentially the psychological structures the individual maintains in order to play out his or her life script.

Upon entering a new group, the individual will have a "provisional imago" with very little differentiation and, in addition to the activity for which the group is formally structured, the individual will probably not feel psychologically secure in structuring time in any way other than rituals. During this phase, the individual's sense of relatedness to the group will be simply that of "participation."

After the individual has been in the group for a brief period and has differentiated a few of the members and has also become aware of their imagoes, the individual will develop an "adaptive imago" and feel comfortable in engaging in pastimes as well. During this phase, the person will develop a sense of "involvement" with the group.

As the group members are further differentiated, the individual will develop an "operative imago" and attempt to get the other group members to adapt to his or her frame of reference by playing games. This phase will produce a sense of "engagement" with the group.

Finally, when the group is fully differentiated, the individual may develop a "secondary adjusted imago" resulting in a new synthesis allowing for intimacy. This final phase will produce a sense of "belonging" with the group. To ensure the survival of the group, it is essential that a majority of the members achieve this final phase.

Since the leader of the group frequently is seen as having the most power, his or her imago is likely to be the most influential in shaping the psychological structure of the group. The other members who join the group are likely to be persons whose own imagoes complement that of the leader. Thus, many social institutions are a reflection of individual life scripts and are structured so as to provide the individuals within the institutions a means for carrying out their life scripts.

As Graham Barnes has pointed out, institutions do not have ego states but do have corresponding elements that result from information within the ego states of the individuals who set up those institutions.[6] Corresponding to the Parent ego state in individuals, institutions have established patterns of belief and patterns of behavior. Analogous to an Adult ego state in the individual, institutions have technologies. In place of a Child ego state, institutions have patterns of feelings and mythologies. Once these institutions are set up with certain defined procedures, they begin to function somewhat independently of any of the individuals involved. This means that if all the individuals within the institution were suddenly to change their life scripts, the institution would continue to function as usual until its operational procedures were also changed. Similarly, the institution's procedures could be changed with little effect on the individuals' life scripts. Thus, effective change must involve both the individuals changing their life scripts and the institution or social system changing its operational procedures on the social and the psychological level.

From this discussion, it can be seen that the intrapersonal, interpersonal, and social systems are all linked by means of the life script to provide psychological support for the individuals involved. This support may be provided through very dysfunctional means (archaic symbiotic games and rackets) which threaten the health and very existence of those involved. Such potentially destructive systems can be changed by changing the life scripts of the individuals involved and the patterns of belief, behavior, technology, feeling, and mythology of the institutions within which the individuals transact. It is important to keep in mind, however, that the psychological support which the old systems provided will not be relinquished until new, more exciting, productive, and secure systems are established or at least foreseen. Therefore, an essential first step in achieving effective change is to change the pattern of stroking an individual receives from the social system from negative to positive. Additional means of eliciting Free Child energy and of providing permission, protection, support, and successful experiences must also be identified and implemented. Otherwise, oppressive reactions are likely to be triggered, since the individuals involved may view the change as a survival issue. The change agent must continually seek to confront all manifestations of dysfunctional Critical Parent, contaminated Adult, and Adapted Child feelings, thoughts, and behavior on whatever level they are encountered, and seek to elicit and reinforce all manifestations of functional Nurturing Parent, clear Adult, and Natural Child alternatives. Any failure to do so will result in a reinforcement of the existing systems.

In summary, whenever a change agent attempts to work with either the intrapsychic, the interpersonal, or the social system without also working with the other two systems, two important dimensions of reality are being discounted and the potential for change will be limited. These three systems are closely tied togther and any change in one will effect significant reactions in the other two. Therefore, maintaining a perspective which links the three systems and developing models for working on all three levels at once will enhance the possibilities for achieving effective and lasting change.

References

1. Vann S. Joines, *A Therapeutic Roadmap,* Chapel Hill, North Carolina, Southeast Institute, 1975.
2. Aaron Wolfe Schiff and Jacqui Lee Schiff, "Passivity," *Transactional Analysis Journal, 1,* no. 1 (January, 1971).

3. Jacqui Lee Schiff, et al., *The Cathexis Reader,* New York, Harper & Row, 1975.
4. See for example Don Jackson and William Lederer, *Mirages of Marriage,* New York, W. W. Norton & Company, 1968, chap. 10.
5. Eric Berne, *The Structure and Dynamics of Organizations and Groups,* Philadelphia, J. B. Lippincott Co., 1963, chap. 12.
6. Workshop at the Southeast Institute, Chapel Hill, North Carolina, June, 1974.

FOURTEEN

THE IMPLICATIONS
OF CULTURAL SCRIPTING
Terri White and Jerome D. White

We think that the way to study a human being is within the entirety of his relationships—intrapersonal, interpersonal, and interfacing with institutions and ultimately with the universe. For this reason, we favor cultural scripting, which leads to seeing cultures as a whole and, consequently, to effecting larger units of change. As new theories emerge for the treatment of individuals and families, or as clusters of techniques are created, they seem to fit within the broad spectrum of cultural-scripting theory assumptions (Figure 1).

Jacob Bronowski reports of a parallel experience, that of viewing man from a more global perspective and of turning from physics to biology only to be confronted by the traditional tendency in biology to focus on details and to study man in terms of his similarities to animals.

> It is something of a shock to think that justice is part of the biological equipment of man. And yet it is exactly that thought which took me out of physics and into biology, and that has taught me since that a man's life, a man's home, is a proper place to study his biological uniqueness. . . . By tradition biology is thought of in a different way . . . the likeness between man and animal is what dominates it . . . . There must be something unique about man because otherwise, evidently, the ducks would be lecturing about Konrad Lorenz, and the rats would be writing papers about B. F. Skinner.[1]

Man is a unique animal indeed. Certainly, part of his uniqueness is that he lives in several generations at the same time, with the past being represented in cultural assumptions (intrapersonally in P_2 and P_1). These cultural assumptions are the interpreted results of psychohistoric events, tested over the generations by a complex set of forces (including archetypal, genetic predispositions). The future may also be represented because of man's ability to fantasize and predict, much of which is based on ongoing experiential data, although this data is subject to a perceiving set or to filtering based on expectations. (Here, the Schiff concept of

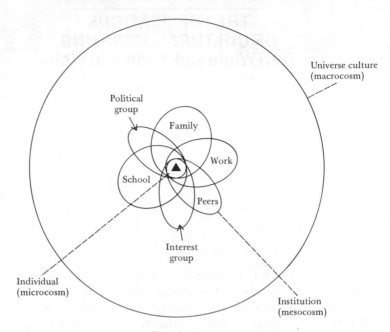

Figure 1
The Cultural Scripting Set: Universe Culture (macrocosm),
Institutions (mesocosms), Individual (microcosm)

"frame of reference" makes the point eloquently, in that C_1 perceives as if all of the data were filtered through the P_2, A_2, P_1, A_1 structure.)

DEFINITION In our experimental book,[2] we were content with defining cultural scripting as "that set of reinforcements or limitations established by the Parent values embodied in the institutions of a culture." By institutions, the definition implies the family—the primary initiator and model—and the interrelated ongoing series of institutions (Figure 2), as well as the value content of the media, the arts, and the entire influencing envelope of modern life (advertisements, fads, "keeping up with the Jones's," subcultural movements). In perceiving the individual as a resultant of the value vectors imposed by a surrounding set of institutions, the Schiffian concept of reinforcement by absence of confrontation around a dystonic behavior is implicit. A value choice is enforced by the absence of modeling and encouragement as well as by an injunction or limiting Parent value.*

---

* Scripting can be effected directly by reinforcement of injunctions that fulfill parental needs or indirectly by not "stopping" the unwanted behavior, e.g., telling a child "be stupid" or *allowing* a child to behave in ways that make him stupid (as *confirmed* by his or her and others' judgment.

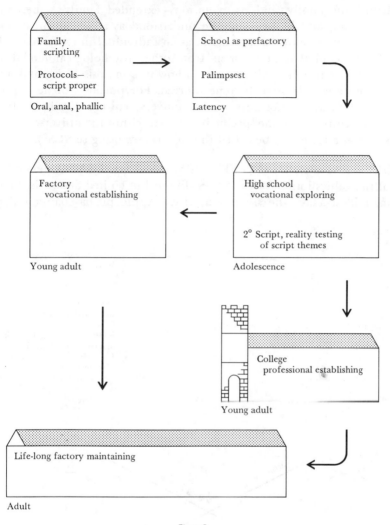

Figure 2
Institutions as Reinforcers of Script

UNIVERSE, INSTITUTION, AND INDIVIDUAL: AN INTERRELATED SET

A main thrust of cultural scripting is the interdependence of the universe culture, the institutions of the culture, and the individual (Figure 1). Much of what is usually defined as clinical pathology, subject disability, or cultural disadvantage springs from an interrelated set of difficulties (as if some gears refused to mesh). As a model, one might see the universe culture as a macrocosm which defines and provides an arena for the microcosm of the individual. From another view, a mass of individuals defined around the same key issues and having the same expectancies molds the universe culture.

Further, the family, and its extensions—extended family, tribe, community, school, and factory—may be understood as a mesocosm at once serving as a universe in miniature and as an individual in extension. The Schiffs' work and that of theorists from other psychological modalities (Laing, for instance) have demonstrated how in symbiosis and grandiosity these separate worlds often become blurred. For purposes of descriptive economy, the interrelationships among universe culture, the institutions within that culture, and the specific individual within the universe culture who serves as a focus will be called the cultural-scripting set (CSS).

A CULTURAL-SCRIPTING SET: LIFE IN THE USA A generalization of the values implied by the CSS—life in the United States—is: mainstream, middle class, the silent majority, "Apple pie-baseball-hot dogs-

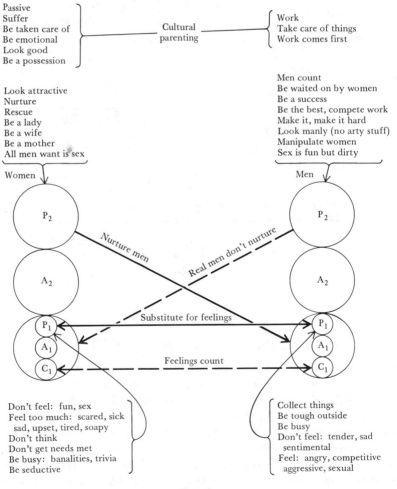

Figure 3
A U.S.A. Cultural Network

Chevrolet USA" (Figure 3). The cultural Parent (P_c) is the persistent set of messages coming from influences within one's milieu. These are parallel to and reinforce the P_2 messages incorporated in the Parent ego states over a lifetime of value orientation by family, school, work, and related institutions in which a Parent authority holds forth (Figure 2). One would expect a close matching of the P_c and P_2 values in an ongoing, functioning society. Individuals who had dystonic values, "don't work" for example, would run counter to the expectancies of the institutions of the universe culture and would suffer the consequences. Those who had syntonic values, "work hard" for example, would be rewarded according to the institutional success ladder. In both syntonic and dystonic values, the behaviors of the individuals would be reinforced consistently, thus effectively limiting the perceiving of options.

There is a story that illustrates the absurdity of the option that runs counter to the universe culture and, thus, to the set of P_2 values. A businessman comes upon an Indian fishing on a river bank and asks him why he doesn't work. The Indian asks why he should work. The businessman goes on to extol the virtues of work, particularly the idea that some day one can make enough money to retire and, then, one can go fishing. The Indian replies, "I'm already doing that!" It occurs to neither one that the other's behavior is an option. That is precisely the function of the values of a universe culture—to maintain expectancies that lead to the preservation of the universe culture.

The injunctions in P_1 vary with the scars of a particular set of Parents' scars sustained in their own childhood from less than perfect parents. Figure 3 injunctions tend to match P_c and P_2 values, such that the needs and wants of C_1 will be minimized. Other injunctions are possible, but these injunctions would be universalized within the culture; that is, one would expect them to be as they are and so they are syntonic. Indeed, their absence would be dystonic, since the culture didn't set up expectations for men to feel tender and women to feel sexual.

CHANGE

A mass change approach to an individual, a group of people, or a portion of a social system would be to design a "new" P_c, a "new" set of cultural Parent influences that would reinforce the change directions which the individual, group, or larger segment decided to modify. In Figure 4, the "old" P_c and the "new" P_c represent alternate influences on the personality of an individual. The "old" is supported primarily by the values in the Critical Parent and also by the habituated behaviors and injunctions of the Adapted Child function,* here represented by the portion of the Adapted Child that the TA observer perceives as overadapted—that is, the

---

* P_1 is the organ from which Adapted Child functions. The use of P_1 as opposed to a functional ego state model is to permit the use of A_1–A_2 alignment in the model.

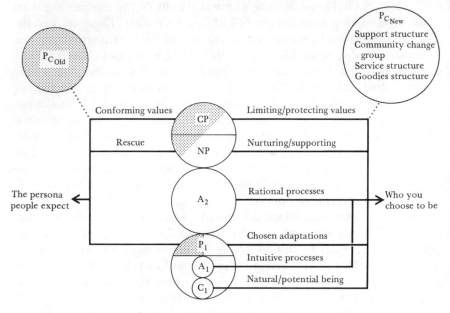

Figure 4
An Educational Change Model

adaptations being more in the service of another than of oneself (following the Schiffian assumption that too much thinking about other people's demands goes into the overadapted response).

The "new" is represented by the bulk of the personality: the NP's care and support of the Free Child (C_1), Adult rationality (A_2), Child intuitiveness (A_1), and the portion of the Adapted Child that does not take care of the self. Within the "new" P_c, there are probably many sources of influence, some of which have concepts that describe their primary function:

1. *Support Structure:* the three or four people an individual uses for support and defining, who are about where she or he is near key change issues.
2. *Community:* a substantial subgroup within an overall culture that supports the new values which change implies. (Examples: Asklepieion, the Schiff Family, Group House, Steiner's radical psychiatry stalwarts, trainees in a large institute.)
3. *Change Group:* the group that supports change and works for change through therapy, information, caring, assorted stroking activities, and so forth.
4. *Service Structure:* a series of services that enrich an individual's life, provided within a society and usually not perceived as important until one moves a physical location or doesn't have money for support. (Examples: the responsive, trusted physician, the reliable food store, the trusted babysitter, the favorite restaurants.)
5. *Goodies Structure:* the treats, things, or people that delight the Natural

Child and can be kept on hand or at a phone call's distance. (Examples: the good novel you want to read, a favorite old movie coming up on TV, a new recipe you want to try.)

Two relatively small portions of the CP and the NP probably have value in support of both the "new" way and the "old" way: respectively, the CP by limiting destructive behaviors, and the NP by buying into a rescue situation, which prevents more fundamental filling of needs and wants. Other functions among ego states are possible and, indeed, probable through the change model (Figure 4), which represents what seems to happen when individual change is undertaken with a P_c change atmosphere.

Another advantage of the change-model approach is that it allows the two systems to operate so that the individual has a choice. The "old" persona may take care of her or him in some situations; in a sense, it did provide a survival style for many years.

FACILITATING CHANGE, ONE TO ONE Many of the change procedures are delivered in a one-to-one relationship in counseling, personnel training, or therapy, so that, within a universe culture encouraging change (the "new" P_c), a heavy emphasis is still made of the personal relationship. In Figure 5, the fundamental transactions are illustrated from the view of procedural effectiveness:

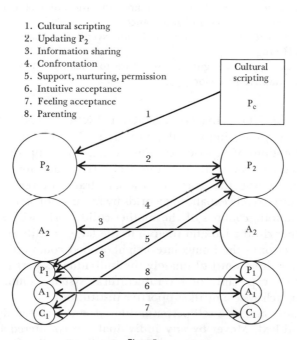

1. Cultural scripting
2. Updating P_2
3. Information sharing
4. Confrontation
5. Support, nurturing, permission
6. Intuitive acceptance
7. Feeling acceptance
8. Parenting

Figure 5
Change Procedures

1. *Cultural scripting:* the supportive change atmosphere, within which the interpersonal procedures take place, forms a congruent, reinforcing envelope of "new" values which facilitate the updating of P_2 values. Updating implies confronting outdated values, filling lacunae (missed or overlooked parenting spaces in the P_2 structure), and reinforcing appropriate operative values. Further, updating implies choosing priorities in values and practicing a benevolent pragmatism.
2. *Updating P_2:* a sharing, modeling, reinforcing process in which the changing person uses her or his P_2 in the updating procedures.
3. *Information sharing:* giving new information as well as putting information already received into a usable perspective. In an increasingly complex society, the gathering and using of information should be a shared function; the fact that the information has been checked out and has worked for the change person makes the data believable. Further, the information is congruent, since it fits the values of the Parent and it satisfies the needs and wants of the Child.
4. *Confrontation:* a limiting and caring transaction that reflects the investment of Parent energy in bringing inappropriate behaviors to an end. Since the individual and the change person have a contract around issues of confronting, the confronting procedure reinforces P_2 values in the individual (P_2-P_2) and sets a model for intrapersonal confronting (individual's P_2-P_1). Potency is a factor of the amount of energy and the consistency with which the therapist acts.
5. *Support, nuturing, permission:* caring and protecting functions of the P_2 are brought to the cause of C_1.
6. *Intuitive acceptance:* feeling and knowing the bond of trust based on experiential Child-to-Child acceptance.
7. *Feeling acceptance:* unconditional, nonexploitative sharing of Child-to-Child feelings.
8. *Parenting:* updating, guided procedure to encourage new, more appropriate, adaptive behaviors.

RESISTANCE TO CHANGES: SCRIPT EXPECTANCIES   The ways in which the young individual perceives the world are based on early biased perceptions of experiences. This is script. It comprises the decisions and expectancies about life that one feels are needed for defending oneself and for setting the world into a safe frame of reference. We will survive in successively expanding worlds by forcing our script expectancies.

The symbiotic confines of the mother-child world will expand to the mother-father-child triad and then onto the larger family community and again further onto the immediate neighborhood community. The extensions will continue until ultimately the individual is part of a larger cultural system or possibly of several cultural systems simultaneously, reinforced in each system by its supportive institutions.

The family acts as a self-perpetuating system once the dynamics have been established. Moves by any individual are countered by resistances and expectancies in the balance of the family. Family systems and their dynamics are accepted as an established truth. The emphasis here is that these dynamics are in keeping with original parental scripting needs and with the cumulative and evolving total family script needs, since each new child and each major family event causes a modest adjustment in the family system. Thus, the family both sets a specific course of behavior for an individual and counters any variant trends.

The family is the first institution involved in cultural scripting. For theoretical purposes, the family has been considered separately,[3] since much of the family's impact lies in the nature of the dependent relationship, particularly the symbiotic bond with mother. In the extrafamilial institutions, the reinforcement is imposed on an already predisposed individual.

Patterns of scarring tend to become universal, either in response to the challenges and deficiencies common to human development (sibling rivalry, tired mothers, symbiosis, and separation anxiety), or in response to culturally characteristic traditions. Patterns of script expectancies within given cultures enable an individual to reinforce his messages; the confrontation of the culturally common script message is rare, since the behavior is accepted as normal.

The possibility of change in an individual's life is limited by his expectancy. The relative uniformity of his culture offers few alternative models. The people who remain within his milieu will seem the same over the years, suggesting that people can't and don't change. Widespread views that substantive change in personality is not possible without massive therapeutic intervention probably reinforce an already pervasive "resigned passivity."

In contrast to the dystonic implication of such passive fatalism, syntonic attitudes limit many people to "successful" behaviors. There is little alternative in the scripting patterns: "Don't take 'no' for an answer," "Find a way, if it takes you all day." The injunction leaves little room for moderation. The heavy syntonic acceptance of academic, business, or athletic success eliminates choice except for the small percentage of "gutsy kids" who kick the script.

AN OLD CULTURALLY REINFORCED SCRIPT: WOMEN'S "DON'T BE IMPORTANT"

The western world's universe culture reflects the expectancies around the role of women. Woman is to serve man as in the Genesis creation statement and is to be defined as successful in terms of the ways in which she functions as wife and mother. This attitude pervades every aspect of culture (religion, myths, literature, art, language), so that within the universe culture a person will perceive a woman's subservience to a man as the natural law. In terms of reality testing, it will pass as a "fact."

The values in the western world vary with the subculture; yet, a universal set of P_2 values paralleling those in Figure 6 could be demonstrated for each subculture. The supportive myths differ, which gives the sub-

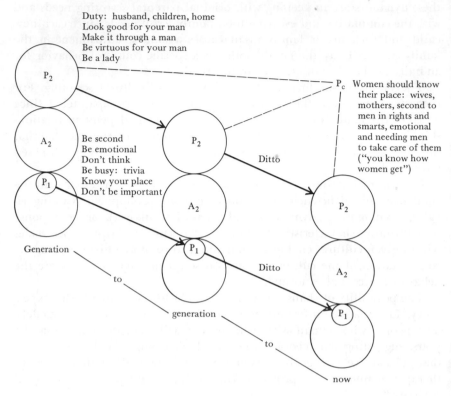

Figure 6
An Old Place: Women's "Don't Be Important!"

cultures their uniqueness (e.g., the Spanish woman's tradition of the virtuous wife redeeming her errant husband; the general Christian tradition of silent suffering in imitation of the Madonna; the pragmatic middle-class tradition of the woman "behind the man").

A MASS CHANGE MODEL: THE EMERGING WOMAN From a change point of view, cultural scripting implies that the most efficient way to promote change for women would be to create a universe culture or, considering the "generation lag," a subculture, since both the old P_c and the new P_c will coexist for decades. In Figure 7, the subculture values are delineated, and these values will be promoted throughout the change community (the media, interest groups, change groups).

The values form a consistent, interrelated CSS, such that any or all of the values are mutually reinforcing. The change person working within the cultural envelope functions as in Figure 5. In Figure 7, some of the thrust for each procedure is illustrated so as to capture the essence of the change interrelationship.

In the new P_c (Figure 7), it seems not a case of women catching up to men, but an issue of women thinking, feeling, and doing "their own

P$_C$ Women can: think and feel
risk and do
be adequate in the "outside" world
be OK with or without a man
be responsible for their own feelings; for their own stroke
giving-getting
make their own success models (don't have to make it like
men make it)
support other women in their growing and changing
(instead of competing)
share with other women (OK too for men to share)
be fun, joyous, smart, exciting, sexual . . . all feelings
are OK
Strokes from women are equal to strokes from men
People are separate: a couple is two, separate, adequate people
choosing to live, work, or have fun together

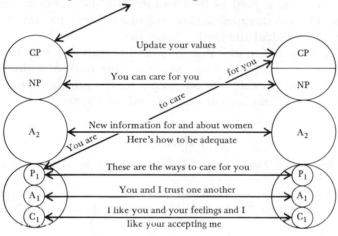

Figure 7
A Mass Change Model: The Emerging Woman

thing" in a changing world. Men are not doing well in terms of intrapersonal satisfactions, although their discomfort with their plight is not as acute as women's. For men, it is more that their awareness level is relatively low, rather than that they are doing "better" in their adjustments to a value-changing society.

CONCLUSION

The energy that we have invested in the cultural scripting model comes from a personal conviction that change is part of life in a rapidly changing world. Skills for dealing with these change pressures and models for mass change are essential to individuals and to responsive leadership. The market for change skills is everyone; the market for therapy (specialized education)* is that small percentage of the population willing to avail themselves of help in the medical model.

* First brought to our attention by Margaret Northcott.

Mass change has the potential to ease the discomfort of entire minorities. Mass change delivery may not have been as obvious in the past; much of the energy of the pioneers in TA application was invested into willing and available subcultures.

It is less important in our model to know where destructive limitation comes from: P_c, P_2, or P_1. The Gouldings' work in redecision and impasse theory enables the therapist to be more effective. The pioneers in script theory and application, too numerous to mention although we all stand on the shoulders of Berne and Steiner, have enabled individuals to understand where they were, where they are, and what they must undo in order to change. Schiff theory has been helpful in giving us "permission" to use Parent effectively, as well as in demonstrating the use of a community structure. The nontherapeutic thrust of our delivery has taken us away and beyond individual and family change delivery.

Finally, the payoff to us is that we, as individuals and as a "decoupled" couple,* are in touch with a *joie de vivre*. Our work over the years has enabled us to incorporate into our own lives the principles that we have shared with our colleagues, our trainees, and our clients.

References

1. Jacob Bronowski, *The Ascent of Man,* Boston, Little, Brown and Company, 1973, p. 411.
2. Terri White and Jerome D. White, *A Transactional Analysis Psychohistory,* Los Altos, California, Goodco Press, 1974 (available Transactional Pubs. ITAA).
3. *Ibid.*

* "Decoupling is our concept for a nonsymbiotic relationship between two people in a primary relationship. Each is separate, adequate, and capable of meeting stroke needs and wants. Each chooses to be with the other. Each of us is autonomous, yet, we can work together and be intimate, often in that oneness that Berne liked to describe as a "crasis."

Toward the end of our decoupling, we were indebted to Ken Mellor for his very insightful information on second-order symbiosis.

IV

Beyond Script Analysis

FIFTEEN

WHAT SHALL I DO TOMORROW?: RECONCEPTUALIZING TRANSACTIONAL ANALYSIS
Fanita English

FINDING TA

Many great theories start out with deceptively simple observations. "Why do apples fall to the ground?" asked Newton. Eric Berne discovered that sometimes he diagnosed better with instant intuition than with pedantic thought. He saw a "mature," respectable lawyer and for awhile it was like transacting with a child. In contrast, while talking with a "totally crazy" psychotic, Berne heard a logical adult. He also found that all of us have ways of oppressing ourselves and/or encouraging ourselves for good or bad purposes with the use of attitudes or a vocabulary that sounds like parents talking to children. He noted that several different systems of feelings, attitudes, and thoughts were taking turns expressing themselves in the Now through the same person, and he recognized that this was a *normal* phenomenon, not a pathological one. Then who or what was directing those different people within us, and could it be that our lives might be better if we could make more deliberate choices as to who or what might steer us when? He told therapists how they might help their patients do just that.

I was an established psychotherapist in private practice when I picked up the book, *Transactional Analysis in Psychotherapy*,[1] just by chance. Berne's message struck me so forcefully that I gulped down the book as if it were a detective story. At last there were answers to some questions that had been puzzling me persistently as a result of my practice.

In Chicago, where I was practicing at the time, none of my establishment colleagues had heard of Berne. I called him long-distance, and a few weeks later, on his way to New York, Berne spent a day with me and four colleagues whom I had hastily recruited.

What followed for me was time in Carmel to learn what I could from Berne and to obtain more formal training in TA from David Kupfer, whom I soon recognized as one of the greatest therapists I had known. I also did some work with Bob and Mary Goulding.

My husband and my friends shook their heads about my continuing passionate interest in TA. It did seem irrational, for it brought my flourishing practice down to almost zero, not only because of my absences in California and the faster termination of my treatment work with patients, but also because I lost my referral sources, all of whom had some connection with the Chicago Institute for Psychoanalysis. They objected to my treating "their" patients in a TA group. And I was even more scorned when *Games People Play* hit the best-seller list and the cocktail circuit. The standard question was how this "simplistic" approach could be effective in dealing with the complexities of human personality.

In retrospect, I am glad that I was thus forced persistently to convey what it was about TA that meant so much to me. At the time such questions troubled me, for my Parent also believed that complications are more honorable than simplicity, and often it was difficult to sustain Berne's answer: "It works." Clearly, my own patients demonstrated significant changes as a result of the contractual TA treatment that I initiated in my practice. It was worth the sacrifice of income and hard-earned prestige.

SCRIPTS AND CONCLUSIONS

MY OWN VIEWS ON SCRIPTS   Although I follow Berne in spirit, some of my new terminology, concepts, and diagrams are at great variance from his and even from my own 1972 essay, "Sleepy, Spunky, and Spooky."[2] From my own clinical experience, I agree with Berne that each of us forms a "script" somewhere between the ages of four and seven, and that it continues to have import throughout our lives. However, I have also found that there are important additions and alternatives to the script that are developed at adolescence.

In contrast to many practitioners, I consider that scripts are valuable assets which evidence one more advantage humans have over other animals. Our scripts *enable* us to blossom, rather than preventing us from doing so, even though they may also contain certain "conclusions" out of early childhood that can be dysfunctional or downright dangerous.

WE ALL NEED A SCRIPT   The child's need for a script reflects an inborn human need for structuring the time, space, and relationships that are ahead of him, so that he can conceptualize boundaries against which to test his ongoing experience of reality.

At about age five, a child awakens to the idea that there is a past and a future, which is a recognition that only humans have. He opens his eyes to a view of chaos; before him and behind him lie the eternity of time and space—there is nothing to hold on to, not even mother! By constructing the outline of a script, he can hold together his hopes, his fantasies, and

his experiences. This becomes a basic structure out of which he can develop a perspective about his life. Thereby he gains a sense of direction
and control and he feels able to steer himself forward into the future even
if the end of the road is not in sight. With a script, he can connect and tie
together his accumulating perceptions, feelings, and thoughts. A script
can facilitate the fantasizing of options in contrast to the disorientation
and confusion that would result from a chaotic view of limitless possibilities.

During the script-structuring age period, the child experiences the intense excitement of being a living human being with ideas. This excitement manifests itself in a flood of "impossible" questions that he persists
in asking, and in increased nightmares. He wants to know: where did he
live before he was born, what happens to people after they die, and does
it happen to mice also? The answers to his questions turn out to be highly
unsatisfactory, and one grownup contradicts another.* How will he reconcile these different answers with all the ideas and images he has gathered
already? Well, at least there's the outline of a script. During the age period
of four to seven, he goes from a little "life story" he may have started out
with and keeps adding and subtracting to it, giving it shape, leaving blanks
here and there, then alternative lines, inserts, footnotes, erasures, and odd
additions. He puts in what he has picked up from his environment and a
jumble of messages and conclusions, positive and negative, that he has accumulated so far. He does this with the mentality of ages four to seven,
during which, as Piaget has shown, data gets organized by means of "syn-
cretic" thinking.³ This means that the child fills out "schemata" of ideas
and/or sets up harum-scarum configurations (Gestalten) of thoughts, observations, and images using illogical juxtapositions, approximations, associations, as well as analogies, fantasies, and magical assumptions about
the forces and objects of his environments. Using the analogy of a the-
atrical script, we can visualize the collected pages of text and illustrations
of the script as representative of Gestalten that are formed and unformed.
Continuing with the analogy, these pages and pictures are bound together
by the existential position that the child established when he was three
years old; it serves as a loose-leaf binder that holds the material together.

In my view, a script is a rather complex combination with some pages
that follow sequentially and some that don't, with ups and downs of content, with magical reversals and magical assumptions that can be positive as well as negative.** Rather than deploring the Child's formation of
a script, I welcome the fact. It is indicative of human creativity that chil-

---

* Ultimately, all the answers add up to Ring Lardner's famous " 'Shut up,' he explained."
** For an example of a creative, totally illogical script story, I refer reader's to Mozart's
The Magic Flute, particularly Ingmar Bergman's recent movie rendering with its un-
explainable reversals of "good" and "bad." For instance, the loving mother who steers
the young man to find his love turns out to be a mean witch, and the bad magician
who has imprisoned the sweet maiden then turns out to be a benevolent dictator.

dren find a way of building an exciting story for themselves during one of the most imaginative stages of their lives. However many irrational elements there may be in a script—including horrible devouring monsters, pitfalls, dangers, and even, in many cases, terrible endings for the unwary hero or heroine—there are also fairy tale elements of excitement, adventure, love, beautiful fantasy, and all kinds of magical tricks and prescriptions as to how calamity can be circumvented and how misfortune can be turned into good fortune. It is these latter aspects that offer clues as to how a person can fulfill himself *through* his script rather than in opposition to it and in fear.

Even a script generated under the worst environmental circumstances contains within itself the Child's own genetic intuitions as to how he might fulfill his inner goals creatively, if certain malevolent fairies and cobwebs can be neutralized. Without a script, the Child ego state would be operating only out of a vacuum of time and space within which there would be no content from which to connect the past to the future, so he would be rootless, like a leaf in the wind. I suspect that certain cases of psychosis represent *lack* of script formation, as a result of which the individual has no background from which to experience the foreground and, therefore, he operates out of a condition of total disorganization.

LOOKING AT SCRIPTS   I shudder when I hear novice trainees blandly imply that a person's script can be defined in one or two sentences and that everything he says or does can be reduced to one or two injunctions or attributions (however useful it may be to recognize also that certain of our life patterns can be monotonously repetitive).

Thanks to Freud we have learned not to discount our daydreams, our fantasies, and even our nightmares. And Jung has demonstrated that they often give us the best insights about what we yearn for and need to express. So does a new look at our script. To get this new look, I have developed the "Four-Story Technique," which I will describe at the end of this chapter. With this technique we gain a good view of the *strengths* of a person's basic script and clues as to how people can get out of traps they may have gotten themselves into. We also work with the fact that people tend to revise and transform parts of their scripts at adolescence, and we evaluate the extent to which these adolescent reactions offer suggestions for new pathways to fulfillment. Therefore, what I call *script analysis* is not necessarily clinical work, though it is often a necessary adjunct for work with certain rigid patients and persons stuck in banal *counterscripts* that they hold on to for fear of their script. (The script itself can never be banal; no five-year-old or adolescent is banal. By definition, "banal" is the opposite of script.) My approach to script analysis is particularly useful for creative people who have curiosity about their untapped resources and who are ready to risk discomfort in exploring these.

THE CHILD CONCLUSIONS   When it comes to the treatment of people who hurt, I do not focus on total "script analysis." There my central clinical emphasis lies in identifying one by one whatever harmful "conclusions" cause difficulties in a person's present-day life. I invite the patient's Adult to evaluate the present-day function of each conclusion we identify. If it is exacting too high a toll, we seek an antidote for the dysfunctional conclusion and we work to get the patient's Child ego state to integrate it and thereby offset the power of the early harmful conclusion. Sometimes such work brings to the surface a whole series of additional conclusions that are attached to the one we work with, and sometimes the process unhinges the individual's defensive existential position, thus generating temporary panic or despair that must be dealt with. However, sometimes the harmful conclusion can be identified and offset rapidly, as an isolated issue.

In my definition, *conclusions* are different from script decisions. Script decisions are made at about age seven, *following* the formation of the script, not before. They can be recalled through verbal or visual memory and thus can be representative of a part of the script. In contrast, conclusions are experienced viscerally, "in the gut," because they were arrived at nonverbally during early childhood, that is, between birth and about age four to five, and many operate as a part of the individual's autonomous functional system. They continue to exist separately within the organism as affect-laden response agents, and usually they are contradictory to one another. They do not lump themselves together into one decision to represent just one guiding principle in a person's life.

A child does not arrive at conclusions simply by the direct ingestion of injunctions or attributions associated with strokes. True, parental messages often do initiate the formation of a conclusion just as they initiate a child's selection of his favorite racket. Even then, a particular conclusion can evolve totally differently from the message of a parent, usually because it represents a combination of messages from different sources. For instance, a person who is chronically withdrawing is not necessarily operating under a "don't be close" injunction, although the net result of his behavior may be that he lacks closeness. He may be operating with a withdrawal racket based on a conclusion that the expression of anger is dangerous.

ENVIRONMENTAL IMPACT ON CONCLUSIONS At all stages of development a child is subject to a collection of environmental forces. These include messages associated with strokes. They also include self-programing tendencies that propel the child to perceive for himself by smelling, tasting, touching, hearing, seeing, feeling, and then *thinking* by means of whatever system of thought operates at each particular chronological stage, intuition being one form of primitive thinking. Many conclusions result from intuitive apprehensions of fears in caretakers, from experiences of excitement and physical pain, from traumatic experiences resulting from going through danger—real or imagined—and from shame or ridicule at the two- to three-year-old age period. A given child's dynamic self-programing tendencies, which are related to different aspects of his genetic endowment, will interact with environmental influences at each stage to form the different conclusions from which he will operate later.

Spitz and others have proved that strokes are essential to survival and that strokes can operate to condition behavior or responses.[4] But it is erroneous to infer from these two separate functions of strokes that *all* early childhood conclusions or decisions result exclusively in obedience to a rigid, systematic, mechanical conditioning process associated with strokes from the Child of a parent. This is a reductionistic assumption that overlooks the fact that there is a multiplicity of drives and responses that are available to a human child at each period of his life.

At each one of his ages, the child is learning (taking *in*) and expressing (throwing *out*), both as a result of his inner drives and in reaction to events and messages around him. At all ages he swings between being both passive and active. And at each stage he is busy *organizing* himself physically, emotionally, and mentally. This is a complicated process that cannot wholly be explained through conditioning or association, or even through stroke theory. He *selects* and *combines* internal or external stimuli with a choice of responding or registering.

At no time are children just passive receptors that get conditioned directly—except that, in infancy, some children actually die of marasmus or other causes if they are deprived of sufficient nutrition and/or strokes. Beyond their very early period, children who survive operate with a "stroke-bank"[5] within their organism. They use their genetic, perceptual, mental, emotional, and physical resources to *process* messages from their environment. In addition, the stimuli that a child registers and elects to respond to are very different at each successive stage of development, particularly at very early stages; the child's needs differ from one stage to another as does his organizing faculties.

Certain crucial conclusions, good or bad, are directly related to strokes (e.g., smiling at mama gets strokes, or banging the crib hard even if it hurts will finally get strokes). There are numerous other conclusions, good or bad, where the direct connection to strokes is so farfetched as to make it useless to understand effectively how the Child will operate later in life. In fact, certain powerful conclusions result from a reaction *against* messages associated to strokes, or from the frequent absence of parental presence. For instance, a conclusion such as "I will only count on me" does not necessarily result from direct "Don't ask" messages. It might be a reaction against too much stroking in infancy that communicated a symbiotic message. It might be reached from being too restrained at the two-year-old stage.

CRITICAL PERIODS AND DIFFERENCES AMONGST CONCLUSIONS   There is a big difference whether a particular conclusion gets reached in infancy, where it could be a step to autism, versus, say, age four or five, where it might lead to distrust or loneliness. A conclusion might also become independent behavior that can be lifesaving at a future time of physical emergency.

The concept of *critical periods* that is used in physiology to evaluate the possible future physical effect of a trauma is also applicable to evaluating significant differences in the effects of comparable messages given to a child at different stages of his development.

The issue of *critical periods* is important not only in relation to the fact that similar messages and inputs will have different impact and meaning at each stage, but also in relation to the fact that similar messages might lead to drastically different conclusions, because each developmental stage represents a different *thinking* system, as shown by Piaget.[6] The thinking process with which a child forms conclusions at each stage of his development varies *qualitatively* according to his age when he forms a particular conclusion. As a result, even if a child has been receiving rather consistent messages during his early childhood, his total Child ego state might maintain, separately from one another, a host of conclusions that can contradict one another. The process whereby one conclusion was established is foreign to the later Child who establishes new conclusions without necessarily reconciling them to the previous ones, and so on; but the previous conclusions are nevertheless retained within the organism, and they can affect behavior or feelings of the grown person's Child positively and negatively. For instance, I carry a conclusion of high trust of strangers (related to my one-to-three-year age period) and another conclusion with high mistrust of strangers (related to later childhood). Currently, I seek to reinstate the earlier conclusion in the hope of offsetting the later one.

Each conclusion can be conceptualized as a configuration which settles within the organism in the structural layer that corresponds to the age of the child when the conclusion was developed. The content of each conclusion varies according to the particular collection of inputs from the environment that was reinforced around the time the conclusion was formed, and according to whatever organizing capacities were available to the child at that time. Thus a conclusion made at eight months related to eight-month-old needs and, being made with eight-month-old physical and mental resources, it will be vastly different from a conclusion made at age four, when the child has been running around and talking to many people. Later in life specific internal and/or external stimuli might revive a conclusion and result in behavior or feelings that may appear contradictory to behavior or feelings that were operating five minutes ago in reaction to a completely different conclusion.

BRIDGES AND CONTRADICTIONS AMONGST CONCLUSIONS

As we develop language, there are some new bridges built to some of the primitive "organismic" Gestalten of conclusions that heretofore existed only separately as visceral feelings or visual imagery. The connection between an earlier, visceral conclusion and a later conclusion that is effected by the use of language may operate in different ways. A child may interpret a metaphor as having literal meaning and use it to reinforce an early conclusion, or else he might reverse it or transform it. For instance, at age two months a baby who picked a "Die" message from his mother's Child but reacted against it by being a demanding baby may survive by getting himself strokes from her Parent and others through insistent howling. He operates with the conclusion "I must demand and make noise to survive." At age four, the phrase "You'll be the death of me," said repeatedly by the mother in response to what is now an irritatingly demanding child, may lead him to conclude that he has magical controlling and destructive powers. Then, depending on what happens later (for example, if mother does get very sick or dies during the child's script age, or even during his adolescence), several different conclusions can be operative regarding energetic behavior. Such divergent conclusions might later manifest themselves through manic-depressive behavior, with omnipotent, daredevil fantasies and behavior alternating with phobic anxiety about his "power" and then attempts to "escape" the conflict by severe withdrawal. Such withdrawal starts the manic-depressive cycle all over again, since the conclusions about being demanding gets reinstated as in the past to ward off the temptation of death through accepting the original "Die" message.

Inherently conflicting conclusions in the Child often lead to subsequent new behaviors that reflect negotiations with the Parent. Alcoholism often starts out from a grown individual's attempt to escape the recurrent turmoil within himself that is generated by contradictory conclusions within his Child when they are stimulated by events in his present-day environment. Advice from the Parent often alleviates this turmoil, but then comes the new need to silence the controlling Parent. Then drinking offers temporary relief from the Parent but brings on the effect of still other conclusions in the Child. Often this would make things better, were it not for the physical damages of alcohol. (Dylan Thomas is an example of the creative writer who performed *better* when drinking than when sober, but the physical effects became disastrous.) In such cases, even if there was a "Don't be" message in infancy, the individual obviously somehow overcame this message in childhood. It is more useful to identify the separate conclusions that he established to *ward off* death and to check out how they worked than to attack the injunction directly. After that it is useful to establish which conclusions contradict one another and to reinforce the useful ones. I have had many cases where "compulsion to drink" simply vanished when the patient saw how he was using liquor to lubricate the internal movement from a message to a conclusion, then to another, contradictory conclusion, and so on (for example, from "Die" to "I'll demand" to "I can kill" to "I'd better hold back because it's too dangerous" to "No! If I hold back I'll be forgotten and die" to "I'll demand" and so on, back through the whole cycle).

One such patient stated (accurately, in my opinion) that he saw how alcoholism had, until this moment, been for him the lesser evil. By enabling him to go through a cycle of expressiveness, anger, and then control through exhaustion and heavy sleep, liquor had temporarily protected him from becoming utterly confused and then "going crazy." In adolescence he had tried to sort out the incongruities within his Child, and he had become the pet of a high school teacher who had seemingly offered "parental help" about his confusion and conflicting feelings. Eventually the patient somehow sensed that he was picking up an episcript to become insane for this teacher. He was a vulnerable recipient for such episcripting because of his particular contradictory conclusions. He escaped becoming "crazy" enough to be hospitalized by making himself unavailable to the process through drinking.[7] By drinking to excess he had found a way both to go through the cycle of contradictory conclusions in his Child and to become stuporous and unavailable to the episcripting influence of his new "parent." Unfortunately, thereby he established the habit of drinking to excess. At age 30 he saw himself as a confirmed alcoholic and entered treatment. From reading he saw himself as scripted to kill himself. The feelings of panic that led to drinking and the pattern of alcoholism evaporated when he recognized that he had not been operating like an animal in response to direct conditioning. He had been trying to orchestrate contradictory conclusions in order to survive rather than to die, and he had been very smart to avoid "help" that might have generated worse consequences.

His previous attempts to redecide about "not drinking to death" had not worked for more than a few months, since, paradoxically, he had been using the liquor in order to maintain and alternate the numerous contradictory conclusions that had kept him alive in childhood, the outstanding ones being: (1) make noise to be cared for—age three months; (2) pull back to live—age 18 months; (3) danger if you explore on your own; (4) danger if you don't take care of yourself independently; (5) rejection if you demand. To stop drinking compulsively, he now had to learn how to alternate safely between expressiveness and withdrawal without feeling scared of these contradictory needs and without needing to drink as a refuge from awareness of his contradictory conclusions.[8]

As the Child grows, many contradictory conclusions can maintain themselves independently of one another without causing undue trouble because of their contradictions. (Example: "It's good to have faith" and "It's good to think for yourself.") Other conclusions will interaffect each other. They might balance each other delicately and neutralize each other, or they might generate conflictive behavior, or they might reinforce each other as a result of additional experiences at later stages of childhood. As in the example above, several conclusions might interconnect into a more complex, seriated pattern of conclusions. So conclusions can operate as "mutually arising causes" or "mutually arising effects" (to use Buddhist phraseology), or they can remain independent of one another. Many also express themselves through a person's script, although as I said before it is impossible to characterize a script as representative of only one or two conclusions or decisions.

SELF-PROTECTIVE CONCLUSIONS Although many of us operate with a number of damaging or dysfunctional conclusions, and although some conclusions can become so harmful that they must be attacked by therapy, let us not assume that all archaic conclusions are harmful or inappropriate for the present, literally or symbolically. For instance, most of us recoil, seemingly by instinct, if we get too close to an open fire, or we avoid gulping down a steaming spoonful of soup, even if our Adult is not on at the moment. Our Child operates with a conclusion which says "It's bad to get burned." We have what looks like an instinctual response against getting burned, although it's not a true inborn instinct. This early conclusion serves us well. It also is useful if we integrate it later into our script with its symbolic meaning. (At the time of script formation the Child has developed the ability to transform images and signs into symbols, although symbol formation is qualitatively different from Adult synthesis. The script includes some conclusions in their literal meaning, and others in both literal and symbolic meanings.)

The original conclusion—"It's bad to get burned"—may have been reached as a result of messages associated with positive or negative strokes, or as a result of experience (touching fire). How it was reached is only of academic interest by the time the person is grown, unless it is interwoven with additional damaging conclusions. What counts is that early conclusions continue to be effective later in life, and if they are useful conclusions that's fine.

GAGIT MESSAGES   Conclusions that may have served useful archaic purposes but are now provoking dysfunctional reactions need to be examined in daylight and updated. Also, if a conclusion that is still necessary was reached too painfully, and if it is associated to an additional, dysfunctional symptom, the separate conclusions may need to be disentangled by means of the Adult's view of reality. For instance a particular child may have arrived at the appropriate "bad to get burned" conclusion through having been burned badly when unsupervised, or by having been punished by burning cigarette butts, or by having been given a "GAGIT" ("Go ahead and get into trouble") message associated to strokes ("Yes, touch the flame, darling, and see if it burns"). He might then carry additional phobic symptoms which are interwoven with the useful conclusion and make it partly dysfunctional. "GAGIT" messages or other crooked messages do not necessarily enforce the messages that came with strokes from the caretaker's Child. Assuming there were additional strokes, even from the same person's Parent, such messages might generate opposite conclusions that prevent the implementation of the original messages. Instead of accepting a "Get burned" or "Get hurt" message, the Child might develop the useful "It's bad to get burned" conclusion. What could develop also are phobic symptoms about fire, excitement, risks, activity, or trusting others, particularly if those others are being friendly! Therefore, it is important for therapists to recognize that certain seemingly dysfunctional symptoms may still serve a self-protective function, since they prevent the person from "automatically" implementing other destructive messages or conclusions that also exist within his Child. For instance, exaggerated fear of fire may represent the Child's attempt to resist operating under a conclusion that says, "I must get hurt to be loved." This does not mean that symptoms should not be confronted, but the therapist does need to be alert to what may lie underneath, lest the cure of a phobia lead to activating a message or conclusion more harmful than the phobia itself.

Thus, in all treatment cases, even those reflecting destructive, "scripty" behavior, the primary treatment task consists in identifying early conclusions clearly and independently of one another and in dealing with them apart from the total script. It is clear that some conclusions set off chain reactions with different sets of additional problems, and that many have affected the script. They must nevertheless be disentangled from one another in treatment. Often it is only by recognizing the most primitive ones that we can understand the later ones that may have appeared reactively.

IDENTIFYING EARLY CONCLUSIONS   Since the primitive conclusions become a part of the Child's organism so very early in life, and since they are not accessible through conscious verbal memory, how is a therapist to identify such conclusions in a grown person? Paradoxically, with training and practice, it is possible to recognize a patient's primitive conclusions rather easily within a standard TA treatment group, and no extraordinary regressive procedures need be used for such purposes, although gestalt therapy work may be necessary in many instances to offer or confirm a diagnostic hunch about an early conclusion or to intervene therapeutically on the primitive level of the Child.

When an early conclusion is stimulated in the Now, it is accompanied by responses of the autonomic system. The patient may or may not be aware of them, but many are evident to outside observation. These are facial or bodily reactions like blushing, tensing, scratching, twitching, blinking, and other reflex-like movements, and, of course, laughter (which is not always gallows laughter).

There are also other circulatory, glandular, "gut," and brainwave phenomena that are not manifested outwardly, except that they are always accompanied by significant momentary changes in the individual's breathing pattern. I have been training myself and my trainees to recognize not only gross facial and bodily responses but, more particularly, sighs and subtle changes in breathing. From these we can infer that there is a sudden "switch" *within* the Child ego state of a patient and that the patient might next be functioning in relation to a conclusion totally different from the one we were dealing with a minute ago. Particular kinds of sighs, slight alterations of voice tone, swallowing, biting the lips, and so forth give clues both to the fact that a new conclusion has surfaced this second and also that we may now be dealing with a different "area of affect" than the one that was influential a minute ago.

AREAS OF AFFECT AND THE SUPERNOW   "Areas of affect" in the Now correspond to the basic drives that lead the child to form conclusions

—namely, inertia, excitement, and survival fear. I will discuss these later as dynamic operational aspects of the total self, rather than as parts of the Child's structure. I have named them Sleepy, Scary, and Spunky.

I have coined the term "SuperNow" for special moments that occur within the framework of transactions or of gestalt "hot-seat" work. Suddenly there is an instantaneous view of the particular age from which the Child is drawing a particular conclusion. At such a moment, I might abruptly stop the flow of whatever else is going on to catch a particular patient's split-second, fleeting reaction to some incidental stimulus, or I might make a point of registering the context of such "autonomic" reactions to establish hunches about what stimulated them. The common denominator between three or four such SuperNow moments occurring around seemingly undramatic issues often leads to identifying a crucial primitive conclusion that keeps surfacing to move a given patient into feelings, behavior, or blind spots that sabotage his fulfillment of what seem like simple goals.

NANCY: CASE EXAMPLE OF ANTIDOTE TREATMENT Before proceeding with more detailed explanations, I will illustrate how one previously undetected conclusion can surface independently of the script, how it can be identified from Now reactions, and how it can be offset by a specific "antidote."

Nancy is a former patient who left treatment three years ago and was doing very well personally and professionally, as I knew from social contact. She came in for an emergency appointment because suddenly she had developed severe insomnia and bouts of anxiety. She said that what had triggered these was a negative year-end evaluation from one of her 30 students. The 29 others had been highly positive. With her Adult, she had recognized that this was an overreaction, and she sought to see the issue in perspective. This kind of reaction to negative strokes was not typical of her nor of what we knew of her script. She was not perfectionistic. She was an experienced teacher. She was not in any way worried about her job or her relationships with her students. Still, she told me, she had been going on and on in her mind about this matter and she had been unsuccessful at stopping this circular train of thought or at dealing with the panic this aroused. When I asked Nancy to quote the evaluation, her composed Adult left; she caught her breath, blushed, stammered, and suddenly I saw a shame-faced two-year-old in front of me breathing jerkily and saying, "Gosh! I could have recited it in my sleep and now I can't remember it!" And she went on rather desperately trying to recall the words of the evaluation.

In my paper on "Shame"[9] I have described how shame experiences at the two- to three-year-old age period have a way of "setting" a conclusion that there is "mortal danger" if there is a recurrence of whatever it is that a child may have been shamed for at that period. The Child ego state carries this conclusion throughout life and will do everything he can to avoid provoking comparable shaming. Should an episode ever occur at some point of that person's life where there is a similarity to the early shaming experience, the Child will "rubberband"[10] right back to that age period and to the panic about "mortal danger" that the body's memory associated to the early shaming. In a grownup, SuperNow indicators of terror associated to shaming at about age two are jerky breathing, blushing, and stammering. These are followed by Adapted Child references to embarrassment, then a switch to the Parent ego state which "scolds" the Child self, often quite indulgently with terms such as "ridiculous" or "foolish." These usually represent *later* parental instructions to the Child, who may have manifested comparable embarrassment in the course of growing up.

Indeed, Nancy took a deep sigh and moved from her panicky two-year-old to her more comfortable Parent, saying, "This is absolutely ridiculous, the test was engraved in my mind!" Because I had witnessed a SuperNow replay of shaming that had probably occurred around the unremembered age of two, I ignored her Parent and asked, "Was there any embarrassment connected to this evaluation?" "Come to think of it, yes," she said. Now she recalled that when she had first gotten the negative evaluation she had not been upset by it, and she had placed it on her desk as a reminder to discuss it with the student later in the day. At lunchtime another teacher (male) came up to her desk to invite her for lunch, and apparently he read something of the evaluation for he teased her about it during lunch. Probably for competitive reasons, since Nancy was known to be a particularly successful teacher, he had kept joking that now he had found her out; her performance was not that great after all! Nancy now realized that it was this teasing that set her off later to obsess about the evaluation and about how she should have "explained herself" to her colleague even though she saw that there was "no point" to justify herself on such a "minor issue."

With this I knew that Nancy must have been shamed by this kind of teasing when she was about two or three years old or her colleague's mild teasing would not have had such impact. Obviously, Nancy was unlikely to remember such an episode but it was clear that she had a conclusion about being in mortal danger if she was ever caught performing badly.

When a therapist identifies a patient's unremembered conclusion by observing the SuperNow reaction, it is often possible to verify the hunch by seeking information from the patient's Adult or Parent.

From whatever she knew of her life and the attitudes of her parents when she was two to three years old, might she have been shamed or ridiculed by them for catching her at what they might have defined as poor performance, I asked. She was puzzled at first, stating that, if anything, she was told that she "always" performed well and was liberally stroked by her mother for precociousness. Then she recalled an anecdote about her childhood that her mother had told her as a funny story and to which so far she had attached no significance. When she was about two, her mother had written to her father, who had been away for a while, that Nancy could now sing foreign-language nursery rhymes. When the father came home in the company of some out-of-town guests, her mother asked her to perform for the company. At that point, Nancy forgot her lines and both her father and the visitors had fun teasing Nancy's mother mercilessly for lying about the accomplishments of her daughter. We can assume that at the time Nancy experienced the teasing as shaming directed at her, hence the subsequent "mortal terror" on being teased by her colleague for her performance. Her sudden forgetting of the text of the evaluation that she had remembered for days probably resulted from a "rubberband" to that episode.

Even if she had not known the particular childhood story that substantiated what I saw, it is by identifying her as a shame-faced two-year-old when I asked her to quote the evaluation that I knew enough to look for the connection to embarrassment. This led her to recognize that it was the *teasing* by the male teacher that had triggered off her overpowering panic, not the evaluation itself, nor her own reaction to it.

Typically, early conclusions generate their own blind spots. Therefore, even as clear-thinking a person as Nancy had only gotten as far as connecting her panic to the evaluation rather than to the subsequent teasing, which she would not have mentioned had I not insisted on checking out the embarrassment. By noting in the SuperNow typical two-year-old "shame" responses, it was easy to diagnose the operative conclusion and move on to treatment instead of floundering around the matter of her reactions to the evaluation itself.

It is useful to note that even so potentially upsetting a conclusion as the one I just described does not necessarily characterize the script. For instance, Nancy's script could not be defined as "Be perfect" or "Don't succeed" or "Don't enjoy." Most of the time she performed well with ease and with plenty of self-acceptance for those occasions when she did not do so well. Nor did she usually get unduly intimidated by men. Although certain reinforced conclusions get included in the script, and a collection of early conclusions will determine the *existential position* at age three, they contribute to the script's pattern only indirectly. There are many others, bad *and* good, which simply maintain themselves independently and coexist with one another. Many are even contradictory to each other. They can remain inactively imbedded in the Child much of a person's life unless they are brought into play by a particular set of circumstances, as in the example with Nancy. By contrast, there are other conclusions which significantly initiate or establish rackets and games.

When a damaging unremembered conclusion is identified, it must be translated into Adult vocabulary in order to find an antidote. With the cooperation of the patient's Adult, the groundwork can be laid for "corrective experiences" that can offset the potency of the conclusion.

Translated, Nancy's early conclusion was that she would be in "mortal danger" if she was ever ridiculed for poor performance, particularly by a man. From previous work with Nancy, I knew that there was no need for special caution in contracting for "antidote" experiences, though more evaluation might be needed in other cases. Nancy agreed to reread the text of the negative evaluation and to brag about it to as many colleagues as she found, particularly male ones. Preferably, she was to recite the text and allow herself to hear any teasing that might ensue. A few days later, she telephoned to report laughingly that she had fulfilled her contract and that the panic had disappeared.

Of course, there are other examples where the identification of a harmful conclusion is not quite so easy, and I might need to use gestalt techniques or engage the patient in doing special exercises. The point I want to underline here is that primitive, pre-script-age conclusions which the patient cannot consciously remember do not necessarily determine the total script, although they might surface under certain circumstances. Also, early unremembered conclusions can be recognized independently as a result of their operation in the SuperNow. They can be translated into Adult language and examined and modified when necessary. Usually all this can be done in conjunction with work in a regular TA group.

SUBSYSTEMS WITHIN THE CHILD

SECOND-ORDER STRUCTURE Conclusions are formed and maintained at different levels in the structure of the organism, and a grownup's Child operating in the Now can switch around and represent some *very different* chronological stages of his Child. As a result, I have found that it is misleading to diagram the second order structure of the Child as C_1, A_1, and P_1, since these appellations imply structural subsystems when they actually correspond to functional aspects of the total Child.

Berne's great discovery was that psychological development does not go by linear progression like physical growth (i.e., that the Child ego state does not just grow *into* the Adult ego state).[11] The Child persists within the grownup as a separate *system* of thought and feeling. Similarly, the second order structural diagram of the Child must represent the fact that within the Child system there are several coherent *subsystems*. These are very different from one another, and they do not necessarily blend into the one system that we later identify as the Child ego state of a grownup.

Before he was seven years old, Johnny did not exist as a C_1, Demon, or as a P_1 Electrode. However, he did exist as a full-fledged baby, then a one year old, a two year old, and so on, and there are photographs to prove it.[12] At different ages, little Johnny had different physical, perceptual, cognitive, and emotional tools which he used to select different stimuli to respond to. With these, he established different conclusions for himself, even though he seemed to be growing gradually from one age to the other. Compare the difference between what interests an infant and what interests a three-year-old; look at the difference between the photographs of Johnny as a baby, Johnny at five, and Johnny at two. Just as the gradual development of the Adult does not erase the *separate* phenomenological existence and function of the Child ego state (and this was one of Berne's great discoveries), so does the advent of age six not erase the fact that a distinct two-year-old Johnny *Child* continues to exist within the six-year-old Johnny. When six-year-old Johnny later operates as a Child ego state within 30-year-old Mr. Jones, there sit within him several other Johnnys representing the several distinctly *different* systems of thought and feeling that Johnny used in his past.

SWITCHES AMONGST SUBSYSTEMS OF THE CHILD

Anyone who knows children will confirm that a six year old can switch between different "systems of thought and feeling" from moment to moment, just the way you and I might switch ego states from one moment to another. Six-year-old Johnny might transact as a two year old one minute, then again as a six year old, then as a one-month-old infant, and then back as a six year old. These switches do not operate in an orderly regressive or progressive fashion, any more than do the ego-state switches of a grownup. TA teaches us how to recognize switches in ego states by differentiating amongst their characteristics in a grownup. Similarly, knowledge of typical behaviors and thought patterns of different ages of children helps a therapist to pinpoint with precision which subsystem of the Child one is dealing with at a given moment, with full knowledge that switches are likely *within* the Child ego state in addition to switches amongst Parent, Adult and Child.

When a therapist attacks a harmful conclusion within a given subsystem, often the Child will switch from that subsystem to another in order to be able to hold on to his archaic conclusion. Just because such switches interfere with therapeutic interventions at certain times, it is a mistake to assume then that the only alternative treatment method is to go for total changes through total regression to previous stages of development. To do this is to follow the precedent of therapy which Berne reversed through his discovery of the value of the Child. In the past, if a person revealed problems in his Child he was treated as a "childish" personality who needed total treatment to become more mature. Rather than assuming that certain behaviors need to be treated through regressing the total person to a particular stage of childhood development, it is possible for therapists to refine their skills to recognize, in the Now, the characteristics and manifestations of each important Child subsystem through which a patient may be expressing himself in the course of treatment. This leads to educated guesses as to what conclusion a patient may be operating with right now, how it was arrived at, what may be done to change it if it is harmful, and how interventions might affect other conclusions that may have been identified previously. This kind of awareness also leads to using the appropriate interventions with split-second timing. Be ready for the next chance if there is a switch. We all know that there is no point in reasoning with a patient when he has switched to his Parent, although it might be very useful to do so when he is in his Adult. Similarly, there is also no point in dealing with a conclusion that exists in one subsystem when the patient has switched to a completely different subsystem of his Child.

As I illustrated with the example of Nancy, identifying the particular subsystem of the Child that is being represented in the SuperNow will offer important clues for guessing at the conclusion that is causing trouble. My intervention with Nancy was effective because I recognized that the upsetting conclusion (shame for being teased about performance) sat in her two-year-old Child subsystem. I enlisted her Adult to evaluate this conclusion but *also* her five-year-old Child subsystem who had a conclusion about the excitement of trying something new. It is by stimulating her five-year-old Child that I got her to accept quickly the challenge of the "antidote" procedure. Had she switched to a helplessly crying Baby subsystem when I suggested the antidote of bragging about the bad evaluation I might first have had to deal with additional, more primitive conclusions, about challenges or fear.

SWITCHES WITHIN CHRONOLOGICAL CHILDREN

The ability to recognize differences in the subsystems of the Child is also useful in working with young children. Four-year-old Johnny does not have a *little Adult* that is four and a *Child* that is two. He can be communicated with better if one distinguishes between a total four-year-old Johnny and a total two-year-old Johnny within him, plus a baby Johnny, etc. Accept that it is OK for him to be one-year-old Johnny at times, with a one-year-old's way of thinking and feeling. It is also OK for Mommy to admit to herself that at times she has more fun playing with cuddly baby Johnny than with question-asking four-year-old Johnny. Dad may enjoy four-year-old Johnny more. Such understanding would prevent the misuse of TA by some parents who now simply use TA vocabulary to communicate time-worn parental adaptive messages. They will tolerate totally regressive Child behavior and feelings "at the right time"—i.e., at bedtime—but otherwise they tell him that it is better to be an *Adult* four-year old than a two-year-old rebellious Child, especially when it comes to obeying parental directives!

WORKING WITH SWITCHES AND CONCLUSIONS

When I work, I like to imagine a little home movie screen above each patient's head on which I see him or her in a scramble of scenes at different ages—maybe at age three, then infancy, then age four, according to whatever Child subsystem is being represented. I expect trainees to become well versed in general early child development, including knowledge of physical stages of growth. I want them to be familiar with Erikson's stages of emotional development and Piaget's stages of cognitive development. I encourage them to practice combining these stages in their heads and to learn what are the functional aspects of the Child ego state that correspond to each stage of development. We practice in identifying, as well as possible, what age is reflected in the operation of another person's Child at a particular moment of stress or pleasure. With such practice therapists can make educated guesses as to strengths or problems at particular critical ages of a person's early childhood. Usually people have been told enough about their early childhood so that they can validate or invalidate specific guesses, even though they cannot consciously remember the messages or experiences that led them to their early conclusions. By having an idea of typical thinking and behavior that correspond to specific ages, the therapist can understand how a particular conclusion will operate now. This is most important in evaluating treatment options, in determining the best treatment antidote, and in knowing how to offer it. In some cases, it is useful for the therapist to know how to move into the particular mental/perceptual system of the particular-aged Child through which a conclusion is operating and to offset it with the appropriately targeted permission. In other cases, like Nancy's, it is sufficient to enlist the patient's Adult and another system of the Child in translating the conclusion and making an antidote contract.

A NEW STRUCTURAL DIAGRAM OF THE CHILD

Because of all the above, I have needed a new diagram to represent the second order structure of the Child. It is necessary both in order to help identify the particular Child subsystem that is active during a given transaction, and to record, in "translated" Adult words, whatever dysfunctional messages or conclusions might be imbedded within that particular Child subsystem. The most obvious way to diagram the inner structure of the Child ego state would be like a cross-section of a tree trunk, which actually has a recognizable ring for each independent unit of its past existence, and significant markings for the equivalents to the tree's "conclusions" within each ring. Figure 1 is my diagram of the second-order structure of the Child. The inner core represents infancy and the subsequent rings represent separately identifiable subsystems that added themselves on as the child grew. Each number identifies a separate subsystem, and each letter indexes a conclusion that has been identified in treatment and is written out in "Adult translation" on an accompanying chart.

With this diagram, we can visualize how different messages, conclusions, or experiences can exist in different layers of the Child ego state, and how messages that were given at, say, age one or two would have had a very different impact and could lead to very different conclusions than even the same kinds of messages or experiences at, say, age five. In addition

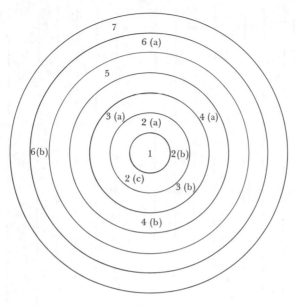

Figure 1

to identifying developmental occurrences, if we visualize such a diagram three dimensionally and think of a grownup's Child as the horizontal cross-section through which one can dip down into a variety of layers, it is possible to conceptualize how a person might be operating in the Super-Now out of his infant Child, then a minute later out of his three-year-old Child, then his two-year-old, and so on.

I am of divided opinion as to whether the Child ego state gets fixated at about age five to seven years, as Berne stated (no doubt under the influence of his psychoanalytic background), or whether it keeps growing past that age. By drawing the layers of the Child in a circular fashion as above, if we want to we can visualize adding more circles to represent later stages of the Child ego state's development beyond age seven, even all the way up to our present age; however, I am inclined to agree with Berne and to assume that, even though we grownups might learn to *use* our Child better, age seven does represent an approximate chronological limit for the development of the Child ego state. Past age seven, the Parent ego state operates as an additional system that can be identified separately, and then, past age twelve, there is the beginning of logical thought, i.e., the smooth operation of the Adult. There is a valid argument to be made for drawing the second-order structure of the Parent and Adult with inner circles representing their own earlier existences within the organism, perhaps with a nuclear "Child" inside. However, in the present context, I prefer to leave these questions open and to revert to the subject of clarifying for patients that the Child ego state is made up of layered, operational subsystems which contain a variety of "conclusions," that the dysfunc-

Name: _____

Developmental age range	Name	Conclusion	Specify whether adaptive or reactive to message/experience
1. 0-3 months	Infant	_____	_____
2. 3-8 months	Baby	_____	_____
3. 8-14 months	Exploring toddler	_____	_____
4. 14 mos.-2 yrs.	Walky talky	_____	_____
5. 2-3 years	Contro	_____	_____
6. 3-4 years	Exister	_____	_____
(Defensive position, rackets)			
7. 4-7 years	Scripter	_____	_____
Theme of stories:	(1)	_____	
	(2)	_____	
	(3)	_____	
	(4)	_____	
Remembered script decisions (ages 5-7 yrs):		_____	_____

Figure 2

Chart A. Subsystems of Child Ego State

tional ones can be identified, and that when we record them we can recognize their different etiology, impact, and possible interaction with one another in the Now.

A CHART FOR CLINICAL PRACTICE ("A") In clinical practice, rather than using the structural diagram of the Child in Figure 1, I find it easier to use a chart with horizontal lines and to conceptualize the layered subsystems of the Child like the geological layers of the earth, where each layer represents its own structural stage and also contains various separately identifiable artifacts and fossils that represent the historical stage of the geological layer. Messages may have entered the geological layer at the time of its formation or they may have erupted from previous layers. They can remain immovably in their spot, or they may surface either separately or in combination with rock formations and artifacts of an even earlier period. Such surfacing results from the operation of external or internal forces ranging all the way from slow erosion to volcanic explosion.

Figure 2 is a model of chart "A" which I use during treatment instead of a script matrix (I keep handy a mimeographed supply). On the chart I make appropriate notations in pencil so the "translation" of whatever conclusions we identify can be refined as treatment advances.

When you look at the chart you will see that each name and number stands for a distinct subsystem of the Child ego state within which there might sit one or more conclusions. Next to each name are the developmental age ranges during which separate conclusions might be reached. I do not claim rigid scientific precision in making distinctions between one subsystem and another, because stages of development overlap onto one another, particularly as the infant grows older. Research and empirical observations have demonstrated that the subsystems I have named correspond roughly to critical markers or signposts in the physical, mental, and emotional development of a growing child. There are significant differences in capabilities and functioning between one stage and another, so that each is a "coherent system of thought and feeling" within which there might lie one or more conclusions, each of which might be very different from previous or subsequent conclusions.

DISTINCTIONS AMONGST CHILD SUBSYSTEMS Before Piaget, mental development was seen exclusively in terms of intelligence and performance, with the additional view that performance was also affected by physical and emotional processes. Piaget has proved that there are significant differences among "typical" methods of thinking at different points of a child's development, regardless of intelligence.[13] The operation of these different processes must be taken into account to understand how an individual might have conceptualized differently what may have been similar inputs from his caretakers at different stages of growth. Also, similar genetic factors operate differently at different stages of growth. There is complex interaction between the child's physical, mental, and emotional endowment and his age-related patterns even when it comes to genetic determinants, let alone environmental factors.

Even today, professionals still tend to think of development in three categories: physical, cognitive, and emotional. There has not been sufficient research done on how these aspects intertwine year by year, although Spitz, Bowlby, and Jerome Bruner are remedying this regarding the first years of life. Researchers and theoreticians in one area of development acknowledge the value of correlating with other areas, but then they get swamped with the multitude of data. Each researcher appears to end up focusing on one area to the detriment of others. For instance, Erikson has emphasized stages of emotional development and Piaget has emphasized stages of cognitive development. And physiologists see the genetically programed stages of physical development as principal agents for all stages. At the other extreme, clinicians often do not account sufficiently for the physical determinants of change even when they recognize the ongoing interaction between emotional and mental development.

In seeking to correlate research on child development from the three different major perspectives, I, too, have felt swamped and have recognized that volumes are needed to correlate the data and spell out the fine-point distinctions between one subsystem and another. For practical purposes, I have limited Chart A to those distinctions among Child systems that rather obviously distinguish one stage of childhood from another, i.e., where there are evident differences in physical skills, in perceptual and mental abilities, and in emotional development. Such differences would stimulate different conclusions at different stages, even to similar stimuli in the same family environment.

To use Chart A, I have taught myself to recognize the typical differences in appearance and manner when a grown person operates out of one subsystem or another. For instance, there is a recognizable difference in appearance and manner when a grown person is crying out of a helpless *Infant Child* than when the same person is crying out of *Contro Child* (that is, controversial, seeking control by temper tantrum), even if the stimulus in both instances is panic.

I invite the reader to train himself similarly, to develop his own acuity of observation in order to familiarize himself with the particular characteristics of one Child subsystem as distinct from another. These become quite obvious when one pays attention to such differences while watching children in nurseries, playgrounds, or, as I do, on board airplanes. The next step is to remember that the age differences, which we distinguish from one another when we watch live children, maintain themselves later as separate entities within the Child ego state of a grownup. These entities do not transform themselves from one into another, the way a child's small bones grow into larger ones. Rather, they remain as separate systems complete with their own idiosyncratic Gestalten of combined feelings and thoughts. These, then, exist as conclusions that are stored within each Child system like so many favorite rattles, teddy bears, dolls, and toy trains that indispensably belonged to the Child at each separate period of his life. They remain there with all their accrued importance, ready to be picked up at moment's notice as the tried and true basic tools for comfort and excitement in response to one stimulus or another that may appear later in life.

CONCLUSIONS WITHIN SUBSYSTEMS

In the space next to each subsystem label on Chart A, I enter whatever important identified conclusions seem to be imbedded within that subsystem. I translate conclusions from primal feelings to formulated language even if it's clear that originally many were set as bodily experiences or as self-programed reactions or responses. Some harmful conclusions exist principally as inhibitions against unwanted feelings or behaviors. These often result from injunctions such as "Don't feel," "Don't use your senses (touch, etc.)," and so on. Sometimes they relate to persistent mislabeling of emotions formerly expressed as behaviors by the child.

It is these categories of conclusions that usually form the basis for *rackets*. Other translated conclusions are more complex and represent an attempt to reconcile two opposite messages. These conclusions lead to a particular sequence of racket-game-racket. (Example: "I'll provoke Mommy —because Daddy likes it—then feel scared after.") This can get replayed as a sequence: (1) rebellious challenges to women (racket); then (2) "Now I've Got You . . ." (game); then (3) fear of women; leading to (4) renewed, now dependent, appeal to women from Child (racket); and so on.

However, it must be remembered that each subsystem also contains many conclusions that are protective; we need not be concerned with these. I also make notations on the chart regarding "antidotes" that prove successful. At the same level as conclusions there is space to enter whatever messages or experiences may have led to a particular conclusion or racket, either "adaptively" (i.e., the message and the conclusion are similar) or "reactively" (i.e., the Child used his resources—genetic or from other stroke sources—to reject the proffered message and to establish a conclusion against it). For instance, "I'm a killer" is a conclusion that can exist in one of the Child's subsystems as a result of an attribution ("You're a killer —I almost died when you were being born"), or it can result from a reactive fantasy *against* a different message such as "Stay with me always." You will note that I have added a line for "Remembered Script Decisions." In my experience, remembered script decisions *follow* script formation rather than precede it. Remembered script decisions can offer significant insights to certain parts of the script if we keep in mind that they do not characterize the person's total script.

ADJUNCTIVE CHART ("B") As an adjunct to Chart A, which is my principal reference point for treatment, I often use the additional Chart B (Figure 3), which is self-explanatory and allows for other data.

Neither of these charts should be used bureaucratically or to stop the flow of treatment. They are simply aids to therapist and patient. Most

Name of patient: _____

	Mother	Father	Other important caretakers during early childhood*
1. From Child ego state:			
a. Nonverbal messages			
b. Verbal or overt messages			
2. From Parent ego state: Instructions (for counterscript)			
3. Typical behavior and/or statements			
a. Re: child			
b. Re: others in household			
c. Re: self			

Family motto (as experienced during grade school period): _____

*List separately with whatever information is available regarding the early age periods when they might have been influential: examples are grandmothers, nurses, older siblings, aunts, uncles, etc.

Figure 3

Chart B. Information about Messages and Instructions

patients are long since cured and gone before all notations are entered, but the headings on the charts do act as useful reference points for diagnosis and treatment, particularly when there are many dysfunctional or contradictory conclusions operating out of the different subsystems of the patient's Child. However, if I note outstanding incongruities in the patient's conclusions, I do ask informational questions such as who the different caretakers were at different stages of very early childhood. Often such information helps to reconstruct the positive or negative influence of additional caretakers such as grandparents, nurses, and older siblings at critical early periods. Patients can usually check out my hunches about early influences by questioning their relatives regarding the roles of difference persons toward them during their unremembered childhood, or, alternatively, by inquiring about significant crises in the lives of their parents at these unremembered times.

Also, I often encourage patients to remember or make up the *family motto* that they consider most representative of their total family during their grade-school years, and I enter it on Chart B. Since this is the period when their Parent ego state is forming, the *motto* gives me ideas about the banal script or counterscript they may be operating on as an alternative to their basic script.

DEVELOPMENT OF SUBSYSTEMS

Here is a brief description of the seven stages and Child subsystems that are listed on Chart A:

(I) INFANT: THE COENESTHETIC SYSTEM (0–3 MONTHS)   Birth! I won't elaborate on theories about perceptions within the womb, or trauma of birth, though it is now known that already before birth the infant's genetic endowment gets influenced by environmental forces. (For instance infants of drug-addicted mothers are born with addiction.)

Infancy starts by taking in a breath of air. Buddhists say that this initiates a debt to the world which is only repaid when the last breath is expired at death. Between his first breath and his last, the individual will or will not develop himself as a "prince." Hopefully, he will bring to fruition his full genetic endowment by becoming creative, joyful about living, and aware of his strengths and limitations. He will become autonomous yet related to others, and, finally, he will gladly transmit the best of his essence to future generations. Much will depend on innumerable environmental variables that immediately converge on the newborn infant (for example, where and to whom he is born makes a big difference). Such variables and many others will continue to influence him in many different ways during his childhood, but always there will be his drive to manifest himself in accordance with his own, unique genetic code. How? "Being is knowing," say the ancient Hindu scriptures, and modern-day geneticists agree.

During his first three months of life, the infant cannot use some of the senses he will use later, such as sight. But he has a special system of perception, which René Spitz calls the "coenesthetic system," whereby "perception and responses take place on the level of deep sensibility and in terms of totalities, in an all-or-none fashion."[14] Reception and the corresponding responses are totally visceral. They are "evoked by signals and stimuli which are completely different from those operating later. . . . The resulting mode of communication is on the level of . . . animal communication." The infant receives signals from his environment as vibrations to his total body, rather than as strokes. He responds to "equilibrium, tension, posture, temperature, vibration, skin and body contact, rhythm, tempo, pitch, duration, tone, resonance, clang, and probably a number of other [signals] of which the adult is hardly aware and which he certainly cannot verbalize." Spitz points out that as adults we no longer consciously use this system of communication because "we have replaced coenesthetic signals by diacritically perceived semantic symbols," so it is difficult for us to conceptualize that infants have the fine "extra-sensory perception" that is later considered a rare gift owned only by "soothsayers, artists, musicians, and nursing mothers." Actually the infant's system is comparable to that of animals, "who know as a matter of course when someone is afraid of them and act without hesitation on this knowledge."

From his meticulous observations, Spitz has deduced that "affective signals generated by maternal moods seem to become a form of communication with the infant. These exchanges between mother and child go on uninterruptedly without the mother necessarily being aware of them . . . below the surface, the ebb and flow of affective energies move the tides which channel the current of personality development into one direction or another."

All this is pertinent to our realizing that during his early months the infant registers through "vibrations" rather than through actual stroking, and he takes in one of two global messages: either "Joy! Come forth into the world!" or "Horrors! Go back to where you came from!" Simply stated, it's "Come forth!" or "Go back!"

Of course, many infants and babies die of marasmus or become autistic from insufficient care or other causes. For the purpose of this chapter, I will exclude such cases and those of physically battered or nutritionally deprived children, and assume "average" American circumstances during childhood. Even so, a high proportion of persons who seem to function well as grownups were the recipients of coenesthetic "Go back" messages through the "vibrations" of their mothers. They flourished anyway, either because they got care and stroking thanks to the mother's Parent and Adult or because they had additional caretakers (father, nurses, grandparents, older siblings) who sent out positive vibrations to the infant when he was held. Still, we must acknowledge the infant's primitive capacity for subtle perceptions of feelings in the mother as a fact of human nature that even takes precedence over the need for strokes. What is important is neither to blame the mother for involuntary communication nor to be squeamish about evaluating the very first emotional message that was absorbed during infancy. Even if it is counterbalanced by other vibrations, many strokes, and later conclusions, good or bad, the early sense either that the world beckons or that it wants you out never quite leaves the organism. Our coenesthetic system of perception and response continues to exist as a kind of mental system that is even more primitive than intuition—which, itself, precedes organized thought.

Erikson tells us that at the first stage of life we establish trust or mistrust,[15] and perhaps this statement suffices. I believe there is a stronger distinction to be made between persons with a "Come forth" imprint, as I call it, versus those with "Go back," in that the former radiate a feeling of welcome wherever they are, whereas the latter radiate the sense of feeling unwelcome. Regardless of all later conclusions, even very damaging ones, persons with a "Come forth" imprint operate with a conviction that life is worthwhile, even if they live in situations of deprivation or stress. They feel lucky and are recognized as such by others. They are "born with a silver spoon." Such persons do, indeed, generate additional luck for themselves because of their basic optimism. "To him who has shall be given" says the Bible, acknowledging the unfairness of life. In mythology, Odysseus is such a lucky hero. The story says that the goddess Athena "loved him from birth." Even though Poseidon, the oceanic "father figure," later sought to destroy him, Odysseus turned his misadventures into a series of successful exploits. In real life such persons need good access to their Adult to stay alive. Often they remain too unconcerned about protection if, during childhood, they also have been supported by "magic thinking." Often they operate with a kind of careless rashness that can ultimately destroy them. (This may have happened with John and Robert Kennedy and other luminaries.)

In contrast, persons who survive the "Go back" imprint may operate with a basic pessimism about life but with a kind of fierce determination to prove their right to live. However, such persons may get themselves into trouble if additional conclusions lead them to keep "proving themselves" in harmful ways; they will fight nonexistence to the absolute limit. Having weathered their biggest crisis—survival in infancy—their coenesthetic system remains perpetually vigilant against the ultimate catastrophe of their own death. Such persons are more attuned than others to picking up hostility, anger, or danger around them. This can serve them well, because they work against it. They, too, must learn to use their Adults lest they go overboard in identifying and fighting enemies. They operate with a great deal of what is called nervous energy, in that their system is perpetually fighting the "Go back" message and they fear relaxation lest it implement the message. Being driven to achievement in order to make their mark often puts them into tense situations that challenge them even further to success. Conversely, like Macbeth, they are driven by a "vaulting ambition" which finally "o'erleaps itself and falls. . . ." Richard Nixon may be such an example, again with due allowance for innumerable additional factors, including many subsequent conclusions.

Note that popular writers have seen "suicidal" tendencies both in John

Kennedy, who emanated a sense of feeling welcome, and in Richard Nixon, who radiated a sense of feeling unwelcome. In actual fact, John Kennedy's "luck" often worked well, as in the PT 109 episode, and as in gaining the Presidency against the odds of being Catholic. Perhaps it also led him to disregard the statistical probabilities of danger, which proved out when he was killed.

By contrast, Nixon survived even the self-made disaster of his career. He may have operated with an inner need to escalate crises and thereby refuel his primitive determination to prove that he could keep "overcoming" the Infant's and Baby's recurrent depressive hopelessness about feeling unwanted in this world.

Because the early coenesthetic experience is so enveloping, it is possible to recognize this early imprint in the people we work with as therapists by awakening our own coenesthetic system to the "vibrations" or "radiations" of other persons. The awakening of our own coenesthetic system can be terrifying at first if we ourselves have been the recipients of "Go back" vibrations. Ultimately we are better off even so, because as grownups we can then draw on the additional resources of our Adult to build on whatever beneficial conclusions exist in our other systems.

It is necessary to remember that persons who radiate "good fortune" and feel "lucky" may also have additional harmful conclusions that may lead to difficulties in life; and that persons who survived "Go back" messages are often the ones most highly motivated to success in the Western world, though sometimes it is at the cost of tremendous effort and tension throughout their lives. Many suffer from insomnia, startled responses, and a multitude of psychosomatic disturbances generated by tension, such as ulcers and high blood pressure. Relaxation or meditation can relieve such symptoms, but characteristically such persons are the ones most likely to get upset by such procedures, even if they clamor for them. This in itself is a diagnostic indicator. I use certain specific meditational techniques for some such cases, but I also work with the Infant panic these generate, and I am careful about the Adult contract.

Even though people with coenesthetic "Go back" messages typically suffer from insomnia, they should *never* be given sleeping pills. Their body is set to fight relaxation so they require increasingly heavy dosages to sleep. Finally the recurrent chemical input overcomes their body's fight against the coenesthetic feeling of not belonging in this world, and thereupon they succumb to death by overdose, because they give up the fight to live. This may have been the case with Marilyn Monroe. In the course of childhood she got many additional harmful messages that reinforced the coenesthetic "Go back" message of her first months, but she fought these valiantly. It is not a coincidence that she herself placed a well-nigh magical value on her body, even though she also sought to cultivate her mind. She might not have given up the fight to live had she not been encouraged to use chemical means for the relaxation she needed. Ultimately, I believe this led her into complying with the death messages she was resisting through insomnia. In a case like this, there should be clear

Adult explanations about how as an infant there was a "survival" need to avoid too much sleep lest she be forgotten and allowed to die. A graduated program of supervised meditational work offers the repeated corrective experience. The grownup body can be allowed to "let go" in a safe place, because she now knows how to get up "out of the crib" when she wakes. Therefore, relaxation would not have the dreaded consequence to the person of being forgotten and getting sucked into the ultimate inertia of nonlife.

(II) BABY: FROM OMNIPOTENCE TO IMPOTENCE (3–8 MONTHS)

At the beginning of this stage, the infant moves from coenesthetic perception to what Spitz calls "contact" perception. Now he registers the physical strokes he receives passively and he also actively uses his own hands and fingers and lips to touch and to distinguish between the feel of one object and another. Following "contact perception"—i.e., the use of touch as his principal form of experience, both passively and actively—the Baby moves on to "distance" perception, i.e., he can now also use sight and hearing to make distinctions. Smiles and frowns which are perceived by sight rather than by touch now acquire the value of physical strokes, and so do specific sounds. This is the beginning of the human ability to manipulate symbolic meanings such as objects that can actually be "handled." When the baby finds that he can smile meaningfully at his mother or that she does not appear instantly when he calls, he discovers that there is a difference between his own volition and that of his mother. She does not always want what he wishes, so the baby establishes conclusions as to what will get him the most strokes. Is it by yelling loudly? By being quiet? By crying in the nighttime or in the daytime? When there's a lot of commotion around, or when the house is still?

During the two to three months that overlap the Infant stage and the Baby stage, all babies, even those who had coenesthetic "Go back" messages, operate with a sense of omnipotence. This is primarily due to their lack of differentiation between themselves and the environment. This leads to the fantasy of being able to control others by their wishes. They can obtain "dream" milk even when they don't get the real thing. This can be noted by watching babies contentedly making sucking motions during sleep. All babies who have survived this far have experienced that they need only to fantasize being fed or diapered, and "it happens"—or if it doesn't, they can dream it.

In addition, they progressively show bodily manifestations which "automatically" elicit responses from their caretakers. For instance, babies will scream in different ways for different results and, if necessary, they will resort to symptoms such as vomiting, rashes, asthma, etc. Even at some cost, they are omnipotent: their bodies know how to make their wishes come true! Caretakers appear and do the right thing.*

---

* Thence came the numerous fairy tales like Aladdin's Lamp, where powerful figures can be ordered around by means of a magic talisman.

However, by the end of this stage—at about six months—along with the primitive differentiation of self comes the rude awakening that neither fantasy nor conclusions will always work. Even in well-cared-for babies there is the experience of pain through teething or colic, and not even strokes can alleviate pain instantly. The baby experiences the opposite of his omnipotence: total impotence, his and that of his caretakers. Despair is the result, total, global "not-OK." Neither he nor his differentiated caretakers have any power over pain. He responds to the despair of total impotence on a continuum between wild screaming rage and silent utter hopelessness, from which he lapses into the withdrawal of sobbing sleep. Melanie Klein refers to this behavior as "six-month-old depression."[16] Spitz also has identified this process that relates to primitive differentiation, and he calls it the "eight-month anxiety."[17] He states that it "marks a distinct stage in the psychic organization." The baby has now lost what Spitz calls his "blissful state." I call it "falling from Paradise."

According to how he is handled during this period, the baby establishes basic conclusions that will determine how the Child will react to the experience of impotence when he encounters it in the future, as is bound to happen to all of us when we run across insurmountable obstacles that give us pain or frustration. As a result of such conclusions, some people react to frustration with variants of rage, high energy discharge, and high activity, reflecting a conclusion at this stage that screaming or agitation works best. Others are likely to go into variants of high passivity, reflecting a conclusion that quietude works best. These conclusions thus trigger off in a grown person "characteristic" responses to pain or frustration. They are also a foundation for the "existential position" within the Child.[18]

(III) EXPLORING TODDLER: THE POWER OF MOBILITY (8–14 MONTHS)

The toddler's new motor power temporarily helps him to overcome functionally (though not necessarily emotionally) the absolute despair he has experienced at the end of the last stage. Bruner has proved that the child's high drive of curiosity exists from birth,[19] but it is at this stage and at the next one that it becomes most evident. The toddler arrives at many conclusions as a result of his own actions, which lead him to excitement, pleasure, and also pain, fear, and moments of real or imagined extreme danger.

Conclusions in this system have a lot to do with excitement, curiosity, experimentation, and the refined use of the senses, particularly touch. If there is insufficient supervision and the toddler keeps hurting himself in rough exploring, there will be conclusions related to fear of new things, or, in reverse, accident-proneness if pain from getting hurt finally gets care. Some toddlers who hurt themselves will develop a yearning for the safe confinement of crib or playpen, and if they also have additional experiences that maintain the early "despair" conclusions, they are likely later in life to push or provoke until they get themselves "safely" incarcerated in a mental hospital or a jail.

Many conclusions of this period are revived again at script-making age and at adolescence in regard to exploration (body or environment) and apprehension, literally and symbolically. Some conclusions relate to the use of the body, sphincter and bowel control, and mastery of self in learning skills. Choices will be made between the drive to explore away from caretakers and the "stroke-security" to be gained for abstaining from adventures. (Later in life all these conclusions will affect behavior in marriage.) It's at this period also that toddlers pick up "GAGIT" ("Go ahead and get into trouble") messages, and phobias and anxieties later in life often reflect reactive conclusions against such messages.

Certain conclusions within this system can be identified by the attitude a given person has in relation to his or her car or other "new" uses of "motor power," and also by how he or she drives.

(IV) WALKY TALKY: DETERMINATION AND IMITATION (14 MONTHS–TWO YEARS)   I have named this system Walky Talky because it corresponds to the stage when the baby has become an active, ambulatory little child. He demonstrates that he has now mastered a wide range of physical skills, including eating with tools, walking, climbing stairs, running, and so on. He has mastered a whole new language, the geography of his home and nearby environment, and he can figure out a great deal about the people around him. As adults, we would consider it difficult to master, within a year, a new language, new sports that involve new skills in finger and body coordination, geography, anthropology, and psychology. But a child simply picks up all these skills and he practices them with a persistent determination that no grownup can match. Mostly, he learns by imitation, which in itself is a new skill. Parents can use the child's new aptitude to teach and to protect him. I still remember my son shaking his finger at the stove and saying "No!" and my relief that finally I did not have to chase after him every second to stop him from getting hurt. However, the child may imitate all kinds of undesirable patterns also. At this age, my daughter was limping up the stairs because I was. (She is now grown and tells me she still has a tendency to do so when under stress.) Children now accept prohibitions: "don't touch," "don't see," "don't hear," "don't think." Many conclusions within this system are equivalent to assimilated messages because this particular Child subsystem is so imitative. This system, and only this system, could be termed P_1, because of the assimilation and "identification with the aggressor" that takes place.

Grownups who overuse their Parent and enter transactions from a stance of Persecutor or Rescuer usually operate out of certain tight conclusions established in this system. It is as a result of specific conclusions in this system that people are more or less willing to accept parental instructions offered verbally later in life.

There are additional conclusions established at this time regarding assumptions about outcomes of activity. These are generated as the child practices all his new skills. Does he get a lot of "Be careful, you'll fall!— See? I told you!" or "Ha, ha, clumsy!" or sarcastic laughter about twists of words, or consistent impatience when he spills, or panic when he runs, or smiles when he is endangering himself? What we refer to as "gallows laughter" usually reflects conclusions in this system as to the danger of using initiative and mastering new skills. Many conclusions in this system need to be offset later in life with permissions about competence, testing out, and using the Adult.

(V) CONTRO: CONTROVERSY AND CONTROL (2–3 YEARS) I have named this period Contro, short for "controversy" and "control." Following the child's tendency to bland imitation of his caretakers at the previous stage of development, the "terrible twos" usher in a new system. This system corresponds to a new stage of differentiation between a child and his caretakers. It is due to his awareness of his new physical and mental powers. He starts "adapting negatively," that is, "wanting" just the opposite of what "they" want for him. Who owns the child's body? Who has the power? Conclusions within this system will affect his later behavior at adolescence, when there are comparable battles between parents and offspring resulting from the new operation of his Adult ego state. Within this system lie the Child's conclusions about the relative power of the Top Dog and the Underdog, and about manipulation.

In this system also lie conclusions related to shame, which is one highly effective way through which even the most negativistic child can be controlled by his caretakers and by the rest of the environment, for better or worse. Much of what is referred to as "cultural scripting" results from inputs into this system.[20] If there has been very much shaming over a large range of areas, there are conclusions of fear and apprehension that are likely to surface powerfully, particularly in social situations, regardless of additional conclusions about how to relate to others that may also exist here. This was illustrated in the case of Nancy given above.

Conclusions that lead to substitution rackets start out in this system and spread out into the next. In my two papers entitled "The Substitution Factor—Rackets and Real Feelings,"[21] I have described how, when the expression of certain genuine feelings is mislabeled, discounted, and/or negatively stroked, children use the power of such repressed feelings to express substitute feelings that are given approval. These substitute feelings are often exaggerations of feelings or behavior that are tolerated by the family at this stage of development. It is during the two-to-three-year-old stage that children learn names for feelings, so there are conclusions in Contro that tell the Child what are approved feelings and what are dangerous feelings. As a result of such conclusions later in life, the individual might "racketeer" for strokes to "approved" feelings both in order to sustain himself and to prevent "dangerous" feelings from surfacing into awareness.[22]

(VI) EXISTER: FORMATION OF EXISTENTIAL POSITION (3–4 YEARS) Berne wrote that a person will operate with one of four potential "existential positions"—i.e., a stance or a point of view through which he experiences himself and others. He gave them the following colloquial labels:

I'm OK, You're OK.
I'm OK, You're not-OK.
I'm not-OK, You're OK.
I'm not-OK, You're not-OK.[23]

To these four categories, I have added what I call a *Fifth Position*— "I'm OK, You're OK-Adult." I distinguish this fifth position from the primitive "I'm OK, You're OK" which every infant is born with according to Berne. The early OK position actually operates as a global, undifferentiated position that involves total fantasized omnipotence. It is primarily a symbiotic "We're OK." By contrast, the fifth position includes differentiation. Optimally, it involves both a quest for autonomy and a sense of our interdependence with others. It represents a recognition both of the lovability and the fallibility in each of us, and contains both idealism and realism. I have elaborated on this subject in my articles, "The Fifth Position" and "I'm OK, You're OK-Adult,"[24] where I pointed out that the development of this position requires adult experience, so the possibility of establishing it is not available to a three-year-old. Nevertheless, I agree with Berne that between the ages of three and four the young child settles into an existential position which becomes the bedrock for his future script, because around that age he develops a need for a point of view for his relationships with others.

By this time, even under the best of circumstances, it is well nigh impossible for a child to sustain the primitive global, undifferentiated "OK" position (I'm OK, You're OK) that he was born with. He has been through pain, such as teething and bellyaches, and through stages of differentiation of self at the Baby stage and at the Contro stage. He has experienced swings of moods; from the fantasized omnipotence of infancy and the rebelliousness of Contro with which he "won" power struggles with caretakers, all the way to feelings of utter impotence when he "lost" battles for control or when he experienced unrelieved pain. At this stage despair, first felt at the end of the Baby stage, threatens to take over once again with its alternations of rage and hopelessness. This can lead him into a position of "I'm not-OK, You're not-OK" that is both furious and desperate. Such a position can only lead to a frantic quest for total omnipotent vengeful destruction of the world, or to a total collapse of the self.

The fact is that existence offers no 100 percent "total solution" (Hitler's term). If a total "not-OK" position is set irrevocably during the Exister stage, I refer to it as being on a *third-degree level* (by analogy to the manner in which doctors grade the damage of burns). An individual with a third-degree "not-OK" existential position will later embark on a globally destructive path if he has the mental and physical capacity to do so, or else he will get himself "safely" locked up in a mental hospital, in jail, or in heroin addiction. He will seek total "control"—either that of his own power over the world (Hitler), or else total control of his person by the world in order to feel "safe" from the besetting dangers he fears in and around him. (After committing one crime after another, Heirens, the notorious murderer of the 1940's, scrawled on a mirror in lipstick, "Lock me up before I kill more.")

DEFENSIVE EXISTENTIAL POSITIONS Fortunately, by age three, the majority of children will have experienced enough stroking and pleasure from experimentation that they can defend themselves from being flooded with the total "not-OK" of despairing impotence or of frantic quest for absolute power. Instead they establish one of two *defensive* existential positions, which I name either: *Type I* ("I'm not-OK, You're OK") or *Type II* ("I'm OK, You're not-OK"). A defensive existential position offers *hope*.* With Type I defensive position, a person can hope that *others* (parents, gods, anyone else) will find solutions; with Type II, a person can hope that he himself will find solutions, even if others can't. Children will develop an "I'm not-OK, You're OK" defensive position if, by age three, they have established a high proportion of conclusions related to helplessness and to being overpowered. In reverse, they will develop an "I'm OK, You're not-OK" defensive position if, so far, they have many conclusions about their power to "make" their caretakers feel good, or angry, or scared, or guilty. So the defensive position represents a resolution for life that follows the battles of either Type I or Type II, and it becomes characteristic of an individual's "personality." A person whose defensive existential position is very tilted one way or another, i.e., third degree, operates in life very rigidly in that position. He then feels compelled to maintain this defensive position without the flexibility of moving to the fifth position for he fears being flooded by total not-OK feelings whereby he would feel even worse than with his rigid defensive position. As a result, the person's script becomes dangerously slanted and nonproductive, for he becomes more invested in maintaining or justifying it than in expressing the creative potentials of his script. Such a person needs treatment, though not necessarily script analysis. The most important part of treatment consists of helping him become aware of the extent to which his position is out of balance, and encouraging him to soften the rigidity of his defensive position. A potentially harmful script can thus transform itself into an exciting and creative one. Techniques of treatment can focus on the manner in which a client "racketeers" for plastic strokes and help in changing his patterns for exchanging strokes. Sometimes gestalt work is required to help a patient recognize alienated feelings within himself and reconcile them with his other, more acceptable feelings. In the course of such treatment, a patient might experience panic from feeling flooded with the despair from which he was defending with his rigid position; so he must be sustained with potent protection until such time as there is more flexibility to his position.

The basic position established at Exister stage is often more important

---

* See the myth of Pandora's Box. There, too, hope is supposed to offset the evils of the world.

than anything else in identifying the direction of a person's life, because the grown person will slant himself and his script one way or the other in accordance with his basic position. Rather than by full script analysis, it is by evaluating the relative rigidity or flexibility of Exister's position in conjunction with the consistency or contradictions of previous conclusions that we can be predictive about the outcome of a person's life. It is to the extent that the grown person can keep realigning himself to the position "I'm OK, You're OK-Adult," regardless of real crises in his life that he can, perhaps, attain "happiness."

In the course of our lifetimes, even after we acquire the ability to operate from the fifth existential position, the majority of us continue to revert on and off to the particular defensive position we selected at about age three. It remains our home base and constitutes our primitive way of distinguishing "good" and "bad," "safe" and "dangerous." At times of stress or emergency, Type I people tend to feel that others are better, righter, smarter, or more powerful than they are, whereas Type II people tend to feel that they themselves are better, righter, smarter, or stronger than others. Type I people tend to shun leadership roles even if they are otherwise highly qualified, whereas Type II people will propel themselves to leadership even when not that qualified.*

RACKETEERING   This is a word I have coined to reflect dyadic transactions in which a *racketeer* involves a partner into giving him contrived strokes in support of his rackets.[25] This is nonproductive on a third degree level, but most of us are likely to do so some of the time on a first degree level. Racketeering reflects a person's defensive position, in addition to reflecting his particular rackets.

A person with a Type I defensive existential position ("I'm not-OK, You're OK") is likely to racketeer as a "Helpless" or "Bratty" Child, seeking ongoing strokes from a Parent. ("I'm so tired, help me," etc.; or—rebellious—"Yeah? Show me.") He will start transactions from a victim or one-down stance, even when he is feeling angry and is subtly persecuting. A person with a Type II defensive position ("I'm OK, You're not-OK") will racketeer as Phony Helpful or Knowledgeable or, then, sometimes Bossy Parent, even when he is covering up inadequacy. He will sound like a Rescuer or a Persecutor from a one-up stance and do so all the more if he feels shaky and scared inside.

Regarding Type II persons who racketeer from what sounds like a Parent ego state as Rescuers or Persecutors, there appears to be a contradiction when I state, as I do here, that their position is established at age three, considering that I have previously indicated that the actual Parent ego state (P_2) does not operate effectively until after age seven. The explanation lies in the fact that Type II racketeers often draw on their Walky Talky Child system to impersonate a Parent, and, later in life, this

---

* The ability to distinguish between these two types of people is essential in hiring or assigning people to jobs in any field.

system aligns itself with P_2. As I mentioned above, the Walky Talky Child system corresponds to what is classically referred to as P_1 in that it integrates imitations of the principal caretaking parent of the 14 months to two-year-old age period.

RELATIONSHIP BETWEEN RACKETEERING, GAMES, AND SCRIPTS Before proceeding on to a description of Scripter, let me digress to discuss the relationship between rackets, games and scripts. My view is radically different from that of many other TA theorists, particularly in regard to what is referred to as the "payoff" of games.

Berne frequently emphasized that the mere fact of repetition or persistence of typical transactions does *not* constitute a game.[26] To qualify as a game, in his definition, the transactional cross that leads to the end of the game must be preceded by a *switch* in the ego state of at least one player. Sadly, Berne died before my contributions to TA on rackets and racketeering. The names of many so-called "games" taken from his early book, *Games People Play*[27] actually represent dyadic racketeering, rather than games. All too often what is loosely referred to as a "game" represents a repetitive quest by a racketeer for strokes to his rackets. The player seeks "payoffs" of stereotyped ongoing strokes within the context of his ongoing transactions with a "hooked" partner. He does not aim to switch his ego state as long as he keeps getting strokes to his racket and support to his existential position.

For instance, continuing transactions with "Gee, you're wonderful" constitute racketeering by a Type I racketeer who operates from an "I'm not-OK, You're OK" position and has found himself a Type II partner who operates from the "I'm OK, You're not-OK" position. Alternately, ongoing transactions on the theme of "I can get it for you wholesale" may constitute racketeering by a Type II player who is seeking the reinforcement of his "I'm OK, You're not-OK" position from grateful partners.

However, even when two complementary partners racketeer with each other, usually one partner has less investment than the other in sustaining ongoing transactions indefinitely. For instance, one player may be racketeering on a third-degree level, and another only on a first-degree level, so the latter soon becomes restless or bored and ready to terminate the complementary transactions, either by crossing them or by walking off. The principal player senses the forthcoming loss of strokes from his partner and, in his distress, switches his ego state. Thereupon, he acquires new, momentary energy with which he "jumps the gun" on his uncooperative partner and crosses the transaction himself. "At least" he has acquired the "consolation prize" of having quit before getting fired, and "at least" has reinforced one or another primitive internal conclusion in the category of "I told you so" or "I knew that good things don't last." This is when the player shows a secret smile, or what is referred to as a gallows laugh. After all, he did get himself a consolation prize even if he has just lost the ticket for the big prize of limitless ongoing strokes to the defensive position that protects him from the total not-OK of despair.

My emphasis, then, is that what are called game players do not initiate games as such. I do not believe that they seek, even unconsciously, to get a *payoff* of bad feelings from a game. Rather, I see what are called game players as persons who carry prohibitions against full awareness of feelings. Thence, rackets and, thence, repetitive attempts to compensate themselves for the awareness that escapes them by racketeering for strokes to their rackets. They switch ego states when they feel that their partner is about to terminate their racketeering transactions. The so-called "game payoff" is only the *consolation prize* that the player settles for when his racketeering fails.

But hope springs up again and, following the crossed transaction of a game switch, a racketeer will start racketeering all over again, either with the same partner or with another.

When two evenly matched complementary racketeers first "find" each other, they contentedly racketeer for quite a while together. This may go on for minutes or for years. Eventually, when one of the partners loses interest in racketeering, a shift occurs around the drama triangle.*

If he senses that his partner is about to leave or cross his transaction, Type I racketeer switches from Child ego state to Parent, and attacks the partner's Child. He moves from Victim to Persecutor. Thereby he acquires his "consolation prize" (*Now I've Got You, You Son of a Bitch*, or *You're Not Much Good*, or *Blemish*, etc.).

For a brief while, he clutches on to his consolation prize and, during this period, he experiences the power of being in the reverse defensive position ("I'm OK, You're not-OK"). This can go on for minutes or for months. But eventually, unless he can move on to "I'm OK, You're OK-Adult," he reverts to his own basic defensive position and starts racketeering all over again from the "I'm not-OK, You're OK" position.

Similarly, when Type II racketeer experiences the real or impending loss of his "one-down" partner, who has gotten tired or exasperated with his helpfulness or bossiness, he anticipates a kick, and, sometimes, he even invites it to *terminate the anxiety* of dread anticipation. Thereupon, there is a switch in his overt ego state; he falls off his perch into the helpless Child spot. He becomes a Victim and blubbers to the Parent of his partner: "What did I do wrong?" or "Why does this always happen to me?"

He, too, thereby acquires a consolation prize in that internally, he says: "I knew it wouldn't last," and for a short while he can relax in the non-

* I refer here to Karpman's brilliant discovery that in life, as in drama, after a character starts a scene with an assigned role of Victim, Persecutor, or Rescuer, "action" proceeds by means of role shifts from one point of this triangle to the next one, so that following a game switch the Rescuer might become the Victim, the Victim becomes the Persecutor, and the Persecutor might become the Rescuer, until there is a new scene within which "action" might generate the next role shift, right on up to the end of the play. See Stephen B. Karpman, "Script Drama Analysis," *Transactional Analysis Bulletin*, 7, no. 26 (1968).

responsible "I'm not-OK, You're OK" position rather than experiencing the persistent strain of justifying his "I'm OK, You're not-OK" position. But he, too, eventually reexperiences the need for strokes and, on the basis of his conclusions, the only "sure" way he believes he can seek them is by moving back to the "I'm OK, You're not-OK" position from which to racketeer all over again as a Rescuer and/or Persecutor.

As we can see, the game switch generates an apparent reversal of a player's usual defensive position, but it is relatively short lived.

Within the Exister sub-system sits the "preferred" defensive position, the only one which each of us experiences as protecting us from total not-OK and the only one from which we have learned to expect strokes; this is what each player soon returns to, ready for the next round of racketeering, for it is the racketeering part of these transactions that structures most of his time, *not* the game switch, which is short lived.

I consider it important to emphasize that it is racketeering that offers the sought-after "payoffs" (albeit exploitative, nonnourishing ones related to childhood conclusions that are anachronistic). Game switches offer only consolation prizes, not payoffs. They result from the player's frustration at receiving insufficient strokes of the kind he learned to go for in childhood when he was needy or deprived of outlets for his feelings.

Nevertheless, the escalation of games in a patient is, indeed, a high danger sign. It implies not only that he cannot sustain himself in an "I'm OK, You're OK-Adult" position, but also that he is less and less capable of sustaining himself even in his defensive position, since his game switches are swinging him back and forth too dizzily from one existential slant to another. A high incidence of game switches is an indicator of increasing frustration and desperation. The individual is experiencing that his manner of racketeering fails to produce the strokes—good, bad, or crooked—that he was accustomed to prior to age three. He does not know how else to get what he needs (creativity and intimacy) because of the very prohibitions about feeling and thinking that generated his reliance on rackets. So his increasing desperation can, indeed, move him to third-degree racketeering, then third-degree game switches, and, finally, to a tragic ending for himself and/or others.

This does not mean that he was escalating games in order to advance his script. Quite the contrary. This kind of escalation *prevents* someone from developing his script fruitfully, and the player's inchoate awareness of this very fact only contributes all the more to the kind of not-OK desperation that can lead to tragedy.

It is on this point that I differ significantly with standard TA theory. I am sure that, even unconsciously, people do not initiate games for the purpose of payoffs and that the script does not represent an ultimate payoff. People seek stroke payoffs from racketeering because it is these transactions that they relied on in childhood at times of stress.

The game switch occurs when the process of racketeering fails and the player feels incapable of drawing on other internal or external resources because of conclusions related to early childhood prohibitions. At that point, the consolation prize of whatever feelings of justification result from the game ending serves temporarily for just that—consolation and justification. This prize becomes the equivalent of trading stamps. Later the player pathetically tries to cash it in for the right to initiate once again an escalated process of racketeering with the same partner or with another. Failing that, he clutches on to his collected trading stamps and eventually, when he contemplates his worthless collection and recognizes that he does not know how to acquire the currency he needs to implement his script within reality, there is nothing left to do but to get to the morgue sooner rather than later.

In short, it is not the player's script that determines his games, rather game switches are the unfortunate results of a player's failure to gain enough ongoing satisfaction from racketeering. And racketeering represents his attempt to obtain strokes for rackets that ward off awareness of the more genuine underlying feelings than he actually needs in order to fulfill his script creatively.

TRAGEDY RESULTS FROM EMOTIONAL IGNORANCE, NOT FROM PREDETERMINED SCRIPTS The early prototype of the script is developed between the ages of four to seven. When a grown patient experiences the "familiar feeling" which characterizes what was classically seen as the "payoff" at the end of a game, he reproduces a childhood feeling, all right, but it reflects a stage of childhood that occurs later than the one at which he developed rackets and racketeering. This latter stage corresponds to periods past ages six or seven when children learn to settle for consolation prizes rather than nothing. This acquired pattern is not directly related to the development or the implementation of a person's script for it occurs *after* early script formation. It simply attaches itself to the movement of a person's life.

I see the escalation of games and their increased interference with the player's ability to fulfill his script successfully as due to *emotional ignorance or blindness* within him. If he remains stuck in his blindness, he "progresses" relentlessly from racketeering to game switches to stroke deprivation to trading stamps; then, again, to racketeering to escalated, speedier switches, and so on, till doomsday. This is, indeed, the pattern of Greek tragedy. The suspense element of these tragedies is that both the chorus and the audience clearly see how the hero/heroine's "tragic flaw" (which I call his emotional ignorance) could be dispelled, but the hero/heroine stubbornly refuses to see it. In the end, he or she fails to bring into fruition all the potentially beautiful elements that the script hints at in the early scenes.

It is not Greek tragedy that necessarily typifies scripts. It is fairy tales and folk tales and all of mythology in many versions. Greek tragedies represent scripts gone sour and, as such, they stand as monumental reminders of the danger of *hubris*—the dismissal of deep, frequently unacceptable feelings within one's self and others which must be taken into account during peace lest they explode later as war. It is emotional ignorance that prevents the hero/heroine from confronting the realities of a grownup's life and death.

Emotional ignorance ties into two staunchly held beliefs in the Child. Each of us carries these to some extent, but they become dangerous when unexamined by the Adult. They are:

1. That it is possible for some people, if not for others, to attain unending happiness; for these lucky ones there is no pain and no death.
2. That such unending happiness can be secured by finding a supplier of unending "home-cooked" strokes in the best style that one ever got or dreamed of as Infant, Baby, or Exister, which are the Child systems most involved with the acquisition of nurture and strokes.

As long as these two beliefs are maintained unshaken by Adult confrontation, the unwary hero or heroine will be involved in a "pursuit of happiness" that remains a mirage—an unreachable dream. He will keep hoping that his script can lead in truth to "they lived happily ever after." It is this very hope that can transform his beautiful fairy tale into something akin to a Greek tragedy. Instead of moving forward in life along a creative script while developing himself as an autonomous human being who takes responsibility for his feelings, he will keep seeking a partner who can impersonate—for a minute or for years—the fairy prince or princess or godmother or elf or brownie who magically "solves" his need for creativity and intimacy by taking on the responsibility for unendingly validating the fantasized "truth" of his childhood beliefs. So, like Don Quixote, he will spend his life and energy racketeering in the quest of this validation. Then, at each disappointment and at each game switch, he will despair more and more until he hits his deathbed.

THE THERAPIST'S TASK   Yet such a sequence need not go on. Perhaps the most important task of a therapist is to disenchant his patients and help them move away from their emotional ignorance. This is a task that wise parents or educators also undertake with their growing children, and that's how people can eventually function out of an "I'm OK, You're OK-Adult" position that permits intimacy, creativity, and love, even though none of these can be sustained without interruption and the fear and sadness of impending death which looms ahead for all of us.

The Child fights off the therapist or parent or teacher who performs this task; he sees him as cruel, he tries to ward off the news that "there is no Santa Claus." And, indeed, moving a person to disenchantment without clobbering him beyond his ability to withstand it is a hard and often painful task. While clutching on to his magic beliefs, the Child does all he can to threaten the solidity of the therapist, parent, or teacher who is challenging his fantasy.

In my opinion, it is the ability to fulfill this task both with strength and with love that is the mark of a good therapist or educator. For it is to the extent that a person has been enabled to exist courageously and lovingly after freedom from emotional ignorance that he can experience the joy of living through a script which represents his own unique creation.

(VII) SCRIPTER: WHAT'S PAST AND FUTURE? (4–7 YEARS)   And now comes Scripter, the Child I described early in this chapter. Suddenly the four-to-seven-year-old child becomes aware of past and future and of a need to chart his existence, to structure time, space, and relationships. He builds on his existential position and, as I described at the beginning of this chapter, he tries to incorporate into his script as many of his conclusions as he can. He deals with a jumble of contradictory conclusions, so he needs a rather complicated story with ups and downs in order to accommodate the huge collection of Gestalten, formed and unformed, that he has accumulated so far. I will elaborate further on Scripter after discussing the forces that have operated to establish the conclusions that are set into the human organism so far.

THE THREE DYNAMIC MUSES WHICH INFLUENCE US

THE MYSTERY OF LIFE   I have indicated that a variety of conclusions get established within the seven subsystems of the Child. What are the dynamic forces that set these conclusions in the first place, and that later motivate a person to operate in accordance with one or more of these early conclusions?

To answer this question, I must digress briefly to considering the mystery of life. Freud posited two oppositional drives: Libido, the Life Thrust (which he based on Eros, the sexual drive, because of the organic drive to procreate), and Thanatos, the thrust to death. Many psychoanalysts later rejected the concept of a "death instinct." They found it distasteful, and they preferred to see a tendency to death as a pathological symptom.

However, Berne stated that he agreed with Freud about a "death instinct."[28] Regardless of the debate on this subject, there is the obvious fact that life emerges *out of* nonlife (inanimate matter). We can then see the forces of life and nonlife by analogy to an electrical charge that sparks inanimate cells of matter and animates them to organize themselves. Thereupon they operate in accordance with whatever are their mysteriously encoded principles until such time as the electric charge runs out and inertia sets in again.

If we recognize that we were pulled out of inertia by what Bergson called the "Elan Vital" (the Thrust to Life), but that, from the moment of birth on to death, the polar force of inertia continues to exert a regressive pull like a gravitational counterforce to life, then we can acknowledge that a part of ourselves is rooted in "nonlife," perhaps all the way down to the mineral antecedents that preceded even our biological evolution. Eventually, when our life runs out, we become mineral matter again, whether we aspire to this condition or not. So death can be seen as a natural reversion *backwards* into the nonlife whence we emerged, rather than as a movement to destruction.

Regarding the Thrust to Life, it is observably true that it maintains itself in two ways: (1) as a thrust to grow and have an individual existence, be it as a weed or as a human; and (2) as a thrust to further the life of the species.

In lower forms of life, both thrusts complement each other and there appears no contradiction between the one and the other. The growth of an individual leads to maturity, which leads to procreation, which in turn generates new individuals, and so on.

Therefore, a narrowly biological viewpoint might support the idea of seeing sexuality—Libido—as being at the root of life in all its forms, without separating out one thrust from the other, particularly since it is indeed true that both life thrusts counterbalance the forces of inertia and/or death. However, as we go up the evolutionary ladder, we note that higher animals not only nurture the young ones they generate, but that some will risk their own lives for their young or for the survival of their group. So, when we consider those species whose survival has resulted from more than simple procreation, we must recognize, not only that there are two separate thrusts for survival (for the individual and for the species), but also that these two thrusts can operate in contradiction with one another, whereby one might take precedence over the other at different times and under different circumstances.

When it comes to humans, this distinction becomes even more crucial because, as a species, we owe our survival not only to the chain of procreation and nurturing of our direct forebears, but also to the chain of exploration and inventiveness that catapulted us all the way from the jungles across oceans and now into outer space. Always there were men and women who felt driven to question and challenge the physical and mental environment that surrounded them—even at the risk of their own lives—for inchoate reasons that even they but rarely saw as species-related. Usually they acted on what they experienced as their own curiosity or playfulness or restlessness or need for "self-expression."

Research with animals has demonstrated that—except for limited instances in chimpanzees, dolphins, and dogs—only humans maintain the tendency to persistent playful excitement past sexual maturity.[29] And, thanks to Berne, we now welcome this tendency when it is manifested through our Child, although it can express itself also through our Parent and Adult (for example, in playing chess). It is this capacity for playful excitement and curiosity that has served the survival of the human species by promoting the risky experimentation and exploration of which our forebears have left us an example in the legacy of their inventions and discoveries.

Our capacity for excitement and our ability to be stimulated by curiosity are the expressions of a species-related urge to transmit the meaning of our individual lives on to future generations in more ways than through procreation and nurture. Our species would have died off if innumerable individuals had not been driven to take risks for creativity or exploration, regardless of concern for their individual welfare or safety. The results of an individual's risk-taking can be generative for others, but that does not turn curiosity and risk-taking into derivatives of sexuality, even though sexuality can also manifest itself through excitement and curiosity. In humans, sexuality is not limited to the procreative urge, as it is in animals. It is one of many channels through which we can express the typically playful excitement that distinguishes human expression from animal expression. Sexual excitement may lead to generativity through procreation and nurture of others. It can also lead to other forms of creative expression by being a way to connect with others and experience our aliveness and our urge to give forth something of our essence, be it in the instantaneous present or in terms of the future. Similarly, the determined, aggressive "crazy" risk-taking behavior of an explorer, an inventor, or an artist can be the expression of his inherent but unacknowledged drive to promote the survival of the species even at the cost of his safety, just as is the lioness's sudden fierce jump at a huntsman in order to defend her young from danger at any cost to herself.

In summary, then, there are not two but three inborn dynamic and counterbalancing drives or forces that affect an individual and express themselves through the various genetically determined channels of a person's mysterious "self."

These three forces are (1) inertia—the pull to nonlife; (2) the drive for individual survival, leading to the quest for nurture and protection from danger; and (3) the drive for species survival, which expresses itself by excitement and by exploratory curiosity, sexual and nonsexual, potentially leading to creativity and the transmission of a broad span of gifts to others in the present and in the future.

THREE FORCES: SLEEPY, SCARY, AND SPUNKY The easiest way to represent these three forces is to personify them as three *Muses* which take turns in influencing us. Until such time as I find the appropriate Greek names, I have given these three Muses the irreverent names of Sleepy, Scary, and Spunky to connote their respective functions and motivational powers within our organism. At any given moment in time or at certain periods of our lives, one Muse is more influential than another, taking the foreground in our "Selves" and relegating the other two to the background until giving way and letting another Muse take primary importance. Each impinges on the others, but each must also operate in conjunction with the others, for all three Muses express their particular function through the same organism, even though each has her own directional pull.

Sleepy represents the pull to inertia; Scary and Spunky represent the opposite twofold pull to life for the individual and the species. However, as was shown above, some of the time, Scary and Spunky also operate at cross-purposes with one another, so that in effect each Muse pulls in a different direction.

In TA we like diagrams as well as colloquial names. Rather than draw the three spirited Muses as figures, I portray them as three ovals that overlap onto each other to signify their interaction. Each Muse has her own area of affect which influences the Self and determines a person's feelings, thoughts, and behavior at a given time either in relation to whatever happens in the present or by "rubberband" to conclusions set in the past.

In Figure 4, the arrows pulling out of each oval represent the directional pulls of each Muse, and next to each arrow are the principal vehicles or modes of expression. Sleepy's arrow pulls regressively downwards to the womb, to inertia, to the all-encompassing cosmos.

Scary's arrow fearfully reaches upwards for nurture, protection, and succor from whatever deities will support the individual's survival.

And Spunky thrusts forward with excitement, fearlessly wanting to explore and express the creativity and sexuality that promote the species.

The plus and minus signs within each oval represent the polar powers and values within each Muse, for each one of the Muses has positive and negative value for us according to the usefulness or harmfulness of the conclusions established within our Child and the proportion of power each wields within us in the day-to-day context of our lives.

The two-pointed arrows within each oval represent the channels of

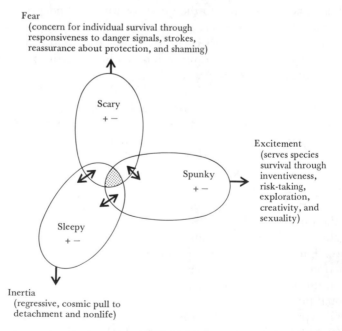

Fear
(concern for individual survival through
responsiveness to danger signals, strokes,
reassurance about protection, and shaming)

Scary
+ −

Excitement
(serves species
survival through
inventiveness,
risk-taking,
exploration,
creativity, and
sexuality)

Spunky
+ −

Sleepy
+ −

Inertia
(regressive, cosmic pull to
detachment and nonlife)

Figure 4
The Three Muses that Motivate the Self for Better or Worse

influence from one Muse to the other in the areas where they overlap, since the Child often experiences a nonverbal pull between the influences of one Muse and another.

The shaded inside core represents the inner self of the individual. It is perpetually affecting the Muses and being affected by them through a process that is not yet fully understood and that we term "growth." It moves relentlessly forward in time according to a genetically determined "clock." Just as this inner clock set us to start walking at about age one, assuming average development, so did it set us to establish our existential position at about age three, our script between ages four and seven, our Parent ego state after age seven, and our Adult after age twelve. The question in life is not whether these processes will happen to a newborn child, but rather how his Muses will successively set and bring forth the conclusions that will determine his feelings, thoughts, and contributions to the processes of the wider world.

In contrast to Sleepy's inertia, it is Scary and Spunky who actively set conclusions within the different systems of the Child. To do so, they use whatever sensory, perceptual, mental, and emotional resources are available to the child at each stage of his development. Intuition is not the prerogative of one Muse—it is available to all three as a mental tool of the Child—but each of them stimulates it in the service of her own function. For instance, Spunky's curiosity leads the Child to use the speed of intuition in order to figure out fast a creative solution to a problem, and Scary's concern leads him to use intuition to figure out fast how he can get an extra stroke. Later in life, it is Scary or Spunky who call forth responses to here-and-now situations in accordance with the conclusions that each has set within each of the Child subsystems. Sleepy also maintains her sway throughout life, particularly during sleep and relaxation.

In addition to having promoted conclusions in the various systems of the Child, each Muse steers the total person in one direction or another at any moment in time by eliciting feelings, thoughts, and behavior that are in accordance with her function, and she buttresses these with whatever formerly established conclusions best seem to serve her task.

Unfortunately, the Muses are often short-sighted or blind to the fast changes of reality as the years move on, be it in the life of the individual or the species. They will often bring forth from the Child old conclusions that sabotage their own functions, or those of the other Muses. For instance, take a luncheon speaker about to make a speech: Scary might bring forth, through his Walky Talky Child, the conclusion that it is dangerous to address strangers—which early conclusion was reinforced throughout his childhood when it had a repeatedly life-saving function during the years that he was growing up in a dangerous neighborhood. He might panic about speaking. But none of the Muses maintains exclusive control for long, so, in this case, the speaker's Spunky Muse might temporarily dislodge Scary along with her inhibiting conclusion and bring on the Adult or another Child system if it happens to contain a different conclusion about speaking to strangers. Eventually this speaker might need treatment to diminish the power of his conclusion about not addressing strangers. The problem might dissolve gradually as a result of a planned or unplanned sequence of "corrective experiences" through which he might discover that he can shift gears between his Muses and that he need not dread being stuck for more than a few minutes if a Scary conclusion pops up.

In all of us at different times one Muse takes precedence over the others, stimulating one ego state or another or one response based on a conclusion in one Child system or another. Most of the time within the person there is an ongoing push/pull between Sleepy and Spunky, Sleepy and Scary, and Scary and Spunky, with the third member of the triumvirate often coming on with extra power if there is a struggle between the other two. To the extent that the three forces are smoothly balancing each other the individual feels "good," i.e., lively, or safe, or else "good and tired" and ready to enjoy sleep. Much of the time the Muses are only precariously balanced with one another, generating physical activity, thoughts, or feelings within what we call the Self. This is "normal"; this is how we know we exist. However, strong imbalance will generate minor or major disruptions in a person, all the way from minor rage outbursts, anxiety or withdrawal, to violence, panic, or severe pathological symptoms such as paralysis or anorexia.

PERSONALITY   What is referred to as our personality reflects the relative power that may have been acquired by one Muse over the others as we were growing up. Thus, a particular Muse may tend to have priority in determining our options for how we structure time, space, and relationships, and for the aspects of our script that we are most likely to implement. (Many aspects of our scripts are never implemented, for better or worse.)

In addition to the different directional forces they represent, Sleepy, Scary, and Spunky also have oppositional active and passive polarities within themselves. Each has particular positive and negative value according to context and according to whatever a given individual or a culture might define as "good" and "right," or "bad" and "wrong." Let us also remember that because the Muses operated throughout the Child's development, each one elicited different parental strokes or discounts for the growing child. This determined different conclusions for different Child systems and the reinforcement of the operation of one Muse or another, however much they might also be interlocked with one another. In fact, it is this interlocking that explains why the Child does not get conditioned simply by taking in messages as undigested wholes. He transforms most messages into conclusions, i.e., combined Gestalten which include a variety of messages, experiences, and reactions because he is perpetually under the sway of the differing internal motivations of his three Muses.

Here are more details about the three Muses:

SLEEPY   Sleepy is the most obvious and the most mysterious of our Muses. We operate through Sleepy for about one-third of our time on earth, yet we cannot account for that time except for a few remembered dreams or through the Adult use of a clock. What do we touch during those periods, and why do we need them? It is difficult to discuss Sleepy's influence without either going into metaphysics or into pedantic sleep research. Empirically and from physiological research, we know that we "sink" into sleep and that we dream. This very sinking has restorative value for life. We do not really know why this has to be so, nor can we logically explain fantasy or regressive or hypnotic phenomena. At those times do we touch archetypal imagery, as Jung assumed? Do we reexperi-ence, each night, the mysterious time that existed before we were born as individuals or as a species, and the time that will exist after we die? Is it Sleepy's function to bridge life and death, the sleep during which we breathe and the final sleep of death—when we will be outside existence the way we were outside before we came out of the womb?

Without dwelling any further on speculation, what we can see every day is that through Sleepy we can withdraw from daily life and relation-ships and we can touch our "zero center" (Perls)[30] either in sleep or by meditative detachment. At times many of us can actually feel the heaviness of what I call Sleepy's "gravitational pull." Tennyson describes it beauti-fully in "The Lotus Eaters." At other times Sleepy also relates us to Peter Pan's extraterrestrial space. In meditation, under hypnosis, or when we dream, we can experience the sense of weightlessness and floating de-scribed by the astronauts who got beyond the earth's gravitational pull. Either way, through Sleepy we can feel detached, uninvolved, without concern about life on earth, our own or that of others. We can relate to the infinity of time and space, not by structuring them, but by experienc-ing a deep oneness with them. Thus Sleepy promotes peacefulness and serenity, which is why meditation can be so valuable. We need ways to withdraw from overstimulation and to pull together our inner resources. Our organism is so set that we cannot survive without sleep. If we fail to allow Sleepy to take over a good chunk of our time, we risk collapse from tension and exhaustion, which would truly lead us to the total inertia of death.

At the other extreme, it is Sleepy who sucks infants into death by marasmus if they have not been sufficiently stimulated to want to live. In grownups, too much domination by Sleepy can lead the person to with-drawn isolation and schizophrenic behavior. Also, there are times when Sleepy's influence can be dangerous for any one of us, for instance when driving a car.

SCARY   It is Scary's function to ward off Sleepy's pull and to promote the survival of the individual by making sure that (1) he gets the nurture he needs to grow on, and that (2) he learns appropriate responses to fear.

Look at the human infant at birth! Utterly helpless! What a contrast to other animals! Except for humans, all young animals either have the instinctive ability to take care of themselves from the moment of birth (fish, for example), or else an instinct that makes them stay physically close to their caretakers for as long as they need care and protection. And fear generates appropriate behavioral responses.

Ducks get imprinted on their mother and follow her everywhere until they are independent, at which time their additional inborn instincts tell them what to do. The baby kangaroo knows how to climb into its mother's pouch at birth and to stay there until it can make it on his own. Even baby monkeys have a "grab reflex" whereby they hang tightly on to their mother's hair as long as they need her, so there is no chance of her leaving them behind when she bounces off.

Not so the human infant. Once the umbilical cord has been cut, the human infant's instinctive reflexes such as sucking, blinking, and screaming do not suffice to ensure his nurture or his protection. He has no physical means to control the contact with his caretakers and thereby force them to take care of him. He is born with the grab reflex of the monkey, but it does not help him hold on to his mother. This reflex is lost a few weeks after birth. He does demonstrate the capacity for fear by having startle responses and by screaming. He even has a coenesthetic empathetic ability to sense fear in his mother and to scream in response to any fear she might be experiencing at a given moment. But neither sucking, startle responses, nor screaming are of any use for nurture or protection from danger unless there are caretakers present who are willing to carry the infant rather than leave him behind to die in the bushes.

So, from birth on, the infant must use psychological means to get his caretakers to "hold on" to him, for he cannot hold on to *them* by himself. It is Scary's job to find these means by programing responses in the child at each stage of his development so that he maintains his caretakers' interest in him to the extent that they voluntarily offer him the nurture and protection that he is incapable of obtaining by himself. If Scary fails in this task, then Sleepy takes over and sucks the child back into nonlife, be it by marasmus at infancy, death from exposure, illness, or accident later on in childhood.

Initially, bodily responses and screaming are the child's only means of expression, so Scary begins by influencing these as calls for nurture or protection. The infant then modulates the patterns he develops in order to obtain as many responses as possible from his caretakers in the form of bodily vibrations or strokes, because these represent the initial reassuring communications from life that "it" can offer nurture and protection. If necessary, Scary will stimulate the recurrence of whatever bodily responses then become the vocabulary of need in addition to screaming. For instance asthma, colic, and rashes all say "Come, tell me you're here to help me survive, I'll pay any price for your presence!"

Persistently, Scary finds every means in the child's power to "tune in," to whatever parental responses promise help for survival. Asthmatic children illustrate pathologically the epic battle that goes on between Sleepy's pull to inertia with stoppage of breath versus Scary's desperate efforts to keep breathing. Asthmatic symptoms have appropriately been labeled "cries for help"—they illustrate that at the early stages of life many children express Scary's sense that even continued breathing depends on continued reassurance that somebody is available out there for help.

In grown patients a history of breathing problems as the only way to survive can be recognized from their breathing patterns when operating out of their Infant or Baby sub-system. Paradoxically, many such patients smoke compulsively later in life in a counterproductive attempt to maintain breathing. They depend on nicotine to stimulate their lungs into breathing because of a Scary conclusion in their Infant system that they will stop breathing unless they keep being stimulated.

As the child grows, Scary urges him to use all his developing resources to establish whatever conclusions for feelings and behavior are most likely to ensure his immediate survival within the particular setting in which he finds himself. Scary carries the instinctive knowledge that it is the Child ego state of his caretakers that is most likely to endanger the growing child, so she gets him to use his growing perceptive and intuitive powers to "pick up" what most pleases the Child ego state of his various caretakers. Under Scary's influence, the Child works to reconcile and combine whatever messages he perceives or intuits from his different caretakers. He develops conclusions about which behavioral responses will best gratify one caretaker without alienating the others, even if this means incurring the wrath of the Parent ego state of one or another. Scary keeps sounding alarm bells within the child's organism to hold him to her task. This is particularly difficult when the child's mobility at Toddler and Walky Talky stages activates Spunky's influence for risk-taking explorations. So Scary has the additional task of trying to prevent the child from actively endangering himself.

In animals other than humans, the fear instinct accurately identifies danger to survival and appropriately prevents them from endangering themselves needlessly. In contrast, children are not born with the instinctive capacity to discriminate realistically about the quality or the degree of any danger. Their fear responses are not proportionate to actual danger or need. For instance, at the Toddler or Walky Talky stages a child might be terrified of an innocuous buzzing fly and might cower near his parents in fear against the "danger." Five minutes later, under the influence of Spunky, he might repeatedly and fearlessly try to crawl into high surf, or try to swallow a sharp object or a poisonous household substance, unlike an animal which ingests nothing hurtful or poisonous in his natural habitat.

So Scary seeks to counterbalance dangers that can be brought on by the child's risk-taking explorations when under the influence of Spunky. She does this by promoting conclusions within the child's organism that generate specific fear-reactions and responses. These have protective values. For instance, it is thanks to conclusions promoted by Scary that we avoid getting burnt. However, Scary can also promote irrational, even paranoid fears by internalizing harmful messages or by maintaining archaic conclusions. Also, Scary may have made the Child vulnerable to shaming for inappropriate or perverse reasons. So she might handicap rather than help the survival of a person if she brings forth archaic responses to shames and fears and allows him to be controlled to his disadvantage as a result of conclusions which she fostered in his Child.

SPUNKY   When we operate through Spunky, we do not recognize the fact that this relates us to the survival of the human species. We simply experience ourselves as alive, excited, sexual, full of "spunk." In fact, we are likely to feel selfish rather than concerned about others.

I pointed out before that humans are the only creatures on earth that are gifted with insatiable curiosity and a form of playfulness for the sake of which they will take "stupid" risks that often run counter to individual survival. Without this tendency, the human species would long since have been extinguished. Both ontogenetically and phylogenetically, curiosity leads to discovery, and discovery leads to creativity and invention. By that I mean that early humans may have discovered the use of tools by fooling around with objects, subsequently inventing the use of the lever and creating the wheel. Similarly, the young child fools around with ashtrays or cups; he discovers, namelessly, complex scientific principles of gravity, form, matter, etc., and eventually, when he grows up, if Spunky's drive has not been too stunted in the process, his own creativity and risk-taking can result in substantial contributions to humanity, often by chance or "for the hell of it," as a seemingly incidental result of his personal Spunky drive. Many of our greatest inventors and explorers were not, in themselves, admirable characters. As individuals many did not care about future generations and were intensely self-involved. Often unbeknownst to them, it is by the very unflinching pursuit of their own goals that they gave great service to the human species.

In everyday life, we are not aware that our capacity for curiosity and our needs for self-expression are aimed at the survival of our species. When we feel excitement or aliveness, when we feel driven to express something inside, be it creativity, emotionality, or sexuality, we do not identify the drive with the survival of the species, but it is because of this force that the need is so strong and that at times we are driven to being rash enough to go counter even to individual survival. Spunky's curiosity manifests itself in the Toddler who wants to crawl into the fire or into the ocean or off the balcony in pursuit of a will o' the wisp, in the explorer who wants to cross yet another territory, or in the inventor who wants to find out "why." Jerome Bruner has proved that infants will even modify their nursing patterns to sharpen the focus of a movie that is being shown.[31] At any age most people can be challenged and dared into taking senseless chances "for the fun of it" when Spunky is on, although at other times Scary won't allow them even to say "boo" in the presence of others.

Spunky, like Scary, sets conclusions in the various subsystems of the Child, but her motivations are excitement and curiosity, not fear. Like Scary's conclusions, some of Spunky's conclusions are effected with inadequate mental tools, and a typical conclusion of Spunky's within a given Child system can be that excitement comes from relentless rashness, or by disregarding warnings, or by cruelty, or by showing off, or by sexual seductiveness, or by challenging others, and so on.

Whether Spunky's conclusions are useful or harmful depends, here also, on the power and/or appropriateness that they have for the person's life; it depends also on the extent to which the individual learns to use his Adult both to translate his creative or exploratory tendencies into concrete achievements and also to evaluate whether and how he will take certain risks. For every Columbus or Lindbergh who successfully crossed the ocean, there are the innumerable Amelia Earharts who died as a result of risk-taking. Similarly, there are the countless young children and adolescents who get killed or maimed as a result of their daring, unaware of the risks they are taking.

Yet life without excitement and risks would be drab indeed—though many people live that way, so much under the sway of conclusions set by Scary that, pathetically, as they grow they experience even a self-criticizing Parent ego state as a relief. With the "help" of this Parent, they develop and maintain a banal counterscript. This inappropriately prevents them from implementing their genuine script through which they could experience their existence as human beings, even if it involves some danger and some pain.

INNER BALANCE   So, even though Scary and Spunky are both forces for life and survival, they keep working to offset each other while also jointly counterbalancing Sleepy, who seeks to detach us from life on earth. Yet Sleepy's influence for detachment is also essential to relieve us from being driven constantly by Scary's vigilance, which can become too anxious, or by Spunky's excitement, which can destroy us through reckless exuberance. Perhaps inner comfort can be represented as the harmonious coexistence of Sleepy, Scary, and Spunky when they cooperate with each other, like three horses jointly pulling a troika.* If one pulls too far, the other two can balance it with their counterforce. Then any one of our ego states can comfortably hold the reins of executive power.

Regrettably in our chemically minded culture, all too often people use medication to move a particular Muse, without recognizing that even if medication seems to activate a reluctant Muse it sets up a different imbalance for later on. Marijuana brings on Sleepy (detachment from everyday life and a sense of "belonging" to the cosmos); tranquilizers bring on Scary (willingness to comply and adapt for the sake of protection or out of embarrassment); and amphetamines bring on Spunky (excitement, accelerated activity, sexual turn-on). LSD also brings on Spunky with her

* A troika is a Russian sled drawn by three horses harnessed in a triangle.

most primitive conclusions, such as the assumption that it is possible to walk on air (which is how dangerous behavior occurs), and alternatively this can also stimulate Scary's panic button and bring on a "bad trip."

One of the reasons for the popularity of liquor is because it temporarily cancels out Scary if she is felt too strongly, particularly when she operates both through Child and Parent. But, after Spunky has had her say with the help of liquor, the organism is exhausted. On comes Sleepy, and to offset the powerful pull to nonlife, Scary comes on with a vengeance the morning after. This provokes a renewed urge to soothe the self by drinking rather than by dealing with the panics that were surfacing as a result of whatever inappropriate archaic conclusions Scary was bringing up in the first place (for example, "It's dangerous to relate, brag, express, think").

Each Muse has her plus and minus value for the development of the individual and the species, for the person's interaction with his environment, for his conclusions, his existential position, the development of his script, his daily transactions, and the manner in which he moves from past to present to future. And each one of the Muses serves the Self for better or worse by shuttling back and forth in time. Scary or Spunky conclusions come in from the past, stimulating responses and projecting the individual forward to the future in accordance with whatever potential directions that are designed by the story line of his script.

Which brings us back to the subject of scripts as I defined them earlier in this chapter.

NEW SCRIPT PERSPECTIVES

SCRIPTS ARE CREATIVE   I remember my excitement when Berne first stated, at the San Francisco Seminars, that scripts should not be thought of only as tragic, and that all of us developed scripts during our childhood. However, I was skeptical about the predictive value of classifying patients by fairy tales or mythological characters, even when the patients identified with these characters. Of course, there are repeated patterns to some people's sequences of rackets and games which can be compared loosely with mythological themes, especially retroactively—for instance, script analysts might say now that Richard Nixon has a Sisyphus script (pushing the rolling boulder up the hill over and over again). But even when one or another of a person's repeated patterns typically fits a well-known story or myth, there are numerous versions of each story, and different interpretations are possible about their outcomes. (For instance, was Oedipus a winner or a loser? He was successful with the Sphinx and lived happily for a long time instead of being killed at birth, and even after he blinded himself he brought honor to his place of burial.)

I became concerned lest script analysis might lead us to pigeonhole people into categories with only minor predictive accuracy—except in cases of extreme pathology, such as someone who was obviously embarked on self-destruction. And even in such cases, might there be undetected aspects of the person's script that he might build on, rather than having to depend on external guidance such as reparenting?

I was looking for a way to become more accurately predictive for a broad range of cases, such as clients who were functioning well and were relatively game-free, but who were experiencing nebulous dissatisfactions with themselves and with their lives that they could not quite formulate. Were these dissatisfactions neurotic symptoms to be cured, or might it be useful to reinforce their dissatisfactions—to help them recognize that there were other, more exciting directions called for by their scripts, and that these might lead to creative expression even if they included risks of certain negative consequences? Could we look at scripts from outside the perspective of pathology, with the assumption that our five-year-old Child might already have been inspired with a valid intuitive sense of how to grow to fulfillment?

About five years ago, to answer such questions for myself, I started using an exercise that became the preliminary design of what is now widely known as my "Four-Story Technique," which I will describe shortly. By now I have used various versions of this exercise, and many additional techniques associated to it, with more than a thousand persons in a broad spectrum of contractual contexts. These persons represent a wide range of ages, statuses, occupations, mental health, creativity, ethnic background, and value systems in the United States, Germany, Yugoslavia, Switzerland, India, and Sri Lanka. In addition, I have received personal and professional reactions and feedback—solicited and unsolicited—from numerous colleagues and trainees who have used various versions of this exercise, with and without my permission.

My experience over the past five years has modified considerably some of my earlier views about scripts. Now I have no question but that every individual carries within himself a script or life plan with which he can guide himself successfully, although many people die without implementing the best parts of their scripts.

SHAPE AND FORM TO THE SCRIPT The Child originally gives form to his script between the ages of four and seven, that is, when he first develops an awareness of past and future on a broader scale than whether Mommy is coming back into the room or not. As the sense of past and future impinges upon him, he raises questions related to the riddle of existence.* The child's awareness of past and future results from the influence of his Spunky Muse, which represents the evolutionary force of

---

* This, I believe, is the central meaning of the story of Oedipus—the confrontation of the Sphinx and the question as to what price must be paid, if any, to master the riddle. In that sense I believe that Freud had aspects of an "Oedipus" script but he episcripted his followers with the piece of it which he couldn't digest, namely the conflicts with his own sexuality. Nowadays we can afford to use the benefits of his genius without accepting his "hot potato" and assuming that all five-year-old conflicts are sexual in origin.

the species and which needs to articulate herself through each member of the species.

The child feels a need for self-determined boundaries and directional guidelines in order to give shape or form to his future life rather than conceptualizing himself as dissolving in space and time. A script gives him the structure with which he can experience his Self as he steps over the threshhold from being simply a creature-in-the-now, like an animal, to being a human blessed or cursed with the consciousness of existence. The chaos of prospective limitless directional options ahead is too threatening; the Child experiences the need somehow to dominate his future life and to develop a map with which to guide himself, the way a traveler in unknown territory might seek a hill from which to survey the land ahead of him in order to draw a tentative map that might orient him on his forthcoming journey. Even if the hill was not very high and he did not see very far ahead and his mapmaking skills were limited, such a traveler would gain a measure of security from his map. It would serve to help him project possible pathways ahead, even if the pathway he then chose took him beyond the landscape he had actually seen from the top of the hill.

At script-making age the child still has difficulty giving manageable shape to his thoughts and feelings. He is in the process of trying to transform the nebulous images of his intuition and feelings into manageable symbols that he can carry in his memory. To do so, he simultaneously uses visual images that are representative only of his personal meanings (for example, a picture of butter means all good food), as well as words or sentences that carry with them culturally determined meanings; but often there is overlapping and confusion, because the four-to-seven-year-old child does not command the culturally accepted symbolic subtleties of language. Often he hears figurative meanings literally, or vice versa, and he adds personal fantasy to literal statements. For instance, he may hear "I'll kill you if you lose my keys" as a literal threat of murder by father; to Dad's literal statement, "I lost the way driving home," he adds imagery about Dad's fear and suffering, how he must have had incredible battles with giants and whatnot. Dad is finally home now only by pure chance, or perhaps by magic intervention, maybe thanks to a talisman that one should always use if one can figure out how.

The child does the best he can with whatever resources are available to give shape to a directional life plan—as does the traveler who is mapmaking in uncharted territory. This is how Scripter latches on to a fairy tale or animal story, or even a distorted news event, to give form to his own story for the future, and this story thereby becomes the initial vehicle through which his life script will express itself. Characteristically, all script stories have ups and downs.

By the time a child is five, he has been exposed to hundreds of episodes, anecdotes, neighborhood and playground scenes, visitors, sayings, old wives' tales, and what have you, not to mention television, nursery school and kindergarten. Even if only a few stories have been read to him, he has a vast array of tales to choose from and combine. This means that even if he uses a "classic" tale to give shape to his script (such as Little Red Riding Hood), it is *his* version that is significant, along with its emphases and distortions, rather than what you and I might read in the story.

For instance the drama of Little Red Riding Hood can have innumerable meanings: it might represent success over great odds, or the value or the lack of value of obedience, disobedience, trust, mistrust, stupidity, danger, help, friendship, relatives; and there are all kinds of triangular rescuer/victim/persecutor transactions involving stand-ins for any number of people to be met later in life. Thus, any number of children might have used the story of Little Red Riding Hood as a vehicle for their scripts, but each one would be seeking to act it out differently in the course of his life, and for each it would be a unique representation of how he was seeking to plot out his destiny.

It is not by coincidence that the most popular fairy tales and myths that have come down to us through the ages, though rather convoluted and illogical to our adult minds, nevertheless seem to make perfectly good sense to children. Almost any one of these complicated tales can give form to a child's script. In reverse, classic tales and myths are the distillates of innumerable individual scripts combined together by the group mind of our species, which also responds to the evolutionary influence of the Spunky Muse.

The Scary and Sleepy Muses also get into the act when Scripter selects a story for his script and when he manipulates its images and words to represent his meanings. For one thing, he draws on the archetypal imagery that Sleepy provides in dreams and fantasy. For another, many of Scary's visceral conclusions are incorporated into the script, in one translation or another (verbal or through imagery). This does not mean that all of Scary's primitive conclusions—or even Spunky's, for that matter—are incorporated into the script, but rather mostly those that were surfacing or were being developed during the four-to-seven-year-old age period. Conclusions are usually represented within the script in the form of magical possibilities for good and evil. The script's directional flow is influenced by the relative power of the three Muses both during the scripting period and during the course of an individual's life.

ADOLESCENT SCRIPT REVISIONS   At adolescence, the implications of the early script surge into semiawareness. One reason for the internal and external battles of that period is the adolescent's attempt to reconcile the intuitive aptitude of his Child with the formal instructions of his Parent and the new, logical faculties of his Adult. Simultaneously, his Spunky Muse presses for the translation of his early script from fairy tales and fantasies into more concrete ideas. His Scary Muse shies at the more potentially dangerous aspects of his script when they are reflected in words and concepts, and she brings up old conclusions to interfere with the process, even though some of these conclusions might generate more trouble by interfering with new life-supporting relationships. (Example, "Don't run off with the princess, or the dragon will get you!").

It is during late adolescence (15–21) that the individual makes crucial decisions regarding his script. He proceeds from the childhood story and elaborates, adds, revises, and adjusts. His Spunky Muse is very active at that time.

Some individuals grapple with life in seeking to implement the exciting aspects of their script, and to the extent that they succeed they experience surges of pleasure and feelings of *success,* regardless of outside evaluation as to whether their lives are happy or unhappy. They experience themselves as fulfilling their destiny. At those times they do not seek therapy, for better or worse.

Other individuals shrink away after adolescence from pursuing their scripts because of Scary's influence in perceiving that this might involve them in struggles and in existential pain. Often they feel, rightly or wrongly, that they have already suffered too much physical pain, or pain from fear while they were growing up, and they want individual safety above all, even if it turns out to be a delusion. They become more and more subject to Scary's old conclusions. For support they clutch on to the banal culturally determined counterscript that most of us develop during the seven-to-twelve-year-old age period, when we acquire the Parent ego state that gives us solid instructions to go by.

IMPLICATIONS FOR TREATMENT The Implication of all the above is that the contractual treatment of persons who are operating dysfunctionally as a result of early conclusions is *not* synonymous with script analysis. Script and conclusions are better worked with separately in the context of separate contracts—although, of course, there will be overlapping of issues. There are different emphases to be made in *treatment,* which involves recognizing dysfunctional conclusions or rackets, and *script analysis* which involves the evaluation of an individual's life course and his creativity. These distinctions must be made clear to the client, and they involve different ways of working.

How a person implements his script is highly influenced by his existential position. The same script implemented through an "I'm not-OK, You're not-OK" position can be destructive, whereas it can be very constructive if implemented through an "I'm OK, You're OK-Adult" position. And, again, it can also be very differently implemented according to what is his defensive position and how rigidly it is maintained.

Here the implication is that the evaluation of a patient's existential position should take precedence over script analysis. As a first priority, there might need to be treatment in regard to certain conclusions. These might affect an individual's behavior and his emotional level, yet they might not even be centrally included, or even evident, in his script.

SCRIPT ANALYSIS An experienced practitioner who is trained in the clinical use of my four-story technique can pick up connecting links between a person's childhood script and its implementation or its repression in his present-day life. A grown person's script also contains substantial additions, revisions, and alternatives from his adolescent period. Some revisions or alternatives are incorporated into the life-patterns that are being lived out by the individual, but very many exist simply as abortive fantasies. Yet, it is these that offer leads as to how a person can fulfill himself better if he happens to be stuck in a banal counterscript. The recognition of this fact has been one of the most surprising by-products of the use of my technique.

As yet there is no totally reliable way to achieve a full analysis of a person's script. But with sufficient time and the assistance of a practitioner who is well trained in the use of the story technique I will describe hereunder, it is possible for a person to gain a reliable perspective about his script. Within each one of us there lie creative script directives that cry to be implemented. These include aspects that were conceptualized at adolescence. With script analysis, as I describe it, a person can guide himself with more mental clarity along directions that are compatible with his intuitive awareness of *Who* he is. This inner awareness is something that all of us carry, whether we acknowledge it or not.

THE FOUR-STORY EXERCISE   Here are the initial instructions I give to clients when we use my four-story exercise. These follow a clear contract about the context and the time to be allotted for script analysis, depending on what goals are agreed upon in advance:—

Write down four stories, in less than fifteen lines each. This is to be done from memory, without checking the original version of the stories. The four are to be:

1. A nursery rhyme or fairy tale or song or animal story remembered from early childhood (under age seven, preferably earlier). (Many people claim they cannot remember any, and this is significant; they are invited to substitute a story they would now choose to tell a four-year-old.)
2. The comprehensible sumary, or an episode, or quotes, from fiction, history, or biography (excluding personal history) that "turned you on" —positively or negatively—during your seven to twelve age period. (From novels, plays, movies, news events, epic tales, poems.)
3. The same is to be done for the 15-to-21-year-old period.
4. A summary or episode or quotes from fiction, history or news events that made a powerful impact on you in the recent past (within the last three years, and preferably within the last year, especially if there has been treatment).

The client is asked to read out loud, exactly as he wrote them, stories (1) and (4). The central themes of these stories are compared and contrasted. Significant common elements between them are almost always startlingly here, even though the content is very different, and the reader may not notice resemblances of themes and patterns until they are pointed out. If work is done in a group, which is a recommended procedure, it becomes evident that even untutored group members can pick up and agree on significant similarities or polarized contrasts between the early elementary story and the sophisticated grownup one. This leads to a few initial hypotheses about some central issues within a client's script.

By limiting the reader to no more than fifteen lines, it is possible to evaluate the relative weight or value he allocates to specific aspects of each story. It is important to deal only with the reader's version and not with the original story, since it is only the reader's version that is significant. (By now I have heard more than a hundred versions of the Three Little Pigs, but the script of one reader of this story varies widely from that of another.)

Subsequently, stories (2) and (3) are read, and it is when we start comparing and contrasting (3) with (1) and (4) that serious script work can begin, subject to what the contract calls for. Quick hunches can be developed in as little as 15 to 20 minutes with this exercise, but solid script work requires several hours of systematic work and must be practiced only under the leadership of an experienced script analyst who is trained in the use of this exercise. My technique depends on collaborative work with the client to clarify the direction in which he has been going in his life so far and to examine both the possibilities to be reinforced and the pitfalls to be anticipated.

Obviously, there are many aspects to be looked at when one takes the time to compare and contrast a series of stories. Beyond getting a sense of their central themes, it is useful to evaluate the relative roles and relationships taken on by the hero/heroine and auxiliary characters. Auxiliary characters, animals and objects, often represent alternate versions of the self, although they also represent people that are feared or yearned for in relationships. Also note abrupt changes or discrepancies in grammar or style. They connote switches amongst the ego states with which the writer relates to his script. Then there is significance to contrasts between first and last lines, between the outcomes of the three stories, between the relative representation of Sleepy, Scary, and Spunky elements, and so on.

Also, there are comparisons to be made with whatever information is available about early conclusions, particularly if the client has previously worked in a treatment context. A deepened view of his script can be achieved by comparing his stories with conclusions listed on Charts A and B (described in connection with subsystems). But this is not an essential procedure.

When I first designed this exercise, I used to ask for only one adolescent story without specifying the age for adolescence. I used to concentrate on similarities and differences between the first and the last story and ask for the adolescent story mostly as a way of getting additional confirmation about the script from the intermediate point between the early childhood story and the present-day story. To my surprise, I found that, whereas usually there were clear parallels and correspondences between the first and the last story, the adolescent story was often at great odds with these patterns. At first I brushed aside this unexpected finding by assuming that the adolescent story simply represented the counterscript and could be disregarded. Later I changed my instructions to the ones given above, separating out the age periods of the stories I was requesting. I found that it is true that story (2) usually represents parental instructions and the counterscript. But that story (3) usually contains transformed and highly dramatic elements of story (1). If story (4) contains tight correspondences to story (2), and if the client is dissatisfied with his current life it is worth examining story (3) quite carefully even if it sounds wild. Often it contains a sense of alternate, more creative ways of living. Some of these can often be implemented if translated into Adult options.

Usually, the individual's satisfaction with his present-day life corresponds to the extent to which there is a directional flow between stories (1), (3), and (4). By contrast high correspondence between stories (2) and (4) and strong discrepancy with (1) and (3) correlates with feelings of dissatisfaction. This has convinced me that the adolescent revisions of a person's script must be taken into account for the fulfillment of a person.

By now I have accumulated considerable additional material on scripts through having used various versions of this exercise and additional techniques (for instance, comparing the rewrites of clients' stories at six-month intervals).

I do want to caution the reader about the fact that this technique is very impactful if used as more than a playful workshop exercise. It should not be used as a tool for change except by experienced practitioners who have had practice in responsible use of this technique. Such practitioners need both specific training and a talent for the kind of intuitive apprehension that is needed to grasp the inner sense of a client's stories. The danger of using this technique is that it can cause severe anxiety in some clients. The significance of any destructive aspects of a person's script must be recognized and dealt with at a level that can be used by the client; otherwise, this exercise can be nonproductive and even damaging. In addition, it is very important to protect certain clients from group members' "laying a trip on them," as people are quite vulnerable after writing and reading their stories.

However, allowing for all the cautions above, we now have a valuable means of helping clients get in touch with their inner sense of direction instead of living lives of psychological "quiet desperation." They can reconnect themselves with the symbolic, convoluted mythological connotations of their childhood and adolescent scripts, and gain therefrom the initiatives and the ideas that were lying dormant within them. They can experience their Selves and live out the potentially exciting drama of their lives. For drama need not turn to tragedy; rather that the very tragedies we seek to avert are often brought on if we deny recognition to the dramatic potentials of our existence on earth.

THE DAY THAT I STOOD ON MY HEAD
by Maurice English

The day that I stood on my head, jumped out of my skin,
Yelled down my throat and covered my eyes with my ears,
The day that I married a witch, tied bells to my tail
And sailed my heart as a boomerang; the day
That I danced on my grave and whistled a jig to my sorrow—
That was today.

What shall I do tomorrow?

From *Midnight in the Century,* Chicago, Swallow Press, 1964.

References

1. Eric Berne, *Transactional Analysis in Psychotherapy,* New York, Grove Press, 1961.
2. Fanita English, "Episcript and the Hot Potato Game," *Transactional Analysis Bulletin, 8,* no. 32 (October, 1969).
3. Jean Piaget, *Judgment and Reasoning in the Child,* Totowa, New Jersey, Littlefield, Adams & Co., 1969.
4. René Spitz "Hospitalism," *The Psychoanalytic Study of the Child,* New York, International Universities Press, 1945, vol. 1.
5. Fanita English, "Strokes in the Credit Bank for David Kupfer," *Transactional Analysis Journal, 1,* no. 3 (July, 1971).
6. Jean Piaget, *The Origins of Intelligence in Children,* New York, International Universities Press, 1952.
7. English, "Episcript," *op. cit.* Space will not permit me to describe the process of episcripting here. Berne considered the theory "a very important contribution to script theory," and I urge the reader to refer to this article in conjunction with this chapter, even though its vocabulary is slightly outdated.
8. Robert Goulding, "Thinking and Feeling in Psychotherapy: Three Impasses," *Voices, 10,* no. 1 (1974), p. 11–13. I have recently become more familiar with the Gouldings' "three levels of impasses" and am glad to find that there is a parallel development in our new approaches.
9. Fanita English, "Shame and Social Control," *Transactional Analysis Journal, 5,* no. 1 (January, 1975).
10. David Kupfer and Morris Haimowitz, "Therapeutic Interventions. Part I: Rubberbands," *Transactional Analysis Journal, 1,* no. 2 (April, 1971), pp. 10–16. The analogy to a "rubber band" for describing the process of snapping back and forth between an episode or feeling in the "now" and a particular moment of the past was first used by David Kupfer, and it is a very important image for working with "conclusions."
11. In Eric Berne, *What Do You Say After You Say Hello?,* New York, Grove Press, 1972. Berne consistently defined ego states as coherent systems of thought and feeling in this, his last book, as well as his other writings. He added that ego states are manifested by patterns of behavior that correspond to these systems.
12. Jean Piaget, *The Child's Conception of the World,* Totowa, New Jersey, Littlefield, Adams & Co., 1969.

13. Piaget, *The Origins of Intelligence in Children, op. cit.*
14. René Spitz, *The First Year of Life,* New York, International Universities Press, 1965.
15. Erik H. Erikson, *Childhood and Society,* 2nd ed., New York, W. W. Norton & Company, 1963.
16. Melanie Klein, *Our Adult World and Its Roots in Infancy,* London, Heineman Medical Books, Ltd., 1963, pp. 1–22.
17. Spitz, *The First Year of Life, op. cit.*
18. Fanita English, "I'm OK, You're OK-Adult," *Transactional Analysis Journal, 5,* no. 3 (October, 1975).
19. Jerome Bruner, Unpublished material at his laboratory, Cambridge, Massachusetts.
20. English, *Shame and Social Control, op. cit.*
21. Fanita English, "The Substitution Factor: Rackets and Real Feelings," *Transactional Analysis Journal, 1,* no. 4 (October, 1971); Fanita English, "Rackets and Real Feelings," *Transactional Analysis Journal, 2,* no. 1 (January, 1972).
22. Fanita English, "Racketeering," *Transactional Analysis Journal, 6,* no. 1 (January, 1976).
23. Eric Berne, "Classification of Positions," *Transactional Analysis Bulletin, 1,* no. 3 (July, 1962), p. 23.
24. Fanita English, "Fifth Position," *Voices, 12,* no. 1 (1976); English, "I'm OK," *op. cit.*
25. English, "Racketeering," *op. cit.*
26. Berne, *What Do You Say, op. cit.*
27. Eric Berne, *Games People Play,* New York, Grove Press, 1964.
28. Berne, *What Do You Say, op. cit.*
29. W. A. Mason, "Scope and Potential of Primate Research," in J. H. Masserman, ed., *Science and Psychoanalysis,* New York, Grune & Stratton, 1968, vol. 12.
30. F. S. Perls, *Ego, Hunger, and Aggression,* San Francisco, Orbit Graphic Arts and Esalen, 1966.
31. Bruner, *op. cit.*

V

Transactional Analysis in Clinical Practice

SIXTEEN

FROM 21 TO 43
Stanley J. Woollams

I am a TA therapist, yet when I am doing therapy, I sometimes go long periods of time without uttering a TA word or phrase. Occasionally I will remark about a discount, a racket, an ego state, or a decision, but not often. So why do I call myself a TA therapist? It is because I *think* TA. Everything I do in therapy centers around a single key TA concept, plus several others that logically develop from it. So even though I may not be using TA labels out loud, I am thinking them and making treatment decisions based on them.

The basic question is: what decisions did the client make about how to live his or her life when growing up that resulted in the behavior and feeling that he or she is having now and wants to change.* These early *script decisions* determined patterns of behavior and feelings that cause present-day problems. I see therapy as a process that facilitates for the client new and desirable patterns of behavior and feelings and thus, in effect, new script decisions. Therefore, I primarily look for information about what the original script decisions were and then use various methods to help the client change in her desired direction. Other important TA concepts I utilize are: contract, ego state, discount, racket, strokes, and the "three P's" of protection, permission, and potency.

The *contract* is crucial. This is an agreement between the client and the therapist about what behavior and/or feelings the client does not like and wants to change to new desirable behavior and/or feelings. Note carefully that the client and therapist agree on the contract. A contract is bilateral. The client must want it and I must like it. It is important that our Adult ego states think the contract makes sense. It also means that the contract must appeal to and turn on the Free Child in both of us. This is especially true for the client. If her Free Child is against the contract, she

---

* Henceforth, when writing about things that apply equally to either sex, I will arbitrarily use feminine pronouns.

will not use her energy to change. As a matter of fact, why should she? Change should be for the Free Child. Developmentally, the Adapted Child makes script decisions because the Free Child cannot get or feel what she wants or needs without undue risk. Therefore, I am interested in helping people get back into their Free Child and out of their substitute behavior and feelings. A strong indicator that a client's contract is from the Free Child is that it not only makes sense to my Adult but that it also feels right to my Free Child. If it does not, I have learned that the client is usually in her Adapted Child. Conversely, just because it feels right to me does not make it a good contract. It must be right for the client too. She may not be interested in what turns on my Child, or it may be that she is just not interested yet ("I am too scared now").

As already demonstrated in the above discussion of contracts, *ego states* are very important. Actually, the accurate diagnosis of ego states is the foundation for good therapy. If I think that the client is in her Free Child when she actually is in her Adapted Child, then I likely will make the wrong intervention and reinforce the wrong behaviors and feelings. A thorough knowledge of the normal development of children will greatly assist in distinguishing between Free Child and Adapted Child (for example, the Free Child when sad cries loudly while the Adapted Child may weep softly). If I think that I am being a Nurturing Parent when I am actually coming on Controlling Parent, then I am likely to be ineffective —or worse. More subtly, if I think I am being a positive Nurturing Parent but actually I am overnurturing (negative Nurturing Parent), I am stopping the client from growing. To facilitate the diagnosis, one can use any of the experiential forms of therapy that have been devised. I use the methods of gestalt, fantasy, encounter, bioenergetics, and cathecting young to get the client into experiencing her feelings more strongly and so be more clearly in touch with the ego state she is in.

It is vital that the therapist be aware of *discounts* or alterations of reality. I am discounting and subtly encouraging your scripty behavior if I see you as a poor soul who is too weak to change and so do not point out your whiny voice or ask you if you accomplished what you had contracted to do. I am discounting if I allow you not to answer my question which I know you hear. We would then be behaving as if our interaction had never happened. A person is discounting (changing reality) every time she is carrying out her script, because she is behaving as if she must carry out decisions made many years before when circumstances were much different. The idea of discounting is similar to the psychoanalytic idea of transference. Both require an alteration of reality. In my first example of discounting, where I saw the client as a poor soul too weak to change, I would probably do so because the client reminded me of some important figure from the past who behaved that way. Thus, I transferred an object from my past into the now as the basis of my discount. A client who incorrectly says "You don't like me" is discounting because, in fact, her mother did not like her and so she has "put her mother's face" on me and is having a transference reaction to me. Therapy, then, is a process to help the client stop discounting, that is, to make new decisions so that she lives in the now and does not transfer faces of the past onto people of the present.

Racket feelings are bad feelings arrived at through discounting and do not lead to useful behavior. There are three basic types of racket feelings and each correlates with a position on the Karpman drama triangle. Persecutor contains the discount, "I am better than you, and/or you are inferior, therefore I may persecute you." The feeling is anger or superiority. Rescuer contains the discount, "I know better than you, and/or you are inadequate, therefore I should help you." The feeling is concern or pity. Victim contains the discount, "I am helpless, and/or you are better than me, therefore you may persecute me or should help me." The feeling is sad or scared. Both the Persecutor and the Rescuer are attempting to ward off being a Victim, which is the basic position. A person in a racket feeling is not only discounting but is also carrying out a negative script.

The concepts of *protection, permission,* and *potency* guide the therapist in setting up an optimal environment for the client to do her work of changing. To change, a client must not only want to change but must also feel it is safe to do so. It is the therapist's job to provide the three P's in sufficient amounts to insure the client's sense of safety. Briefly put (I will discuss this later), the therapist provides protection by setting up a structure of therapy to protect against physical and emotional harm. Permission to change is given when the therapist lets the client know that it is OK to break out of her script and to behave and feel in the new desired way. Finally, the permission and protection must be done potently so that they are believable.

Strokes are units of attention. Clients come for therapy because they are practiced at getting more negative strokes than they like and because they want to learn to get positive ones. It is the therapist's job to help the client learn this skill, and she can promote this by her own judicious use of both positive and negative strokes.

HOW I GOT FROM THERE TO HERE

The way I go about helping the client change her script is shaped by my own developmental history as a person and as a therapist and by a few particular principles I have developed regarding theory and practice. To illustrate how I do therapy, I will describe my development and discuss along the way the issues I consider to be important.

I was brought up like all the therapists I know—to be a Rescuer—and, again quite typically, to be hard working, to have the desire to accomplish something worthwhile, and, finally, to be curious. I resolved this by going to medical school with the intention to be a psychiatrist. In medical school and during my year of internship, I learned to be reasonably comfortable about being responsible for the people I was caring for. This did not help my rescuing tendencies, but it did teach me to be thoughtful about what I was doing and it prepared me for the TA concept of protection. My medical background also helped my future potency as a therapist, since the physician is trained to be in charge, to lead, and to see that something gets done. Unfortunately, medical school and internship also reinforced my Work Hard pattern.

I then went on to psychiatric residency training. Both my medical school and residency training were at the University of Michigan. Coincidentally, at the very beginning of my training I was assigned to a service where group therapy was an important part of the program. So I started out with equal emphasis on both group and individual therapy. This helped me avoid the usual prejudice against group therapy that most psychiatrists have.

It has been my experience that the greatest resistance a client has to group therapy—or more specifically to working on a particular issue in group—is the therapist. If the therapist believes that individual therapy is superior and so does not expect the client to work on more than superficial issues in group, then group work can go no deeper since the therapist sets the pace and tone for the group. If the therapist has specific areas, such as sex, transference issues, working-through, and the like, that she believes should not or cannot be worked on in group, they will be avoided. All the therapist has to do to sabotage her group is not to respond to a particular statement, or more blatantly to say "Let's work on that in the individual session," or merely to agree with the client when she says "I can't talk about that here." I have found that the great majority of people (95 percent) will work in group just as well and often better than in individual therapy. Group therapy has several advantages over individual:

1. There is opportunity for more and varied transference reactions.
2. Support for working through transference reactions to the therapist is available from peers.
3. Help to the therapist for her countertransference problems is directly available.
4. What the client does with other people is immediately observable, so information is directly available about ego states, transactions, games, etc.
5. More support to work on particular problem areas (sex, assertiveness, parents, etc.) is available, since someone else in the group almost always has a similar problem.
6. After one person has gotten into a strong feeling about something, it is easier for the next person to do so (contagion).
7. More sources of information about external issues as well as what is going on in the group are available.
8. "Working through" a particular problem can occur right in the group. When a client makes a decision for a new behavior, there are people right there to practice on.
9. Support between sessions is available from other group members and the therapist does not have to be the sole giver of support.

10. More strokes are available for everyone.
11. There is less pressure on the client and less time wasted.

In individual therapy the client ordinarily "works" for 50 minutes or some arbitrary length of time, even though she may have stopped doing something useful after ten minutes. In group, the therapist can go on to someone else while letting the client think on her own and come back a second or third time to the client when she is ready to do further "work."

Much of the concentration, intensity, and individual attention available in individual therapy is available in group also if the style of working with one client at a time on his or her individual contract is generally followed. Some of the advantages of a process group (one that primarily pays attention to the interaction between the members) are lost this way. However, in a well-functioning group it is more efficient to stress individual work. I see almost all of my clients in group as their primary mode of treatment. I see a few also in individual therapy because they need the added contact (protection) and can use the time profitably. An occasional client is seen individually because the group is experienced as too upsetting. For example, one client experienced all the needy people in group as being just like his family, and so he would not get anything for himself.

PSYCHOANALYSIS

My residency training of three years was psychoanalytic in orientation. This was very helpful because the dynamic approach within the psychoanalytic developmental framework taught me much about people. I also learned a great deal about listening and observing. I especially remember the permission I received during this time from one of my teachers—Andrew Watson, MD—to use my own creative thinking (my Little Professor) and not just to "go by the book." I also began my personal analysis, which lasted six years. From this experience I learned several things. Primarily I took in some additional Nurturing Parent from someone who for a long time listened comfortably to me saying foolish and (I thought) terrible things. I also learned a great deal of patience for allowing the process of change to occur. That has been most helpful. Thus, I am not too inclined to "hurry up" my clients and I do not bug myself when they do not change rapidly or as fast as they "should" (according to the experts and the writers in the field). On the other hand, I felt that the psychoanalysis had been too slow and that I could have moved faster with a different style of intervention. Specifically, I was aware of a lot going on in my body that seemed unattended to.

Thus, after I finished my residency and completed two years of servitude with the Air Force, I was ready to learn some new things to help people and myself change. Eric Berne was traveling in my area. I heard him lecture and got turned on to his interesting ideas of ego states and games and to his clever ideas of how to intervene in scripts. Coincidentally, I soon discovered that Claude Steiner was working in the same hospital

I was, and so I asked him to do a group with me. This we did for several months until he returned to California. This experience, although brief, was positive, and so in 1965 I joined the International Transactional Analysis Association. However, with Claude Steiner gone, and since the TA I had learned was essentially for the "head," I turned my interest elsewhere.

First I went to "encounter" and the humanistic movement. I worked with George Bach and learned, among other things, about marathons, which I now use extensively both in therapy and in teaching. Although at first my marathon experiences had little provision for sleep, I now do marathons lasting from two to seven days with regular breaks for meals, play, and sleeping. Because of a later influence from TA (with the Haimowitzes and the Gouldings), I am not interested in breaking down defenses by lack of sleep but instead want to provide an opportunity for clients to let go safely of defenses. A marathon provides for this because of the prolonged chance to work on a problem in a positive environment containing many strokes. An individual in once-weekly therapy will tend to go back to her usual defensive patterns of behavior between sessions until she slowly (usually) establishes a new pattern that not only satisfies her but also works. In psychoanalysis, the client attends three to five times per week and this frequency is important in adding to the protection she experiences. The marathon even more strongly enhances protection. Partly because of this I have extended my regular group sessions to five hours in length so that clients have a longer period of time to feel safe to work on their contracts and to establish new patterns of behavior.

HIGHLIGHTS OF ENCOUNTERING

Within the encounter movement there is a wide diversity of styles, but there are several common elements that are important. There is permission to be creative and to use one's unique talents. I believe that the talent and personality of the therapist is the crucial element in helping others to change.[1] There is no system that has all the right answers. Therefore, instead of everyone learning how to do therapy in one way, it is important for each individual to be exposed to many different styles so that each therapist can develop her or his special talents. One of the things I especially like about TA is that since it is a general theory describing human behavior, it can have techniques from any other system used comfortably within its framework.

Also from encounter, I got my first permission to touch my clients. From my psychoanalytically oriented training, and from Eric Berne too, I had learned not to touch my clients. Touching would interfere with the transference; it would create countertransference; it would foster dependency; and so on. From encounter and, later, from gestalt, bioenergetics, and many subgroups within TA, I was given permission to question this and to change my mind. Actually, to state the obvious, touching is normal. Not to touch, then, is abnormal and therefore likely to cause transference distortions. If I do not ever touch a client, she may very likely see me as a withholding, cold parent, and it may be harder to get over that transference because there might be too much reality to it. This is particularly true for a client who had a parent who did not touch her. To touch certainly may stir up countertransference problems, especially if I have problems touching people. If I had been uncomfortable touching or being touched by my father or my mother, I can easily have problems touching my clients. Also, if I am uncomfortable touching females (males) because of my sexual desires or fears, then again, I may well have trouble touching my clients. Not to touch may avoid that, but it will also be artificial and limit my ability to help my clients work through many issues:

Being close to others

Liking their own bodies (children like their bodies and how they function because their parents liked their bodies and did not teach them to be disgusted with them)

Feeling secure and trusting

Existing (babies learn that they exist from the physical strokes they receive in the first year of life; they also learn the limits of their bodies and that other bodies exist in response to being touched all over)

The therapist essentially is in a parent position in relationship to the client. Even if we intend otherwise, the client will make it so. The client's problems stem from decisions made during childhood and it is her scared and unhappy Child who comes for help. Thus, therapists should do for clients what good parents do. Good parents get their own needs (sexual, nurturing, and otherwise) met from people other than their children. When they are with their children, they are not there to get but to give what is needed—caring and strokes, help for growth, and information. A good parent does not have a sexual relationship with her children, but she will appreciate their sexual growth. A therapist, then, who takes care of her own needs outside of the therapy situation can safely touch, hold, play with, and stroke her clients and deal with their reactions. It is true that their reactions may sometimes be quite intense, since the more active, involved, and nonpassive the therapist is, the more intensely the client is likely to respond. In effect, I am saying that the transference reactions are often stronger. This is true not only with touching but with many of the other overt and real behaviors of the therapist. If these are at all like a real or fantasized figure from the client's past, the transference reaction may occur more quickly and intensely than if the therapist had been more of a "blank screen." I must be prepared to deal with these intense reactions if I use such stimulating methods, and to frequently examine myself, with the aid of the group if necessary, to make sure I am not having a countertransference problem—that is, if I, not the client, am distorting. The primary rule for touching is that it is OK and a good idea if it will facilitate the accomplishment of the contract without creating another problem that the client will not want to solve.

As a part of its stress on the here-and-now, a major method of encounter is to act out in the therapy situation whatever the client is thinking or feeling. This allows the person to express herself through her body. From my work with encounter and later with gestalt and bioenergetics, I have become convinced that our life experiences are recorded not only in our brains but also in our bodies. A client may talk about her fear of assertiveness and experience that moderately, but when she is asked to get out of her seat and actually physically confront members of the group in an assertive way, she is likely to experience her fear fully and perhaps get back to an early scene where she made a decision to placate instead of assert. If a client has trouble getting into a feeling in the course of working on a contract, you might have her:

Arrange her body in a position that goes with the feeling
Exaggerate that position
Do it in front of a group member
Say something negative, assertive, or argumentative to that person
Express whatever she is saying increasingly loudly

By doing these, she will very likely get into her feeling and fully express it and so may finish an old experience that accompanied the feeling and be ready to make a redecision. As each client works on her contract, it is possible to create specific encounters involving other group members. To facilitate doing that it is useful to be aware of the many standard experiments that have been devised.[2] They are also useful in a general way to "warm up" a group and to get people in touch with their bodies and aware of problems they have in dealing with other people.

WHAT I GOT FROM THE GOULDINGS

While developing my skills with encounter, I was still interested in using a clearer language and theory than what psychoanalysis offered. So in May, 1970, I journeyed to California to study with Bob and Mary Goulding and to thoroughly try out TA. This was a turning point for me, since my experience with the Gouldings convinced me to become a TA therapist. I found TA theory to be essentially clear (only a few foggy areas), concise, and relatively free of jargon. I only had to learn three ego states, the three P's, strokes, decision, racket and game (along with Persecutor, Rescuer, and Victim), and script. And, Hallelujah!, my clients could understand it too. Their Adult ego states were acknowledged as being as good and as useful as mine, so we could talk together as equals about their psyches. They could read the literature and get ideas for change. They could work on their own and talk to their spouses, children, and friends in a useful language. This is one of Eric Berne's greatest accomplishments. I have serious reservations about theories that have a large number of complex idiosyncratic words. The colloquial nature of TA words is a plus, since they are short and appeal to the Child. However, I think even TA has a few words that are not very useful and so I ignore them. Even some of the useful ones have their problems. For example, racket, although a useful concept, is frequently misused because of the word itself. A racket sounds "bad" and many people think they have committed a sin if they discover they have been in their racket. So instead of working on what their Free Child wants, they give themselves a hard time for "goofing up" again. The phrase "substitute behavior or feeling" is not pejorative and nicely describes what a racket is, but it is cumbersome. I suggest a prize for the person who invents a better term.

I also learned from the Gouldings the marvelous value of positive stroking!

From them, too, I learned about *decisions* and *redecisions*.[3] The awareness of the decisions we made as children, which resulted in our life plans or scripts, leads to the notion that we therefore can make new decisions—redecisions—*now* about how we are going to live. This has the tremendous advantage of focusing the client's work. What is the contract? What was the original decision that is causing the present problem? What is the client telling herself and doing now to maintain that decision? What does she need (protection, permission, information, etc.) to make a new decision? Will she make the new decision? How will she carry it out? When? What did she think or do to avoid carrying it out? What does she now need to get or to do to assist her in carrying out her new decision? Perhaps make a new decision about something else? Once she is regularly carrying out her new decision successfully, is she interested in working on something else (a new contract) or in terminating therapy?

Each step of treatment is clear, since everything the client works on should relate to one of the above steps. By the way, it is important that clients and therapists understand that when clients make a redecision they have not promised anything to anybody. It is not a Child-to-Parent transaction by which the client is now obligated to perform and should feel bad when she does not. Many clients and therapists get angry (or disappointed or sad) when new decisions are not perfectly carried out. A redecision is an *intention*. The Child, along with the Adult's understanding and perhaps the Parent's approval, intends to carry out a new behavior and to give up an old one. Like any new step a child takes, it will probably occur haltingly and perhaps always with room for improvement. In no case does it become an obligation. It is not done to please a parent but only to please the self.

Something I learned from several different people in TA (Eric Berne being the first) is the value of the Parent ego state. It is all right to have one and to use it in therapy! It is all right to admit to having opinions and to express them! This gives the therapist the free opportunity to give permission and to do it potently—a combination which is a powerful tool to effect change. To tell a client directly, "It is all right for you to express your feeling!" will sometimes facilitate movement into a new behavior much faster than any other intervention.

I FIND PERLS: GESTALT

In the year or so preceding my work with the Gouldings, I had learned some gestalt theory and technique (originally developed by Fritz Perls[4]). With the Gouldings, I fully integrated gestalt into my armamentarium. Gestalt is another system of therapy which provides access to the messages of the body. A whole new language is available in addition to the usual verbal statements of the client. By paying attention to every movement and posture of the client's body and by asking the client to "be" that part of the body and to speak as that part, one can discover and therefore work through otherwise hidden material. The woman who says "Of course I love my husband" while twirling the ring on her finger is directed to "Speak for your hand twirling your ring." Her response: "I feel caught by him, I wish I could get away." A man in family treatment had great difficulty in getting along with his son. Nevertheless he was talking about how he was going to behave differently. While saying this, he was lightly tapping one of his fingers on the arm of his chair. I asked him to "be" his finger and do what it wanted to do and then to speak for it. He began by tapping his finger more vigorously, then by pounding his fist, and finally while doing this, shouting that he hated his son and was jealous of him. In each of the above instances, I might have been able to obtain the same important information by talking directly with the client but generally it would have taken much longer. Also, by experiencing it so strongly clients cannot help but accept the existence of a hidden part which often they previously had not been aware of.

Gestalt also emphasizes the here-and-now, so that nothing is talked about but instead is experienced NOW. If a client is angry at her mother, she does not talk about that to the therapist or to the group, she "puts"— or imagines—her mother in front of her and talks to her directly. This is called the empty chair technique, since an empty chair often is used for the fantasized person. By talking to mother now, the client tends to re-create very quickly whatever scene is meaningful to her—with all the attendant feeling. She may regress to early ages and experience episodes where she received powerful negative messages to which she responded with script decisions. At this point, with the help of the therapist and her own now fully developed Adult, she may come to a new decision. Gestalt not only opens up the language of the body for investigation, but also provides some powerful tools to help reintegrate it. Anything can be put on the empty chair and the process tends to intensify and focus. I will give an abbreviated example:

> *Client:* "I have a headache I want to get rid of."
> *Therapist:* "Put your headache on the chair and talk to it."

Client: "Why are you hurting me?"
Headache: "I've got you and you are not going to get away."
Therapist: "Respond to that."
Client: "I am scared of you, go away!"
Headache: "I won't. I hate you!"
Therapist: "Who is saying that to you?"
Client: "My father."
Therapist: "What will you say to him now?"
Client: "You are not going to get me anymore. I'm done with you!"
Therapist: "How do you feel now?"
Client: "Great! My headache is gone!"

In addition to the above, I use gestalt methods to investigate directly a person's interpersonal interactions, games, rackets, and script. For example, a man who is talking about the difficulties he is having with his wife (who is not present) is asked to put her on the empty chair and to talk with her. While he had been talking *about* the situation it had sounded as if she were quite unreasonable, but when he talked *to* her in the other chair we noted his angry tone and provocative manner. Also, when he took her chair and answered, she sounded scared and unsure of herself. The Persecutor–Victim relationship became clear and his game of *Blemish* was unmistakable—even to him! Chairing is also an excellent way to clarify script messages. I find it useful to focus the work by having the client state the issue in as direct a way as possible. If done in a less structured way, the client may avoid the issue, since her Adapted Child is afraid of the truth.

Alice said she wanted to die and did not know why.

Therapist: "Put your mother on the chair and tell her you want to die."
AC: "Mom, I want to die."
Mother: "Now don't you talk that way. Let's go shopping."
AC: "Mom! I want to die."
Mother: "Now stop your fussing. You will upset your father!"
AC: "Mom! Don't you care about me?"
Mother: "You be quiet now! Go out and play."

The "Don't bother me" message that Alice had known about was really a "Don't be" as indicated by the level of discounting, and the confrontation with mother clarified this for her. A similar conversation with father also demystified his message. To summarize, the empty chair technique is basically an enactment in fantasy of a thought or body statement. When combined with TA it adds a potent method to get to script redecisions. Last but not least, it is very interesting to do and often a lot of fun. The creativity of my Little Professor is given full rein.

A year or so after my time with the Gouldings I began learning about another system that concentrates on the messages of the body—bioenergetics—which was developed by Alexander Lowen.[5] His notion is that the actual structure of the body is, in part, determined by the environmental forces that play upon it. Thus, the structure of my body expresses my script. The term "bodyscript" has been coined by Ressler[6] to describe this.

In therapy one may challenge the client's "body armor" by placing her in various stressful positions while maintaining a free flow of breathing. At the same time she may say or yell out something pertinent, like "I hate you" or "Don't leave me." All of this tends to evoke script material and provides opportunity for making redecisions along with changing the body structure.

IS REPARENTING THE ANSWER?

At around this same time, I was learning about a new development in TA that has a somewhat psychoanalytic heritage. This is *reparenting* and was developed by Jacqui Schiff.[7] In this system, the client cathects young, in other words, decides to be little at a specific age that is pertinent for the resolution of her contract, and meanwhile relates to the therapist as parent. Among other things, this facilitates the formation of a new Parent ego state.

The Parent ego state is being formed from the moment of birth and continues to be formed throughout life. The Parent is our version or recording of what our parent figures did. What I record is based on my vulnerability as well as my estimate of the parent figures' power and their importance to me. As a child, I am quite vulnerable and my parents are quite powerful and important to me, and so I take into my Parent most of what they do. As a grownup client, I am not nearly so vulnerable and the therapist is not nearly so powerful or important (a fuller exposition is to come later in this chapter). However, if I decide to be little and to make the therapist a parent figure as a part of our contract, then I increase my vulnerability and enhance the therapist's power and importance. New Parent messages are more likely to be taken in and so my Child has a new supportive source to turn to. Also, during the process of reparenting my Child may feel more safe trying out new behaviors and can be reinforced while doing them. I can make a redecision with a new Parent in my head to say it's OK, and my Adult, which was observing, can say it's real and it makes sense. It is like the "corrective emotional experience" of Alexander and French.[8] Reparenting, then, has the potential to increase the potency of the intervention. Also, the level of protection is high, since during the time of reparenting the client is being taken care of in a way appropriate for whatever age she is cathecting. Therefore, the permissions are given in an environment of high protection and high potency, which is ideal.

In spite of this, reparenting is not the panacea for all our ailments. The client may not let herself be any more vulnerable to new messages than with other methods, and if so she will still resist change in her usual ways. The technique also tends to ask more of a commitment of time and energy from the therapist, and this I often am not willing to do. It tends to provoke stronger transference reactions. These, on the one hand, may be productive, since working them through may be an important aspect of changing and fulfilling the contract. On the other hand, however, there are likely to be some stormy treatment sessions, which are a lot of work and unless dealt with successfully can end with a negative result. Reparenting can provoke stronger countertransference reactions. With the client so stirred up, it is more likely that the therapist will overreact. And, with the client cathecting young, it is easier for any Rescuing tendencies in the therapist to manifest themselves, so that a hard game of *I'm Only Trying to Help You* might ensue. It must be remembered that nurturing by itself is not enough to cure anybody or to have them change their script. Most clients, if not all, do not wish to take full responsibility for their own behavior. With a reparenting contract the therapist may be seen as the giving parent they always wanted, one who would solve all their problems. This can result in strong Victim/Rescuer and Victim/Persecutor interchanges.

I find it extremely helpful to check out regularly how my Child is feeling about what is going on. Am I feeilng pushed? Does what the client wants feel right? Do I feel like giving it or saying it? Am I being asked to give more than I contracted for? Not only is it bad for me to allow myself to be discounted, but it is bad parenting and bad therapy. If I ignore my Free Child, the client will record in her Parent that it is OK to ignore your own needs and later on get mad, sad, or scared about it. Also, if my Child is being discounted, the client is probably in scripty behavior. If I continue on with nurturing or whatever I am doing, I will inadvertently reinforce the behavior.

Schiff *et al.* have said, "Symbiosis occurs when two or more individuals behave as though between them they form a whole person. This relationship is characterized structurally by neither individual cathecting a full complement of ego states." Unfortunately they go on to say, "Symbiosis is a natural occurrence between parents and children."[9] This latter statement confuses *normal dependency* with symbiosis.[10] In healthy parenting neither party need or should exclude an ego state. Parents often do exclude one or two of their ego states and so invite their offspring to enter into a symbiotic relationship and not grow up. This is not normal and occurs only when parents are misinformed, tired, ill, or upset and involved in their own scripts. Good parenting, as well as good therapy and good reparenting, requires that all three ego states of both parties be taken into account and dealt with to avoid discounting and being in script. Whether as a therapist or parent, I function best when my Child feels OK and taken care of, my Adult thinks what I am doing makes sense, and my Parent approves.

Another problem to keep in mind is that the ordinary neurotic or character-disorder client can recathect Adult within a few seconds to a minute or so of her deciding to or of being directed to. The client with deeper pathology (especially the psychotic or schizophrenic client) may have more trouble and should be given more time. The therapist should be especially careful in letting such a person cathect young unless they have made a clear agreement that the client will recathect Adult when asked to.

With these warnings in mind, I find reparenting to be a very useful method. It can be used as a diagnostic procedure, since an individual, when being little, will act out their Child directly, thereby showing their scripty behavior; and it is another way for a person to get directly to what is going on through their body and to do something about changing in the process.

To do reparenting, it is essential to know the stages of normal development of the growing child. For me, my medical school experience and treatment of children have been valuable. Also, psychoanalytic theory as well as all the other research done on child development by Piaget and others is important. Within TA, Jacqui Schiff[11] has done the pioneering work and has outlined what the growing child needs to accomplish at each stage of development. Raising my own children has been the most informative thing for me and is the experience I recommend to therapists most of all. Failing that, then I suggest getting as much experience as possible being around kids of all ages who are not overadapted.

When to reparent is an important question. First, decide when it is timely to give permissions, because the two are interrelated. Giving a permission is, in many respects, like giving a small dose of parenting. No matter which of the three ego states the therapist sends the permission from, it will be received, if effective, as though from a parent and so will be recorded in the client's Parent while being reacted to in her Child. The Child may make a new script decision if the permission is successful (Figure 1). There are two good times to give a permission message. The first is when the client wants one. Often a simple permission may help move someone past an impasse easily and other types of intervention will be

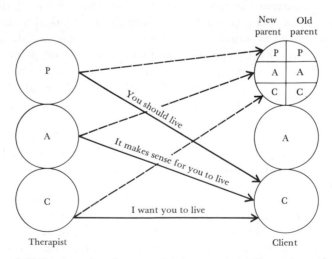

Solid lines show where the message is being sent, where it is reacted to, and where a decision is made. Dotted lines show where the message is recorded.

Figure 1

unnecessary. If the client is not in her Adapted Child but is in her Free Child, the transaction can be very effective. The second time that permission makes sense is when the client has very little or no positive Controlling or positive Nurturing Parent available to permit some new behavior. In these circumstances the client usually has severe problems dating from the first 18 months or so of development. Her Adult may work at programing the new permission (this is self-reparenting,[12] an excellent technique), but if the negative Controlling Parent is strong she will have great difficulty succeeding. A permission from a new Parent source who is respected and seen as important by the client may make the difference by providing an option to the client's Child. The same comments apply to reparenting. Reparenting is OK to do when the client wants it and when she is not being a Victim, provided it will help achieve the contract and the therapist is willing to spend the necessary energy. Reparenting is likely to be most useful when the problems are most severe and will require the greatest effort on the part of the therapist.

A permission transaction may only take a few seconds; similarly a reparenting contract may last for only a few minutes. Or it can be as long as a session and occur every time the client is in session; it can be made for up to 24 hours a day for a specified period of time while the client is living separately, or it can be a lifetime contract with the client living separate from or with the therapist-parent. The last mentioned possibility is the most potent intervention and most enhances the three P's. The contract should be carefully worked out. The therapist should check within herself on how much she is actually willing to do and if she is having a magical rescuing fantasy.

Permission-giving and reparenting do not reduce the client's autonomy if used within the framework of a contract. The client decides what she wants and if she will take in new Parent messages. If she does she has new choices available to her. The therapist does not loan the new Parent messages to the client. The client either takes them in or does not. The major danger is from a therapist who gives permissions or reparents to enhance her own importance or sense of belonging, and so attempts to tie clients to her in a parent-child symbiosis. As always, it is vital for the therapist to get her needs met outside of the therapy situation.

What the therapist-parent does may sound simpler than it is. Essentially, it is to respond to the cathected little person in a way that is appropriate for her age. Many people who had to grow up quickly will act older than is reasonable for their age. That can be changed most effectively while they are in a position to be taken care of. A four-year-old who sits silently in a corner needs to be brought into the group in a caring way. A six-month-old infant who is hungry needs to cry and get a bottle. Discounts of age-appropriate behavior are watched for and responded to. The therapist-parent is active not passive. It is very interesting, sometimes fun, and often rewarding.

The last system of therapy that I have studied is behavior therapy.[13] It is a system that pays special attention to behavior, defines closely where the person is and where she wants to go, and specifies ways of getting there with the proper reinforcements. Inadvertently we are all behaviorists, since all therapists one way or another are in business to assist clients to change their behavior, so that a careful study of behaviorists' principles and methods is well worthwhile. Many standard TA methods already are essentially behavioral. The use of the egogram,[14] the stroking profile,[15] the discounting chart,[16] and the practicing of options[17] all lead to behavioral contracts. TA and behavioral therapy will have a long history together.

THE FOUR RULES OF THERAPY

What I have done so far is to describe the basic ingredients of the kind of therapy I do and some attendant principles. What I am going to do next is to discuss a few more principles of theory and practice that I think are important. Finally, I will discuss the general issue of why people change and how we can help them do so.

I will start with what I call the First Rule of Therapy. *The therapist should, both during and after therapy, feel OK.* This, by the way, is analogous to a first rule of parenting. As I have said before, a good therapist as well as a good parent takes good care of herself and does not discount any of her ego states. She does not Rescue and Try Hard, or feel guilty and become a martyr. It is true that if she follows this rule, she will provide a good model for her clients and probably do good therapy. Do not use this as the reason for following the rule. Follow it because it is right. It is all right for you to take care of yourself and to come first!

The next three rules of therapy are about priorities in therapy and will be carried out best when the first rule is being followed. With that in mind, the Second Rule of Therapy is: *deal with the structure of the relationship between the therapist and the client before anything else.* This does not mean just at the beginning of therapy but at all times. Where and when the session meets, what the people sit on, how much the clients pay and when, and what rules are followed for group procedure (no one hits anyone, for example), all must be handled before much that is useful can occur. The therapist is the leader of the session and like a good parent should have opinions and set the conditions and framework for the relationship. This sets up a safe situation and, if done potently, will provide a good environment for change. If any of the conditions of the structure are violated, further testing of the limits is likely and safety is reduced. If this occurs on the part of one person in a group, the other members, too, may digress from working on their contracts so as to check out the structure. The looser the structure the more a client needs to provide her own. A client with early developmental problems, who therefore has a loose internal structure, will have a greater need for a secure external structure with clear boundaries. If a client is not changing in therapy, it may be because she does not believe that the structure of the therapy situation can handle her. Here are several examples of violations of structure that should take priority over everything else: (1) Missing a session; (2) Throwing a hard object; (3) Running out of the session; (4) Not paying the agreed fee; (5) Therapist breaking or not enforcing any of the rules.

The Third Rule of Therapy is: *deal with the transference or countertransference before dealing with the content of the contract.* This overlaps somewhat the second rule inasmuch as transgressions of the structure are often due to transference issues. Since transference is putting the face of someone from the past onto someone in the present, the client's perception of whatever is occurring is distorted. Thus, working on a content issue such as taking in positive strokes will not be successful while the client sees the hated image of a sibling on the stroke giver. The therapist may elect not to overtly deal with the transference at the time, preferring to let it intensify so that when it is pointed out the client will be likely to understand it better. Or the therapist may have the client double-chair the transferred figure and deal with the impasse that way. The important thing is that the therapist is aware of what is going on and selects a way to deal with it. If a client is not changing although ostensibly working on her contract, one of the likely possibilities is that she is in an unrecognized transference bind. On the other hand, possibly the therapist is in a countertransference bind and so is not responding to the client in appropriate ways.

The last and Fourth Rule of Therapy is: *deal with here-and-now problems that exist between the participants (including the therapist) and with other major life events before dealing with the content of the contract.* This is especially important if the therapist has as her style one-to-one therapy in the group and so tends not to focus on interaction between members. Many new groups need a period of time where the interaction among the members is the primary focus. This gives everyone a chance to get to know each other and the leader without revealing too much too fast. Structured exercises for everyone can facilitate this sense of comfort. They can be encounter, gestalt,[18] bioenergetics, or TA. Among the latter, one can do life script questionnaires with script matrixes, egograms, and stroking profiles. This is especially useful with adolescents and others who tend to come to therapy with much overt resistance, such as referrals from courts and jails, and spouses and parents of those who are labeled the identified client. Life events to pay attention to are such things as death in the family, divorce, injury, and even birthdays.

TEASING APART THE EGO STATES

Berne's[19] great contribution was his notion that there are three major ego states or groups of feelings and behavior patterns and that each can transact internally or externally with another ego state. When the ego states are subdivided into their components by doing a second-order structural analysis, it becomes quite clear that there are many potential sources for transactions.

Figure 2 shows how people can behave in many, and even contradictory,

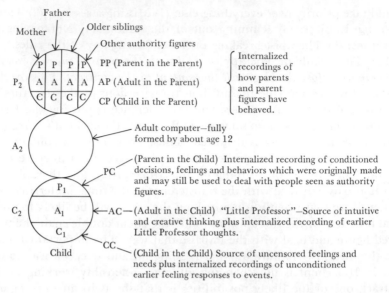

Figure 2
Second Order Structural Analysis

ways. Actually it should be further elaborated in a time dimension. Both the Parent and the Child are recording from birth on, and so each may contain a different statement about a subject from several different ages. Furthermore, the structural diagram can be subdivided in a descriptive way. I find it helpful to think in terms of a three-dimension diagram with the descriptive (or functional) diagram on top of the structural diagram. Thus, each part of the Parent can function in either a Nurturing or Controlling way and the Child can behave in either a Free or Adapted manner, and any of the parts can behave either positively or negatively. The Parent (Father's Child) may say "I love you" (positive Nurturing) *and* "I hate you" (negative Controlling). The Little Professor may say "I want to belong so I'll take care of people" (Adapted Child) *and* "This is how to do it!" (Free Child). It is important not to assume that just because the Child or Parent ego states have spoken once that that is it.

A young child because of her vulnerability needs to please the grown-ups caring for her. She must respond to the variety of messages coming her way with behavior that will satisfy the big people and allow her to stay in the system until she is old enough to leave it. Any behavior we observe in a client today was in all probability somehow reinforced when the client was small. Therefore, one of the parent's ego states will have given off a pertinent message and with proper exploration the client can discover it. This means that "rebellion" rarely occurs; ordinarily, there will have been a message from a parent fostering it.

Fifteen-year-old John ran away from home a lot and during these times he stole cars and drove all over the country. His mother was ostensibly horrified, and John insisted he hated his mother and would not do a single thing she wanted. After one of his runaways, John was apprehended and he and his mother were brought together. Mother at first scolded John for what he had done and John scowled in response. Then mother said, "Well, I can't do anything with you. You're just like your father." (Father had left her years before.) "It is just as well you go off on your own." Thus, by attribution ("You're just like your father") and by direct permission, she gave messages to John to run away. Then she said to John with a smile on her face, "What did you do? Tell me about it." John then entered into an animated conversation with his mother describing his exploits. Her Child was turned on by his behavior! So to please her in all these ways he would run away. It was very important for John to become aware of this so he could decide for himself how *he* wanted to behave.

Caveat: Do not accept the superficial socially acceptable message. Look for the message that is supporting the feeling or behavior. It is there! When the client becomes aware of it she experiences new options to make decisions for herself.

When a client is not changing—or is getting worse, for that matter— she may have an undiscovered "Don't be" message scaring her. It might even be a well-known one that the client and the therapist believe has long ago been taken care of—i.e., redecided. Actually, if the old "Don't be" was very potent, the client will likely revive it at each major step in therapy. This happens because, when a client redecides to live and even says "I will never kill myself no matter what!" she is not thinking about or experiencing all the eventual possibilities. So when she says "no matter what" she may not really mean it. It is like a child who promises something but then does not carry it out because she does not understand all that the promise entails. Another important reason this happens is that some people erect rigid boundaries between different parts of themselves. This occurs especially in people with early developmental problems; they feel "split" into sections that do not communicate with one another. Thus, one person decided from her five-year-old Child ego state that she would never kill herself, but her two-year-old Child was not listening. Finally the two-year-old decided it too, but then it developed that the one-year-old had not been listening and that part needed to redecide. Whenever a client makes a major breakthrough, it is important to provide additional protection, since the Child will tend to be scared of changing and may shortly be tempted to go back to the old patterns of behavior.

FORMATION OF EGO STATES

How are the ego states formed? This area is the cloudiest in TA and different theories abound. Keeping in mind that these are theories and so are likely to be at least in part wrong, I will briefly present my version. It will be useful to refer to the second-order structural analysis diagram (Figure 2) for nomenclature. Berne[20] talks of a psychobiological structure, implying that the origin of the ego states is based in our physiology. With that in mind, it appears that at the time of birth the infant is all Child ego state (C_1) and is full of needs and feelings. Soon, probably in the first two months, some evidence of thinking (mostly intuitive and creative) occurs (A_1). How do P_1 and P_2 form? I am aware of no conclusive evidence that the Parent ego state is based in physiology. In "lower" animals there is evidence of parenting instincts but not so in humans. Therefore, it is likely that we somehow manufacture the Parent. Since it is crucial for the child to please others to get along and survive, it is useful for her to make a record of what the important things are that happen to her. This recording is called the Parent (P_2). It is available at any time for feedback as to how the child should behave. Later on, P_2 is handy since it can also be used to parent other people. It slowly accumulates information and can be added to at any time. At the same time, another part is being manufactured to carry out decisions for getting along made by C_1 and A_1. This is P_1 and since it is carrying out a lot of "shoulds" and "musts" is called the Parent in the Child. I do not put any parent recordings in the Child, since it makes more sense to me to keep all the parent information in the Parent (P_2) and all the child information and decisions in the Child. What is in the Child is the *reaction* to what the parents do. What the parents *do* is in the Parent (P_2). The Parent (P_2) therefore contains both the Nuurturing Parent and the Controlling Parent.

As the child is growing a new kind of thinking develops that is increasingly logical and able to deal with abstractions. This ability parallels the final growth and development of the nervous system and is complete by around the age of twelve; it is called the Adult ego state (A_2). The early intuitive kind of thinking (A_1) still is available at all ages. Figure 2, then, contains C_1, A_1, and A_2, which are based on the development of the nervous system and body, plus P_1 and P_2, which are constructs of the Child.

The energy of the individual is still primarily in the Child (C_1 and A_1) and from these sources some variable amount is invested in P_1 and P_2. A_2, since it is based in our nervous system, may have energy of its own. If it does it does not have a great deal, because it is clear in working with clients that decisions made in the Adult (A_2) do not carry a lot of power if the Child is in opposition or not yet convinced. The Child clearly uses the Adult (A_2) in making decisions and redecisions of its own, and perhaps the primary energy of the Adult (A_2) is given to it by the Child. At any rate, until the Child has made a decision and become comfortable with it, one cannot expect the person's behavior to be thoroughly changed or believe that the contract is really completed.

As noted in Figure 1, the parents' messages are reacted to in the Child, the decisions are made in the Child, and the script is carried out by the Child. Therefore, all types of script messages—positive and negative, permissions and injunctions—should be diagramed as going to the Child. Figure 3 is a typical script matrix[21]—for simplicity only the negative constricting messages are shown. The so-called counterscript messages should

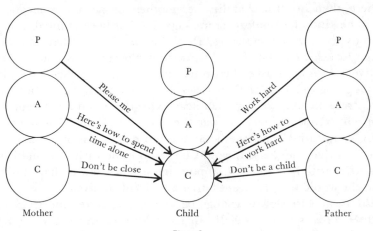

Figure 3
Script Matrix

not be directed to the Parent (P_2) as in the Steiner matrix,[22] since the Parent is a recording of what parents do and is neither a place where decisions are made for a life plan nor where such a program would be activated. It is the place where reminders about what one should do come from, while the Child is the place where those reminders are reacted to.

In an earlier publication[23] I stated that the counterscript often is not in opposition to the script. Instead, the two usually are in agreement, and the counterscript actually fosters the script (Figure 3). For all those times that the messages from the Parent of the parents actually are serving to reinforce the script, I suggest we do not use the term counterscript—since that implies something working against the script. Instead the term *subscript*[24] appears more accurate. This secondary script is indeed subsidiary to the primary script and closely related to it, since it subtly fosters the primary script. On those occasions when the Parent messages offer a true alternative to the script, then the use of *counterscript* is appropriate.

When a client appears improved, a question that should arise is: has she made a redecision and changed her script? ("I will live no matter what!")

Or has she chosen to follow a counterscript available to her? She may be out of script for the moment but the force of the script messages may be biding their time. ("I am not going to think of dying. My father said it was OK for me to have fun and that is what I am going to do.")

Or has she gone into her subscript where she may look temporarily better but actually is still gathering data that she is not OK? ("I am going to try really hard this time to please people so that I can be with them. Then I won't want to die.")

When a client is not changing, look for the influence of messages coming from a different part of the script matrix. If a client has been working on redeciding about her father's "Don't be" message to her and getting nowhere, then in all probability her mother—or possibly someone else—gave some kind of a reinforcing message that has been ignored.

Trudy was aware of a strong "Don't be" from her father, and in spite of what looked like a lot of good work on her part, she was not making an effective redecision. I asked her to tell her mother in the empty chair that she was going to tell her father that she was not going to kill herself. Her mother responded by saying, "Oh dear! Now don't you upset your father! What will happen to me?" It was then clear to Trudy that she was not dealing with father's message because of an early decision to take care of mother, so that she, herself, would be given some caring by mother. She had to deal with her fear of disappointing mother and perhaps losing her before she would fully confront father and decide to live.

Also, people are slow to change because change often means giving up strokes.[25] This is true especially in second-degree (moderate) and third-degree (severe) losers' scripts, where the client's Controlling Parent and/or Adapted Child closely monitors the Child's behavior, feelings, and thoughts. These people are used to a great deal going on in their heads and rarely, if ever, experience periods of quiet and peace. If, because of therapy, they do have such an experience, they often will react with fear as if something is wrong. Actually, as far as their Adapted Child is concerned, something is. Their Parent, whom they believe they need, is temporarily gone. Often in therapy one instructs a client who is changing and giving up an old behavior pattern to establish a new pattern so that she will be getting at least as many strokes as before. This is not practical in the scripts I referred to above, because the number of internal negative strokes that the client is used to getting is so high that no system of positive strokes can possibly compete. To change, the client must give up getting so many strokes and such constant attention. Instead she must believe that positive strokes are potentially available so it is not necessary to escalate interactions to get a large quantity of negative strokes quickly. Furthermore, without all the internal negative stroking, she is open to the strokes that are actually available from the external world. Also, when it is "quiet" in her head, her Free Child can be creative and express what she wants and enjoys. Fewer strokes will allow for more pleasant strokes.

EARLY SCRIPT DECISIONS: WHY CHANGE?

The basic issue in therapy is: why do people change? Or, better yet, why do people choose to change? Why are they willing to change their patterns of behavior or make redecisions and new life scripts for themselves? There are two important factors: first, an individual must be motivated to change; and second, she must feel safe enough to do it.

Motivation results from three factors. First, is the person dissatisfied with her present behavior or feelings and, second, does she want to behave or feel a new way? The Free Child freely expresses her dislikes and wants, but in many people one or both of these have been suppressed. The therapist can help the client learn that it is OK to be dissatisfied and become aware of new wants and to use this information in making contracts for change. The four levels of discounting[26] of problems are important in this regard (as they are in all phases of treatment). Take the example of a person who is not close to anyone:

> *First,* does she know that not being close to anyone is a problem? That it is all right to be unhappy about that and to want to be close to someone?
>
> *Second,* does she know that it is a significant problem? That it is not a small issue and is worthy of being given serious attention?
>
> *Third,* does she know that it is solvable? That other people have been able to do something about getting close?
>
> *Fourth,* does she know that she, herself, can do something about this? That she is not bad or defective and so can change?

A therapy group helps, in that some group members will actively demonstrate that not being close is a real problem, that it is significant and solvable, and will inform the client that it is all right and possible for her to change too.

The third motivational factor is the desire to please others, especially those others who are the source of strokes. Basically, this comes from the Adapted Child. If the therapist or group is seen as an important source of strokes, this will enhance motivation and promote change.

Safety is the other major issue. Originally, an individual makes her script decisions because she believes she must if she is to get along with the big people in her life. She is motivated by the threat of her parents' displeasure, their rejection, and even annihilation. Most script decisions are made by age five, and in especially negative scripts the major decisions are made by age two. The following are the reasons why the young child is so vulnerable:

1. She is very small, a child in a land of giants. The difference in strength of two people is determined by taking the fourth power of the ratio of their respective levers, such as arms. The average adult female is twice as tall as the average two-year-old and is therefore 16 times as strong ($2^4 = 16$). Thus, even when a parent does not intend to be hurtful, one of her movements can easily be experienced as such by the small child.

2. She is not yet able to think well. Her Adult ego state is rudimentary and her thinking is quite concrete and magical. She cannot handle large amounts of anxiety, and information must be given to her clearly, concisely, and simply.

3. Parents essentially "own" the data about the world. Until she is three, and often four or five, the little girl gets most of her information from her parents. Parents often do not pass on to their young children much information about what is happening. They don't reveal that Mommy is mad at Daddy, and so the child can easily believe that Mommy is mad at her or that she has caused the problem between Mommy and Daddy.

Also, parents define reality for the child. If parents say "You are no good," she has little choice but to believe it, since her parents know everything and she does not yet have an Adult ego state that can figure such things out.

4. She has no option to leave home and find a better place to live. She is stuck, and must get along in that environment.

Thus safety and the immediate reduction of anxiety are the primary reasons for making the all-encompassing script decisions. As she grows older, she carries out her script in order to maintain the semblance of being safe. Each time she experiences stress, she tends to turn on (cathect) her old Child tapes and behave just as that scared little girl thought she had to. She also follows her script because it gets her strokes. Everytime she behaves or feels in a way her parents rewarded, she gets strokes. The strokes which the substitute behaviors and feelings provide are a powerful, secondary motivation for continuing in the same way and not changing.

The first task of treatment is to focus the client's motivation (as discussed earlier) and then arrive at a contract for change. Here the knowledge of the normal development, needs, and feelings of infants and children is helpful. When a client says she wants to work on being strong and not needing anyone, the therapist knows that this is an Adopted Child wish (pleasing an internal Parent) and that more likely her Natural Child wants to be close to someone but is afraid. In all probability in the past she was picking people to relate with who were likely to hurt her (with the end result of proving that she was right in deciding to be distant).

THE CONTRACT

The next step is to accomplish the contract. Essentially, as I said earlier, this means helping the client feel safe enough to change.

It should be noted that the client is not vulnerable to the therapist in the same way as the child was to the parent:

1. Often now there is no size difference, so the real childhood fear of physical assault is much less. There are definite differences in status however, and so the client may easily fantasize being smaller, as though she were a child again. On the other hand, some clients are fearful they may hurt the therapist. So the specific size of each person (client and therapist) is still pertinent—especially in therapies where people touch each other. To have a stated rule against people getting hurt physically will increase the sense of safety.

2. After the age of 12, clients have a fully developed Adult and so can think much better than when they were making their original script decisions. This is a very crucial change and is a major factor in increasing the feeling of safety for clients. Many people change their behavior on the basis of new information alone. School, books, television, and movies help a great many people change who never come to a therapist. Many first-degree (mild) games and scripts are changed with the proper input, and many second-degree (moderate) and third-degree (severe) games and scripts can be interfered with by information to the Adult

that the Child cannot refute. In these latter instances, with contamination out of the way, it is then possible to find out what the Child needs in order to feel safe enough to change.

3. The therapist, unlike the parent, does not have all the information. However, if she uses a therapy system with a complex system of beliefs and language, it may appear that she has all of the answers and may put the client one-down. Ordinarily, this does not happen with TA, but a therapist who plays *Blemish* can operate in any system.

4. The client has the option to leave and doesn't have to stay with a particular therapist. Many will stay, though, and behave like stuck children. Thus, it may be important in stalemated therapy for the therapist to suggest to the client that she find someone who will be better for her.

In summary, the client is less vulnerable to the therapist than she was to her parents. Therefore, she is less likely to respond to messages of the therapist than she was to messages of her parents. This is a major reason why therapy takes as long as it does in second-degree and third-degree situations. In these, the client is too scared to trust quickly the information and concern of this new someone who is acting differently from her parents. Before she can be listened to safely, the therapist must be seen to be at least as powerful and believable as the original source of the negative messages, and this may take quite a while.

The client arrives at this conclusion in two ways, which may go on simultaneously:

1. By checking out the therapist in many different ways (such as telling secrets, asking questions, and revealing feelings) and watching to see whether she provokes anger, disgust, impatience, fear, or whether she is instead accepted.

2. The therapist usually helps the client face the feared situations and scare feelings in *gradually increasing amounts*. The client tends to feel safer in the beginning anyway, since (*a*) a big person (*b*) labeled as "helper" (*c*) says it is OK to change in the desired direction (after all, the therapist has accepted the contract—a big advantage in having specific contracts) and then (*d*) suggests specifically how to do it.

CHOOSING THE METHODS OF THERAPY

"How to do it" means the many different types of therapy that exist. Each has structure and techniques to facilitate change. Each provides for varying levels of safety and gradualness. Some clients will do well in any or all of them. Others will do best in only one or, perhaps, two of them. Thus, it is very helpful for the therapist to be skillful in several. The following are some important examples.

A. Various kinds of behavior-modification techniques (desensitization, token systems, etc.) help the client feel safe by allowing her to face her fears gradually—perhaps even first in fantasy. This is basically the idea of shaping: first, start something (such as a new behavior) a little at a time and build onto what has been accomplished at each step of the way. By changing in easy stages she finds out she does not hurt, so her Child feels OK and her Adult gathers information that being different is possible and makes sense. After doing the new behavior enough times, she may then decide to keep it up and that the old system is unnecessary. This is called a redecision.

B. Encounter is similar, but here the feared behavior is acted out in the here-and-now with other people. If done too abruptly, this may produce adverse reactions.

C. Gestalt therapy is also similar, but here the feared behavior is faced in fantasized interchanges—often with the original negative message-givers.

D. Psychoanalysis—specifically the analysis of transference—is similar, but here the feared behavior is repeatedly faced in the here-and-now with a a new person (the therapist) whom the client, out of her own awareness, thinks is treating her as her parents did.

E. In transactional analysis the feared behavior is faced in the here-and-now, usually in a group, with special attention paid to ego states, transactions, games, and scripts.

F. For reparenting, the feared behavior is faced in the here-and-now, usually many times, with the new parent-therapist.

To effect the maximum safety for the client and to best utilize the above treatment methods, the proper doses of protection, permission, and potency are necessary. All methods of therapy offer some feeling of protection, since a high-status therapist, who purports to know what she is doing, overtly acts in the client's behalf. Any therapist who behaves with caring and concern is giving protection. The frequency of sessions and the therapist's availability by phone are important for the feeling of safety to work on particular contracts. The behaviorist is protective by carefully working out a hierarchy of feared situations, so that each increment of change will not cause undue anxiety. The client cooperates in preparing the hierarchy and so she always knows what will happen next. This also removes the magic (which is often scary) from the therapy. In general, by limiting the scope of the contract, the client will feel safer and so she will be more likely to accomplish it. Then, after the original contract has been accomplished, she may make a new contract that will go further.

The gestaltist who allows her client to hit gives protection by having pillows available so that no physical harm will occur; the office should be arranged so that the client can move and do what she needs to do without getting hurt. The transactional analyst will not push for change around a "Don't be close" decision without first having made sure that the client does not have a "Don't be" injunction that she was gathering stamps to cash in on (since the therapist knows that the client needs to have a clear decision to live as a foundation for any other changes). The marathon leader offers protection by being available for a long period of time to help the client work through a problem. The therapist who uses reparenting gives a great deal of protection by saying that, during the time of the contract, she will take care of the client's age-appropriate needs and then following through with what she agreed to do.

All methods of therapy offer permission (or suggestion to change). Some do this covertly, others quite overtly. By agreeing to a contract and then by receptively listening to various previously unmentionable secrets and fears, permission is given to change. Stroking, or responding positively to every change for the better, is a very important permission for maintaining that change and for fostering further changes. The therapist who is open about what she is thinking and feeling gives permission to be unguarded by modeling. The group therapist, who brings together a variety of people, offers many different examples of options of behavior, which is permission-giving. Those therapies that suggest specific new behaviors give considerable permission. The behaviorist who says "Face the phobia," the gestaltist who says "Yell at your mother," the encounterer who says "Show her what you are feeling," and the transactional analyst who says "It's OK for you to grow up and take care of yourself," are all giving overt, strong permissions. Those therapies that give strong behavioral permissions should also emphasize strong protection—not only physical, by having a safe place to work, but also emotional. Quick changes in behavior are sometimes followed by feelings of despair, pain, and fear. The therapist should not discount this but should be available to assist the client to find new and more appropriate behaviors, while seeing that the client's scared Child is asking for what it needs (strokes, more permissions, reiteration of the facts, etc.). Protection also is given by only giving those permissions that fit clearly within the agreed-upon contract.

All methods of therapy require a potent therapist, one who is not seen as wishy-washy, ambivalent about change (especially regarding the target behavior), or personally ineffectual. Instead, potent means strong, knowledgeable, clear, concise, and definite. It means that all three of the therapist's ego states—especially the Child—believe in what is occurring. Those therapies that offer strong permissions for behavior change—such as gestalt, bioenergetics, encounter, transactional analysis, and reparenting—require considerable potency on the part of the therapist, so that the client will believe it is safe to follow through on the suggestions.

What will help a person to change is very much the same as what will help a child to grow: positive regard, acceptance, understanding, concern, useful information, and assistance in facing stress. These come from the positive Nurturing Parent, the positive Controlling Parent, the Adult, the positive Free Child, and the positive Adapted Child of the therapist. Things that get in the way of growth are: aloofness, disdain, put-downs, overprotection, putting up with put-downs, fear, and misinformation. These come from the negative Nurturing Parent, the negative Controlling Parent, the uninformed Adult, and the negative Adapted Child.

The therapist's task, then, is to behave in growth inducing ways while focusing the client's motivation and promoting her sense of safety so that she will achieve her contract and arrive at a new life script. At this time I can do this best with TA as my theory plus the techniques offered by a wide variety of systems.

References

1. See also Morton A. Lieberman, Irvin D. Yalom, Matthew B. Miles, *Encounter Groups: First Facts,* New York, Basic Books, 1973.
2. William C. Schutz, *Joy: Expanding Human Awareness,* New York, Grove Press, 1967; H. R. Lewis and H. S. Streitfeld, *Growth Games,* New York, Harcourt Brace Jovanovich, Inc., 1972.
3. Robert Goulding "New Directions in Transactional Analysis: Creating an Environment for Redecision and Change," in Clifford J. Sager and Helen Singer Kaplan, eds., *Progress in Group and Family Therapy,* New York, Brunner/Mazel, 1972.
4. F. S. Perls, *The Gestalt Approach and Eyewitness to Therapy,* Ben Lomond, California, Science and Behavior Books, 1973.
5. Alexander Lowen, *Bioenergetics,* New York, Coward, McCann & Geoghegan, Inc., 1975.
6. Adrienne Ressler, "Bodyscript," Ann Arbor, Michigan, Huron Valley Institute, 1975.
7. Jacqui Lee Schiff, "Reparenting Schizophrenics," *Transactional Analysis Bulletin, 8,* no. 31 (1969); Jacqui Lee Schiff and Beth Day, *All My Children,* Philadelphia: J. B. Lippincott Co., 1970.
8. F. Alexander and T. French, *Psychoanalytic Theory: Principles and Applications,* New York, Ronald Press, 1946.
9. Jacqui Lee Schiff, *et al., The Cathexis Reader,* New York, Harper & Row, 1975, pp. 5–6.
10. Stanley J. Woollams and Kristyn Huige, "Normal Dependency and Symbiosis," submitted for publication.
11. Schiff, *The Cathexis Reader, op. cit.,* pp. 32–48.
12. Muriel James, "Self-Reparenting," *Transactional Analysis Journal, 4,* no. 3 (July, 1974).
13. Arnold Lazarus, *Behavior Therapy and Beyond,* New York, McGraw-Hill, 1971.
14. John M. Dusay, "Egograms and the Constancy Hypothesis," *Transactional Analysis Journal, 2,* no. 3 (July, 1972), pp. 37–41.
15. James McKenna, "Stroking Profile," *Transactional Analysis Journal, 4,* no. 4 (October, 1974), pp. 20–24.
16. Ken Mellor and Eric Schiff, "Discounting," *Transactional Analysis Journal, 5,* no. 3 (July, 1975), pp. 295–303.
17. Stephen Karpman, "Options," *Transactional Asalysis Journal, 1,* no. 1 (January, 1971), pp. 79–88.
18. John O. Stevens, *Awareness: Exploring, Experimenting, Experiencing,* Moab, Utah, Real People Press, 1971.
19. Eric Berne, *Transactional Analysis in Psychotherapy,* New York, Grove Press, 1961.
20. Eric Berne, *Principles of Group Treatment,* New York, Oxford University Press, 1966.
21. Stanley J. Woollams, "Formation of the Script," *Transactional Analysis Journal, 3,* no. 1 (January, 1973).
22. Claude Steiner, "Script and Counterscript," *Transactional Analysis Bulletin, 5,* no. 18 (April, 1966).
23. Woollams, "Formation of the Script," *op. cit.*

24. Stanley J. Woollams, "Subscript Instead of Counterscript," submitted for publication.
25. Stanley J. Woollams, "When Fewer Strokes Are Better," *Transactional Analysis Journal, 6*, no. 3 (July, 1976).
26. Aaron Wolfe Schiff and Jacqui Lee Schiff, "Passivity," *Transactional Analysis Journal, 1*, no. 1 (January, 1971), pp. 71–78.

SEVENTEEN

RECYCLING THE PAST
FOR A WINNING FUTURE
Lois M. Johnson

Many people learn to stifle, more or less painlessly, their emptiness, frustration, hopelessness, fear, and other feelings; they become accustomed to disregarding their own wants or needs.

A kindling of desire to improve one's self-image may be provoked when others who are significant change their attitudes and behaviors. When that happens, the first modification in additude is to value one's self as an OK person. The principles of transactional analysis give a person a rational method for examining and understanding his or her behavior. Body education provides a new capacity for feeling alive in an emotionally deadened world. Feeling, seeing, knowing can lead one to renounce superficial human relationships.

As a teacher, trainer, and therapist, I am not a wizard nor am I omnipotent. I give information, respond to behavior, report my observations and my intuitive hunches; and each person is responsible for getting what she or he needs or wants. "What do you want for you? What will you change to get what you want? When will you put that plan into action? How will you know when you've reached your goal?"

Meg is a representative case: "I want to find out who I am! I want to stop being depressed. I want the world to be right."

Meg was quiet, withdrawn, and resistive to experiential exercises on the first day of a workshop dealing with sexuality, vision, and feeling. The second morning she confronted the writer. "I've been angry with you since yesterday. I've got a splitting headache and I didn't sleep all night!" "What does being angry with me do for you, except give you a headache and ruin a night's sleep?" I asked.

Meg said, "What a dumb question!" Then, "I'm afraid of being found wanting. What hurts is not being willing to be close or care about anyone." She paused. "You make me look at my decisions, goals. You said I need to love my own warts and I don't!"

A letter came from Meg one week later: "It's like it's too much to expect that you would care about me—so I don't know how to respond or to react. Close relationships scare me because I fear becoming passive or demanding. Why have I continued to just survive? It's not enough to just survive. If it's OK, if there's room, I'll be at the workshop next weekend. Thanks."

BLOCKING THE CONTRACT FOR CHANGE

Attempts to improve one's self-image often occur sporadically. The failure of short-lived efforts is due to internal criticism and/or external coercion. Internal criticism floods the personality from the internalized Parent ego state, which reminds the self of "shoulds," "have to's," "musts," and "ought to's." This criticism may be combined with petulant reminders of "After all I've done for you," "How ungrateful and selfish you are," "What will people think," or "You're not my little girl anymore."

The Cultural Parent ego state is coercive and affirms the internalized Parent ego state by underlining society's accepted and expected patterns of behavior. Some persons use the Cultural Parent ego state to excuse their unauthentic self; others use the internalized Parent ego state. History offers examples of men and women who found ways to become autonomous and authentic while living within educational and religious institutions that sought to suppress nonconformist tendencies and to eliminate spontaneous drives that allow self-responsibility.

SUCCESSFUL CHANGE

Everlean is an "Aid to Dependent Children" mother. She is seeking to improve her feelings about herself and to find a meaning in living. Her classmates at Lake Michigan College (Institute of Professional and Paraprofessional Studies, Benton Harbor, Michigan) are drop-outs from high school, unemployed day parolees from the county jails—blacks and whites seeking Associate of Arts degrees so as to be able to get jobs as "aides." They are enrolled in Psychology for Living class, a basic introduction to TA. I see her scrunched posture, lack of dentures, hair concealed with a well-worn scarf. I see hopelessness in her eyes and her weariness, and I marvel that she made it to class. TA is a contractual discipline, I explain to them. I am here to give you information and answer your questions, and you are responsible for getting what you want for yourself. I want a written contract from you. List three things you want for you in the next 15 weeks. Everlean's contract reads: "I want to get rid of my black language so I can be respected. I want off ADC. I want to find out who I am." I accept only the last item as a contract. In class, she listens intently, asks for clarification when she doesn't grasp the meaning of basic TA theory. She uses her own experiences to recheck her understanding.

The fourth week in class, her trudge has more bounce. Her face is glowing, her eyes sparkle as she announces in a clear voice, "It works! TA

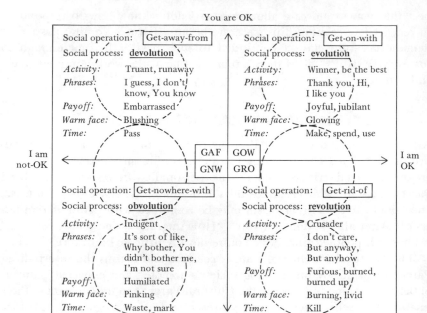

You are OK

Social operation: Get-away-from

Social process: devolution

Activity:	Truant, runaway
Phrases:	I guess, I don't know, You know
Payoff:	Embarrassed
Warm face:	Blushing
Time:	Pass

Social operation: Get-on-with

Social process: evolution

Activity:	Winner, be the best
Phrases:	Thank you, Hi, I like you
Payoff:	Joyful, jubilant
Warm face:	Glowing
Time:	Make, spend, use

I am not-OK ⟵ ⟶ I am OK

| GAF | GOW |
| GNW | GRO |

Social operation: Get-nowhere-with

Social process: obvolution

Activity:	Indigent
Phrases:	It's sort of like, Why bother, You didn't bother me, I'm not sure
Payoff:	Humiliated
Warm face:	Pinking
Time:	Waste, mark

Social operation: Get-rid-of

Social process: revolution

Activity:	Crusader
Phrases:	I don't care, But anyway, But anyhow
Payoff:	Furious, burned, burned up
Warm face:	Burning, livid
Time:	Kill

You are not-OK

Figure 1
Transactional Analysis in
The OK Corral

THE OK CORRAL is the diagram for classifying the outcomes of the events in your life: *GET-ON-WITH, GET-AWAY-FROM, GET-NOWHERE-WITH* or *GET-RID-OF. YOU CAN CHOOSE* how you want a situation to come out **BEFORE** the end of it. Not all events can end in a get-on-with. To have a get-on-with for some events you can choose for others to come out in one of the other three ways. You cannot get-on-with everybody and everything. Healthy people use each one of the four ways at least once a day.

One person's get-on-with is also the other person's get-on-with.

One person's get-away-from is the other's get-rid-of AND vice versa.

One person's get-nowhere-with is the other person's get-nowhere-with.

SOCIAL PROCESS: Long range trend of a person's or a group's life.

The arrow points on the four sides show there are four kinds of strokes a person can give: I Am OK, I Am Not-OK, You Are OK, You Are Not-OK. One person strokes the other, gives words (gestures and touches) to move (stimulate) the other, AND MORE; to move the other person to the extent that first person gets words given back, to complete one transaction. Whatever else, while transactions are continuing the parties are negotiating the answer to the psychological-business questions of "What are we to do with each other?" and "How is this going to come out?" For the persons involved, the ending will come out in one of the four corners of their respective OK Corrals when they have arrived at a psychological-level form of (mutual) agreement about each person being OK or Not-OK.

"I Am OK" is drawn to the right, "I am going ahead."

"I Am Not-OK" is to the left, "I am going backward."

"You Are OK" is the upper arrow point, "I look up to you; think well of you; admire you."

"You Are Not-OK" is the lower arrow, "I look down on you; think poorly of you; give you a put down."

When used for named people, put the first person's name on either end of the horizontal axis and the second person's name on either end of the vertical axis.

People form alliances, friendships. The "I Am OK (or Not-OK)" becomes a "We" after "I" and "You" have negotiated to become a "We;" "You" recruit "Me" or "I" recruit "You," either way. The "We" now dealing with others. The others can be a "You (singular or plural)," "He," She," Named Person, "They" or Named Group. Then the "We" are listed on either end of the horizontal axis instead of "I" and the other party on either end of the vertical axis.

"*You Are OK (with me)*" *Strokes:* "Either way (you take it), you are OK with me!" "It's on me!" "Treat's on me!"

"*I Am OK (with me)*" *Strokes:* "Either way (you take it) I AM OK!" "It's on you, if you will be OK with me or not!"

"*I Am Not-OK (with me)*" *Strokes:* "It's because of me!" "It's my fault!"

"*You Are Not-OK (with me)*" *Strokes* (the jeers, put downs and psychological rackets): "It's because of you!" "It's your fault!" ("It's ALL MY FAULT," means "It's your fault!").

All four forms of strokes (dynamics, arrows) are useful.

Transactions of games are built of combinations of the four forms of strokes; they have more than one stroking (dynamic) arrow.

To keep from crossing a transaction, to have a complementary transaction, start your response with (a dynamic) an arrow 90 degrees either way from the arrow point of the last thing said to you.

F. H. Ernest, Jr., M. D.

works. I got five grown young'uns living with me. I was looking at me— then at them. So, after last class, I goes home and begins to figure. I got so much. I take what I needs to get what I want for me. The rest I split five ways. At supper, I gives each of them young'uns their share. I tells 'em, I quit cooking, shopping, doing your laundry. Make do or get your selfs a job." She covers her empty mouth as she laughs gleefully. "My oldest said they never should of let me go to school. And I said I was going and gonna keep going."

Utilizing TA in everyday problems requires reducing the psychological and scientific information to a common denominator. The OK Corral (Figure 1) is a diagram which catalogues and deciphers; it can be used like a Geiger counter to disentangle realistic goals from the script lifestyle.

The final paper for students is their own OK Corral (Figure 2). Goals for Getting-On-With are set at six months, one year, three years. How students might sabotage these goals is dealt with in Getting-Away-From, Geting-Nowhere-With, and what needs to be in the Getting-Rid-Of.

To the OK Corral I add the game drama triangle and rackets, and I insist on closing doors to the options: (1) to go crazy, (2) to commit suicide, and (3) to kill someone else. The only open option is to Get-On-With.

As she presented her OK Corral, Everlean added the structural diagram in G.O.W., Child-contamination in the G.A.F., double contamination in G.N.W., and Parent contamination in the G.R.O. quadrant (note structural diagrams in Figure 2).

At the beginning of the second semester, Everlean entered class with full dentures, new hair style, straight posture, and she invited the students to call her Evelyn. She said, "My Momma didn't know how to spell. Her

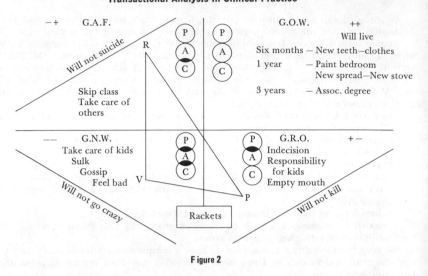

Figure 2

talk was black. White folks didn't take much care. Everlean is a goof. I've been following what my name said, being my Ever-lean-on-me name. I've decided Evelyn is my name and what my Momma wanted me to be named. Nobody is gonna lean on me forever." Evelyn (Everlean) achieved changes and reached short-term goals. Her redecisions about archaic attitudes, feelings, and outdated information produced a healthy amount of self-esteem. However, I was aware that somatically she had a propensity to sabotage herself.

In TA, clients recall and work with their experiences, childhood decisions, rackets, script injunctions, and games; but blocking, which occurs in body musculature—defined by Reich as "armoring"—is seldom dealt with. It is this armor that provides the propensity for self-sabotage. I question the long-term therapeutic value of cognitive therapy techniques when used alone. The body musculature holds recorded history—i.e., armor—and it demands independent attention. The human mind is a thinking substance in intimate association with the body. Relief from neurosis, or "cure," happens when mind and body are congruent in redecision.

Therefore, I choose an approach which acts from the foundation of transactional analysis theory. This foundation is augmented by emotional release work which includes the RADIX process as developed by Charles R. Kelley, Nathaniel Branden's sentence-completion technique, and Edward C. Whitmont's creative use of Jungian dream analysis. Feathered in at appropriate times are phototherapy, vision improvement, Tai Chi, and clay work.

TREATMENT METHODS

Beth, her husband, and her son were referred to me after extended therapy had resulted in no consistent change. Beth had made several redecisions to give up her script injunctions, "Don't trust," "Don't be close," "Don't see what you see." Her redecision work had neither eliminated her automatic reactions nor resulted in her giving up games and rackets. Cognitively, she had redecided to trust, be close, and see reality; her mind accepted that change, words left her lips, but her body armor kept her a "nonwinner."

What does refusing to accept reality do for you?" I asked. Instantly, her respiration pattern changed. She shifted to short gaspy breaths, her chest became immobile, the floor of her mouth (the underchin) was taut. Her jaw was rigidly clenched and her eyes held fear and pain.

"Let your breathing become full, gentle, and rhythmic. You stop your feelings from full expression by counterpulsating. By changing your natural breathing pattern, which pulsates through your body, to a tight, short pattern of counterpulsation, you stop the feelings. You've armored in chest, throat, and mouth. That's one way to deny reality."

Her breathing changed slowly. She appeared cautious and apprehensive as she allowed the full breathing to develop.

"Let your eyes be closed, relax your eyelids, breathe fully, surrender to your feelings, and recall a time when you first felt as you did just now. Keep breathing full, let your jaw be loose." Beth relaxed perceptibly.

"My brother, Ronnie, is dying. He's in another room," she said. "I'm about three. Mom and Dad are kneeling by the couch praying and I'm in the middle. They've got their arms around me and I feel happy! Happy because they are holding, touching me. I'm supposed to be sad, and I'm happy."

Beth's guilty feelings about her joy at being close, not feeling sad, were the seed from which one part of her body armor developed. Beth was happy when another brother was born, and her mom and dad were ecstatic with joy. He was named Ronnie because "Momma said he'd come back to us." As Beth related the rest of the scene her breathing pattern reverted to the shallow, short counterpulsating breaths. The old patterns of armor were again evident to the entire group.

Beth joined the Body Education group. She got in touch with her body and listened to the language her body spoke. Surrendering to the feelings she had blocked and armored herself against for more than 40 years, she became aware of an episcript that had been given to her, which she had accepted and was passing on to her children.

I do not expect a client to free herself or himself of script, games, rackets, or childhood decisions until both body and mind have integrated information and are capable of being congruent. For each blocked thought, there is also a blocked emotion. Therefore, it is imperative to move from conceptual to experiential and to develop an awareness which moves inward and outward. Along with basic transactional analysis, body education—learning to breathe fully and to have eye-to-eye contacts—is an integral part of teaching people how to regain constructive control of their own body and mind.

To get in touch with the function of visual perception, a group member is invited to "be your eyes." Here are two exercises to illustrate:

"I'm Bruce's eyes. I've been stopping Bruce from seeing what's ahead. That can be very scary. So, I only use my energy to let Bruce see what's two feet in front, then Bruce feels safer."

"I'm Viola's eyes. I've been keeping Viola busy looking far ahead into the future. I don't want Viola to see what is in front of her. When she does, she wants to kill herself. She gets so desperate about her fat. When I block out Viola's here-and-now, I take the pressure off needing to change what's up front."

Interpersonal relationships most often suffer from what I call the Talk-Wait (or T-W) syndrome. To achieve awareness, it is imperative to listen to one's own body-mind barometer, which registers and predicts emotional fair weather or storms. I fantasize that on my forehead are three letters, W, T, and R, and that a tiny switch can be directed to the desired position. I talk and then my friend talks. With this exchange, I can switch to W (Wait for sound to stop) and get busy in my head about what I will say next. What intelligent remark can I make? As soon as the sound of another voice stops, I switch back to T (Talk). I have the option to turn on R (Record), to listen, and then respond to what was said.

When the T-W syndrome is contributing to unresolved problems, I combine Eric Berne's Intimacy exercise[1] with Branden's sentence-completion technique. The sentences provide the springboard from which, spontaneously, the unspoken thoughts and phrases are catapulted into the here-and-now.

Two people sit facing each other, knee to knee. Eye-to-eye contact will be maintained throughout the experience. One person will talk and one will listen, neither responding nor thinking about what to say, but listening, breathing fully, and keeping eye contact. The talker completes the root sentence with a different ending each time. The sentences relax conscious control, helping to remove the censor from the mind, allowing the inner privy self to speak.

The individual is requested to repeat the root sentence and to add new endings at least five to ten times. The endings need not be right, wrong, or make sense; they can be fantasy endings. The root sentence might be one of the following:

I am a person who . . .
Ever since I was a child . . .
One of the things I wish you knew about me . . .
One of the crooked ways I ask for help is . . .
It's hard for me to admit . . .
If I knew you wouldn't laugh, I might tell you . . .
If you knew how lonely I am . . .
If I knew no one would ever find out . . .
One of the steps I could take to solve my problem . . .

If I would breathe deeply and feel my own energy . . .
If I gave myself the right to enjoy life . . .
I like you when . . .
I don't like you when . . .
If any of what I've been saying is true . . .
I'm becoming aware that . . .
When I'm ready to accept what I'm learning . . .

Other sentence completions are specifically geared to deal with sexuality, vision, childhood, and specific feelings.

These root sentences can be used in a multitude of situations. An example is Liz, a psychiatric nurse. She has enrolled in a class to get to know herself. Her contract is to stop fantasizing or intellectualizing and develop a warm and intimate fulfilling relationship with her husband. She frowns most of the time, sits hunched on the edge of her chair, pokes her husband to be sure he has gotten the notes on the lecture down in "their" notebook. He whispers in response to the poke. Liz gets up and starts for the door. "I've got a slight headache," she explains in a whiny voice, "mostly I'm very nauseated right now."

I ask her to stand where she is and complete a sentence I will give her. "OK," she nods her head.

"Repeat the root sentence I will give you at least five times. Don't think, let the words come, make up an ending. You're not required to be honest or to make sense." She agrees by nodding, her face is lined with discomfort.

"I can't stomach . . ."

She swallows and begins, "I can't stomach the truth. I can't stomach knowing. I can't stomach myself inside, I can't stomach taking care of myself, I can't stomach hearing what you tell me, I can't stomach being afraid, I can't stomach how I waste my time, I can't stomach not being loved."

She stops, her hand goes to her head—her face begins to ruffle in smiles. "My headache is gone and my stomach feels much better." As she returns to her seat, tears are tenderly caressing her cheeks.

Some people do not have the courage to stop, think, feel, and act. Transactional analysis provides cognitive information to expedite and increase courage. The elasticity to move, turn around, change lifestyles is often caught and held taut. Body education and emotional release work allow for loosening awry necks, stiffened backs, immobile chests, and tight raspy throats.

In three to six months after the often maligned older adults enter the body education program at Michigan Center, they are looking younger, their bodies are more supple, and their minds are actively listening to their own body barometer and to others. They change lifestyles. They seek new and realistic goals. The gold watch, memories of the retirement banquet, and fears of loneliness are replaced.

FAMILY WORKSHOP TECHNIQUES

To paraphrase observations of Margaret Mead, it takes three generations of sharing, enjoying, loving, fighting, setting forth lifestyle models to rear children adequately. At Michigan Center many workshops include children along with young adults, moms and dads, grandmas and grandpas, singles, divorced persons, and celibates. Observing, listening, choosing to be a partner in Berne's intimacy experience, the youngster shares fears, anger, and dreams with an older adult and reciprocates by listening, learning, and accepting that growups have problems too.

In family worshops, I use a "Responsibility-Space Contract Form." Each member fills out his or her own space and puts into the "Our space" what he or she wants to share. Later the items of conflict in "Our space" will be negotiated. Each person examines carefully his own column to be sure it is inclusive and adequate. The parents finish their column, then use the self column as they develop a contract with each child. Many couples are surprised when they see there is no specific space for them to share, except as time is accidentally freed up. They have no commitment to each other without external demands. One family discovered that Mom and Dad had *no* time which belonged to them. No sharing space. They decided that 10:00 PM to 7:00 AM would be theirs. All family or sibling problems would be dealt with before 10:00 PM or after 7:00 AM, except emergency illness. "We looked at each other the first night

Jan (mine)	Ours	Bill (yours)
Cleaning, cooking	Money for college	Bowling, golf
Shopping, laundry	Expenses—two kids	Hunting and fishing
Housework	Big purchases	My job—teacher
New job—MSW	Season car care	Yard work—my car
My car		
Tennis	Wed., 5:00 P.M.–	*Alternate shopping*
	7.00 A.M., Thurs.	
Ceramics	Sat., 2:00 P.M.–	*Own laundry of*
	7:00 A.M., Mon.	*Sports togs*
Friday nights		
		← 3½ hours
4 hours →		← 2 hours
1 hour →		← ½ hour
1 hour →		

(Italics are items added to equalize original facts.)

Figure 3

and asked, 'What do we do now?'" Always invaded by offspring asking for nonemergency assistance, they had not had time structure for their own relationship.

Culling from the techniques of Virginia Satir and Carl A. Whitaker, and from the skills I developed working with families in a court setting, it appears evident that clearly defined Responsibility-Space Contracts can be the first move in eliminating *Uproar, Let's You and Him Fight, Harried,* and many other games.

Jan came to therapy to find a way to get a friendly divorce. Bill came to be sure his point of view was not misrepresented (Figure 3). At first glance, Jan had no fun time or activities for her Child ego state. Bill bowled Monday, Tuesday, and Thursday evenings or played golf—as the season allowed. Jan sat home and sulked. Before the kids went away to college, she had them to do things with. Now she was lonely. Lack of planned shared time also was evident, so they reached a compromise on time to be set aside for each other. Jan joined a local tennis club and also reawakened her talent for ceramics. Eventually, emergency situations required default on "Our time." Bill wrote in his first owed time: $3\frac{1}{2}$ hours; Jan followed suit. Then they totaled up the hours they owed each other and went away for a long weekend. Three years later I received a letter: "We're celebrating our 25th Anniversary."

PERSONAL EXPERIENCE WITH OFFENDERS

All too often, the nonconformist or the law violator is discarded and discounted. I recall my first brush with society's warped, termite-infested view when I began family groups in the Juvenile Court setting. I was told, "They are beyond help when they get to Juvenile Court." No person is beyond help when he is respected as a human being; that means, when he is respected in spite of his overt behavior.

It is not a waste of time to train, teach, and do therapy inside the barred windows, electrically controlled doors, and sterile day rooms of detention homes, jails, or prisons, because inmates are not beyond help. Many, however, are prevented from receiving help.

To regain membership in the human race requires involvement in a process of change. Accepting confrontation, learning new options, changing language patterns, and discarding archaic information, experiences, or feelings are part of the process. Law violators who begin to change inside the walls are better equipped than their counterparts who get a pat on the back and a sardonic "Hope you learned your lesson" when they are paroled or released onto the street. One pertinent fact about offenders is that they rarely have a model of a Nurturing Parent ego state. They know well the controlling, judgmental, critical Parent. What's this Nurturing Parent? They question the need, the validity of Nurturing and ask, "Won't I become a sissy?"

Permission-Protection-Potency are the tools which Liladee V. Bellinger uses to inoculate inmates so they can grow and develop their own Nurturing Parent ego state.

> The Natural Child inside of us knows his or her own specialness. The Child has fun, enjoys life, feels OK about himself and the rest of the world. We're born with all the feelings, spontaneity, creativity, enthusiasm, and power we need to go where we want to go.
>
> Your Nurturing Parent loves you, cares for you because you are. The Parent gives you permission and support and provides information on the safeness of the person you choose to be—with no strings or "ifs" attached.[2]

In the day room or group room, inmates collect Nurturing Parent information. An emergency kit is created and stocked with antidotes, antitoxin, information such as ways to stroke yourself at all times, how to handle difficult or threatening situations and keep your name off the docket. Bob is an example:

Bob was given a life sentence. After years of marking time (Getting-Nowhere-With), he entered a treatment unit at a federal prison. He decided to eliminate the options to go crazy, commit suicide, or kill someone. He was immersed in daily group work. He began to read, study, and apply basic TA to his own life within the "joint." Three years later, as he was being examined for Clinical Membership in ITAA in the sterile day room at the prison, he said, "I'm asking to be transferred to a youthful offender facility so's I can teach them about better options."

Gene has been in for five years. He can receive no visitors and no mail, yet he pretends he's not really an inmate. Confronted by his peers, Gene faces choices for change.

"I'm here!" He finally admits his incarceration. "My family sold me out. They said, 'Better you, you're young and we've got families to care for.'"

When Gene gave up his earlier decision to "get even," he began to grow, to change, and to plan how he would deal with reality when he was back on the streets.

At the Midwest TA Conference in Chicago in 1974, I was walking through the lobby when I spied a familiar face. "Hi, Gene. How are you doing?" I recognized a strange confusion inside of me as we hugged. I pulled back and looked at Gene. "You're out!"

"Yep, I'm out and I need strokes. My family has only negative strokes to give me—so I come here to get a vault full of positive strokes so I can keep growing. I'm never going back to the joint." And he hasn't.

Mary is 14 years old, a juvenile delinquent, according to society's yardstick. Charged with a felony, her case could be named to Circuit Court. "A lost soul," according to the social worker, "a malingerer, liar, cheat." Many other derogatory adjectives come from all sorts of grownups who experienced her behavior as grossly inconvenient to their preconceived expectations.

Her mother is a social climber, working hard at keeping the status quo. Her father, an army veteran with a military school background, customarily demanded instant obedience. Her older brother, a runaway from home, is considered a disgrace to the family and is never spoken of.

"I learned to survive by being quiet, by never talking back, by working, cleaning, by saying please and thank you. Then, my boyfriend touched me, held me, and said, 'You're beautiful.'"

I hear her dilemma. "Here are three circles I want you to look at: Parent-Adult-Child. Which one do you allow to run your life? How will you change?"

At the preliminary hearing, I learned she had *never* said no to her parents. I asked them, "How did you expect her to learn to say no if she never practiced? You've reared a yes-woman. What will you do?"

Seven years later, Mary flies in to take me to dinner. She's been a deputy of a sheriff's staff for two years while in a junior college, and she gives me a picture of herself taken by the sheriff's car. "Thanks for TA" is inscribed across the front of the picture.

OUR DREAMS

Seldom are clients aware that one function of visual perception is to look to see what is inside, to observe how the Child screens out those visual pictures which disturb and create panic and screens in those pictures which develop joy and creativity. Dreams tell it like it is and compensate for the usual one-sided conscious view of pictures created and directed by the Natural Child and the Little Professor.

The dream usually points out that "making progress" is not enough. Berne emphasizes that the best hope of getting a clear picture of the "script-set" is through dreams.[3] Transactionally, the dream is an exact replica of the client's way of life. As the dream is retold, many things fall into place.

From childhood, dreams are often discounted by parents with statements like, "It's only a bad dream, go back to sleep," "You had a nightmare—there's no lion in this room, no man at the window, so go to sleep." The Child ego can decide early in life *not* to recall dreams. Research indicates that the nondreamer is deprived of health and of a healthy source of subconscious-level information. So those who appear healthy and claim they do not dream are usually *not* recalling the dream.

"If you were to dream, what might be happening?" is a technique which brings into the here-and-now the awareness of the denied dream.

As a therapist, I want to be able to see the pictorial dream, find the "script-set." Then I am able to focus in, to see the message from the Child ego state. For example, here is a dream related by a client:

I am walking down a hall, a very ordinary hall. White walls, brown woodwork, and French doors on the left side open into rooms. There's one set of French doors that are wide open, folded back against the wall on each side of the doorway.

I look into the room. There's a girl on the floor, face down. There's a corsage of roses near the right side of her head. She's wearing a green ruffled dress, black high-heel dancing shoes.

I say, "She's dead." Nobody shot her, she's not stabbed, but she's dead, and there's no blood. Sad, I think, and as I started walking down the hall, I woke up.

I use Jungian dream analysis as practiced and taught by Edward C. Whitmont.[4] Using this technique, I do not have to deal with all the different items in the dream. The script-set is the picture of the girl on the floor—no blood and the feeling the dreamer has of death.

"How old is the girl on the floor?"

"Oh, 20, 23, maybe 16!"

"When did you kill the party girl inside of you? When did you decide she couldn't play?"

Hands cover the face of the client and between sobs, "It was wicked to dance."

"Will you redecide to give her life now? And how will you accomplish that rebirth?"

The client enters body education to learn where she has armored in her musculature to prevent her body from being able to dance—a pelvic block which reinforces the script injunction that she is aware of cognitively.

I find Jungian dream analysis crisp, focused, and productive. I learned from Berne to look for the pictorial script-set in the dream. What had been removed from reality is pictured and examined in the present.

One justification for holding on to script-sets (recurring dreams) is the fear that the subsidy—that is, crooked or manipulative strokes—will be lost. Without a strong Nurturing Parent inside one's own personality structure, starvation appears imminent. To avert the fear of starvation, emergency strokes must be made available to the client. We are our own dream maker and, to be free of the script-set, a log of dreams is a way to collect important facts about how we live. Forget about what your friend dreams; look at your own dreams. What is the information you've already stored in the unconscious? How will that information assist you in learning to take care of your happiness, nurture your new growth, and strengthen the roots of redecisions? Follow the dream even when it leads you away from the path of timid souls, away from archaic injunctions and experiences.

Problems never stop so long as living is merely an activity. Were I at my wits' end, I would want to know that the person offering to lead me through unfamiliar dark feelings or remote unfathomable thoughts has been that way before. I would want to know that the therapist has delved into his or her own darkness and that the options, clarifications, and information offered me has been found, by experience, to work effectively in his or her own life. My Child ego state renounces the Parental "Do as I say, not as I do" and "because I said so" kind of education or therapy.

References

1. Eric Berne, "Social Dynamics: The Intimacy Experiment," *Transactional Analysis Bulletin, 3,* no. 9 (January, 1964), p. 113; Eric Berne, "Research: More About Intimacy," *Transactional Analysis Bulletin, 3,* no. 10 (April, 1964), p. 125.
2. Liladee V. Bellinger, *Keep on Trucking Manual,* Schoolcraft, Michigan, and Watsonville, California, Trucking Pub. Co., 1974.
3. Eric Berne, *What Do You Say After You Say Hello?,* New York, Grove Press, 1972, p. 174.
4. Edward C. Whitmont, *Symbolic Quest,* New York, C. G. Jung Foundation, 1969.

EIGHTEEN

ENJOYING EVERY MINUTE
John Gladfelter

No one ever told me that the development of a private practice is a highly individual and personal adventure for which there are only the guides of one's own growth, change, and learning as indicators. I'm not sure that if someone had told me twenty years ago about private practice as an adventure I would have believed him. I'm not sure that twenty years ago such individual choices as I have were possible, but I find that as I view my history as a therapist I am pleased and excited. I am pleased by the impressive people I chose as teachers and models and excited by the here-and-now pleasure of doing therapy and teaching it as a profession. My section of this book is a chronicle of my growth, my here-and-now, and my views of the future.

METAMORPHOSIS: PROFESSOR TO THERAPIST

My earliest exposure to therapy was through a group therapist, W. Sterling Bell, who was a resident in psychiatry while I was a psychology intern; we embarked on doing group therapy with little preparation but our own enthusiasm as students and our reading of the group therapy literature of the 1950s. We both soon learned that reading was not enough, and we sought out others in the community and region who had similar interests. We both discovered and became actively involved in a local study group and a regional organization, the Southwest Group Psychotherapy Society. The influence of that association on group therapists in the region is described by David Mendell.[1] Mendell beautifully portrays the contributions to the organization of a wide range of national and international group therapists. Personally, I found the input of enormous value in allowing for selectivity in approach, theoretical stance, and practical applications. I found that for me the views of Milton Berger, with his emphasis on uses of television, and those of Cornelius Beukenkamp, with his emphasis on the value and integrity of the person, to be the most important in my own development. My own personal growth in Beukenkamp's private therapy group was a primary factor in my moving into private practice from academia and my choice of being exclusively a group therapist. Although I had been trained in a variety of other modalities, including nondirective and psychoanalytic therapy, I found myself limited by the individual approach.[2]

I discovered that for me the learning and doing of group therapy depended on doing a number of groups; within a short time in private practice I was seeing 15 groups per week with a very limited number of individual appointments. Group size was usually limited to eight or nine people, so that during a week I was seeing an average of 125 patients. I realized later that I was taking an unusually large number of groups compared to other group therapists, but no one had told me what the usual number was or that doing group therapy was supposed to be difficult or hard work. I found it exciting but also puzzling, for I was aware that many of the traditional notions about psychoanalytic group treatment had a limited clinical application over a wide range of patients.

Time and economic demands on patients were severe unless I chose to limit my practice to those who could afford the time and money for my help over a three- or four-year period. From my active involvement in the Southwest Group Psychotherapy Society, the Dallas Group Psychotherapy Society, and the American Group Psychotherapy Association I was aware that there were new, adventurous, and exciting ideas being talked about and experimented with and that opportunities for new methods in group therapy were available. These connections also enabled me to fully claim my identity as a group therapist and move into my combined identity as a teacher and a therapist. The teaching and learning model combined with experiential learning as provided by the group therapy organizations further encouraged my exploration of new methods and new approaches.

While still a university professor, I had read Eric Berne's first two books[3] and had been impressed by the direct way he had addressed himself to therapeutic issues. Although his ideas impressed me, I could not see an effective direct application of them to the group therapy methods I knew, and so it was not until I met Berne at the American Group Psychotherapy Conference in San Francisco in 1965 that I reconsidered his views and mine. Although my contact with Berne was brief, I was able to talk to others in the San Francisco area who were using transactional analysis and who recognized this approach as having great merit. The limitations of distance and the uniqueness of applications of transactional analysis meant that I would have to delay my learning at the source and learn what I could through the annual workshops available through the American Group Psychotherapy Association.

I continued to read Berne's other books[4] as they were published and my continued contact with Robert Goulding stimulated my further interest in transactional analysis. As a result of my continued consultation with a local educational foundation, I had the good fortune to influence it to invite Berne as the speaker for the annual spring workshop. I was both pleased and surprised when Berne agreed to come and was encouraged by the enthusiasm of the attendees at that conference in the spring of 1970. This enthusiasm led to the beginning of a study group which met on a regular basis until the regular seminar in Dallas was formed. In the fall of 1970 Robert Goulding and Mary Goulding were the workshop leaders for the annual Southwest Group Psychotherapy Society in Oklahoma City and were the major impetus for me to begin using transactional analysis in my treatment groups. As a result of the Gouldings doing a one-week workshop in Dallas the following year, I was well on my way to incorporating and developing my practice in an entirely new way. I completed my basic reorientation to group therapy as a result of a Clinical Membership training contract with Harry Boyd and a Teaching Member training contract with John O'Hearne.

My reorientation to group therapy was an emancipation for me from a disorganized practice and from the stress caused by my feeling overly responsible *for* rather than *to* the people who were in treatment with me. They were very well aware of the changes going on in me and were pleased with these changes. At the same time, they experienced considerable anxiety which seemed mostly related to their fears of abandonment. I realized that I very much wanted to teach after leaving academia and had been instrumental in the development of group therapy training programs for the Dallas Group Psychotherapy Society. I decreased the size of my practice from 15 groups to nine groups and added training groups to replace them. I also made a major modification in time with my treatment groups so that I saw them for three two-hour sessions per month with a week or two in between each month for vacation for them and me. This time economy has proved beneficial for group members and has given me free time to take care of me.

A NEW DIRECTION

The transition period was important for me because it forced me to rethink many of my notions about group therapy, psychopathology, current treatment approaches, education, personal time economy, and my personal stance as a teacher and therapist. I discovered that a great portion of my professional training was a waste of time and energy. I found that I could no longer identify myself with my profession of origin and that my views were in agreement with what is sometimes called the fifth profession, psychotherapy.

My meetings with Berne were brief but important to me for they enabled me to see him in relation to his approach and to the field of therapy. To me he was a warm, open man. He was also a person who could muster great personal charisma with an audience. At the same time he could be highly abrasive with an audience that was antagonistic or disinterested. He obviously liked to teach, to play, to have fun, and be the person that he was.

Berne spoke to the therapist in me that wants to do the very best, most potent, rapid, and effective work with a client. He was interested in discovering practical ways to help patients to change. His emphasis on competency was of particular importance to me both as a teacher and practitioner, since I had been seeing the field of therapy as avoiding basic issues in this area. His insistence on training standards for both teachers and students was valuable to me. His belief that competency was a demonstrable commodity that could be evaluated and scaled gave heart to my own convictions that gross negligence, fuzzy thinking, irresponsibility, and incompetency were closer to the norm. His emphasis on helping the patient get what he or she wants was exciting and refreshing to me after long years of hearing patients judged as stupid and helpless. His condemnation of case conferences, grand rounds, and case discussions was important to me after having spent many years in a teaching setting where trivia and tradition ruled. Indeed, it seemed to me that Berne was doing a kind of conceptual housecleaning for clinicians that was long overdue, and that he was providing at the same time a wide range of powerful tools and handy household hints.

TOOLS FOR CLINICIANS

Berne's theoretical system has much to offer the practicing clinician. The system was firmly founded on psychoanalytic research and teaching and at the same time represented a clear break from the traditional methodology of psychoanalytic psychotherapy. From the conceptual foundations of the system to its more esoteric views, transactional analysis is an open system which allows maximum creativeness and inventiveness on the part of the user. At the same time, there are inherent limits on conceptualizing beyond clinical experience and observable behavior. Berne wisely developed a language which would enlist both interest on the part of the reader and thinking on the part of the researcher and clinician. His careful selection of words of one and two syllables to describe phenomena went a long way in encouraging patients as well as therapists to be interested in his work. At the same time Berne was careful to delimit the range of meaning of his words by basing them in observable, describable, and verifiable behavior. It is often, in fact, this remarkable economy of communication that is criticized as being simplistic, superficial, jargonistic, and rather silly.

Transactional analysis as a treatment system seems to be one of the most practical and useful of any of the systems available. Berne does not tell his audience at any point in his writings that they can learn to do TA by reading his books and articles. In fact, one of my standing amusements is watching a clinician who has had no training in transactional analysis attempt to use the treatment method. Much of the disillusionment about transactional analysis that I hear comes from people who have tried to use the methods without previous training. Otherwise responsible clinicians seem bent on criticising and nitpicking with the transactional approaches when they have had little or no supervised experience in using TA. I suspect their difficulties arise from the problems of making real changes in themselves and growing into a new approach that directly conflicts with old learning and old experiences. I found myself in a number of major dilemmas in relearning therapeutic approaches to patients' problems and I came to view a number of assumptions about treatment in a new light.

Clinical treatment methods, as Berne well knew, depend on training and supervision by a competent trainer and are not communicated in writing. The theoretical system is available in writing but the applications and cognitive stance are not. Doing transactional analysis from the book is much like building a house from a book. I'd rather not see the house thus built and I would rather not meet the patient treated by the book. For the person who would attempt to treat himself with transactional analysis, I would suggest that anyone who treats himself psychologically has a fool for a patient. The most common misconception I see among some therapists is that they can use the language of transactional analysis effectively in treatment without employing the treatment modality. I seriously doubt that the language by itself is useful for change in patients. This misconception leads largely to disillusionment in treatment for both patient and therapist.

In presenting transactional analysis Berne was presenting a remarkably sophisticated treatment approach that has a wide range of behavioral applications. It seems likely that he developed this approach out of his own discouragement with "analytically oriented" psychotherapy and his awareness of a need for a treatment based on both analytic principles and the observable behavior of people. In transactional analysis the full range of emotional and behavioral human experiences is effectively described and evaluated in terms of individualized treatment approaches. This view of human experience readily lends itself as a comprehensive conceptual umbrella under which a wide range of current psychological treatment methods can be subsumed without doing injustice to the method or to transactional analysis. Transactional analysis is often described as being a "head"' system of treatment, and yet gestalt treatment, primal therapies, and body methods can easily be conceptualized with this system. A facet of Berne not often emphasized is that he was a researcher in the best sense of the word. His achievement in systematically working from basic clinical data to concepts and then validating or invalidating data and concepts is a cornerstone in behavioral science. Of basic importance to me is that Berne, in making major extensions in theory, carefully adhered to basic psychoanalytic theory without doing injustice to clinical evidence. From one perspective, transactional analysis can be seen as Berne's contribution to psychoanalysis; he made an important area of human understanding comprehensible and useful. Berne was ever mindful of the need for clear, precise, and careful communication even though he was critical of the common usage of the word "communication."

INFLUENCES: CONTRIBUTIONS OF THE GOULDINGS AND OTHERS

Robert Goulding was the first therapist that I saw using transactional analysis. I had known Bob for a number of years and had come to know him as an open, direct, caring person and was impressed by him as a professional and responsible member of a number of organizations. It was also clear to me from the beginning of our meetings that he was a growing person who had a thorough investment in living as fully and as enthusiastically as possible. I did some personal therapeutic work for myself with Bob as therapist and I became aware of how easily and effectively change was possible. That work made me aware of my need to investigate further about treatment, transactional analysis, and gestalt therapy. That therapeutic experience was also important because I came to know Mary Goulding, who was working with Bob at the time. The two of them enabled me to make a major change for myself.

Bob and Mary Goulding are important individuals in the field of therapy. No one has done more than they to involve people in transactional analysis training; they also represent the melding of gestalt training into transactional treatment in a way which gives a therapist great potency in facilitating change. Bob has been an important innovator in transactional analysis as well as an integrator. His past extensive medical experience has been effectively used as a base for his work as a therapist and clinician. Bob is also a remarkably talented teacher who has devoted a massive amount of time, energy, and resources to the creation of a teaching environment at Mt. Madonna. Many of the teaching models used currently throughout the country in teaching transactional analysis were modeled after those developed by the Gouldings. They bring to the field a base of history in the development of transactional analysis derived from their experiences with both Eric Berne and Fritz Perls. They also have remained politically active in group treatment and have influenced training and membership standards. Mary Goulding holds an important role in the development of effective role models for women as therapists and as politically active people in the professional world as well as the *real* world. She also has been a creative force in the treatment of women and the problems of loss, and in developing the concepts of Parent. Bob and Mary have been important people in my own shaping and growing as a therapist. Mary's ease of style, clarity of understanding, gentle support, and directness of confrontation have been major influences in my therapeutic skill. Bob's directness, inventiveness, firm patience, openness, and smoothness have also been valuable resources for my own treatment armamentarium.

I believe that Bob's development of redecision[5] and impasse resolution[6] and his work with phobias[7] and depressions are landmarks of creativity in transactional treatment. I emphasize with my students that these developments are important basic tools for cure in a wide range of areas where previous modes of treatment were lengthy, difficult, and marginal in value. Although the basic theory for these innovations is in print, the learning therapist would be wise to get experience with supervision in using these methods, because they are potent, effective, and dangerous if used by neophytes. I believe that the dangers are largely the discouragement and confusion to the client that result if these highly valuable tools are used ineptly.

Claude Steiner has been an important influence on my own growing ideas about change and the manner in which it comes about. In particular, I am as concerned as he is about the influence of the medical model in helping people. I also find his views and treatment methods with alcoholics[8] of particular usefulness when working with this problem.

The work of Jacqui Schiff and others[9] is of special value when doing basic confrontation work as a therapist. Their theoretical formulations and research are useful when working with individuals who are considered psychotic. Their views of contract work are also quite helpful. Many therapists who have learned transactional analysis have avoided confrontation techniques because they fear the potential for games. There is no doubt that games are possible, but I doubt that anyone well trained and supervised in truly potent confrontation techniques would easily give them up. Ways of handling such situations have been well developed and are effective in developing Adult functioning in the patient. Parenting and reparenting also are major contributions of Jacqui Schiff to treatment in transactional analysis. This approach, although developed in the context of working with severely disturbed patients, is also important in working with less disturbed patients. Modifications of reparenting have been very useful to me in enabling patients to move beyond cure.

William Holloway and Martha Holloway have provided a cogent theoretical and experiential foundation for contract work in transactional analysis. Their contributions[10] have heavily influenced my own thinking in the creation and working through of many types of contracts. I find their elaboration of redecision and early decision formulations[11] a solid foundation in the learning and process of change contract work.

Harry Boyd was heavily influential in my developing an economy of style in treatment which I thoroughly enjoy and which gives maximum therapeutic potency for a length of time. His emphasis on stroking in treatment has been of major importance to me as a therapist.

My final polish as a transactional therapist came from John O'Hearne, whose scope of transactional treatment and the entire breadth of group therapy is without parallel. John's ability to teach, supervise, and support the growth in therapists is remarkable. He is highly effective in applications of transactional analysis in a number of areas other than treatment. John was most influential in my learning to use transactional approaches without the language of transactional analysis.

VALUABLE CONCEPTS

My transition from doing existential psychoanalytically oriented group therapy to doing transactional analysis group treatment did not result from failure in what I was doing. I found that people did change in group therapy, that people were pleased by what they got in treatment, and that I could easily have continued doing what I was doing for as long as I chose. I know that many group therapists have continued to follow a traditional approach and have been unwilling to change in spite of recent innovations. That certainly is their choice and until research evidence provides conclusive proof that other methods are more effective, they probably will continue as they are. My choice grew out of a series of decisions relating to personal growth and practical issues in the entire field of psychological treatment. In the field of psychotherapy, waiting for research evidence is a lifetime proposition. My own personal growth resulted in my confirming for myself that I liked to teach, learn, do research, and enjoy more free time for myself. That growth and growing process enabled me to find the most compatible context for teaching and learning outside the oppressive and stultifying atmosphere of the modern American university. My choice of becoming a Teaching Member in the International Transactional Analysis Association and my becoming a field coordinator for the Fielding Institute have become valuable outlets for the scholar that is in me. At the same time my decision came about because of important issues in the field of helping people which I find have been largely ignored. I abhor the trade-unionism which is taking place in the professional helping fields as a result of licensing, health insurance, and malpractice concerns. The needs, hopes, pains, and desires of our patients become lost in our attempts to legislate competence, responsibility, and caring for people. In my work as a therapist and teacher I confront myself regularly with four basic questions and from my answers I evaluate what I must do and what I must teach. The questions are as follows:

1. How can a helper of people survive and grow best as he ages?
2. How can a helper of people effect major changes in the well-being, lifestyle, awareness, and growth of people he helps?
3. How can a helper of people effect major changes in problem areas of society such as violence, poverty, aging, and death?
4. How can a helper of people effect changes in world attitudes, world behavior, and history?

Presumptuous as these questions might sound I believe that therapists bear responsibilities for these issues because we are at the grass roots of change in people, and the people who change with us change the world.

I see in transactional analysis a number of strong arguments for the values and positions that are inherent in its theory and practice. My reasons lie in the simplicity, the organized and open-ended modeling, the linguistic emphasis, the teachability, the contractual viewpoint, the compatibility with other existing therapeutic models, and the utility of the approach. I will discuss each of these reasons briefly and give some practical values for each.

I like the *simplicity* of transactional analysis, for it allows me the greatest freedom to work and the greatest freedom for others to be aware of themselves. I can explain the entire system in a matter of minutes to a bright adult and he can find usefulness and applications for it in his everyday life. His awareness of ego states, games, and scripts in his own life and the lives of others around him is potent information. The simplicity makes for rapid and effective use. The one- and two-syllable words make for a conciseness which children understand also.

I like the emphasis on an *organized model,* for it allows the information which the person already has to be useful to him and applicable in a variety of ways. It allows the person a greater latitude for making predictions about behavior on both an immediate and a long-range scale of time. The organization gives a sense of degree and dimension which is useful in applications of change methods. Because the model has a place for diverse notions such as time, reinforcement, change, repetitive behaviors, culture, cognition, affect, and learning its utility is enormously enhanced. There is the further advantage (or irritation to some people) that the model offers an easy way to understand each person and his behavior, rather than the "Oh, we are all so terribly complex" vista so often presented by other psychologies.

Transactional analysis is an *open-ended* model and is so organized and structured that it can encompass a wide variety of existing personality theories and behavior concepts. I find it just as easy to talk about Piaget from a transactional point of view as about reinforcement theory, behavior modification, dream work, culture, shock, anthropological concepts, and moral development.

The *linguistic efficiency* of transactional analysis and the care exercised in using language in treatment have been very valuable to me. Concepts and words are carefully defined and linked to observable and objective phenomena and thus they carry greater potency when used in treatment. When I talk of "Parent ego state," the patients I work with have a reasonably clear notion of what I am talking about. The use of the word "stroke" rather than its rough equivalent in psychology—"reinforcement" —is an economy of three syllables and an advantage in clarity.

I find that most of my patients can read one or more books in transactional analysis and have a good working knowledge of the concepts and ideas. My use of explanation and clarification further informs and teaches the basic ideas. The ease with which people learn basic transactional analysis demonstrates the utility of its ideas and the effectiveness of its use for change. The patient is always capable of understanding what is going on in his therapy and the therapy of other people in the group. I do not believe that insight and awareness are of major importance in treatment, but they are valuable in giving the patient hope and encouragement for what he is doing to change.

The *treatment contract* in therapy is of great value to me as a therapist and to the patient, because it promotes active and full commitment to treatment goals and places proper emphasis on the need for change. I confront patients with the fact that they are paying me to help them and that the way I can help them is through exploring with them and helping them decide what it is they want to change. This decision for change takes time but it is of paramount importance to me that a client has opportunity during every session to get full value for money and time. "What do you want to change today?" is a constant question to be raised with every client every session. The contract becomes the vehicle by which the client can recognize his responsibility as a client and I can claim my responsibility as a therapist. The use of a contract makes clear to the patient on a regular basis that I will and can help him to do more than make progress, chat, or play *Ain't It Awful*.

I find the *compatibility* of transactional analysis with other current behavior and treatment models particularly useful. It is already clear for many therapists that gestalt therapy is well conceptualized with second-order structural diagrams. I readily use many of the behavior modification methods because I find the notions easily applied in stroke economy terms. Reality therapy and rational emotive approaches also are highly congruent and easy to incorporate into a transactional frame of reference. I find Piaget's concepts readily translatable into my thinking about the development of Little Professor and Adult ego state concepts. At the same time I find much of my earlier psychoanalytic thinking highly relevant to transactional diagrams.

I like the *utility* of transactional analysis and I appreciate having something to do when a patient wants to change. I remember past experiences in case conferences and treatment planning sessions; I and others held forth on what each patient needed and often there was the feeling that all patients got the same prescription and plan. Certainly the patient was not a part of the planning session for we were solidly convinced that we knew what was best for him. I find now that my task as a therapist is to have available for use with a client a variety of methods, approaches, experiences, exercises, experiments, and actions which will enable him to make the kinds of changes that he wants. This means that when the patient says "I want to stop being depressed and I want to stop now," I have something that I can do and offer instead of reflecting, reacting, reinforcing, and rebuffing. The further advantage which is enormously reinforcing for continuing to use transactional analysis is that I now see the patient giving up his depression in the present and in the group. He enters the group session depressing himself and he leaves the same session no longer depressed. This form of rapid utility is also important for other group members because it gives them hope and encouragement to continue working to make the changes they want.

TREATMENT METHODS: THE CONTRACT

The treatment methods that I find most useful in my practice are contract work, permission, impasse resolution, redecision, parenting, treatment operations, television, and growth work. I will describe my approach to each of these methods and emphasize that since I do only group work, all of these methods are utilized in group treatment. There are other occasional methods used, but I find that this list covers most of the time-structuring in the group.

My contract work begins when I make the first contact with the patient, whether it be by phone or by direct contact during intake. As clearly as I can I establish with the person what it is that he wants and then I make the decision as to whether or not I will treat him. That decision will depend largely on whether I have what he wants and whether I want to treat him. I believe that most patients come not for treatment but instead for some sort of magic. My task is to assist them in formulating a decision on what changes they want to make. I still find it puzzling that so many people who come for therapy have little concept or notion about change and often have given up all hope or wish for alteration of their lives. In contract formulation the patient arrives at what alterations he wants to make in himself in terms of both feeling and behavior, and those alterations become the fabric for a series of contract work sessions. I see contracts as being of six types and those types often serve to move the patient into change.

An early contract that I may offer is a tourist contract. It is an opportunity for the patient to attend one session merely as a spectator to learn about the group treatment experience and at the end of the session to make a decision for himself about treatment. This experience often serves as a springboard for further contract choices.

A second contract form is an exploration contract, in which the individual has the opportunity for a limited time, usually five minutes, to talk about himself, what he is feeling and what he wants. At the end of this time, I expect him to formulate what it is that he wants for himself and to make some kind of change contract. I use this type of contract with caution, because it can lead to a variety of detours in treatment such as catharsis and abreaction. If the patient moves in that direction, I will stop him and press for a change contract. My experience with catharsis and abreaction is that they are ways the Adapted Child in the patient is able to protect himself from change and enlist stroking from the therapist and other group members for feeling bad and being clever in avoiding change. At the end of five minutes I ask the patient to summarize the material he has explored and say what he would like to change now.

There are occasions when exploration readily moves the patient into making a clear change contract.

A third contract I use, which often precedes a change contract, is an information contract. This is valuable because it often assists the Adult of the patient to evaluate what is happening and what the possible solutions and changes are. Questions of information can usually be differentiated from game operations because they come from the Adult in the patient and are simply and clearly asked. Information for the patient may come from other group members as well as from the therapist and often take the form of clarification, support, reassurance, and new data. An information contract might be, "Do people in the group think that I look or sound depressed?" Another information contract might be one related to change data such as, "Is it possible for me to be not depressed at all any more?" It is the task of the therapist to evaluate the information contract to avoid the possible games and loss of time.

The change contract is the core of treatment in transactional analysis and is basic to change in feelings and behavior in the patient. Change contracts are stated in clear, simple, and positive language and are here-and-now statements. The patient says, "I will give up my scare right now and feel excited and enthusiastic about my work." Many change contracts are statements at the end of working through rather than at the beginning. Also, change contracts often are a result of treatment operations and represent the culmination of much previous work in treatment. Change contracts may result from dialogue from the Parents in the person's head or may come about as a result of other treatment work such as permission or impasse resolution. The statement of the change contract is important for both patient and group as a crystallization of treatment work and an experience of Adult confirmation of change.

The awareness contract is designed to enable the patient to experience his physical and emotional experiences in the group and use these as data for further change.

The experience contract is an opportunity for the patient to disobey the "Don't think" and "Don't feel" injunctions and use Adult functioning to process and evaluate how he wants to change. Again, experience contracts are time limited, ten minutes or so, and must lead to Adult data-processing of the experience and options for change. The experience contract can also lead to games and must be carefully monitored and stopped if the patient moves to catharsis or abreaction. An experience contract might begin with the patient stating that he is not aware of having any feelings, or that he is aware of having much physical stress but no accompanying emotions. I then say to the patient, "Will you allow yourself to relax and pay attention to whatever you are feeling, physically or emotionally? When you are aware of feelings, will you talk about them?" When the person has been able to report his feelings, I ask for a possible change contract.

The last form of contract I use is a practice contract. This is a contract often involving homework or practice in situations both in and out of the group. The content of the contract has to do with behavior which the patient wants to change, and the practice contract allows the person to practice immediately in the group. This often means use of psychodramatic techniques in the group to enable the patient to have experience before he explores the behavior outside the group. The patient wants to confront his boss and ask for a raise. I ask him to do this either with a group member being the boss or with the fantasized boss in the group. He then has the opportunity to play with the words he will use, edit, and relay and thereby gain maximum experience in changing his behavior. I like to employ assertiveness exercises on occasion in the group to allow further practice of new and different behaviors. The practice contract is dependent on the patient operating from his Adult ego state and being able to evaluate and use the new learning experiences from the group.

New group members are given early opportunities to practice contract work and to be aware of the potent effects of contracts. I tell them that I believe more often in what people do than in what they say, and that truly effective change depends on the saying and the doing being congruent. Thus, early in the group I give patients the opportunity to effectively say "No, I won't" and "I refuse," so that they are aware that they have choices and can protect themselves in group treatment from contracts that are not in their best interests. I am careful to use clear language in the offering of contracts, so that "Can you?" or "Would you?" becomes "Will you now?" I believe that the therapist serves best as a coach and assistant for the formulation of early contracts. He must, however, be operating from his own Adult and not from his Nurturing Parent at that time. The contract work offers real hope to individuals who come for help and have little experience with the accomplishment, satisfaction, and completion of tasks. Positive stroking for completion of contracts is basic and necessary for further effective contract work. The most delightful part of early contract work is clarifying what the patient wants or feels. The change the patient makes via contract work, from saying "I guess maybe I might want to not feel bad much" to "I will be aware of what I feel and decide whether I want to change how I feel by next session," is a potent result of good contract work with the patient.

The first group session for the new patient is very important, because it provides a model for subsequent sessions and must provide basic information for later use. The patient becomes aware of the positive stroking atmosphere of the group and the warmth and caring that is a part of the group experience. He also is aware of the care and value that is placed on contract work as a basis for working through and changing. He experiences himself talking with the therapist and others about himself and experiences their positive attitudes about such openness and disclosure. In that first session he meets other people in different phases of treatment and becomes aware of how change has affected the thinking and feelings of other people. He experiences the importance of time-structuring and the care with which the therapist allows each person to work without at the same time becoming competitive. He becomes aware of how much work is done in a short time with little room for disruptions, tangential wanderings, chaos, and confusion. At the end of the first session I ask the new member whether he has any questions for me or for other members of the group. He is given ample opportunity and time to get responses from all group members and a chance to experience briefly the social interchange of the group.

Videotape recordings are important in my treatment groups, and I use instant replay as a way of verifying and validating contract statements of patients. I also give careful attention to body language, since it gives important data as to whether the contract is an Adult contract or an Adapted Child contract. On occasion I have had a patient make a contract while keeping his fingers crossed behind his back. (Needless to say the contract thus made was not kept.) I look for the variety of ways the person may negate what he is saying, such as winks, crossed fingers, tongues in cheek, and negative head shakes. Depending on the Adult available in the patient, I may or may not confront these negations and continue to work. If the client is negating the contract I may stop, assuming that, for whatever reasons, he is not ready to change.

CLOSING THE ESCAPE HATCH

I believe that effective treatment with transactional analysis must lead off with the closing of escape hatches, and I do so with all patients. This means that the client must make a commitment to himself never to kill himself, never to go crazy, and never to kill anyone. This may seem a strange way to start off treatment, but I have found through experience that even the best-educated, most sophisticated, and most comfortable patient may be harboring the options of suicide, craziness, or murder and must give them up before contracts, decision, redecisions, and changes are fully effective and potent. I ask the patient to make the statement for himself that says, "I will never kill myself, either accidentally or on purpose, no matter how bad I feel and no matter how bad things get." I also ask him to make the commitment to himself that he will never reconsider his decision. I ask him to make that same statement to himself about going crazy and about murdering anyone. I emphasize that he is making a statement not to me or anyone else but to himself, and that it is not a promise but a commitment. I find that promises are often a part of the ready repertoire of the Adapted Child and can be made and broken easily. The person is allowed and encouraged to use his own words in the commitment, but the content must be monitored carefully for sneaky Child loopholes. For the patients in which escape hatches are already closed or never open, the statements are not difficult to make. When I see a patient object or get into strong feelings about the statement, his feelings are solid data about an open escape hatch.

Even though a patient closes escape hatches, I do not believe that they are permanently closed until he has made major script changes, and that means redecision work. I do occasionally check escape hatches even after closing, because I find that circumstances in people's lives often (to them) necessitate desperate measures. I often recheck when I find that the patient is refusing to work, getting into bad feelings, or negating the contracts he makes. When I encounter someone who will not close an escape hatch—and that escape hatch is frequently suicide—I make a decision as to whether or not I believe there is immediate danger. If there is danger I push for hospitalization; if there is not, I carefully store data about the person so that I continue as first priority the closing of that escape hatch. I rarely have a patient who does not close all escape hatches during the first two sessions.

When I am aware that a patient is reluctant to close escape hatches, I assume that he has had much difficulty in protecting himself while growing up and that the closing of the hatches will provide some immediate temporary relief of bad feelings. I tell the person that this relief is an important part of change and that he must continue in treatment for a period of time lest he assume that he is through. Resistance to closing escape hatches often foretells early termination and a reluctance to make any significant changes, particularly when there is no immediate danger of suicide, craziness, or murder. I find this particularly true when I am working with people who are in a troubled marriage and the suicide threat still has effectiveness in the relationship.

ENCOURAGING SELF-PERMISSION

I see permission in transactional analysis from a number of viewpoints, and I follow the notion that most but not all permission must come from the person himself and not from me. This does not mean that I will not give permission, but I believe that when I do I may impede the autonomous choices of the patient, and I am strongly opposed to doing that. I believe that patients must learn about the Parents in their head and learn how to give themselves Parental permission. They first must learn about the nonpermissiveness of the Parent ego states which they acquired from their parents and how unreasonable this Parent can often be. Much permission work is founded on basic permission to think, feel, listen, and learn. This is often the result of redecision work, but it also can be done with multiple chair work as well. The best permission work culminates in statements of "I will" or "I won't" and "I will decide and choose." Permission is often best demonstrated in the group through each group member talking, thinking, and feeling as he works. It is also an integral part of the charisma of the therapist for him to demonstrate his freedom to think, feel, listen, intuit, and communicate openly and actively and thus tacitly convey what permission is about. Permission also is best done in a here-and-now manner so that if the patient gives himself permission, it is demonstrable immediately in the group. The immediacy of the experience gets stroking and reinforcement for the patient to continue the permission. There are important times when I do give permission, and this is often to make clear to the patient that I support some significant Parent material which he has and which is useful and valuable for him in daily functioning. That permission comes in the form of a statement from me that I too believe strongly in certain values and practices which should continue. The permission from me usually comes at a time when I believe that the patient is in confusion or under outside pressure and needs support and reassurance from me about his behavior.

GETTING PAST THE IMPASSE: FIRST, SECOND, AND THIRD DEGREE

Bob Goulding's article on the three impasses in transactional treatment states concisely the three ego-state models, the methods they are based on, and the theoretical formulations of the processes. In some ways the first-degree impasse resolution is similar to what others call decontamination. I follow a conceptual format in decontamination, for which there are four steps. I first enlist whatever Adult ego state is available in the patient, with requests for attention, concentration, and awareness. I look for signs of escalating passivity, increasing bad feelings, or confusion, and if I see none I continue with the second step, which is focusing on the patient's awareness of feelings, Parent messages in his head, body signals, or other data of which he is aware. If he is willing to move to this point and continue Adult data-processing, I move to step three, which is his claiming for himself the responsibility for whatever he is feeling, thinking, experiencing, or doing. If he is able to be aware that he is in charge of what he thinks, feels, or experiences, I then ask him to review for himself what he has just done and to be aware that he is in charge and can, with practice, change any part that he wants. If the patient has followed to this point he may also be aware of how he originally learned the contamination, how it helped him in the past, and how it is supposed to help him in the present. An example of such contaminations are "feeling that I should work hard" or "feeling that people don't like me." Resolution of these contaminations gives the patient awareness and control of his behavior, so that if he decides to work hard it is an autonomous choice and not a "should" or a "feel I should." If the patient stops himself at any of the steps, I stroke him for the work he has done and ask him to confront me with a statement of "I won't go any further," thereby claiming his potency either to stop or to work in therapy, as he chooses. At this point I may stop working with him or continue, depending on how much of his rebelliousness I experience and how much he is trying to please me. Since I usually work for short periods of time, I am most likely to stop and work with him later in the session.

The first-degree impasse resolution is an exciting experience for the patient because he becomes suddenly aware of the amount of power he has been using against himself. It is very valuable work in the group; other group members will frequently do important coat-tailing on this work. This impasse resolution often frees the person to do and feel many new things. First-degree impasse work should be followed by second-degree impasse work and the patient must be cautioned to take care of himself. Patients who experience freedom from their impasse are not aware that this block was a protection from an early injunction and that they can be in danger if further work is not done. This kind of treatment work is relatively easy to do but is best done gently, rapidly, and clearly. Most of this type of work can be done in from ten to fifteen minutes or less.

Second-degree impasse work is redecision work and to me has the greatest effect in enabling people to make changes in their lives. Contrary to some notions, redecision work can sometimes be done very early in treatment with maximum benefit. I usually get into redecision through focusing on major rackets that I hear being talked about by the patient. The patient may not be aware that he is talking about the long-standing chronic bad feelings when he talks about his physical symptoms, his fatigue, his feeling "out of," and the like, but spotting the racket is often the beginning of doing redecision work. It is also well advised to consider the basic injunction that the patient is obeying by feeling bad. Escape hatches now need to be closed for clear, potent, and decisive work. It is at this point that the therapist's Adult and Parent are important allies for the Little Professor and Adult of the patient. The beginning of second-degree impasse work is best done from a contract for change. That change usually means giving up bad feelings but it also means having good ones as an alternative. I often ask the patient what he will replace his anxiety or depression with. I point out to him that if he has been depressed, he has been structuring from 40 to 60 hours per week with bad feelings and that he will need to structure that time in other ways. Bad feelings seem to be an important adjunct to time-structuring, and I suggest that patients make some choices as to activities that will enable them to feel good. I ask them to make a fun list of eighty-five activities they can do for fun that don't cost anything. This fun list is useful to someone who has decided to stop depressing himself and feel good.

One of the interesting aspects of redecision work is that early decisions to feel bad serve not only a blackmail function for the Child but also an important caretaking function. It is as though the Child experiences or is aware of pain in the parent and chooses to feel bad and obey the injunction to avoid what he might anticipate as catastrophic consequences of disobedience. He, the Child, also is operating, as Piaget notes,[12] from a position of intuitive thought, thinking that he is somehow in charge of the parent's bad feeling. He bargains to feel bad instead of the parent in the hope that, by taking care of the parent, things will be made better for him. Sadly enough, the Child gets confirmation of his thinking by the parent changing, but not for the reasons that the Child believes. When working with the second-degree impasse, it becomes clear how a little boy or girl at an early age made an unfortunate choice and remained stuck with that choice. When reviewing the thinking processes of children from Piaget's point of view, it becomes evident that the cognition of the four- to six-year-old is heavily magical, and is rarely updated or revised as far as relationships and feelings are concerned. This review or update is the focus of the second-degree impasse resolution.

Third-degree impasse work is one of the most elegant and creative innovations of Bob Goulding and carries with it some of the finest change work possible. It is with this work that I believe the demon mentioned in transactional writings can be finally put to rest. This work involves early choices and decisions which we made on our own without help from our parents and which can be resolved rapidly and effectively. In doing third-degree impasse work with a patient from another culture, I found that, indeed, his work with a demon he believed to be within himself gave him the option to give it up and be aware that he had chosen the demon for some important early self-protective reasons. He was both surprised and delighted to find that he could be free of a demon that his culture had taught him was permanent and unchangeable. Third-degree impasse work has proved very useful in work with somatic symptomatology, magical process, vague bad feelings, and processes that the patient experiences as out of his control. It is wise, however, before undertaking any third-degree impasse work, to check that the patient is in good physical condition and that the work you are doing is not on real physical pathology. Be sure the patient is doing all he can from a medical standpoint before undertaking the psychological part.

STROKING FOR CHANGE

The notion of stroke economy as described by Steiner[13] has been a practical point of departure for me in treatment, and I like to use stroking in a variety of ways. In keeping with a paper by Harry Boyd,[14] I like to offer a rich source of strokes to both beginning members as well as older members in a group. This means that touching as well as verbal stroking are basic and necessary as a part of the group's transactions. In particular, I focus on the stroking of a new member for his willingness to come to a group session and talk, and the courage he shows by being open and vulnerable. I stroke as often as I can for "being" rather than "doing" and I encourage group members to stroke the new member. I might say to a new group member, "I hear how scared you feel right now and I like your willingness to stay and talk about yourself." Other group members will often respond to the new member by sharing their own first experiences in the group and saying to the new member, "I am aware of your being scared and I like you for staying and being a person who wants to change." Most experienced group members have learned how to stroke and get strokes in the process and so are willing to enrich the stroke level of the new person until he is able to respond with good feeling.

Skill in stroking depends on the therapist operating from a caring position and working within a strict semantic base. Potent strokes depend on the care with which words are linked together to become a stroke. This means that the therapist must be knowledgeable in words that have discount or conditional value and avoid them or use them with great care. If the therapist listens to the words of the patient and recognizes the value system in which the patient lives, he can give strokes that are potent and valuable. I find that for people who have difficulty accepting strokes, a succession of stroking statements is useful. Usually the person may be able to discount three or four stroking statements in a sequence but rarely more than that. It is also important in learning effective stroking to be able to decline the discounts that the patient gives in response to strokes. I emphasize to my trainees that the reason for stroking on the part of the therapist is that it feels good to do, and that if stroking is done to get return from the patient, then the therapist should not be stroking. My way of saying it is that the patient is not paying me to take care of me and my feelings. He is there because he needs help and I am the expert at helping to change what he wants changed. I do believe it is important that the therapist accept strokes from patients and learn to feel good about them. The modeling of stroke acceptance is important information for the patient. The rule of thumb for me in stroking other people is that I will stroke them so carefully and specifically that they will have to work very hard to discount and thus very often they will not discount.

I have eight criteria by which I evaluate stroking statements, and though these criteria are far from rules they convey the basic intent that is important in stroking. First, it is important that the word "I" be used to begin a stroking statement; using one's own person and potency are valuable to the other person. "I like you" has greater potency than "You are likeable." Second, I prefer to use the word "you," or even better, the person's favorite name when stroking him. I would be likely to say, "Jimmie, I really like your taste in the colors you choose for your clothes," rather than "That's not a bad looking suit." Thirdly, stroking statements are best kept to very simple statements. "I like your bright smile" has much more potency than something like "Your current visage is rather pleasant to look upon." Fourth, stroking statements should be given slowly and clearly while looking directly at the person you are stroking. To demonstrate this, experiment with saying something stroking to one person while looking at another. Fifth, strokes should be constructed with transitive verbs as often as possible. "I experience you as an exciting person" carries more power than "I felt that you were an exciting person." A sixth criterion is that strokes are most potent when they are in the present tense. Thus, "I liked your smile" is not as effective as "I like your smile." A seventh criterion is that strokes that describe specific attributes and characteristics are easier for the person to hear, understand, and use. When I say to a person, "I enjoy the clear, loud, and happy laugh you have," he can process that for greater good feeling than a statement which says

"Your laugh is OK." The last criterion is to avoid conditional modifiers as much as possible. Statements such as "I like your smile a little" give little positive stroke value to the person. Potent and effective stroking requires straight Adult work. The greatest asset for the therapist doing stroking is his freedom to see, hear, and experience the other person. Good practice for learning this is to practice stroking one's self.

POTENTIAL BEYOND CURE

I am particularly interested in one aspect of transactional analysis that might get lost in the richness of many aspects of the method. I am interested in patients going beyond cure. I mean that once people are fully able to experience their own good feelings and involve themselves in intimacy, I offer options which have to do with being the star or princess in their growth potential. In some transactional analysis literature it often sounds as if the patient once cured is through with change. My interest and emphasis is that people be the very best they want to be and that they have that capability within them. I am willing to explore with them via fantasy trips the exciting and fulfilling possibilities they may have. I approach them from my Adult with clear cautions that they experience what I am suggesting not as Parent but rather as Little Professor. I like to work with the person until he becomes aware of how he stops himself, discounts himself, limits himself, and avoids the real excitement, enthusiasm, curiosity, and power that he has inside. When he completes the fantasy work, I stroke him for being willing to take such an adventure and encourage him to do further personal exploration. Much of this work seems to be supporting Little Professor operations of curiosity, magic, fantasy, play, and excitement and giving permission to use these abilities. Sessions in which this kind of work is done are important to other group members and encourage others to explore their own potential.

I like to do dream work with a transactional point of view and regularly incorporate what I have learned from my gestalt colleagues. I believe that most dreams carry within them implicit contracts for change. When I work with a patient and his dream, I pay attention to the goals and changes implicit in the dream and work toward fulfilling the contract with the person. I use the not-OK miniscript diagram[15] as a way of diagraming a dream as the patient tells it. When I have completed the diagram on the basis of the material I have heard, I then check with the person as to whether the elements I have written on the blackboard are in keeping with the feeling and content of the dream. When the diagram has been verified, I offer the opportunity to play with it and ask for alternative options for drivers, stoppers, vindictive Child, and the final bad feelings. When this has been done I explore with the patient the OK miniscript alternatives for allowers, go'ers, and OK feelings. When an alternative diagram has been suggested, I ask the person to rewrite his dream in the way which pleases, excites, or interests him and then ask how this dream script diagram approximates any current events and experiences in his life. From this application the person often finds solutions or contracts for change which are important to him.

At other times in dream work I diagram the dream on the basis of statements from different ego states. Then, using second-order structural diagrams I fill in the statements on the diagram and ask the person to do multiple chair work to resolve to his satisfaction the dilemma or impasse created in the ego-state diagram. Again, the result is often a contract for change which then can be worked on. I rarely work on a dream longer than 15 minutes using these approaches, and I rely on the person to decide if the result has been useful and, if not, how it might be valuable in developing a contract. In my practice I also use the more traditional methods of working with dreams as developed by gestalt therapists. I do customarily conceptualize the dream content in terms of the script matrix of the patient and consider possible treatment options as they relate to the evolving script pattern.

USES OF VIDEO IN TREATMENT

I was doing work with video replay before I worked and trained in transactional analysis, and it has not been surprising to me that television has dovetailed superbly into the new and useful things I do now in treatment. Video has been even more useful to me in working from a transactional approach, and there is hardly any aspect of the approach which does not benefit from the incorporation of video. Since the point at which I passed my Clinical Membership examination with videotape segments of therapy, I have been actively developing ways to use television to enhance and improve my treatment approaches. I will briefly review a number of areas where I find video of particular value. I emphasize, however, that introduction of video depends on solid training in both video and transactional analysis before full clinical application. Effective therapeutic use requires ongoing supervision to achieve the most potent application of the technique. The therapist needs to be totally familiar with the equipment and its operation, before introducing it in his work with patients. Learning in the group is possible but difficult and often it takes time away from the treatment process. The therapist must become so skilled that doing treatment with video as an adjunct becomes as second nature as driving a car. I strongly discourage use of technicians in the operation and application of video in treatment. The technician prevents the therapist from learning how to integrate video into his approach; good video pictures may result, but they are of little or no use to the therapist in the process of doing therapy.

I urge people who use video to buy the simplest equipment and play with it before they use it in treatment. I also urge that they become comfortable with their own video image before they begin using the equipment in the group. At this point a good supervisor can aid the therapist in learning about himself. Most therapists when first seeing themselves in therapy become aware of much heavy Critical Parent material in their heads about their appearance, their behavior, and their work. This inevitably takes working through before effective use can be made of the equipment. This process is important for it allows the therapist to learn how to work through problems that are very similar to what the patient will be working on later when video is used in the group. If this is not done, the therapist will find himself unwilling to use video equipment and will discount its usefulness in the treatment process. It is important to inform the group of your intention to use video in treatment and allow them some time to become accustomed to the equipment. Video units currently available are relatively foolproof, simple to operate, highly stable, and, with the exception of the monitor, small in size. Cost of videotape and the basic cost of equipment are also much less than the average buyer might think. I will be presenting a wide range of applications and methods which are specific to transactional analysis and video in a book I am now writing.

The areas I will discuss here are recognition of ego states, contract work, permission, and game analysis. I anticipate that the reader will have some basic familiarity with transactional concepts and the imagination to picture the physical setup that faces the new patient. Since the patient has seen me briefly in an intake session, he already has some basic awareness of the physical setting and the equipment.

When a new member enters my group room he is confronted with ample chairs, a large video monitor, a camera, and microphones. He is given ample opportunity to ask questions, to see himself on the monitor, and to explore with me whatever feelings he has about the video image. Very early in the group experience he will see me working with other individuals and will see the work involved in teaching ego states. I believe that it is much easier for individuals to learn to recognize Parent, Adult, and Child ego states from video than from any other modality. I can stop and replay, still-frame, and replay segments of behavior showing facial expressions, sound segments capturing the tone and quality of voice that accompany the expression, and ample evidence to describe a particular ego state. The frown of the Parent, no matter how fleeting, is recapturable and replayable. The amount of showing and replaying, however, is strictly dependent on the individual who is on the screen and if and how he wants to use the data. Although all of the work I do is videotaped, the segments that are replayed are at the choice of the individual who is working. Since I use a single-hour videotape reel, over and over, there is no storage or retaining of any material that is taped in the group. If I find a particular piece of data on the tape that might be useful, I ask the person to consider whether or not he wants the data input. If he elects to see what is on the video tape, he has control over how much and when. When he sees himself on the screen he can become familiar with his own image and incorporate data about his appearance which has not been available to him previously.

The limitation is that if he has little Adult ego state available, there will be little input of data. I monitor the patient's ability to use the information and will not give feedback when he is obviously into bad feelings. Even then, however, video input may enable him to cathect his Adult ego state and observe himself with some effectiveness. When he sees himself he begins to recognize that the messages he gives with his face often are incongruent with what he says or what he is doing. He also learns to recognize his body position, his posture, and his movement as useful data about himself. In particular, when he is talking about himself, he can see the same image that others see and be more aware of their responses to him. Contaminations of ego states become apparent to him when he sees himself talking about painful or difficult material with a smile on his face. He can see and hear the prejudicial statements he makes and be aware that what he has considered to be Adult data has a definite Parent flavor. In the process of seeing himself he also becomes aware of the potential for modifying his presentation of himself to others in a way that is his choice and the result of life history.

I find video replay a vital part of contract work and very useful to the patient. I tape and replay the segment of contract work that contains the clearest statement of the contract. I then ask him, if he chooses to, to evaluate the validity and workability of the contract. With this material the patient is often able to change the contract so that it is what he wants and does not contain the Adapted Child loopholes which are often a part of early contract work. I ask him to check with other group members for their feedback about the contract. It becomes clear to the patient that some contract work is really not of Adult choosing but is heavily Parent-dominated, and that he can modify his work to protect himself and get what he wants. He may find that there are elements he might want to salvage from the contract which are in keeping with his Adult choice. The video image captures many of the discounts that invalidate the contract. The wink, the negative nod of the head, the head tilt, and the shrug are only a few of the ways in which people invalidate their choices to protect themselves. I may, if I believe the person to be particularly rebellious at the time, ask him to make a contract for the now and to make no further contracts for the session. A replay of this sort of contract will make clear where the person is in terms of ego states and what he is likely to do in that session. When the contract is made and if it seems to be a good one, I find that replay will give valuable Adult ego state support for the contract statement and clarification. It is usually potent support, because the patient gets to look himself in the eye as he makes the contract and to see and hear the contract statement from himself in replay. Each of the six types of contracts mentioned earlier is important to review on video. I find that video is of interesting use to the patient because he sees his own face larger than life; I zoom in when he is talking and his face fills the large monitor. He gets to see and watch carefully the qualities and motility of his face in a way never before possible. If he is operating from his Adult when he is doing this, he often gains important information that only he would find useful. He may note similarity between his expression, tone, or emphasis and that of a parent or grandparent. This data may further enable him to modify and clarify the kind of contract work he chooses to complete. Often the patient discovers the Parent contamination in the contract by what he sees and hears. He may also discover the social contract he is choosing rather than the personal change contract which is what he wants. If there are discounts in the contract statement, he is able to hear them and make the changes that he wants.

Permission work with video is often much fun because the permission is replayable and restateable in a way which the patient chooses. He has ample opportunity to give permission to the image on the screen and then hear the permission replayed. He now can also recognize whether or not he is accepting the permission. In permission work, as with other video work, the face seems to have primary importance. I find, however, that by slowly zooming in and out I can find other body data which is congruent or incongruent with the patient's words. When I see hands, legs, body position, or body movement which does not go with the permission, I give the person the option of viewing the behavior and processing the data. Revealed by the inconsistencies of the person's appearance are germs of impasses or contaminations of which he is unaware. I want to emphasize that the therapist who uses video is not in the position of knowing what body language means. Each of us comes from a different family, a different region, and a different culture and much of body language is highly individual. Body language belongs to the person and is not to be used against him; he has the choice of using or not using the information. The popular books on body language are dreadfully astray and serve to amuse readers but certainly not to inform them. In permission work, the patient decides the meaning of his body language and has the option to adjust and modify the permission he gives himself in his own unique way. I have found that video replay also adds, by its very nature, reinforcement and protection to the permission. The individual can often use his own Parent to give the permission and the hearing of that permission in replay is powerful support. Several replays of such information are useful to the patient and to other group members who can see the value of this treatment operation.

Game analysis with video in group treatment is infrequent, because the incidence of games in the group is very low and because analysis of a game is time-consuming. I analyze a game when it is clear that a game has been played and when I can use both the blackboard for game moves and videotape replay for selecting segments to demonstrate each move of the game. Since many of the games that occur involve me, I use a second camera to record my behavior and use a split screen for recording both images. I do not knowingly play games in my treatment groups and often the only portions I have available are the con and gimmick sections. These help the patient in learning to avoid games.

When I have a married couple in a treatment group, I usually arrange two cameras so that I can record any games that might occur. They are more likely to play games than other members in the group, and I then can replay the game as a part of either person's contract and give clear, precise information for game analysis. I find game analysis particularly useful for couples and urge them to evaluate the games that have evolved as an important segment of their lives. Many times a single game evaluation stops the game but leaves them with little to say to each other. A useful operation at this point is to explore their stroking of each other in ways that are straight and positive.

Game analysis with video demonstrates how the game is used to get into the bad feeling racket of the person through negative strokes. He can watch his face, note his game moves, see ego-state shifts, and see the emergence of the racket. Thus, he often discovers information that he can use to avoid the game and get the kind of strokes he wants in another way. He also sees in the games old family patterns and messages which he may not have been aware of before. I caution people that when they look at their games to view themselves with their Adult ego state. If they are in a Parent ego state, they may become highly critical of themselves and use the data to feel bad. I find that game analysis with video has echo effects and that over a several-day period the patient will recall and replay in his own head the material he saw on the video tape. I stress the need to give himself permission to be the way he is until he chooses to make a contract for change. To give the patient protection, I often suggest that he view limited segments of the game at one time and give himself permission to recognize his behavior without harassing himself about it.

Whether the patient does script work, redecision, or game analysis, I am cautious as to how much and what the person wants to see and use. Showing video images can be heavily gamey if the patient does not have a clear contract for work and for the use of the video content. Confrontation with video images is valuable but it also can be destructive; it can hurt, frighten, and anger unnecessarily. Much depends on the therapist's skill, wisdom, and tact as to how useful and effective video work can be. I find it an important tool when I use transactional analysis in a group.

CURRENT BASIC TREATMENT ASSUMPTIONS

As a result of my training and work in transactional analysis and my experience with it as a treatment modality, I have changed much of my basic orientation to helping people; I am pleased by the changes, as are the people I work with. For much of my professional life I have worked as a psychologist following what some people describe as a medical model. However, I find that I no longer support or believe the assumptions of that model and have replaced it with a model which is more congruent with a psychological or humanistic social model. The assumptions I now make differ in both degree and substance and only coincidentally parallel the assumptions of the medical model. My current treatment assumptions are based on these basic notions:

1. The individual manifesting problems is reacting to a self-created internal psychological environment that is a result of time and experience.
2. The manifestations of his difficulty are observable, describable, and modifiable to the degree the person is aware and chooses.
3. All of his behavior is contextual and had adaptive and protective service in the past and has adaptive value in the present.
4. Early emotional and learning experiences in the past form the basis for current difficulties.
5. Treatment is based on basic learning and emotional experiences that are within the capacity of all individuals.
6. All individuals have within them the capacity to change and be aware to the degree that they choose.
7. All psychological difficulties have their origins in a personal and social setting and changes must occur in the same context to enable the individual full range of choices for growth.

With these basic assumptions, my stance as a therapist is no longer disease-oriented or dependent on a position of responsibility for patients. I am now responsible for myself as a therapist and responsible to the people I help to give them the services they desire to the best of my ability. People who come to me for help are capable of making choices and decisions for themselves, and as a therapist I must offer my skills, knowledge, and assistance to them in a fair, responsible, and reasonable manner. My choices, decisions, responsibilities, and methods are not those of a medical practitioner nor are they based on the medical model. I respect and appreciate the physician's role and practice, and I refer people to him because many people that I see are not skilled or even careful in taking care of their physical selves. At the same time, the difficulties that people come for help with are not totally physical or totally psychological. When people seek my help I carefully inform them that I have no skills or expertise in any form of medical knowledge or care, and that they must be aware that I am capable of helping them solve and resolve their emotional, learning, and psychological difficulties. I urge them to consult a physician on a regular basis and from him I learn of any possible organic bases for their problems.

CHOOSING THE PATIENT AND VICE VERSA

Before seeing anyone in treatment I do a 15-minute intake during which I establish for myself whether or not I have services to offer the client, whether he or she sees value in the services I offer, and whether or not I want to treat the person. I arrive at a basic script formulation of the patient in the first five minutes on the basis of his primary rackets. I then enter into contract bargaining to determine what he wants to be cured of, whether what he wants is in my area of expertise, and whether it is possible. I make my decisions within the first ten minutes and then use the balance of the time to orient him to group treatment and to the group he will be entering, and to answer whatever questions he may have. I also give him a biographical inventory to complete and bring back. This inventory will give me basic background information on him and more than enough history. I negotiate with him on the fee, since I use a sliding scale of fees and the negotiation is an important part in his taking care of himself. From this session I arrive at what he wants to be cured of as I hear it, and I check with him as to the validity of what I perceive. If we cannot arrive at a general treatment contract, I suggest that he see someone else or spend some time considering what I have said and see if it is possible for him to decide what it is that he wants from me.

During the intake process I inform prospective patients that I am a group therapist and believe that this treatment modality is superior to individual methods. The patient has the option of choosing to work with me in group treatment or to find another therapist. I usually do not make referrals to other therapists, because I believe that the client is quite capable of finding someone on his own who is compatible with himself and his views. My choice of doing group treatment exclusively is based on a series of conclusions that group treatment is more rapid, potent, comprehensive, and satisfying to patients than individual approaches. Also during the intake process I inform the patient as to time of group treatment sessions. I practice in the late afternoon and evening because most of the people I work with are employed during the day. I believe that I am obligated to people who come to me to make the process and experience as easy and as feasible as possible. There are enough obstacles, both reasonable and irrational, for people not to get psychological help, and I do as much realistic accommodation as I can with time arrangements and sliding-scale fees.

All of my group sessions meet three times per month and allow an interlude of a week or two between monthly sessions for people to consolidate their treatment process and gain some distance from the treatment situation. I believe that the treatment process can be very seductive and enticing for people to be at ease, feel good, and change, but it is not a situation to make a permanent part of one's life. I want people to be in treatment for as brief a period as possible, and I believe that the week or two interval gives the person an opportunity to decide whether he is getting what he wants, whether he has completed treatment, and how well he is functioning with the changes he is making in himself. If the client makes the decision for treatment with me, I immediately begin work on closing all escape hatches and focus on decontamination and change. This might occur in the intake session or might take a session or two in the group.

An important factor not mentioned thus far is that I believe that my charisma as a therapist is an important factor in treatment. This means that I give care to my appearance, my office décor, my approach to patients, and the treatment methods I use. These are all valuable ways of creating charisma.[16] My behavior as a social creature in my area and community is an important factor in how my patients and prospective patients see me, and I give careful thought to newspaper articles about me, television appearances, and other ways I may or may not convey the kind of appearance I want to give as a therapist.

ADVANTAGES OF TA IN TREATMENT

As a result of my working and training as a transactional therapist I view many of the problems of my community and society as issues in treatment. I am convinced that many of the people I work with have difficult life script problems with money, and I work with them toward a change in what I think of as their "poverty scripts." I have developed a series of treatment tactics and notions as to how people develop problems with money and how they might change and have the kind of economic well-being they choose. I also find that many young people have developed "stupid scripts," or life choices which prevent them from reading, learning, and training or educating themselves in a way that is to their greatest life advantage. Again, I have developed a number of treatment tactics directed toward helping people learn in a manner compatible with their life choices. I like to work with old people because I find them so ready for change and so capable and effective in making the kind of life changes they want. I particularly like to help people cure themselves of retirement. Retirement is a particularly malevolent social and personal process which encourages people to give up, become bored, cease work, distance themselves, and die. In the area of psychosomatic difficulties, I believe the treatment I now do with such patients is far superior to any I have done in the past because it allows the patient a greater range of responsibility for himself and it gives the physician who is treating him a sense of being a real part of the treatment process. The patient does not experience himself as being discounted for the physical process and can claim real awareness of how he is a part of the physical difficulty. The sense of being in control of his body and being able to care for it is an important change.

I believe that there are a number of basic advantages to the use of transactional analysis in treatment that I recognize and that my patients recognize. I realize that arguments can be raised about the relative merits of each of the advantages, and until there is hard evidence through research such as that of Lieberman et al.[17] I will continue to work within this treatment approach.

I will mention briefly the ten advantages that I find mentioned by clients and experienced by myself in the use of transactional treatment.

1. The patient experiences a rapid cessation of difficulties or distress, often within days or weeks. I am convinced that the approach is the most rapid treatment of recent devising.

2. As a result of rapidity, the cost to the patient is markedly less.

3. Patients can be gainfully employed, come to me after their work hours, and not carry a psychiatric diagnosis. The social stigma is not necessary from a transactional viewpoint.

4. The length of treatment is decidedly less than in other forms of treatment. Average stay in my groups is about nine months.

5. Patients find transactional analytic groups a positive, informative, and pleasant experience.

6. The patient recognizes his role as an active and knowledgeable participant in the change process. He knows what is happening in his treatment and how.

7. The patient likes the responsibility that he has for changing or not changing. He claims the potency of the work he does in treatment and recognizes how fully he is responsible for his change.

8. The patient finds the learning and developing of caring relationships a particular advantage of transactional treatment.

9. The patient finds the "no blame" quality of transactional analysis a positive view to adopt about his family and his social life.

10. The patient finds that his therapy not only helps him to make the changes in his life that he has wanted, but it gives him cognitive skills to integrate with his awareness of his working situation, his family, his community, and his country. His therapy gives him useful skills in raising his children, relating to his wife, working with his boss, being politically active, and enhancing his life in ways he may not have thought of before.

The advantages for the therapist of a transactional approach are those that I have recognized for myself and for others as they have talked about their experiences as therapists. As a teacher of transactional analysis, I have many therapists who make the transition to TA as an integration of a wide variety of previous training and learning experiences. I am not an advocate of the "true believer" position for transactional analysis or any other form of therapy. I want therapists in training to be growing people who are willing to use what works for them, and to add to and integrate all of the skills they already have. I do not want them to throw away any useful technique. The advantages that I find for using transactional analysis as a core conceptual system are related to both practical and conceptual issues. Gradually, research will provide the answers.

1. The transactional treatment approach will enable the therapist to make an early decision as to whether the patient wants to change. People who are looking for new experiences or new friends, for proof that they are helpless or a place to dump their woes will not last long in this kind of treatment group.

2. The therapist will be free of the responsibility for clients. Night calls, weekend calls, emergencies, and crises take on a new perspective in the treatment process, and the transactional therapist now can order his life in a way that benefits him and the people he chooses to treat. I have not had night or weekend calls from patients in about three years now. I have yet to have a client who believed that I was either uncaring or indifferent because of my not being available at all times. I do realize

that I am very selective about whom I treat. I realize that many of those people who might have had night and weekend emergencies had the wisdom to select a therapist who needed them.

3. I find that the doing of transactional treatment is a pleasurable experience for me. I like the potency that I experience in myself, the fun I have in doing good therapy, the fun I have in playing with the people in my groups, and the joy in watching change in those people. I further enjoy the freedom I have at night, on weekends, and on vacation, knowing that the people I work with are taking care of themselves.

4. I find a real advantage in watching people change and grow rapidly. I can validate quickly new treatment methods, new ideas, and new approaches in a way not possible before. Each person becomes a new challenge for me because I can recognize his power to change and find ways to enable him to use that power for his own gain.

5. There is a real sense of accomplishment for me in therapy which I did did not have before I acquired transactional approaches. People come for help, they change and leave with what they wanted. Patients no longer "make progress." They change.

7. I find the most important advantage to me has been my own sense of awareness and change, my need to change, and my sense of growing. I experience people who use this approach as committed to continued change and growth for excitement, fun, involvement, and caring.

The liabilities or shortcomings of transactional approaches to treatment are those in common with any treatment methodology of the past or present. I do believe that the people in this field have been mindful of those shortcomings and have developed measures or adjustments to correct the problems. I will enumerate the problems I see and suggest possible options to be considered.

From early in its development transactional analysis was a popular notion and got television, newspaper, and press coverage. This popularization has led to a number of misconceptions by professional people and laymen alike. Many naive professionals believe that they can do transactional analysis from reading Berne's writings or from brief treatment experiences. The truth is that solid supervision and training are prerequisites for using any new or innovative technique. Some laymen believe that they can read themselves into psychological health.

Transactional analysts from the beginning recognized the need for careful evaluation of trainers and trainees and began the most comprehensive series of training standards and evaluations of any treatment approach. Membership levels were and are contingent upon the therapist's demonstration before peers of her or his ability and competence to do treatment in a manner equal to established standards. This field of treatment has been consistently committed to upgrading standards by giving attention to quality of treatment, focusing on ethical standards, maintaining and reevaluating goals for professionals in training, and providing social bases for the careful evaluation of new and better treatment capabilities.

Research bases for transactional analysis have been broad and thorough and yet have lagged behind the rapid growth of the treatment approach. Unfortunately the base for research in this country has evolved into a politically oriented structure where sources of money are tied to governmental strictures; funding for innovative studies is nil. In particular, issues of privacy, confidentiality, and subject protection are so ominous that only the most naive researcher would dare venture into this forbidding territory by asking people what they think, feel, believe, or want. However, research in transactional analysis is nevertheless moving on rapidly. Although much of it will be available only through professional workshops and meetings, it is available to the interested and searching practitioner.

References

1. David Mendell, "The Southwest Regional—A Community of Therapists," *Group Process, 6* (1974), 5–20.
2. John Gladfelter, "The Liabilities of Individual Psychotherapy," *Group Process, 6* (1974), 5–20.
3. Eric Berne, *Transactional Analysis in Psychotherapy,* New York, Grove Press, 1961; Eric Berne, *Games People Play,* New York, Grove Press, 1964.
4. Eric Berne, *Principles of Group Treatment,* New York, Oxford University Press, 1966; Eric Berne, *Sex in Human Loving,* New York, Simon & Schuster, 1970; Eric Berne, *What Do You Say After You Say Hello?,* New York, Grove Press, 1972.
5. Robert Goulding, "New Directions in Transactional Analysis: Creating an Environment for Redecision and Change," in Clifford J. Sanger and Helen Singer Kaplan, eds., *Progress in Group and Family Therapy,* New York, Brunner/Mazel, 1972.
6. Robert Goulding, "Thinking and Feeling in Psychotherapy: Three Impasses," *Voices, 10,* no. 1 (1974), 11–13.
7. Robert Goulding, "Curing Phobias," *Voices, 11,* no. 1 (1975), 30–31.
8. Claude Steiner, *Games Alcoholics Play,* New York, Grove Press, 1971.
9. Jacqui Lee Schiff et al., *The Cathexis Reader,* New York, Harper & Row, 1975.
10. William Holloway and Martha Holloway, *The Monograph Series,* Medina, Ohio, Midwest Institute, 1973.
11. William Holloway and Martha Holloway, *Change Now!,* Medina, Ohio, Midwest Institute, 1973.
12. Jean Piaget, *The Origins of Intelligence in Children,* New York, W. W. Norton & Company, 1963.
13. Claude Steiner, *Scripts People Live,* New York, Grove Press, 1974.
14. Harry Boyd, "Strokes and Risks," *Transactional Analysis Journal, 3,* no. 2 (April 1973), p. 16.
15. Taibi Kahler with Hedges Capers, "The Miniscript," *Transactional Analysis Journal, 4,* no. 1 (January 1974).
16. John Gladfelter, "The Unchangeable Core vs. Charisma," *Voices, 10,* no. 4 (1975), pp. 68–69.
17. Morton A. Lieberman, Irvin D. Yalom, and Matthew B. Miles, *Encounter Groups: First Facts,* New York, Basic Books, 1973.

NINETEEN
THE SEVEN COMPONENTS
OF REDECISION THERAPY
John R. McNeel

For the two years of 1974 and 1975 this author researched one weekend workshop marathon done by Robert Goulding, MD, and Mary Goulding, MSW, of the Western Institute for Group and Family Therapy in order to determine if people changed as a result of that event. The treatment modality for this workshop was a combination of transactional analysis and gestalt therapy with an emphasis placed on making redecisions. The evidence that the group of 15 people attending this workshop changed was substantial from the statistical measures used. The measures that were used in this study were the Personal Orientation Inventory (POI) which contains 12 subscales, and the Personal Growth Checklist (PGC) which contains 5 subscales. The POI is an instrument developed by Shostrom in 1964 which purports to measure self-actualization. The PGC is an instrument which was developed by the researcher in 1974 for this study and purports to measure behavior change. These measures were administered just prior to the workshop and three months following the workshop. The group as a whole showed change exceeding the .05 level of significance on 10 of the 12 subscales of the POI (exceeding the .01 level on 7 of these). The group as a whole subjectively experienced change in their own behavior as indicated by exceeding the .05 level of significance on all 5 scales of the PGC (exceeding the .01 level on two of these). These findings are also substantiated from interviews administered to each participant before and after the workshop. During the post-interview participants were able to talk specifically of changes made as a result of specific pieces of work done during the workshop.

The above facts indicate that this three-day workshop was instrumental in helping these people change substantially. In order to gain more specific knowledge about what actually helped these people to change, the author included in the original research a complete transcript of the workshop. Each piece of work in the workshop was identified as to type. There were three basic types of work done during the weekend. These were identified as: (1) contract work; (2) impasse clarification work; and (3) redecision work. There were also some pieces of work during the workshop which were unidentified as to type. The types of work done were obtained by using six independent raters who watched the entire weekend. The raters judged each piece of work done by the participants as being one of the above three types. By the end of the weekend there had been 86 pieces of work identified. Twenty-one of these were seen as contract work, 25 of these were seen as impasse clarification work, and 31 of these were seen as being redecision work. Nine pieces of work were undetermined as to type.

Because this writer is deeply interested in what brings about change, he began to study the transcript from the point of view of seeing if he could discover what were consistently repeated patterns carried out during the workshop. From this intensive study of the transcript he discovered 43 specific techniques or types of interventions (hereafter referred to as "elements") which were used throughout the workshop. Working with an assistant, he divided these into seven components: (1) Emphasis on personal power and responsibility; (2) Fostering a nurturing environment; (3) Leaders' modeling behavior; (4) Separating myth from reality; (5) Confrontation of incongruity; (6) Particular techniques; (7) Procedural rules. Taken together, these seven categories can be seen as what is done in redecision therapy, and in this case very effective redecision therapy.

Below, each of these components will be discussed, including the elements that make up each one. In the original text of the research the reader is referred to specific pages where he can find examples of the various elements in order to see how these concepts are employed in the actual process of therapy. For the benefit of readers of this [chapter] the writer will include one example from the text following each element. The seven components can be seen as *what* is valuable in this type of therapeutic experience and the elements that make up each category can be seen as the *how* to create each one of these components.

EMPHASIS ON PERSONAL POWER AND RESPONSIBILITY

The issues of personal power and responsibility are central to the idea of redecision therapy. The Gouldings operate from the simple yet profound assumption that each individual is responsible for his life and is in possession of adequate power to carry out that responsibility. Personal power and responsibility are often subtly denied and it is the task of the therapist to help the client be aware of that fact and claim his power.

RESPONSIBILITY   Outside of his awareness, a client will often describe himself as being the victim of events or circumstances. In this presentation he will often disclaim any active responsibility for having participated in his own dilemma. This attitude towards one's existence is often communicated in very subtle ways, such as using passive rather than active verbs. The Gouldings counter this by consistently asking people to claim responsibility for their existence and their behavior.

> *Tom:* I really have to think about the other times that . . . it did happen this time.
> *Mary:* OK. So will you be aware that a piece of you picked her, that she didn't just fall through the skylight in your apartment? (*Laughs.*)
> *Bob:* You've got part of you that says, "It happened," see.
> *Tom:* Did I say, "It happened"?
> *Bob and Mary:* Yes, yes.

OWNERSHIP OF POWER In order to change, one must know he has the power to change. During the workshop people often referred to their accomplishments as if they had just happened. In those situations, the Gouldings asked people to claim the power that was involved in accomplishing their goals.

> *Gwen:* I've had a lot of awareness through the past three or four years. And I'm astounded at how everything is being pulled together. Um, last night and this morning, what's going on.
> *Bob:* You pulled things together?
> *Gwen:* Pardon?
> *Bob:* How you pulled things together?
> *Gwen:* Yeah, I'm really pulling them together.

CONFRONTING "YOU MAKE ME FEEL" A common ploy to deny responsibility for experience is the use of the statement "You make me feel." The content of this statement implies that one human being controls the experience of another human being. In confronting this statement, the Gouldings invite their clients to be aware of the power they have to direct their own lives and control their own feelings.

> *Christine:* In our small group, um, I was telling them that, um, I'm avoiding working and—I'm not sure why I'm feeling so strongly (*faint voice*), but, uh, and I said that it wasn't all my fault that Gene doesn't share with me really made me feel different.
> *Mary:* You make me feel different? (*softly*).
> *Christine:* Yeah. . . .

OWNING PROJECTIONS The Gouldings often invite people to own their own beauty or strength by inviting them to personalize a pleasant remark which was made referring to something outside of them. An example of this would be changing the statement "This is a beautiful day" to "I am beautiful." Throughout the transcript the Gouldings constantly looked for ways in which people could feel good about themselves and their existence.

> *Sherri:* Yeah. Those are really nice.
> *Bob:* Yes, you are.
> *Sherri:* Yeah. I really am!

USE OF THE PRESENT TENSE   It is not uncommon for a client to deny his experience by removing himself from the present. This is done by ruminating about the past or making up intentions about the future. To counter this the Gouldings invited participants to experience both past scenes and future scenes in the present, as if they are taking place in the here-and-now. This helps people to experience more power over their lives and to see the availability of options.

> *Bob:* OK. Go on with that.
> *Janie:* I'm going to be . . .
> *Bob:* Put it in the present tense.
> *Janie:* OK.
> *Bob:* I am great.
> *Janie:* I am great.
> *Bob:* Say it again.
> *Janie:* I am great.
> *Bob:* What do you experience?
> *Janie:* (*Laughs.*) Sure. I am great.

SPEAK UP   A common way to deny power is to speak so softly that no one can hear. To counter this, the Gouldings encourage people to speak loudly enough to be heard by everyone in the room.

> *Mary:* I'm available.
> *Steve:* I woke up this morning feeling all warm and fuzzy.
> *Mary:* (*shouting*) My guess is nobody but you and me are going to hear you!

CAREFUL USE OF "WILL YOU?"   Being interested in the use of personal power, the therapists were careful throughout the workshop to ask questions in such a way that the client responded in a powerful manner, i.e., "I will" or "I won't." Being interested in powerful responses, they were careful to precede questions concerning action on the part of the client with clear, precise, unambiguous phrases such as "Will you?"

> *Mary:* Will you come here and answer that?
> *Sharon:* (*Moving to empty chair.*) I don't know.
> *Mary:* Make it up. I'll bet you do know.
> *Sharon:* (*Pauses.*) I have to speak as my mother?
> *Mary:* Yes. Will you be mother?
> *Bob:* We're asking if you're willing to.

WORD CONFRONTATION/WORD CHANGE   One of the most used techniques throughout the workshop was that of word confrontation and word change. This can be seen in two ways. Often the therapists will change the wording of the questions they are asking the client in such a way as to reinforce the client's feeling responsible for himself. At other times, the therapists will confront the client when he uses words which surrender power. Some specific types of word confrontations are discussed below.

Often a client will say "can't" and sound powerless, rather than using the more accurate "won't" and sound powerful and be aware of his power. Therefore, clients are often invited to change their "can'ts to won'ts."

> *Christine:* I clicked. Last time I was at the marathon, Coyote, I had that hunger for the mother love that I never can go back and get. You know my mother can't show love. And . . .
> *Mary:* I didn't know.
> *Bob:* Won't.
> *Christine:* Won't. Well, yeah.

A common displacement of power is to give an outside source credit for one's experience. An example of this is the statement "It makes me feel good," rather than the existentially more accurate "I make me feel good." Throughout the transcript the Gouldings consistently asked people to own their responsibility in either making a mess of their lives or making heaven of their lives by substituting "I" for "it."

> *Christine:* Because . . . and I, you asked me at that time what I wanted to do about it and I realized that I couldn't get it from her and I said, "Well, I'll get it from Gene." And do you remember I went over and I crawled in his lap? And I got love from him. I came here today and I . . . he's getting tired of that, that needing, me needing him so desperately, and I came here and I'm just going to love myself instead. (*Crying.*) It's really neat.
> *Mary:* Yeah. Would you be willing to substitue "I" for "it" and see how you go with that?
> *Christine:* Yeah. I'm really neat to figure that out.

The word "try" often implies a refusal to complete an act. This is particularly true in the area of psychotherapeutic contract. In confronting the word "try," the therapist will invite the client either to agree to complete the proposed project or to state clearly his refusal to do so. To draw attention to this concept, Dr. Goulding rang a large cow bell each time someone used the word "try" in a way that denied power.

> *Martha:* I'm just trying to . . .
> *Mary:* Do you know about trying?
> *Bob:* Did she say try? (*Rings cow bell.*)
> *Martha:* Is that your try bell?
> *Bob:* That's my try bell. (*Laughs.*)
> *Mary:* Like think of the difference between trying to throw and throwing. Or trying to shit and shitting.
> (*All laugh.*)
> *Bob:* (*To Mary*) You are delightful.

In the POI, the synergy subscale measures one's ability to see the opposites of life as equal. This value is reflected in the transcript when the Gouldings invited people to change their "buts" to "ands." Even though this is not directly related to the issue of power and responsibility, it is included here with the other word changes. This technique invites people to deal realistically with themselves and the world by inviting them to see that two conflicting situations can exist at once, such as hate and love.

> *Chrissie:* I think I'm going to make some difference because I'm learning to stroke myself. I'm going to make differences in my life. But I have a couple more minor things that I want to work on.
>
> *Bob:* Will you say "and" instead of "but"?
>
> *Chrissie:* Did I say "but"?
>
> *Bob:* Uhhuh.
>
> *Chrissie:* And I have a couple more minor things that I'd like to work on either tonight or tomorrow.
>
> *Bob:* Does that feel different to you when you say "and" instead of "but"?
>
> *Chrissie:* Yes, uhhuh.
>
> *Bob:* What's the difference?
>
> *Chrissie:* Well, "and" means I still accept myself, it's OK to keep stroking myself and still have something to work on.

FOSTERING A NUTURING ENVIRONMENT

The Gouldings put emphasis on the importance of creating an environment in which people can change. They create the necessary therapeutic climate by encouraging a nonjudgmental, nurturing environment. By stroking good feelings and encouraging fun and pleasure, they create an environment in which people feel secure enough to risk feelings and experiences ordinarily denied. This quality of trust was seen in the large number of times people allowed themselves to experience deep emotion in the group setting. It is important to note that the participants shared these experiences not only with the rest of the group, but also with some 25 observers who were watching the workshop.

STROKING STRENGTH AND HEALTH Throughout the workshop, the Gouldings emphasized that they were more interested in people being healthy than in being sick. They demonstrated this by taking every opportunity to congratulate the participants for new behaviors and new feelings which demonstrated health to them.

> *Bob:* What are you doing with your left hand?
>
> *Chrissie:* What are you talking about?
>
> *Bob:* What are you doing with your left hand?
>
> *Chrissie:* Stroking me.
>
> *Bob:* Yeah.

ON THE SIDE OF THE "CHILD" The Gouldings quickly establish themselves as allies with their clients. This alliance is created by statements and actions on their part which tell the client that he will not be judged by them. This nonjudgmental alliance is fostered by demonstrations of caring and by indignation at past injustices done to the client when he was a child. In such a way, the Gouldings establish themselves as firmly being on the side of the "child" inside the client.

> *Mary:* Any reason for treating a child with such cruelty is not obvious.
> *Ralph:* I did it, and to this day . . .
> *Bob:* Did you hear what Mary said?
> *Ralph:* No.
> *Mary:* I said, "The reason for treating a child with such cruelty is not obvious." I hear that you're down on yourself because you accepted their really sadistic evaluations. Of course, little kids wet the bed when they're in a strange house. And other times. So the first order of priority for you is to start being nice to you.
> *Bob:* Somebody needs to be.
> *Ralph:* This is true.
> *Bob:* If you aren't, who's gonna?

STROKE-RESTROKE   Often people who are not used to hearing compliments or nice things said to them will not respond when offered a compliment. In order to ensure that people hear positive evaluations and absorb them, the Gouldings will often repeat a positive stroke to ensure that the person has heard.

> *Bob:* I'd like you to be aware that you're a very sharp guy, in or out of the doctor's office.
> *Ralph:* Well, the thought occurred to me then that . . .
> *Bob:* Believe me?
> *Ralph:* Yeah. Yeah.

USE OF HUMOR   Throughout the workshop an atmosphere of nurturing was encouraged by the use of humor. By their own enjoyment of life, the therapists encouraged the participants to enjoy themselves also.

> *Mary:* What's your smile saying?
> *Sam:* I'm just admiring you.
> *Mary:* Thank you. That's not a "just"! (*Laughs.*)

NOT LAUGHING   Caring is also communicated by not laughing at things which are not funny for the person involved. Outside of his awareness, a client will often laugh and encourage others to laugh about things which are tragic for him. The Gouldings refuse to laugh at gallows humor and encourage the participants to refuse also.

> *Bob:* You discount a little bit. I said, "You're amazing," and you said, "I amaze myself." Are you willing to say you're amazing?
> *Steve:* I'm amazing.
> *Bob:* Yeah. What do you experience with that?

Steve: OK. Now the last time I was here . . .
(*Loud laughs.*)
Mary: I'm not going to laugh. I hear you getting a lot of strokes for continuing to discount yourself a little bit.
Steve: I wasn't aware of that.

SELF-HARASSMENT TO SEX FANTASY This is a delightful technique in which the Gouldings invite participants to replace self-harassment with a pleasurable sex fantasy. This is a particularly effective exercise for an obsessive, compulsive person who can always manage to find one more thing to feel bad about.

Christine: When things are going good, I find things to feel badly about.
Mary: What do you want to do? When you start yourself thinking about victims, do you want to stay with thinking about victims or do you want to think about something else?
Christine: (*Pauses.*)
Bob: Right now, close your eyes and have a sexual fantasy.
(*Laughs.*)

LEADERS' MODELING BEHAVIOR

By their actions as well as their words, the therapists communicate the values that they hold. In turn, their behavior deeply influences the nature and tone of the workshop.

PATTERNING Throughout the workshop, the Gouldings present themselves as aggressively healthy. As much as anything else they do, this is a therapeutic intervention. By vigorously demonstrating excitement about life they create an environment of permission.

Sherri: And I feel really good. And . . . (*still crying.*)
Bob: Anything else you want to tell her?
Sherri: (*Pause-cries.*) I guess, I guess it's OK. It's really OK if I feel like this.
Mary: Guess?
Sherri: I know it is.
Bob: Well, if not, I'm the world's biggest sinner! (*Laughs.*)

TRACKING The climate of professional competence is greatly enhanced by the frequent evidence that the Gouldings "track" with one another at a high degree of regularity. Evidence of this ability to track with one another is seen in the number of times that they say virtually the same statement at the same time to a client.

Mary: Meaning he had sex play with you?
Janie: Yes. My original father.
Bob: How did you know that?
Janie: I remember.
Bob: Do you really?

Janie: Yes, I do. It's a little bit fuzzy, but I can remember some things. And my greatest feeling was to see . . . all I ever heard from my mother was the bad things that had happened to me and the bad type of person he was, and when I was 20 . . .

Mary and Bob: That's how come you still remember.

QUESTION-REQUESTION   A frequent issue in therapy is that of self-importance. Throughout the transcript the leaders modeled their own high regard for their own importance. One way in which they do this is to refuse to be discounted. This refusal can be seen when they re-ask a question that the client has not answered.

Bob: Will you say to father, "I cried enough"?
Janie: Dad, I don't like myself this way and I'm not going to be this way.
Bob: That's not what I asked you to say. I asked you to say to him, "I've cried enough." Start with that.

SEPARATING MYTH FROM REALITY

Many people carry with them a mythical view of reality in which they misperceive facts. In the setting of psychotherapy, most myths take the form of beliefs about being responsible for the experience of someone else. People who experience the world as they did when they were five years old are not seeing reality. Throughout the weekend, the Gouldings helped people to see how they had misperceived themselves or the world by relying on information gathered in childhood.

SEPARATENESS   Important for any client is the understanding that he is separate from other people. Some people grow up feeling responsible for their parents' experience as if there is some umbilical cord attaching them together. Believing this, the client then behaves in such a way that he believes will keep the other person from feeling bad. The issue of separateness is also important in those instances where one person feels he will die if denied access to another person. Throughout the weekend the Gouldings encouraged people to see themselves as separate and self-sufficient.

Sharon: I think I have more guilt from later years as far as making my mother unhappy about my weight. Now, mind you, I was never more than 10 to 15 pounds overweight . . .

Mary: Isn't that interesting how your mother let her happiness depend on what you put in your mouth? Has that ever struck you as a very strange thing?

EXPOSED MYTH   Exposing a myth generally takes the form of countering a long-held belief, such as the "naturalness" of feeling bad, or the sense of causing someone else to feel negative emotions. Often such myths are assumed and acted on largely outside the person's awareness. In the transcript, myths such as these were aggressively confronted with statements such as, "Are you aware that you just said that you made her feel? That's not possible."

> *Sharon:* Well, not really. Let me explain a little bit about my family.
> *Bob:* No! I want you to be aware of what you say. You said you made your mother unhappy.
> *Sharon:* Yes.
> *Bob:* That's where I see your guilt being piled up for a long time. You actually believe that.
> *Sharon:* That I made mother unhappy? Oh, yes, of course, I mean that has been what I have been believing . . .
> *Mary:* And you're still believing that?
> *Sharon:* (*Pauses.*) Um. Yeah.
> *Mary:* Will you see your mother for just a minute and ask her something? (*Mary places empty chair in front of Sharon.*) OK. There's one question I want you to ask her. Ask her what she was unhappy about before she had you to blame it on.

MAGIC OF THE RACKET   Long-held negative feelings can take on a magical quality. A hypothetical example of this would be, "If only I feel bad enough long enough, then maybe my mother will love me." In the transcript, whenever this magical quality to negative feeling was encountered it was challenged.

> *Steve:* And now I look at the paper and when the stock market goes down I get depressed and get trapped in a money game. And if this is being a man, I don't want any more part of it.
> *Mary:* So what do you think of doing about that issue? Would you be willing at first to see the paper with the stock market listed on it and tell it, "If you only knew how depressed I am you'd bounce up"?
> *Steve:* If you only knew how depressed I am you'd bounce up and stay up. And split and double.
> *Mary:* So if you can't make it rise by feeling bad, have you some alternatives? Using that groovy part of you from graduate school.

PRESENT IMPASSE AND OLD SCENE   In order to separate the past from the present, the Gouldings help people to see how they still experience reality the same way they did when they were little. In doing this, they demonstrate to the person how his present impasse is actually related to an old scene. Once the person begins to understand that he "will not be sent away to boarding school" if he has fun, then he begins to separate his past situation from his present experience.

> *Bob:* What do you experience with that?
> *Harold:* I experience . . . I'm taking a chance of losing my job. I guess. You don't think so?
> *Bob:* No.
> *Mary:* I can appreciate how very, very careful you had to be as a kid, because they were crazy.

Harold: You mean my folks?

Mary: Yeah. Absolutely crazy. And I would stroke you for being so careful and also so guarded back then. And my guess is that sometimes you exaggerate the importance of keeping the peace now. Like I think it would be perfectly fine if someday your wife is in a big old sulk and you just walked out and got in the car and drove off and did your shopping and came home. But a piece of you forgets that she's not that crazy person that was back there when you were a little kid.

Harold: You mean I'm hanging onto something that isn't anymore.

Mary: Yeah.

Bob: Yeah. You're still behaving as if everybody in the world is out to get you. In a minor way, not a major way.

Mary: Like I really doubt if he'd fire you for saying "I disagree."

Harold: No, he wouldn't, I guess.

Mary: OK.

Harold: Besides he can't.

Bob: (*Laughs.*)

Mary: See how a piece of you still acts a bit as if you were that quite helpless kid in that quite crazy family?

WAITING FOR SOMEONE ELSE TO CHANGE Clients are sometimes in a wating game with someone from their past: "If only father had talked to me more . . . " In this situation the client needs to realize that he is waiting for somebody in his past to change. This has a distinct mythical quality and is not uncommonly connected to rackety feelings.

Sam: I want to have fun with it. I want to enjoy it. I want it to be everything it possibly can be. And I don't want to hear any more from any of you about it. And I don't want any of you anymore, uh, to give me any crazy ideas about it. I just want to be me and find what I want and and to get what I want.

Mary: They're going to give you lots more crazy ideas. The Pope hasn't changed a bit because of what you said. So what are you going to do about that? You're wanting. You're still telling them to change. Go away, to not bug you.

CONFRONTATION OF INCONGRUITY

In psychotherapy the client will often offer two communications at one time, one verbal and one nonverbal. It is important for the therapist to see both of these forms of communication as equally important. These incongruities are seen in head shakes that go with a "yes" answer, smiles that go with tragic stories, and decisions that lack action. Throughout the workshop Bob and Mary modeled clarity and did not shirk from confronting the participants with their demands for specificity.

SPECIFICITY/CLEARNESS Throughout the workshop, when the Gouldings did not understand words or phrases that the client was using, they would not go further until they had clarified what the person meant.

Martha: I want to feel more secure in what I'm doing.

Mary: OK. How would you test out with anybody here your security, lack of security in your new way?

Bob: Before that, I'd like to know what "secure" means.

Mary: Yeah. I don't know what any of the words mean.

Bob: Does secure mean that even if they don't like you in your new way you're going to stay with it?

Martha: Absolutely. I intend to.

HEARING LITERALLY By one definition, psychotherapy is largely the process of accurate hearing. Whenever a client would allude to anything that was in the least way tragic for him during the workshop, the Gouldings heard this literally and confronted it as such, even though the client may have intended to be "flip." By such listening the Gouldings help clients be in touch with tragic tendencies in their own lives that they would ordinarily overlook.

> *Carol:* I made some decisions that I'm not responsible for all those six million Jews, and, uh, that I can still have good things without having to feel guilty about it.
>
> *Bob:* Uh. Hold it. Hold it. What you said was, "I can have all those goodies, or do all those goodies without having to feel guilty about it." Doesn't say anything about dropping the guilt?
>
> *Carol:* Oh, well, yeah. I'm not going to feel guilty about them.

DISCREPANCY OF BODY LANGUAGE Often a client will say "Yes" with his mouth and shake his head "No," or vice versa. When that occurs, the Gouldings ask what the nonverbal message is saying, or will ask the client to make the nonverbal gesture congruent with the verbal message.

> *Sherri:* And I'm sorry you don't like it, and I like it.
>
> *Mary:* True?
>
> *Sherri:* Well, I'm trying to convince myself *(laughs)*.
>
> *Bob:* OK. So will you say it like this, "I like it" *(indicates to her that she shook her head "No" as she said "I like it")*?
>
> *Sherri:* Did I do that?
>
> *Bob:* You say it like this, "I like it." Will you do it like this, "I like it"? *(Changing position.)* That's the part your mother says, the part that goes like that.
>
> *Sherri:* And I like it.

DISTINCTION BETWEEN THINKING/FEELING It is not uncommon for people to confuse thinking and feeling. The most frequent confusion is for a client to offer a thought when he has been asked for a feeling. When the Gouldings encounter this confusion, they make clear that the client is giving a thought instead of a feeling and ask for a feeling. In this way, the people begin to distinguish their thoughts and their feelings and become more congruent in their responses.

Sam: Uh, I have intelligence and, uh, determination (*pause*) and, uh, feelings. And I think I'm a creative person.

Bob: What are you experiencing?

Sam: There isn't any more.

Bob: That's what you were thinking. What were you experiencing? What were you feeling? (*Long pause.*)

Sam: Scared.

CONFRONT PARENT CONTRACT   During the workshop, anytime a client would set a goal that he "should do" or "better do" the Gouldings would confront this as a "parent" contract. Doing this they would then go on to seek those things that the person wished to do that were more congruent with his natural desires.

Sharon: Um—somethimes it's being dissatisfied with a situation. Sometimes it's being angry at the children. And sometimes it's because the vacuum cleaner breaks and I'm having company. You know those are forms of being upset to me.

Mary: My problem with your contract is it's not yours, it's your mother's. And, I'm hearing a Cinderella thing in terms of your upset. That naturally you're supposed to be upset—that's the state of things, but you're not supposed to eat so that your mother can do something. And my guess is that when the marathon's over you'll gain three pounds.

PARTICULAR TECHNIQUES

It is interesting to note particular techniques that were used throughout the weekend.

GAME ANALYSIS   The function of game analysis is to show people the maneuvers they go through in order to end up feeling bad. This information can help people change their behavior.

Bob: You got the choice of hanging them up in the morning or hanging them up at night. Who the hell cares? (*Chuckles.*)

Chrissie: Yeah. Maybe it's not that. Maybe what I'm really saying is that sometimes I handle situations the way I want to and sometimes I don't. And I get mad at myself when I don't.

Bob: That's the game.

Chrissie: It's a game?

Bob: Sure. It's a one-handed game, but it's a game. Here's Chrissie, and there's Ma, back when you're a little kid, see?

Chrissie: Yeah.

Bob: I forgot to hang up the clothes.

Chrissie: Or I didn't handle the situation. Whatever it was.

Bob: I'll stay with clothes, that's the one you're on. I'm treating it as if you were a kid. Please bawl me out.

Chrissie: And she does.

Bob: The secret message.

Chrissie: She won't do it. She'll pick up my clothes instead.

Bob: That's not what you're doing. What you're doing is saying, "OK," and bawling yourself out. It's a one-handed game. And you don't hang them up in the service of bawling yourself out when you come back. Otherwise, who cares?

TWO-CHAIR   During the marathon there were literally dozens of examples of two-chair work by the Gouldings. This is a technique that was popularized by the gestalt therapist Fritz Perls. This technique is particularly helpful in aiding the participants to own all parts of himself.

Mary: How would your father respond to that? Would you be him? (*Softly.*) Sit in that chair for him.

SAY GOODBYE TO THE PAST   Some people drag a negative past around with them like a ball and chain. The concept of saying goodbye to the past has to do with letting go of negative memories or the wish for never-realized positive experiences in the past.

Jim: (*Teary*) I'll never know.

Bob: Furthermore, it doesn't make a damn bit of difference.

Jim: Yeah, you're right.

Bob: You know something, Jim, the time has come for you to say goodbye to your past.

Jim: Yeah.

Bob: You've been dragging it through the mud now for years.

FANTASY   Fantasy techniques were used during the marathon in two ways. One is to focus on past events and bring them into the present, and the other is to focus on future events and bring them into the present.

Mary: OK. Uh, I'd like to start with some experiential things we do and then tie it into a bit of theory later. So would you shut your eyes and go back through time, and what's the meanest thing mother, father said and/or did to you when you were a little kid? What's the scene, and what were they feeling and what were your feelings? When you are in touch with a scene, come on back.

TALKING TO PARENT PROJECTIONS   During two-chair work the Gouldings would often talk to the person while he was playing his mother or father as if he were that person from his past. This technique is a powerful vehicle to introduce the person to the inner experiences of his parent. The subsequent appreciation for his parent's experience helps the person to forgive any seeming injustices and to make separation.

Bob: Will you do a little bit more experimenting with me? Sit over here and be your mother. Start with high school. "We moved so you could go to high school." You are mother, say that to . . .

Mary: What's your name, Mother?

Carol: Marsha.

"TILT" This technique consists of saying the word "tilt" when a client would make a statement which he believed was true, but was indeed false. This is a nonjudgmental word which simply tags the event. Statements which implied that one person was responsible for another person's feelings would often draw the response of "tilt."

> *Christine:* Oh, set myself up, or do something that makes people mad at at me, or not . . .
>
> *Bob:* Tilt! What you said was, "I do something that makes people mad at me." I don't know any way you can make me mad at you unless I decide to get angry.

CONFRONTS "YOU KNOW" During the workshop the Gouldings would sometimes confront the statement "You know" with the statement "No, I don't know." The end function of this was to help the person hear his "You know" and to see if he was glossing over some of his feeling experience with that phrase. Another important aspect of this confrontation is to interrupt a move by the client to establish a symbiotic relationship with the therapist. That is, the only way a therapist can "know" what one feels is to be a part of that person.

> *Christine:* You know my mother can't show love. And . . .
>
> *Mary:* I didn't know.

USE OF HUNCH Throughout the workshop the Gouldings made generous use of their hunches. In doing so they often facilitated for someone the connection between past influences and present behavior.

> *Patsy:* Um, yes. I'd like to, I'd like to know what I want. I get confused easily and I'd like to be able to dintinguish what I want from what other people want of me.
>
> *Mary:* Did your mother used to pick your clothes out when you were little?
>
> *Patsy:* Umhum.
>
> *Mary:* And what happens if you walk in the store and say I want that dress.
>
> *Patsy:* Um. That's not you.

"OF COURSE" TECHNIQUE The "of course" technique invites people to act with assurance about their natural desires or experiences, rather than with reticence, such as "I like sex, of course!" or, "I feel sad my dog died, of course."

> *Mary:* You see, "maybe" is the way you can keep other people acting like you said your mother did, thinking for you. Telling you who you are and how you feel. As long as you say "maybe" you can usually find some damn rescuer in the world who will say you're absolutely right, or it isn't that way, it's this way, some kind of icky parent thing. Would you be willing to substitute "of course" for "maybe" in your sentences?
>
> *Irma:* Of course (*laughs*).
>
> *Mary:* Feel the difference?
>
> *Irma:* Yes.

Mary: So go ahead, of course.
Irma: I'm not really too sure where to begin.
Bob: Of course.
Irma: Of course, right.

TAPE RECORDER Throughout the workshop the tape recorder was used a great deal so that participants could hear the kinds of things they would say, often outside of their awareness. An especially important phrase to play back to clients is a statement starting with the word "You." This is very often a verbatim quote from someone in the past, "If you have fun, you'll get in trouble."

Mary: Well, I just heard, "I don't want to hurt him, he's a nice guy." It's longer than that, but it still doesn't give an example of how you protect him. (*Plays tape again.*)
Bob: OK. Do you hear what we're talking about?
Mary: Like pretend I'm a travel agent, OK?, behind my desk and you come in and say, "I want to go somewhere." Or, "I have just as much right to go somewhere as anyone." OK?
Martha: Yeah.

PROCEDURAL RULES

This section contains procedural rules which are important in setting the tone for weekend workshops at the Institute.

NO GOSSIP RULE This rule simply means that no participant can talk about someone who is not in the room and cannot talk about someone who is in the room as if he were not there. If the participant wishes to make comment about someone, he must make that comment to the person.

Mary: I'm going to call a halt on that because they're not here to speak for themselves. And, uh, I don't think it's cricket to bring them in. Most kids in the long run would rather live with people who are happy than when they are unhappy, and I feel we can't talk about them.

TIME LIMIT This rule simply states that under no conditions will the therapist work beyond a specified stopping time. The strict adherence to this rule encourages participants to be responsible for getting their goals accomplished during the time allotted.

Irma: I'd like to work.
Bob: I may stop. I will stop if it gets to 12 o'clock and you haven't finished.
Irma: OK.

SPECIFIC ENVIRONMENTAL RULES These are four rules given to participants at the beginning of workshops at the Western Institute. These rules have the two-fold purpose of providing the participants with a pro-tected environment in which to grow and to establish guidelines for optimal use of time during the weekend.* (1) No violence or threats of violence. The value of this rule is obvious. (2) Sex only with your attending partner. The function of this rule is to encourage one to spend time focusing on one's concerns rather than playing various seductive games. (3) No alcohol or mind-altering drugs. There are two purposes for this rule. One cannot work clearly if he is not thinking clearly and it is often important for someone to learn of his ability to enjoy himself without altering his state of consciousness with chemicals. (4) Stay on the property during a three-day marathon. In order to give themselves optimum opportunity to work and grow, participants are encouraged not to interrupt their experience by leaving the Institute.

* No examples are given of these rules in action. They are added for reader interest.

TWENTY

THE BEST OF TWO WORLDS: A PSYCHOANALYST LOOKS AT TA
Robert C. Drye

"What's a nice psychoanalyst like you doing in a place like this?" is a frequent question from both psychoanalytic and TA friends. ("This" is teaching TA theory and therapy.) My answer: "I made a decision to have the best of two good worlds." A story goes with this answer. In 1969 I was part of the psychoanalytic world and having trouble deciding where to commit myself professionally. Advice and site-visiting didn't seem to help and, despite having no serious financial or personal restraints, I couldn't decide.

I was at the American Group Psychotherapy Association meetings in 1969 only because they were held in New York. I wasn't very happy about the group therapy I was supervising (using group process notions), and Warden Rimel, a friend of mine, liked TA. I went to a workshop on TA given by Bob and Mary Goulding; I told Bob Goulding this story and he said, "Oh, you like to stew." (Note that this interpretation has no word with more than four letters.) Inside me I could feel lights going on all over the place as I connected with the work I had done during my analyses. I suddenly experienced myself as someone stewing, not as someone who was the victim of an obsessive neurosis. I could decide, even if I was deciding to stew! Here was a system I wanted to know more about.

SOME SYSTEMS THAT WORK

I have always liked systems that work. I started out learning to be a chemical engineer at Massachusetts Institute of Technology and switched into pre-med as a researcher, an Arrowsmith rather than a chemist. When the photometer didn't measure the phosphorous correctly and the guinea pig died in vain, I concluded I had not the skill or patience to be Arrowsmith, whose last words were "and probably we'll fail!"[1] After all, doctors' human patients get better. In medical school, I was intrigued with the patients from psychiatry (the first real patients we saw in our first year) and the psychoanalytic system that could explain some of their behavior—which I applied to myself in the same way I applied the physical pathology I was learning: "I know it's anal" in the same way as "I know I've got a melanoma." I walked around Bellevue Psychopathic for a month with a few psychiatric patients who were partly mine, but I was learning mainly internal medicine. Psychiatry and internal medicine were systems that worked.

I was still interested enough in psychiatry so that, in 1953, when the U. S. Army offered me first a one-way subway ticket to the induction center and then offered four months training in neuropsychiatry, I was ready. They had a system called military psychiatry, and it worked. Some of the men in a regiment under fire will develop battle fatigue. This is a syndrome where the soldier is disoriented, stuporous, panicky, agitated, or has bizarre physical symptoms. More soldiers develop battle fatigue as the stress continues. If they are sent back from the combat area to a hospital, most of them only recover partially, and many end up still nervous in a Veterans' Administration hospital. If they get treated in a quiet place close to the front line and if they are told they'll be back to duty shortly, most of them go back to duty and never need a hospital. The number of men who develop battle fatigue can be reduced by a system that includes good training, good leadership, and good support. This system can be learned and practiced in a few months. Again, psychoanalysis was the system that provided the theory to make some sense out of the conflict inside an individual soldier: fear of death vs. shame at abandoning his buddies. The soldier with battle fatigue is no longer able to mediate the conflict as a result of the collapse of the ego. The system also has some social dimensions, particularly how the group can provide support and direction to carry an individual soldier through a crisis.

Al Glass, then head of Military Psychiatry at the Army Medical Service School, made the following social suggestions for the therapist in the system: "The first thing to do on a new post is go to the Officers' Club bar. Do the same soldiering the line people do and you'll get on fine. Don't evacuate anybody unless there is no way they can do some duty; on the other hand, don't keep somebody on duty just because you have to stay too." These suggestions were easy to follow, since I wanted to soldier anyway. The system worked fine in the paratroop division where I spent most of two years. I met the staff people I needed to work with and had their backing on my controversial recommendations. For instance, I was usually against punitive treatment or discharge of soldiers whose personality difficulties got them in conflict with their commanding officers in a peacetime army (often after creditable combat service). My expectations that most troubled soldiers would feel better completing service than getting a discharge seemed to help them finish service. Psychoanalysis, again, seemed helpful in understanding those soldiers with more chronic anxiety or anxiety not related to the military.

THE DEVELOPING PSYCHOANALYST

I decided I enjoyed doing psychiatry and I went to Chicago in 1955. There, psychoanalysis was readily available to psychiatric residents as part of a program: the Chicago Associated Psychiatric Faculties, composed of several training centers, and the Psychoanalytic Institute. From 1954, when I successfully applied for residency training and a training analysis, until 1965, when I graduated from training myself, "the Institute" always meant the Chicago Institute for Psychoanalysis. (A training analysis is one conducted by an analyst approved by the American Psychoanalytic Association to analyze a possible future analyst.) The Chicago Associated Faculties delivered what they promised. I had a variety of teachers, many of them famous analysts such as Franz Alexander. There were also many psychiatrists (some also analysts) including L. J. Meduna, one of the inventors of shock therapy; Roy Grinker, who wrote on neurology, psychosomatic illness, and military stress; and Frances Gerty, who understood professional organizations. All were excited and curious, finding things that might work or did work or would work if we just knew a little more. I began my own training analysis by taking a piece out of each day to struggle with my own anxiety. My analyst instructed me to "Lie on the couch and report whatever comes into your mind. If you get uncomfortable you may sit up, but note what you were thinking about at that point." Following her instructions, I lay down and reported for 50 minutes, first four times and then five times a week. From time to time she commented on what was happening. The general sequence of interpretations was behavior in the analyst's office to behavior outside the office to historical antecedents. "Sounds like you are getting angry in here. . . . How are you afraid I will react to your anger? . . . You are afraid of your angry patients; could you be feeling angry yourself? . . . You are afraid I will disapprove of your anger as you thought your mother did. . . ."

There were three goals within the treatment. The first was to develop my skills as a self-observer. The second was to assist the gradual development of the transference neurosis in which my feelings towards her and my anxiety about those feelings were more important than my anxieties elsewhere, which then, indeed, might subside even before I understood them. I would be repeating the original scenes I had difficulty with as a child, and my current anxiety would be related to her as a participant (in my head) rather than simply as a listener and observer. I might assign her several parts, such as comforter and punisher (hopefully for my minor rather than major sins). These transferences (or resistances to change by definition, since I wanted to relive the old scenes rather than experience new ones) changed over time as I related to her in various scenes and as various people. Because of the multiple scenes and the multiple parts, no one insight—no one linking of the present with the past—would change much in me. I observed that as I got more in touch with my own rages, I was less anxious. At times I felt I was responding to outside situations entirely beyond my control, such as angry patients in my practice or the stresses of my own growing family. At other times I was aware that, in reaction to experience in the analysis, I perceived or even arranged outside situations to happen in particular ways. For instance, I might say something provocative to an angry patient rather than be angry at my analyst.

The third goal was working through each of these patterns over and over so that I could gradually separate the present from the past and become aware of my present strengths. In contrast to my childhood doubts I could deal directly with the situation. This is expressed in the psychoanalytic model as increased flexible control by the ego of aggressive impulses with less superego disapproval. My analysis contained many resistances in addition to the transference: compulsive talking to get away from the feeling of the moment; arriving late to decrease my working time and to express some rebelliousness, and also to protest what I experienced as the somewhat impersonal behavior of my analyst. These resistances, often out of my awareness, were understood by paying attention to them as they occurred. I terminated my analysis in three and a half years with my anxiety substantially and permanently reduced and with an awareness of some unfinished business which I wanted to defer.

I helped most of my own patients with bits of what I was learning from teachers and myself. Repeatedly in case conferences I was asked "What's working?" In 1957, in a seminar that focused on the messages sent and returned, Grinker said "Look at transactions," neither discounting analytic terminology nor using it.[2]

Part of my residency experience was at the Chicago State Hospital. What I had learned in the army worked at Chicago State too: I could expect people labeled hopeless to follow the label and they did; I could expect them to rise up and use their "Adult" and they did.[3] After taking my residency at the University of Illinois and Michael Reese, I went to the University of Chicago on the Student Health service. This was like combat psychiatry again, with contracts for a maximum of five treatment sessions and the expectation of quick results. Morton Lieberman, then a staff psychologist in student health, suggested we start a small student group for students who seemed to need a longer period. After leading two of these groups, and having had group-leading experience at Chicago State, I was suddenly a group therapist—my ticket to my meeting with Bob Goulding ten years in the future. By now I had worked, sweated, and worried with a lot of patients; some were better, and some were not. I knew a woman whom I could have understood much better had I analyzed her. My analyst said, "That's the first time I've heard you excited about using analysis yourself." I regarded as odd those people who had failed to apply for training as analysts; those who had applied and been turned down, I saw as lost souls who of course would reapply. When I was accepted for training right out of residency in 1958, I was marked as an upcoming young man.

We were psychiatrists or behavioral scientists. Joan Fleming, the Dean, welcomed us with the hope we'd be analytic scholars. Every other weekend we spent Friday and much of Saturday in theory classes and clinical seminars. Year by year we read our way through Freud and his more modern colleagues. We considered dreams in detail and theory and in normal and abnormal psychology. We also presented our work as analysts. Somewhere in that first year we were assigned our first patient (called a control because we met with a supervisor weekly and the analysis was under his or her control), and when our supervisor thought we were well along we could add another. Between the second and the third patient, the Education Committee considered our progress. If it approved, we could analyze privately and expect to go on to graduation. If not, we had to improve our work and reapply later for a third case. The first two patients were referred by the Institute's social workers and paid a nominal fee; our third and fourth controls paid closer to private rates.

By this time I had tied up at least 12 to 16 working hours a week at very low or reduced fees, plus two to four hours for supervision. The experience was tremendously burdening and exciting, but wives and families were often distant spectators. "Does teacher make you read all those books?" my daughter asked me. The requirements were: (a) five years of classwork; (b) one completed case; and (c) a fourth case well started. All of us expected to prepare for at least a year (reviewing five years or more of work) so that we could answer five essay questions in three hours. Supposedly nobody flunked the exam (or did they?), but the hazards along the way were real. Referral for more personal analysis after completing the first analysis was commonplace, or the candidate might return to treatment for his or her own reasons, as I did.

Obviously, I wanted to be an analyst even at high personal and financial cost. Tuition was $1000 a year; supervision after the third year cost extra, although I knew my teachers worked for cut rates, too. As I drove by friends playing tennis on my way home to study, I remember saying to myself, "Nobody put you here but you." The decision seemed inevitable; for me analysis was the only good game in town.

NONANALYTIC INTERESTS

At the same time, other currents were flowing. I had switched from the university to the new Illinois State Psychiatric Institute in 1959. First, I was Director of two psychiatric wards. After two years, I became Director of Education, responsible for the psychiatric residency program and for the overall direction of training in the state hospitals. I took as a workable challenge the improvement of training in the state hospitals (11 of them; 50,000 patients). Jules Masserman, the first Education Director, had already designed a plan for consultants from Chicago to go to the state hospitals.[4] As each floor at ISPI was sponsored by a training center, so each hospital could be. This did not prove entirely practical, since some schools had more resources than others, but all hospitals and one of the training schools for the retarded got consultant teams, and I began to learn the importance of contract negotiation.[5] I have many good feelings about my work there and the people I worked with: Lester Rudy, the first Director, now Chairman at the University of Illinois; Jack Weinberg, the current Director; Jackson Smith, now Chairman at Loyola; and Percival Bailey, a neuropathologist and friend of the mentally ill.

The department itself was in a state of flux; community psychiatry had arrived. Beginning in 1966, the zone centers designed to provide community-supported treatment were real buildings; and under the leadership of Harold Visotsky, experiments were possible. Patients would move out of the hospitals back into the community to be handled by follow-up clinics strategically located in each zone of the state. Students from the ISPI programs rapidly took scattered positions throughout the network of zone centers. The state hospitals were suddenly poor brothers, and even within ISPI the community program for the black ghetto next door and the Mexican district beyond began to preempt resources and energies traditionally reserved for teaching and psychotherapy. In reaction, even some of the former opponents of analysis began to speak favorably of learning vs. service. Then came a financial crunch, after years of relative affluence, and Visotsky was replaced by an accountant.

I found many of the crises to be opportunities and a great way to get acquainted with myself. The social issues of racism, war, and civil rights were right in our laps in literal fire and smoke; even before 1968, Chicago blew up repeatedly. But I had begun looking elsewhere, partly from nostalgia for the East and partly out of general fatigue with administration. We had helped develop the state hospital program. I had been encouraged by my contacts with dedicated teachers and dedicated caretakers in the hospital, stormy as these contacts sometimes were. However, the endless minor details of scheduling, budget preparation, staff interviewing, and other aspects of personal administration consumed more time and energy than I wanted to commit to the new planning that I knew ought to go into the zone centers (community psychiatric models). I was intellectually but not personally committed to doing the organizational development work necessary to making the new programs work. I had at one time been quite interested in organizational development, which was a major issue with each state hospital consultant contract. In 1963 I attended the basic laboratory of National Training Laboratories at Bethel, Maine. I led T-groups within ISPI that looked at our organization. And the one time I heard Eric Berne speak, in the late sixties, his topic was hospitals as organizations. I had invited him as a guest speaker for our staff and trainees, knowing little about him except that he was supposed to be interesting on this subject. He was brilliant, but so acid that, although I agreed with what he said about organizations that are organized for the staff rather than to deliver services, I felt caught rather than helped.

I resigned as Director of Education and began looking openly for a change of scene. I worked for a year for two black community organizations in our catchment area. It was in 1969 and I had a few TA tools, so I was struggling with contracts and noticing Parent ego states all over the community. I had heavily reinforced my first good impression of Bob and Mary Goulding by attending a one-week workshop in Carmel. There I made the acquaintance not only of TA but of gestalt. I regard gestalt as a powerful set of techniques for increasing awareness, focusing associations, and evoking early scenes, rather than as a complete psychological system. I use it within the context of TA, my general rule being to use a gestalt exercise only with a contract.

I made a decision to go to California, where Bob Goulding knew something I didn't know yet, just as Grinker went to Vienna to see Freud. There I planned to practice analysis and, with the Gouldings, add to my understanding of TA and gestalt. I think it is important to say that I went into TA not to get away from analysis but to supplement it.

TA IN TEACHING PSYCHOTHERAPY

Consider my dilemma as a teacher before I knew about TA. I am responsible for a psychiatry training program. I honestly believe psychoanalytic theory is the best system for explaining human behavior. I want my students to do psychotherapy, which I believe is important, and to understand some patients even if the therapy isn't directly curative (for instance, one of my residents could go into a catatonic patient's room, tell him, "That's OK, John, you don't have to go home this weekend" and watch him unwind). I have to use a system based on a way of working different from the way the residents worked. Psychoanalysis is a theory developed to explain what happens when someone lies on a couch several hours a week and free-associates both here and now (whats the focal conflict) and over periods of time (the rise and fall of resistances), and develops and resolves the transference neurosis. I have years to cure the patient and days to understand a conflict. Besides, my patient is a volunteer and is generally able to manage most of his affairs between sessions, care for himself, and stay out of the hospital. Now I set out to teach psychotherapy to a resident who doesn't have the years of psychoanalytic training and experience, who is dealing much of the time with patients who are less able to manage their lives and may have been sent into a hospital against their will; some may belong to that group of patients who classically do not respond well to verbal therapy, or they may come from a social background where talking about feelings isn't typical behavior. The resident who has enthusiasm and eagerness to learn and who uses his Little Professor can often help patients, but he doesn't have a clear language from psychoanalysis to describe what happens between him and his patients. In addition, he has to learn to master his own feelings, the anxieties generated by sudden massive contact with other peoples' troubles, external and internal. (The residents often entered into their own personal therapy or analysis, but to get the results of this might take a long time; a resident who isn't hurting personally often won't start therapy merely to become more efficient at his or her work.)

TA provides important answers to several of these problems. Parent-Adult-Child and transactions offer a teachable/learnable vocabulary for interpersonal transactions. Psychoanalysis, designed to explain largely intrapersonal phenomena, particularly conflict, doesn't do this. The resident (or other student therapist, for whom the difficulties are even greater) can describe what he sees with some confidence. He does not have to resort to labels of inferred phenomena. Secondly, a treatment goal can be expressed in terms of social control first and of script later, which can be fairly sharply defined as two separate operations. I recall our nursing director saying with considerable disappointment, "I see a lot of improved behavior around here, but not much personality change," which I understood to mean no change in internal relationships, such as the reworking of old ego-superego-id balances or the changing of defenses; in other words, no psychoanalytic changes! This social control approach was congruent with the general goal in a public mental hospital of rapid return to part-time hospital or outpatient care, whether hospital or "community" based. The social control and script notions lend precision to treatment goals. With clearer goals, the student therapist can notice what works and how various interventions help each patient. His own behavior in relationship to the patient can also be described with TA. He can practice working from various ego states and get in touch with his own rackets. The resident may still need therapy to get out of the racket that interferes with his work, but may be able to do this in a marathon or in short-term TA therapy. Longer-term therapy, including analysis, might still be recommended if brief therapy is not effective and/or if the resident wishes more extensive therapy for self-understanding.

If teaching individual therapy was difficult, I felt that teaching group therapy would be nearly impossible. (A luncheon speaker at the AGPA meeting where I met Bob and Mary Goulding seriously suggested that to do "group psychoanalysis" a therapist needed not only full psychoanalytic training, including a training analysis, but full group psychoanalytic training, including personal group psychoanalysis!) Yet we relied heavily on group programs. I used patient/staff meetings in designing many of the ISPI hospital living arrangements when the hospital opened, and in managing ward crises such as an assaultive patient or patient/staff tensions that were blocking treatment. Every resident and many other student therapists began leading groups soon after their arrival, and, by the third year, the residents not only had one or more outpatient therapy groups but used patient/staff meetings as part of their technique during the state hospital assignment.

GROUP PROCESS

Fortunately, I had a partially manageable model,[6] an extension of the focal-conflict idea from psychoanalysis to a group. Could a group be considered an organism whose total communications would be understand-

able as one side or another of a particular conflict? For instance, a hospital
ward group:

> *A:* Dr. Drye, what can I do about John? He's been keeping us all awake at
> night.
> *B:* Oh, A, you know Dr. Drye never answers questions.
> *C:* Impossible to get a straight answer around here!
> *A:* Well, I'm still worried about John, but if I'm supposed to figure it out
> myself . . .
> *Drye:* Sounds like you'd like some help but you're doubting I'll respond
> the way you'll want.

"You" refers to the group, not just A, since all speakers have said something related to A's opening request. Note I don't say help *with John*
since neither B or C referred to John, and I'm predicting that there may
be another ward problem more serious than John that people won't raise
until they find out what I do when they ask for help with John. My diagnosis of the conflict is, wish for help from ward chief *versus* fear of my
disapproval. Resolution: Talk about problem but don't deal with me
directly. This approach works as part of a system for ward management.

For example, I clearly expect the group members to work out their own
solutions to ward problems including the amount of help they may need
from me, and this approach was successful in that the group members met
that expectation. The system partly works as a system for teaching
problem-solving. Here the goal is that the patients will carry the skills
learned in the group into whatever problem-solving situations are relevant
to them outside. While this reflects a general confidence of the therapist
that people can solve their problems, I became aware that, for me, this
was not sufficiently precise. I couldn't tell if it worked for a particular
patient or not, unless I clarified contracts, and as I began to clarify contracts, I began to notice in the group what the patient was doing about
contracts and what he wasn't, rather than gathering the data necessary to
make overall conflict interpretations. My understanding of the group process leader is that he listens, like an analyst with an individual patient,
and when he can formulate the conflict in a way he believes the group can
hear, he makes some comment. As with other labels, getting people to
define what they do is important with "group process." Some people say
"I use group process" when they mean having the entire group do things
such as warm-up exercises, which can be used in a variety of groups, including TA. One belief I do share with some group process leaders is that
detailed attention to the composition of the group is not terribly important unless the task of the group requires certain people to be present.

I had become aware of contracts in my psychoanalytic training[7]—although some analysts de-emphasized contracts, since the presenting com-
plaint might turn out to be less important as the analysis proceeds. As a
supervisor I frequently first heard about a patient or a group of patients
after the therapist had been working for months under one or more previ-

ous supervisors. I found "What are your goals?" a powerful question to focus discussion of the information the therapist had already collected. Once I had heard about contracts through TA, I began to use contracts as being more precise than goals, since the contract includes not only what changes the patient wants to make, but also the time frame and therapist's activities.

TA AS AN EFFECTIVE SYSTEM

I hope by now I have established myself as a sort of Renaissance man of psychiatry while revealing the several ways I have encountered and liked TA. Now I want to come back to what I believe really tests the workability of any system: the tough problems in our field. I have already referred to tough-teaching problems, and how I believe TA helps with a number of problems in teaching psychotherapy through its concepts of ego states, transactions, rackets, and contracts. If I can more rapidly teach someone how to do effective therapy, that is a real advantage. Can the therapy itself be more effective? With whom? With what kinds of problems? And in whose hands? I have the impression that many patients are likely to respond to practically any confident empathic therapist regardless of technique if the therapist is interested in problem-solving and not merely in pathology. My army and student health experiences at the beginning of my training reinforce this belief.

In Chicago I analyzed eight patients contractually with the following results: five patients completed their contract and terminated satisfied; time varied from four to six years. Two patients left dissatisfied, one after six years, one after six months. One patient interrupted at three years, when I moved to California, with partial completion of a contract. I felt, and still feel, considerable satisfaction with these results and continue as a psychoanalyst because of them. My current indications for psychoanalysis are:

(1) Persistent impasses despite reasonably well-conducted TA therapy, including use of gestalt therapy, particularly if the patient has an obsessive, compulsive, phobic, or conversion neurosis, or related personality disorders.

(2) Some patients with brief but stormy eruptions of archaic Child (borderline syndrome) which disrupt problem-solving despite an apparently available Adult. Here the level of distrust and distancing based on early decisions may be so severe that they need a more continuous relationship, as in psychoanalysis. So far only one of the borderline patients I am working with in California is being seen in a modified analysis.

(3) Patients with major narcissistic disorders, where narcissistic transferences can be more clearly observed in several sessions a week. Narcissistic disorder here means difficulties in managing self-esteem, shame, and admiration or idealization of others. (I will comment on this briefly later.)

(4) A strong personal preference, based on previous useful experience

with psychoanalytic psychotherapy or the desire to know oneself in depth as well as to obtain relief. Menninger commented that improved psychotherapies which would be faster than psychoanalysis would be found, but that analysis would remain important for therapists and educators because of the increased self-knowledge they would obtain.[8] Naturally, a TA therapist will consider the possibility that such a leisurely approach might be part of a loser or nonwinner script.

As a psychotherapist, I saw about 20 patients, many of them with completed contracts, over a period of 11 years. Some of them I worked with off and on for most of the period. Comparing these with the patients I saw after my first two years of using TA exclusively, I couldn't be sure which results were better, but I was sure that with TA I worked more easily and with a clearer sense of what I was doing. As I think about my last three years of practice, my position is about the same. I am not tremendously more effective with office psychotherapy *by itself,* individually, or in groups, but I am impressed with my greater ease and occasionally faster contract completion. Moreover, for some patients I have a new tool, the TA-gestalt marathon, which I find very effective. (For a discussion of this, see John McNeel's chapter in this book.) I now know better how to deal with suicide. Bob Goulding's system really works in an emergency room, a clinic, or a private office.[9] I started out at Illinois State Psychiatric Institute, right after my first TA workshop, telling the Outpatient Department to send me the next eight patients that come in. These I treated in front of the group therapy committee after I had taught my colleagues an introductory course in TA. (Talk about "Look, Ma, no hands!" The first patient began, "Since I committed suicide 6 weeks ago . . .") The group ran for ten months with no suicides or serious attempts and with completion of about half the contracts, although one man had to be hospitalized. This convinced me that I could work effectively with a wide variety of patients in a TA group, but that not every patient could complete his contract in eight months in a group that met once a week.

I am also aware that with my methods, even as I increase my experience and training, I am not always able to successfully work with particular patients. I explain this to myself as: (1) technical inadequacy to be remedied by further advances; no-suicide decisions turn out to be important in treating some phobias;[10] (2) certain syndromes are defined almost by their difficulty, for example, borderline states, schizophrenia, certain depressions, certain phobics and compulsives, antisocial personalities, addicts. For instance, an alcoholic could be defined as somebody whom a therapist will have trouble helping to stop drinking, or a borderline patient is someone who makes a therapist more anxious than a neurotic patient does, but less anxious than a schizophrenic patient does.

I believe syndromes are useful categories despite the real but secondary dangers of labeling. Within any category, I am aware of great ranges of difficulties, assets, possible contracts, and "curability." Take borderlines as an example. I have worked with Grinker to make this syndrome easier to describe. Our experience was that no one receiving routine outpatient therapy during the years of the study changed significantly.[11] Since I have been in California, I have worked with six such patients extensively; all have completed at least one important contract, defined as changing their personal, social, and/or occupational situation in a major way. I do not as yet feel much confidence that I can work with alcoholic or addict patients in the office. However, I am cautiously impressed by the results of a residential program (Satori) that I observed at the Palo Alto Veterans Administration hospital. A group of veterans, who had all failed in another drug abuse program, achieved 50 percent success in stopping the use of heroin without using methadone. Of those who did use methadone, 85 percent stopped using heroin. This program used contracts, script analysis, and decisions, as well as non-TA methods. I do not feel that Alcoholics Anonymous usage means a failure in working with alcoholics, since I agree with Berne that social control in this area is worthwhile in itself, and I have few successes using TA with alcoholics without also using AA.

As I did before I knew TA, I continue to have both successful and unsuccessful experiences with patients I label schizophrenic. I do not consider myself competent to use the Schiff approaches as yet, although I am slowly getting more knowledgable about them. I am impressed with the power of the Schiff ideas, particularly discounting and frame of reference. The questions I am asking are: are their results reliable only with the kind of massive input the Schiffs describe in their earlier writings? What might be happening in patients with whom they don't succeed? I am aware that some therapists seem much more talented than others in working with schizophrenics; an intensive personal commitment seems to be required. I also believe that there are still unknown biological factors which somehow need to be included in the treatment plan for some patients. For instance, one of my patients did not respond to my best skills. I included her husband in the treatment plan. I then prescribed tranquilizers and she seemed worse. She had had a similar episode many years before and had responded to 18 electric shock treatments. I am reluctant to recommend a course of more than a few shock treatments to anyone, but out of desperation, I gave her a similar course, and she began to improve at the fourteenth treatment, exactly as she had done years before.

The most interesting issue to me in any new technique is the management of resistance. When Freud decided to analyze resistance instead of overpowering it by head pressure or dissolving it by hypnosis, he changed the focus of the therapist's investigation from the original conflict around which the patient had developed this particular system of not changing, to the ways in which the patient was stopping himself from changing. Looking at this resistance as an active process, as in discounting or as in my work on the Rebellious Child ego state,[12] often leads to change. Resistance can also be understood as the following of injunctions. "I don't understand" can be a response to a "Don't think" injunction. The anxiety experienced as someone approaches an underlying conflict can be understood as a signal that one is moving against an old decision that resolved the conflict between the injunction and other forces, including the wishes of the Free Child. The dynamics of the resistance often can be brought alive by gestalt techniques. This formulation is an almost exact parallel to the psychoanalytic formulation of the signal function of anxiety.

Without reviewing the injunction/decision process as described by Goulding,[13] the decision about how to handle the thoughts and feelings that are related to the wishes countered by an injunction can be seen as a lifesaving and stroke-preserving action. The decision, elaborated through fantasy into the script, helps the patient get to where he is today although it may not make him happy. Stewing enabled me to gain time when I experienced direct action as dangerous. I appeared to obtain some magical successes by stewing; I often managed a situation well after worrying. The Little Professor notes the success and thinks the stewing may have helped. Besides, a stewer can delay rebelliously, while ostensibly "making progress" on the problem. I hesitate to abandon such a strong defensive position. Technically, this means that when patients report resistance, I invite them to get in touch with it, with the original scene that goes with the resistance, and with the decision made at the time. For instance, writing, originally a torture for me, was associated with school assignments or Christmas thank-you letters. It had to be done right! Although, to my surprise, teachers occasionally liked my more casual efforts. In Joan Putz's workshop on writing I recently learned I could write spontaneously from Child and leave Parent and Adult for editing by deliberately thinking of all the restrictions I have on my writing (be a scholar, leave plenty of space, don't use "I" so much) and by deciding to drop the injunctions when writing the first draft. Depending on the stroking I get for this article, I may move toward more freedom and probably more writing, or I may return to an exclusively scholarly position. This working-through process is necessary to establish new working styles which don't fit the script.

TRAUMA OR DECISION

One final theoretical remark. I believe there is enormous potential leverage in the decision model, because it steps outside the victim notion of psychopathology. Neither Freud[14] nor Berne committed themselves on this issue. In one of his last papers Freud said:

> But it is a "construction" when one lays before the subject of the analysis a piece of his early history that he has forgotten, in some such way as this: "Up to your nth year you regarded yourself as the sole and unlimited possessor of your mother; then came another baby and brought you grave disillusionment. Your mother left you for some time, and even after her reappearance she was never again devoted to you exclusively. Your feelings toward your mother became ambivalent, your father gained a new importance for you," . . .[15]

Now, whether this scene is reconstructed from the analysis via the patient's behavior towards the analyst, or whether it is directly recalled during the analysis, or reached by use of a TA or gestalt technique, I still have the choice of considering the patient a victim of the experience of the new baby and his mother's withdrawal, or as someone who creatively decided to switch to father. The second position gives the patient more sense of power to change.

As I listen to the terrible stresses people have survived, I believe in the notion of trauma, an overwhelming stimulus which cannot be managed without permanent psychologic change. Again, Freud wrote:

> The thesis that neuroses and psychoses originate in the ego's conflicts with its various ruling agencies—that is, therefore, that they reflect a failure in the functioning of the ego, which is at pains to reconcile all the various demands made on it—this thesis needs to be supplemented in one further point. One would like to know in what circumstances and by what means the ego can succeed in emerging from such conflicts, which are certainly always present, without falling ill. This is a new field of research, in which no doubt the most varied factors will come up for examination. Two of them, however, can be stressed at once. In the first place, the outcome of all such situations will undoubtedly depend on economic considerations—on the relative magnitudes of the trends which are struggling with one another. In the second place, it will be possible for the ego to avoid a rupture in any direction by deforming itself, by submitting to encroachments on its own unity and even perhaps by effecting a cleavage or division of itself. In this way the inconsistencies, eccentricities and follies of men would appear in a similar light to their sexual perversions, through the acceptance of which they spare themselves repressions.[16]

Reference to the ego submitting to encroachments on its own unity sounds like a function of the Adapted Child. Through the creativity of the Child, people "spare themselves repressions." Freud seems to be describing what the Child does to master the event, namely, to develop systems for dealing with the threat of a recurrence of the traumatic experience, particularly the use of anxiety as a signal. When, as a trainee, I became anxious about a patient's anger, I would be tempted not to go to work, externally protecting myself from the patient, internally protecting myself from awareness of my own potential rage. This system is elaborated in detail by Berne in *Games People Play*.[17] Berne talks about solutions as decisions, but they are so heavily influenced by the child's situation that the child's creativity is minimized. I prefer to see myself and my patients as having that creativity then—and now—for change. I use the following metaphor for teaching the patient: A patient comes in saying, "I was run over by a truck—see the tire marks?" If he appears to roll in still holding onto the tire, I will ask if he wants to hold onto it and for what? To keep the tire marks bright and shiny? I invite him to shift from Victim to Decider.

I would like to see a prospective study comparing results of TA therapists using and not using the redecision model, with an equal amount of working-through time in each case. In the meantime, I will continue to use the decision/redecision model in my own practice.

NOW AND THE FUTURE

I hope my excitement in this paper has come across, as well as my recognition of unfinished business in myself and in the field of psychotherapy. The piece of business I will work on is how childhood experiences of the first four years can be effectively brought to the awareness of both client and therapist, and how these experiences affect later problem-solving. Clinical evidence from psychoanalysis suggests that very small children do not have cohesive pictures of themselves or others, but do have part representations on their Child tapes. Following Kohut's reports,[18] I believe that understanding these partial pictures and the ways the developing child succeeds and fails in getting these together will help in learning about and reaching a life position of I'm OK, You're OK. Kohut's work on narcissism, particularly on self-esteem and idealization as normal developments of narcissism, is having a considerable impact on my thinking, including permission to use lots of "I."[19]

References

1. Sinclair Lewis, *Arrowsmith,* New York, Harcourt, Brace & Company, 1925.
2. R. Grinker, H. MacGregor, K. Selan, *et al., Psychiatric Social Work,* New York, Basic Books, 1961.
3. R. Wadeson, R. Drye, and P. Greene, "Development of an Active Therapeutic Program on a Chronic Ward," American Medical Association—*Archives of Neurology and Psychiatry, 80* (1958), pp. 363–373.
4. Jules Masserman, "Psychiatric Residency Training for Public Institutional Service," *American Journal of Psychiatry, 119* (1963), pp. 1038–1044.
5. P. Seitz, E. Jacob, H. Koenig, *et al.,* "A Coordinated Consultant Team for Remote State Hospitals," *Archives of General Psychiatry, 8* (1963), pp. 283–288.
6. Dorothy S. Whitaker and Morton A. Lieberman, *Psychotherapy through the Group Process,* Chicago, Aldine Press, 1964.
7. Karl Menninger, *The Theory of Psychoanalytic Technique,* New York, Basic Books, 1958.
8. *Ibid.*
9. Robert Drye, Robert Goulding, and Mary Goulding, "No-Suicide Decisions," *American Journal of Psychiatry, 130,* no. 2 (1973), pp. 171–174.
10. Robert Goulding, "Thinking and Feeling in Psychotherapy: Three Impasses," *Voices 10,* no. 1 (1974), pp. 11–13; Robert Goulding, "Curing Phobias," *Voices, 11,* no. 1 (1975), pp. 30–31.
11. R. Grinker, B. Werble, and R. Drye, *The Borderline Syndrome,* New York, Basic Books, 1968.
12. Robert Drye, "Stroking the Rebellious Child," *Transactional Analysis Journal, 4,* no. 3 (July, 1974), pp. 23–26.
13. Robert Goulding, "New Directions in Transactional Analysis: Creating an

Environment for Redecision and Change," in Clifford J. Sager and Helen Singer Kaplan, eds., *Progress in Group and Family Therapy*, New York, Brunner/Mazel, 1972.

Robert Goulding and Mary Goulding, "Injunctions, Decisions, and Redecisions," *Transactional Analysis Journal, 6*, no. 1 (January, 1976), pp. 41–48.

14. Sigmund Freud, "On Constructions," (1937), in James Strachey, ed., *The Standard Edition of the Complete Psychological Works of Sigmund Freud*, London, Hogarth Press, 1953, vol. 22, pp. 255–269.

15. Sigmund Freud, "Neurosis and Psychosis," (1924), in James Strachey, ed., *The Standard Edition of the Complete Psychological Works of Sigmund Freud*, London, Hogarth Press, 1953, vol. 19, pp. 149–157.

16. *Ibid.*

17. Eric Berne, *Games People Play*, New York, Grove Press, 1964.

18. Heinz Kohut, *The Analysis of the Self*, New York, International Universities Press, 1971.

19. Robert Drye, "Psychoanalysis and TA," in Muriel James, ed., *Techniques with Transactional Analysis for Psychotherapists and Counselors*, Reading, Massachusetts, Addison-Wesley, 1976.

TWENTY-ONE

PILGRIM'S PROGRESS
John J. O'Hearne

When I first met transactional analysis, I did not like it. I put down the journal article[1] before I finished reading it. It was too mechanistic for me. I felt as if they were trying to reduce the puzzling grandeur of a human being to three little circles on a page. After all, I had spent thousands of dollars for my own training and supervision and many years in learning about these complicated human beings. I wasn't about to reduce all that to three little circles!

When I first met Eric Berne at a meeting of the American Group Psychotherapy Association, we shared a table at a dinner dance along with six other people. That evening I admired his way of looking out for himself. I was a good boy and stayed politely at the table, since I "knew" that I should stay and dance with the women. I still have a vivid memory of Eric stretching his neck and looking through his thick glasses all around the room while he turned his head slowly from one side to the other. He reminded me of a periscope sticking up through the water. Evidently what he saw looked good for soon he left the table. I didn't see him again for many years.

In the mid-1960s Kansas City had a few psychoanalysts and a few psychiatrists who had very, very large hospital practices. The great majority of the rest of us had varying exposures to what was called—often euphemistically—psychoanalytically-oriented psychotherapy. Those of us in this majority group saw patients both in office and in hospital. As a member of this majority group, I believe it is fair to say that I was regarded by some as "Mr. Group Psychotherapy of Kansas City." From this vantage point I could introduce new methods of group treatment into the mental health community in my area. I did this when I asked Robert L. Goulding to come to Kansas City in 1968 and, with me, to introduce transactional analysis to a group of fourteen psychiatrists, one internist, and one teacher of psychiatric nursing.

Since 1968, I have become better known as a psychiatrist who integrates

TA and gestalt therapies with more traditional forms of psychotherapy. When I have taught various group psychotherapy societies and in various medical schools, members of the audience have told me they like to hear of my evolution as a psychotherapist. Many of them have found similarities between my maturation as a therapist and their own. Because of these experiences, I shall share the story of this evolution with you. Since my maturation as a psychotherapist could only have taken place as I further matured personally, I shall include some personal details.

SOME BACKGROUND NOTES

My childhood is replete with positive scripting to be a leader. I was the first-born child, followed by four sisters. As a youngster my curiosity was encouraged. As I grew my ability to question and challenge was encouraged, provided I stayed within boundaries of propriety. I was a painfully shy teen-ager until I found that I could talk well enough so that others would listen. I started becoming president of small organizations in the ninth grade.

I did well in college and went to medical school on a full-tuition scholarship, courtesy of the Kellogg Foundation, for the first 12 months. After medical school I took a rotating internship at Denver General Hospital and felt glorious finally to be a doctor. I love being a doctor. As early as my internship, I was paid to teach others. In my two years of Army service as a doctor, I had the good fortune to go through the Army School of Military Neuropsychiatry for four months. It was more valuable than a year of psychiatric residency training. There I first met psychoanalytic concepts and was enthralled with them. They explained everything! I acquired confidence at that school largely from the experience and training. They also taught us how to answer the question, "What are your qualifications as a psychiatrist?" The answer was: "I am a psychiatrist by order of the Surgeon General."

Soon after entering active service in the Army we were given forms on which to rank our preferences for specialization. I ranked them in this order: Neurosurgery, Neurology, and Psychiatry.

However, my experiences in the Army and my introduction to dynamic psychiatry were almost sufficient to induce me to forget my earlier interest and beginning expertise in neurology and neurosurgery. Besides, one of my mentors in the Army had told me that I would never become a neurosurgeon. I asked him why and he replied, "You're not that much of an S.O.B. You can't be that mean."

When I began my psychiatric residency under the tutelage of Frank G. Ebaugh at the University of Colorado in Denver, my Army experience stood me in good stead. I already had some expertise with psychiatric patients. I felt comfortable with them. I was extremely fortunate not only to have this recognized, but to be introduced to projective testing by Donald G. Glad, Chief of Psychology at that hospital. I was further fortunate in being asked if I would like to teach mental hygiene for the Extension Division of the University of Colorado in outlying parts of the state. Since I liked to travel and to teach, I willingly accepted. I was then asked to teach child psychology and adolescent psychology. From these activities I acquired a good idea of the developmental and maturation sequences of human beings, This was of extraordinary value to me as I learned psychiatry. I also remembered and began to use a pre-med course concerning the history and philosophy of religions.

Early in this first year of residency, I asked Dr. Ebaugh why we did not have group psychotherapy at the University of Colorado. I had had an introduction to it in the Army and had participated in some of it, particularly what would now be called staff development. Dr. Ebaugh replied that it was too soon after the war and that it was a new specialty. He offered to pay my airplane fare to a group psychotherapy convention in New York, if I would pay my other expenses. I jumped at the chance.

At this American Group Psychotherapy Association meeting in January, 1949, one of "hot" subjects was: should psychotherapy groups have both male and female therapists so that the transference could be split between them? I also remember hearing, as dogma, which patients should not be put into group psychotherapy. I was struck that the presenter of this opinion evidently had no research findings with which to back up his opinion.

When I reported on this conference in Denver, the report generated enough enthusiasm that Glad and I were authorized to begin psychotherapy groups there and to do research on them. Happily, I was allowed to work with Glad for an entire year of my residency. In exchange for this privilege, I did the forensic psychiatry for that medical center for a year and occasionally taught medical students. During the year I learned a great deal about research methods, and we began curing some paranoid schizophrenics who were thought to be incurable. The "we" included Lillian Plattner, who came to the university six months after I did. We liked working and playing together so much that we were married fourteen months later.

After finishing my residency I stayed on in the lowest faculty position, instructor. I passed my American Board of Psychiatry and Neurology exams in December, 1951. By then I was the proud father of our first child. Lillian interrupted her residency training in psychiatry, after completing two years, in order to be a full-time mother and homemaker.

I began to consider a "training" psychoanalysis for myself, since I had heard that they made for better psychiatrists, but there was nothing available in Denver at that time. I left the University of Colorado in February, 1952, to accept an offer in Kansas City to help plan and open an acute-treatment psychiatric receiving center. The fact that Lillian had gone to medical school in Kansas City and liked it was an important factor in my decision.

My major concern about Kansas City was that it might be too far south for me. Too far south meant too much heat and humidity, and bigotry besides, which I had experienced while growing up in the South. I survived the heat; the humidity was not that bad. We blew apart some of the bigotry. We planned and opened a psychiatric hospital situated between two general hospitals—one for white people and one for black people. In planning our Psychiatric Receiving Center, we decided that we could not possibly administer it efficiently on the basis of separate-but-equal facilities. So we integrated, opening in 1954. I am happy to say that at the end of one year's operation the only person who had been called a "nigger" was a white woman who had been called that in disgust by a black woman. Part of the success of this venture lay in the staff development work that I had instituted.

MY PERSONAL ANALYSIS

The hospital opened in 1954. By that time I was in my Freudian psychoanalysis. My analyst was a very kind, patient woman who became ill and died after I had been working with her for five years. Before her death she vacated her office and saw patients in her apartment living room. I was asked if I would like to rent her office. By that time I was deciding whether to take a position as psychiatric consultant for the Southern Conference Education Fund or to go into private practice. I elected to go into private practice and to use my old analyst's office.

By the time my analyst died, I had introduced both staff development and group psychotherapy at the Veterans Administration Hospital in Kansas City. Several years later I reasoned that, as my analysis had helped me become a better therapist to individual patients, then I should consider becoming a patient in a psychotherapy group, since I was doing and teaching group psychotherapy. Alexander Wolf in New York City, a leading pioneer in psychoanalytic group psychotherapy, offered me the rare opportunity to sit in with him in one of his therapy groups one evening. The next week I returned to New York and sat in a group with another pioneer, Milton M. Berger.[2] I chose to become a pilgrim and commute to New York from Kansas City once a week by propeller airplane and to work with Dr. Berger. A part of the reason for my choice lay in the fact that he belonged to a group that was endeavoring to teach their methods of group psychotherapy to trainees. I saw him for one individual session and a group therapy session in the morning, and followed this with a supervisory session with another analyst in the afternoon and a session which their group taught in the evening. Then I would go to the airport and return to Kansas City. About three weeks after I started, Dr. Berger and I decided that I could be in two therapy groups with him on the same day.

This was one of the most stimulating experiences so far in my professional career. Berger's training had been in the Horney school and he had then a heavy emphasis on existentialism with some interest in Zen Buddhism. This was an entirely new dimension of therapy to me. It fitted many of the things I had thought that therapists should do. It was the first therapy I had seen that I believe could be called humanistic. Berger in his approach was much "looser," warmer, and more human than my prior analyst. I rapidly grew in tolerance of both my patients and of my own impulses. Berger's emphasis on nonverbal communication[3] fitted in with an interest I had already developed in that area. The longest 17 minutes I have ever spent was when I lay on the couch in his office in an individual session and he let me know I did not have to talk for his benefit. I stayed silent for 17 minutes, during which I worked through a very important, unfinished bit of my analysis that no amount of talking could have ever done.

I continued with supervision from a psychoanalyst, Harold Meyers. I also had the great good fortune to be a member of a group of three psychiatrists that met twice a month with this same supervisor. Not only was I impressed with his knowledge, skill, and precision, I was impressed with his and the group's ethics. Dr. Meyers regarded himself as a part of the community and felt he should contribute something back to the community—he met with us for no fee. As for the ethics of the group, I could never identify a single case anyone discussed in spite of the fact that I knew many of their patients.

DIRECTIONS IN MY PRIVATE PRACTICE

I began my private practice in the fall of 1953 and in 1956 started the first psychotherapy group in private practice in Kansas City.

About 1964, Donald Glad had come from Denver to the Psychiatric Receiving Center and we again were working together in the field of group psychotherapy.[4] Through him I learned of the National Training Laboratories in Bethel, Maine. In 1965, I went there for two weeks' basic human relations or T-group training. I could easily spot people who had had successful psychotherapy and I urged the administrators there to have separate T-groups for them. I learned something about group dynamics but still primarily from the viewpoint of group psychotherapy. I believe that I often influenced my group there to move in the direction I desired. (In so doing, I was only called "Little Hitler" once.) This was another step in my learning that my previous theory might be all right—but it also might not be. For example, I learned that to sit beside, and take the hand of, someone in severe grief did not lead to all sorts of wild, dangerous activities. While it was not pertinent to psychoanalysis, it was pertinent to the type of work I was doing with patients. At last, I began to be clear that I was not a psychoanalyst, was not trained to be one, and did not want to be one. I am a more active, less formal person. I like more intense, more open communication, and more equality between me and my patients. I am not talking about pulling down my psychic zipper to let the patient know all about me.[5] I believe that to deny my status as a trained psychotherapist is not possible, even in theory. An existential psychotherapist once said that he recognized that it was his job to serve as a mountain guide for the patient. He could not pick up the patient's feet and move them; he had not been over this particular mountain before. But he knew a lot about mountains from previous training and experience. I liked this viewpoint and began to study more existential approaches to treatment.

After working in this direction a while, I told Don Glad that I was enjoying my work with groups, especially since my patients were getting well, but that when students asked about my theoretical frame of reference, I could not tell them with the same clarity I had had a few years earlier. I asked him to use his particular skills in rating interpersonal behavior and tell me whether I was Freudian, Sullivanian, or what. He observed my work and then said, "There are elements of many theorists but, basically, you are simply John O'Hearne."

In about 1967 Lillian and I went to a couples' group sponsored by NTL and run in Kansas City by Erving Polster and Sonia Nevis, both from Cleveland. This was a very good experience for us.

By this time our four children were in school full-time. Lillian returned to training in child psychiatry to finish her residency. She did this by going half-time for two years. When she started seeing children as patients in a limited private practice, she did not have the aid of social workers, which had been freely available in her training. To have employed them privately would have almost doubled the cost to the family. She did not like that. For a while, she saw the children three times, then the parents once. She was extraordinarily skillful in getting children to change. The parents were more difficult. She then asked if I would help her learn more about adult psychiatry, with which she had had little contact now for a number of years. I told her I thought it would be profitable for her to go to an NTL T-group session for ten days, and she went to what must have been one of the most disastrous sessions they ever had, with at least one psychotic, and an incident of a man being slammed up against a board by the associate trainer in one training group. She was not enthusiastic when I brought up the possibility of our learning something new.

LEARNING TA AND GESTALT   The something new was transactional analysis and gestalt therapy. When I met TA, I felt it was too mechanical and too reductionistic. However, on the Program Committee of the American Group Psychotherapy Association, I became acquainted with Robert L. Goulding. Goulding had studied with Eric Berne and did not seem to reduce people to three little circles. I talked with Bob about my going to California for a three-day weekend of TA with him and Mary. I also discussed with him the possibility of going to Esalen Institute to work for a week in a dream seminar with Frederick (Fritz) Perls. Bob's response was, "Fritz is older than I am; I plan to be around a lot longer than he. If you can only do one, I would definitely recommend you study with Fritz."

Lillian and I decided to study with Fritz. However, Bob and Mary were doing a TA weekend which ended on Sunday afternoon and the session with Fritz began later that same Sunday in the evening. We decided to attend both sessions. We were off now on a pilgrimage together.

We were impressed with the strict rules that Bob and Mary had about no drugs, no alcohol, no hitting, and no sex between participants at the marathon unless they already were having sexual relations together. I saw how he used nonverbal communication and knew that my particular interest and skills in those areas would be highly useful in TA. Before the three days were over, I was clear that I had found something that fitted me well. I had already discovered on my own the split between the grown-up part of the person and the childlike part of the person. What I had not before discovered was what Frank Ernst called Berne's most significant invention, the Parent ego state—the idea that the influences of our parents and other important caretakers are recorded as on videotape in the old part of our brain, that they are subject to instant recall and frequently influence our behavior from second to second.[6] I saw very quickly that those reductionistic three little circles were much easier to deal with than the philosophical constructs of ego, id, and superego. The simplicity and orderliness of the TA approach appealed to me in somewhat the same way as had the orderliness of the central nervous system when I was studying neurology.

When a man in the marathon talked about his rage in the past, and how he had held this in instead of killing somebody, I suddenly broke into tears. I was as surprised as anyone else. When I finished I knew that I was sobbing with relief that no matter how much rage I had felt, I had never killed anybody with it. When I felt this tremendously deep relief and compared it with the times that I had been in both individual and group psychotherapy before—with all the emotions that I had felt there—I knew that I had discovered something enormously important for me. I had some other fantasies which gave me quick, deep insights into responses that had been characteristic of me. I thought: if I can get to these depths in three days, compared to the years I have spent on them before, couldn't I also do the same for my patients in a much shorter period of time than previously. My answer was an unqualified yes.

Bob and Mary's technique included having each person go around at the end of the marathon and say goodbye to other people there in whatever way they wished. Upon my leaving this first TA marathon I decided to say my goodbyes nonverbally, since I had been rather verbal during parts of the marathon. I made one piece of art. In so doing, I clarified for myself much about games. There was one man who had led Bob on a merry chase several times during the marathon. Nonverbally I got him to kneel down in front of Bob, put his right thumb on his nose, and wave the fingers at Bob while he put the other hand near his anus and waved similarly with that. He and the group erupted with laughter because I had shown the closed circuit in which he maintained himself in his *Yes,*

But game. At last I could understand what games were by seeing them rather than by trying to understand them out of the encyclopedic *Games People Play.*[7]

ESALEN AND FRITZ PERLS

Immediately after we had finished saying the goodbyes at our first TA marathon, Lillian and I drove to Esalen in a car borrowed from Bob Goulding. The setting was beautiful. Our first evening session with Fritz Perls began at 7:00 PM. I was shocked at the way in which he so clearly and so powerfully revealed that his were not the ethics that I had come to associate with being a physician. He told us his "Gestalt Prayer": "I am not in the world to live up to your expectations. You are not in the world to live up to mine. I do my thing and you do yours, for I am I, and you are you. Amen."

Furthermore, he said, "If you decide to go crazy here, that's not my responsibility. If you decide to drive off the cliff and kill yourself on the way home, that's not my responsibility. I do not see people individually. I work in the workshop only."

I thought many people were afraid of this brilliant man. Most people in the workshop did not speak up while he was working in the early part of the week. He very quickly let us know that most of the comments people made in psychotherapy groups helped the person stay in his childlike fear that he could not support himself; accordingly, they then would play roles and be phony or would scare themselves with the prospect of all support being removed if they were to become self-sufficient. In TA parlance, Perls said in effect, "Don't help people in the group. You are likely to play a game, such as *I'm Only Trying to Help You.* And you will help them avoid doing their own growing." Even though his orientation and technique were vastly different from mine, his directions were clear. Since his method was so different, I found it easy to follow his directions.

To watch Fritz Perls in action was to watch a consummate artist. His sense of timing was fantastic. At times he seemed to be actually asleep, but instantly would rouse if the person working actively needed him. If people were playing helpless games, he might stay with them for a while or he might ask them to go back to their seat. Sometimes he would do this kindly; sometimes not so kindly.

He did many things I did not expect him to do. For example, it was not rare for him to walk up to a woman in the workshop, kiss her, and put his hand on her breast. I learned a lot about the gestalt approach by watching him do this. If he had done the same thing in private with a woman he did not know well, she might have protested more. Instead, most of them smiled. What he had done was to change the background against which the foreground actions were seen, thus changing the entire gestalt. He was more action-oriented and his sense of theater was sharper than with any therapist I have ever seen. For example, when I occupied the famous "hot seat," an empty chair to his left, and started to tell a dream I had already examined during my psychoanalysis, I was rapidly surprised. I had dreamed this dream at approximately 11 years of age when I broke my arm. The dream occurred during gas anesthesia. When I started to tell the dream, he reminded me to tell it in the present tense. I began, "I am on a narrow cot with no arms, no head, and no feet to the bed. The bed is revolving rapidly around a tall, greased pole." At this point he interrupted and said, "Dance the pole." I looked at him in astonishment, laughed and went to the center of the room. I danced around, coming up from the floor in a spiral going faster and faster. I stopped and continued the dream. "At the top of the pole sits King Kong." Fritz said, "Be King Kong." I said, "Be King Kong?" He said, "You were scared of King Kong, scare the people here like you are King Kong." I went around growling, roaring, and flailing my arms. Nobody was scared. I finally began to laugh. He said, "You see, you are already integrating this part which you had disowned. Are you scared now?" I laughed, "No." He said, "Put King Kong out here [on an empty stool in front of my chair] and talk to him." I did. Then he said, "Change places and be King Kong." I did that. As I kept up this dialogue, changing seats appropriately, I found that King Kong was lonely, not frightening. With this integration Fritz directed me to return to my chair and devise a way to get me and King Kong down the pole. At first I felt puzzled, then remembered what my analyst had told me on numerous occasions: "You dreamed the dream. You wrote it." I imagined some controls on the head of the bed upon which I now sat and slowly I brought King Kong and me back to earth. As I did I felt a sadness. I could not distinguish whether it was mine or King Kong's. I finally decided it was King Kong's, because now he would have to go to a zoo and would not be able to scare people and would be lonely because he was separated from them and was all locked up. At that point I felt much calmer. Fritz asked me to close my eyes and to go to a pleasant place. I imagined myself to be on the beach, feeling the sand, seeing the waves, feeling and hearing the wind. I felt very calm. Fritz gently said, "Open your eyes." I did. What an amazing experience! At the far end of the room, Lillian suddenly seemed to pop out in vivid three dimensions while the other people were so much in the background that they could have been figures painted on the wall. Nobody else in the room was of much significance to me then. I felt very close to her. Fritz then smiled and said, "You have had a minisatori. You lost your head and came to your senses in the fantasy in being on the beach. You see your wife more clearly." I felt entirely relaxed. A much different feeling than I had had when I worked on this same dream in psychoanalysis. In fact, only at that moment did I realize that the greased pole was the pole which pushed the operating table on which I had had my gas anesthesia up to an appropriate height, very much like pushing a barber chair or a car on a grease rack up to the desired height. I had completed the gestalt—with no interpretations. This method was a far cry from the phallic preoccupations which I had tried to make fit this dream in psychoanalysis.

I was surprised at the rapidity with which Fritz would move in when someone gave him an appropriate clue. For example, I took the hot chair again during the week and said, "I want to clear up a problem which has whipped me for a long time." He immediately said, "Sit out here and whip you." I looked at him in astonishment but by then already knew what he meant. I moved to the stool, sat in front of the cushioned chair, started beating on it with both hands. In a very short while he said, "Do you notice any difference in your two hands?" I said, "Yes, my right hand hits much harder than my left." He said, "Have them speak to each other." I did, and ended up with my right hand saying, "I am strong, aggressive, and at times can be full of rage." He said, "What is your left hand doing?" I looked down and saw that my left hand was entirely covering and cradling my right fist. He said, "Now speak for the left hand." I had my left hand say, "I am gentle, sensitive, soft. I am powerful enough to restrain you." At that point I again felt very quiet and relaxed. He smiled and said, "What was the problem which has beaten you?" I told him about being anxious while piloting a light plane, totally alone, and that my anxiety was greatest as the plane left the ground. He said, "Get your plane ready for take-off, pilot it down the runway, and leave the ground." I acted this out. As I pretended that the plane was leaving the ground, I became anxious. Fritz showed me that I was becoming anxious because external support was not there for me. He said, "Now climb the plane up to whatever altitude you like." I told him that I frequently became anxious when I exceeded 3000 feet. He said, "Go to 3000 feet." I did and was calmer. He said, "Are you afraid now?" I said, "Yes, I have some fear that I may crash the plane." He smiled and said, "Crash it." I made loud engine noises and pushed the wheel forward. As I did so, I really "got with it" and crashed the plane. I had leaned so far out of my chair that my head was on the ground. He said, "Where are you?" I said, "St. Peter's Square." Everyone laughed. He said, "Where is your head?" I said, "On the ground, in the crash." He said, "Where is your ass?" I erupted in laughter and said, "Facing the Pope." With the laughter, I decided I was not comfortable standing almost on my head and decided to return to my seat.

When people would stand primarily on one leg while addressing the group, Fritz would help them become aware that they were only partially supporting themselves. I experimented with standing first on one leg, then the other, having a dialogue between my two legs. I learned a great deal about how sturdy I could be on my own legs and that I also wished for support from outside. At the same time, I had rebelled against an excess of this in my childhood. I made many such good integrations for myself in that week there.

I saw Fritz get involved in psychological games where he wanted to rescue someone with whom he felt friendly. I felt better when I saw even heroic leaders make mistakes. Among my many surprises in the week was an incident in which a woman in the hot seat became very angry with him and started to beat on him with her fists. He merely ducked his head a little bit and did not even raise his arms. I was seated next to the hot seat and I reached over and grabbed her. He said, "Let her go." I was astounded. I did. Now she was angry with me, not him. Once, before the week was over, I was in a small leaderless group with her and she tried to push me through a plate-glass window. Outside the window was a drop-off onto rocks far below. At one point in this struggle I had my foot in her crotch. I suddenly realized that I could hurt her a great deal if I gave a quick kick. I decided not to. I kept her from injuring me and held her until she quieted down. Others in the group did not assist. Afterward I did some very fruitful thinking about the women and girls toward whom I had felt resentment, and I actually "let go" of the unnecessary burden of carrying around resentment which I no longer felt served any purpose. Again, none of this had been touched deeply in any of my previous treatment.

I learned other things there too. I learned that Fritz could have strong sexual feelings and perhaps overt sexual activity with some of the women in his groups without destroying his effectiveness. Lillian and I had some extra talking time by drinking wine with him on quiet evenings. He told us that he saw psychotherapy as the method of getting people to wipe their own ass. I added, "Without resenting it." I saw our difference then. I still believed in working through; he did not. Yet he did know that one workshop, even with minisatories and completed gestalts, would not work like magic.

Lillian and I loved talking together about our many peak experiences in California and about our new ways of seeing the world. In contrast, we had not discussed our psychoanalyses with each other. Not only did we talk about our new shared experiences, a check of my calendar shows that we shared more family activities following our introductions to TA and gestalt therapy than in the years before these introductions.

SHALL WE MOVE TO CALIFORNIA?

Shortly after our return from California, the clock measuring our lives sped up. It began with a telephone call between Bob Goulding and me. I told him how much we had profited personally and professionally from being in the workshop with him and Mary and how much we enjoyed getting to know them. Bob replied that this was mutual. In our subsequent discussion, he said that he would like to discuss the possibility of my coming to California to practice jointly with him! That was not beyond my wildest dream. It *was* my single wildest dream. Both Lillian and I had discussed the possibility when we returned home. One of our first thoughts concerned our four children, who were doing well in school and for whom the move would be a sizable readjustment. Later we thought it would be a sizable readjustment for us also. That did not deter us.

With this encouragement from Bob, we needed to see first about getting our medical licenses in California. Accordingly, we rushed through the application process. That left us approximately one month's time to study for the California Board of Medical Examiners. I thoroughly enjoyed this review. I enjoyed most of my one-hour oral examination. They asked me questions about psychiatry, a little pelvic surgery, and how to treat someone for a heart attack. Lillian told me that her examination concentrated almost exclusively on psychiatry. After that we went up to Carmel to spend three more days with the Gouldings and look over the area as a place to live. It looked great to both of us as far as climate and friendship with Bob and Mary were concerned. We made arrangements for other times to share with them. Meanwhile, I studied TA and gestalt approaches diligently.

For years I had been using nonverbal methods and what came to be called encounter techniques. Gestalt theory helped me to see why such techniques worked, and I became creative in inventing more such techniques. The books by Perls and associates showed more art than science.[8] I already had my own art of therapy. Gestalt therapy was more difficult to conceptualize and to teach as a science. In contrast, Berne's books and articles were masterpieces of clarity—sometimes with a pedantic flair. When I began to apply TA to my practice, I found it necessary to stop and think or to draw out the transactions on paper before I understood them well enough to draw them on a board. Often, I would use a gestalt method and only later draw it out in TA fashion. This method was a happy one for me. I could finish a bit of therapeutic work such as helping a patient finish or close a gestalt. In this, feelings were often discharged and relative peace followed. Then we could talk about such things as the racket he was in or the injunction he was influenced by or the script he was following. Only later did I find that Eric was right when he stressed structural analysis, the delineation of three primary ego states of each person. I made mistakes in analyzing games, even scripts, before delineating these ego states. Now I respect Eric's wisdom and check for the three ego states—Parent, Adult, and Child—before proceeding further.

Our next TA time came in October, 1968, when Bob Goulding came to Kansas City to lead the first TA marathon here with me. It was a smashing success. Some of the people present almost immediately started making plans to go to California and learn more with Bob and Mary. Many of these "pilgrims" made such trips and did learn enormous amounts. I am convinced that by starting "at the top," primarily with psychiatrists and those well accepted by them, we avoided much of the difficulty that many training centers have encountered.

In December I returned to California to co-lead a TA workshop with Bob and Mary and afterward to watch their training activities. At my request, Bob had arranged appointments for me with Eric Berne and with

David Kupfer, who shared Bob's office. Bob had given both of them instructions to tell me everything they knew about him. I shall never forget Bob's frankness with me and the frankness with which he encouraged others to speak to me about him.

I was very pleased when Eric told me that he would be glad to supervise some of my work if I moved out there.

When I drove with some of Bob's trainees to Eric's San Francisco seminars, I was doubly glad that I had already met him. I did not see him when I walked into his large group room. I started to sit down front, as is my wont. Several people snickered. When I asked why, I was told that those seats were more or less reserved for senior members of the seminar. Thereupon I moved to the rear of the room.

At five minutes after the appointed hour a hush descended on the room and shortly thereafter Eric entered by the back door. He did this in an unostentatious fashion, but the ritual was so marked that I immediately thought of the priest coming out of the sacristy door to say Mass. This was further heightened when Claude Steiner put a long microphone right in front of Eric as he seated himself. Jack Dusay was making a presentation on the treatment of psychotic people. In the ensuing discussion I was delighted when Eric said, "Let's call on Dr. John O'Hearne, who has recently had an article published on this subject."[9] I was so caught off-guard with this that I instantly "forgot" almost all the TA I had learned and discussed the issue in conventional non-TA terms.

After the meeting I wanted to get to know Eric better and, of course, to "pick his brains." He very tactfully and without words let me know that that part of the session was over. As I listened to him talk, particularly with Claude Steiner, Steve Karpman, and Jack Dusay, I was impressed by the number of big words and puns that were being used. I also had a feeling that they were trying too hard to make the funnies happen. Yet, I decided that it was their seminar and their friendship and I was looking in from the outside.

Upon my return to Kansas City, Lillian and I spent a long evening discussing reasons to accept or not to accept this remarkable offer from Bob to move to California. We finally decided not to move. Why? I was tired of pioneering. I had pioneered in coming to Kansas City to plan, open, and administer an acute-treatment Psychiatric Receiving Center. I had gotten the training program accredited for three full years by the American Board of Psychiatry and Neurology. I had introduced group psychotherapy into Kansas City and felt the loneliness of that until some of my colleagues gradually began to work with groups. I realized that if I moved to California I would once again need to build up my practice. I had a thriving one in Kansas City. My only competition in Kansas City was from other psychiatrists. Here, I often turned away patients and speaking invitations. In California there would be many so-called healers of various sorts, and I did not like the idea of that. Lillian said she would go with me to California if that was my decision. Her reluctance was twofold. She wanted me to live longer and spare myself the stress of starting a new practice again. Also, we were concerned about our children's welfare. Not only would they have to move from their schools—where they were doing so well—but they would be confronted with the problem of drugs in California. The latter turned out to be a very naive consideration, as proved by the fact that the drug situation in Kansas City became as bad within three years as I had thought it was in Carmel. The openness and frankness of Bob and his family, friends, and colleagues in talking to me about the pros and cons of moving there is a treasure that I shall never forget.

NEW ADVANCES WITH TA

In March of the following year I did my first TA marathon with Lillian. In June I did my first such marathon with my friend, Louis H. Forman, with whom I had shared an office when I first entered private practice. Lou was one of three psychiatrists I had allowed to come into my psychotherapy groups as assistant therapists to see what it was like to be in a therapy group, to learn something about it from watching, and to learn from me after the sessions were over. He had had a good psychoanalysis and good analytic training in Chicago. By now Lillian and I had begun to question the value of our respective psychoanalyses when we saw how much faster TA worked.

In August, 1969, I had Irma Shepherd come from Atlanta to Kansas City to lead a TA-gestalt workshop for three days with me. I was very comfortable with her and noticed she used a gestalt approach that was her own, not a carbon copy of Fritz Perls's. I saw some encounter techniques skillfully used and began to understand why encounter leaders—if they were good—should certainly know a lot about gestalt approaches. This workshop was so successful that Irma came back the next year.

One of the demonstrations she used was firm contact between the two hands of one person and the forehead and back of the head of a second person. As she was demonstrating this to me, I could feel a tremendous surge of warm feelings. The strength and support which she gave my head were so remarkable that I instantly regressed to a feeling of being safely cradled. When she tilted my head forward, I felt like vomiting. I remembered instantly that this was how both my parents had held my head when I would vomit as a child. I knew then that body contact was something that no amount of verbal psychotherapy could supplant. After the workshop with Irma I understood regression in the service of the ego more than I had ever understood it before. Now I was not afraid to help some people quickly *regress*, in full confidence that they could equally quickly *progress*.

I accepted an invitation from one of the largest churches in the area to talk on the myths of marriage and the games married couples play. This was my first large public presentation of TA theory. I related TA to myths of marriage and games married couples play. The word-of-mouth advertising following this session must have been good. The church was entirely filled for the second session. Now I had a tool with which I could have fun, help people have fun, see things as they were from a new viewpoint.

In 1970 I passed my Clinical Member exam given by the International Transactional Analysis Association and spent more time studying with Bob and Mary.

In my last telephone conversation with Eric Berne I invited him to the University of Kansas as a guest lecturer. He declined. I heard later he had said that when he made such trips, actually three days were taken from him: two for travel and recovery and one for delivering the address itself. In this last telephone conversation he was warm and cordial and I shall never forget him saying, "With your continued interest you ought to become a Teaching Member." I'm glad to say I did.

The TA in my world really began to pop in 1971. I gave a presentation on "Good Grief" at the ITAA Summer Conference. The central theme of this paper, which was never published, lay in the fact that no one in TA seemed to be doing any "working-through." By this I mean bringing up the patient's desire and looking at it from different viewpoints and seeing that, in the vernacular, "You just can't get there from here"; then, working this through by looking at the fact and the frustrated feelings time and again, helping the individual into his grief. I believe that it is common in TA to overlook the fact that the Child made some original decisions but drove underground his grief at not being loved in his preferred way by the significant parent people in his life. I believe that working-through is essential even after a redecision is made, so that the Child in the patient can forever give up the wish to be loved in the way that he would most like to be loved. I have seen many therapists have patients hit couches and yell and scream out in rage; the only therapists I have ever seen help patients to thoroughly work through their grief have had prior psychoanalytic supervision.

A very significant development for my life in TA occurred in this year. I met James H. Morrison, a management psychologist. Jim talked with me about TA and agreed to give me three hours to present an introduction to TA in a management update program for Hallmark Cards. He took a big gamble, since he scheduled me to give five such presentations locally for Hallmark. Happily, these five went so well for the junior managers that the senior managers of Hallmark asked us to give them similar presentations. I found business ethics and attitudes different from those in the clinical setting. Big business insists on good training techniques. Professional schools could learn a great deal by going to such conferences and watching the skill with which big business and its consultants teach and train employees. I learned never to give long lectures for business groups. Now I use slides, exercises, activities, more discussion from the floor.

While doing this work with TA, I was still active nationally in the American Group Psychotherapy Association, including serving a term as president. I led many workshops for AGPA on utilization of nonverbal methods in group psychotherapy. I also began to introduce TA into my work and found that the two blended beautifully. In essence, I gave the group permission to be aware of what their senses told them and to use their senses differently. I had previously participated in AGPA panels such as "The Case for Interaction Versus Insight," in which I presented the case for interaction.[10] The next logical step was to touch patients, something which had been almost forbidden in some of my previous training. Knowing TA enabled me to wonder why it had been tabooed and to question whether this was appropriate. I decided that, of course, it is inappropriate to touch the patient under certain circumstances but equally inappropriate not to touch him or her on others. Accordingly, I presented a paper, "How Can We Reach Patients Most Effectively,"[11] at the January, 1971, AGPA meeting.

I put together my ideas for the November, 1971, meeting of the World Congress in Psychiatry in Mexico City, where I presented a paper on "To Touch or Not to Touch"[12] and participated in the skilled TA panel at the International College of Psychosomatic Medicine in Guadalajara, Mexico.

In July, 1972, Dr. Fujiro Ikemi invited me to come to Japan as keynote speaker for the Psychosomatic Society of Japan. This is the world's largest such society. It differed from similar societies in the United States by having specialists from many different branches of medicine. Most of those I am familiar with in the United States have been composed mainly of psychiatrists, internists, physiologists, and psychologists. I also taught the Japanese Society of Medical Psychotherapists an introduction to TA and was pleased to provide a similar introduction to TA in Dr. Ikemi's medical school, the University of Fukuoka. (He and some of his colleagues are now members of the ITAA. They have already published several books on TA in Japanese.)

In 1973 we had Erving Polster come to Kansas City. I had the great opportunity of co-leading a group with my warm friend and highly esteemed colleague, Helen Durkin, when she and I joined leadership in one of her therapy groups. After that I spent several days in Vermont with H. Peter Laqueur, getting my first formal practical introduction to multifamily group therapy.

MY DIFFERENCES WITH OTHERS IN TA

I did not find Ernst's article about the OK Corral helpful until one day when I recognized that a patient and I were getting nowhere. I relearned some of Ernst's concepts.[13] Now I spot such patients faster. I may refuse to work with such patients if they are in "get nowhere" situations. Not infrequently, this is enough of a surprise that they enter effective treatment with someone else.

I believe that a *redecision* alone does not provide adequately for working through the grief the Child feels at giving up his long-held wish that he will someday be loved in just the way he wants, providing he obeys the injunction given by the Child of one or both of his actual parents. I compare this to someone telling an eight-year-old child that he will never be able to get his mother or father to love and approve and recognize him in the way he'd like best of all. Such a statement would be frightening or saddening to a youngster. I believe the grief of such a discovery may take four to six months to be adequately worked through.

Concerning the Schiff material on *discounts*,[14] I do not believe that anyone can discount me unless I let them do it. This is not true of infants, of course. I do not know enough about *reparenting* to believe that it can actually happen. Lillian believes in it. I withhold judgment on the effectiveness of this technique until I have known more people treated with it. In a few cases, I have wondered if this approach might help some reparenters remain symbiotic with their patients. On the other hand, I know of some very sick people who are being kept outside of institutions by good workers in this same field. I am also inclined to believe that a therapist who firmly believes in the efficacy of his approach is often more likely to be successful than one who is using his technique with less evangelistic zeal.

My view is that the Parent is recorded on videotape and that we can update it by adding new material. What is called reparenting is often Adult thinking that a loving parent would respond differently and then the individual talking to himself from his Adult. This sounds much closer to Eric Berne's original concept of structural analysis than to so-called self-reparenting. I remain open on these issues. As I learn more about them, I may change my mind.

I do not use Berne's formula for games except for teaching purposes.[15] It is too complicated. I much prefer the Kupfer-Goulding definition of a game. I do use structural analysis, redecision, then working-through.

I use the *miniscript* a great deal.[16] I believe this is the newest frontier in TA. It lies on the boundary between TA and behavior therapies. I have attended three seminars on the miniscript and have co-led a fourth one with Taibi Kahler. I like his clarity in thinking and his interest in building a theory that people can use in their own artistic ways. I especially like his sharp distinctions between structural and functional analysis. This clarity aids greatly in keeping TA simple. I do not believe that Kahler understands and uses the concept of grief and its working-through adequately; therefore, I believe there will be a very few "Wow" experiences with miniscript users until this is integrated into their theory and practice. In my hands, the working-through time of my patients seems to be shortened when I use the miniscript well, and I teach it much earlier in treatment.

I have no patience with those who like to dissect TA further into small pieces. One of its beauties is its simplicity. So who cares what color stamps the patient collects? I don't. I want to know if he and the world around him value them positively or negatively. I have little interest in seeing how much further we can divide the scripting process. I prefer to keep

TA as Eric founded it—simple enough for patients to understand. I like to have them help us.

I do not believe that there is only one way to help a patient get well. Many years ago, I thought there was only one—psychoanalysis. Now, I know there are many such roads. I also believe that skilled psychotherapists share a great deal in their work, even if they do not in their theory. After I made a presentation on nonverbal methods at an International Congress on Nonverbal Methods in Psychotherapy in 1974, a psychodramatist there told me, "You are a psychodramatist." When I recently described some of my work with patients to a couple of expert TA therapists who are interested in bioenergetics, I was told, "You are using a lot of bioenergetics in your work." People from classical psychotherapeutic backgrounds often feel relieved to see me utilize some of what I learned before TA.

LEARNING TA SKILLS

Some of my difficulties in learning TA centered upon my going back to the old ways that I had been taught, for which I had paid so much money, and for which I had had many role models. Reading TA helped. Reading gestalt did not help much until the publication of Shepherd and Fagan's book, *Gestalt Therapy Now,* and the Polsters' book, *Gestalt Therapy Integrated.*[17] I tended to use gestalt as a gimmick until I understood it theoretically; then I could make up my own gestalt experiments.

Most helpful to me in learning were the TA marathons I attended. Here I saw role models—mainly Bob and Mary Goulding—working smoothly and efficiently together. I learned by watching Muriel James and others demonstrating their styles of working at summer ITAA Conferences. However, since TA does not require a dogmatic adherence to any one particular style or theory, I was content to develop and use my own style.

One of my greatest difficulties in becoming skillful in using TA concerned those patients whom I had previously seen two or three times a week, and in whom there were some manifestations of transference neurosis. I had previously wanted this for the treatment of certain conditions in a few patients. In TA a transference neurosis is not desirable. I had not desired the transference neurosis in most of the group psychotherapy which I had done before TA. I agreed with some experts who said that the transference neurosis is probably not analyzable in group psychotherapy. I would see these people individually or in individual and group treatment concurrently. With them I would adopt a neutral (later I learned it was pseudo-neutral) expression and wait for the patient. This developed his leadership hunger, and as the patient was deprived of strokes he regressed to earlier levels of development.

None of this was needed in TA. TA gave me the tools to prevent, with relative ease, formation of such neuroses. Even with TA they are more difficult to cure than to prevent.

Before TA, when I was referred patients who had been treated by other therapists with analytic orientations, I would usually look for another way to treat the patient—for example, group psychotherapy, particularly including some nonverbal methods. Now if the patient has been treated by a TA therapist and referred to me, I still may use TA in many cases. I will want a very clear contract and to know the games this person played with the previous therapist. I may use many nonverbal communications, such as mentioned earlier, particularly for those who play the game of Psychiatry.

I aim for the same things Eric Berne aimed for, namely, to be sure there are three primary ego states and that the patient can move from one to the other flexibly. I prefer the patient to have a relatively clear idea of his goal, though I do not insist on a contract in every case. I tend to look for the patient's feelings in order to get him to express them. He can understand and work through feelings (mainly grief) later.

Does TA cure everybody? No. Does it cure almost everybody? Yes. In the past I have seen statements made that monosymptomatic phobias should be referred to someone who uses a form of behavior therapy. I see very few of such patients. Almost all of the ones I do see have severe early oral problems underneath the symptoms. I have cured mild phobias mainly with structural analysis. The patients' changed behavior leads to so many good feelings and such different feedback that they stay cured without the necessity for deep working-through. If their problems are long standing, and with severe oral-level fixation, I know the treatment is going to take longer and be more complicated. To date, I have not used Bob Goulding's method of treatment in phobias and am looking for the opportunity to do so. Bob makes skillful use not only of redecisions but of here-and-now change, just as Freud insisted upon the patient's practicing the action of which he was most phobic.[18]

Though I seldom need them, I do not hesitate to use medications for patients with anxiety and depression.

As for technique, I still use many nonverbal methods. Instead of talking *about,* we demonstrate what *is.* Instead of talking about things which have happened in the past or are going to happen in the dreaded future, I encourage and sometimes insist that my patients speak in the present tense; this fits in well both with gestalt and with TA. If they are using big words, I ask them to speak in terms that an eight-year-old child can understand. If they do not, I will use video or audiotape feedback or ask them to write on the board what they are telling me. This is particularly important in clarifying a patient's goals.

I have recently heard it said that it is not necessity that is the mother of invention, but, rather, it is the knowledge of other people's inventions. So I find it with some techniques in TA. For example, if an individual or a group is "stuck" (highly resistant), I may use Muriel James' approach of asking them if they have any opinions, thoughts, or feelings about what is going on. Or, I may have each individual in the group write on the board his name and what he wants to accomplish before he leaves the group that day. For the same purpose, I may ask patients to imagine that our time to work today is now over. Then I ask, "How are you feeling as you leave here today? Did you get what you came for today? If not, what will you have to do between now and the time you leave?" I may utilize my past training and say something like, "Sometimes people come here for one thing and en route to that goal they lose sight of the goal and think they want something else—for example, my approval or disapproval. Let's check on this." Sometimes I find that, in spite of the best TA therapy that I can do, I must use the latter approach to deal with some resistances that patients have.

EXAMPLES OF MY CLINICAL WORK

In 1962, I described a man in group treatment in a mental hospital.[19] This man announced that he was the son of God, and shortly after another patient announced that he thought he was an Indian chief; I replied, "That's our boys; nothing but the best." There was, naturally, group laughter. At that time I noted that humor may be a very valuable tool with which to help patients gain further distance from their delusions, provided that humor is well integrated into the personality of the therapist. I noted also that technique is not the motive force in the therapy of any patient. By this I meant that in order to be authentic with a patient, the therapist should be as fluent with his technique as an expert typist is with a typewriter. In TA language, he must have the knowledge of the Adult, the caring and limiting of the Parent, and the ability of the Child to see things as they really are. He must also have the ability to shift quickly and appropriately from one to another ego state (something which I believe should be a prerequisite for becoming a TA therapist). If the therapist is going to have much fun while working and to be an appropriate role model for his patients, I believe he will not only recognize ulterior transactions but will also deliberately, on occasion, use them. In this respect I disagree with those who recommend that therapy be done from the Adult. In spite of what some say, I have not seen any TA therapist who stays entirely in his Adult when working with patients, clients, or workshop members.

Here is one of the nonverbal activities I use: I have people stand at two arms' length from each other then slowly advance until they are one arm's length apart where they stop and examine their feelings; then move so close that their faces are blurred, and then put their cheeks near each other. Many of these people reach out for the other person in a comfortable way when they are this close. I ask if they can argue at that range. Most cannot. I ask if they notice the smell of the other person and most do not. Utilizing TA, I ask them if something in their head told them not to smell or if there was no smell there. Then I ask them to go back to being five inches or less apart and see if they can detect a smell. The majority of them can. This graphically illustrates for them how they blind themselves to the inputs of their senses in obedience to some Parent tapes.

People who have been taught not to need anything from other people show this, and their injunctions can be spotted easily in a trust circle or a blind walk. In a trust circle people stand close around a participant who stands in the center with his or her feet together, knees stiff, and eyes closed. I give the person a slight push and the person to whom he falls pushes him back to another member in the group. This is done very well with music from Ravel's "Bolero," although, of course, it can be done without sound. In a blind walk, a patient is blindfolded by his own consent and led by a partner for a period of ten minutes. Some of the partners have Nurturing Parents who are firm enough to control and provide many interesting sensory inputs. Others stay straight Adult. At the end of the first walk, or even at the time that both partners have had an opportunity to be led blindfolded, they then debrief, and the knowledge of the ego states can once again be reinforced.

A man in a psychotherapy group said that he felt like he was at the bottom of the well. He had repeatedly discussed this with his individual therapist. He seemed stuck at this point. Talking about visualizing the bottom of the well did not work. I asked him to sit on the floor in the middle of the room and surrounded him with group members. He then looked up as if he were at the bottom of the well and said that nobody had a rope long enough to reach him. I pointed out that he had not raised his hands. Actually, he raised his eyes only a little toward each of us. He then decided none of the ropes would be long enough except mine. He did not know whether he could trust me to reach down to him with it or whether I would. I pointed out his decision to remain swimming in the well rather than to try us out. Then, shifting from the visual imagery of the well bottom, he became verbal and said that he thought maybe he could begin to trust us. I told him not to rush it, that he had lived satisfactorily at the bottom of the well, even though his life had been restricted—and that as his trust developed he would reach out and find that some people could be trusted. You may note from this example that I rely heavily upon Erikson's scheme of human development.[20]

I find that combining TA with the nonverbal interests and activities I had had earlier leads me very quickly to injunctions. When a man in a group talked about how much he'd like to have a raise and how difficult it was for him to ask for it, I pointed out that he seldom asked us for anything in the group, even the time to talk. He agreed, and I asked if he had been trained not to ask for what he needed. He documented this. He had previously felt rage as he thought about his depriving parents. To help him into his rage again would not help him work it through nearly so rapidly as another exercise. To rage and to understand does not equal behavioral change. His trouble at the moment was not rage; he needed to *ask* and not avoid asking by raging. I asked if he would go around the room and ask each person if he could get some small change from their purse or pocket. He blushed and said he would. He began to take the money. I told him again that the directions were to ask and that asking was a very crucial issue for him. His mixed feelings as he sat down with a handful of small coins was a peak experience for him. On the one hand, he liked having them and jingled them; on the other, he felt he should give them back to the people. I forbade this. He then said that he should keep them for himself. He blushed and the tears then began to flow. I felt no necessity to do any more uncovering of the original injunction, "Don't need." I am happy to say that he asked for and got his raise within two months. The working-through that he needed lay in the area of raging *because* he had to ask.

When a psychotic woman started another *Kick Me* game, I saw that she would be kicked. Verbal intervention did not suffice. I asked her if she would like to come over and sit by my chair. She sat on the floor by my chair and I put my hand on her shoulder. She began to cry. The group asked why she hadn't told them what she felt and she replied that she had not been taught to do that. This is a prime example, I believe, of permission and protection.

When a psychotic woman in a group began to "talk crazy" again, I asked her if she would like to come over and sit at my feet. She did, and when she started it again, I put my knees over her shoulders so that she was firmly reminded that someone else could control her. She started talking crazy again and I said, "Shhhh." She relaxed and while other group members talked, she played with my shoelaces like a little child. After a while, she said that she had enough. Someone asked her, "Did that really help you?" She said, "Yes, now I can be quiet." Furthermore, at that time she did not get a kick.

Sometimes I prescribe a nonverbal activity if the person is willing to make the experiment. For example, I was treating a man with whom I was careful to have no contract because I was convinced that if I did he would guarantee we would not get to the goal. Accordingly, I treated him without a contract. He was addicted to negative strokes. When he received three positive strokes in a rush, he became nauseated and pale. I helped him out by supplying the negative and he said with relief, "Whew! I needed that." In the process of weaning him from his self-destructive way of life, he began to develop some trust with people in the group. Even before I read Eric's posthumous book, *What Do You Say After You Say Hello?*[21] the over-and-over character of this man's script was so clear that we talked together about his being like Sisyphus who pushed the rock up the hill until he almost got to the top. Part of his developing trust in the group was first in thinking that one woman in the group might be trusted to hold his rock while he rested. As he began similarly to trust other people in the group we noted his increase in trust. I asked if he thought it would be safe, in the group setting, for him to receive something. He thought so. He had been twisting his neck and said it was stiff. I asked if he would be willing to lie on the floor and have a backrub. He laughed with embarrassment and said, "Not you." I said, "No, not me; how about some of the women here in the group?" He agreed and I asked two women if they would give him a rub on the back of his neck and shoulders. He laughed at this and within a few minutes, while he was getting the backrub, he started to say that he had had enough. To this one of the women said, "Be quiet, you have not either." He laughed and relaxed. While this was going on, one of the two women said to the other, "I've never shared a man with a woman before." People in the group laughed and she said, "No, I don't mean that way. I didn't get to share my dad with my mom and at times I know I won't willingly share my husband with my daughters. This is a new experience for me!"

Those of you familiar with gestalt approaches will see that we are completing gestalt here. We are also giving permission and protection for patients to violate the injunction with which they have lived for many years.

When I first started giving permission in TA, I knew that the patients were going to experience some anxiety and/or depression as they gave up the wishes and dreams that they had had for so many years—the dream wishes of being loved in an ideal way by the frustrating parents.

When I give permission to the patient to violate the injunction, or when he decides to violate it, I tell him that he is going to be sad or scared at giving up what he has dreamed for for so long. Then I tell him that he may get scared sometimes, especially when he feels most alone. "Here is my telephone number; you may call me, and I'll help you remember. I know it's scary for the little Child in you to look up at someone two or three times your size and say to them in effect, 'I know I can never please you.' If you feel scared or even begin to have any trouble thinking or remembering what we say here today, here is my telephone number. Call me. However, my Child gets sleepy just like yours, and may I ask that you try to have your emergencies before 10:00 PM." So far I have only gotten one telephone call from such a patient after 10:00 PM.

EVOLUTION OF TRAINING PROGRAM

Every year since 1971, Lou Forman and I have taught a weekly session of four hours over a period of a year.

We knew from other training centers that it might be difficult to attract physicians, particularly psychiatrists, into TA training programs. We thought that if we first took many other helping professionals into our group, we might have trouble attracting physicians again, particularly psychiatrists. This proved to be a wise decision. We have since been invited to present introductions to TA to many different groups of physicians in this area as well as to the Missouri State Medical Association.

In the subsequent years of our 200-hour training program, we have admitted other helping professionals. In 1975, building upon my experience in presenting TA to business and industry groups for approximately one month a year, we invited three men in positions of leadership in business to join our year-long training program. We are not training them to be TA therapists. We tell people, "We will help you to do what you are now doing better by training you in TA. We will not prepare you for a profession that you do not already have." For instance, we will not take a schoolteacher or a business person and train her or him to be a TA therapist. We will train psychiatrists, psychologists, social workers, ministers, physicians, counselors with master's or doctor's degrees to be psychotherapists. We have already encountered a decrease in the number of physicians enrolling for our course.

This course still requires a minimum of 200 hours. We still use peer-group treatment and supervision as one of our training methods. We also insist upon tape-recorded work or actual direct treatment of patients under our supervision. Concerning peer-group treatment, I believe that if the group get to know each other well over a period of time—such as one week to one month in residence—then peer-group treatment may be "real enough." The peer-group treatment in our weekly training group is good practice. However, it seldom compares with the Notre Dame game of patient treatment.

I enjoy comparing psychoanalytic treatment methods with newer treatment modalities, such as TA and gestalt and nonverbal methods. I have the great pleasure of doing this in a weekly group at the University of Missouri's School of Medicine in Kansas City. Here another psychiatrist and I meet in the center of a large room with a group of patients. We are surrounded by trainees, most of whom are in their third year of training in the use of group psychotherapy. Their knowledge of TA covers a broad range, from zero to fairly expert. The other psychiatrist and I treat the group. At the end of an hour and a half, we are joined by the trainees who have been in the background and silent up until now. At the end of that time anyone may say anything they wish. Here we differ from Eric Berne's staff-patient-staff group, primarily in that we give patients and trainees an opportunity to talk together.[22] The advantage of this over Eric's method is that the patient is not left with misunderstandings or bad feelings resulting from what a trainee has said about him. He gets equal time. Trainees seldom believe my statement, "In the second group you may say anything that you wish." They are convinced that their words can almost literally destroy a patient. Patients have similar attitudes, but usually within three months they are talking about the trainees and what they like and dislike about them, often in a very protective way because they are afraid that they will "hurt" the trainees.

We have prevented some damage in our training groups. Here I am particularly concerned about the danger of suicide. Some people may learn the body of knowledge that is represented as TA and the techniques associated with it and still know very little about psychopathology, clinical diagnosis, and follow-up. One sample of this was a social worker who talked about a client referred to her with depression. We asked if he had threatened suicide and found that he had. The worker said, "Oh, he won't kill himself. I have a no-suicide contract with him." While the article by Drye and the Gouldings has saved the lives of many people, I believe that placing complete confidence in a no-suicide contract is about as safe as jumping into a whirlpool while wearing a miraculous medal and hoping for the miracle. Diagnosis must continue throughout treatment.[23]

MY FUTURE

I will continue to teach through AGPA and its affiliate societies and the International Group Therapy Association. I shall continue to teach in business and management. I am working actively with Dr. Ray Parmley in the Department of Anesthesiology at the University of Kansas Medical Center in management science for health professionals. In this we weave TA together with other approaches to management science.

Lillian and I share between us a half-time job at the new six-year combined premedical and medical school of the University of Missouri at Kansas City. In this program students enter directly from high school to a six-year program. At the end of that they graduate with a BA and MD degree. When we work with some of these students on an intense basis, we actually feel "high." They are very stimulating and we like the work.

I shall continue working with Lou Forman, Lillian, and other colleagues in our year-long training group if enough professionals continue to want such training.

I shall carry on my work with individual and group psychotherapy, seeing individuals, couples, and families. Lillian and I expect to continue to work with couples with sexual problems. I shall continue to learn and do multifamily group therapy. I doubt that I shall do treatment of social networks like families, neighborhoods, or communities. I may work with social networks in medical schools, business settings, or organizations. Here I can use TA more than if I treated a family as part of a social network comprising relatives and neighbors as well.

FUTURE OF TRANSACTIONAL ANALYSIS

Transactional analysis is simple.

It has many advantages. Patients can understand it and can help in their own treatment. They always can know what is going on in the treatment. Children can understand it and remind their parents. Family therapy and couple therapy are easier by far with TA, particularly when aided by the principles of general systems theory. TA usually provides a quick resolution of symptoms, less regression, and fewer magical expectations. It is useful in decathecting Parent when teaching new ideas to people who have previously worked another way, as in business, or believed in another way, as in sex education. Many of its concepts may be expressed in the form of cartoons. I use these in almost all of my teaching.

Berne's concepts of group dynamics differ from many others published in this field.[24] I find them very useful, particularly when I am called upon as consultant in macrosystems, such as a large organization of volunteer members with a paid central office staff, or in large businesses.

I fear that TA will gradually become more left-wing. The right-wing, conservative, clinically trained people do not need the credentials of ITAA behind their names. Some, like Lillian and me, will join for interest, learning, and stimulation. I fear that the number of people who want to change careers by trying to become psychotherapists, believing that they can get there simply by learning TA, will increase.

I believe that some businesses will continue to hire people to orient them to TA and that some of these people will know what they are doing. They will know their limitations as well as their assets. They may interest a great number of people in TA. The same thing will continue to happen in churches and perhaps even in Parent-Teacher Association meetings.

I am told that Eric Berne predicted that the ITAA would not survive beyond ten years. I do not believe that the organization will dissolve or split within the next several years. Like the American Medical Association, it may have meetings for all of its members with some special meetings for those with special interests. It may form divisions, as the American Psychological Association has done. Each division represents separate interests but all remain members of the large group.

I believe that ITAA will continue to spread rapidly in the rest of the world and that these non-USA organizations will experience their own divisions. This time of rapid growth outside the USA is fascinating to watch. I hope that as the ITAA matures it will resemble a family, all of whose members are maturing, and that we will see varying viewpoints presented rather than a forced homogenization of viewpoints. The ITAA is the most exciting group with which I have ever been involved. I hope it remains so.

References

1. Eric Berne, "Ego States in Psychotherapy," *American Journal of Psychotherapy, 11* (1957), 292–309.
2. Max Rosenbaum and Milton Berger, eds., *Group Psychotherapy and Group Function,* New York, Basic Books, 1963.
3. Milton Berger, "Nonverbal Communications in Group Psychotherapy," *International Journal of Group Psychotherapy, 8* (1958), pp. 161–178.
4. Donald G. Glad, *Operational Values in Psychotherapy,* New York, Oxford University Press, 1959.
5. John O'Hearne, "Therapeutic Utilization of Nonverbal Processes in Group Therapy," in *Group Therapy and Social Environment,* Bern, Switzerland, Hans Huber, 1975, pp. 695–699.
6. Franklin H. Ernst, "The Diagrammed Parent—Eric Berne's Most Significant Contribution," *Transactional Analysis Journal, 1,* no. 1 (January, 1971), pp. 49–59.
7. Eric Berne, *Games People Play,* New York, Grove Press, 1964.

8. F. S. Perls, *Gestalt Therapy Verbatim*, Lafayette, California, Real People Press, 1969.

9. John O'Hearne, "Some Methods of Dealing With Delusions in Group Psychotherapy," *International Journal of Group Psychotherapy, 12* (1962), pp. 35–40.

10. John O'Hearne and Donald G. Glad, "The Case for Interaction," *International Journal of Group Psychotherapy, 19* (1969), pp. 268–277.

11. John O'Hearne, "How Can We Reach Patients Most Effectively?" *International Journal of Group Psychotherapy, 22* (1972), pp. 446–454.

12. John O'Hearne, "To Touch or Not to Touch," paper presented at Fifth World Congress of Psychiatry, Mexico City (1971).

13. Franklin H. Ernst, "The OK Corral: The Grid for Get-On-With," *Transactional Analysis Journal, 1,* no. 4 (October 1971), pp. 33–41.

14. Aaron Wolfe Schiff and Jacqui Lee Schiff, "Passivity," *Transactional Analysis Journal, 1,* no. 1 (January 1971), pp. 71–78.

15. Eric Berne, *What Do You Say After You Say Hello?*, New York, Grove Press, 1972.

16. Taibi Kahler with Hedges Capers, "The Miniscript," *Transactional Analysis Journal, 4,* no. 1 (January, 1974), pp. 26–42.

17. Joen Fagan and Irma Lee Shepherd, *Gestalt Therapy Now,* Palo Alto, Science and Behavior Books, 1970; Erving Polster and Miriam Polster, *Gestalt Therapy Integrated,* New York, Brunner/Mazel, 1973.

18. Robert Goulding, "Curing Phobias," *Voices, 11,* no. 1 (1975), pp. 30–32.

19. O'Hearne, *loc. cit.*

20. Erik H. Erikson, *Childhood and Society,* New York, W. W. Norton & Company, 1963.

21. Berne, *What Do You Say . . . , op. cit.*

22. Eric Berne, "Staff-Patient-Staff Conferences," *American Journal of Psychiatry, 125* (1968), pp. 286–293.

23. Robert Drye, Robert Goulding, and Mary Goulding, "No-Suicide Decisions," *American Journal of Psychiatry, 130,* no. 2 (1973), pp. 171–174.

24. Eric Berne, *The Structure and Dynamics of Organizations and Groups,* Philadelphia, J. B. Lippincott Co., 1963.

VI

Overview of Transactional Analysis

TWENTY-TWO

WHAT TRANSACTIONAL ANALYSTS WANT THEIR CLIENTS TO KNOW*
Stanley Woollams, Michael Brown, and Kristyn Huige

Transactional analysis (TA) uses four major methods to understand and predict human behavior: (1) *structural analysis* aids in understanding what is happening within the individual; (2) *transactional analysis* describes what is happening between two or more people; (3) *racket* and *game analysis* provides understanding of the transactions that lead to bad feeling payoffs; and (4) *script analysis* assists in understanding the life plan that an individual is following.

STRUCTURAL ANALYSIS

Each person has three functional parts called *ego states* (Figure 1). Eric Berne, the founder and primary developer of TA, defined an ego state as "a system of feelings accompanied by a related set of behavior patterns."[1] The three major groupings of these sets of feelings and behaviors in people are named *Parent* (P), *Adult* (A), and *Child* (C). (When capitalized, these words refer to ego states, otherwise they refer to persons.)

The *Parent* ego state consists of attitudes, perceptual styles, and behaviors taken in from outside sources, primarily parents. It is a recording of the individual's perception of what significant figures in his life have done. Descriptively, the Parent functions in two ways—*Nurturing* (NP) and *Controlling* (CP)—and contains a collection of moral and value judgments, both positive and negative. The Parent also contains an attitudinal style, such as being a caring person or an angry person. The Parent may express itself directly, in which case the person acts just as one of his parent figures acted, or indirectly as an influence on his Adult or Child ego state (Figure 2).**

---

* For an expanded version of the ideas presented here, see Stanley Woollams, Michael Brown, and Kristyn Huige, *Transactional Analysis in Brief*, 3rd ed., Ann Arbor, Michigan, Huron Valley Institute, 1976.

** We have alternated the gender of pronouns throughout the text, instead of writing as if everyone is male. We realize that this, too, is artificial, but nevertheless we think it is an improvement over the traditional way.

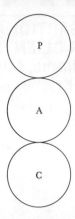

Figure 1
Structural Diagram

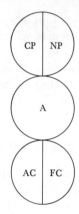

Figure 2
Functional Diagram

The *Adult* ego state objectively appraises reality. To do so it gathers, stores, and uses information from all sources, including the external world and one's other ego states (Child and Parent). The Adult uses this information to make statements and estimate probabilities. The Adult is often called the *Computer* because it functions like a digital computer, i.e., it computes logically, and without feeling, the data it has taken in. If the Adult has inaccurate or insufficient data it will not make accurate statements. The nervous system is not fully developed at birth and develops gradually while the child grows. Logical thinking probably does not begin until late in the first year of life and only slowly increases until full abstract thinking is available by around age 12. It is at this age that the Adult becomes fully functional.

The *Child* ego state consists of all the urges and feelings that come naturally to the individual. Different impulses and feelings become available at different ages. Thus, an infant has certain innate feelings and wants which change, at least through adolescence, as his nervous and hormonal systems develop. In addition to these natural or inherent feeling states, the Child also consists of a recording of his early feelings and how he reacted to them. For descriptive or functional purposes, the Child may be divided into two parts: *Adapted Child* (AC) and *Free Child* (FC). The Adapted Child is expressed when the individual uses automatic patterns of behavior which enable him to get along with and get some kind of attention from the "big people" in his life. The Free Child expresses himself spontaneously without concern for the reactions of the parents of the world.

As an illustration of ego states, a 16-year-old boy, observing a pretty girl, might go through the following dialogue: "She looks like a slut [CP], but perhaps she really is a nice girl [NP]. I think there's a good chance she would go out with me [A]. She really turns me on [FC], but she'll see I'm really no good, so I might as well go away [AC]."

In addition to the descriptive method, ego states may be analyzed structurally, providing what Berne calls the *"psychobiological structure."* For fuller understanding, it is useful to do what is called a second-order structural analysis, in which the Parent and Child are broken down into smaller divisions. Figure 3 shows the second-order structure of an eight-year-old. To illustrate the formation of the Parent, he is shown taking in and recording his perception of his mother's behavior and messages in his Parent ego state.

At the time of birth, all that exists is the Child in the Child (C_1). This is the source of the individual's energy and it consists of innate wants and

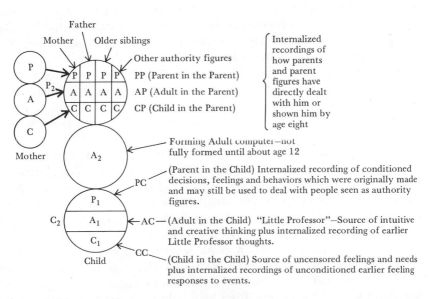

Figure 3
Second Order Structural Analysis of an Eight-year-old

feeling states. It is from here that the desires and feelings of the individual are expressed. As the person grows he retains recordings of how he spontaneously felt in response to what happened around him and to him. For the first two months or so the chief learning and responding mechanism is the conditioned reflex. By the third month the infant appears to respond to the outside world with some kind of thinking process. This primitive thinking mechanism is called the Adult in the Child (A_1) or *Little Professor,* essentially a nonverbal system based on intuition. The infant somehow "knows" how the important people around him are feeling and responds directly to that. It is also the source of creative thinking. These abilities are retained in the growing individual unless they are suppressed by parent figures who are upset when (1) their child knows how they feel, or (2) he creates new and different methods or things. In response to the events occurring in his life the growing child has many feelings and thoughts. As a result of these reactions he makes decisions as to how to best get along with the parent figures upon whom he is dependent. These decisions are the basis for patterns of behavior and feeling which, through repetition, become automatic. The structure that results from these decisions is called the Parent in the Child (P_1). This part often functions in close association with the Parent (P_2), looking for and setting up the negative and positive responses to which it has become accustomed.

As mentioned earlier, the Adult ego state slowly forms its logical capacities and is fully developed by around the age of 12. It seems likely that the Adult is not a fully autonomous ego state but rather functions mostly in conjunction with one of the other ego states from which it gets its energy.

Second-order analysis of the Parent shows recording of the Parent, Adult, and Child of the person's mother, father, older sibling(s), and any other individuals who functioned in any kind of parental capacity. Cultural and ethnic messages may be acquired from any of these sources. New information can be assimilated into the Parent at any age. It is probably the Child who decides what goes into the Parent, since this seems to be correlated with (1) how vulnerable the individual is and (2) how impressed he is by the other person. Thus, a person who is seen as being quite potent may be taken in as new Parent, while one who is not seen as powerful may be completely ignored.

The complexity of the second-order analysis of an individual explains why a person may respond in many different ways to a single stimulus. During every moment of life the individual is simultaneously recording two things: (1) in his Parent he records what significant others are doing; and (2) in his Child he records what he is feeling (C_1), thinking (A_1), and deciding (P_1) about what is happening. Also, as he grows older he may record in his Adult information about what is happening. In addition to these recordings, which are available for playback at any time, the individual can respond in the here-and-now from his Adult with logical thinking about what is happening, from his Little Professor with some creative thinking, or from his Child in the Child with a new urge or feeling. The choice of which ego state he will use in a given situation is influenced by his lifestyle, or life script, which will be explained more fully in a later section.

DIAGNOSIS OF EGO STATES   When a particular ego state is in executive control of the personality, that ego state is said to be *cathected*. There are four ways—behavioral, social, historical, and phenomenological—to determine which of a person's ego states is cathected at a given time.

The awareness of *behavioral* clues is often the most useful, especially until the client himself is able to report accurately on what he is doing. A person's words, voice, dress, posture, and attitude, as well as other clues, help determine which ego state he has cathected. Typical Parent words contain value judgments, Adult words are clear and definable; the Free Child speaks up for himself. Slogans for living and phrases that begin with "you" usually come from the Parent. For instance, "I want to go to the movie tonight, but you know you can't always go out and have a good time," shows an individual beginning with an "I" statement from his Child but then switching to his Controlling Parent with a "you" followed by a slogan. The posture of the Adult tends to be erect without any tilting of the body in any direction while a sideways tilt of the head may indicate that the Little Professor is psyching out a situation. The Little Professor may be either Free Child (functioning without fear of parental figures) or Adapted Child (psyching out the best way to get along). If a person is crying silently, he is usually in his Adapted Child, since the Free Child makes a lot of noise when upset.

Noting the kinds of transactions a person has with other people will give the *social* diagnosis. A person coming on from an Adapted Child position and saying "I'm helpless" is likely to elicit responses from another person's Parent, either Controlling or Nurturing. Personal responses to other people also provide clues to help identify ego states. For example, if you are aware that you want to have fun with someone, he is probably in his Free Child. If you are inclined to respond from your own Adapted Child, he probably is in his Parent ego state. If you respond with a fact, he is most likely in his Adult ego state.

Historical diagnosis is made by checking into the past. Recalling that in the past you were in a very similar situation with feelings similar to those you are now experiencing will let you know that you are in your Child. If your father or mother gestured and talked just as you are doing now, you are probably in your Parent.

A *phenomenological* diagnosis is made when a person examines his own feelings. He can look inside himself and experience whether he is in his Child, Adult, or Parent. To help him do this, he can use various techniques, such as a gestalt technique, to go back and relive an old scene, thus directly experiencing the ego state involved.

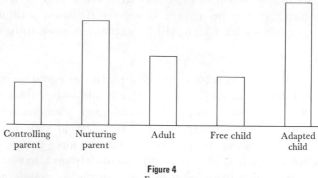

Figure 4
Egogram

EGOGRAMS   A person learns to respond from certain ego states at certain times in order to get what he wants. Different people tend to spend varying amounts of time and energy in different ego states. These tendencies are illustrated by *egograms*.

Egograms were developed by John Dusay as a visual representation of how the individual appears to others. They depict the amount of psychic energy found in each ego state relative to the others. Egograms and the constancy hypothesis (which holds that the amount of psychic energy within a person is constant) imply a physiological approach to psychotherapy. Thus, if a client takes away some of the energy he is putting into his Controlling Parent, he will have more energy available to his other ego states. Also, if a client builds up his Nurturing Parent, he will take energy away from other ego states.[2]

Egograms are best done by the Little Professor, who intuitively is aware of how other people are behaving. When a number of individuals are asked to draw egograms of a single person there is a good deal of agreement. If the person's own egogram differs from how others see him, he may be in a game and discounting how he really is coming on. A person can also draw an internal egogram (how the individual feels inside). The internal and external diagrams may be quite different.

In the egogram in Figure 4, the individual is highest in the Adapted Child, with Nurturing Parent next. The Controlling Parent is lowest. He expects people to take care of him and do what he wants. His Free Child is low, so he does not go after much of what he really wants but instead demands what Nurturing Parents have told him he should have. In addition, this person nurtures other people a great deal so that his Adapted Child will feel he deserves to belong.

PSYCHOPATHOLOGY

An emotionally healthy individual is able to cathect the ego state of her choice. She chooses that ego state which appears to her to be most func-

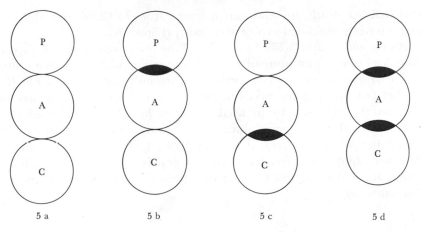

5 a   5 b   5 c   5 d

Figure 5

tional in the situation, i.e., the Parent for nurturing someone, the Adult for solving a problem, and the Child for having fun and getting close. She has available an Adult ego state that contains accurate data upon which she estimates probabilities to make appropriate decisions and carry them into action.

Parent prejudices and Child fears do not masquerade as Adult information in the healthy individual. Psychopathology is present when ego boundaries break down and the Adult becomes *contaminated* by the Parent and/or Child and the Adult does not correct or check out misinformation.

Figure 5a represents the uncontaminated Adult. A Parent-contaminated Adult (Figure 5b) results in prejudices ("Women don't think; they're flighty"). A Child-contaminated Adult (Figure 5c) results in phobias and delusions ("Cats are scary"). The Adult can be contaminated by both Parent and Child (a person hears words from his Parent and expresses fears about them from his Child, Figure 5d).

Exclusion is another type of psychopathology. Exclusion occurs when one ego state dominates the person's behavior. This may be evidenced in various ways. The Constant Parent (Figure 6a) may be very preachy and authoritarian (some ministers and career military personnel). The Constant Adult (Figure 6b) is someone who has excluded feelings and seems to function like a breathing computer (some mathematicians and engineers). The Constant Child (Figure 6c) may be someone who always plays and entertains others (the typical good-time Joe). Also, the psychotic individual may be in a confused Constant Child ego state.

Some people use only two ego states while excluding the third. This may occur as a defensive maneuver when a confused, crazy Child is excluded in an effort to maintain functioning, as in Figure 7a. The Parent or Adult also may be excluded. The person with an excluded Parent may behave irresponsibly and without conscience (Figure 7b). If a person has excluded her Adult, she may switch from Parent to Child with thoughts and behaviors unrelated to objective reality (Figure 7c).

Aaron and Jacqui Schiff have shown how the development of psychopathology results from unresolved *symbiotic* relationships, i.e., two people behaving as though between them there are only three ego states.[3] If a mother fails to meet the needs of her own Child ego state, she may become overly responsive to the needs of her child. The young person does not learn to think properly, since she is not allowed to fully develop or cathect her Adult or Parent. When this person grows up, she may attempt from her Child to manipulate others into gratifying her unmet needs and wants, and fail to be aware of her own power to get her needs met in a direct manner.

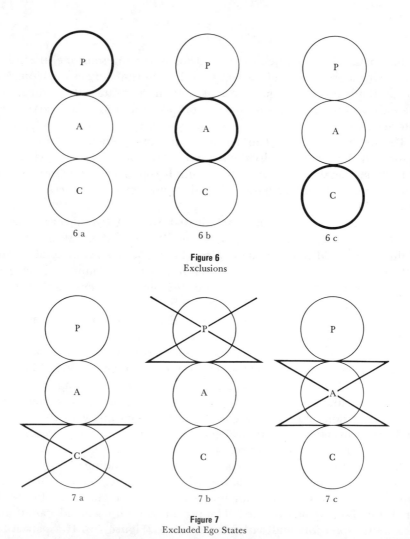

Figure 6
Exclusions

Figure 7
Excluded Ego States

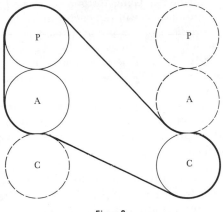

Figure 8
Symbiosis

Another person might have a mother who, herself, is very needy, enveloping, and almost devouring. This person might decide to exclude her Child, remaining Constant Parent in order to protect her Child from being swallowed up. She may take on her mother's role in symbiotic relationships and go through life thinking for others and telling them what to do, discounting or refusing to be aware of her own Child's needs and wants. It is evident from Figure 8 that the psychopathology involved consists of the individual's decision not to be a whole person without the psychological or real presence of another individual. It is also evident from the diagram that in this type of relationship only one person has thinking (Adult) available to her and only one person attends to her own feelings and needs (Child) at any one moment in time. Often in symbiosis there is no thinking going on and the relationship is purely Parent to Adapted Child.

An infant comes into the world as a helpless being whose only means of communicating her need for food or comfort is her cry. For the infant to develop normally the usual process is: the infant cries, the parents hear the cry, respond to it, and most likely discover and resolve the child's problem. If the parents *discount* the child by responding more to their internal world of prejudices and feelings instead of to the actual external reality of what is happening to the infant, the child will develop pathological ways of relating to the world. There are four levels of severity of discounting, and within these levels a person can discount in three areas: *oneself, others,* and the *situation.* The four levels are:

1. The *existence* of a problem (baby cries and parents go to sleep). This is a total discount and the most pathological. It involves blocking an awareness of a stimulus from the baby (others) which could lead to the definition and solution of the problem.
2. The *significance* of the problem (baby cries and parents say she is always fussy at that particular time of day). The baby is acknowledged as ex-

isting but the situation is being discounted. A problem must be seen as significant before a person will put energy into solving it.

3. The *change possibilities* of the problem (baby cries and parents claim that there is no way she will be satisfied). The parents are aware of a problem, acknowledge that it is important, but believe that it has no solution. Since they do not look for other ways to respond, they discount the baby (others).

4. *Personal abilities* (baby cries, the parents know it is a problem, that it can be solved, that others could handle it, but see themselves as incapable of dealing with it). In this instance the parents are likely to get someone else to do something.

In order to discount in any of these ways the parents would have to be operating either: (1) from a misinformed Adult, or (2) from a contaminated Adult, or (3) by excluding the Adult and cathecting an unhelpful Parent or Child. For example, mother may respond in a helpless, whiny Child ego state, failing to cathect or energize her thinking capacities. Mother is excluding her Adult, failing to take in necessary information (baby is wet and cold) to help her solve the problem. Her Child may insist that she's helpless and inadequate while her Parent may call her useless and no good. Or mother may be operating from a Parent-contaminated Adult, with Parent tapes masquerading as accurate Adult information (e.g., "It is better to let babies cry themselves to sleep than to pick them up"). In both of these instances the parents may think they are gathering more proof that their behaviors were Adult programed when baby finally adapts by giving up and stopping her crying. The exclamation at this point is usually, "I knew nothing was wrong; she's stopped crying." The child's adaptation thus reinforces the parents' discounting.

When the baby cries and her needs are not met, she may escalate as a reaction to being discounted (for example, she may scream more loudly). The child may then make an unhealthy life decision based on being discounted. If she repeatedly has to escalate feelings, she may decide not to experience her feelings and to be passive as she relates to the world. Or she may decide that her needs will be met only after she tolerates a great deal of frustration. If the child is still discounted, she may develop other pathological ways of relating, such as games and rackets, which she substitutes for her original needs. Thus, she makes a *decision* to give up the Free Child feeling, need, or want which began the process. These decisions determine a person's *script* or life plan. For example, a child who does not get the loving attention she needs and wants may learn to accept negative attention or punishment as a substitute. Or, in more extreme cases, a child may learn to discount hunger by not allowing herself to experience or feel stomach contractions when she has a physiological need for food. Instead, she substitutes confused, Adapted Child behavior, such as withdrawal and rocking, rather than experience the discomfort of her need not being met.

All script behavior is motivated primarily by the Adapted Child and involves a discount of at least one of the individual's ego states. Thus, the person will enter into symbiotic relationships with other people. It is said that the mechanism that maintains symbiosis is discounting and the justification for that discounting is *grandiosity* (or exaggeration). In other words, to discount a here-and-now situation one must exaggerate something to make it appear like the old scene where she made the original script decision. Often a person will say or experience "I can't stand it" as she discounts herself.

The discounting mechanism the person uses to maintain the belief system that supports her script and her way of conceptualizing herself and others is *redefining*. When she hears or perceives information discordant with her frame of reference she is apt to discount its existence or interpret it so as to support her own belief system.

There are four styles of *passive* behavior that a person may use to establish a symbiotic relationship. None involves thinking through a problem to a solution while taking into account all of the ego states.

1. *Do nothing* means that psychic energy is used to inhibit responses and thinking (when asked to pick up something she dropped, she instead stands still and looks sullen).
2. *Overadaptation* is psyching out what she thinks others want of her and adapting to this fantasy. She is anxious to please and identifies others as parent figures who are more important than she and whose needs and wants are her responsibility to figure out (the person who wants to be held but will not ask because she assumes the other person will not want to). This type of passive behavior is not the same as the nonpassive, conscious behavior called adaptation, which involves thinking and deciding to comply because it makes sense to do so.
3. *Agitation* involves the use of energy in purposeless, non-goal-oriented activities (smoking, pacing, rocking, jiggling, hair twirling, talking incessantly, etc.). Mild and even moderate agitation often can be stopped by making the person aware, and the Adult then may resume functioning. Or, one may put words to the behavior and discover what message is contained in it. More severe agitation is usually best dealt with by getting the person to respond by Parent direction or stroking ("Just sit down, no one is going to hurt you"). A confrontation without support for the Child may result in escalation to violence, since the severely agitated person is experiencing a threat to a symbiotic relationship (real or imagined).
4. *Incapacitation and/or Violence.* These behaviors are in the same category, since they both involve a refusal to think and problem-solve at a high level and the environment often must take over. Behaviors may include getting sick, fainting, going crazy, attacking someone, etc.

The substitute behaviors (games, rackets, etc.) directed by the Adapted Child are the person's compromise with her world and often keep her alive by providing strokes, even if it means she has to be miserable to get them. Infants express needs and generally let their feelings be known. Many adults have long since forgotten their Free Child needs. Sometimes a person, usually when in a substitute behavior, will cycle back to her Free Child without confrontation. However, because she does not feel OK, she will tend to discount her own need or feeling and quickly return to her familiar game or racket. In treatment it is important to confront the discounting of these needs and to help the client to think and to figure out how she is substituting pathological behavior for Free Child needs or feelings.

LIFE POSITIONS

Each person has inherent wants, needs, and feelings. The early experiences of the individual, including whether or not these needs are met, play a deciding role in the establishment of that person's *life position* (also called *basic position* or *existential position*). The life position influences how the individual thinks, feels, acts, and relates with others. There are four basic life positions:

1. I'm OK, You're OK.
2. I'm OK, You're not-OK.
3. I'm not-OK, You're OK.
4. I'm not-OK, You're not-OK.

The OK Corral, developed by Franklin Ernst, Jr., depicts the four life positions as well as attitudinal stances which accompany each position (Figure 9).[4]

When an infant enters the world, he probably is in the healthy number-one position—I'm OK, You're OK. As long as the child's basic needs are met, he will remain in this position. Persons in this position reflect an optimistic and healthy outlook on life, freely relate with others, and assume a "get-on-with" stance in their dealings with other persons and the environment. If, however, the child's needs are discounted through chance or neglect, he may enter position number two, three, or four. Persons may

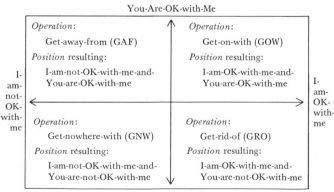

Figure 9

also move into not-OK positions as a result of learning from significant others, either through modeling or by being stroked.

If the young person is severely neglected, abused, or oppressed, he may decide that it is others, not himself, who are not-OK. When this happens, he may assume position number two, I'm OK, You're not-OK. Commonly, one of his parents modeled the position for him. For example, most child abusers were themselves abused as children. This position is often called the paranoid position, since persons in this position are often extremely distrusting, blaming, or hateful. They may deny personal difficulties, feel cheated, and react toward the world with anger or frustration. Their general stance in dealings with others is a "get-rid-of" position.

Position number three, I'm not-OK, You're OK, is referred to as the depressive position and is the most frequent in American society. If his needs are not met, the young person may decide that "I'm not-OK." Persons in this position often feel stupid, inferior, ugly, or inadequate. Depression, guilt, and/or distrust of others may also accompany this position. Persons in this position have great difficulties accepting compliments, and generally take a "get-away-from" stance in their dealings with others and the environment.

Position number four, I'm not-OK, You're not-OK, is assumed by persons who were miserable enough in their youth to have decided that neither they nor anyone else is worthwhile or valuable. This is the "give-up" position, and persons who have assumed this position often wind up in prisons, mental institutions, or morgues. These persons generally assume a "get-nowhere-with" stance in their dealings with other persons and the environment.

Once a person has assumed a basic life position, he tends selectively to perceive the world in ways that will maintain that position. In reality, most people are not fixated in a single position but rather move from one position to another at different times with different people. For example, a man may assume an arrogant I'm OK, You're not-OK position at home with his family, while feeling and acting inadequate (I'm not-OK, You're OK) with his boss, and yet be relaxed and outgoing (I'm OK, You're OK) with his friends at his country club. The position in which an individual spends the greatest proportion of his time is called his life position. Positions are assumed as a result of a decision made when the person was very young and lacked adequate Adult information. Like any other decision, this can be changed. Since all persons are in fact OK, all of the not-OK positions can be thought of as unhealthy delusions. Helping people to reassume the healthy life position is one of the major goals of transactional analysis.

STROKES

Each person must satisfy the basic need of stimulus-hunger. A *stroke* is a unit of recognition, a form of stimulation. Research indicates that infants require physical stimulation (touching) in order to survive and grow.

Without physical stimulation the infant may become seriously crippled or die. It apparently makes no difference whether the physical stimulation invokes pain or pleasure, only that the infant is physically stroked. From this research and other observations, the general rule is that a negative stroke is better than no stroke at all.

Strokes can be physical, verbal, or nonverbal. As a person grows older, she discovers new ways to exchange strokes. The need for stimulation becomes, at least in part, a need for recognition. Also, since physical touching is frowned upon by much of our society, there is added incentive for a person to learn to accept other forms of stimulation. Words, smiles, gestures, touch, and other forms of recognition are accepted as strokes. Since the need for strokes is inherent, exchanging strokes is one of the most important of all human activities.

Strokes can be positive or negative. A positive stroke is one which carries a "You're OK" message and usually results in good feelings. A negative stroke is one which carries a "You're not-OK" message and may result in unpleasant feelings. Since each person in a transaction is free to exercise options regarding which strokes she will give and receive, the ultimate responsibility for how a person feels lies in herself; e.g., negative strokes can be accepted, in which case bad feelings may result, or they may not be accepted, in which case there will be no bad feelings (Figure 10).

Strokes also can be unconditional or conditional. An unconditional stroke is a stroke for *being*, whereas a conditional stroke is a stroke for *doing*. It is possible, then, to think of strokes in four categories, examples of which are given below:

POSITIVE UNCONDITIONAL: "I like you."
POSITIVE CONDITIONAL: "Thank you for rubbing my back."
NEGATIVE CONDITIONAL: "I don't appreciate your sarcasm."
NEGATIVE UNCONDITIONAL: "I hate you."

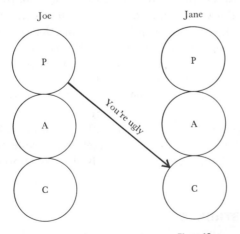

Option A: "I'm not-OK (ugly), Joe is right and I feel bad."

Option B: "I'm OK and I feel good about myself regardless of Joe."

Figure 10
Options with Negative Strokes

Conditional strokes, both positive and negative, are often used to modify the behavior of other persons. Used appropriately and consistently, conditional strokes provide a powerful tool with which persons are taught healthy adaptive responses. For example, a mother gives her child a positive, conditional stroke by exclaiming that it's great when she has used the toilet, and she gives her negative, conditional strokes (scolding) when the child has bowel movements on the floor.

Since strokes are necessary for survival, a person will do whatever she thinks necessary in order to receive the strokes she needs. A person will develop a style of giving and receiving strokes based on her life position. A person who feels OK about herself and others tends to seek out exchanges of positive strokes. A person who feels not-OK about herself and/or others tends to seek out negative strokes that will increase her not-OK feelings. When positive unconditional strokes are not given to or accepted by an individual, she will seek out the other kinds of strokes.

TRANSACTIONAL ANALYSIS

People communicate with each other by means of *transactions*. A transaction is an exchange between two persons, consisting of a stimulus and a response between specific ego states. Transactions can be simple, involving only two ego states, or complex, involving three or four ego states. A conversation consists of a series of transactions linked together. Whenever an individual initiates a transaction (or responds to a stimulus from another person) he has a number of options as to which ego state he will use and to which ego state in the other person the stimulus will be directed. The healthy individual is autonomous in his choice of options and chooses to initiate or respond from the ego state he judges to be most useful in a given situation. There are three kinds of transactions—complementary, crossed, and ulterior—and for each there is a corresponding rule of communication.

A *complementary* (*uncrossed* or *parallel*) transaction is one in which the stimulus and response vectors (communication paths) are parallel so

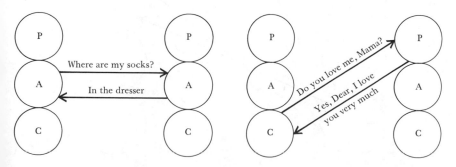

Figure 11
Complementary Transactions

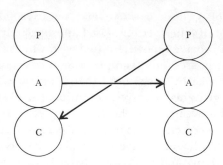

Adult to Adult: "Where are my socks?"

Parent to Child: "Can't you do anything
for yourself?"

Figure 12
Crossed Transactions

that only two ego states are involved (one from each person). More specifically, a complementary transaction must meet two criteria: (1) the response comes from the same ego state as that to which the stimulus is directed, and (2) the response is directed to the same ego state from which the stimulus is initiated (Figure 11). Complementary transactions can occur between any two ego states. The *first rule of communication* is that as long as the vectors remain parallel, communication may continue indefinitely.

A *crossed* transaction occurs when the communication lines are not parallel and do not meet the above criteria. The *second rule of communication* is that when the communication is not parallel a breakdown (sometimes only a brief, temporary one) in communication results and something different is likely to follow (Figure 12).

Sometimes a crossed transaction (and communication breakdown)

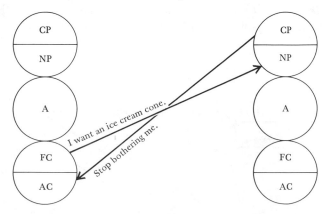

Figure 13
Crossed Transaction

occurs even though it appears that the two conditions for a parallel trans-action are met. To clarify this, it is necessary to divide the Parent and Child ego states into their descriptive parts. This demonstrates that they are functioning as if they were two separate ego states, and thus the requirements for a crossed transaction are fulfilled. (Figure 13).

In ordinary social conversation, parallel transactions are most useful. However, in therapy and at other times when it is desirous for someone to change his mind or think differently, it is necessary to effectively cross transactions. A client says he is a poor soul and can't figure out what he needs to do. He is in his Adapted Child and hoping to hook a Nurturing Parent response. It is necessary for the therapist to exercise his options and respond from a different ego state to break off that flow of transactions and so motivate the client to switch ego states.

The therapist could respond to the above from his:

a. Free Child   "Wow, you really are in bad shape! What are you going to do?"

b. Adult   "You are capable of figuring out what you need to do."

c. Positive Controlling Parent   "Stop discounting yourself and figure out what to do!"

Any one of these crossed transactions will break off the original communication (second rule of communication) and perhaps hook the client into a different kind of response. After the client is in his Adult or Free Child it is then appropriate to use complementary transactions to reinforce the Adult and/or Free Child behavior.

Ulterior transactions can be *angular* or *duplex*. An *angular transaction* involves three ego states and occurs when messages are sent simultaneously from one ego state of the initiator to two ego states of the respondent.

In the example in Figure 14, the salesperson provides Adult informa-

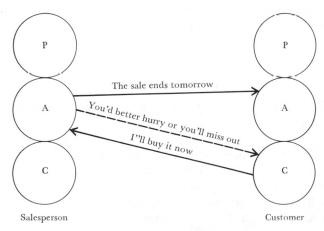

Figure 14
Angular Transaction

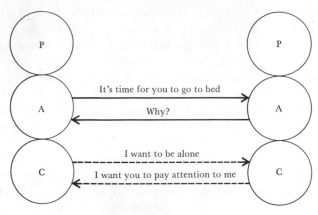

Figure 15
Duplex Transaction

tion to the prospective buyer. However, he simultaneously sends a secret message to the customer in an attempt to "hook" the latter's impulsive Child and quickly close the deal. The secret message is nonverbal and is referred to as the *psychological message.* The Adult-Adult stimulus is overt and is called the *social message.* The respondent may reply from any of his ego states. In the example in Figure 14, the salesperson was successful in "hooking" the customer's Child.

A *duplex transaction* involves four ego states, two in each person. During the course of a duplex transaction, two conversations are occurring simultaneously, one on the social level and another on the psychological level (Figure 15).

The *third rule of communication* states that the outcome of the transactions will be determined on the psychological level. Often the only persons aware of the ulterior transactions are the participants themselves. Ulterior transactions are not necessarily dishonest, but at times the secret message may be used to set people up for games and their ensuing negative payoffs.

TIME-STRUCTURING

The need for individuals to structure time is called *structure-hunger.* This can be thought of as an extension of *stimulus-hunger,* since the need for stimulation requires that persons establish situations in which strokes can be exchanged. How a person structures her time depends upon how OK she feels about herself and others, the kind of strokes she is seeking, and other learned patterns of behavior. There are six ways of structuring time, and each has advantages and disadvantages. They are listed below in ascending order from the lowest emotional involvement:

1. *Withdrawal:* When a person withdraws, she is mentally removed from others. This can be done alone in one's room, at a party, or while walk-

ing down a crowded street. Daydreams, fantasy, and meditation are all forms of withdrawal. When a person withdraws, she is choosing to shut others out, relying on herself for positive or negative stroking. Withdrawal is usually safe, requires little emotional investment but generally provides minimal stroke yield.

2. *Rituals:* A ritual is a safe and predictable exchange of strokes in which persons behave toward one another in a fixed manner. Rituals may be brief and simple, such as an exchange of "Good mornings," or long and complex, such as a religious ceremony. For many people, these predictable exchanges provide important maintenance strokes.

3. *Pastimes:* When people are not trying to accomplish a goal but are only "talking about" something, usually one of their favorite subjects, they are engaging in a pastime. "Bull sessions" and other semiritualized conversations may supply a relatively large number of strokes, usually pleasant, without risking closeness. Common examples of pastimes include "General Motors" in which people discuss automobiles, and "Betty Crocker" in which people talk about cooking recipes.

4. *Activities:* When one's energy is directed to external sources (objects, tasks, ideas, etc.) the person is engaged in an activity. Work, hobbies, and chores are common examples; hence, most people spend a great deal of their waking hours involved in activities. Activities produce strokes in many ways. When a job is well done, positive strokes often are obtained in the form of praise from friends, relatives, or the Parent within the person. Negative strokes may be received if a person does a job poorly, is self-critical of her work, or chooses to work with people who find fault easily. Strokes also come from direct rewards like school grades, trophies, and paychecks, and some people use their rewards as their major source of strokes. If the activity involves body movement or thinking that is fun or creative, the Child experiences this as positive stroking.

All these first four ways of structuring time can be done from any of the ego states. For example, while withdrawing, a person can have either a scary or pleasant Child fantasy, an interesting Adult fantasy as she plays with numbers in her head, or a Parent fantasy of "how awful kids are nowadays." Besides being used for their own value, rituals, pastimes, and activities often are used in selecting people for the more involved ways of structuring time—games and intimacy.

5. *Games and Rackets:* A psychological game is an ongoing series of complementary ulterior transactions that lead to a well-defined, predictable outcome. A racket is not only the bad feeling payoff which occurs at the end of a game, it also is often an ongoing series of complementary transactions containing constant bad feelings, and so it, too, is a way of structuring time. Games and rackets will be described in more detail in the next section.

6. *Intimacy:* Intimacy is the most rewarding of all the ways of structuring time. It is also the most difficult to define. Intimacy involves the sharing of feelings, thoughts, and experiences in a relationship of honesty and trust. There is a straight, spontaneous exchange of strokes, in the here-

and-now, with no ulterior motives, no exploitation, and no other way of time-structuring present. The Free Child is always involved during intimacy and open to whatever happens. The intimate experience may be physical or emotional, pleasant or unpleasant, real or imagined. Although intimacy provides the highest stroke yield, people often avoid intimacy because they see it as risky and unpredictable. When a person feels and knows that she is OK, she will seek out friends to be open and intimate with.

The amount of time spent and strokes received in each way of structuring time will vary a great deal from person to person. One person may derive most of her strokes in withdrawal by having frightening fantasies, another in ritualized exchanges or by pastiming superficially, and still another by working very hard. Some get most of their strokes in games—especially from the bad feeling payoff—and a few get many strokes in intimate relationships. A person's script (life plan) determines how she will spend her time and which ego state she most often uses. If she does not want to get close to others, for example, she may spend a lot of time withdrawing or in rituals and perhaps playing games resulting in distance. If she does not want to feel, she may stay mostly in her Adult and choose fantasies, rituals, pastimes, and activities that primarily use that ego state.

RACKETS AND GAMES

Rackets and games have a great deal in common. Both are substitute ways of getting strokes, both are learned systems, and both require a discount of the self and/or the other person. The Adapted Child substitutes these learned behaviors for spontaneous Child feelings that were discounted or not permitted. The two are somewhat different in that a game is a process using ulterior transactions that end with a racket feeling. A racket, however, also can be a process using complementary transactions that include the bad feeling.

RACKETS   Some families have rules against sadness or grief because they think it denotes weakness, but on the other hand they think it is all right to be angry. Children in those families often learn to suppress their sadness and to show an angry façade. Other families say, "Don't be angry, smile instead," and their children learn a quite different façade. By smiling, they produce strokes from the Parent inside of them for being good children. These feelings are called racket feelings since they are an indirect or manipulative way of getting strokes and do not lead to any useful action or result. A person's natural tendency is to have a feeling, express it, be done with it, and then go on to something else. If he is sad and it is against the rules to express sadness, he will substitute a racket feeling. This will produce strokes but not satisfy or finish the original feeling, so he will tend to go on indefinitely with the substitute feeling.

Racket feelings often seem manipulative, artificial, repetitive, stereotyped, and lacking in authenticity. Any feeling may be a racket and cover up a spontaneous Free Child feeling. Anger, sadness, confusion, fear, guilt, helpfulness, superiority, and other feelings all can be used as substitute ways of getting strokes. Each person will tend to have one favorite racket feeling and will use that feeling in many different situations. To illustrate, each person driving down an expressway may be experiencing his familiar racket feeling. If seven such people were asked to report their feelings, each might report a different feeling even though they were all in the same situation:

> Driver number 1 is angry at the other drivers.
> Driver number 2 is sad about the crowded expressway.
> Driver number 3 is confused with all those cars around him.
> Driver number 4 is afraid about driving.
> Driver number 5 is guilty for causing the crowded expressway.
> Driver number 6 helpfully defers to all the other drivers.
> Driver number 7 feels superior to the other poor drivers.

When a person's feeling is not a racket, that feeling will make sense for the situation and the person will do something that will finish the feeling, i.e., get off the expressway, vote for funds for a better expressway or a mass transit system, slow down, or do whatever would be reasonable for the situation.

There are three ways in which racket feelings are learned:

1. When a parent models it for a child (mom shows daughter that a woman should be quiet and sad by being quiet and sad herself).
2. By being stroked (reinforced or conditioned) when he displays the feeling. (A child may decide on an anger racket because he gets most of his strokes when he is angry or obnoxious. His parents may not pay attention to him when he is feeling good and doing well.)
3. By a parent telling a child what to feel or think. (An angry child is told, "You're not mad, you're just tired.")

An individual can be in a racket, and so be discounting, from one of three major positions. This is best demonstrated by using Karpman's drama or game triangle. The basic roles are: *Persecutor* (P) ("I am better than you, you are inferior"); *Rescuer* (R) ("I know more than you, you are inadequate"); and *Victim* (V) ("I am helpless, you are better than I am").[5] (Figure 16.)

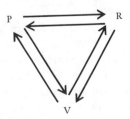

Figure 16
Drama or Game Triangle

Each person knows and has a favorite role and will look for other people to exchange strokes with to complement his position. If a Persecutor talks to a Persecutor they will likely pastime, but if the Persecutor finds a Victim they can exchange strokes of greater intensity. There are two types of Victims: those who look for Persecutors and those who look for Rescuers. Some, of course, will settle for either one, and others persist until they find both.

A person may be in his racket without interacting with others and may stroke himself internally.

A's Parent says to A's Child: "You goofed again."
Child responds: "I'll try harder."

This is a Persecutor-Victim exchange.

If another person becomes involved, the transactions between the two are parallel and can continue indefinitely.

A says: "I goofed again."
B responds: "That's all right. You tried."

This is a Victim-Rescuer exchange.

A person may be into a racket during most of his waking time and, as Fanita English points out, he begins playing games only when he perceives that his racket strokes are no longer forthcoming, that the other person is refusing to continue.[6] At that time, he may switch game-triangle roles and play a game to keep the strokes coming in. Thus, a person may begin in the Victim position, crying and moaning about how hard life is and how inadequate he is. While he has a sympathetic listener the transactions can continue indefinitely. However, when the listener tires of the Victim's Adapted Child whining and decides to leave, the original Victim might switch to being a Persecutor, castigating his listener for not really caring about him. In switching from one racket position to another, he collects another stroke payoff and perhaps even influences his listener to stay.

GAMES When people communicate on more than one level at the same time, and when the results of their transactions lead to bad feelings, they are playing a game. A psychological game is defined by Berne as "an ongoing series of complementary ulterior transactions progressing to a well-defined, predictable outcome." The predictable outcome, or *payoff*, consists of bad feelings for each player. A bad feeling is any feeling that occurs because of a discount—either of the self or someone else. This ranges from a Victim's sadness or confusion, to a Persecutor's anger or triumph, to a Rescuer's concern or pity. People are often amazed that after having engaged in pleasant stroking for a period of time, they suddenly are aware of an emotional climate which is tense, hostile, sad, or otherwise unpleasant. Their amazement stems from the fact that games are played without Adult awareness, so that the bad feeling payoff comes as a surprise. Games are noted by their repetitive occurrence, always beginning with a discount and always ending in bad feelings.

Games are learned patterns of behavior, and most people play a small number of favorite games with various persons and in varying intensities. Game players intuitively seek out and find partners for complementary games, and it is in marriage and other close relationships that most games are played to the greatest intensity.

First-degree games are played in social circles with anyone willing to play and generally lead to mild upsets. A mild game of *Seducto* can be basically exciting and fun. A man and woman enjoy an evening of flirtation with each other, one turns the other down at the end of the night, and both feel slightly uncomfortable.

Second-degree games occur when the players go after bigger stakes, usually in more intimate circles, and end up with a bigger bad feeling payoff. Here, the come-on may even last for several days until a blatant sexual advance is met with a strong rebuff. The woman leaves angry and justified that "all men are no good," while the man, who is playing *Kick Me,* feels hurt and rejected by yet another woman.

Third-degree games involve tissue damage and the players may end up in the jail, hospital, or morgue (if, for example, the woman shoots the man to defend her honor).

Games also vary in the length of time that passes while they are being played. A short version of a game may take only a few seconds from start to finish, while longer versions may last weeks, months, or even years.

People play games for these reasons:

1. To structure time.
2. To acquire strokes—positive strokes may be acquired in the early moves of the game, and negative strokes always accompany the payoff. A "good" game might be thought of as one that produces many more positive strokes in the early phases of the game than negative strokes resulting from the payoff.
3. To maintain a racket.
4. To keep others around when racket strokes are running out.
5. To confirm parental injunctions and further the life script.
6. To maintain the person's life position by "proving" that self and/or others are not-OK.
7. To provide a high level of stroke exchange while blocking intimacy and maintaining distance.
8. To make people predictable.

GAME ANALYSIS   There are several ways to understand the dynamics of a game. One way is illustrated by the symbiosis diagram (Figure 17).

A game, like a racket, involves a symbiotic relationship and begins with a *discount*.

A discounts his Child needs or feelings ("Let me take care of you," is stated verbally while he suppresses that he's tired and wants to rest).

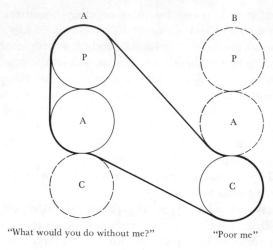

Figure 17
Symbiosis Game Diagram

B discounts his Adult's ability to solve problems and his Parent's guidance in taking care of himself (and so says, "Yes, take care of me!").

A is playing "What Would You Do Without Me," while *B* is playing "Poor Me."

Each individual is responding to a situation by ignoring the reality of what is happening and how the other person feels, and by dealing exclusively from an internal frame of reference (with what is going on in his own head). Discounting can only occur when Adult thinking is avoided and actual Child needs or feelings are ignored. Any person can stop discounting and refuse to play games by acknowledging his Child needs or feelings and choosing appropriate means to have them met.

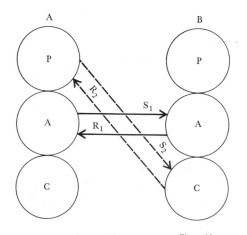

S_1: "Can I see you tonight?"
R_1: "Yes, come over later."
S_2: "I'll teach you a lesson."
R_2: "Come and kick me."

Figure 18
Transactional Diagram of a Game

Another way to illustrate games is depicted in the transactional diagram in Figure 18.

The two persons in Figure 18 are sending dual or ulterior messages. While their Adult ego states are discussing a rendezvous (social message), *A*'s Parent and *B*'s Child are setting up a situation (by a covert or psychological message) which will lead to bad feelings. The game becomes apparent when ego states are switched and the psychological message becomes overt and bad feelings are experienced by both players. *A* is playing *Now I've Got You, You SOB* while *B* is playing *Kick Me*. The transactional diagram illustrates that both partners must be willing to play a game in order for the game to continue. Robert Goulding lists seven steps necessary for a game:

1. An ostensible stimulus, usually Adult to Adult (social message);
2. A psychological stimulus (secret message);
3. A response to the secret message;
4. A payoff of bad feelings;
5. A statement about self;
6. A statement about others;
7. The game is played without Adult awareness (if the participant is aware of the psychological level of communication, he is maneuvering or manipulating the other, not playing a game).

The Karpman game triangle illustrates still another way of understanding games. Persons who play games are discounting while assuming the role of Persecutor, Rescuer, or Victim. Any one player knows all the roles and may switch from role to role as the game progresses or as he goes from one game to another. Most people, however, have a favorite role and spend most of their time in that position. A game occurs when at least one of the players switches positions on the triangle, thereby providing a negative stroke payoff for each player in the game. Note the many switches in the following example.

A wife may start out ostensibly as a helper by saying "What's troubling you, dear?" to her husband. However, when he tells her he's just lost his job, she may switch to a Persecutor and put him down for being stupid and lazy. Her game is *Now I've Got You, You SOB*, while his game is *Kick Me*. The game triangle may also be used to show switches to other games. To carry on the above example, if the husband seems upset, the wife may switch to Rescuer and say, "I was only trying to help you." When he looks better she may switch to Victim and say, "Why does this always happen to me?"

The final transaction of each game has served as the overt stimulus to the next game, which is brought out when the next switch of ego states, or game-triangle position, occurs (Figure 18).

The game formula, defined by Berne, describes the flow of a game:

Con + Gimmick = Response ⟶ Switch ⟶ Crossup ⟶ Payoff

(The underlining was added by the authors to illustrate that the three last events often occur simultaneously.)

CON: *A*'s desire to play a game is initiated by a discount (his con). "Let me help you," is given verbally, while the nonverbal message is "You're inferior to me."

GIMMICK: *B* also discounts (and reveals the part of him that is interested or hooked by the con, which is his gimmick) and responds to the secret message. His verbal response is "Help me." The nonverbal message is "You're right, I am inferior."

RESPONSE: A series of social messages follows, usually Adult to Adult (*A* "helps" *B* by telling him what to do).

SWITCH: Each player switches ego states and the secret messages become apparent. *A* says, "You can't be helped. You really are inferior." He now shows that he is a Persecutor and not a helper. *B* says, "This proves it. I really am no good."

CROSSUP: A moment of confusion is experienced by each player. *B* may momentarily wonder, "What happened? I thought he was trying to help me."

PAYOFF: Bad feelings are experienced by each player. *A* feels superior after having played *Now I've Got You, You SOB* and *B* feels depressed after having played *Kick Me*.

Games provide many strokes for some clients, and lifelong patterns of stroking are not easily given up. Initial confrontations of games and/or rackets often frustrate the client, who may escalate the pattern by crying louder or by threatening to leave or to hurt himself. The therapist encourages the client to learn new and more satisfying ways of acquiring the strokes he needs and wants while using one or more of the following methods.

One is to provide the client with Adult information concerning the game(s) the client is playing, how it fits into his script, and how the moves of the game progress to a bad feeling payoff. The therapist does this by allowing a game to be played out or described, asking the player how he feels after receiving the payoff, and diagraming the moves. With this information the client, especially if he is playing a first-degree game, can learn to avoid the payoff, and can change how he relates to others.

Another way to treat game players is to work directly with the client's racket feelings, pointing out their repetitive occurrence and the client's responsibility for feeling the way he does. Finally, find out what the suppressed Free Child feeling is and encourage him to express it. When the client gives up the racket feeling he will likely give up the game moves that accompany it.

A third way to stop game-playing and rackets is to confront the opening discount and encourage the client to think about what he is discounting. As the client becomes aware of what is really going on within himself he may choose to stop discounting and give up the ensuing game or racket.

In general, the task of the therapist is to help the client become aware of and express in a useful way the Free Child need or feeling that he has been discounting.

STAMPS

Many people collect feelings in order to justify their behavior. These collected feelings are called *stamps,* because they are saved up and cashed in just like trading stamps. Stamps can be collected for bad feelings as well as for good deeds.

Bad feeling stamps may be accumulated whenever a person is in his racket feeling or receives the negative payoff at the end of a game. For example, a henpecked man refuses to deal with his anger when his wife criticizes him. Instead, he feels sorry for himself and collects stamps. After five years or so he may cash in his stamps to justify beating her up, leaving the marriage, or some other behavior.

Good deed stamps are collected when a person feels a need to justify his behavior by doing good things. A hardworking doctor may work for many years until finally he decides it is all right to take a short vacation.

Some people save only one kind of stamp, but most people collect both kinds. An alcoholic may justify a weekend binge by cashing in bad feeling stamps ("I've had such a hard week, I deserve a drink") or good deed stamps ("I've done really well lately, let's celebrate and have a drink").

Stamps are collected by people who feel not-OK about themselves and/or others and want to avoid taking responsibility for their behavior. Some people cash in their stamps regularly for small prizes (missing a day of work or failing a test), while others save them up for bigger prizes (divorce, suicide, homicide). Stamps are unnecessary and are used to keep a person from being autonomous by maintaining his racket and forwarding his script. The healthy individual deals with his feelings, wants, and needs as they occur and does not collect stamps. One of the goals of TA treatment is to help the client give up his existing stamp collection and stop collecting them thereafter.

SCRIPTS

A script is a personal life plan *decided* upon by each individual at an early age in reaction to her interpretations of external events. A young child is extremely vulnerable to parental influence. First, she is very small compared to her parents; second, she does not yet have a fully formed Adult ego state to help her understand what is going on; third, she often is not given much information about what is going on; and fourth, she has no option to leave and find a better place to live. The above factors contribute significantly to the powerful effect of parental messages.

It is generally true that people do not love as strongly as they hate, so a moment of hatred may overshadow hours of love or caring. Thus, the negative messages that come to the baby from her parents are especially powerful. Every child must receive some positive messages or she will not live. If the positive strokes are given unconditionally—for example, "I love you," then they function as *permissions* and do not limit the person in any way. If the positive strokes are given conditionally—for example, "I love you when you smile," they lead to adaptations in getting along with people. Thus, the person may be limited or scripted (although in this instance the script is benign). The negative messages (called *injunctions*) are taken in more powerfully and may form the basis for a destructive script. This may not occur if some other important person gives the child permission to ignore the injunction or to find a way to avoid it. Unfortunately, most injunctions from one parent are reinforced by injunctions from the other parent, since two people who decide to live together usually have mutually complementary scripts. Script decisions are probably formed in the following sequence. The Child in the Child (C_1) reacts with feelings to the input it receives. The Little Professor (A_1) then works out what it thinks is the best way to obtain strokes, positive or negative, so that the little person will not be rejected or killed. The Parent in the Child (P_1) then carries out the plan or decision.

Berne described several types of script patterns that people tend to follow:[7]

1. Persons with "Never" scripts never get to do or have what they most want—their Parent forbids it ("Sex is bad, stay away from it").
2. Those with "Always" scripts are in an opposite position. They must keep on doing the same thing—such as working, moving about and never settling down, living with a particular person ("You made your bed, now lie on it!"), etc.
3. "Until" or "Before" scripts insist that the person must wait until a certain time or do something before she can have a reward ("If you're real good and have all your work done, then you can play").
4. "After" scripts set one up for trouble after a particular milestone ("After forty, life is over," or "After you're married, life is full of obligations"). The first people get fat and forget about sex after forty, while the second group get married and collect obligations such as mortgages, in-laws to care for, and children whom they react to as burdens.
5. A person with an "Over and Over" or "Almost" script never quite succeeds; e.g., the businesswoman who never finishes her work ("I almost get the job done but the phone keeps ringing").
6. An "Open-Ended" script does not tell a person what to do after a certain time. Instead, without giving options for later on, it stresses very heavily what the person is supposed to do earlier. Thus, some women flounder after their children grow up and leave home, and some men are at loose ends after they retire.

If the life plan produces mostly negative strokes, it is a *loser's* script. If the script has a tragic ending, it is called an *hamartic* script. People with loser's scripts have serious problems that often require the attention of lawyers, therapists, or jailers. If the strokes are evenly distributed and not highly charged, the person has chosen a *banal* or *nonwinning* script. These people play it safe and avoid highly charged situations, such as Child-to-Child intimacy. A typical male banal script is a hardworking businessman who uses his Adult a lot, but does not get much closeness for his Child. A typical female banal script is a hardworking housewife who functions a great deal in her Nurturing Parent (with both her children and her husband) and does not use her Adult (except to run the house) or her Child to get close to others. If the strokes are mostly positive, then it is a *winner's* script. If our hero and heroine have mostly received permissions to live and grow and think, they are not script-bound and will basically do what they want if it makes sense for them.

PERMISSIONS AND INJUNCTIONS Each growing child needs a series of permissions to fully develop her or his capacities. The earlier the need for a permission, the more important it is. For every permission not given there is a corresponding injunction. In the following discussion we are indebted to Robert and Mary Goulding's work on injunctions[8] and to James and Barbara Allen's idea of a progression of permissions.[9]

1. The first permission needed for the growing infant is *to exist* and belong in the world. Beginning at the moment of birth, and perhaps before, the infant receives verbal and nonverbal messages from her parents as to whether or not they really want her around. If she is ignored, or handled perfunctorily, at a distance, stiffly, or with rage, she is not given permission to live. This infant has received a "Don't be" message. The basic permission to live occurs in the first year or two. However, a "Don't be" injunction can be given later—at any age, for that matter—by such statements as "Go away!" and "I wish you'd never been born." If the individual is lovingly touched and cared for, then this basic permission to live is given. If she does not have permission to live, she will not have a foundation from which she can successfully deal with her other problems. She may be trying, for example, to assert herself or to get close to other people, but if she has a "Don't be" message, she will be gathering proof, out of her awareness, that she really should not exist. Therefore, the absence of this basic permission to exist should be carefully looked for in every person, especially those who are depressed or who are not changing in therapy or who belong to a family where someone had died from suicide or a psychosomatic equivalent such as overwork. It is very useful for such a person to make a no-suicide decision, which means a decision for herself that she will not, under any circumstances, ever kill herself. In the beginning, this decision may be made predominantly from the person's Adult. However, to be completely free of this or any injunction, the new decision must ultimately be made and accepted within the Child.[10]

2. Permission *to have and be aware of one's own sensations:* Beginning with birth the individual needs responses to and acceptance of the basic bodily sensations, such as hunger, pain, cold, warmth, and touch. If this does not occur, the injunction "Don't feel" (sensation) is given. Some individuals grow up without an awareness of hunger, and eat only because

they see other people eating or because they learn that one eats at certain times of the day. Other individuals will not have a real awareness of hot, cold, or pain and consequently get injured frequently.

3. Permission *to feel:* From the early months of life, infants have feelings such as joy, despair, fear, and anger. If these are not discounted by the important parent figures, the baby has permission to express her own feelings. Otherwise, she learns to feel only what other people want her to feel, that is, a racket feeling, and she has received the injunction "Don't feel."

4. Permission *to think:* Beginning at around the age of two to three months, when the Little Professor (A_1) begins to appear, the individual needs permission to think. By responding reasonably to the young child, by not discounting how she reacts, and at a later age, not discounting what she says or what she wonders about, her parents and other important people give her continuing permission to think instead of a message that says "Don't think."

5. Throughout childhood, a person needs to receive permission *to be emotionally and physically close to others.* If a parent is remote and fearful of touch, the message of "Don't be close" is given. Often, verbal messages are given that it is dangerous to get close to: (a) members of the opposite sex, (b) members of the same sex, (c) spouses, or (d) anyone. A parent who is a hard worker and rarely around is nonverbally giving her children a "Don't be close" message.

6. Permission *to be who you are:* Usually by the age of three, each one of us knows what sex we are and whether or not that is all right. All our basic physical attributes should be approved of, not only sex, but race, size, color of hair, etc. Often a female is given a "Don't be you" message, because in her family or culture a boy is seen as more valuable. A male may be told by his mother not to be who he is because he reminds mother of her ex-husband. Individuals whose sex was not approved of often have confusion rackets.

7. Permission *to be whatever age* the individual is: Often parents who are either upset by small children, or who wish the child would quickly grow up so the child can take care of herself or her parents, transmit the message, "Don't be a child." Other youngsters are given "Don't grow up" messages, since their parents would be upset if they were to grow up and leave. Some children get both.

8. Permission *to succeed:* Many "Don't make it" messages stem from a parent's fear that her children will outdo her. This parent would be jealous of, or dislike her child's success because that would make it clear how the parent herself had failed. These "Don't make it" messages may be global and designed to stop the individual from succeeding in all ways, or just in certain ways, such as in work or in sex.

Another important way in which injunctions are transmitted is by identification. If mother says to son, "You're just like your Uncle Joe," then all of Uncle Joe's attributes have been passed on in one large injunction (which may include several or all of those in the above list). If Uncle Joe died an alcoholic in the gutter somewhere at age 30, then the son may take this on as his life script. However, if his father says, "No, you're not just like your Uncle Joe," that may be taken as permission to ignore mother's injunction.

The original dramatic experiences involving the injunctions are called the *protocol*. Injunctions may be handed down by anyone. The more powerful and important the person who gives the injunction is seen as being by the child who receives it, the more repeated the experience, the more intense the strokes that accompany the injunction, the more likely it will be that the injunction will be effective and a script *decision* will be made by the child in response to the injunction. In general, it is not possible to eliminate the effect of an injunction nearer the end of the list when there is an injunction earlier that has not yet been cleared away, relieved, or replaced by a permission and a *redecision*.

A *script matrix* is a diagram showing a person with his two parents and their messages. Added to this matrix can be any other important person, such as an older sibling, or other people who gave strong cultural messages that have been influential in the person's life. Figure 19 shows a typical script matrix.

The messages coming from the Child of the parents are the most potent, and it is these messages that stimulate the primary script for the individual. Messages that come from the Parent ego state of the parents have to do with moral judgments and values, and form the basis for a secondary script, or what is commonly called the *counterscript*. Often the counterscript messages will reinforce the script messages and so are actually not in

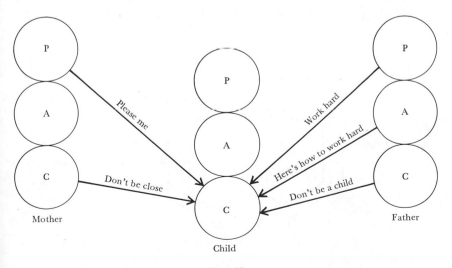

Figure 19
Script Matrix

opposition to each other as the name implies. Thus *subscript* is a better term. The messages are socially acceptable, however, and are statements that the parent's are willing to tell their friends and relatives about. A "Be independent" message may be given from the Parent, for example, but it will actually reinforce a "Don't be close" message that has been given from the Child. Or, a "Work hard" message may come from the Parent and reinforce a "Don't feel" message from the Child. Other typical subscript messages are "Be a good boy," "Be quiet," "Don't be selfish," etc. On other occasions messages are in opposition to the script messages and offer a real alternative and so are really counterscript. Often an individual who suddenly improves has only switched from his script to his counterscript or subscript. Since the counterscript only avoids the script and the subscript fosters the script, it may only be a temporary improvement.

In the script matrix in Figure 19, all of the script. counterscript, and subscript messages are directed to the Child of the client. *Decisions* regarding how a person will lead his life are both made and carried out in the Child. While these messages are directed toward the Child ego state, they are simultaneously recorded in the Parent ego state and thus form the individual's Parent (see Figure 3). Later, even though the individual will be living away from his parent (who may even be dead), he will have internalized these messages and will continue to carry them with him and be influenced by them (unless he decides to ignore or change his Parent).

The script depicted in Figure 20 with "Don't be close" and "Don't be a child" injunctions as well as "Work hard" and "Please me" subscript messages, resulted in a decision by the individual to become a businessman, work very hard to please others, and not have a close relationship with anyone. His father further contributed to his decision by teaching him to work hard in order not to have fun. This information came from father's Adult ego state and is called the *program*. He does not allow

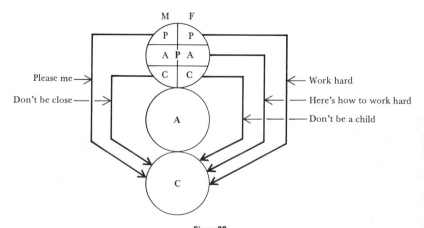

Figure 20
The Same Person Experiencing Internalized Messages

himself to have fun or to pay attention to his own feelings because that was disapproved of when he was a child. He must, instead, pay attention to what other people want and help them get it. His favorite games are *I'm Only Trying To Help You* and *Kick Me,* while his racket is depression.

MINISCRIPT   The *miniscript,* developed by Taibi Kahler with Hedges Capers, focuses on the minute-by-minute process by which a person furthers his script.[11] It is assumed that scripty behavior begins when a person places a condition on his OKness: "I'm OK *if* I can *Be Perfect, Be Strong, Hurry Up, Try Hard,* or *Please (Someone).* These five messages are called *drivers* and represent the not-OK parts of counterscript or subscript. These drivers allow the person to avoid temporarily the bad feelings of his script. Each driver can be observed behaviorally in words, tones of voice, facial expressions, gestures, and postures. Drivers last for only a short period of time, after which a person may return to nonscripty behavior, switch to another driver, or escalate into one or more racket feelings. The miniscript triangle in Figure 21 shows how the sequence may progress. Note:

1. The sequence always begins with a driver. It may stop there.
2. If the sequence continues, the person moves to his *stopper.* The stopper is derived from the injunction and is the feeling the person tries to avoid through driver behavior. When a person is in his stopper, his life experience is "I'm not-OK, You're OK." He feels guilty, inadequate, stupid, etc.
3. Once the sequence reaches the stopper level, the person may stay there, escalate to Vengeful or Final Miniscript Payoff position, return to a driver, or return to nonscripty behavior. This will depend upon his life position and the strokes available in each situation. Although all persons experience all three positions (Stopper, Vengeful, Final Miniscript Payoff), an individual will spend most of his time in the one that corresponds to his basic positions, since that's where he collects his favorite bad feelings. However, racket feelings are experienced and stamps are collected at each of these three positions. They may be collected in any order (note the arrows in the triangle) and to whatever intensity is called for by the script.

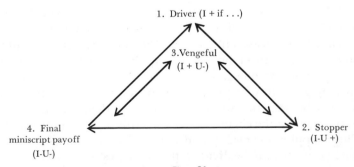

Figure 21
Not-OK Miniscript Triangle

4. The *Vengeful* position is an attempt to avoid painful feelings by blaming someone else. Here the person's experience is "I'm OK, You're not-OK" and he feels angry, righteous, triumphant, etc.

5. The *Final Miniscript Payoff* position is one of futility ("I'm not-OK, You're not-OK"). He may feel unloved, hopeless, rejected, etc.

In general, people of the same sex who are close to each other will have the same primary drivers, while those of the opposite sex will have complementary primary drivers, for example, Be Perfect with Please Me. In addition to starting the script process in a person, drivers invite others into their scripts. If a person goes into driver behavior, the person he is talking to will usually respond with driver behavior of his own. Either or both then may escalate to racket feelings. If the first person stays out of scripty behavior, the second will usually do likewise. Focusing on healthy, non-scripty behavior is especially important for therapists and others in the helping professions.

The following shows the *allowers* needed to stop each driver.

Drivers	*Allowers*
Be Perfect	Be yourself
Hurry Up	Take your time
Try Hard	Do it
Please Me	Consider and respect yourself
Be Strong	Be open and get needs met

The following correlates drivers with the script types with which they are most often found.

Script	*Drivers*
Never	Try Hard
Always	Be Strong, Hurry Up
Until	Be Perfect
After	Please Me
Almost	Please Me + Try Hard

TREATMENT

CONTRACTS   A treatment *contract* is an agreement between the therapist and the client to accomplish a clearly stated goal. The final outcome is clearly defined and measurable, so that the therapist and the client, as well as other people, will know when it has been reached. Normally, an individual will work on one contract at a time and focus his energies on that particular goal. In order for treatment to be effective, the contract should be made between the Adult ego state of the therapist and the Adult and Child ego states of the client. The client's Adult provides relevant data anl the Child supplies the energy and motivation necessary for change.

Treatment contracts can be divided into two types: *social control* (changing behavior), and *autonomy* (changing the script). A social control contract involves setting a goal to change a specific behavior or attitude. This can be accomplished by increasing Adult awareness and exercising Adult control or by reinforcing healthy adaptations. Autonomy is achieved when the Child ego state has been deconfused and unhealthy script decisions are replaced with new decisions for personal growth.

In order for a treatment contract to be valid, four basic requirements must be met: mutual consent, valid consideration, legal object, and competency.[12] *Mutual consent* implies that the client and the therapist are in agreement as to the goals, means, and predictable outcomes of treatment. *Valid consideration* means that there is an exchange of goods or services between both parties. The therapist gives his time, skill, and knowledge in exchange for money or objects (art works, poems, essays, etc.). This exchange helps avoid the establishment of a hidden Parent-Child relationship. *Legal object* requires that the contract be pursued by legal and ethical means toward legal and ethical ends. *Competency* requires that the therapist be adequately trained and experienced to perform what he purports to do, and that the patient be competent to enter into a valid treatment contract.

The following are examples of contracts that a therapist and client might agree to work on for the client: "to stop drinking alcohol"; "to stop destroying my body and take care of myself"; "to stop smoking cigarettes"; "to make my own decisions about my personal relationships"; "to hold a steady job for one year"; and "to make three new friends."

The contract should be stated by the client, accepted by the therapist, and acknowledged by the client. If a therapy group is to be the method of treatment used, it is important for group members to be aware of each person's contract. The treatment contract delineates the responsibilities of each person involved and places the ultimate responsibility for personal change with the client. It also provides a "roadway" for charting, measuring, and reporting the client's movement toward his goal. When the client has extended the contract primarily from his Adapted Child or Parent ego state, or when treatment is not following the goals of the contract, resistance to change is experienced. The alert therapist heeds this signal to return to the original contract or to ask for a new one. Stating clear contracts, working them through, and reaching personal goals is itself a therapeutic procedure.

THE THREE P'S: PROTECTION, PERMISSION, POTENCY   The effective transactional analyst employs three basic treatment concepts to assist the individual to make a redecision and accomplish his contract.[13] The therapist must offer the client adequate *protection*. Protection from physical harm during treatment is accomplished in several ways. First, the office is designed and equipped to be a safe place for the client's Child to come out and do what he needs to do. Second, if it's appropriate, priority is given to working on the client's making a decision not to kill himself or to hurt himself. The client may need protection from the reactions of his Controlling Parent ego state and the therapist should keep alert for that possibility. An offer of protection implies that the therapist is qualified and willing to effect cure, and that he will be available if or when needed throughout the course of treatment. The therapist offers the protection necessary for the client's scared or confused Child to try out new behaviors and experiences. Once an impasse is broken and the client gives up a game, racket, or part of his script, he may experience despair, a sense of aloneness with a feeling of "Where do I go from here?" This is especially true at the time of any major redecision or change in behavior. The therapist does not discount this feeling, but rather assists the client in finding new and more appropriate behaviors while checking to see that the client's scared Child is asking for what it needs (such as more permissions, reiteration of the facts, etc.). Without this protection, the client may revert to old patterns and be entrenched more solidly than ever in rackets, games, and other scripty behaviors.

Since the client arrived at his script decisions under pressure of parental injunctions and since he continues to respond to the pressure of his Parent ego state, *permission* to change from a new Parent source is very useful and perhaps even necessary. This new source may be any influential person(s) the individual encounters. It may be a therapist or the members of a therapy group. Depending on the client's current level of functioning, he may need permission to exist, to feel, to think, to be close, to be himself, to be his age, or to succeed. Permissions always carry the statements "I'm OK, You're OK" and "It's OK to change." The intent of a permission is to lift the restricting injunctions in order to realign the individual with his original script-free Free Child. Each person knows best what permissions he needs. The most effective permission is simultaneously communicated from all three ego states, as in the example in Figure 22.

In order for a permission to be effective it must be delivered with *potency*. The life script is a powerful force, decided under heavy parental

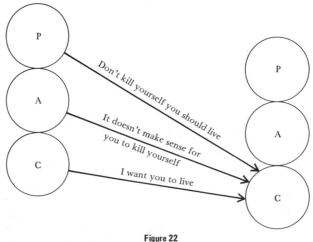

Figure 22
Permission

pressures and reinforced by many years of games, rackets, and non-problem-solving behaviors. Permissions must be given with a potency at least equal to that of the original injunctions. Potency lies in the timing of the intervention, as well as in the emphasis with which the permission is given. The potent therapist communicates his willingness and capacity to effect change and demonstrates strength in handling difficult therapeutic situations.

The most effective interventions are given by a therapist who has all three of his ego states actively involved in the therapeutic process. When the therapist has Parent values that promote the client's well-being, Adult information regarding what the client needs, and a freed-up Child that allows him full use of his strength, creativity, and intuitive powers, he is capable of delivering permissions potently while offering protection.

METHODS Regardless of which methods or techniques the therapist chooses to employ, the treatment goal remains the same: to help the client to attain and maintain the objectives of his contract(s) while moving toward autonomous living.

Structural analysis is used to increase the client's awareness of his ego-state functions and to encourage him to experience and utilize the ego states most useful for him in each situation. *Transactional analysis* helps the client define his interactions with others and exercise options. *Game and/or racket analysis* helps him become aware of the games and rackets he uses. Discounts are confronted and Adult information is provided until the client chooses to give them up.

Script analysis is a more extensive form of treatment and generally takes longer than the above methods. The goal is to identify the client's unsatisfactory life plan and help him to close it down and "put a new show on the road." The client may work through earlier life experiences to determine what early decisions are standing in his way, and then make new life decisions. This process is called *redecisions therapy*.

To make *redecisions* for change, it is useful for the client to know his script. Script information may be obtained in various ways. Check lists are available which ask questions such as:

"What were the nicest and worst things that your parents said to you?"
"What is your earliest memory?"
"What is the family story about your birth?"
"How were you named? What was your nickname?"
"Describe your mother; describe your father."
"What is your favorite fairy tale, story, or song?"
"How long do you expect to live?"

The gestalt therapy technique of double-chairing, in which a person talks to feelings he may have or to his "mother" or "father," can also help bring out needed information and move the client through the impasse of early script decisions.

Reparenting is a form of treatment introduced by Jacqui Schiff with specific reference to the treatment of schizophrenics.[14] A number of therapists also are providing new parenting for nonpsychotic patients. In this form of treatment, the therapist contracts with the client to be his new parent. The length of time this contract will run varies from a few minutes to a lifetime, and the therapist's time investment may vary from one session per week or less to 24 hours per day. Reparenting is a form of treatment that requires much skill and knowledge and a high energy investment. With these factors in mind, and since most therapists have some tendency to rescue others, special care ought to be taken in establishing these contracts.

The reparenting of psychotic patients most often involves their totally giving up their old Parent and starting over again with a new parent. Starting over ordinarily requires the client, when in a therapy situation, to regress to the stage in infancy or childhood prior to the traumatic situations that led to his psychopathology. He is encouraged to reexperience the trauma and release the feelings that he has never expressed. When this occurs, the therapist provides a new, healthy, parenting experience to replace the original pathological parenting. The person once again works through developmental levels as an infant would: needs are now felt, expressed, and met, allowing the child to move on to the next emerging need. The person grows with each new experience, and he does not remain fixed in the early dependent states. When his needs are met, he simply moves on as does the normal infant. Also, if his young needs are met, he will have much better Adult functioning to maintain himself, even while working through the early experiences. From this, it appears that when the Free Child has his needs met he provides, or releases, energy to the Adult.

Nonpsychotic clients also may want to go back to specific early scenes by cathecting (or deciding to be) whatever age is pertinent and have corrective experiences with different parenting. They do not regress or get rid of their old Parent in its entirety. They exchange some of their old Parent tapes for new ones. A reparenting contract maximizes the feeling of protection and allows for permission to be given most meaningfully with heightened potency.

References

1. Eric Berne, *Transactional Analysis in Psychotherapy*, New York, Grove Press, 1961.

   Eric Berne, *The Structure and Dynamics of Organizations and Groups*, Philadelphia, J. B. Lippincott Co., 1963.

   Eric Berne, *Games People Play*, New York, Grove Press, 1964.

   Eric Berne, *Principles of Group Treatment*, New York, Oxford University Press, 1966.

   Eric Berne, *Sex in Human Loving*, New York, Simon & Schuster, 1970.

   Eric Berne, *What Do You Say After You Say Hello?*, New York, Grove Press, 1972.

2. John Dusay, "Egograms and the Constancy Hypothesis," *Transactional Analysis Journal, 2,* no. 3 (July, 1972).
3. Aaron Wolfe Schiff and Jacqui Lee Schiff, "Passivity," *Transactional Analysis Journal, 1,* no. 1 (January, 1971); also see Jacqui Lee Schiff, et al., *The Cathexis Reader,* New York, Harper & Row, 1975.
4. Franklin H. Ernst, "The OK Corral: The Grid for Get-On-With," *Transactional Analysis Journal, 1,* no. 4 (October, 1971).
5. Stephen Karpman, "Fairy Tales and Script Drama Analysis," *Transactional Analysis Buletin, 7,* no. 26 (April, 1968).
6. Fanita English, "Rackets and Real Feelings," *Transactional Analysis Journal, 2,* no. 1 (January, 1972).
7. Berne, *Sex in Human Loving, op. cit.*
   Berne, *What Do You Say, op. cit.*
8. Robert L. Goulding, "Decisions in Script Formation," *Transactional Analysis Journal, 2,* no. 2 (April, 1972); Robert Goulding and Mary Goulding, "Injunction, Decisions, and Redecisions," *Transactional Analysis Journal, 6,* no. 1 (January, 1976), pp. 41–48.
9. James R. Allen and Barbara Ann Allen, "The Role of Permission," *Transactional Analysis Journal, 2,* no. 2 (April, 1972).
10. Robert Drye, Robert Goulding, and Mary Goulding, "No-Suicide Decisions," *American Journal of Psychiatry, 130,* no. 2 (1973), pp. 171–174.
11. Taibi Kahler with Hedges Capers, "The Miniscript," *Transactional Analysis Journal, 4,* no. 1 (January, 1974).
12. Claude Steiner, *Scripts People Live,* New York, Grove Press, 1974, pp. 243–250.
13. Pat Crossman, "Permission and Protection," *Transactional Analysis Bulletin, 5,* no. 19 (July, 1966); Claude Steiner, "Transactional Analysis as a Treatment Philosophy," *Transactional Analysis Bulletin, 7,* no. 27 (July, 1968).
14. Jacqui Lee Schiff and Aaron Wolfe Schiff, "Reparenting Schizophrenics," *Transactional Analysis Bulletin, 8,* no. 31 (July, 1969).

THE AUTHORS

Graham Barnes, MDiv
Clinical Member and Teaching Member and Vice President, ITAA
President, Southeast Institute, Chapel Hill, North Carolina
Adjunct Lecturer, Department of Psychiatry of the University of North
    Carolina School of Medicine
Member, American Group Psychotherapy Association

Michael Brown, PhD
Clinical Member and Teaching Member, ITAA
Director of Training, Huron Valley Institute, Ann Arbor, Michigan
Member, American Psychological Association

Robert C. Drye, MD
Clinical Member and Teaching Member and Member, Board of Trustees,
    ITAA
Member, American Psychoanalytic Association
Staff, Western Institute for Group and Family Therapy, Watsonville, Cali-
    fornia
Lecturer in Psychiatry, Stanford University, Stanford, California

John M. Dusay, MD
Clinical Member and Teaching Member and Past President, ITAA
Fellow, American Psychiatric Association
Assistant Clinical Professor, University of California School of Medicine,
    San Francisco, California

Fanita English, MSW
Clinical Member, American Association of Marriage and Family Coun-
    selors
Clinical Member and Teaching Member, ITAA

Clinical Director, Eastern Institute for TA and Gestalt, Philadelphia, Pennsylvania
Fellow of the American Group Psychotherapy Association
Founding Member, Jean Piaget Society
Member, International College of Psychosomatic Medicine
Clinical Member, International Group Psychotherapy Association

John Gladfelter, PhD
Clinical Member and Teaching Member, ITAA
Fellow and Director of the American Group Psychotherapy Association
Private practice of psychotherapy, Dallas, Texas

Robert L. Goulding, MD
Clinical Member and Teaching Member, ITAA
Co-Director, Western Institute for Group and Family Therapy, Watsonville, California
President, American Academy of Psychotherapists
Fellow and Retiring Secretary of the American Group Psychotherapy Association
Fellow, American Psychiatric Association

Martin G. Groder, MD
Clinical Member and Teaching Member and Vice President, ITAA
Chairman of the Board and Founder, Asklepieion Foundation
Assistant Clinical Professor of Psychiatry, Duke University Medical Center, Durham, North Carolina

Wiliam H. Holloway, MD
Clinical Member and Teacher Member and 1976–1977 President, ITAA
Co-Founder and Co-Director, Midwest Institute for Human Understanding, Medina, Ohio
Fellow, American Psychiatric Association
Fellow, director, and former officer of the American Group Psychotherapy Association
Diplomate, American Board of Psychiatry and Neurology
Past President, Ohio Psychiatric Association and Tristate Group Psychotherapy Association

Kristyn Huige, MSW
Clinical Member and Teaching Member, ITAA
Associate, Huron Valley Institute, Ann Arbor, Michigan

Lois M. Johson, MA
Clinical Member and Teaching Member and Member, Board of Trustees, ITAA
Director, Michigan Center, Inc., Schoolcraft, Michigan

Instructor, Lake Michigan College
Consultant U.S. Civil Service, U.S. Bureau of Prisons

Vann S. Joines, MDiv
Clinical Member and Teaching Member and Member, Board of Trustees, ITAA
Vice President, Southeast Institute
Clinical Member, American Association of Marriage and Family Counselors

Taibi Kahler, PhD
Clinical Member and Provisional Teaching Member, ITAA
Director, Human Development Institute for the South, Little Rock, Arkansas

Ken Lessler, PhD, ABPP
Clinical Member, ITAA
Director of Human Resource Consultants, P.A., Chapel Hill, North Carolina
Faculty, Southeast Institute, Chapel Hill, North Carolina
Diplomate in Clinical Psychology, American Board of Professional Psychology

Ruth McClendon, MSW
Clinical Member and Teaching Member and Member, Board of Trustees, ITAA
Associate of the Western Institute for Group and Family Therapy, Watsonville, California
Member, Board of Directors, American Group Psychotherapy Association
Associate of the Pacific Center for Family and Personal Therapy, Aptos, California

John R. McNeel, PhD
Clinical Member and Teaching Member, ITAA
Co-Director, Palo Alto Branch, Western Institute for Group and Family Therapy, Palo Alto, California
Adjunct Faculty, Southeast Institute, Chapel Hill, North Carolina

John J. O'Hearne, MD
Clinical Member and Teaching Member and Member, Board of Trustees, ITAA
Past President, American Group Psychotherapy Association
Member, Board of Directors, International Group Therapy Association
Clinical Professor of Psychiatry, University of Missouri at Kansas City, School of Medicine

Jacqui Lee Schiff, MSSW
Clinical Member and Teaching Member and Member, Board of Trustees, ITAA
Director, Cathexis Institute, Oakland, California

Jon Weiss, PhD
Clinical Member and Teaching Member and Member, Board of Trustees, ITAA
Director, Rocky Mountain TA Institute, Littleton, Colorado
Private practice of psychotherapy, Littleton, Colorado

Laurie Weiss, MA
Clinical Member and Teaching Member and Member, Board of Trustees, ITAA
Executive Director, Rocky Mountain TA Institute, Littleton, Colorado
Private practice of psychotherapy, Littleton, Colorado

Jerome D. White, PhD
Clinical Member and Teaching Member and Treasurer, ITAA
Director of Psychological Services, Peninsula Institute, Palo Alto, California

Terri White, MA
Clinical Member and Provisional Teaching Member, ITAA
Marriage & Family Counselor
Director of Programing, Peninsula Institute, Palo Alto, California

Kenneth L. Windes
Clinical Member and Teaching Member, ITAA
Director, Asklepieion Foundation

Stanley J. Woollams, MD
Clinical Member and Teaching Members, ITAA
Director, Huron Valley Institute, Ann Arbor, Michigan
Member, American Group Psychotherapy Association
Past President, Wolverine State Group Psychotherapy Society

THE INTERNATIONAL TRANSACTIONAL
ANALYSIS ASSOCIATION

In 1958, Eric Berne began a series on ongoing meetings in his office in San Francisco. The original title for this group was The San Francisco Social Psychiatry Seminars, and it was granted a charter by the State of California on May 19, 1960, as a nonprofit educational corporation. The seminar offered alternative approaches to earlier types of psychotherapy and later, as the theory developed, it took the name The San Francisco Transactional Analysis Seminars.

In 1964, the International Transactional Analysis Association (ITAA) came into existence to promote the understanding of transactional analysis and to provide appropriate training and certification of TA therapists. Currently, the Association has more than 10,000 members throughout the world.

The International Transactional Analysis Association insists upon high standards and demonstrated competence for those who offer treatment, counseling, teaching, or consultation in transactional analysis.

Only persons who have attained the advanced membership levels in the ITAA are authorized to call themselves transactional analysts. These levels of membership are: Special Fields Member (SFM), Clinical Member (CM), and Teaching Member (TM). A Teaching Member with competence primarily in clinical work is called a Clinical Teaching Member (C TM). A Teaching Member with competence in nonclinical fields is called a Special Fields Teaching Member (SF TM). A Special Fields or Clinical Member who has been approved by ITAA to pursue Teaching Membership is called a Provisional Teaching Member.

The international headquarters of the International Transactional Analysis Association is located at 1772 Vallejo Street, San Francisco, California 94123, Telephone (800) 227–4242 or (415) 885–5992.

INDEX